Contents

GW00497772

Understanding wild flowers

In earlier centuries it was for the usefulness of flowers more than for their beauty that people went out into the fields and woods to look for them. Most medicines were made from plants, and it was necessary for collectors to know them well; for many of the medicines were said to be effective only if the plants were collected at a particular time, from a particular place, in a particular way. Wild flowers' leaves and roots provided a natural food supply; their petals and fruits were crushed to make dyes and cosmetics; and many plants were thought to possess powerful magic, giving protection against all manner of evil in a superstitious age.

The magic of flowers abides, but now it is the flowers' turn to require protection. The sight of a woodland carpeted with bluebells in spring, or the sudden discovery of a cluster of cowslips in a meadow or hedgerow, offers a timeless salve to man's spirit and renews for a moment his power to wonder. But modern methods of agriculture have made cowslips and many other wild flowers much rarer than they used to be; children can no longer run out into the meadows in spring and come back with their baskets full to make cowslip-balls from the blossoms. Flowers require man's protection if they are to continue to afford him delight; and to protect them, and to enjoy them to the full, it is necessary to know them by name and to understand how they grow.

There are some 2,500 species of flowering plants native to Britain. More than 550 of these are illustrated in this book, including all the species most commonly encountered, and a selection of rarities. A few of the plants are technically shrubs because they have woody stems, but they are rarely thought of as anything but flowers. These include heather, bilberry, dyer's greenwood and roses.

The book includes some of the readily recognised species of grass or sedge, whose flowers are specially adapted for pollination by the wind and therefore lack the showy petals of flowers which are pollinated by insects. Non-flowering plants such as ferns, horsetails and mosses are not included.

The naming of flowers

The common names by which many plants are known seem to echo in their lyrical extravagance some of the natural beauty of the flowers themselves. Sun spurge, shepherd's purse, fat hen, field penny-cress – even common, so-called weeds often have names which trip off the tongue like ancient charms. Sometimes the original meaning of the name is lost in antiquity. Sometimes the name describes a quality of the plant, or the use to which man once put it. Woundwort was used to dress wounds, for example, while fleabane got rid of fleas and soap was made from soapwort.

However, the common names of plants are frequently misleading. They vary from place to place, and sometimes the same name is applied to different plants in different places. Ground elder is known by many names, including goutweed, bishop's weed and pope's weed. A bluebell in Scotland is not the same flower as a bluebell in England, where the Scottish flower is usually called a harebell. Only the scientific names of flowers are always the same – in all parts of Britain and throughout the world, the bluebell remains *Hyacinthoides non-scriptus*, and ground elder is *Aegopodium podagraria*.

The scientific system of naming plants was devised by the 18th-century Swedish naturalist Linnaeus, in order to clarify this confusion about names and to simplify the study of nature in all its forms. The first part of the scientific name defines the genus to which the plant belongs – the group of similar plants such as *Viola* (violets) or *Primula* (primroses). The second part of the name describes the species – a group of virtually identical, usually interbreeding plants. Thus the sweet violet is called *Viola odorata*, Latin for 'scented violet', and the dog violet is *Viola canina*, a literal translation into Latin of the common name.

Most scientific names are based on Latin or Greek as international languages, and often, as in the case of *Viola odorata*, the specific name describes some particular attribute of the plant. For instance, the plant may be upright, *erectus*, creeping, *repens*, or drooping, *pendula*; the colour of its petals may be white, *alba*, yellow, *lutea*, red, *rubra*, purple, *purpurea*, or blue, *caerulea*. The name may describe where the plant usually grows – in a meadow, *pratensis*, an arable field, *arvensis*, a wood, *sylvatica*, by the sea, *maritima*, on sand, *arenaria*, on a mountain, *montana*, on a wall, *muralis*, in a marsh, *palustris*, in water, *aquatilis*, or both on land and in water, *amphibium*. Many other names record the practical value of the plant. It may be edible, *edulis*, a crop plant, *sativa*, used by apothecaries, *officinalis*, valuable for healing wounds, *vulneraria*, for treating dysentery, *dysenterica*, for getting rid of stones, *saxifraga*, or for mending broken bones, *ossifragum*.

When one genus of plants closely resembles another, or several others, they are grouped together in a family. Daisies, dandelions and thistles all have flower-heads composed of many separate, petal-like parts called florets. They all belong to the daisy family, *Compositae*, one of the largest of all families of flowering plants.

Occasionally the same species of plant shows slight but distinctive variations from one area to another. Bladder campion, *Silene vulgaris*, is a tall plant inland, but when it grows by the sea it is shorter, with larger flowers. The coastal plants are recognised as a separate subspecies (abbreviated ssp.), and the scientific name given to the plant is *Silene vulgaris ssp. maritima*, commonly known as sea campion.

On rare occasions two species of wild flowers cross-fertilise to produce a hybrid. The hybrid shows characteristics of both parent species, and is often more vigorous than both. An × placed before the species name indicates that the flower is a hybrid. Blue comfrey, *Symphytum × uplandicum*, for instance, is a hybrid between common comfrey and rough comfrey.

How to use this book

As the first step towards wild-flower identification, the key on pages 10–15 groups the flowers described and illustrated in the book according to obvious identification features such as the shape and colour of their petals and the arrangement of their leaves. Having identified from this key the group to which an unfamiliar plant belongs, turn next to the pages indicated to identify the species.

Each illustrated page includes a painting of a whole plant, and smaller paintings of parts of the plant which are useful identification features. For still greater clarity, parts may be shown magnified, the degree of magnification being shown as [× 3], for example. A photograph shows the plant as it typically appears growing. However, wild flowers are living things, and one found in the field may vary slightly in colour or shape from the specimen illustrated.

The flowers are arranged in their family groups, so that similar-looking plants are usually found close together. In certain groups, such as parsleys, the most easily confused species are contrasted in special 'look-alike' keys, on a grey background.

Sometimes a species of wild flower varies in its appearance from one part of the country to another; mountain pansy, for instance, usually has yellow flowers in Derbyshire and purple flowers in Scotland. In these cases both forms are illustrated. A species closely related to the main flower on a page, and differing from it only in points of detail, is shown with a separate heading.

How to identify flowers

When a flower has been identified once, it should be possible to recognise it at a glance on subsequent occasions just by its size, colour and character; but in the beginning, a quick glance is never enough. Flower identification requires time and patience. It is necessary to look closely at the flower's petals, to see how many there are or how they are attached; the leaves may offer identification clues; it may also be necessary to examine the sepals outside the flower and the stamens or other parts inside it.

The parts of a flower

The study of flowers has a language of its own, and knowing the right names for the parts of a flower is the first step towards naming the flower itself.

PETALS These may be all the same size and shape (called 'equal petals' in the identification key), or different shapes and sizes (called 'unequal petals'). In some flowers, such as daisies, the parts which look like petals are complete flowers in themselves, called florets. A few flowers, such as nettles, have no petals at all.

SEPALS Most petalled flowers have green sepals outside the petals. These begin life as a protection for the flower bud. Sometimes the sepals are the same colour as the petals.

STAMENS These are the flower's pollen-bearing organs, and grow inside the flower.

STIGMA This part of the flower's female organs receives pollen from the stamens.

FLOWER Flowers grow in many different ways – with stalks or without them, at the end of the stem or scattered along it, singly or in groups or clusters called flower-heads.

LEAVES Some leaves are straight-edged, others are lobed, toothed or divided into separate leaflets. They may be scattered about the stem, grow in pairs or clusters from the same point on the stem, or all grow from the bottom of the stem.

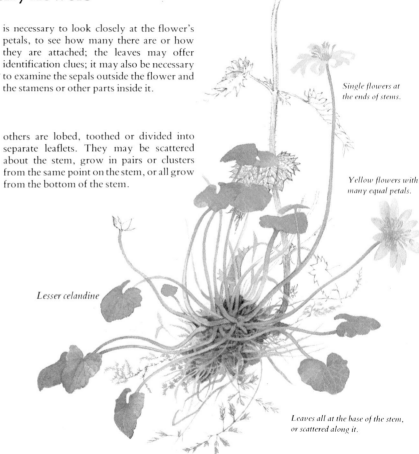

Single flowers at the ends of stems.

Yellow flowers with many equal petals.

Lesser celandine

Leaves all at the base of the stem, or scattered along it.

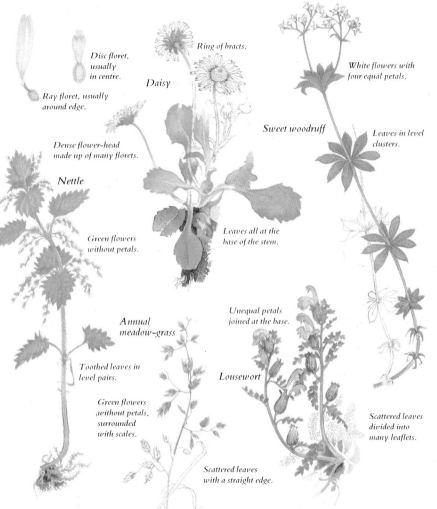

Disc floret, usually in centre.

Ray floret, usually around edge.

Ring of bracts.

Daisy

Dense flower-head made up of many florets.

White flowers with four equal petals.

Sweet woodruff

Leaves in level clusters.

Nettle

Green flowers without petals.

Leaves all at the base of the stem.

Annual meadow-grass

Toothed leaves in level pairs.

Unequal petals joined at the base.

Lousewort

Green flowers without petals, surrounded with scales.

Scattered leaves with a straight edge.

Scattered leaves divided into many leaflets.

Using the identification key

In the identification key in the following pages, the flowers described in the main part of this book are divided into ten groups, based on distinctive characteristics such as the shape of the flower-head and petals and the way the leaves grow from the stem. Each group is sub-divided according to features such as petal colour or leaf shape.

To identify a flower, examine it closely and proceed through the key to discover to which group it belongs. Then turn to the pages referred to in that section, and study the illustration on those pages until the particular species is found.

Increasing familiarity with the features identifying each group and sub-group of flowers will make the key quick and simple to use. The ten groups are:

1 WATER PLANTS.

2 NON-GREEN PLANTS.

3 PLANTS WITH FLOWERS IN UMBRELLA-SHAPED CLUSTERS.

4 PLANTS WITH DENSE FLOWER-HEADS MADE UP OF MANY FLORETS.

5 PLANTS WITH UNEQUAL PETALS, AND LEAVES IN LEVEL PAIRS OR CLUSTERS.

6 PLANTS WITH UNEQUAL PETALS AND SCATTERED LEAVES, OR LEAVES ALL AT THE BASE OF THE STEM.

7 PLANTS WITH EQUAL PETALS AND SCATTERED LEAVES, OR LEAVES ALL AT THE BASE OF THE STEM.

8 PLANTS WITH EQUAL PETALS, AND LEAVES IN LEVEL PAIRS OR CLUSTERS.

9 PLANTS WITH GREEN OR BROWN FLOWERS, WITH OR WITHOUT PETALS, WITH LEAVES IN LEVEL PAIRS OR CLUSTERS.

10 PLANTS WITH GREEN OR BROWN FLOWERS, WITH OR WITHOUT PETALS, WITH SCATTERED LEAVES OR LEAVES ALL AT THE BASE OF THE STEM.

1 Water plants

Plants which grow in the water have some leaves floating or all leaves submerged.

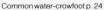
Common water-crowfoot p. 24

Water violet p. 224

Some leaves floating

Buttercups pp. 24–25
Water-lilies pp. 28–29
Water starwort p. 165
Marsh pennywort p. 170
Amphibious bistort p. 205

Water-plantain p. 370
Frogbit p. 373
Broad-leaved pondweed p. 374

All leaves submerged
River water-crowfoot p. 25
Water-milfoils p. 164
Water violet p. 224
Greater bladderwort, lesser bladderwort p. 280
Canadian waterweed p. 372
Curled pondweed p. 375

2 Non-green plants

Plants which obtain their food from other plants, or from decaying humus, have no leaves on their stems, and no green pigment; their stems are pale yellow or red.

Common dodder p. 249

Yellow bird's-nest p. 219
Common dodder, great dodder p. 249
Broomrapes pp. 278–9
Bird's-nest orchid p. 396

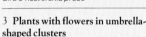

3 Plants with flowers in umbrella-shaped clusters

The tiny, stalked flowers are in umbrella-shaped clusters, or umbels. Each flower has five petals, five sepals and five stamens.

Sanicle p. 171
Parsleys pp. 173–96 (look-alikes compared pp. 168–9)

Hogweed p. 195

Flower-head

Umbel: top view

Umbel: side view

4 Plants with dense flower-heads made up of many florets

Each petal-like part making up the flower-head is a complete, small flower called a floret. Some species, such as the dandelion, have ray florets; others, such as tansy, have disc florets; while daisies have both. A ring of small, green leaf-like bracts surrounds the flower-head.

Field scabious p. 322
Chicory p. 357
Sea holly p. 172
Daisies pp. 324–69
Teasels pp. 320–3
Thrift p. 221

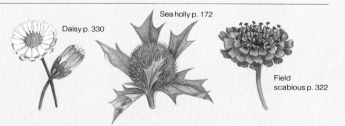
Daisy p. 330
Sea holly p. 172
Field scabious p. 322

5 Plants with unequal petals, and leaves in level pairs or clusters

Heath milkwort p. 61
Lesser periwinkle, greater periwinkle p. 231
Figworts pp. 265–6, 268–71, 274–7
Vervain p. 282
Mints pp. 283–304
Honeysuckle p. 315
Red valerian p. 317

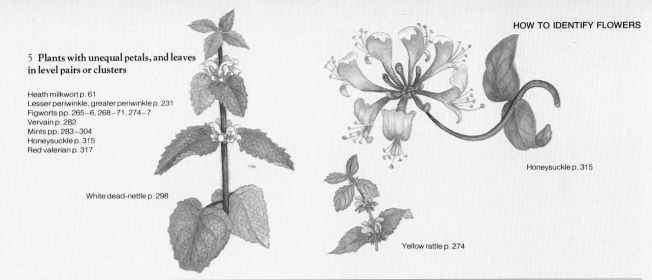

Honeysuckle p. 315

White dead-nettle p. 298

Yellow rattle p. 274

6 Plants with unequal petals and scattered leaves, or leaves all at the base of the stem

Flowers with a large upper petal, two side petals, and two lower petals joined to form a keel
Peas pp. 107–32

Leaves with a straight edge
Weld p. 60
Common and heath milkwort p. 61
Rosebay willowherb p. 161
Viper's-bugloss p. 248
Figworts pp. 262–3
Common butterwort p. 281
Flowering-rush p. 371
Daffodils pp. 388–9
Irises pp. 390–1
Orchids pp. 393–4, 397–402

Leaves toothed, lobed or divided into leaflets
Wild pansy p. 65
Lousewort p. 273
Fumitories pp. 36–37
Violets pp. 62–65
Wild mignonette p. 60
Himalayan balsam, orange balsam p. 106
Figworts pp. 263–4, 267, 272–3
Lords and ladies p. 403

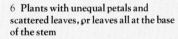

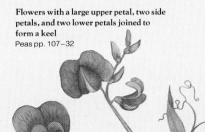

Narrow-leaved everlasting pea p. 132

Heath spotted orchid p. 401

Lousewort p. 273

Wild pansy p. 65

11

7 Plants with equal petals and scattered leaves, or leaves all at the base of the stem

Flowers with four petals
Common meadow-rue, lesser meadow-rue p. 27
Poppies pp. 30–35
Cabbages pp. 38–59 (look-alikes compared pp. 38–39, 49)
Roses pp. 137, 143
Heathers pp. 216–17

Charlock p. 42

Flowers with five petals; fruit a cluster of four dark nutlets enclosed by sepals
Forget-me-nots pp. 238–47 (look-alikes compared p. 238)

Wood forget-me-not and fruit p. 247

Flowers with five pink petals; leaves toothed, lobed or divided into leaflets
Common mallow, musk mallow p. 96
Roses pp. 135, 145–6
Bilberry, cowberry p. 216
Common wintergreen p. 218
Bird's-eye primrose p. 222
Bogbean p. 237

Dog rose p. 145

Field poppy p. 30

Flowers with five yellow or white petals; leaves with a straight edge
Lesser spearwort p. 23
Stonecrops pp. 148–9
Grass-of-Parnassus p. 155
Round-leaved sundew, great sundew p. 156
Brookweed p. 230
Black nightshade p. 253

Biting stonecrop p. 148

Flowers with five purple or blue petals; leaves toothed, lobed or divided into leaflets
Orpine p. 147
Nightshades pp. 252, 254
Bellflowers pp. 308–11

Nettle-leaved bellflower p. 308

Flowers with three, six or more than six petals
Lesser celandine p. 26
Sundews p. 156
Crowberry p. 220
Water-plantain, arrowhead p. 370
Lilies pp. 376–8, 380–3
Wild daffodil p. 388

Lesser celandine p. 26

Flowers with five pink, purple or blue petals; leaves with a straight edge
Pale flax, perennial flax p. 99
Docks pp. 204–5
Thrift, sea-lavender p. 221
Bindweed p. 250
Deadly nightshade p. 255
Harebell p. 310

Pale flax p. 99

Flowers with five white, yellow or red petals, and more than ten stamens; leaves toothed, lobed or divided into leaflets
Buttercups pp. 18, 21–23
Roses pp. 133–40, 144–5

Meadow buttercup p. 21

Flowers with five white, yellow or red petals, joined at the base, and ten or fewer stamens; leaves toothed, lobed or divided into leaflets
Navelwort p. 150
White bryony p. 157
Primroses pp. 222–3
Bindweeds pp. 250–1
Black nightshade p. 253
Figworts pp. 260–1

Aaron's rod p. 260

Primrose p. 222

Flowers with five white or yellow petals, separate at the base, and ten or fewer stamens; leaves toothed, lobed or divided into leaflets
Wood-sorrel, sleeping beauty p. 105
Saxifrages pp. 151–3
White bryony p. 157
Serrated wintergreen p. 218

Wood-sorrel p. 105

8 **Plants with equal petals, and leaves in level pairs or clusters**

Flowers with two or four white, pink or purple petals
Traveller's-joy p. 20
Procumbent pearlwort p. 81
Allseed p. 97
Willowherbs pp. 160, 162–3
Heathers pp. 213–15
Bedstraws pp. 312–14

Cross-leaved heath p. 215

Sweet woodruff p. 313

Flowers with four blue petals
Figworts pp. 270–1
Gentians pp. 235–6

Field gentian p. 235

Flowers with five petals; fruit with a long beak and five segments
Crane's-bills pp. 100–4

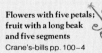

Meadow crane's-bill and fruit p. 100

Flowers with five yellow petals
Common rock-rose p. 66
St John's-worts pp. 67–69
Primroses pp. 226–7

Common rock-rose p. 66

Flowers with five white petals
Pinks pp. 70–86
Spring beauty p. 88
Fairy flax p. 98
Primroses pp. 225, 228–9

Greater stitchwort p. 79

Flowers with five blue or purple petals
Loosestrifes pp. 158–9
Blue pimpernel p. 228
Lesser periwinkle, greater periwinkle p. 231
Gentians pp. 234, 236

Marsh gentian p. 234

Flowers with five pink or red petals
Pinks pp. 70–86
Centaurys p. 232
Valerians pp. 318–19

Common centaury p. 232

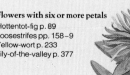

Red campion p. 70

Flowers with six or more petals
Hottentot-fig p. 89
Loosestrifes pp. 158–9
Yellow-wort p. 233
Lily-of-the-valley p. 377

Hottentot-fig p. 89

9 Plants with green or brown flowers, with or without petals; leaves in level pairs or clusters

Plant growing from the branch of a tree, with a leathery stem and leaves, and white berries
Mistletoe p. 166

Mistletoe p. 166

Leaves with a straight edge
Pinks pp. 81–82, 87
Goosefoots pp. 93, 95
Opposite-leaved, alternate-leaved golden saxifrage p. 154
Common twayblade p. 395

Procumbent pearlwort p. 81

Climbing plants, with leaves toothed, lobed or divided into leaflets
Traveller's-joy p. 20
Hop p. 211

Hop p. 211

Leaves toothed, lobed or divided into leaflets
Opposite-leaved, alternate-leaved golden saxifrage p. 154
Dog's mercury, annual mercury p. 197
Stinging nettle, small nettle p. 210
Common figwort, water figwort p. 265
Wood sage p. 303
Moschatel p. 316

Stinging nettle p. 210

10 Plants with green or brown flowers, with or without petals, with scattered leaves or leaves all at the base of the stem

Flower-head with a broad hood
Lords and ladies p. 403

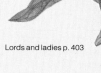

Lords and ladies p. 403

Climbing plants
White bryony p. 157
Ivy p. 167
Black bindweed p. 204
Black bryony p. 392

Black bryony p. 392

Flowers form cyathium (with stamens and a stalked ovary), surrounded by four glands. Cut stems exude milky juice
Spurges pp. 197–9

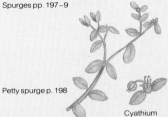

Petty spurge p. 198

Cyathium

Plants with woody, stiff stems
Bog myrtle p. 212
Butcher's-broom p. 379

Bog myrtle p. 212

Leaves with stalks attached to centre of leaf-blade
Navelwort p. 150
Marsh pennywort p. 170

Marsh pennywort p. 170

Leaves deeply toothed or divided into leaflets
Buttercups pp. 19, 27
Swine-cress, slender wart-cress p. 52
Roses pp. 141–3
Sheep's sorrel p. 206
Buck's-horn plantain p. 305
Daisies pp. 343, 347

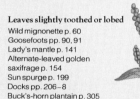

Pineapple weed p. 343

Leaves slightly toothed or lobed
Wild mignonette p. 60
Goosefoots pp. 90, 91
Lady's mantle p. 141
Alternate-leaved golden saxifrage p. 154
Sun spurge p. 199
Docks pp. 206–8
Buck's-horn plantain p. 305

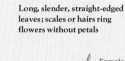

Common orache p. 91

Long, slender, straight-edged leaves; scales or hairs ring flowers without petals

Female flower

Branched bur-reed p. 404
Reedmace p. 405
Sedges pp. 406–14
Grasses pp. 415–31

Reedmace p. 405

Broad leaves with a straight edge
Goosefoots pp. 90, 92
Spurges pp. 198–9
Curled dock, broad-leaved dock p. 208
Wall pellitory p. 209
Deadly nightshade p. 255
Plantains pp. 305–7
Solomon's-seal p. 376
Orchids pp. 393, 395, 398

Hoary plantain p. 307

Long, slender leaves with a straight edge; flowers with petal-like lobes
Weld p. 60
Annual seablite p. 94
Knotgrass p. 204
Plantains pp. 305–6
Daisies pp. 332–3
Rushes pp. 384–7

Jointed rush p. 384

Flower

15

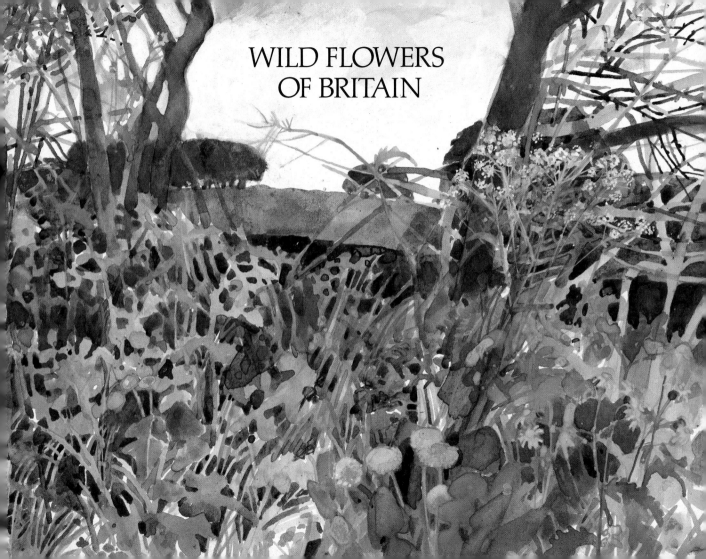

WILD FLOWERS
OF BRITAIN

A hairless plant with usually upright stems. It has large leaves, dark green and shiny; the upper leaves are stalkless and clasp the stems.
12–24 in. (30–60 cm); flowers Mar.–July.

Leaves growing from the base are heart-shaped and have long stalks.

Flower is a bright golden-yellow, with many stamens.

Ripe capsules split down one side to release seeds.
[Actual size]

Marsh-marigold is common in wet wood-lands, fens, marshes and ditches in all parts of the British Isles.

Marsh-marigold *Caltha palustris*

As early as March, with snow still on the ground, marsh-marigolds may often be seen lighting up windswept marshes and damp woods with their brilliant golden flowers and bright green, glossy leaves. The plants continue flowering well into summer, and are at their most luxuriant in partial shade.

Some marsh-marigold flowers are as much as 2 in. (5 cm) across, with as many as 100 stamens. Numerous insects, including many species of fly, visit the flowers for their nectar and pollen; an insect crawling over the stamens becomes covered with pollen and so pollinates the flower. Plants growing on high land in the north of England and in Scotland have smaller flowers, growing from stems sprawling on the ground.

The plant's common name of kingcup is derived from the Old English *cop*, meaning a 'button' or 'stud' such as kings once wore. In many parts of the British Isles, farmers used to hang marsh-marigolds over the byres of their cattle on May Day to protect them from the evil-doings of fairies and witches. Some writers believe that marsh-marigolds were the flowers referred to by Shakespeare when he wrote in *Cymbeline* that 'winking Mary-buds begin to ope their golden eyes'.

Ripe capsules
split open to
release seeds.
[Actual size]

Globe-shaped,
yellowish-green
flower often has a
reddish border.
[Actual size]

Nectary is
about half as
long as the
stamens; there
are five to ten in
each flower. [× 2]

A stout-stemmed plant with numerous
flowers. The lower leaves are long-
stalked and evergreen. Up to 32 in.
(80 cm); flowers Feb. – Apr.

The plant is most likely to be found in
woods and scrub on chalk and limestone
in south and west England, and Wales.

Stinking hellebore *Helleborus foetidus*

This is an uncommon woodland plant, and not easily detected
even where it does occur. Although it flowers before much else
is in bloom – as early as February, even when there is snow about
– its yellowish-green petals are inconspicuous. The disagreeable
smell which gives the plant its name attracts early bees and other
insects to its nectar. When the foliage is crushed, it emits an even
more vile, fetid odour.

Another unusual feature of the hellebore is the way its seeds
are dispersed by snails. Each seed has a white ridge along one
side, which produces an oil attractive to snails. The snail eats the
oily matter but discards the seed, which then sticks to its slime
and is carried to a new growing site.

Parts of both Britain's native hellebores were once used to
make dangerously violent purgatives for killing worms in children. The practice was abandoned, for in addition to removing
the worms the hellebore often killed the patient as well. An
infusion made from the plant was also used for delousing and
treating boils, but this treatment also proved fatal on more than
one occasion. In the Victorian language of flowers, hellebore
represented calumny, or malicious slander.

Green hellebore
Helleborus viridis

The flowers of the rarer green
hellebore are flat, without reddish petal tips. It grows in moist
woods, mainly on limestone.

19

Each head contains numerous plumed seeds. [Actual size]

Plume is a long, feathery style flowing from each seed. [× 2]

The clematis brightens hedgerows, wood margins and scrub on chalky soil in southern England and Wales.

Each leaf has three to five leaflets. The leaf-stalk twists around twigs and branches of other plants. [Actual size]

Flower has long stamens, and is hairy on outside. [Actual size]

A woody climbing plant with opposite leaves, which grows by twining itself around other plants; here it is shown climbing on dogwood. Up to 100 ft (30 m); flowers July–Aug.

Traveller's-joy *Clematis vitalba*

The name of traveller's-joy was given to this clematis by the 16th-century English botanist John Gerard because, he said, he found it 'decking and adorning ways and hedges where people travel'. Today it is still a familiar sight in southern Britain, instantly recognisable by its woody climbing stems and sprays of white or greenish flowers smelling sweetly of vanilla. The plant uses its twining leaf-stalks to climb up trees. The thick stems, sometimes 100 ft (30 m) long, hang from the treetops like jungle lianas.

The small flowers of clematis do not have true petals. Even the showy blue or reddish clematises grown in gardens provide their display with coloured sepals.

When the fruits ripen, the reason for the plant's other popular name, old man's beard, becomes apparent. The seeds sit in clusters on the ends of the flower-stalks, each with a long feathery plume and together resembling a growth of curly white hair. The dried stems were once smoked by young boys, hence another old name for the plant, 'boy's bacca'. Beggars used to arouse sympathy by rubbing their legs with fresh twigs, as an irritant in the sap produced the appearance of ulcers.

A plant with numerous leaves divided into two to seven lobes. Unlike some other buttercups, the middle lobe is not on a separate stalk. Flowers are bright yellow, sometimes paler yellow or even white. The plant is growing with marsh bedstraw and grass. 12–36 in. (30–90 cm); flowers May onwards.

Bulbous buttercup
Ranunculus bulbosus

The base of the stem is swollen, and each leaf has a stalked middle lobe. The sepals are bent back. This plant flowers earlier than the meadow buttercup, from Mar.–June, and prefers drier grassland.

Sepals are erect, spreading as the flower opens, but not bent back. [Actual size]

Fruits are numerous; each has a short, hooked beak. [Actual size]

The plant creates a yellow carpet in damp meadows throughout the British Isles, and invades gardens.

Meadow buttercup *Ranunculus acris*

Often reaching 36 in. (90 cm) in height, this is the most majestic of our three most common buttercups (meadow, creeping and bulbous). It has always been a traditional sight of the British countryside, and survives today despite increasing use of weed-killers. There is hardly a meadow that does not become a blaze of buttercup yellow between May and July; in exceptional years the display may last until October. They are popular with children, who hold the flower under each other's chins to discover if they like butter. All buttercups contain an unpleasant chemical which is poisonous to cattle; fortunately, most cattle avoid eating them, so cases of poisoning are rare.

There are some fanciful beliefs associated with the medicinal properties of buttercups. According to one, the roots when ground up with salt could cure the plague. The mixture was said to cause blisters which drew out the disease. Buttercups hung round the neck in a bag were thought to cure lunacy.

The name buttercup dates back only to the late 18th century. Before that, the flower was known as butterflower or crowfoot – a name now restricted to white-flowered species growing in ponds, streams and rivers.

A wide-spreading plant with creeping runners, which root at intervals. The long-stalked lower leaves are divided into three lobes, the middle lobe projecting beyond the others on a short stalk. All leaves are hairy. 2–20 in. (5–50 cm); flowers May–Sept.

[Actual size]

Celery-leaved crowfoot
Ranunculus sceleratus

This species has much smaller flowers, lacks runners, and has hairless lower leaves without a stalked middle lobe. The fruits form an elongated head.

[× 5]

Smooth fruits with short, curved beaks are clustered in a globe-shaped head.

[× 2]

Flowers are borne singly or in clusters. Sepals are erect.

Creeping buttercup is a common weed of arable and disturbed land, damp pastures and roadsides all over Britain.

Creeping buttercup *Ranunculus repens*

Farmers and gardeners look on creeping buttercup as by far the worst pest of all forms of buttercup, for it is an invader of meadows and lawns on a massive scale. Its runners spread in all directions, every few inches putting down roots and developing clusters of leaves. In this way the original plant may very soon cover a broad area of ground. Unless every last scrap of the plant is extirpated, it can quickly ruin a good lawn.

In a damp meadow grazed by cattle, a takeover by creeping buttercup can be disastrous. Because it is unpleasant to the taste and probably a little poisonous, cattle refuse to eat it, so, as the grass around is removed by grazing, the buttercup has room to spread. It cannot be eradicated by hand because of the scale of the task, and ploughing it in only chops up and spreads the runners, so creating thousands of potential new plants.

Celery-leaved crowfoot is much more poisonous to cattle, reducing their milk supply when it does not actually kill. All parts of the plant are acrid, and readily produce sores on the skin if handled. It is nearly as widespread as creeping buttercup, but prefers waterlogged places on rich soil. The name celery-leaved is a corruption of the Latin name *sceleratus*, 'vicious'.

A plant with upright or creeping stems which often root at intervals. Stems are mainly hairless, often reddish and slightly branched. The leaves vary in shape but are usually spear-shaped, the lower ones stalked, those at the top stalkless. 2–20 in. (5–50 cm); flowers May–Sept.

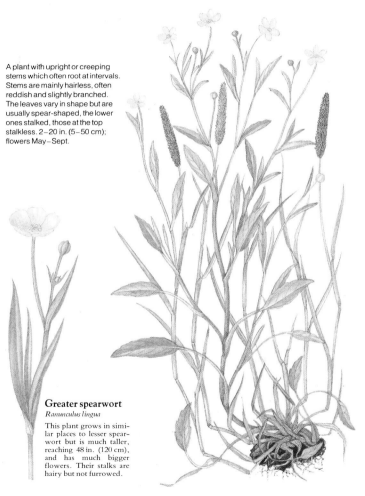

Fruit [×5]

The fruiting head is globe-shaped. Each fruit has a very short, blunt beak. [×5]

Flowers are borne singly or a few in a cluster; the stalks are furrowed and slightly hairy. [Actual size]

Lesser spearwort is a common plant of wet or marshy places, ditches, ponds and lakesides throughout Britain.

Lesser spearwort *Ranunculus flammula*

The two spearworts are in reality no more than buttercups with leaves that are narrow and spearhead-shaped instead of being lobed or deeply divided like those of other plants of the family. Lesser spearwort, which is commoner than greater spearwort, has the buttercups' bitter, acrid sap that readily causes blisters. At one time beggars smeared it on their skins to raise sores that would attract sympathy and coins from passers-by; the sap was applied with a limpet shell, the sharp edges of which would make the shape of the sore more distinct.

Lesser spearwort has killed cattle and sheep that have eaten it. The sap contains greater concentrations of the poisons common to all buttercups than any other of the family, except celery-leaved crowfoot. Used in moderation, however, it has medicinal value. Some doctors claim that the distilled sap of this plant is more effective in producing instant vomiting, in cases of internal poisoning, than any other substance: the lesser poison drives out the greater. The botanical name *flammula* probably refers to the inflammation of the skin or digestive tract caused by the sap. Greater spearwort is also potentially dangerous, but is less likely to cause harm as it occurs in more scattered localities.

Greater spearwort
Ranunculus lingua

This plant grows in similar places to lesser spearwort but is much taller, reaching 48 in. (120 cm), and has much bigger flowers. Their stalks are hairy but not furrowed.

23

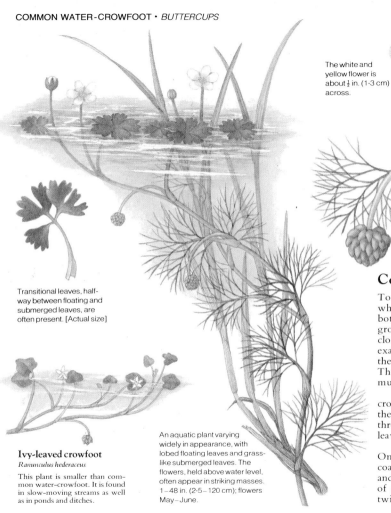

The white and yellow flower is about ½ in. (1·3 cm) across.

The short-beaked fruit is hairy when young. [× 5]

The fruit-stalks curve downwards into the water, bearing globe-shaped heads. [× 2]

Transitional leaves, half-way between floating and submerged leaves, are often present. [Actual size]

Ivy-leaved crowfoot
Ranunculus hederaceus

This plant is smaller than common water-crowfoot. It is found in slow-moving streams as well as in ponds and ditches.

An aquatic plant varying widely in appearance, with lobed floating leaves and grass-like submerged leaves. The flowers, held above water level, often appear in striking masses. 1–48 in. (2·5–120 cm); flowers May–June.

Common water-crowfoot grows in ponds, streams and ditches all over Britain – except for mountainous districts.

Common water-crowfoot *Ranunculus aquatilis*

To the casual observer, buttercups which grow in water and which have white leaves are, simply, water-crowfoot. To the botanist, however, water-crowfoot is a collective name for a group of nine very similar plants which, when looked at very closely, are found to be quite different from each other. For example, if a random handful of water-crowfoot is taken from the water the chances are that it will have two sets of leaves. There are the round ones which float on the surface, and the much-divided, feathery ones which are submerged.

In three plants of the water-crowfoot group – ivy-leaved crowfoot, three-lobed crowfoot and round-leaved crowfoot – the submerged leaves are usually absent. In three others – thread-leaved water-crowfoot, river water-crowfoot and fan-leaved water-crowfoot – the floating leaves are missing.

The three remaining crowfoots have both kinds of leaves. One of them, brackish water-crowfoot, grows only in brackish coastal water. The other two – shield-leaved water-crowfoot and common water-crowfoot – are much alike. But the flowers of shield-leaved water-crowfoot are almost an inch across – twice the size of those of the common water-crowfoot.

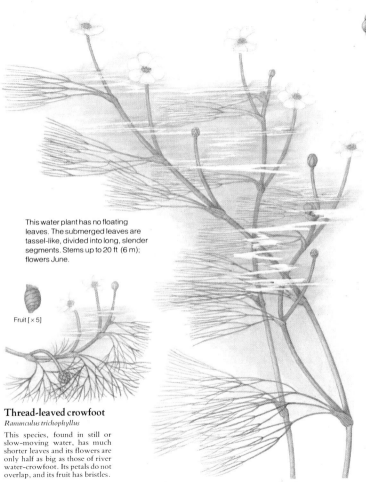

This water plant has no floating leaves. The submerged leaves are tassel-like, divided into long, slender segments. Stems up to 20 ft (6 m); flowers June.

Fruit [× 5]

Thread-leaved crowfoot
Ranunculus trichophyllus

This species, found in still or slow-moving water, has much shorter leaves and its flowers are only half as big as those of river water-crowfoot. Its petals do not overlap, and its fruit has bristles.

The fruit is hairless [× 5]

The fruit heads have stout stalks and often project above water. [× 2]

The white flowers, ¾–1¼ in. (2–3 cm) across, have overlapping petals and are held above the water.

River water-crowfoot is a common plant of swift-flowing water throughout England, Wales and southern Scotland.

River water-crowfoot *Ranunculus fluitans*

Poets have long been inspired by plants of the *Ranunculus* family, and the 19th-century Dorset dialect poet William Barnes paid tribute to the river water-crowfoot in the same way that Wordsworth immortalised the lesser celandine. He celebrated the plant in a poem which spoke of its small, fair face studding the River Frome with white. Concerned for the plant's future, Barnes warned that it was in danger from the 'water man', who would wade the river with his deadly blade and 'slay thee even in thy bloom'.

Fast-flowing water is the river water-crowfoot's sole domain, and its leaves are streamlined to lower resistance to the water's movement. The submerged leaves of other crowfoots are more or less circular and seldom more than 3 in. (7·5 cm) across. But those of the river water-crowfoot are very narrow and are often up to 12 in. (30 cm) in length, with long, thread-like segments.

Unlike the river water-crowfoot, the thread-leaved crowfoot dislikes turbulent water. Its flowers have the conventional five petals, as opposed to the river water-crowfoot which often has as many as eight.

On some plants tiny bulbils form where the leaves join the stems.

The heart-shaped leaves grow on long stalks. The solitary flowers are yellow, sometimes fading to white, and are often seen growing with bluebells. 2½–6 in. (6–15 cm); flowers Mar.–May.

Sometimes the dark green leaves bear dark or light markings. [Actual size]

Single fruit, containing seed. [× 2]

The fruiting head contains numerous fruits, each with a minute beak. [× 2]

Each flower has 8–12 petals and three sepals. [Actual size]

The lesser celandine is very common in damp, shady places, woods, meadows and gardens all over the British Isles.

Lesser celandine *Ranunculus ficaria*

One of the earliest of Britain's wild flowers to appear is the lesser celandine, which often carpets woodlands with a broad splash of gold in spring. William Wordsworth so admired the flower, which grows in abundance in his beloved Lake District, that he wrote a whole poem about it. It begins:

There is a flower, the lesser Celandine
That shrinks, like many more, from cold and rain
And, the first moment that the sun may shine
Bright as the sun himself, 'tis out again!

A carving on Wordsworth's tomb in Grasmere churchyard depicts the unrelated greater celandine, which does not close up in dull weather like the celandine of Wordsworth's poem.

The flower was mentioned in print in Britain more than 200 years before Wordsworth, when the 16th-century herbalist William Turner wrote that it 'groweth under the shadowes of ash trees'. In the Faroe Islands, lesser celandine was introduced as a medicinal herb, and it still survives there in churchyards.

The 17th-century herbalist Nicholas Culpeper used the plant to treat his own daughter for the so-called 'king's evil', or scrofula, and claimed that it cured her in one week.

The leaves are dark green above, paler below, and divided into numerous segments. [× 2]

The lower stem-leaves of this tall plant have stalks, but the upper ones are stalkless. Flowers are in dense clusters. 24–48 in. (60–120 cm); flowers June–Aug.

Lesser meadow-rue
Thalictrum minus

This species is more slender and wiry. It has drooping stamens and 3–15 brown fruits to each flower. The plant is locally common in the north.

Three dry fruits develop from each flower. [× 2]

Flowers have four small, white sepals and many erect stamens, which make the clusters appear yellow. [× 2]

Common meadow-rue is widespread mainly in the south and east, but is also found in Scotland and Ireland.

Common meadow-rue *Thalictrum flavum*

Although it is pollinated by bees and flies – as well as by the wind – the common meadow-rue has no scent to draw insects from a distance, and no nectar for them to feed upon if they do come to the flower. Visiting insects also find that the common meadow-rue, unlike many plants, has no platform of petals to act as a landing spot – although one is provided by the stamens, which are rigid and upright and enable insects to walk across them.

The features of the flower that do attract insects are the numerous bright yellow, feathery stamens in each flower. Their colourful appearance is enhanced by the way in which the flowers are bunched together. So much pollen is produced by the fluffy-looking flowers that even if no insects visit them some of the pollen may be blown onto the stigmas, so ensuring a crop of fertile seed for the following year.

The flower's foliage is thought to be harmful to cattle, although the roots and leaves act as a useful purgative in man. This may have been the origin of the meadow-rue's alternative name of meadow rhubarb, for rhubarb has long been valued as a laxative. The scientific name *thalictrum*, from the Greek *thallo*, 'to flourish', probably refers to the plant's wide distribution.

The plant is anchored by a stout underground stem. Flowers and all leaves float on the surface.

The fruit is globe-shaped and covered with scars where the stamens have fallen.

Leaves are more or less circular, green above and often reddish beneath. The large flowers have numerous petals and four shorter sepals. Flowers June–Aug.

Sepals are green on the back and white inside.

The large flowers of the white water-lily blossom on the surface of still water of lakes and ponds throughout Britain.

White water-lily *Nymphaea alba*

To Elizabethan poets and apothecaries, the water-lily was 'nenuphar', a word corrupted from the Sanskrit *nilotpala*, describing another water plant, the Indian blue lotus. For poets, the bloom of the white water-lily – the largest flower in the British flora – was a symbol of purity of heart. For apothecaries, the plant was the source of oils and distillations of nenuphar, used in the treatment of skin blemishes and sunburn, baldness and feminine disorders.

The underwater stems are fleshy and grow as deep as 6 ft (1·8 m) below the surface of ponds and slow-moving rivers. These stems were once eaten as a delicacy, and are sometimes still served as a food in parts of northern Europe.

Some local English names for the white water-lily approach the beauty of its bloom. In Cheshire it is called 'lady of the lake', and in Wiltshire and Dorset it is known as 'swan among the flowers'. But the beauty is transient. The flowers, on stems up to 9 ft (2·75 m) long, open only towards midday and close again, sinking partly below water, as evening approaches. There are usually more than 20 petals; those nearest the centre of the flower are stamens.

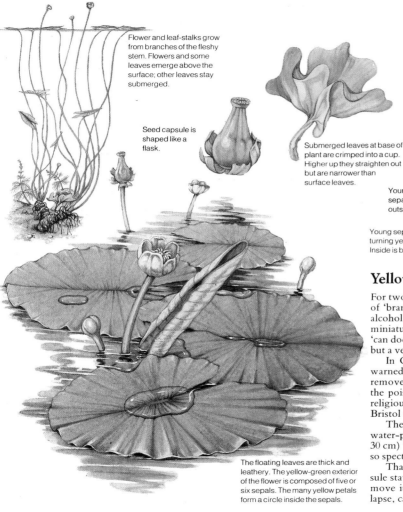

Flower and leaf-stalks grow from branches of the fleshy stem. Flowers and some leaves emerge above the surface; other leaves stay submerged.

Seed capsule is shaped like a flask.

Submerged leaves at base of plant are crimped into a cup. Higher up they straighten out but are narrower than surface leaves.

Mature flower

Young sepal, inside.

Young sepal, outside.

Young sepals are green on outside, turning yellowish-green later. Inside is bright yellow.

The floating leaves are thick and leathery. The yellow-green exterior of the flower is composed of five or six sepals. The many yellow petals form a circle inside the sepals.

The yellow water-lily is a plant of still and slow-flowing water, found in water-gardens as well as in the wild.

Yellow water-lily *Nuphar lutea*

For two good reasons the yellow water-lily has earned the name of 'brandy bottle' – its flowers exude a distinct aroma of stale alcohol, and its seed capsules have a remarkable resemblance to miniature bottles of spirits. In medieval days the plant was called 'can dock', for in those days can did not mean the modern tin can but a vessel of pottery or metal used to contain liquids.

In Classical times, and again in medieval France, doctors warned their patients against the yellow water-lily: they said it removed the sexual drive – it was 'the destroyer of pleasure and the poison of love'. Perhaps it was to encourage celibacy that religious stone-masons carved the flowers in the roof bosses of Bristol Cathedral and Westminster Abbey.

The yellow water-lily has the biggest leaves of any British water-plant, measuring as much as 16 in. × 12 in. (40 cm × 30 cm) with stalks up to 9 ft (2·75 m) long. The flowers are not so spectacular, being only 2–3 in. (5–7·5 cm) across.

Thanks to air bladders in its tissues, the brandy-bottle capsule stays afloat for a while, allowing moving water or birds to move it to a new flowering site. Eventually the bladders collapse, causing the seeds to sink and take root in the mud.

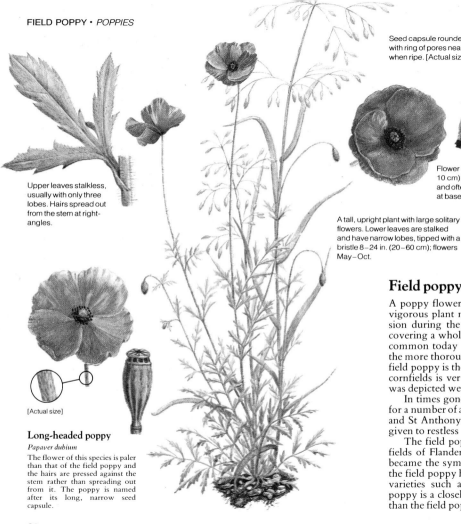

Upper leaves stalkless, usually with only three lobes. Hairs spread out from the stem at right-angles.

Seed capsule rounded, with ring of pores near top when ripe. [Actual size]

Flower 3–4 in. (7·5–10 cm); petals overlap and often have blotch at base.

A tall, upright plant with large solitary flowers. Lower leaves are stalked and have narrow lobes, tipped with a bristle 8–24 in. (20–60 cm); flowers May–Oct.

Field poppies add colour to roadsides and the edges of cornfields in most of the British Isles, except for the far north.

[Actual size]

Long-headed poppy

Papaver dubium

The flower of this species is paler than that of the field poppy and the hairs are pressed against the stem rather than spreading out from it. The poppy is named after its long, narrow seed capsule.

Field poppy *Papaver rhoeas*

A poppy flower sheds its petals after only a single day – but a vigorous plant may produce more than 400 flowers in succession during the summer. The once-familiar sight of poppies covering a whole cornfield with a blaze of red is, however, less common today because of the use of selective weedkillers and the more thorough cleaning of seed corn. Another name for the field poppy is the corn rose, and the association of poppies with cornfields is very ancient: Ceres, the Roman goddess of corn, was depicted wearing a wreath of field poppies.

In times gone by, parts of the poppy were used as remedies for a number of ailments including various aches and pains, gout and St Anthony's fire. A syrup produced from the petals was given to restless infants to make them sleep.

The field poppy was probably the species that grew on the fields of Flanders after the battles of the First World War and became the symbol of Remembrance Day. Colour variants of the field poppy have been cultivated to produce familiar garden varieties such as the Shirley poppy, while the long-headed poppy is a closely related wild species that grows further north than the field poppy.

Flower ¾–2¼ in. (2–5·5 cm); petals, dark at base, do not overlap at edges.

Seed capsule oblong, with thick ridges and few bristles. [Actual size]

A smaller, less-upright plant than field poppy. Leaves near the base have stalks and narrow lobes, tipped with a bristle. Hairs are pressed close to the stem. 6–20 in. (15–50 cm); flowers May–July.

Upper leaves stalkless, with longer, narrower lobes.

The pale poppy is a common weed of cultivated ground, especially on sandy soils in southern England.

[Actual size]

Bristly poppy

Papaver hybridum

The seed capsule of this species differs from that of the pale poppy in two respects: it is globe-shaped, and it is covered with stiff yellow bristles.

Pale poppy *Papaver argemone*

Of the many varieties of poppy that spring up in disturbed or ploughed soil, the pale poppy is the earliest to flower. Where poppies survive in cornfields, the pale poppy is more likely to be seen among barley on sandy soils, while the field poppy prefers the heavier soils on which wheat and oats are grown. The rarer bristly poppy, *Papaver hybridum*, is largely confined to soils on chalk or limestone in southern and eastern England.

The poppy's unusual seed capsule acts like a pepper-pot, shedding seeds as the stem is shaken by the wind. These seeds can lie dormant in the soil for many years, germinating only when the soil is turned over. Like all poppies, the pale poppy exudes a sticky latex from cuts in the stem, leaves and fruits. This contains various alkaloids that have been used in small quantities in herbal remedies. Because these alkaloids are poisonous and grazing animals are wary of them, poppies often survive where other plants have been eaten.

In folklore, a poppy petal was used as a test of faithfulness in love: the petal was placed in the palm of the hand and struck with the fist, and if it produced a snapping sound it indicated that the loved one was faithful.

The big, globe-shaped capsule has a characteristic fluted cap. [Half actual size]

A very upright plant; the leaves are broad, with shallow-toothed lobes and short stalks. Flowers are very big, up to 7 in. (18 cm) across. 12–36 in. (30–90 cm); flowers June–Aug.

The leaves are bluish, the upper ones stalkless and clasping the stem. [Half actual size]

Petals sometimes have dark markings at the base.

Although it grows in the wild all over Britain, this poppy has usually escaped from gardens or fields where it was cultivated.

Opium poppy *Papaver somniferum*

Despite its association with drug addiction, the opium poppy is an old friend of mankind and has long been grown as a valuable farming plant. It was known, for instance, to the Stone Age lake-dwellers of Switzerland, who probably grew it as a food. Even today the seeds of the opium poppy, which are not narcotic, are baked into bread and cakes, particularly in central Europe. The seeds are also crushed for the oil they contain, which is used as a salad dressing, for cooking, for burning in lamps and in the manufacture of paint, varnish and soap.

The opium poppy was once widely cultivated in parts of Britain, and plants found growing wild nowadays are usually remnants of old crops or escapes from gardens. The large, showy flowers make it a popular ornamental plant.

Only very occasionally is the variety that is used for making narcotics found growing wild in Britain. Opium and the other pain-killing drug codeine are extracted from it. Morphine and heroin are derivatives of opium. Because of the narcotics it contains, the plant was named *somniferum*, after Somnus, the Roman god of sleep. The word opium comes from the Greek and has the prosaic meaning of 'vegetable juice'.

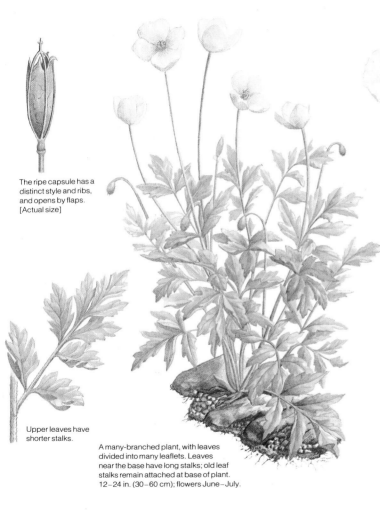

The ripe capsule has a distinct style and ribs, and opens by flaps. [Actual size]

Upper leaves have shorter stalks.

A many-branched plant, with leaves divided into many leaflets. Leaves near the base have long stalks; old leaf stalks remain attached at base of plant. 12–24 in. (30–60 cm); flowers June–July.

Flower is yellow, and lacks dark blotches.

This poppy is found in damp, shaded woods and rocky places, mainly in Wales and south-western England.

Welsh poppy *Meconopsis cambrica*

The yellow Welsh poppy, which can still be found in damp woods and rocky places of the Welsh uplands, has been taken from its native habitat and cultivated as a garden flower over much of Britain. However, it frequently escapes from custody and grows wild again, often close to the gardens where it was tended, but sometimes further afield under hedges or on wasteland.

The Welsh poppy was never exclusive to Wales: it is also a native of south-western England, western Ireland, France, Spain and Portugal. But it was first identified in Wales and classified by Linnaeus, the great 18th-century Swedish botanist, as *Papaver cambricum* (literally 'Welsh poppy'). A later botanist decided that it differed slightly from other poppies because its seed-pod released seed through slits and not through the familiar pepper-pot head of the opium and field varieties. The new name he gave it, *Meconopsis*, means 'looking like a poppy' in Greek.

This poppy's closest relatives are natives of the world's highest mountains in Tibet; one *Meconopsis* has been found at 19,000 ft on Mount Everest. The spectacular blue poppy is one of these Himalayan species brought to Britain for gardens.

33

The seed capsule is very long and thin.

Upper leaves have less-prominent lobes than lower leaves, and clasp the stem. [Actual size]

The lowest leaves are stalked and hairy, with toothed lobes. 12–36 in. (30–90 cm); flowers June–Oct.

The ripe capsule splits, leaving the seeds embedded in the wall.

The horned poppy adds colour to shingle banks all round the coast of Britain, except in northern Scotland.

Horned poppy *Glaucium flavum*

Of all British seashore plants, yellow horned poppy is by far the most colourful, bearing bright yellow flowers about 3 in. (7·5 cm) across. In the autumn the flowers are succeeded by long narrow seed-pods, sometimes reaching 12 in. (30 cm) in length and resembling the pods of some members of the cabbage family rather than those of cornfield poppies. The sap is orange-coloured and smells foul. In Britain the plant grows on the coasts, preferring shingle beds, although it will grow on sand and cliff tops. It is a native of Europe and western Asia.

The horned poppy used to be in demand for its medical properties, and in Hampshire was known as squatmore: in Old English, a *squat* was a bruise and *more* meant a root. However, it is a dangerous plant to handle, for all parts of it are poisonous and if eaten it can affect the brain.

Old records preserve a curious story about the horned poppy, dating from 1698. A man made himself a pie of horned poppy roots under the impression that they were the roots of sea holly. After eating the pie he became delirious and fancied that his white porcelain chamber pot was solid gold. He broke the pot into bits in the belief that he owned great treasure.

Seeds are black with a white appendage. [× 6]

The flowers, less than an inch across, grow in clusters.

The stems are leafy; the leaves have rounded leaflets, the terminal one usually being three-lobed. 12–36 in. (30–90 cm); flowers May–Sept.

The slender seed capsules split from the bottom upwards. [Actual size]

Leaves are almost hairless and blue-green beneath.

This plant of hedgerows, banks and walls is common all over the British Isles except northern Scotland.

Greater celandine *Chelidonium majus*

Orange-coloured sap from the greater celandine has been used in Asia for burning away warts and corns since the early days of Chinese civilisation. At great risk to the sight of the patient, this caustic liquid was also prescribed for removing soreness and cloudiness from the eyes.

The origins of the name of celandine were described in the 1st century BC by Pedanius Dioscorides, who travelled widely as a surgeon with the Roman Army. He said the name, derived from the Greek word for the swallow, might be linked with the plant's flowering time, which coincided with the arrival of the swallows; alternatively it could stem from the belief that mother swallows used the sap to restore the sight of their blinded young.

Greater celandine is not related to the lesser celandine but is a member of the poppy family, although an unusual one; with its yellow flowers and long seed-pods, it looks more like some members of the cabbage family. It shares with hellebores the use of an oil gland on its seeds to ensure that they are carried far afield. Snails feed on hellebore seed-oil and take away the seed stuck to their bodies. In the case of greater celandine, it is ants which feed on the oil and carry off the seeds.

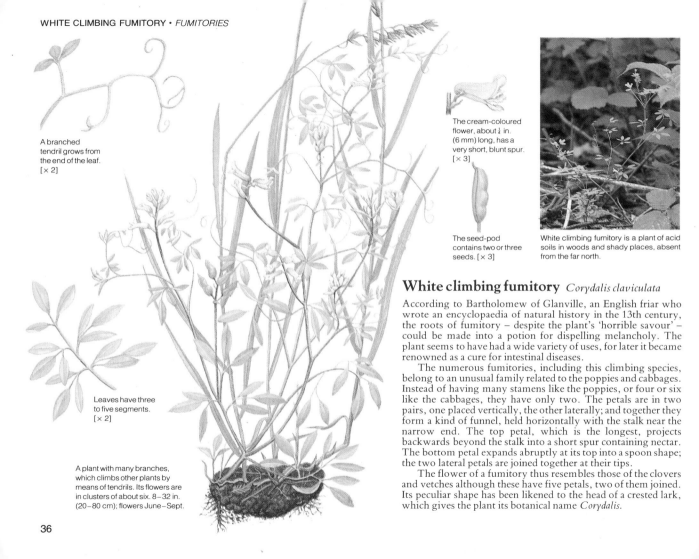

A branched tendril grows from the end of the leaf. [× 2]

Leaves have three to five segments. [× 2]

A plant with many branches, which climbs other plants by means of tendrils. Its flowers are in clusters of about six. 8–32 in. (20–80 cm); flowers June–Sept.

The cream-coloured flower, about ¼ in. (6 mm) long, has a very short, blunt spur. [× 3]

The seed-pod contains two or three seeds. [× 3]

White climbing fumitory is a plant of acid soils in woods and shady places, absent from the far north.

White climbing fumitory *Corydalis claviculata*

According to Bartholomew of Glanville, an English friar who wrote an encyclopaedia of natural history in the 13th century, the roots of fumitory – despite the plant's 'horrible savour' – could be made into a potion for dispelling melancholy. The plant seems to have had a wide variety of uses, for later it became renowned as a cure for intestinal diseases.

The numerous fumitories, including this climbing species, belong to an unusual family related to the poppies and cabbages. Instead of having many stamens like the poppies, or four or six like the cabbages, they have only two. The petals are in two pairs, one placed vertically, the other laterally; and together they form a kind of funnel, held horizontally with the stalk near the narrow end. The top petal, which is the longest, projects backwards beyond the stalk into a short spur containing nectar. The bottom petal expands abruptly at its top into a spoon shape; the two lateral petals are joined together at their tips.

The flower of a fumitory thus resembles those of the clovers and vetches although these have five petals, two of them joined. Its peculiar shape has been likened to the head of a crested lark, which gives the plant its botanical name *Corydalis*.

The long, slender leaves are deeply divided. The segments are flat.

Flowers are pink, with dark-tipped petals. [× 2]

The fruit is a globe-shaped nutlet containing one seed. [× 2]

The common fumitory grows on cultivated ground and by roadsides all over the British Isles, especially in the east.

Common fumitory *Fumaria officinalis*

Fumitories are such odd little plants that they are rarely confused with any others. One curiosity is that they provide nectar for insects in the short spur at the back of each flower; but apparently the nectar is not attractive, for insects seem to ignore it, and the flowers usually pollinate themselves. The fumitories are plants of arable, bare and disturbed sites, and are familiar cornfield weeds throughout the country.

The name of fumitory is derived from a medieval Latin word meaning 'smoke of the earth'. Pulling a fumitory from the ground demonstrates one good reason for this description, as the roots give off an acrid, gaseous smell recalling the fumes of nitric acid; this is the origin of the North American name for the plant, 'fume-root'. The name is also descriptive of the way the plant spreads its bluish-green foliage over the surface of the soil in the manner of dispersing smoke. Lastly, if the sap is allowed to get into the eyes, it will make them water as if they were affected by smoke.

Ramping fumitory is more common in the western parts of Britain than common fumitory. It has flowers less than two-fifths of an inch (1 cm) long, and its bottom petal is narrower.

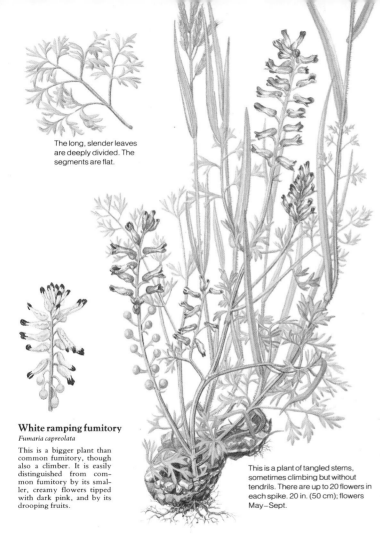

White ramping fumitory
Fumaria capreolata

This is a bigger plant than common fumitory, though also a climber. It is easily distinguished from common fumitory by its smaller, creamy flowers tipped with dark pink, and by its drooping fruits.

This is a plant of tangled stems, sometimes climbing but without tendrils. There are up to 20 flowers in each spike. 20 in. (50 cm); flowers May–Sept.

37

YELLOW-FLOWERED CABBAGES

Because of their four-petalled, cross-shaped flowers, plants of the cabbage family are known as crucifers. Their long seed-pods are divided by a thin wall down the centre. This chart identifies six of the most easily confused yellow-flowered crucifers.

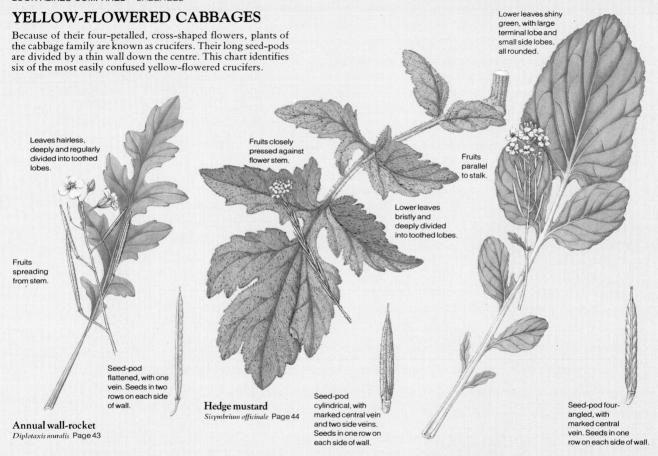

Lower leaves shiny green, with large terminal lobe and small side lobes, all rounded.

Leaves hairless, deeply and regularly divided into toothed lobes.

Fruits closely pressed against flower stem.

Fruits parallel to stalk.

Lower leaves bristly and deeply divided into toothed lobes.

Fruits spreading from stem.

Seed-pod flattened, with one vein. Seeds in two rows on each side of wall.

Hedge mustard
Sisymbrium officinale Page 44

Seed-pod cylindrical, with marked central vein and two side veins. Seeds in one row on each side of wall.

Annual wall-rocket
Diplotaxis muralis Page 43

Seed-pod four-angled, with marked central vein. Seeds in one row on each side of wall.

Common winter-cress
Barbarea vulgaris Page 46

Leaves grey-green, roughly hairy, with large toothed terminal lobe and much smaller lateral lobes.

Leaves hairless and deeply divided into regular lobes.

Fruits widely spreading from stem.

Fruits spreading from stem.

Charlock
Sinapsis arvensis Page 42

Seed-pod cylindrical with three to five veins and large beak. Seeds in one row on each side of wall.

Seed-pod short and oblong. Seeds in more than one row on each side of wall.

Marsh yellow-cress
Rorippa islandica Page 45

Fruits closely flattened against stem.

Leaves grass-green and hairless, with large terminal lobe and smaller lateral lobes, all toothed.

Black mustard
Brassica nigra Page 41

Seed-pod cylindrical, with marked central vein. Row of seeds each side of wall.

Seeds are round to oval in shape. [× 2]

Fruit has up to eight seeds in the 'waisted' and jointed pod.

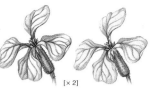

[× 2]

Petals are lilac, yellow or white, with dark veins.

Stems are rough and hairy. Each leaf has up to four pairs of widely spaced leaflets. The plant is shown growing with poppies. 8–24 in. (20–60 cm); flowers May–Sept.

Wild radish is common throughout England, where it can be a nuisance on arable land, but is rarer in Scotland.

[× 2]

Sea radish

Raphanus raphanistrum ssp. *maritimus*

Each leaf of this rarer seaside sub-species has numerous leaflets, crowded and overlapping. The fruit usually has two or no more than three seeds. Flowers are yellow, except in the Channel Islands, where they are white.

Wild radish *Raphanus raphanistrum*

By any name this persistent annual is one of the most irksome weeds of arable land: it is detested by northern farmers under the name of 'runch', while southern farmers curse it as 'cadlock' or 'white charlock'. The name white charlock is appropriate only in south-east England, where the flowers are white. Further north and west, they are usually lilac with dark veins on the petals, while in the Isle of Man, the Hebrides and northern Scotland they are bright yellow.

Although not an ancestor of the garden radish, wild radish is a relative, as can be clearly seen on the rare occasions when the garden radish is allowed to flower and produce seed-pods very similar to those of the wild radish. Those pods are distinctive and rather curious, even for this eccentric plant family. About 2 in. (5 cm) long, they contain up to eight roundish seeds. Between each seed, the pod is constricted and jointed, resembling a string of beads. As it ripens, each seed, together with its own portion of the pod, breaks off and falls to the ground.

Sea radish is a coastal plant confined to the drift-line and cliffs all round the British Isles. Its seed-pods do not readily break up when ripe, as those of the wild radish do.

The four yellow petals are twice as long as the sepals. [× 2]

The long seed-pods hug the stem.

The pods grow upright with a short beak. [× 2]

Rounded seed is dark brown in colour. [× 5]

An upright plant with stalked leaves, bristly at the base of the plant, smooth and narrow higher up. It is often seen growing with poppies. 24–36 in. (60–90 cm); flowers from May onwards.

Black mustard is still cultivated in some areas. Elsewhere it has become a weed of waysides and waste places.

Black mustard *Brassica nigra*

Black mustard was being used as a condiment more than 2,000 years ago, and the Roman author Columella, writing in the 1st century AD, spoke of eating the leaves of the plant pickled in vinegar. In France, it was not until the 13th century that cooks began to grind up the peppery seeds and mix them with must (partly fermented grape-juice), to make *moût-ardent* (burning must), or *moutarde* as it soon became known.

Black mustard and the milder white mustard are still grown to make the condiment in France, but British manufacturers found that the seed of rape, a related plant, produced a mustard more to the liking of their customers. It is this crop that now paints great splashes of yellow across the countryside in early summer, while fields of black mustard are rarer.

The plant is called 'black' mustard because its seeds are brownish-black outside; when ground up they make the familiar yellow powder and sauce. This has long been one of the most popular folk remedies for all sorts of ailments. Well into this century, people with colds used to soak their feet in hot mustard baths, and mustard poultices are still used to relieve muscular pains and chest ailments.

The sepals spread out horizontally below the yellow flower. [× 2]

[× 5]

Seeds grow in two separate rows, one in each half of pod. The round seeds are a dark red-brown.

A roughly hairy plant; pods are held away from the stem. The plant is shown growing with poppies and the oval-leaved sun spurge. 6–18 in. (15–45 cm); flowers May–July.

The seed-pod is cylindrical, with a long beak. [Actual size]

This common and persistent weed of arable land is found on field margins, roadsides and wasteland all over Britain.

Charlock *Sinapis arvensis*

The golden glow of charlock covering a young cornfield may stir the heart of a visitor to the countryside. But the only emotion it is likely to arouse in the farmer is fury; for this dogged, choking weed is one of the most ancient pests of arable land, especially when crops are spring-sown. The seed output of a single charlock plant is prodigious, and to add to its menace, it is extremely long-lived. Seeds brought to the surface after 11 years have been shown to grow quite freely, and there are records of 50-year-old pastures being ploughed up and turning into a yellow sea of charlock – the only possible assumption being that the seeds had been buried half a century earlier, when the corn fields in which they had grown were allowed to revert to grassland.

Today charlock appears to be succumbing to selective weed-killers, but farmers still do not know for certain that the enemy of their ancestors has finally been defeated.

Like many plants which are now treated only as weeds, charlock was once used as a food. Early in the 18th century it was sold on the streets of Dublin for use as a boiled vegetable, and in the Hebrides this use persisted many years later.

Petals are twice as long as the sepals, which spread slightly.

The fruit makes an angle with the shorter, spreading stalk.

The annual wall-rocket is common in southern England, but rarer in northern England, Wales and Scotland.

[× 10]

The fruit is cylindrical, with a short, slender beak. Each fruit contains two rows of yellow-brown seeds.

A plant with unbranched stems and lobed leaves that form a rosette at the base. It is shown growing with ragwort and grass. 6–24 in. (15–60 cm); flowers May–Sept.

Annual wall-rocket *Diplotaxis muralis*

Crush a stem of annual wall-rocket in the hand, and the juices will give off vile-smelling sulphuretted hydrogen – the 'rotten eggs' chemical used by schoolboys in stink-bombs. It is one of only two members of the cabbage family with this disagreeable trait; hence its alternative name of 'stinkweed'. In fact, stinkweed is a more accurate name than annual wall-rocket, since the plant can be either annual or biennial. In spite of the name, however, the flowers of the plant exude fragrance. This attracts bees and other insects, which fertilise the flowers in summer.

Although widespread in Britain, the plant is usually confined to waste and disturbed ground, especially where there is sandy soil, and it is rarer in the north. Sometimes it may be found growing on old walls, a habit shared with the perennial wallrocket, a related plant with the same unpleasant smell.

Annual wall-rocket is the smaller of the two, with a rosette of lobed leaves at the base of the stem, and narrow, cylindrical seed-pods, held out on long stalks at an angle with the stem. Perennial wall-rocket is much taller and bushier, with larger flowers. It has no rosette at the stem base, but leaves appear in a thick cluster higher up the stem and below the flower spike.

43

Seeds are orange-brown, roughly oval. [× 10]

Fruits are ribbed and hairy, each with a short beak. They overlap, pressed closely against the stem.

Flower-heads elongate as the fruits form.

Flowers are small, with petals less than twice as long as the sepals.

Flowering stalks branch widely from a rigid, bristly stem. It is shown growing with poppies. 12–36 in. (30–90 cm); flowers May–Sept.

Hedge mustard is widespread in Britain on waste ground and arable land, at roadsides or in hedgebanks.

Hedge mustard *Sisymbrium officinale*

In the 16th century, Guillaume Rondelet of Montpellier claimed to have given a choirboy the voice of an angel by the use of hedge mustard. Since then, French actors, politicians and singers have employed infusions of this plant as a gargle and medicine to improve their vocal performance. The dramatist Racine advised Boileau, the 17th-century man of letters, to take hedge mustard when he lost his voice. Because of the pungent taste, the concoction was flavoured with liquorice or scented honey.

In Britain, hedge mustard did not enjoy such renown. Although piquant, it does not possess the powerful flavour of ordinary mustard, and in the kitchen it was usually reserved for making a sauce served with salt fish. However, the sap was mixed into a syrup with honey or treacle as a cure for asthma.

Hedge mustard is common all over Britain and can be recognised by its branches protruding almost at right-angles to the stem, while its seed-pods grow erect and are hugged against the stem. The flower-head is at first rather flat-topped with tiny, yellow flowers opening around the edge. As the plant grows older, the stalk lengthens, the flowers which opened first are left at the bottom, and the latest appear at the top.

Petals are the same length as the sepals. [× 5]

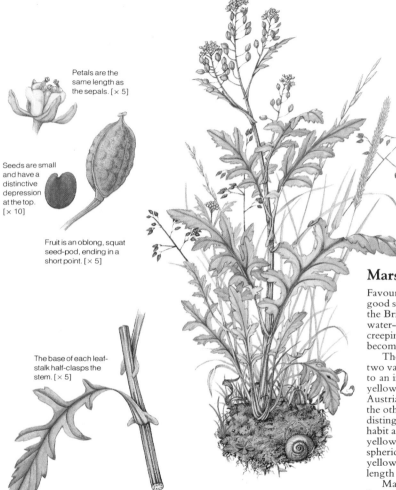

Seeds are small and have a distinctive depression at the top. [× 10]

Fruit is an oblong, squat seed-pod, ending in a short point. [× 5]

The base of each leaf-stalk half-clasps the stem. [× 5]

An erect plant with a hollow stem and strongly lobed leaves. The lower leaves are stalked, but the upper ones may be stalkless. 10–24 in. (25–60 cm); flowers June–Sept.

Marsh yellow-cress is found on pond sides and river banks throughout the British Isles, occasionally in drier places.

Marsh yellow-cress *Rorippa islandica*

Favouring a site that is under water in winter but dries out in a good summer, marsh yellow-cress is not surprisingly a native of the British Isles. It can be found on river banks, sand-banks and water-meadows subject to occasional flooding. Like the related creeping yellow-cress, alongside which it often grows, it can become a nuisance in gardens, particularly in damp spots.

The plant is a relative of the white-flowered watercresses, two varieties of which are sold as salad food; but it belongs itself to an inedible group with yellow flowers. Three other sorts of yellow-cress are to be found in Britain. One of these, the Austrian yellow-cress, is only occasionally seen near ports, but the other two are quite common. Creeping yellow-cress can be distinguished from the marsh species by its more sprawling habit and by its much longer and thinner seed-pods; and greater yellow-cress has petals of a deeper yellow shade and almost spherical seed-pods on stalks at least twice their length. Marsh yellow-cress has oblong seed-pods on stalks of about the same length as the pods.

Marsh yellow-cress is also known as Iceland watercress, from its botanical name. It is visited by flies and small bees.

45

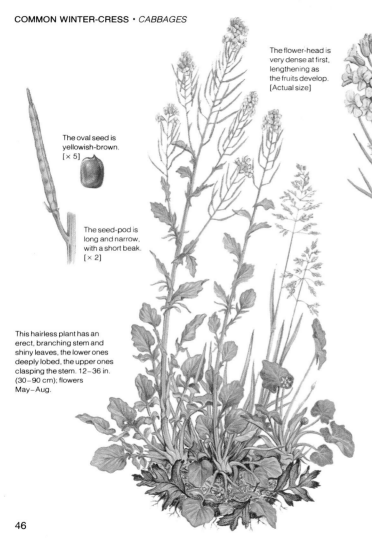

The flower-head is very dense at first, lengthening as the fruits develop. [Actual size]

The oval seed is yellowish-brown. [× 5]

The seed-pod is long and narrow, with a short beak. [× 2]

Petals are about twice as long as the sepals. [× 2]

This hairless plant has an erect, branching stem and shiny leaves, the lower ones deeply lobed, the upper ones clasping the stem. 12–36 in. (30–90 cm); flowers May–Aug.

This cress is common in hedges and beside streams and other damp places in much of Britain; it is rarer in Scotland.

Common winter-cress *Barbarea vulgaris*

Saint Barbara is the patron saint of gunners, miners and quarry-men – all vulnerable to danger from explosives – and winter-cress was dedicated to her because its leaves were widely used in covering and healing their wounds. As if in recognition of this honour, the plant is always bright and green on St Barbara's Day, December 4, when most other growth is brown and withered. In France the plant is known as *barbarée*; and the connection with the saint is maintained in the botanical name.

The leaves of winter-cress, shiny and green, resemble those of watercress and in the past were often eaten in salads, providing a rich source of vitamin C. But their rather bitter taste put them out of fashion, and in Britain they have been superseded by new varieties of watercress. However, in some parts of the world, including Sweden and North America, winter-cress is still eaten.

Winter-cress is not to be confused with the white-flowered winter-cress of commerce, a form of watercress. To make this distinction clear, it is sometimes known as land cress, an appropriate name since it is as much a plant of waysides and hedgerows as it is of streamsides and ditches.

A plant with at least one erect, branched leafy stem. The bottom leaves are stalked, the upper ones stalkless. It is shown growing with poppies. 6–36 in. (15–90 cm); flowers June–Aug.

The petals of the flower are roughly twice as long as the sepals. [× 2]

[× 10]　[× 2]

The fruit is square in cross-section, and downy; the seeds are pale brown.

Treacle mustard is found both on cultivated and waste ground. It is common in southern England, but rarer in the north.

Treacle mustard *Erysimum cheiranthoides*

In the 16th century, herbalists recommended the use of the treacle mustard plant as a remedy for insect and animal bites, and to counteract poisons. That is the source of its common name, for 'treacle' is a corruption of the ancient Greek word *theriaki*, meaning an antidote to poisonous bites. The plant was reputedly effective on its own, but its healing powers were increased when it was made into Venice treacle, a concoction that included several other herbs. The seeds of the treacle mustard were also given to children to drive out intestinal worms: hence its alternative name of wormseed mustard.

Treacle mustard is a close relative of the Siberian wallflower, planted in many British gardens. It is more distantly related to the ordinary wallflower which, although it is not a native, grows wild in some parts of the country, particularly along the cliffs near Dover in Kent.

At first glance, treacle mustard resembles several other yellow-flowered plants – for example, the charlock or stinkweed. But its leaves are smooth edged or have shallow teeth and its seed-pods look square when cut across. The young flowerhead is flat-topped, with the flowers in a neat ring.

Wallflower
Cheiranthus cheiri

This introduced species can be distinguished from treacle mustard by its fruit, which is round in cross-section, and hairy.

47

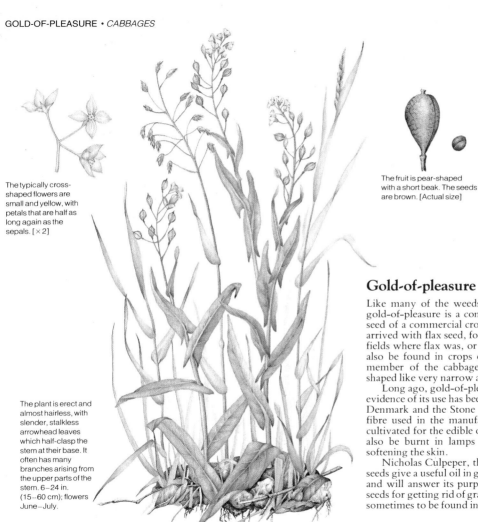

The typically cross-shaped flowers are small and yellow, with petals that are half as long again as the sepals. [× 2]

The plant is erect and almost hairless, with slender, stalkless arrowhead leaves which half-clasp the stem at their base. It often has many branches arising from the upper parts of the stem. 6–24 in. (15–60 cm); flowers June–July.

The fruit is pear-shaped with a short beak. The seeds are brown. [Actual size]

Rubbish dumps and crop fields are the habitats of gold-of-pleasure. It occurs sporadically throughout Britain.

Gold-of-pleasure *Camelina sativa*

Like many of the weeds of Britain's cornfields and gardens, gold-of-pleasure is a continental invader, brought in with the seed of a commercial crop. It is probable that gold-of-pleasure arrived with flax seed, for it is found growing wild mainly near fields where flax was, or still is, cultivated. Occasionally it can also be found in crops of lucerne and corn. Unusually for a member of the cabbage family, gold-of-pleasure has leaves shaped like very narrow arrowheads, which clasp the stem.

Long ago, gold-of-pleasure was itself widely cultivated, and evidence of its use has been found dating back to the Iron Age in Denmark and the Stone Age in Hungary. It produces a tough fibre used in the manufacture of brushes, but it was mainly cultivated for the edible oil extracted from its seeds. This could also be burnt in lamps or used cosmetically as a means of softening the skin.

Nicholas Culpeper, the 17th-century herbalist, wrote: 'The seeds give a useful oil in great quantity, little inferior to olive oil, and will answer its purpose very well.' He recommended the seeds for getting rid of gravel in the kidneys. Nowadays they are sometimes to be found in bird-seed mixtures.

PALE-FLOWERED CABBAGES

Many members of the cabbage family have very similar, small white or near-white flowers. Four of the commonest can be distinguished from one another by examining the leaves and the shape of the seed-pod, and looking to see if the plant is hairy.

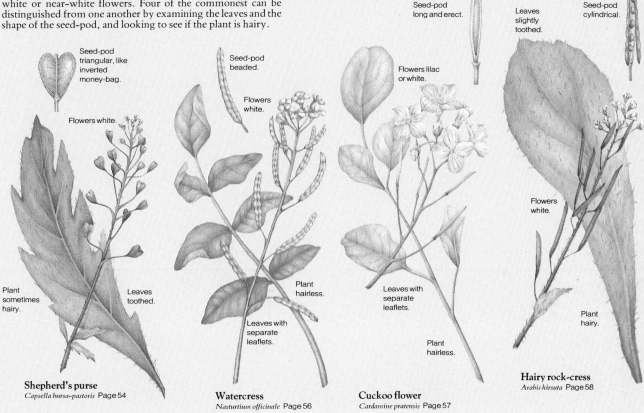

Seed-pod triangular, like inverted money-bag.

Flowers white.

Plant sometimes hairy.

Leaves toothed.

Seed-pod beaded.

Flowers white.

Plant hairless.

Leaves with separate leaflets.

Seed-pod long and erect.

Flowers lilac or white.

Leaves with separate leaflets.

Plant hairless.

Leaves slightly toothed.

Seed-pod cylindrical.

Flowers white.

Plant hairy.

Shepherd's purse
Capsella bursa-pastoris Page 54

Watercress
Nasturtium officinale Page 56

Cuckoo flower
Cardamine pratensis Page 57

Hairy rock-cress
Arabis hirsuta Page 58

49

[Actual size]

[× 2]

Fruit is stubby with short, thick stalk, and contains one or two smooth, yellow-brown seeds.

Flowers are purple, lilac or white, with petals twice as long as sepals. [Actual size]

Sea rocket is widespread on the higher levels of sandy and shingle beaches in all parts of the British Isles.

A bushy, untidy, hairless plant with a branched stem and fleshy, lobed, shiny leaves. The buoyant fruit is dispersed by tides and sea currents. 6–12 in. (15–30 cm); flowers June–Aug.

Sea rocket *Cakile maritima*

In company with prickly saltwort, sea rocket can form a narrow but distinct line of vegetation along the top of a beach. It prefers the drift line of a sandy beach, but occasionally may be found on dunes, or even on shingle. The drift line is one of the least appealing parts of a beach, often marked by driftwood, seaweed and litter. Its rather dismal aspect, not helped by the presence of unattractive saltworts and sometimes oraches, is relieved only by the bright white, pink or pale lilac flowers of sea rocket.

The leaves, fleshy and succulent, conserve every drop of fresh water that the roots can find. Sea rocket can tolerate being buried by sand, and its creeping roots and prostrate stems sometimes accumulate sand around them, forming miniature dunes. The plant is, however, only an annual; it regenerates itself with the help of the tide, which carries the seeds away and throws them up again elsewhere.

Of the four kinds of sea rocket that grow world-wide, three occur on seashores, but the fourth is found only in the central Arabian Desert. This suggests that the two habitats have much in common. Certainly both desert and drift line are as a rule desperately short of fresh water.

Front view Side view

Fruit is oval and smooth, with a pronounced beak at the top. [×3]

Stems are upright, often branched from the ground. Stem leaves are narrowly triangular, without stalks. The plant is seen growing among curled dock, dandelion and grass. 6–36 in. (15–90 cm); flowers May–Aug.

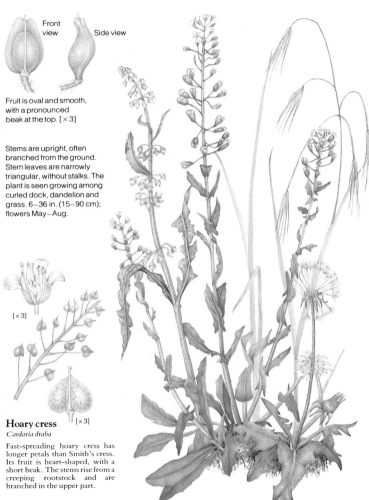

[×3]

Hoary cress [×3]
Cardaria draba

Fast-spreading hoary cress has longer petals than Smith's cress. Its fruit is heart-shaped, with a short beak. The stems rise from a creeping rootstock and are branched in the upper part.

White petals are half as long again as the sepals. The stamens have violet anthers. [×5]

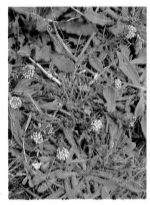

Smith's cress grows in arable fields, on dry banks and by roads and paths in England, Wales and southern Scotland.

Smith's cress *Lepidium heterophyllum*

Sir William Hooker, the first director of the Royal Botanic Gardens at Kew, gave this plant its alternative botanical name of *Lepidium smithii* – Smith's cress – in honour of the British botanist Sir James Edward Smith (1759–1828). It is, in fact, a plant of many names, for it is also known as 'Smith's pepperwort' and 'hairy pepperwort', being similar in appearance to the pepperworts, which belong to the same group of plants.

The pepperworts are so called because some of them have a peppery taste. Some members of the group have been cultivated, among them garden cress (the cress of 'mustard and cress') and dittander, which was once grown as a condiment; but Smith's cress is a weed of arable land.

Hoary cress, too, is a weed of ploughed fields, rapidly spreading and troublesome. According to one story it was brought to Britain in the hay used to stuff the mattresses of British soldiers wounded in the Walcheren campaign of 1809. It is said to have been dumped in a Kentish field and ploughed in by a farmer, from whose land it eventually spread throughout Britain. At one time its seeds were ground as a substitute for pepper, hence its alternative name of hoary pepperwort.

Fruits have a wart-like surface and are broader than they are long, with short stalks. Each fruit contains only one or two seeds, which are small and pear-shaped. [× 5]

Each tiny white flower has four petals that are longer than the sepals. They grow in clusters opposite a leaf. [× 5]

Swine-cress is found on waste ground and well-trodden places throughout southern Britain, but it is rarer in the north.

Slender wart-cress
Coronopus didymus

Leaves of this related species are more deeply divided than those of swine-cress. The plant is hairy, and the petals of its flowers are shorter than the sepals, or sometimes absent. The fruit has a notch at the top, and is shorter than its stalk.

A greyish, low-growing, hairless plant, with small, finely divided leaves. 2–12 in. (5–30 cm); flowers June–Sept.

Swine-cress *Coronopus squamatus*

To judge from this plant's various English names – swine-cress, hog-cress and sow-cress – it would seem to be associated with pigs. But there is no evidence that the animals are particularly fond of it – even though it grows in areas in which they might grub around for food. It is more probable that the name is derogatory. The plant was once used in salads as a substitute for watercress and, with its inferior taste, it was thought to be fit only for pigs.

Although swine-cress is a relative of the garden wallflower, it is unlike that plant in almost every respect. The only clue to their relationship lies in the arrangement of the flower parts – especially the four petals arranged in a cross. Swine-cress is a low-growing plant with finely divided, greyish leaves. Its flowers are borne in small clusters in the angle formed by the stem and the leaf-stalk. Its alternative name, wart-cress, comes from the tiny, rounded fruits which have a wart-like surface.

Swine-cress is native to Britain, but slender wart-cress was introduced from South America. It is just as widespread – particularly in the south of England – and also grows on waste ground and trampled places.

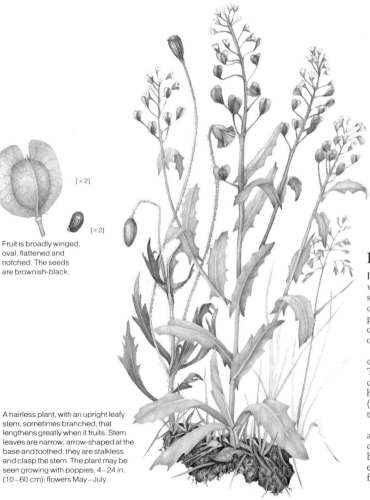

The four white petals of the tiny flower are twice as long as the sepals. Flowers are stalked and grow in clusters at the tops of stems. [×2]

Fruit is broadly winged, oval, flattened and notched. The seeds are brownish-black. [×2] [×2]

The ripe yellow fruit of field penny-cress make a bright display on wasteland throughout most of Britain.

A hairless plant, with an upright leafy stem, sometimes branched, that lengthens greatly when it fruits. Stem leaves are narrow, arrow-shaped at the base and toothed; they are stalkless and clasp the stem. The plant may be seen growing with poppies. 4–24 in. (10–60 cm); flowers May–July.

Field penny-cress *Thlaspi arvense*

In Britain, this weed got its name from the shape of its fruits, which were thought to resemble a penny. It is, in fact, closer in size to the new penny than to the old one after which it was called. In Germany, the weed is called *feld pfennigkraut* (field pennywort) – after the *pfennig*, a copper coin worth one hundredth of a mark – and in France it is called *monnoyère*, from the old French word *monnoie*, 'money'.

Among the four penny-cresses found in Britain, field penny-cress is the only one that has a circular, or almost circular, fruit. The other three plants – perfoliate penny-cress, alpine penny-cress and garlic penny-cress – have fruits that are either round or heart-shaped. The fruit of the field penny-cress is about ½–¾ in. (1–2 cm) in diameter. It is flat, broad-winged and has a notch at the top.

The seeds of field penny-cress probably came to Britain as an accidental accompaniment to seeds for field crops. When crushed, the plant has a strong, unpleasant smell and is avoided by herb-eating animals. Vigorous efforts have been made to exterminate the field penny-cress on agricultural land, but it still flourishes abundantly.

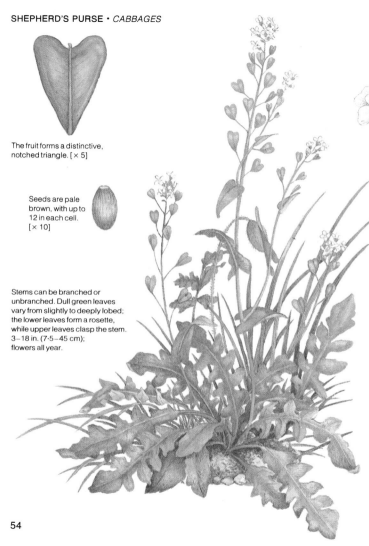

The fruit forms a distinctive, notched triangle. [× 5]

Seeds are pale brown, with up to 12 in each cell. [× 10]

Stems can be branched or unbranched. Dull green leaves vary from slightly to deeply lobed; the lower leaves form a rosette, while upper leaves clasp the stem. 3–18 in. (7·5–45 cm); flowers all year.

Small, white flowers cluster at tip of stem; petals are up to twice as long as sepals. [× 5]

This persistent weed grows on wasteland and in fields and gardens over much of the world, including Britain.

Shepherd's purse *Capsella bursa-pastoris*

In 1657 William Coles wrote of this plant in his book *Adam in Eden*: 'It is called Shepheard purse or Scrip [wallet] from the likeness the seed hath with that kind of leathearne bag, wherein Shepherds carry their Victualls into the field.' In Dutch paintings of that period town and country folk can be seen with just such bags slung from a belt round their jerkins. If the seed-pods of the plant are picked when ripe, the seeds tumble out – again suggesting a purse, this time with coins in it.

The alternative name of 'mother's heart' given to the plant in parts of England and Scotland derives from a trick played by children both in Britain and on the Continent. An unwitting child would be asked to pluck a seed-pod, and when it broke open, he would be accused of breaking his mother's heart.

Shepherd's purse is a remarkably successful weed, growing throughout Europe and much of the rest of the world, even as far north as Greenland. There are few British gardeners who do not have to cope with its persistent invasion of flower beds, paths and drives. Although visited by small insects, it is self-pollinated and, because of this, distinctive variations tend to establish themselves in particular localities.

The small flowers are white or lilac. [× 2]

The plant is hairless, with long-stalked, fleshy leaves. The leaves are heart-shaped or kidney-shaped, and the lower ones form a loose rosette. It is shown growing alongside thrift and sea campion. 4–20 in. (10–50 cm); flowers May–Aug.

English scurvygrass
Cochlearia anglica

This species has slightly toothed leaves. The flowers are white or pale mauve and bigger than those of common scurvygrass.

Seed-pods are globe-shaped. [× 2]

The rounded seeds are reddish-brown. [× 5]

Common scurvygrass grows on sea-cliffs, shores and salt-marshes around the British Isles, but rarely grows inland.

Common scurvygrass *Cochlearia officinalis*

Scurvy is a disease caused by prolonged deficiency of vitamin C, usually obtained from salads, fresh fruit and vegetables. In the days of sailing ships, when sea voyages often lasted for months, sailors were often afflicted with scurvy through their prolonged diet of salt pork and dried biscuit. They had to endure eruptions of the skin all over the body, extreme tenderness of the gums, swollen limbs and foul breath. Scurvy was prevalent even on land, because of dietary deficiencies. Herbalists were triumphant, therefore, when they discovered that scurvygrass, which has a high content of vitamin C, prevented the disease.

To be effective, vitamin C treatment must be regularly maintained. In 17th-century England it became the fashion to take a glass of scurvygrass water every morning, just as many people drink orange juice for the same purpose today. The leaves were also made into a beer called scurvygrass ale.

The second half of the name of scurvygrass is a misnomer: the plant is in fact a member of the cabbage family and not a grass. English scurvygrass is an equally rich source of vitamin C, but it did not grow so well and had to be gathered by hand from marshes along the Thames estuary.

55

White petals are nearly twice as long as sepals. [× 2]

The oval seeds are covered with small depressions. [× 10]

Fruits are cylindrical and slightly pinched around each seed. [× 2]

Watercress is cultivated in beds in shallow rivers. It also grows wild in lowland streams and ditches and on mud.

Watercress is a hairless, creeping water plant with hollow stems. Leaves are divided into many leaflets, which stay green all year. 4–15 in. (10–38 cm); flowers May–Oct.

Watercress *Nasturtium officinale*

The sharp flavour of watercress has earned it the name of 'tang-tongue' in Yorkshire, while its pungent aroma provides the generic name of *Nasturtium*, from the Latin *nasi tortium*, 'nose-twisting'. Few plants are richer than watercress in vitamin C; as long ago as the mid-17th century the herbalist Nicholas Culpeper described the plant as 'powerful against the scurvy and to cleanse the blood and humours'.

It was not until 1808 that commercial cultivation of watercress began – at first in Kent, but soon spreading around London. No improved strains have been developed, and the plants grown commercially are identical to those found wild in streams and ditches throughout Britain. So wild watercress can safely be eaten, provided care is taken not to pick plants growing in stagnant water or streams flowing through pasture-land; lying in such places may be the eggs of the liver fluke, a parasitic flat-worm that destroys the livers of sheep and can also find a home in man.

Surprisingly, the older shoots of watercress, with a slight burnish on their leaves, make the best eating – young shoots tend to be rather tasteless.

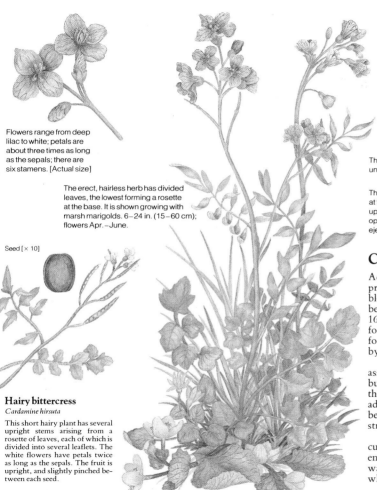

Flowers range from deep lilac to white; petals are about three times as long as the sepals; there are six stamens. [Actual size]

The erect, hairless herb has divided leaves, the lowest forming a rosette at the base. It is shown growing with marsh marigolds. 6–24 in. (15–60 cm); flowers Apr.–June.

Seed [× 10]

Hairy bittercress
Cardamine hirsuta

This short hairy plant has several upright stems arising from a rosette of leaves, each of which is divided into several leaflets. The white flowers have petals twice as long as the sepals. The fruit is upright, and slightly pinched between each seed.

The seed is unwinged. [× 5]

The fruit has a short beak at the top, and stands upright on a long stalk. It opens explosively to eject seed. [Actual size]

Cuckoo flower is a pretty wild flower, common in damp pastures and by streams throughout the British Isles.

Cuckoo flower *Cardamine pratensis*

According to John Gerard, the 16th-century herbalist, this pretty springtime flower was called cuckoo flower because it blooms 'for the most part in April and May, when the Cuckoo begins to sing her pleasant note without stammering'. Another 16th-century explanation relates the name to 'cuckoo-spit', the foamy substance with which the plant is often covered. This foam has actually nothing to do with cuckoos, but is produced by the nymphs of a bug called the frog hopper.

The spring blooming of cuckoo flower has led to folklore associations with milkmaids, their smocks and the Virgin Mary, but there are other, less pleasant associations. In Austria it was thought that anyone who picked the plant would be bitten by an adder before the year was out; and in Germany some people believed that bringing it indoors would cause the house to be struck by lightning.

Probably because of its more sinister connections in folklore, cuckoo flower was little used in medicine. It is, in fact, safe enough; the leaves may be eaten in salads as a substitute for watercress, as may those of hairy bittercress, a close relative which grows on waste ground.

57

The white petals are twice as long as the sepals. [× 2]

This erect, usually unbranched, hairy plant has a long spike of flowers. Lower leaves form a rosette; the stalkless upper leaves clasp the stem. 6–24 in. (15–60 cm); flowers June–Aug.

[× 2]

Common wall cress

Arabidopsis thaliana

This plant, also hairy and white-flowered, has slightly toothed, narrow leaves which do not clasp the stem. Fruits are stiff and stand out from the stem.

The slightly winged seed is reddish brown. [× 10]

The fruits are cylindrical, and pressed close to the stem. [× 2]

Hairy rock-cress grows throughout the British Isles on chalk slopes, dunes, hedgebanks, walls and rocks.

Hairy rock-cress *Arabis hirsuta*

Hairy rock-cress hides a world of fascinating fine detail under a humdrum appearance. At first sight, this undistinguished-looking plant, so widespread in Britain's hills and fields, seems hardly worth another look; but take a powerful magnifying glass to the stems and leaves of *Arabis hirsuta*, and a forest of tiny hairs springs into focus. The same is true of some other members of the *Arabis* genus, for though only this species bears the name *hirsuta*, meaning 'hairy', its relatives can be hairy as well.

The shapes of the hairs vary amazingly from species to species. Those of hairy rock-cress are stiff and forking, like the frame of a child's catapult; charlock has simple, single-stemmed hairs; on dame's violet the two types are mingled. The hairs of other plants have three, four or more points; those of one – treacle mustard – actually lie flat, being anchored in the middle.

Common wall cress, like hairy rock-cress, grows on walls and sandy soils in Britain. One of its peculiarities is that when the pods are ripe they are likely to burst on being touched. This scatters the seeds far afield. An alternative name for common wall cress is thale cress, from the German botanist Johannes Thal, who described it in the 16th century.

Fruits are ribbed, cylindrical pods, curving at the base. [× 2]

This erect, usually unbranched plant has stalked leaves, hairy on the underside. The lower leaves are heart shaped and form a rosette; upper leaves are triangular. 8–48 in. (20–120 cm); flowers Apr.–June.

The white petals are about twice as long as the sepals. [× 2]

The horn-shaped seed is almost black. [× 5]

Garlic mustard is a common plant in shady wood margins, hedgerows and alongside walls throughout Britain.

Garlic mustard *Alliaria petiolata*

Garlic mustard is the only British member of the cabbage family to give off the unmistakable, pungent smell of garlic. All the other plants that smell like it, such as leeks, onions and garlic itself, are members of an entirely unrelated family, that of the lily (*Allium*). The scientific names for both genera are derived from the Latin word for garlic.

An alternative name for garlic mustard is hedge garlic, and it also has many colourful folk-names. 'Jack-by-the-hedge' obviously alludes to its habitat, while 'poor man's mustard' indicates its culinary uses. Like many of the wild cabbage family garlic mustard makes a tasty condiment. In the 17th century it was recommended as a flavouring for salt fish. It can also be made into a sauce for eating with roast lamb, or salad.

All parts of the plant, including the roots, give off a strong odour. The small white flowers have a rather unpleasant aroma which attracts midges and hoverflies, although the flowers usually pollinate themselves. In June the pale green caterpillar of the orange tip butterfly (*Anthocharis cardamines*) can be found feeding on the long green seed-pods, from which it can hardly be distinguished.

59

The upright, hairless stem has few if any branches. Flowers are in a spike, and the lower leaves are narrow, arranged round the stem in a rosette. The upper or stem leaves are oblong, with wavy edges. Weld is shown growing with grasses and a poppy. 20–60 in. (50–152 cm); flowers June–Aug.

[Actual size]

Wild mignonette
Reseda lutea

This plant is shorter than weld, growing only 12–24 in. (30–60 cm) tall, and has a more branched stem. It has divided leaves, and flowers with six sepals and six divided petals.

The yellow-green flower has four sepals and four divided petals.

Seeds are dark brown, smooth and shiny. [× 2]

The fruit is ovoid or globular in shape, and upright. It is divided into three or more sharply pointed lobes. [× 2]

Weld flourishes on open ground, especially on chalk. It is found throughout Britain, though it is rare in the north.

Weld *Reseda luteola*

Weld was one of the ancient trio of plants used by medieval dyers – woad for blue, madder for red and weld for yellow. All three had, in fact, been used long before the Middle Ages, and weld was a dye known in Stone Age Switzerland. When crushed and soaked in water, it yields a liquor which produces a brilliant, pure and fast colour in wool and other fabrics. Although it is a native British plant, the demand from the fast-growing English woollen industry in medieval times was so great that weld had to be imported from France; it took 3–6 lb of weld plants to colour 1 lb of cloth.

Eventually, cultivation developed in Britain on a large scale; the plant was grown in Kent, Essex and Yorkshire until recent times, continuing to compete for many years with the new chemical dyes. Nowadays weld is an outcast in waysides, wasteland, field margins, walls and limestone quarries.

Seen from a distance, weld is an impressive plant, up to 5 ft (1·5 m) tall. It has the curious property of being what scientists call heliotropic – that is, it moves with the sun. When the flowers open in the morning, they face east, but by the late afternoon they have turned west.

The fruit is
very flat. [× 2]

The stems have many
branches and are woody
at the base. All leaves
alternate up stem. The
plant is shown growing with
the pinkish-purple flowers
of wild thyme, and tall tufts
of quaking grass.
2–4 in. (5–10 cm); flowers
May–Sept.

The flower has three
tiny green outer sepals
and two big, bluish
inner sepals, which all
but conceal the tube of
the petals. [× 2]

Petals are usually longer
than the coloured sepals
and joined together, the
lower one fringed. [× 2]

Common milkwort grows on heaths,
dunes and grasslands. Flowers may be
blue, mauve, pink or white.

Heath milkwort
Polygala serpyllifolia

A smaller plant than common
milkwort; the lower leaves are
opposite and the bluish sepals are
longer than the petals.

Common milkwort *Polygala vulgaris*

According to Classical and Renaissance writers on the medicinal
properties of plants, an infusion of milkwort was supposed to
increase the flow of a nursing mother's milk. Only common
milkwort ever has white flowers, but both it and the related
heath milkwort can have pink, mauve or blue flowers. These
four possible colours account for the milkworts' Irish folk-name
of 'four sisters'.

They are abundant plants but few people take the trouble to
examine them closely. This is a pity, for their flowers are among
the most unusual in Britain. A flower's sepals are normally
small, green and insignificant, but the two inner sepals of
milkwort are much larger than the three outer ones, and are
brightly coloured – most often blue, but also pink or white. In
common milkwort, the inner sepals are usually shorter than the
petals, but in the heath milkwort they are longer.

Inside the flower there is more to reward the close observer.
The stalks of the eight stamens are joined together to form a
tube, and united with this tube, one on either side, are two tiny
petals. On the lower side of the flower lies the third petal; it, too,
is joined to the stamen tube, but it is larger, and fringed.

The flowers are bluish-violet or white; the spur is lilac or pale violet. [Actual size]

The fruit is a rounded hairy capsule, remaining closed until after it has fallen to the ground. [Actual size]

Creeping runners grow from the rosette and root.

At the base of each hairy leaf-stalk is a pair of leaf-like stipules, fringed with gland-tipped hairs. [× 2]

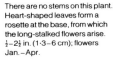

There are no stems on this plant. Heart-shaped leaves form a rosette at the base, from which the long-stalked flowers arise. ½–2½ in. (1·3–6 cm); flowers Jan.–Apr.

White-flowered sweet violets also grow in hedges and planted woodland over most of the British Isles.

Sweet violet *Viola odorata*

The heady fragrance of sweet violet has been the scent of love for thousands of years. As the flower of Aphrodite, goddess of love, it so enraptured the Greeks that they made it the symbol of Athens. The oil distilled from its petals is used today to make scent, toiletries and flavourings – even a very sweet liqueur called *parfait amour*.

In less sanitary days the flowers were strewn on the floors of cottages and churches to sweeten the air and conceal the musty smell of damp – even though the scent of sweet violet is lost almost as soon as it is detected. It was, indeed, this very property that made it so effective: the flower produces with the scent a substance called ionine, which quickly dulls the sense of smell, so that not only does the scent of violets vanish, but other odours too. This can be proved by sniffing the flower until the scent is lost, then holding it away for a moment before sniffing again: the scent will return until the ionine does its job once more.

The sweet violet is the easiest to recognise of all British violets – and there are about nine species, excluding those commonly called pansies. It is also the only violet to have scented flowers.

The flowers are usually blue-violet, with a much paler spur. [Actual size]

At the base of each hairless leaf-stalk is a pair of leaf-like stipules, with long, slender teeth on their margins. [× 2]

The triangular seed capsule opens to shed its seeds before falling from the plant. [Actual size]

This violet has leafy flowering stems and no runners. The long-stalked leaves are heart-shaped, those at the base of the stem forming a rosette. 1–8 in. (2·5–20 cm); flowers May–June.

The common dog violet grows in woods, hedges, pastures, heaths and rocky areas throughout the British Isles.

Heath dog violet
Viola canina

Although resembling common dog violet, this plant has less markedly heart-shaped leaves and no basal leaf rosette. The stipules have fewer, shorter teeth and the flower usually has a yellowish spur. It grows on heaths and fens all over Britain.

Common dog violet *Viola riviniana*

To country folk there are only two kinds of violet: the scented sweet violet and the scentless dog violet. Dog, in this context, is a derogatory term that is often used for wild flowers to distinguish an inferior form from relatives that are superior in some way. Other examples are dog rose (a rose which is not cultivated in gardens), dog's mercury (the useless relative of annual mercury, which was a folk medicine) and dogwood (a shrub with berries that are not fit to be eaten).

Dog violet as a traditional English name for the flower dates only from the 16th century, when the herbalist John Gerard translated it from the Latin, *Viola canina*. In fact this was a name devised by the Swedish naturalist Linneaus not for the dog violet most common in Britain, but for the the heath dog violet. This is common in Sweden, but in Britain is less usual than *Viola riviniana*.

Common dog violet closely resembles pale wood violet (*Viola reichenbachiana*) which, however, has lilac petals and a darker spur and is common in the south and east of England. Unscented violets have a variety of local folk-names, including 'blue mice', 'pig violet' and 'shoes and stockings'.

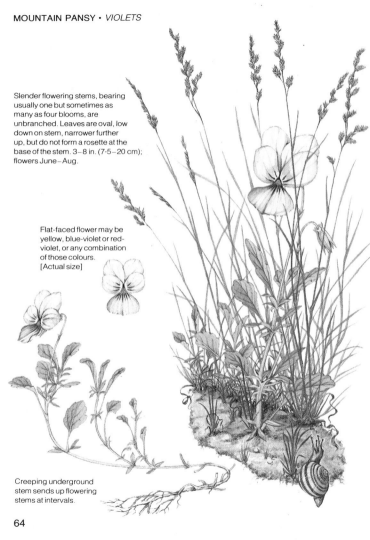

Slender flowering stems, bearing usually one but sometimes as many as four blooms, are unbranched. Leaves are oval, low down on stem, narrower further up, but do not form a rosette at the base of the stem. 3–8 in. (7·5–20 cm); flowers June–Aug.

Flat-faced flower may be yellow, blue-violet or red-violet, or any combination of those colours. [Actual size]

Creeping underground stem sends up flowering stems at intervals.

Leaf-like stipules at base of leaf-stalk are divided into slender lobes.

Fruit capsule splits into three parts to release ripe seeds. [Actual size]

Mountain pansy favours grassy areas or rock ledges in hill country, from Wales and the Midlands northwards.

Mountain pansy *Viola lutea*

Although the flowers of the mountain pansy show the same kind of colour variations as the wild pansy, the two are not likely to be confused. The mountain pansy, as its name implies, shows a marked preference for upland homes, usually on lime-rich soils: it is found in every county north of a line from the River Severn to the Humber.

Another distinction between the two plants is that while the different colour variations of the wild pansy grow together, each colour of the mountain pansy predominates in a different area. Thus in Derbyshire and Yorkshire the yellow type is commonest, but in upper Teesdale and in Scotland – especially on Ben Lawers – the purple form is dominant.

At one time, garden pansies were forms of wild pansy bred and selected for size of flower and variety of colour. Today's garden pansies, however, were derived from a cross between the wild and mountain pansies and probably a third, foreign pansy. The mountain pansy in its pure form has always been a failure when planted in gardens. As long ago as the 16th century, the herbalist John Gerard complained of the difficulties encountered in cultivating the mountain plant.

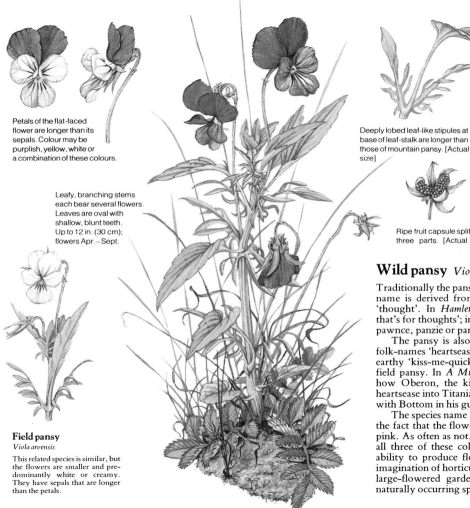

Petals of the flat-faced flower are longer than its sepals. Colour may be purplish, yellow, white or a combination of these colours.

Leafy, branching stems each bear several flowers. Leaves are oval with shallow, blunt teeth. Up to 12 in. (30 cm); flowers Apr.–Sept.

Deeply lobed leaf-like stipules at base of leaf-stalk are longer than those of mountain pansy. [Actual size]

Ripe fruit capsule splits into three parts. [Actual size]

Wild pansy grows readily throughout Britain on cultivated and waste ground, short grassland or coastal dunes.

Field pansy
Viola arvensis

This related species is similar, but the flowers are smaller and predominantly white or creamy. They have sepals that are longer than the petals.

Wild pansy *Viola tricolor*

Traditionally the pansy is a symbol of remembrance: its English name is derived from its French name, *pensée*, which means 'thought'. In *Hamlet*, Shakespeare wrote: 'There is pansies, that's for thoughts'; in the playwright's time the name was spelt pawnce, panzie or pancye.

The pansy is also associated with love, accounting for the folk-names 'heartsease', 'love-in-idleness', and the rather more earthy 'kiss-me-quick', which the wild pansy shares with the field pansy. In *A Midsummer Night's Dream*, Shakespeare told how Oberon, the king of the fairies, squeezed the juice of heartsease into Titania's eyes in order to induce her to fall in love with Bottom in his guise as an ass.

The species name *tricolor* means three-coloured, and refers to the fact that the flowers may be yellow, violet-blue or (rarely) pink. As often as not, however, a combination of two, or even all three of these colours may be found in one flower. This ability to produce flowers of various colours has caught the imagination of horticulturists, who have produced the familiar, large-flowered garden pansies by means of hybridising the naturally occurring species.

Flower's outer sepals are tiny compared with the inner ones.

Leaf has dense white hairs on the underside and leaf-like stipules at the stalkless base.

Hairy casing of globe-shaped fruit splits into three teeth.

Branches sprawl from a woody base, often taking root to form new plants. It is shown growing with grass and bird's-foot-trefoil. 2–12 in. (5–30 cm); flowers June–Sept.

The common rock-rose grows on scrub, rocky places and grassland in most of England, Wales and southern Scotland.

Common rock-rose *Helianthemum chamaecistus*

Thoughtless people who tear up armfuls of wild flowers from the fields and hedgerows will be wasting their time in picking the attractive rock-roses. They have no scent, and almost as soon as they are gathered their thin, delicate petals fall off.

This plant not only lacks fragrance: it also lacks nectar. Insects visit the flower, however, to gather the abundant pollen, some of which is brushed off on the next flower they visit. But if this lure fails to entice the insects, the rock-rose has recourse to another device. In wet weather and at night it closes its petals, so pushing the pollen-covered stamens onto its own style, thus ensuring self-pollination.

The rock-rose is not a rose and does not much resemble one with its yellow flowers and densely hairy leaves. Its generic name of *Helianthemum*, meaning 'sunflower', can also be mis-leading; it was probably given because the flowers open only in the sunlight. Usually the flowers are a uniform buttercup col-our, but there are several variations including sulphur-yellow and white, and some forms with orange spots at the base of each petal. Garden rock-roses, developed by hybridisation of various wild kinds, are even more varied in colour.

Young fruits are red and fleshy. [Actual size]

Ripe fruit is black. [Actual size]

Petals are as long as the sepals; there are numerous stamens. [Actual size]

A shrub-like, branched and semi-evergreen plant, with large stalkless leaves and few flowers in each cluster. 16–40 in. (40–100 cm); flowers June–Aug.

Rose of Sharon
Hypericum calycinum

This species is a low-growing plant with very large, solitary flowers. It is commonly planted in gardens.

A native flower, the tutsan grows in damp parts of woods and hedges throughout the British Isles, but is rare in the north.

Tutsan *Hypericum androsaemum*

Before the age of modern medicine, leaves of tutsan were laid across flesh wounds to help them to heal. The plant has genuine antiseptic properties. It derives its name from the Anglo-Norman *tutsaine* (*toute-saine* in modern French) meaning 'all-wholesome' or 'all-healthy'.

Owing to confusion with the shrub *Agnus castus*, tutsan acquired another reputation in the Middle Ages – that of inducing chastity in members of both sexes. Men in pursuit of this virtue would drink infusions of the plant and women would spread twigs of it under their beds.

When fresh, the leaves of tutsan have no particular smell, but a day or so after drying and for four years or so thereafter they emit a subtle, pleasant odour, which is likened to that of ambergris, the costly scent-base found in the intestines of certain sperm whales. Because of this aroma, tutsan is also known as sweet amber. Its dried leaves have been used as scented bookmarks, particularly in prayer books and Bibles. Like the rose of Sharon, the other shrubby St John's-wort common in Britain, the tutsan is easily recognised by its many prominent stamens bristling like pins in a pin-cushion.

67

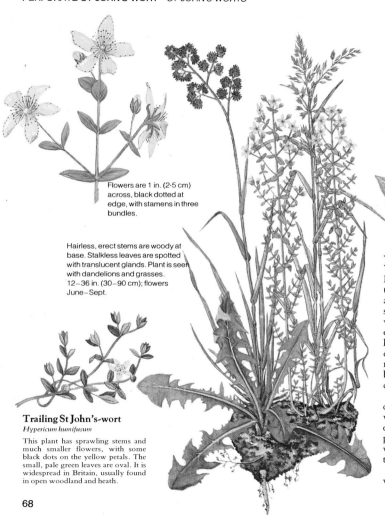

Flowers are 1 in. (2·5 cm) across, black dotted at edge, with stamens in three bundles.

Hairless, erect stems are woody at base. Stalkless leaves are spotted with translucent glands. Plant is seen with dandelions and grasses. 12–36 in. (30–90 cm); flowers June–Sept.

Trailing St John's-wort
Hypericum humifusum

This plant has sprawling stems and much smaller flowers, with some black dots on the yellow petals. The small, pale green leaves are oval. It is widespread in Britain, usually found in open woodland and heath.

The fruit is a three-celled capsule surrounded by the withered remains of the flower. [× 5]

[× 10]

The stem has two narrow wings running along its length.

Perforate St John's-wort is common on grassland, hedgebanks and open woods in Britain, especially on chalky soils.

Perforate St John's-wort *Hypericum perforatum*

During the Crusades, the Knights of St John of Jerusalem used this St John's-wort to heal the wounds of Crusaders. This was in accordance with the so-called 'doctrine of signatures', which said that a plant could cure the ailments of the part of the body which it resembled. But perforate St John's-wort does not outwardly resemble any part of the anatomy: its supposed magic lies in the fact that when a leaf is held up to the light it is seen to be covered with translucent glands resembling punctures, which medieval folk saw as 'wounds'. According to the doctrine, because the leaf appeared to be punctured it was capable of curing wounds – especially those received in battle.

Perforate St John's-wort was also esteemed for its power to drive away devils and evil spirits. In medieval times, the plant was hung in windows and doorways to prevent Satan and his emissaries from entering. If a woman thought herself to be possessed by a devil, and when Christian prayers had failed to work, all she had to do to free herself was to place leaves from the plant on her bosom and strew them throughout her home.

Unlike the perforate St John's-wort, the trailing St John's-wort does not flourish in lime-rich soil.

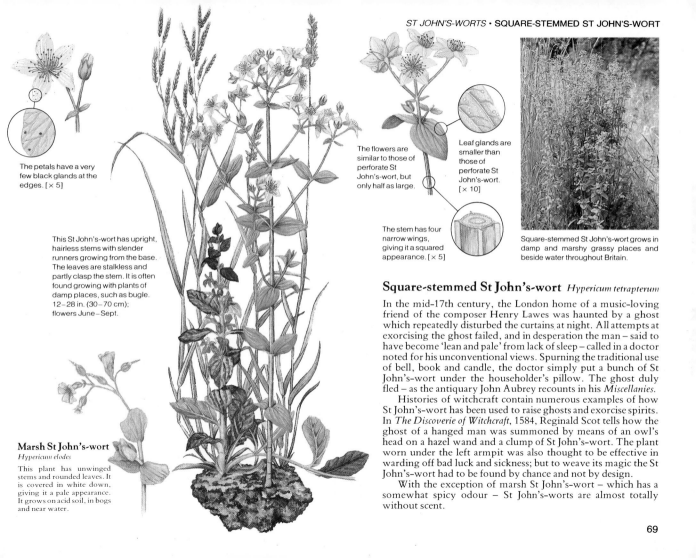

The petals have a very few black glands at the edges. [× 5]

This St John's-wort has upright, hairless stems with slender runners growing from the base. The leaves are stalkless and partly clasp the stem. It is often found growing with plants of damp places, such as bugle. 12–28 in. (30–70 cm); flowers June–Sept.

The flowers are similar to those of perforate St John's-wort, but only half as large.

Leaf glands are smaller than those of perforate St John's-wort. [× 10]

The stem has four narrow wings, giving it a squared appearance. [× 5]

Square-stemmed St John's-wort grows in damp and marshy grassy places and beside water throughout Britain.

Marsh St John's-wort
Hypericum elodes

This plant has unwinged stems and rounded leaves. It is covered in white down, giving it a pale appearance. It grows on acid soil, in bogs and near water.

Square-stemmed St John's-wort *Hypericum tetrapterum*

In the mid-17th century, the London home of a music-loving friend of the composer Henry Lawes was haunted by a ghost which repeatedly disturbed the curtains at night. All attempts at exorcising the ghost failed, and in desperation the man – said to have become 'lean and pale' from lack of sleep – called in a doctor noted for his unconventional views. Spurning the traditional use of bell, book and candle, the doctor simply put a bunch of St John's-wort under the householder's pillow. The ghost duly fled – as the antiquary John Aubrey recounts in his *Miscellanies*.

Histories of witchcraft contain numerous examples of how St John's-wort has been used to raise ghosts and exorcise spirits. In *The Discoverie of Witchcraft*, 1584, Reginald Scot tells how the ghost of a hanged man was summoned by means of an owl's head on a hazel wand and a clump of St John's-wort. The plant worn under the left armpit was also thought to be effective in warding off bad luck and sickness; but to weave its magic the St John's-wort had to be found by chance and not by design.

With the exception of marsh St John's-wort – which has a somewhat spicy odour – St John's-worts are almost totally without scent.

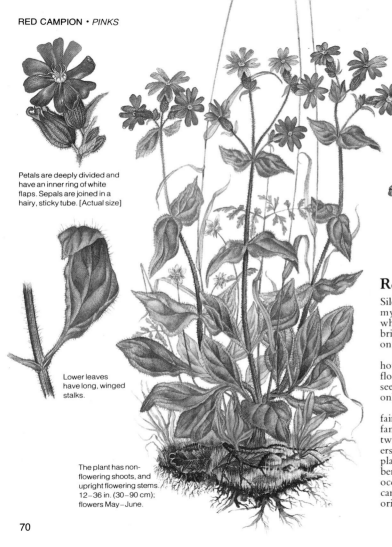

Petals are deeply divided and have an inner ring of white flaps. Sepals are joined in a hairy, sticky tube. [Actual size]

Lower leaves have long, winged stalks.

The plant has non-flowering shoots, and upright flowering stems. 12–36 in. (30–90 cm); flowers May–June.

Female flower has five styles but lacks stamens. [× 2]

Capsule is about as long as the sepals, with a broad mouth. [Actual size]

Abundant in most areas of Britain, red campion is usually found on rich soils at the edges of woods or in hedgerows.

Red campion *Silene dioica*

Silenus, the drunken, merry god of the woodlands in Greek mythology, gave his name to *Silene dioica*, the red campion, which enlivens woods and hedgerows all over Britain with its bright red flowers and even climbs mountains to establish itself on screes and cliff ledges.

The second part of its scientific name, *dioica*, means 'two houses', and refers to the fact that each red campion plant has flowers of one sex only, so that two plants are needed to make seed. Female flowers have no stamens, while male flowers have only a small, non-functioning ovary. Both are scentless.

White campion is a similar plant, although its flowers bear a faint scent at night. It grows mainly on arable land, where it is a familiar weed; but when it grows alongside red campion, the two will often hybridise, the resulting cross bearing pink flowers as might be expected. However, unlike many hybrids, the plant is completely fertile and will often hybridise with members of the parent strains. This is called back-crossing. When it occurs, all shades of colour from red through pink to pure white can be found, and it is often difficult to tell which plants are the original red and white campions.

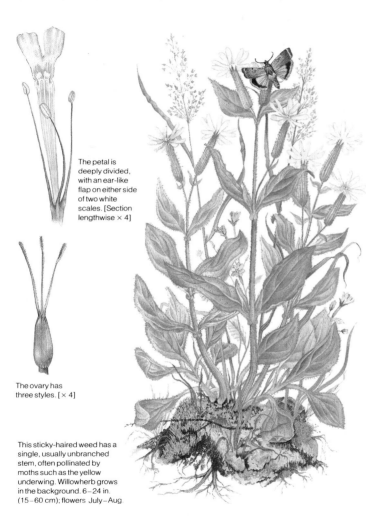

The petal is deeply divided, with an ear-like flap on either side of two white scales. [Section lengthwise × 4]

The ovary has three styles. [× 4]

This sticky-haired weed has a single, usually unbranched stem, often pollinated by moths such as the yellow underwing. Willowherb grows in the background. 6–24 in. (15–60 cm); flowers July–Aug.

Petals roll up during the day. Sepals are joined in a narrow, sticky tube. [× 2]

The capsule teeth curve back to release the seeds. [Actual size]

Night-flowering catchfly grows on arable land or among bricks and rubble, all over Britain except for the far north.

Night-flowering catchfly *Silene noctiflora*

During the heat of the day, the busy insect life of field and wasteland passes this plant by: its petals, a dull yellow-green on their undersides, are rolled up inconspicuously towards the centre of the flower. But between five and eight o'clock on a summer evening – or even earlier if the temperature falls low enough – the petals unroll to expose their rosy upper surfaces, and a sweet clover-like perfume suffuses the air.

The night-flowering catchfly is one of the very few plants in Britain that opens its flowers at dusk, and moths in particular are attracted by it. No sooner has any small night-flying insect landed on the plant than it finds itself temporarily anchored to the stem by sticky hairs. These make it certain that pollen will adhere to the insect when it goes into the flower. Although small insects often get trapped by the sticky stems, the catchfly does not eat them as the sundews do.

Although the plant has bisexual flowers, they cannot pollinate themselves because the anthers produce their pollen several days before the stigma is ready to receive it. Pollen to fertilise a flower has therefore to be brought to it from another flower by an insect or by the wind.

The six-toothed
fruit capsule is
globe shaped.
[Actual size]

Each ovary has
three long styles.
[× 2]

Stems are erect, usually hairless,
with drooping flowers on every stem.
The plant is seen growing with red
dead-nettle and grass. 10–36 in.
(25–90 cm); flowers May–Aug.

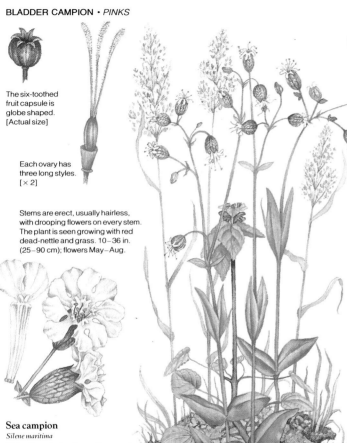

Petals are deeply
lobed and have
minute scales.
[Actual size]

Bisexual flower

Female flower

Flowers are male, female or
bisexual. Sepals are joined in a
bladder-like tube. [Actual size]

Bladder campion flourishes on both
waste and cultivated land in most parts of
the British Isles, but is rarer in the north.

Sea campion
Silene maritima

This subspecies has fewer flowers in each cluster than the bladder campion and larger scales on
its petals. It has sprawling, non-
flowering stems and grows
mainly on cliffs and shingle by
the sea.

Bladder campion *Silene vulgaris*

Bumble bees have learned to cheat the bladder campion to
extract its nectar. To ensure pollination, the plant has a particularly deep flower with the nectar as much as half an inch below
the top of the petals; as a result even long-tongued bees and night
moths have to exert themselves to reach it. But instead of
settling on the petals, bumble bees have taken to biting through
the base of the flower and drawing the nectar out through the
hole – a process which does nothing to help pollination.

In most British campions, the sepals are joined to form a
straight-sided or slightly bulging tube, but in the bladder campion this tube is inflated like a balloon, and it is this feature that
gives the plant its common name. Unlike the similar-looking
white campion, bladder campion has bisexual flowers (in addition to its rarer male flowers); but the sexes in each flower
mature at different times. Although the flowers are open day
and night, it is only in the evening that they begin to emit their
pleasant, clove-like scent.

The slightly waxy, bluish-green foliage of the bladder campion was recommended in the last century as a table vegetable,
being said to smell strongly of fresh green peas.

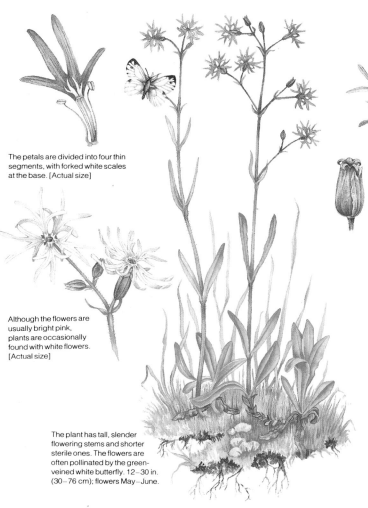

The petals are divided into four thin segments, with forked white scales at the base. [Actual size]

Although the flowers are usually bright pink, plants are occasionally found with white flowers. [Actual size]

The plant has tall, slender flowering stems and shorter sterile ones. The flowers are often pollinated by the green-veined white butterfly. 12–30 in. (30–76 cm); flowers May–June.

The reddish-brown sepals form a tube with short teeth below the flower. [Actual size]

Five short teeth bend back to open seed capsule. [× 2]

Ragged-robin brings a splash of bright pink to marshes, wet meadows and damp woodland throughout Britain.

Ragged-robin *Lychnis flos-cuculi*

To country girls of an earlier age, ragged-robin was a plant to be taken very seriously. It was one of the many British wild flowers – including the three common buttercups, marsh marigold and columbine – to be given the additional name of bachelor's buttons. West Country girls, in the 16th century, used to pick the flowers several at a time, give each the name of an unmarried local boy, and tuck them under their aprons. Whichever flower opened first was said to identify either the boy the girl should marry, or the one who wanted to marry her.

The name of bachelor's buttons has been applied to almost any plant that has double flowers, or tiny flowers gathered into tight, ball-like heads that resemble old-fashioned cloth buttons. Another name that ragged-robin shares with several other plants – such as red and white campion and greater stitchwort – is thunder flower. Children believed that if they picked the flower thunder and lightning would occur.

The genus name of *Lychnis* is Greek for rose campion, a garden flower related to ragged-robin. The species name of *flos-cuculi* is Latin for cuckoo-flower, a third name that this plant shares with other wild flowers.

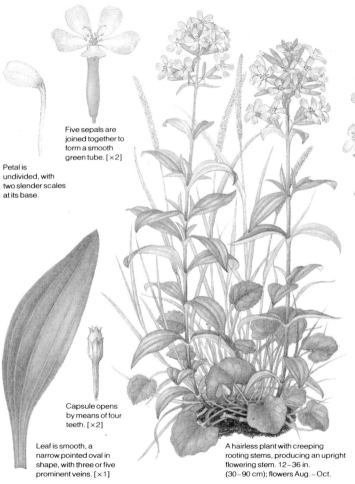

Five sepals are joined together to form a smooth green tube. [×2]

Petal is undivided, with two slender scales at its base.

Capsule opens by means of four teeth. [×2]

Leaf is smooth, a narrow pointed oval in shape, with three or five prominent veins. [×1]

A hairless plant with creeping rooting stems, producing an upright flowering stem. 12–36 in. (30–90 cm); flowers Aug.–Oct.

Flowers, pink or white, are in compact clusters. [Actual size]

This plant is common on wasteland, in hedgerows and in woods, by streams and roads or near villages.

Soapwort *Saponaria officinalis*

When bruised and boiled in water, the green parts of soapwort produce a lathery liquid, once widely used for washing wool and woollen cloth. For this purpose it was grown close to woollen mills; and much of the wild soapwort visible today, lining hedgebanks with drifts of pink, is growing near to the fields or gardens where it was once cultivated commercially. It is thought that soapwort was brought to parts of Britain in the Middle Ages from the Continent, where it was widely used in the woollen industry; but its presence by streams in the West Country, far away from human habitation, suggests that there at least it may have been a British native.

Although soapwort makes a poor substitute for modern soap, it is possible to wash with it, and some French herbalists recommend it as a shampoo for delicate hair. A poisonous substance called saponin is contained in the leaves and roots, but in spite of this, extracts of the plant have been used in many herbal remedies for gout, rheumatism and skin diseases.

Soapworts are sometimes cultivated in gardens for their showy flowers, usually pink and single but occasionally white or double. A delicate scent attracts hawkmoths.

74

Fruit is as long as sepals or longer; four teeth open to release the seed. [×2]

Lower leaves and those of non-flowering shoots are blunt.

Deptford pink
Dianthus armeria

Non-flowering shoots are absent, and flowers are in dense clusters.

A plant with non-flowering stems and upright flowering stems. The flowers form open clusters. 6–18 in. (15–45 cm); flowers June–Sept.

Petals are toothed, pink with pale spots. [×2]

Maiden pink is a local plant of dry banks and hill pastures throughout Britain, and is also grown as an ornamental flower.

Maiden pink *Dianthus deltoides*

This pretty flower seems to have got its name from its delicate colour, reminiscent of a maiden's blushes, and its coy habit of closing its petals during overcast weather. But some authors insist that the name is a corruption of 'mead-pink', a pink which grows in meadows. It does not grow very commonly today.

The common name of another fairly widespread pink, the Deptford pink (*Dianthus armeria*), is the result of confusion by early botanists. Towards the end of the 16th century the herbalist John Gerard recorded: 'There is a little, wilde creeping Pinke, which groweth in our pastures ... especially in the great field next to Detford.' From his description it is obvious that the flower he was referring to was the maiden pink; but later editions of his book printed his text with an illustration of *Dianthus armeria* and the name Deptford pink. The mistake has been perpetuated to this day.

The *Dianthus* family is represented in gardens by many different sorts of pinks, carnations and sweet williams, and maiden pink itself is available for growing as a biennial. The heavy, clove-like scent is a characteristic of these flowers, which are pollinated by butterflies and moths.

FOUR COMMON PINKS

There are two groups of pinks: the first includes pinks and campions, while the second includes chickweeds and sand-worts. Four closely similar species in the second group can be distinguished by the shape of their flowers and fruit.

Petals not notched and shorter than sepals. [× 2]

Six teeth open to release seeds. [× 2]

Petals not notched and shorter than sepals. [× 2]

Eight to ten teeth open to release seeds. [× 2]

Petals deeply notched and twice as long as sepals. [× 2]

Ten teeth on fruit open to release the seeds. [× 2]

Petals deeply notched, about as long as sepals. [× 2]

Five teeth open to release seeds. [× 2]

Thyme-leaved sandwort
Arenaria serpyllifolia Page 83

Upright chickweed
Moenchia erecta Page 80

Field mouse-ear
Cerastium arvense Page 77

Chickweed
Stellaria media Page 78

A low, hairy-stemmed plant; the non-flowering stems are sprawling and the flowering stems more upright. The leaves are narrow and lance-shaped. The plant is shown growing with hoary plantain and grass. Up to 12 in. (30 cm); flowers Apr.–Aug.

Flower is white, with petals deeply divided and twice as long as the sepals. [Actual size]

The fruit is a cylindrical capsule with ten teeth. [× 2]

This mouse-ear is widespread on dry, chalky, or slightly acid grassland, banks and waysides, except in eastern Britain.

Field mouse-ear *Cerastium arvense*

The name mouse-ear has been used to describe many British wild flowers, but their connection with mice and their ears is not at all obvious to the eye. The aptness of the description is realised, however, on touching the plants: all have short, downy hairs on their leaves, which can be likened to those on the ear of a mouse.

The first plant to which the description was applied was the mouse-ear hawkweed – a plant related to the dandelion, which was called *muos ota* (Greek for 'mouse-ear') by the Classical writer Dioscorides. Fifteen hundred years later, in the 16th century, the name mouse-ear was applied to a group of more than a dozen British plants of the genus *Cerastium*.

Another characteristic shared by all the British mouse-ears, including field mouse-ear, is a seed capsule that is longer than it is wide and that only releases seeds in dry air, so ensuring dispersal by the wind. The capsule is often curved, not unlike the horn of a cow. The Greek for horn is *keras* and this word, in its Latin form of *Cerastium*, was adopted as the botanical name of the mouse-ears. The word keratin, the horny substance of horns and hoofs and human nails, comes from the same root.

Common mouse-ear
Cerastium fontanum ssp. *triviale*

This species is similar to field mouse-ear and grows on the same dry terrain; but it has much smaller leaves, and petals and sepals the same length. [Actual size]

77

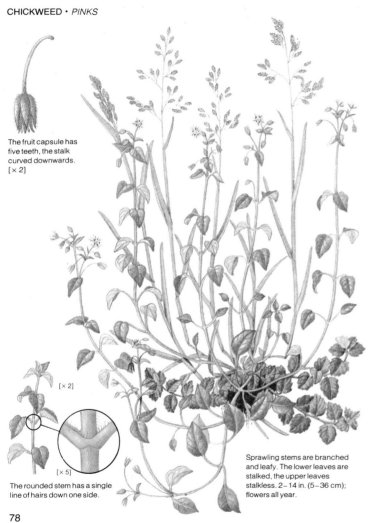

The fruit capsule has five teeth, the stalk curved downwards. [× 2]

[× 2]

[× 5]

The rounded stem has a single line of hairs down one side.

Sprawling stems are branched and leafy. The lower leaves are stalked, the upper leaves stalkless. 2–14 in. (5–36 cm); flowers all year.

The flower has deeply divided petals about the same length as the sepals, and has three to eight stamens and three styles. [Actual size]

The small, star-like flowers of chickweed are a common sight of waste and cultivated land throughout the British Isles.

Chickweed *Stellaria media*

The botanical name *Stellaria* means 'little star' – and a glance at the flower from above shows why it is so called. Each of its five tiny white petals is deeply notched, producing a star with ten points. The plant is small, with weak stems that tend to straggle along the ground. But its disarming looks are misleading, for it is a widespread and prolific weed loathed by every gardener. Part of the problem is that it flowers freely at all times of the year, producing countless tiny brown seeds.

The plant's common name is also appropriate, for chickens, goslings and cage-birds all relish its greenery and seeds. Some people hold that feeding chickweed to birds is a waste; they claim that it is the tastiest and most tender of all British wild plants that can be eaten as salad vegetables.

A curious feature of chickweed, and a ready means of identification, is the single line of hairs that runs the length of the stem. As a drop of dew settles on the stem, it runs along the line of hairs until checked by a pair of leaves. Here some of it is absorbed through the hairs, and the rest runs on down the stem to the next pair of leaves. The water absorbed is retained by the plant as a reserve against times of drought.

A straggly plant with angled stems. The shorter stems are flowerless and the longer stems bear white flowers. It often uses other plants such as grasses for support. The leaves are stalkless, narrow and long-pointed. 6–24 in. (15–60 cm); flowers Apr.–June.

Lesser stitchwort
Stellaria graminea
This species has narrower leaves and much more deeply divided petals. It is common in woods, grassland and heaths in most parts of the British Isles.

The fruit is a globe-shaped capsule on an upright stalk. [× 2]

Petals, divided for half their length, are longer than the sepals. There are ten stamens. [Actual size]

Greater stitchwort is a plant of woods and hedgerows, found all over the British Isles except the Shetlands.

Greater stitchwort *Stellaria holostea*

In common with many shade-loving plants, greater stitchwort does not last long once it has been picked. Furthermore, the stems of this attractive hedgerow flower are very weak, needing the support of surrounding vegetation to reach any height, and snap easily at the point where the leaves are attached. According to the ancient 'doctrine of signatures', if the stems snap as easily as they do in this plant, they must clearly help to heal broken bones: indeed, the Greek words *holos* and *osteon* that make up part of the botanical name mean 'whole' and 'bone'.

The common name, however, refers to a different use made of the plant – that of easing 'stitches' in the side and similar pains. A preparation of stitchwort and acorns taken in wine was the standard remedy. Although greater and lesser stitchwort often grow together throughout the British Isles, and look very much alike, lesser stitchwort was not thought to have any medicinal properties.

Along with white campion and field poppy, among many other wild plants, greater stitchwort was at one time regarded as a 'thunder flower', the picking of which was believed to provoke thunder and lightning.

The main stem is upright. Branches sprouting from base, bent at first, later become upright. It may be partially obscured by the leaves of sea bindweed and common storksbill, and overshadowed by the tall spikes of red fescue. 1–5 in. (2·5–12·5 cm); flowers Apr.–June.

Seed-pod is about same length as sepals, its opening surrounded by eight teeth. [× 2]

The pointed green sepals have white margins. Petals are undivided, and shorter than sepals.

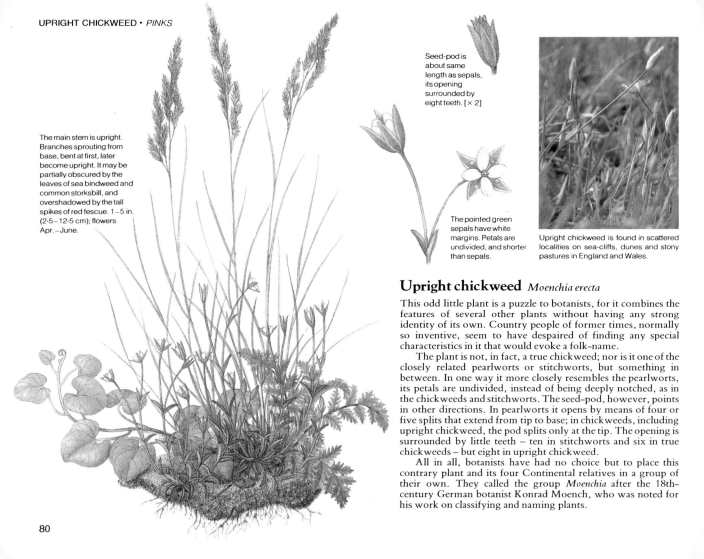

Upright chickweed is found in scattered localities on sea-cliffs, dunes and stony pastures in England and Wales.

Upright chickweed *Moenchia erecta*

This odd little plant is a puzzle to botanists, for it combines the features of several other plants without having any strong identity of its own. Country people of former times, normally so inventive, seem to have despaired of finding any special characteristics in it that would evoke a folk-name.

The plant is not, in fact, a true chickweed; nor is it one of the closely related pearlworts or stitchworts, but something in between. In one way it more closely resembles the pearlworts, its petals are undivided, instead of being deeply notched, as in the chickweeds and stitchworts. The seed-pod, however, points in other directions. In pearlworts it opens by means of four or five splits that extend from tip to base; in chickweeds, including upright chickweed, the pod splits only at the tip. The opening is surrounded by little teeth – ten in stitchworts and six in true chickweeds – but eight in upright chickweed.

All in all, botanists have had no choice but to place this contrary plant and its four Continental relatives in a group of their own. They called the group *Moenchia* after the 18th-century German botanist Konrad Moench, who was noted for his work on classifying and naming plants.

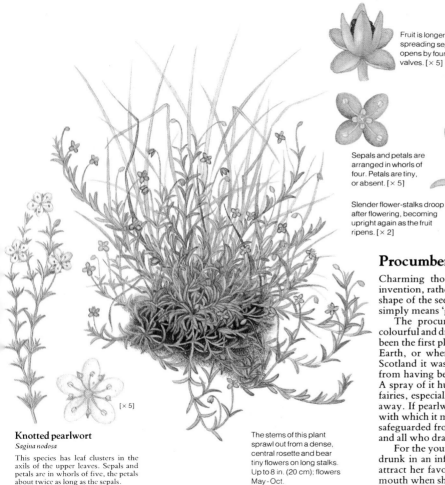

Fruit is longer than its spreading sepals, and opens by four blunt valves. [× 5]

Sepals and petals are arranged in whorls of four. Petals are tiny, or absent. [× 5]

Slender flower-stalks droop after flowering, becoming upright again as the fruit ripens. [× 2]

Procumbent pearlwort is common throughout Britain on lawns, banks and grassy verges and beside footpaths.

Procumbent pearlwort *Sagina procumbens*

Charming though it is, the name pearlwort is a botanist's invention, rather than a folk-name. 'Pearl' probably refers to the shape of the seed-pod or unopened flower, while 'procumbent' simply means 'growing along the ground'.

The procumbent pearlwort's name gives no clue to its colourful and dramatic role in legend and magic. It is said to have been the first plant on which Christ set his foot when he came to Earth, or when he rose from the dead. In the Highlands of Scotland it was supposed to have derived supernatural powers from having been blessed by Christ, St Bride and St Columba. A spray of it hung from the door lintel gave protection against fairies, especially those who made a practice of spiriting people away. If pearlwort were stuck in a bull's fore-hooves, the cows with which it mated and the calves and milk they produced were safeguarded from ills. If a cow ate the herb, its calves and milk, and all who drank the milk, were also protected against fairies.

For the young village maiden, pearlwort brought a bonus. If drunk in an infusion, or used merely to wet the lips, it would attract her favoured lover; and if a piece of it were in the girl's mouth when she kissed him, he was bound to her for ever.

[× 5]

Knotted pearlwort
Sagina nodosa

This species has leaf clusters in the axils of the upper leaves. Sepals and petals are in whorls of five, the petals about twice as long as the sepals.

The stems of this plant sprawl out from a dense, central rosette and bear tiny flowers on long stalks. Up to 8 in. (20 cm); flowers May - Oct.

Flowers grow
from bases of
leaves and in
the forks of
branches. Male
and female
flowers grow on
separate plants.

Leaves are
fleshy and
stalkless.
[Actual size]

Female flower has
minute stamens
and petals. [× 2]

This fleshy plant has
flowering and non-
flowering shoots growing
from creeping stems.
2–10 in. (5–25 cm);
flowers May–Sept.

Male flower has
no style. [× 2]

Fruit lets seed
escape by
movement of
three teeth. [× 2]

Sea sandwort is found all around the
coasts of Britain, binding the sand and
helping to form dunes.

Sea sandwort *Honkenya peploides*

This lowly plant stands in the first rank among the defenders of
Britain's shores, holding and rebuilding them against the in-
roads of the sea. Few plants can survive the rigours of life on the
seashore, but sea sandwort is so adapted to this habitat that it can
colonise bare, salty sand and grow on shifting dunes.

Unlike most seashore plants, sea sandwort is not a drab,
greyish colour but grows in extensive carpets of bright, glossy
green. Its low-growing stems give little indication of the strong
root system that supports them. Once the plant is established on
sand, although still only a few inches high, it starts to act as a
windbreak, so that sand piles up on its windward side to form
the beginnings of a dune. The plant's habit of creeping outwards
makes the windbreak all the more effective, and for a while at
least the shifting sand is stabilised under a dense carpet of closely
woven stems and thick, fleshy leaves.

If the wind changes its direction, causing sand or shingle to
pile up on top of it, sea sandwort can adapt. As the stems are
buried, they send new shoots upwards until they emerge into
the light of day. The old shoots die back from their base, the new
shoots root afresh and a new surface carpet is laid above the old.

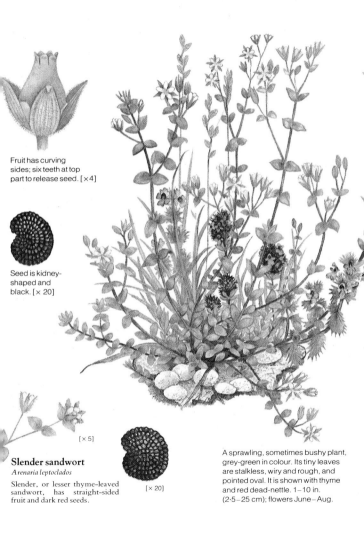

Fruit has curving sides; six teeth at top part to release seed. [×4]

Seed is kidney-shaped and black. [×20]

Petals are not divided, and are shorter than sepals. [×5]

This sandwort is found throughout Britain, except in the far north, inhabiting walls, cliff-tops, chalk downs and arable land.

Thyme-leaved sandwort *Arenaria serpyllifolia*

In the struggle for existence, the big and showy plants are not the only winners. Many small and insignificant species manage to survive simply by remaining lowly and little sought after for fodder or decoration. A highly successful exponent of this method of survival is the thyme-leaved sandwort, a drab, unimpressive plant with small flowers and usually an untidy, sprawling growth, which prospers in every county of Britain and Ireland. In appearance it is not unlike the common chickweed, although none of its leaves is stalked, its petals are not divided and it is less often a weed of garden beds.

Thyme-leaved sandwort is an odd little plant, rarely more than 2–3 in. (5–7·5 cm) in height, yet often quite bushy. It has tiny, grey leaves and a flower never more than a third of an inch across, with small, white petals smaller than the sepals. According to some authorities, animals are deterred from eating the plant by poison produced in its stems and leaves; certainly it is a fact that rabbits will not feed on it, and as a result it can often be found growing around their burrows.

Because of its similarity to thyme-leaved sandwort, slender sandwort was long overlooked as a separate species.

[×5]

Slender sandwort
Arenaria leptoclados

Slender, or lesser thyme-leaved sandwort, has straight-sided fruit and dark red seeds.

[×20]

A sprawling, sometimes bushy plant, grey-green in colour. Its tiny leaves are stalkless, wiry and rough, and pointed oval. It is shown with thyme and red dead-nettle. 1–10 in. (2·5–25 cm); flowers June–Aug.

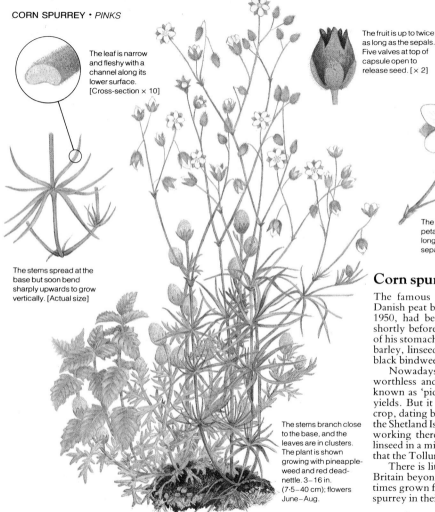

The leaf is narrow and fleshy with a channel along its lower surface. [Cross-section × 10]

The stems spread at the base but soon bend sharply upwards to grow vertically. [Actual size]

The stems branch close to the base, and the leaves are in clusters. The plant is shown growing with pineapple-weed and red dead-nettle. 3–16 in. (7·5–40 cm); flowers June–Aug.

The fruit is up to twice as long as the sepals. Five valves at top of capsule open to release seed. [× 2]

The five undivided petals are slightly longer than the sepals. [× 2]

Corn spurrey is a common plant of waste ground throughout Britain, often invading crops as a troublesome weed.

Corn spurrey *Spergula arvensis*

The famous Tollund man, whose body lay preserved in a Danish peat bog for at least 1,500 years before it was dug up in 1950, had been eating a gruel containing corn spurrey seed shortly before he met his death by strangulation. Examination of his stomach contents showed that the dish had also contained barley, linseed and the seeds of gold of pleasure, pale persicaria, black bindweed, fat hen and heartsease.

Nowadays corn spurrey is considered to be no more than a worthless and tiresome weed of cornfields – in Norfolk it is known as 'pickpurse', because of its disastrous effect on grain yields. But it has had a long and respectable history as a food crop, dating back to pre-Roman days. At one time, for instance, the Shetland Islanders ground the seeds into meal; archaeologists working there have found corn spurrey mixed with oats and linseed in a mixture intended for human consumption, showing that the Tollund man's diet was not exceptional.

There is little to suggest that corn spurrey was cultivated in Britain beyond the 16th century, but in Europe it is still some-times grown for fodder; sheep are fond of it and cattle with corn spurrey in their feed are said to produce richer milk.

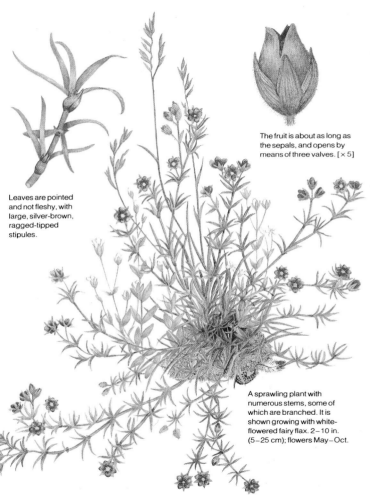

Leaves are pointed and not fleshy, with large, silver-brown, ragged-tipped stipules.

The fruit is about as long as the sepals, and opens by means of three valves. [× 5]

The pink, star-shaped flower has five undivided petals which are slightly shorter than the sepals. [× 5]

A sprawling plant with numerous stems, some of which are branched. It is shown growing with white-flowered fairy flax. 2–10 in. (5–25 cm); flowers May–Oct.

Sand spurrey is common on lime-free ground in most of Britain, except Ireland and northern Scotland.

Sand spurrey *Spergularia rubra*

As its name suggests, sand spurrey is found in open sandy or gravelly places, especially where the soil is lime-free. Of the several species of spurrey present in the British Isles, sand spurrey is the only one which grows inland. The others – Greek sand spurrey, corn spurrey, sea spurrey, greater sea spurrey and cliff spurrey – are only found near the sea, either in sandy turf or on walls and high places.

Sand spurrey has three styles on top of the ovary – as do all the spurreys except the corn spurrey – and it is classed in the group known as *Spergularia*. Corn spurrey has five styles, and botanists have placed it in a genus of its own called *Spergula*. The sand spurrey has pinkish flowers, which accounts for its Latin adjective *rubra*, 'red'.

Together with the other spurreys, sand spurrey is noted for its distinctive, triangular stipules. These are little flaps of tissue found at the base of the leaf-stalk of certain plants. Usually they are so small as to be scarcely noticeable, but those of sand spurrey can measure as much as one-third of the length of the leaf. Normally stipules are green, but the sand spurrey's stipules are silver, turning brown, and have jagged edges.

The leaves have three nerves; the upper ones are almost stalkless.

The fruit is rounded and shorter than the sepals. It opens by means of six valves. [× 5]

The star-shaped flower has five petals, which are shorter than the sepals. [× 5]

A plant with trailing stems, upright flowering shoots and flowers on long stalks. It is shown with ground ivy. 4–16 in. (10–40 cm); flowers May–July.

Three-nerved sandwort is a common plant of woodland clearings over much of Britain, especially on rich soils.

Three-nerved sandwort *Moehringia trinervia*

Three conspicuous veins, or nerves, beneath each leaf identify this plant and help to distinguish it from other sandworts, stitchworts and chickweeds which are in the same family. The family also includes pinks, campions and catchflys, all of which usually have opposite leaves, five sepals, five or more petals, five or ten stamens and two to five styles.

The small, white-flowered members of this family are so much alike that they are easily confused with one another. But the sandworts have undivided petals, whereas the petals of chickweeds and stitchworts are forked. There are three groups of sandwort: *Minuartia*, which has long, narrow leaves; *Arenaria*, which has short, round leaves; and *Moehringia*, of which three-nerved sandwort is the only member and the largest plant of the three.

The seeds of three-nerved sandwort, though tiny, have an oily appendage which makes them attractive to ants. The plant is the only sandwort which grows in woodland, and ants collecting the oily seeds play a large part in its dispersal. It is widespread on well-drained, nitrate-rich soils in most parts of Britain, but less common in Scotland and Ireland.

Each pair of leaves is joined by the scaly leaf margins.

The plant has branched stems with short hairs. The flowers are in clusters, or solitary in the forks of the stem. The white-flowered common chickweed is shown growing at the base of the plant. 1–10 in. (2·5–25 cm); flowers June–Aug.

The fruit is a dry nut, hidden by the sepals. [× 3]

The flowers have no petals, one to ten stamens and two styles. [× 3]

Annual knawel grows throughout Britain on waste and cultivated ground, especially on sandy or gravelly soils.

Annual knawel *Scleranthus annuus*

The thin, thread-like stems of this tiny plant have given it the English name knawel, which comes from the German meaning 'a tangle of threads'. There are two kinds of knawel, annual and perennial, but the annual knawel is the most common, occurring in dry, sandy and gravelly places, and in corn fields.

The plant is so small it is easily overlooked, but it can be identified by its wiry, bushy appearance, narrow pointed leaves and greenish petal-less flowers measuring little more than $\frac{1}{6}$ in. (4 mm) across. The pointed green sepals have a narrow white border.

Knawels belong to a group of six plants characterised by their one-seeded fruits, and although they are now classed as members of the chickweed family they were once regarded as a family on their own. One of the group, coral necklace, appears only in the south of England. It has a reddish stem, rounded leaves and tiny white flowers and is similar to the rupture-wort and smooth rupture-wort. The other plant in the group, strap-wort, is a rare seashore plant with long narrow leaves which are not in pairs. The petals are white and the white-edged sepals sometimes have a maroon centre.

87

The flowers have two sepals and five white petals, slightly notched. [×5]

Basal leaves have long stalks. One pair of joined leaves completely encircles each long flowering stem, so that the flowers appear to grow from a green bowl. 4–12 in. (10–30 cm); flowers May–July.

Seed is black and shiny. [× 10]

The seed capsule is surrounded and hidden by sepals. [× 5]

Spring beauty grows on disturbed ground, waste land and cultivated ground. It is scattered throughout Britain.

Pink purslane
Montia sibirica

The stem leaves are unstalked, but not joined as in spring beauty. The flowers are bigger with more deeply notched, delicately hued pink petals.

Spring beauty *Montia perfoliata*

Many plants have been transported from Europe to North America, but the delicate spring beauty, with its pretty white flowers, has crossed the Atlantic in the opposite direction. It comes from the Pacific coast, and was not spotted in Britain until 1852. In America it was also called Indian lettuce and miner's lettuce, and was considered to be both nourishing and tasty. American Indians, in particular, prized its bulbs as a food source, and the tender foliage was boiled and eaten.

Spring beauty prefers sandy soils to heavier, darker soils. Gardens, therefore, are not usually afflicted with it as a weed. The plant is easily recognised by its leaves which – apart from those at the base – are stalkless and fused in pairs. Because of this, the flower-stems appear to grow up through the middle of a single leaf – a condition which botanists call perfoliate.

At first sight, spring beauty and the related pink purslane appear to have very little in common. The purslane's flowers are pink and much bigger, and the leaves are separate. But their similarity is revealed on the back of the flowers. Unlike the rather similar chickweeds and spurreys, spring beauty and pink purslane have two sepals instead of five.

Trailing stems bear narrow, upward-curving, fleshy leaves which are triangular in cross-section, often reddish towards the tip. The many-petalled flowers are magenta or yellow. 3–4 in. (7·5–10 cm); flowers May–Aug.

Five leaf-shaped lobes surround the fruit, which is fleshy. [Actual size]

The hottentot-fig is a plant of cliffs, banks and dunes, used for binding sand near the sea in south-western England.

Hottentot-fig *Carpobrotus edulis*

When gardeners or countryfolk use the botanical name for a flower, they sometimes transform it into an attractive English form. For instance, kew-weed, given the scientific name of *Galinsoga*, became known as gallant soldier. Hottentot-fig is another example, for when it was first introduced to Cornwall, it brought with it the cumbersome early botanical name of *Mesembryanthemum*; but the locals had a way with such tongue-twisters and turned it into the delightful Sally-my-handsome. *Mesembryanthemum* means 'midday flower', and refers to the habit of some species, such as the Livingstone daisy of gardens, of opening up only in full sun.

The Hottentots were nomadic tribesmen of south-west Africa, who ate the big, fleshy fruit of this perennial plant. It was introduced to British gardens in 1690, but now it flourishes only near the sea in Devon and Cornwall and around Dublin.

Many-petalled flowers such as the hottentot-fig are rare among wild plants in Britain, which usually have only four, five or six petals. The flowers of the daisy family, including daisies and dandelions, appear to have many petals, but in fact each of them is a small but complete flower.

89

The stem is hollow. [Actual size]

The flowers have four to five greenish petal-like segments. [× 10]

Seed capsule is positioned vertically, not hidden by segments. [× 10]

Leaves are broad and triangular, powdery-white when young. The flower spike is leafless except at the base. 12–20 in. (30–50 cm); flowers May–Aug.

Good King Henry is found all over Britain on sites rich in nitrogen, especially road-sides, farmyards and rich grasslands.

Good King Henry *Chenopodium bonus–henricus*

Despite its very English-sounding name, Good King Henry is a translation of the German *Guter Heinrich*, or 'Good Henry'. Henry was not a figure in German history but probably an elf – like the Robin who features in various English plant names. The word 'King' was added in this country, but the name does not refer to a specific monarch. The 16th-century herbalist John Gerard wrote that the plant grew in 'untilled places, and among rubbish neere common waise, olde walls, and by hedges in fields'. It is a handsome plant with tall, greenish-yellow flowering tops, and it can still be seen on some medieval sites.

There are some 15 different types of goosefoot growing in the British Isles, and of these the Good King Henry is the only perennial. It is also the only one with broad, arrowhead-shaped leaves. The leaves and young shoots used to be boiled and eaten as a green vegetable.

A far tastier kind of wild spinach is fat hen – another goosefoot – which grows on any waste or disturbed ground. Its use in Britain as a food has been traced back to the Bronze Age in Sussex and Scotland. Along with Good King Henry, this plant has now been replaced as a vegetable by cultivated spinach.

Fat hen
Chenopodium album [× 10]

The lower leaves of fat hen are broad but not triangular; the upper leaves are narrow. The flower spike is leafy. Fruit is positioned horizontally, and hidden by petal-like segments.

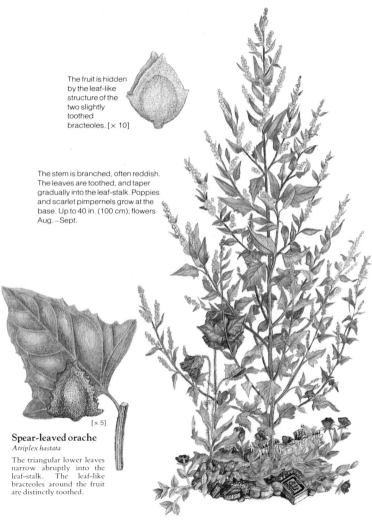

The fruit is hidden by the leaf-like structure of the two slightly toothed bracteoles. [× 10]

The stem is branched, often reddish. The leaves are toothed, and taper gradually into the leaf-stalk. Poppies and scarlet pimpernels grow at the base. Up to 40 in. (100 cm); flowers Aug.–Sept.

Spear-leaved orache
Atriplex hastata

The triangular lower leaves narrow abruptly into the leaf-stalk. The leaf-like bracteoles around the fruit are distinctly toothed.

[× 5]

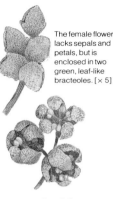

The female flower lacks sepals and petals, but is enclosed in two green, leaf-like bracteoles. [× 5]

In male flowers the green sepals and petals are alike. [× 10]

Common orache grows widely in cultivated and waste ground near the sea coast over most of the British Isles.

Common orache *Atriplex patula*

The garden form of orache (or orach) was served until quite recently as a table vegetable resembling spinach. But although it grows easily and quickly and provides a shelter belt for less hardy plants, it has gone out of favour and is now treated as a weed, despite a high content of vitamin C. Its reputation as a mild laxative may have brought about its downfall.

The oraches are close relatives of the goosefoots and are distinguished only by their flower structure; goosefoot flowers are usually bisexual, while those of the orache are either male or female. Since the flowers are very small, it is not easy to spot this difference, but the two plants have a distinguishing mark which can be detected with the naked eye. Each flower of goosefoot is surrounded by about five small scales which do not enclose it; in the oraches, the flower is enclosed by two green, leaf-like structures, up to half an inch long, called bracteoles. Common orache is similar enough in appearance to fat hen to share this name in certain parts of the country.

Spear-leaved orache often grows together with common orache, but is rather less common. Its botanical name of *hastata*, from the Latin *hasta*, 'spear', describes its triangular leaves.

91

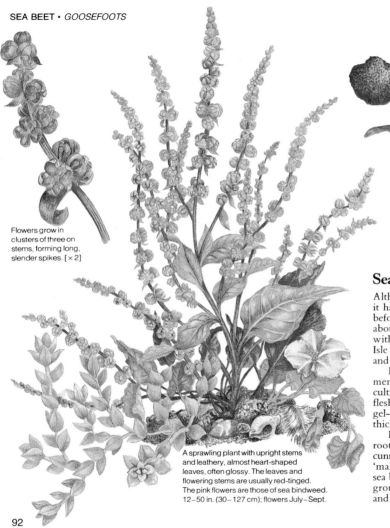

Flowers grow in clusters of three on stems, forming long, slender spikes. [× 2]

The seed is enclosed by the thickened, brown flower segments. [× 5]

The flower has five greenish segments containing the yellow stamens and styles. [× 5]

As its name implies, the sprawling, hairless sea beet can be found on most shores round the coasts of Britain.

A sprawling plant with upright stems and leathery, almost heart-shaped leaves, often glossy. The leaves and flowering stems are usually red-tinged. The pink flowers are those of sea bindweed. 12–50 in. (30–127 cm); flowers July–Sept.

Sea beet *Beta vulgaris* ssp. *maritima*

Although wild sea beet was not recorded in England until 1629, it had probably been growing in these islands for some time before that. Cultivation of the plant began in the Middle East about 2,000 years ago, when efforts were made to breed strains with bigger and fleshier roots and more nourishing leaves. In the Isle of Wight the plant was called sea spinach or wild spinach, and cottagers boiled its leaves and ate them with bacon or pork.

Despite its somewhat ordinary appearance, sea beet is a member of a very large and economically important group of cultivated vegetables – the goosefoots. Among the plants with fleshy roots, the family includes beetroot, sugar beet and mangel-wurzels; while the leafy variety includes spinach and the thickly stalked chard-beet.

In the 16th century, the herbalist John Gerard grew a beet-root to a height of 12 ft (3·6 m), and assured the 'curious and cunning cooke' that the root was 'good and holsome' and would 'make thereof many and divers dishes both faire and good'. But sea beet is usually a sprawling plant whose stems lie flat on the ground. It has small, greenish flowers and large, leathery leaves, and is one of the few shore plants that survives in salt spray.

The fruit is enclosed by a pair of three-lobed knobbly bracteoles, joined nearly to the top. [× 5]

Female flower has no sepals or petals, but styles project from two enclosing bracteoles. [× 5]

Male flowers are borne in clusters. They have one whorl of sepal-like segments only. [× 5]

The stems sprawl at the base, then turn upright. Leaves are elliptical and untoothed, powdery silver-green in colour. Up to 32 in. (80 cm); flowers July–Sept.

Sea-purslane thrives in salt-marshes in England and western Scotland that are covered by the tide.

Sea-purslane *Halimione portulacoides*

Sea-purslane has to be tough, for it survives in that most forbidding of habitats, the salt-marsh. Such plants have to tolerate high concentrations of salt around their roots; they also have to endure twice-daily flooding by the tide, and biting, drying winds sweeping across the exposed flatlands. Appropriately the plant's generic name is *Halimione*, Greek for 'daughter of the sea'.

The plant grows most abundantly along the edges of the deep, muddy creeks that cut through salt-marshes; these creeks can often be spotted from a distance by the silvery foliage of the little bushes of sea-purslane that line them. This silver sheen is created by tiny, papery scales, too small to be seen with the naked eye, on the surface of the leaves.

The scales on the leaves of sea-purslane are filled only with air, not sap, and they are dead when the leaf reaches maturity. Their function is to retain a layer of moist air against the leaf's surface, so protecting it against the drying effect of salt water. The scales also serve to reflect the sun's heat at low tide, preventing the plant from drying out through exposure. Plants grow underground winter-buds to help them survive.

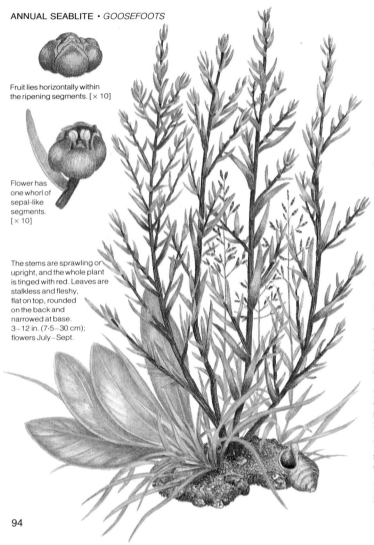

Fruit lies horizontally within the ripening segments. [× 10]

Flower has one whorl of sepal-like segments. [× 10]

The stems are sprawling or upright, and the whole plant is tinged with red. Leaves are stalkless and fleshy, flat on top, rounded on the back and narrowed at base. 3–12 in. (7·5–30 cm); flowers July–Sept.

Flowers grow at the junction of leaf and stem. [× 2]

Annual seablite grows on seashores and in salt-marshes round most of the British coast and up the Severn estuary.

Annual seablite *Suaeda maritima*

For most plants, sea-water is a poison. Those which can flourish in its presence are called halophytes, a word which comes from the Greek and means 'salt-loving', although a better description of most of them would be salt-tolerating. There are two sorts of halophytes: those which can put up with an occasional splashing of sea-water, the 'spray halophytes', and those which survive regular immersion by the rising tide, the 'true halophytes'. The annual seablite is a true halophyte, which is covered by the tide twice daily; moreover, this is a case of a true salt-lover, for the plant seems to have a definite need for sea-water, although it does like a well-aerated soil and usually grows on sandy seashores. By contrast shrubby seablite, its perennial cousin, flourishes on soils free from salt.

The seablites were among the seaside plants which used to be burned to produce an ash known as *barrilla* (the Spanish name for saltwort or its ashes). This provided an impure form of sodium carbonate, which was once used to make a poor-quality glass.

The name 'blite' is an old English word derived from the Latin for spinach or orache. In the 15th century, English herbalists used the name blite for the plant now known as fat hen.

Each segment bears several flowers, with two stamens and two feathery styles.

Perennial glasswort, a tussock plant on salt-marshes and pebbly shores in southern England, is difficult to uproot.

Prostrate glasswort
Salicornia ramosissima

This related species often has purplish-red stems. Each flower has only one stamen but three styles.

Segmented flowering branches form on sprawling stems. Each segment, dark green at first but turning yellow, is a pair of fleshy leaves fused around a woody stem. Up to 12 in. (30 cm); flowers Aug.–Sept.

Perennial glasswort *Arthrocnemum perenne*

For centuries glassworts were used in the manufacture of glass. The succulent stems of this seashore plant were gathered at low tide, dried and burned in heaps; the crude ash, which is high in soda, was then fused with sand to make a rather poor quality glass. Other seaside plants, such as saltworts, were often used for the same purpose. The process, probably introduced from Europe in the 16th century, was discontinued when much purer forms of soda became available.

Glasswort is also known as marsh samphire and, like other coastal plants called samphires, it can be eaten lightly boiled or pickled in spiced vinegar. The production of these pickles is still very much alive in East Anglia and elsewhere along the North Sea coast, and in some places is on the increase.

There are many sorts of glasswort, all with jointed stems resembling miniature cacti. The most common are annual plants: they include prostrate glasswort. Perennial forms are represented in Britain only by *Arthrocnemum perenne*. The main differences between the two types are that perennial glasswort is woody at the base, and difficult to uproot, while prostrate glasswort is never woody at the base and is easily uprooted.

Wrinkled nutlet is brownish-green. [× 2]

The heliotrope-pink flower is 1–2 in. (2·5–5 cm) across, with five narrow, dark-veined petals. [Actual size]

The round fruits, called 'cheeses' after their shape, contain many nutlets. [Actual size]

Common mallow grows widely on road-sides and waste ground all over the British Isles, but is rarer in far north.

Common mallow *Malva sylvestris*

The common mallow of dusty roadsides and waste ground has some famous relatives – the lordly hollyhock, the exotic hibiscus, and the cotton plant. On its own merits it has long stood high in popular esteem, both for the beauty of its big, rose-purple flowers and for its value as a food and medicine. As early as the 8th century BC, young mallow shoots were eaten as a vegetable; and the practice persisted into Roman times. The orator Cicero complained that the dish was giving him indigestion; the poet Martial used it to dispel his hangovers after orgies; and the naturalist Pliny found that mallow sap mixed with water would give him day-long protection against aches and pains.

In medieval days, when there was widespread belief in the efficacy of love-potions, mallow had a reputation as an anti-aphrodisiac, promoting calm, sober conduct. More recently, mallow leaves were used to draw out wasp stings, and the gummy sap was made into poultices and soothing ointment.

It was the fruit rather than the flowers that caught the popular imagination, and nearly all folk-names for mallow refer to the ring of nutlets – 'Billy buttons', 'pancake plant' and 'cheese flower' are examples.

Musk mallow
Malva moschata
This species has kidney-shaped leaves at the base and deeply divided stem leaves. Flowers are 1–2 in. (2·5–5 cm).

Leaves at the base are rounded; stem leaves ivy-shaped. 12–36 in. (30–90 cm); flowers June–Sept.

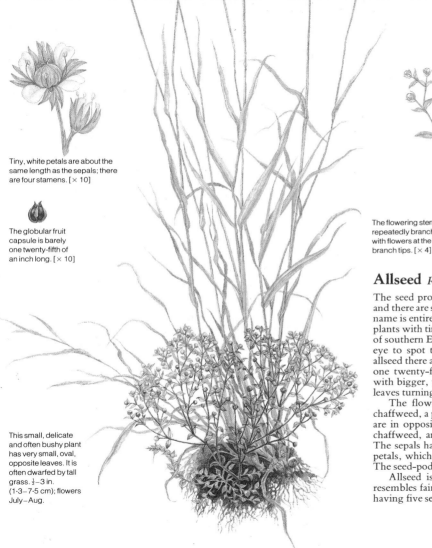

Tiny, white petals are about the same length as the sepals; there are four stamens. [× 10]

The globular fruit capsule is barely one twenty-fifth of an inch long. [× 10]

This small, delicate and often bushy plant has very small, oval, opposite leaves. It is often dwarfed by tall grass. ½–3 in. (1·3–7·5 cm); flowers July–Aug.

The flowering stem is repeatedly branched, with flowers at the branch tips. [× 4]

Allseed grows on damp patches on heaths and grassland. It is widespread in scattered localities throughout Britain.

Allseed *Radiola linoides*

The seed production of this diminutive plant is so enormous, and there are so many fruits on it in the autumn, that its common name is entirely appropriate. Allseed is one of a number of small plants with tiny flowers that are found particularly on the heaths of southern England. They are inconspicuous and it takes a keen eye to spot them below other, bigger plants. In addition to allseed there are chaffweed, with pink or white flowers less than one twenty-fifth of an inch (1 mm) across; yellow centaury, with bigger, yellow flowers; and mossy stonecrop, with fleshy leaves turning bright red in autumn.

The flowers of allseed are scarcely bigger than those of chaffweed, a plant it closely resembles from a distance. Its leaves are in opposite pairs, not on alternate sides of the stem as in chaffweed, and its thread-like stems are repeatedly branched. The sepals have two to four little teeth at the tip, and the oval petals, which are about the same length as the sepals, soon fall. The seed-pods have four compartments, each with two seeds.

Allseed is a close relative of the flaxes and most closely resembles fairy flax. The flaxes differ from allseed, however, in having five sepals and petals instead of four.

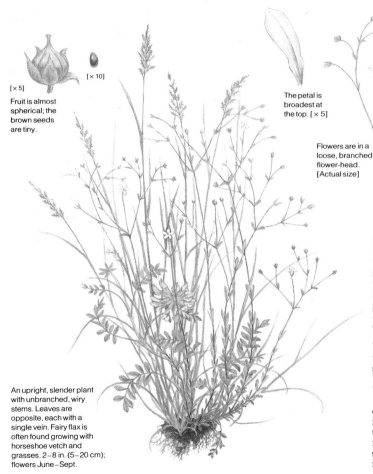

[×5]

Fruit is almost spherical; the brown seeds are tiny.

[×10]

The petal is broadest at the top. [×5]

Flowers are in a loose, branched flower-head. [Actual size]

The flower has five narrow white petals. [×2]

An upright, slender plant with unbranched, wiry stems. Leaves are opposite, each with a single vein. Fairy flax is often found growing with horseshoe vetch and grasses. 2–8 in. (5–20 cm); flowers June–Sept.

Fairy flax is common throughout Britain on well-drained soils, including grassland, heaths, moors and fenland.

Fairy flax *Linum catharticum*

With its delicate, white flowers carried on slender, wire-like stems, this diminutive plant looks like the stitchworts or sandworts of the chickweed family, rather than the big, blue-flowered flaxes, grown for the manufacture of linen or to adorn gardens, which are its close relatives. Its small size has often been linked with the use of the word fairy in its name, but this connection is unlikely.

In fact the plant's name dates back to the Middle Ages, when belief in gnomes, elves and fairies was strong and they were thought to be not dainty sprites but redoubtable, powerful spirits of the countryside. West Country names for this plant – 'lady's flax' and 'lady's lint' – and the Highland or Irish name, 'fairy woman's flax', all give it associations with fairy magic.

Although gentle in appearance, fairy flax displays quite different characteristics when used as a medicine. An infusion of its bruised stems, gently simmered in wine, was once widely used as a purgative, giving rise to its alternative name of purging flax and its botanical name of *Linum catharticum*, which has the same meaning. But the effects of this potion were so violent that it had to be discontinued.

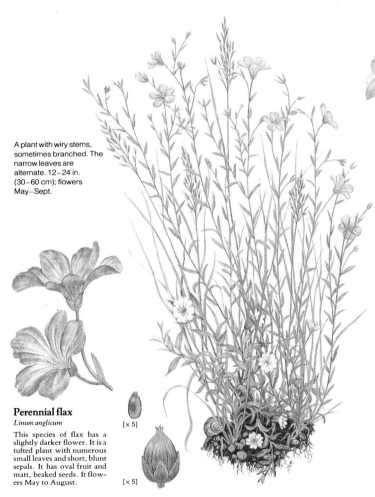

A plant with wiry stems, sometimes branched. The narrow leaves are alternate. 12–24 in. (30–60 cm); flowers May–Sept.

Perennial flax

Linum anglicum   [× 5]

This species of flax has a slightly darker flower. It is a tufted plant with numerous small leaves and short, blunt sepals. It has oval fruit and matt, beaked seeds. It flowers May to August.

[× 5]

Sepals have a fine point. [× 2]

The fruit is cone-shaped; the seed is shiny, oval and without a beak. [× 5]

Pale flax grows in grassy places, especially near the sea. It is common in the West Country, and occurs in the north.

Pale flax *Linum bienne*

Wrappings for Egyptian mummies were made 5,000 years ago from the stems of a plant related to the pretty blue flower which blows today along the west coasts of England and Wales. Cultivated flax – a similar plant to pale flax but slightly larger – has been used for the making of linen since time immemorial; its botanical name, *Linum usitatissimum*, means 'flax that is very much used'. Long before the pharaohs of Egypt built the first pyramids, flax had been known in the Middle East. In later centuries it clothed almost every civilised society, until it began to be ousted by mass-produced cotton in the 19th century.

Linen is made by retting, or soaking, the flax stems in water and then beating, cleaning and combing out the fibres. Nowadays it is largely reserved for better-quality cloth and high-grade writing and cigarette papers. Cultivated flax used to be widely grown in Britain but is today rarer than pale flax.

Probably an even more ancient use of flax was for its food-oil, obtained from crushing the seeds. Today flax seeds are still used in some human foods, and more frequently in cattle-cake, and the purified linseed oil is an important ingredient of some paints, varnishes and putty.

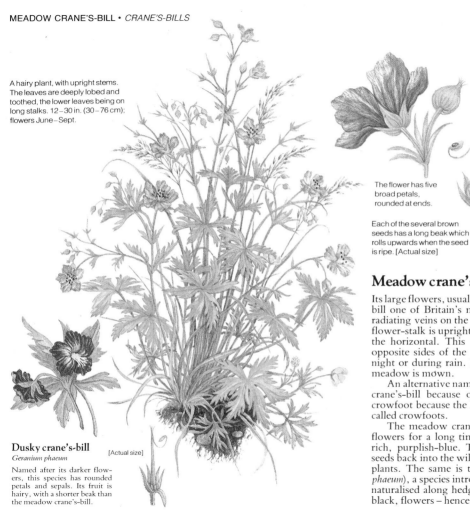

A hairy plant, with upright stems. The leaves are deeply lobed and toothed, the lower leaves being on long stalks. 12–30 in. (30–76 cm); flowers June–Sept.

The flower has five broad petals, rounded at ends.

Each of the several brown seeds has a long beak which rolls upwards when the seed is ripe. [Actual size]

Ranging in colour from bluish to soft purple, this crane's-bill is locally common in meadows over most of Britain.

Meadow crane's-bill *Geranium pratense*

Its large flowers, usually a soft violet, make the meadow crane's-bill one of Britain's most distinctive wild plants. The darker, radiating veins on the petals guide bees to the nectar. In bud the flower-stalk is upright, but as the petals unfurl, the stalk dips to the horizontal. This is because the cells grow unevenly on opposite sides of the stalk. The flower-stalks droop lower at night or during rain. Plants may flower a second time when a meadow is mown.

An alternative name for this species is crowfoot crane's-bill – crane's-bill because of the 'beak' over the seed cluster and crowfoot because the leaves resemble those of buttercups, once called crowfoots.

The meadow crane's-bill is often planted in gardens, as it flowers for a long time; a double form produces pompons of rich, purplish-blue. These garden plants often disperse their seeds back into the wild, extending the range of the more showy plants. The same is true of the dusky crane's-bill (*Geranium phaeum*), a species introduced from central Europe which is now naturalised along hedges and roadsides. This has dark, almost black, flowers – hence its second name of 'mourning widow'.

Dusky crane's-bill
Geranium phaeum   [Actual size]

Named after its darker flowers, this species has rounded petals and sepals. Its fruit is hairy, with a shorter beak than the meadow crane's-bill.

Fruits are smooth and downy, with a smooth seed. A seed is shown breaking away from the beak on its long, spring-like style. [Actual size]

Flowers grow in pairs. Sepals are oval and pointed and petals deeply notched. [Actual size]

Common in hedgerows, wasteland and field margins in the south and east, this plant is rarer elsewhere.

A downy plant with upright stems and rounded leaves, lobed about halfway to the midrib. It is seen growing with dandelions and grasses. 9–24 in. (23–60 cm); flowers June–Aug.

Mountain crane's-bill *Geranium pyrenaicum*

Crane's-bills are so named because their pointed fruits resemble the beak of a crane, a stork-like bird. The scientific name, *Geranium*, comes from the classical Greek *geranos*, meaning a crane. Each section of the fruit has a long, thin style running up the outside of this beak. When the seed is ripe, the style suddenly flicks up like a released spring, throwing the seed for distances of up to 10 ft (3 m) from the parent plant.

The mountain crane's-bill, also known as the Pyrenean or hedgerow crane's-bill, is in Britain restricted to the lowlands. However, it does grow in the mountains of southern Europe, including the Pyrenees, where it is thought to have spread originally from the Caucasus. Mountain crane's-bill is possibly not a native of Britain, as it was not recorded here until 1762. Until relatively recently, the species was not very common, but over the last 50 years it has become widely naturalised, especially in neglected churchyards.

The *Geranium* species of the British Isles are quite distinct from the scarlet-flowered garden plants generally known as geraniums. These belong to the genus *Pelargonium*, which includes the ivy-leaved and scented-leaved geraniums.

101

Pointed sepals are covered
with dense hair; the five petals
are deeply notched. [×2]

Fruit
[×10]

Seed
[×10]

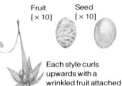

Each style curls
upwards with a
wrinkled fruit attached
and ejects the seed.

This plant is common in Britain in fields,
wasteland and sandy places up to
1,750 ft (535 m) above sea level.

Dove's-foot crane's-bill *Geranium molle*

Some of the most delicate plants of grassy banks are the pink-flowered crane's-bills, which owe their name to the characteristic pointed shape of their fruits. The flowers are visited by various insects, but since the male stamens and female stigmas are held together, the flowers pollinate themselves.

The soft hairy down that covers the roundish, lobed leaves of dove's-foot crane's-bill distinguishes the plant from shining crane's-bill, with its smooth waxy leaves, and also gives it the species name of *molle*, from the Latin *mollis*, 'soft'. Its common name of dove's-foot derives from the fanciful resemblance of its leaf to the bird's foot. In the autumn, and when the plants are growing in a dry place, the leaves often turn bright red; this colouring is due to the production of red pigments called anthocyanins, which also tint some tree leaves in autumn.

Dove's-foot crane's-bill was well known to early herbalists, and in the 16th century John Gerard prescribed the plant as a cure for ruptures. His remedy was a complex one, requiring a powder to be made from dried plants of the crane's-bill and then strengthened with the powder of nine oven-dried slugs. The mixture was then added to claret and drunk.

Shining crane's-bill
Geranium lucidum

The stems of this species are upright and almost hairless; leaves are glossy, the sepals end in a bristle and the petals are not notched.

A softly hairy plant with purple to
lilac flowers on semi-erect stems
branching from the base. Leaves are
rounded. 4–16 in. (10–40 cm);
flowers Apr.–Sept.

Stems branch from the base, some upright and some sprawling. The fern-like leaves have three to five lobes. 4–20 in. (10–50 cm); flowers May–Sept.

[×5]

Pink flower has rounded petals, without notches. The fruit is slightly wrinkled, but the seed is smooth.

Herb-robert is widespread throughout Britain in shady spots on hedgebanks, rocks and walls or in woods.

Herb-robert *Geranium robertianum*

In the Middle Ages there was a widespread belief in the 'doctrine of signatures'. This meant that any plant with curative properties would reveal the divine purpose for which it was intended through its shape or colour. In the case of herb-robert, the hairy stems and leaves turn a fiery red in autumn or when the plant is growing in dry, exposed situations. It followed, according to the logic of medieval times, that herb-robert should be used in the treatment of blood disorders; in particular the leaves were employed to staunch the flow of blood.

The 'robert' of the plant's name is believed to be a corruption of the Latin *ruber* meaning red; but it may have been derived from the name of Robert, an early Duke of Normandy, for whom a celebrated medieval medical treatise was written.

The poet William Wordsworth found herb-robert an attractive plant and wrote: 'Poor Robin is yet flowerless, but how gay with his red stalks on this sunny day.' But not everyone would agree with him. The leaves produce a strong, disagreeable odour, and in some districts the plant has been given the name of 'Stinking Bob'. An unusual form of the plant with stems growing close to the ground is found on shingle beaches.

Cut-leaved crane's-bill
Geranium dissectum

The stems are sprawling and hairy. Leaves are deeply divided into five to seven narrow lobes. Petals are notched. The fruit is smooth but the seed is pitted.

The petals are longer than the sepals. [Actual size]

The long-beaked fruit splits and twists from the base, each segment carrying a seed. [Actual size]

Common storksbill flourishes throughout Britain in dry grasslands and fields, in gravel pits, and in sandy seaside areas.

Common storksbill *Erodium cicutarium*

This common plant of the British coastline is remarkable for its ingenious and elaborate method of planting its seed. The fruit is a cluster of five narrow segments, each carrying a seed and together formed into the long beak-like structure which gives the plant its name. When the fruit becomes ripe, the beak splits and each of the five strips twists into a corkscrew-ended shape with a seed attached. The seed flutters to the ground with this corkscrew attached as a long tail. With changes in humidity, the corkscrew changes shape, either unwinding or screwing itself up tighter – movements which cause the seed to burrow into the ground. Backward-pointing hairs prevent the seed from re-emerging until it is about the right depth in the soil, when the twisting ceases.

Common storksbill is also extraordinary in the short life of some of its flowers. Opening in the morning, they may be pollinated and have dropped their petals by midday.

There are two other storksbills growing mainly by the coast, the sea storksbill, *Erodium maritimum*, which has undivided leaves, unlike common storksbill; and the musky storksbill, *Erodium moschatum*.

Sea storksbill
Erodium maritimum

The leaves of this species are not divided into leaflets, as in common storksbill. Petals are shorter than sepals, or completely absent. Beak of fruit is shorter.

The stems of this plant can be erect or prostrate, and are usually hairy. Leaves are composed of two rows of leaflets of varying shapes. Up to 20 in. (50 cm); flowers May–Sept.

This creeping plant produces tufts of leaves directly from the rootstock. Each leaf has three wedge-shaped leaflets. 2–6 in. (5–15 cm); flowers May–Aug.

Solitary flowers, each borne on a long stalk, are white, veined with lilac or mauve, with blunt sepals. [Actual size]

Wood-sorrel is common in most parts of Britain, in woods, hedges and other shady spots, and on high ground.

Wood-sorrel *Oxalis acetosella*

Wood-sorrel has managed to spread itself across the length and breadth of the British Isles, despite a curious reproduction system. It produces two sorts of flower. The first, carried on a slender stem, is the familiar, usually lilac-veined spring flower of woodland floors, drooping at night or in the rain to protect the pollen. Abundant nectar attracts bees and beetles, but for all this, it produces very little seed. The second sort of flower, borne prolifically in summer, is carried on a short stalk close to the ground and seldom opens. These flowers pollinate themselves, and produce most of the seed for the next generation.

The leaves of wood-sorrel resemble those of the clovers; and in fact this is one of the plants claimed to be the shamrock used by St Patrick to illustrate the doctrine of the Trinity. The three leaflets fold down at night, giving rise to the local Dorset names of 'sleeping beauty' or 'sleeping clover' for the related species *Oxalis corniculata*.

The generic name of *Oxalis* refers to the sharp, acid taste of the leaves, which contain calcium oxalate. As early as the 14th century these leaves were used to add flavour to salads and green sauces, and were cultivated for that purpose in gardens.

Sleeping beauty
Oxalis corniculata

Instead of solitary flowers, this species bears a loose head of one to six yellow flowers with pointed sepals. Its fruit is cylindrical and hairy.

105

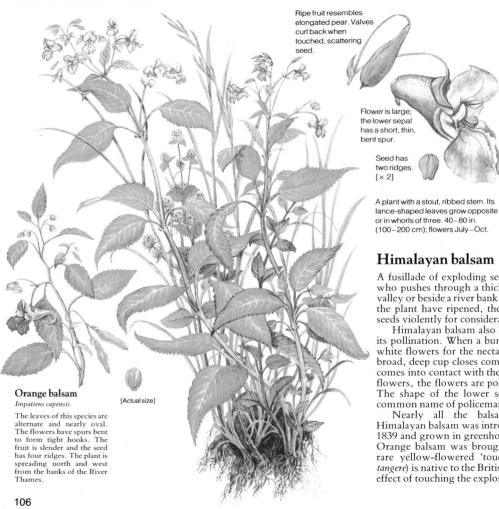

Ripe fruit resembles elongated pear. Valves curl back when touched, scattering seed.

Flower is large; the lower sepal has a short, thin, bent spur.

Seed has two ridges. [× 2]

A plant with a stout, ribbed stem. Its lance-shaped leaves grow opposite or in whorls of three. 40–80 in. (100–200 cm); flowers July–Oct.

Himalayan balsam flourishes on river banks and in waste places. It is common in scattered localities throughout Britain.

Orange balsam
Impatiens capensis

[Actual size]

The leaves of this species are alternate and nearly oval. The flowers have spurs bent to form tight hooks. The fruit is slender and the seed has four ridges. The plant is spreading north and west from the banks of the River Thames.

Himalayan balsam *Impatiens glandulifera*

A fusillade of exploding seed capsules may shower the walker who pushes through a thicket of Himalayan balsam in a moist valley or beside a river bank. For when the green seed capsules of the plant have ripened, their sides spring back, throwing the seeds violently for considerable distances.

Himalayan balsam also has a foolproof method of ensuring its pollination. When a bumble-bee visits the purplish-pink or white flowers for the nectar contained in the lower sepal, this broad, deep cup closes completely round the insect. As the bee comes into contact with the male and female parts of successive flowers, the flowers are pollinated and the fruits start to form. The shape of the lower sepal has given the plant its other common name of policeman's helmet.

Nearly all the balsams are naturalised 'foreigners'. Himalayan balsam was introduced from its Asiatic homeland in 1839 and grown in greenhouses before it escaped into the wild. Orange balsam was brought from North America. Only the rare yellow-flowered 'touch-me-not' balsam (*Impatiens noli-tangere*) is native to the British Isles; both its names arise from the effect of touching the explosive seed capsules.

The long pod twists open suddenly when ripe, scattering seed. [Actual size]

Deep yellow spikes of flowers grow along tips of shoots. [Actual size]

Dyer's greenweed grows in grassy places on clay and chalk soils in England and Wales, but only rarely in Scotland.

Dyer's greenweed *Genista tinctoria*

This small shrub, related to the broom, derives its name from the yellow dye obtained from its flowering stems. Flemish immigrants, in the 14th century, were the first to make use of the dye as a means of turning cloth green; they soaked the cloth in the dye, then dipped it into a vat of blue woad. The colour became known as Kendal green, after the Cumbrian town where it was developed.

Dyer's greenweed lacks the spines typical of its genus, but petty whin, the other widespread British species, does have spine-tipped branchlets. A variety of dyer's greenweed found in parts of Cornwall and Dyfed grows flat on the ground and produces hairy pods. All these plants are members of the pea family and can be recognised by their distinctive flowers and fruits. The flowers have a big upper petal called the standard, two side petals known as wings and two lower petals, joined along their edges, known together as the keel.

The seeds produced by this family are housed in pods which may be straight, curved or coiled and contain one or more seeds. Most pods split open suddenly and eject the ripe seeds, scattering them well away from the parent plant.

Petty whin
Genista anglica

This species has a spiny stem and much smaller leaves than dyer's greenweed. It grows on dry moors and heaths all over Britain, flowering May to June.

A small deciduous shrub with smooth green stems, resembling a dwarf broom. The leaves are stalkless and undivided. 12–28 in. (30–70 cm); flowers July–Sept.

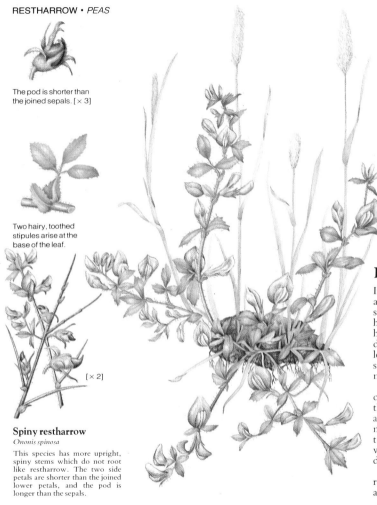

The pod is shorter than the joined sepals. [× 3]

Two hairy, toothed stipules arise at the base of the leaf.

[× 2]

Spiny restharrow
Ononis spinosa

This species has more upright, spiny stems which do not root like restharrow. The two side petals are shorter than the joined lower petals, and the pod is longer than the sepals.

The side petals are about as long as the joined lower petals, or keel. [× 3]

The trailing stems of restharrow often root at intervals towards the base. The plant is common near the coast and is shown growing with sand cat's-tail grass. 12–24 in. (30–60 cm); flowers June–Sept.

Restharrow grows in rough, grassy places throughout Britain, especially on chalk and limestone and on sand-dunes.

Restharrow *Ononis repens*

In the days before tractors, restharrow was a source of great annoyance to the arable farmer. Its matted stems and deep roots slowed considerably the progress of a horse-drawn plough or harrow; the plant's common name means literally 'to stop the harrow'. There was another reason why restharrow was heartily disliked by farmers: it tainted milk, butter and cheese. The leaves when crushed give off a strong, unpleasant, goatlike smell, and cattle that eat the leaves give tainted or 'cammocky' milk: 'cammock' is one of the plant's folk-names.

The underground stems of restharrow were, in the past, considered a great delicacy by children in the north. They dug them up and chewed them like liquorice; hence the plant's alternative common name of wild liquorice. The plant had many medical applications in the 17th century: it was used to treat kidney disorders; the outer part of the root taken with wine was considered a useful treatment for gallstones; and the powdered root was applied externally to clear up ulcers.

Common restharrow occurs throughout Britain, but the related spiny restharrow is limited to clay or chalky soils in south and south-east England.

YELLOW-FLOWERED PEAS

Members of the pea family are recognisable by the distinctive form and arrangement of their flowers, pods and leaves. In some species the leaf consists of only three leaflets, while others have several pairs of leaflets.

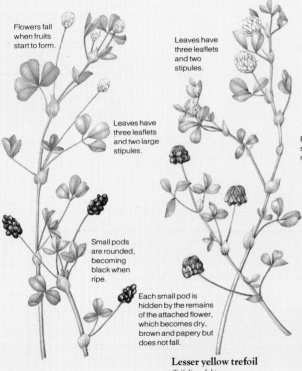

Flowers fall when fruits start to form.

Leaves have three leaflets and two large stipules.

Small pods are rounded, becoming black when ripe.

Each small pod is hidden by the remains of the attached flower, which becomes dry, brown and papery but does not fall.

Leaves have three leaflets and two stipules.

Flowers fall when fruit starts to form.

Pods are straight and many-seeded.

Each leaf has three leaflets on a stalk and two stipules close to the stem.

Flowers fall when fruit starts to form.

Pods are wavy, breaking into one-seeded, curved segments.

Each leaf has several pairs of leaflets, and two small stipules.

Black medick
Medicago lupulina
Page 112

Lesser yellow trefoil
Trifolium dubium
Page 114

Bird's-foot-trefoil
Lotus corniculatus
Page 119

Horseshoe vetch
Hippocrepis comosa
Page 118

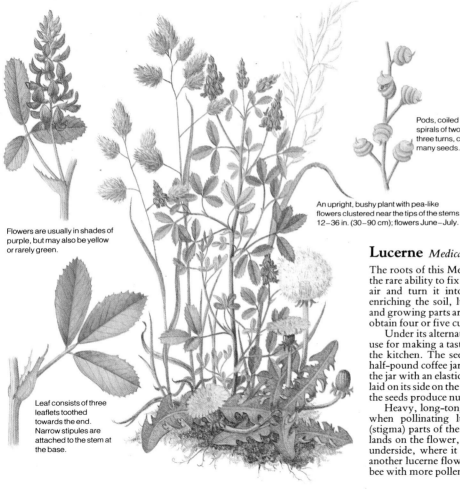

Flowers are usually in shades of purple, but may also be yellow or rarely green.

Leaf consists of three leaflets toothed towards the end. Narrow stipules are attached to the stem at the base.

Pods, coiled in spirals of two or three turns, contain many seeds.

An upright, bushy plant with pea-like flowers clustered near the tips of the stems. 12–36 in. (30–90 cm); flowers June–July.

Lucerne has naturalised itself all over Britain near fields where it was grown as a crop, especially on roadsides.

Lucerne *Medicago sativa*

The roots of this Mediterranean native bear small nodules with the rare ability to fix nitrogen – that is, to take nitrogen from the air and turn it into an essential plant food. In addition to enriching the soil, lucerne makes valuable fodder, as its seeds and growing parts are rich in vitamins and proteins. Farmers can obtain four or five cuts of the crop in a year.

Under its alternative name of alfalfa, the plant has come into use for making a tasty garnish to salads, which can be grown in the kitchen. The seed is soaked in a glass container such as a half-pound coffee jar; then muslin is fastened over the mouth of the jar with an elastic band, the water is drained off and the jar is laid on its side on the window-sill. Dampened and drained daily, the seeds produce nutty-tasting seedlings in a few days.

Heavy, long-tongued insects trigger an unusual mechanism when pollinating lucerne. The male (stamen) and female (stigma) parts of the flower are held under tension. When a bee lands on the flower, the stigma is released and strikes the bee's underside, where it picks up pollen collected previously from another lucerne flower. At the same time, the stamens dust the bee with more pollen for carrying to the next plant.

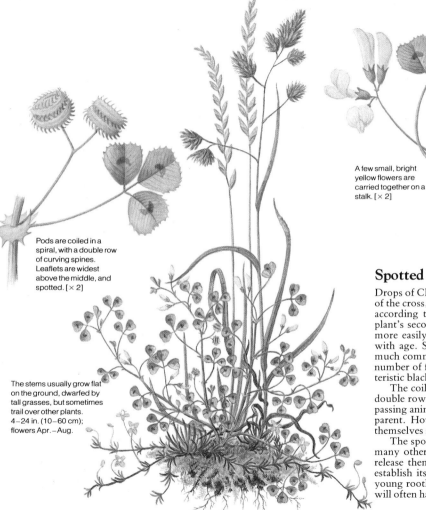

Pods are coiled in a
spiral, with a double row
of curving spines.
Leaflets are widest
above the middle, and
spotted. [× 2]

A few small, bright
yellow flowers are
carried together on a
stalk. [× 2]

The stems usually grow flat
on the ground, dwarfed by
tall grasses, but sometimes
trail over other plants.
4–24 in. (10–60 cm);
flowers Apr.–Aug.

Spotted medick grows in pastures and
other grassy places, especially on sandy
soil in the east and south.

Spotted medick *Medicago arabica*

Drops of Christ's blood, falling on to clover growing at the foot
of the cross, gave this plant the characteristic spots on its leaves,
according to an old folk belief. The same belief explains the
plant's second popular name of Calvary clover. The spots are
more easily noticed on older leaves as they become brownish
with age. Spotted medick can also be distinguished from the
much commoner black medick (*Medicago lupulina*) by the small
number of flowers in each head; in addition it lacks the characteristic black pods of this species.

The coiled pods, produced from May to September, carry a
double row of spines, which enable them to cling to the fur of a
passing animal and so get carried for planting far away from the
parent. However, other species of medick manage to spread
themselves successfully with smooth and disc-like pods.

The spotted medick's pods contain several seeds, but unlike
many other pods of the pea family, they do not split open to
release them. Normally only one seed in the pod manages to
establish itself as a new plant. When the seed germinates, the
young rootlet pierces the wall of the pod, and a flowering plant
will often have the old pod attached to its root.

111

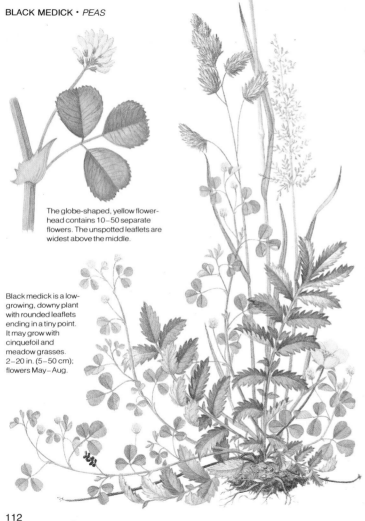

The globe-shaped, yellow flower-head contains 10–50 separate flowers. The unspotted leaflets are widest above the middle.

Black medick is a low-growing, downy plant with rounded leaflets ending in a tiny point. It may grow with cinquefoil and meadow grasses. 2–20 in. (5–50 cm); flowers May–Aug.

Petals do not stay attached to the kidney-shaped seed-pods, which coil and turn black.

Black medick is common in grassy places, especially in south-eastern England, but it is rare in Ireland.

Black medick *Medicago lupulina*

The name of this common roadside plant has nothing to do with doctors or medicine. It means plant of the Medes, the ancient Middle Eastern people whose legal system, as adapted by their Persian conquerors, made the 'Laws of the Medes and the Persians' respected throughout their lands. The name was given by the Romans in Classical times to lucerne, a crop much cultivated in western Asia, and over the centuries its scope has been enlarged to include relatives like *Medicago lupulina. Lupulina* means 'hop-like', probably referring to its similarity to hop trefoil rather than to the hop used in brewing.

Black medick can be confused with hop trefoils *Trifolium dubium* and *Trifolium campestre.* But unlike them it does not retain dead, papery flowers when in fruit, and it has a tiny, sharp tip in the middle of the rounded end of each leaflet. Its characteristic black pods do not split open to release the single seed; instead the germinating seed forces a young rootlet through the pod wall.

This is one of the plants sold on St Patrick's Day as shamrock. Other plants which have claims to be shamrock are hop trefoil, white clover and wood sorrel. Black medick is still cultivated as animal fodder in some European countries.

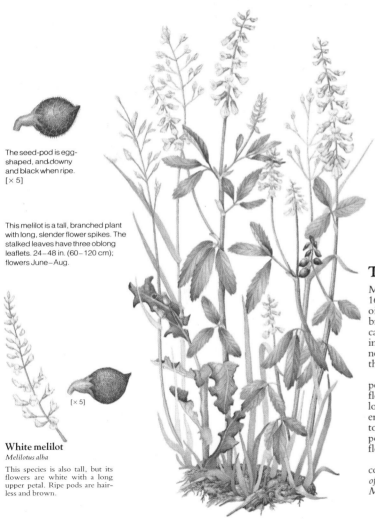

The seed-pod is egg-shaped, and downy and black when ripe. [× 5]

This melilot is a tall, branched plant with long, slender flower spikes. The stalked leaves have three oblong leaflets. 24–48 in. (60–120 cm); flowers June–Aug.

White melilot
Melilotus alba

This species is also tall, but its flowers are white with a long upper petal. Ripe pods are hairless and brown.

[× 5]

The flowers have deep yellow petals of about equal length and hang downwards on the stem.

The tall melilot grows in waste places, by roadsides and in woods. Generally common, it is rarer in the north of Scotland.

Tall melilot *Melilotus altissima*

Melilots were introduced to Britain from the Continent in the 16th century, probably by herbalists, who used them to make ointments and poultices to reduce swellings, blisters and bruises. As late as the 19th century an infusion of the flowers in camphorated spirit was widely used as a wash for tired and inflamed eyes. When dried, melilots give off a pleasant smell of new-mown hay, owing to the aromatic substance coumarin in their leaves and stalks, which is also found in various grasses.

Melilots are a rich source of wild honey, and are commonly pollinated by large insects such as hoverflies and bees. In each flower, the stigma and stamens are held stiffly inside the joined lower petals. The weight of a big insect landing on the flower is enough to press the lower petals downwards, so that the stigma touches the underside of the insect's body and is fertilised by the pollen there, which has been carried from a previously visited flower.

Tall melilot has pods with net-like markings, while another common yellow-flowered species, the ribbed melilot, *Melilotus officinalis*, has ribbed pods. White melilot or Bokhara clover, *Melilotus alba*, has brown, hairless pods.

113

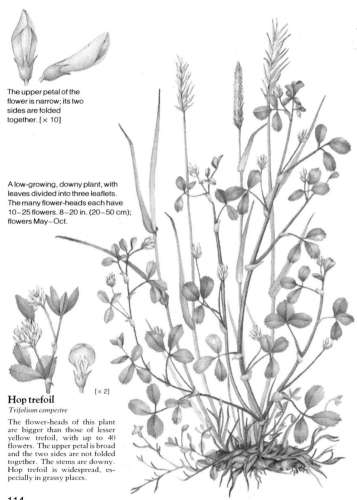

The upper petal of the flower is narrow; its two sides are folded together. [× 10]

A low-growing, downy plant, with leaves divided into three leaflets. The many flower-heads each have 10–25 flowers. 8–20 in. (20–50 cm); flowers May–Oct.

Hop trefoil
Trifolium campestre

The flower-heads of this plant are bigger than those of lesser yellow trefoil, with up to 40 flowers. The upper petal is broad and the two sides are not folded together. The stems are downy. Hop trefoil is widespread, especially in grassy places.

[× 2]

The seed-pod is hidden by a brown, papery, dead flower; the whole head looks like a hop. Each pod has a single seed. [× 2]

Lesser yellow trefoil is common in grassy places, especially banks and pastures, in Britain, but rarer in the far north.

Lesser yellow trefoil *Trifolium dubium*

According to many patriotic Irishmen, the lesser yellow trefoil, with its three leaflets joined in one, is the shamrock used by St Patrick to explain the Holy Trinity to the people of Ireland; and this is the plant that Irishmen wear as a national symbol on St Patrick's Day. The exact identity of the shamrock has long been a mystery. The Irish *seamróg* means 'little clover'; the lesser yellow trefoil (meaning 'three-leaf') fits this description, but claims that it is the true shamrock have also been made for white clover, black medick, watercress and wood sorrel.

The lesser yellow trefoil is probably the commonest of the hop trefoils, so named because their brown fruiting heads look like the tiny heads of hops. It is called 'lesser' because it has smaller flower–heads and is less showy than the true hop trefoil (*Trifolium campestre*).

In flower, lesser yellow trefoil can be confused with black medick (*Medicago lupulina*), but medick, unlike any trefoil or clover, has a sharp point at the tip of each leaflet. Once the flowers ripen the species are easily told apart, as the flowers of black medick fall off to reveal coiled, black pods, whereas hop trefoil flowers remain attached, covering straight, brown pods.

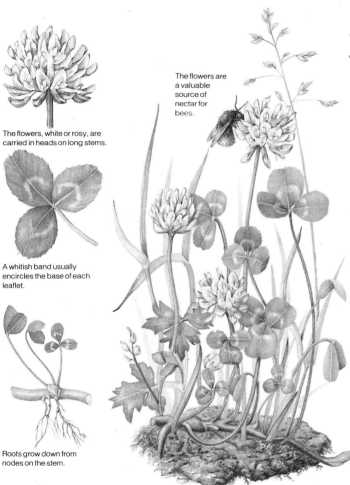

The flowers, white or rosy, are carried in heads on long stems.

A whitish band usually encircles the base of each leaflet.

Roots grow down from nodes on the stem.

The flowers are a valuable source of nectar for bees.

The dead flowers remain folded over the hanging seed-pods.

The stems creep along the ground and take root. The hairless, trefoil leaves with three leaflets are on long, upright stalks. 20 in. (50 cm); flowers June–Sept.

White (or Dutch) clover grows in grassy places everywhere in the British Isles, and especially on clay soils.

White clover *Trifolium repens*

The creeping stems of white clover, taking root as they progress, make this a troublesome plant to eradicate once it establishes itself in garden lawns. It also has a persistent rootstock, which may last for many years. Some white clover plants produce a chemical in their leaves which yields prussic acid when eaten by animals, and in sufficient quantity this can cause poisoning. Fortunately the unpleasant taste will deter the animals if other food is available.

Abundant nectar is contained at the bottom of the deep tube formed by the petals. Usually only long-tongued insects such as bees are able to reach it. White clover is especially valuable to bee-keepers, as it is one of the first flowers to produce 'main-flow' nectar for bees after the dandelion and sycamore supplies run out. Once the flowers are fertilised, they fold down over the young pods. Occasionally one flower is left standing upright and is known among country people as the 'old maid'.

With its long stems supporting the flower-heads, white clover is unlikely to be confused with any other clover except perhaps the alsike clover, which usually has pink flowers, lacks whitish marks on the leaflets and has non-rooting stems.

Reddish-purple flower-heads rise stalkless from a pair of leaves at the end of a stem. [Actual size]

Dead flowers stay on the fruiting head, concealing the small seed-pods.

Narrow, pointed leaflets with a pale V-band identify the red clover, here growing with buttercups and grasses. Up to 24 in. (60 cm); flowers May–Sept.

Red clover is common throughout Britain in pastures and other grassy places. It is widely cultivated as animal fodder.

Zigzag clover
Trifolium medium

The flowers are similar in appearance to those of red clover, but their heads stand on stalks. Narrow, spiky sheath-like stipules stand out from the branched, zig-zag stem. Leaflets are less rounded and do not have a clear V-band. [Actual size]

Red clover *Trifolium pratense*

On the roots of red clover are tiny nodules containing bacteria which are able to fix nitrogen – that is, to turn the plentiful nitrogen of the air, which plants cannot absorb directly, into salts which are essential for plant growth. Experiments are being made to transfer the colonies of bacteria to other plants; if wheat, for instance, could be made to fix its own nitrogen, it would bring farmers huge reductions in their fertiliser bills. In the meantime, farmers prize red clover as a crop which can be harvested for fodder or ploughed in to enrich the soil.

A delicate scent attracts long-tongued flies, butterflies and moths to the flower-heads, but in most fields the main pollinators appear to be bumble bees, based on nearby nests in hedgerows, wooded areas and waste ground. If their hives are placed close to the clover field, honey bees are equally effective collectors of nectar; red clover is often known as 'bee bread'.

In country districts the flowers of the red clover are made into a potent wine, and in the past they were used in a syrup for the relief of whooping cough. The curiously shaped leaves, and particularly the rare four-leaved clovers, were worn traditionally to bring luck and ward off witches and warlocks.

The flowers are borne in cylindrical heads up to 1 in. (2·5 cm) long. The stalks are as long, or longer, than the leaves. [Actual size]

The fruiting heads are elongated, and dead flowers persist. The reddish teeth of the sepal tube spread widely and are clothed in white hairs.

An upright plant with flower-heads on slender, upright stalks. Stipules at the base of the leaf have long bristle-like points. May grow with wall pepper and grasses. 4–8 in. (10–20 cm); flowers June–Sept.

Hare's-foot clover grows throughout Britain in dry, grassy places, particularly near the sea and on sandy soils.

Hare's-foot clover *Trifolium arvense*

The name clover is probably derived from the Latin *clava*, meaning 'a club', and the triple leaves of the *Trifolium* genus resemble the mythological three-lobed club of Hercules. This is also the origin of the clubs suit in playing cards. The name hare's-foot clover refers to the soft, downy heads of the flowers, which have the shape and texture of a hare's foot.

The distinctive flower-heads stand erect on stalks; they are cream in colour, with a pinkish tinge caused by the reddish pointed teeth of the sepals, which are masked by a covering of long white hairs. Each pod contains a single seed. At one time, hare's-foot clover was common in Britain on arable land, as the name *arvense* – 'of arable land' – suggests. In other European countries, Asia and North Africa it is still found in this habitat. In the British Isles, however, hare's-foot clover has been cleared away with improved agricultural practices and a general tidying up of waste areas. The species is now more commonly found in grassy areas on sandy soil.

Crimson clover was introduced from the Mediterranean. It was cultivated as animal feed, and is now occasionally found naturalised on grassy banks near fields in which it was planted.

Crimson clover
Trifolium incarnatum

The stipules at the base of the leaf of this species are papery. Flowers are crimson – or sometimes pink or white – in heads up to 2¼ in. (6 cm) long. Hairs on sepal tube are white or brownish.

117

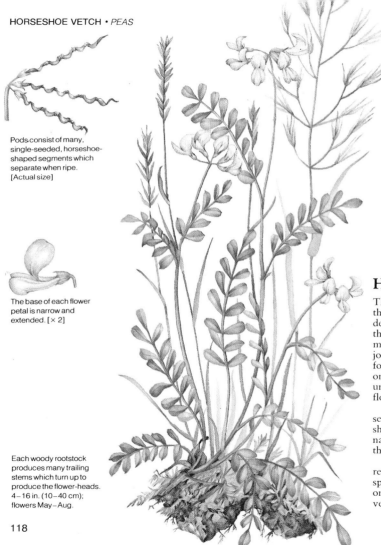

Pods consist of many, single-seeded, horseshoe-shaped segments which separate when ripe. [Actual size]

The base of each flower petal is narrow and extended. [× 2]

Each woody rootstock produces many trailing stems which turn up to produce the flower-heads. 4–16 in. (10–40 cm); flowers May–Aug.

Each leaf has two rows of leaflets; a terminal leaflet; and two tiny stipules at the base.

Horseshoe vetch favours chalky or lime-stone soil on dry pastures and grassy cliffs. It is common except in the far north.

Horseshoe vetch *Hippocrepis comosa*

The golden mat of horseshoe vetch that spreads itself beneath the feet of the walker on downland turf, hides a subtly and delicately fashioned natural mechanism for the perpetuation of the species. The heavy-bodied bumble bee and honey bee are its most common pollinators. The weight of a bee landing on the joined lower petals is enough to cause the group of stamens to force a string of pollen through a hole at the end of the petals and onto the insect. At the same time, the stigma touches the underside of the bee where there may be pollen from another flower that it has already visited.

The ripe pods break up into three to six horseshoe-shaped segments, covered with minute, reddish-brown spines. It is the shape of the pod segments that gives the plant its common name. Similarly, the scientific name *Hippocrepis* is derived from the Greek for 'horseshoe'.

The heads of the golden flowers are sometimes striped with red, as in the bird's-foot-trefoil. Both growing in grass, the two species can be confused at first sight, but bird's-foot-trefoil has only two pairs of leaflets and a terminal leaflet, while horseshoe vetch has 4–15 pairs of leaflets and a terminal leaflet.

The leaves appear to have only three leaflets, but in fact another pair of leaflets is carried close to the stem.

Pods twist and split, each releasing several seeds.

Solid stems trail from a woody rootstock. Flowers are carried in stalked heads. The plant is shown among meadow grasses and mosses. 4–16 in. (10–40 cm); flowers June–Sept.

Bird's-foot-trefoil grows abundantly on pastures, roadsides and dry grasslands in all parts of the British Isles.

Large bird's-foot-trefoil

Lotus pedunculatus

Stems of this related species are hollow and stand more upright. Underground stems form new plants. Large bird's-foot-trefoil favours damper grasslands and bogs throughout Britain.

Bird's-foot-trefoil *Lotus corniculatus*

'Lady's shoes and stockings', 'crow-toes', 'God Almighty's thumb and finger' – the folk-names that this plant has attracted are remarkable both for their number – there are more than 70 – and for their diversity. Their number is, perhaps, accounted for by the fact that the plant is so abundant and showy. The folk-names are so varied because, without the exercise of too much imagination, the flowers can be seen as shoe-shaped, and the ends of the pods as resembling fingers, toes and claws.

Bird's-foot, in the plant's common name, reflects this resemblance to a bird's claw. Trefoil suggests that the leaves have only three leaflets each, but there is in fact an extra pair of leaflets carried close to the stem. The red streaks or flushes sometimes seen on the yellow flowers give the plant the alternative common name of 'bacon-and-eggs'.

The caterpillars of the green hairstreak and dingy skipper butterflies feed on the bird's-foot-trefoil. Butterflies visit the flowers for nectar, but it is unlikely that they bring about pollination. The means of pollination is the same as for the horseshoe vetch, and calls for an insect such as a bee or wasp to force the pollen and the stigma from the joined lower petals.

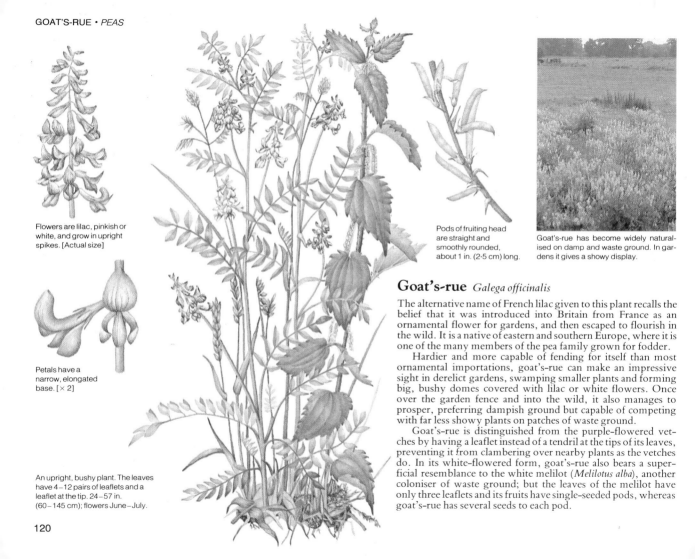

Flowers are lilac, pinkish or white, and grow in upright spikes. [Actual size]

Petals have a narrow, elongated base. [× 2]

An upright, bushy plant. The leaves have 4–12 pairs of leaflets and a leaflet at the tip. 24–57 in. (60–145 cm); flowers June–July.

Pods of fruiting head are straight and smoothly rounded, about 1 in. (2·5 cm) long.

Goat's-rue has become widely naturalised on damp and waste ground. In gardens it gives a showy display.

Goat's-rue *Galega officinalis*

The alternative name of French lilac given to this plant recalls the belief that it was introduced into Britain from France as an ornamental flower for gardens, and then escaped to flourish in the wild. It is a native of eastern and southern Europe, where it is one of the many members of the pea family grown for fodder.

Hardier and more capable of fending for itself than most ornamental importations, goat's-rue can make an impressive sight in derelict gardens, swamping smaller plants and forming big, bushy domes covered with lilac or white flowers. Once over the garden fence and into the wild, it also manages to prosper, preferring dampish ground but capable of competing with far less showy plants on patches of waste ground.

Goat's-rue is distinguished from the purple-flowered vetches by having a leaflet instead of a tendril at the tips of its leaves, preventing it from clambering over nearby plants as the vetches do. In its white-flowered form, goat's-rue also bears a superficial resemblance to the white melilot (*Melilotus alba*), another coloniser of waste ground; but the leaves of the melilot have only three leaflets and its fruits have single-seeded pods, whereas goat's-rue has several seeds to each pod.

The curved pods break into single-seeded segments when ripe.

The first leaflets are often close to the stem and curved backwards.

Each flower-stalk carries several small blossoms in leaf-like bracts. [× 4]

Stems are finely hairy, some sprawling flat along the ground. Flowers are white, veined with red, on thread-like individual stalks growing from thick common stalk. 1–18 in. (2·5–45 cm); flowers May–Aug.

Bird's-foot prefers well-drained soils on sand and gravel. It is common throughout Britain, except in the extreme north.

Bird's-foot *Ornithopus perpusillus*

The heads of its slightly curved, pointed pods, which resemble birds' claws, give this plant its name. Bird's-foot trefoil has similar pods but bears much bigger flowers and quite different leaves. Bird's-foot can also be easily distinguished from the vetches, as its leaves have a leaflet rather than a tendril at the tip. Another characteristic feature of bird's-foot is a leaf-like bract growing immediately beneath the cluster of flowers. The small, white and red-veined flowers normally pollinate themselves.

Unlike most British species of the pea family, bird's-foot has pods which do not split open to release their seeds. Instead, the pods break into pieces at the narrow parts between seeds, so that one seed remains in each segment.

Although bird's-foot is a native British species, it is more common in continental western Europe as far east as Italy, Poland and southern Sweden. There are several other related species in Europe, but only one of these, *Ornithopus pinnatus*, is found in Britain. This species is particularly common in the Channel Islands and the Isles of Scilly. *Ornithopus pinnatus* has fewer leaflets than common bird's-foot, has yellow flowers, and lacks the leaf-like bract beneath the flower clusters.

121

The flower-heads have leaf-like bracts, and are carried on a long stalk. Flowers go brown as they fade. [Actual size]

The terminal leaflet of a leaf is much larger than the others. [Actual size]

Sepals are purple-tipped and woolly, enclosing the pod. [Actual size]

Kidney vetch is a more or less upright plant, with silky leaves and stems. It is shown growing with sheep's-fescue. Up to 24 in. (60 cm); flowers June–Sept.

Dry grassland is this plant's favoured habitat. It grows throughout Britain, most commonly by the sea.

Kidney vetch *Anthyllis vulneraria*

In the Middle Ages the kidney vetch was known throughout Europe as a herb that would speed the healing of wounds. Its species name, *vulneraria*, comes from the Latin *vulnus*, meaning 'a wound'. Its common name, kidney vetch, refers to the old idea that it could also cure kidney diseases, the belief stemming from the fact that its flower-heads are kidney-shaped.

Local names for the kidney vetch include 'butter-fingers', 'fingers and thumbs', 'double pincushion' and 'lamb's foot'. In some regions, such as Dorset, Yorkshire and East Anglia, it is called 'lady's finger'. This name describes the silky, finger-like bracts; the small leaves or scales that appear just below the flower-heads.

The flower of the kidney vetch is a rich source of nectar, but only the most powerful insects, like bumble bees, are able to force open the large, stiff petals to extract it. The small blue butterfly, a common species on the chalky grasslands where the kidney vetch flourishes, lays its eggs on the plant, which is the main source of food for its caterpillars. The flowers of the kidney vetch are found in many colours: yellow, orange, red, purple and occasionally off-white.

The downy, toothed pod contains one seed, and does not split open. [Actual size]

The flowers are bright pink or red, often with purplish veins, and are carried in conical spikes. [Actual size]

Sainfoin is often found on chalk and limestone grassland in southern England and Wales.

This is an upright, often branched plant. Its leaves consist of 6–14 pairs of leaflets and a terminal leaflet. Here it grows with sheep's-fescue. 4–32 in. (10–80 cm); flowers June–Aug.

Sainfoin *Onobrychis viciifolia*

The name sainfoin comes from French, *sain* meaning 'wholesome' and *foin* meaning 'hay'. For many centuries sainfoin has been cultivated as fodder for cattle, especially on the Continent. Some early botanists mistakenly attributed the name to a mythical Saint Foyne. Although the plant now flourishes in Britain, especially on the chalk downs of the south, it is doubtful whether sainfoin is a native plant; it is more likely to have been imported from central Europe.

The 17th-century herbalist Nicholas Culpeper suggested that, since sainfoin was said to increase the milk yield in cows, it should be boiled up and given to nursing mothers. Sainfoin had other, purely medicinal uses: it was a cure for 'stranguary', a painful disease of the bladder; the leaves were made into a poultice for drawing out boils and, pulped and mixed with oil, were thought to induce sweating.

A local name for sainfoin is 'cock's head' or 'cock's comb', owing to the distinctive shape of its spiny pods, which were thought to be like the head of a cockerel. The flowers, striped with a glowing magenta-pink, are some of the most spectacular seen in Britain.

123

FIVE PEA-LIKE PLANTS

Many members of the pea family have leaves divided into numerous leaflets and flowers borne in long heads. Five species superficially similar in many respects may be distinguished by their characteristic leaf-tip, flower colour and seed-pod.

Flowers pale purple.

Leaf has branched tendril at tip.

Leaf has leaflet at tip.

Flowers blue, lilac or white.

Leaf has leaflet at tip.

Flowers creamy or greenish.

Flowers crimson or bluish.

Pod smooth and straight, with up to six seeds.

Leaf has short point at tip.

Flowers bright pink or red.

Leaf has leaflet at tip.

Pod rounded, toothed and downy, with one seed.

Pod smooth and straight, with six to ten seeds.

Pod smooth and straight with many seeds.

Pod smooth, curved and divided lengthwise, each half with many seeds.

Bush vetch
Vicia sepium Page 127

Goat's-rue
Galega officinalis Page 120

Milk-vetch
Astragalus glycyphyllos Page 125

Bitter vetch
Lathyrus montanus Page 130

Sainfoin
Onobrychis viciifolia Page 123

The smooth, curving pods are divided lengthwise by an internal wall, each half containing several seeds. [Actual size]

Many flowers are carried together on a stalk, which is shorter than the leaves. [Actual size]

Milk-vetch raises its zigzag stems in rough, grassy places on chalk and limestone; it is absent from Ireland.

This straggling plant has smooth, trailing stems and many hairless leaflets. It is distinguished from other vetches by its heads of large flowers of a dirty cream or greenish-cream colour. It is shown growing with small scabious and ox-eye daisy. 24–40 in. (60–100 cm); flowers July–Aug.

Milk-vetch *Astragalus glycyphyllos*

Goats that ate this plant were commonly believed to yield more milk: hence the name of 'milk-vetch'. It grows in scattered localities throughout Britain, but is easily overlooked as its greenish-cream flowers blend with the colour of its foliage. The straggling stems bend each time they give rise to a leaf, and the resulting appearance is a characteristic zigzag.

Growing among tall grasses, often on a woodland floor, the plant can be mistaken for other sorts of vetch, but it lacks the tendrils at its leaf-tips. Milk-vetch is a plant of temperate climates, occupying most of Europe as far east as the Caucasus but rare as far south as the Mediterranean.

Milk-vetch is also known as wild liquorice, but this is not the plant used as a laxative and to flavour confectionery. Commercial liquorice is made by pulping the roots of a related species of the pea family (*Glycirrhiza glabra*) and condensing the juice. Another British plant known as wild liquorice is the restharrow (*Ononis repens*), whose underground stems used to be chewed as were the roots of true liquorice, and possibly the milk-vetch was at one time put to similar use. The botanical name *glycyphyllos* derives from the Greek and means 'sweet stem'.

125

Sepals are joined at the base in a tube covered with short blackish hairs. [× 2]

Short pods, containing six or seven seeds, are inflated and covered with white hairs. [Actual size]

Purple milk-vetch grows on chalk and limestone, and on dunes and other sandy areas, chiefly in eastern Britain.

A plant with almost upright stems and many leaflets covered with soft whitish hairs. Several purplish flowers are carried on each stem, well above the leaves. 2–14 in. (5–36 cm); flowers May–July.

Purple milk-vetch *Astragalus danicus*

William Shenstone, the 18th-century poet and essayist who spent every penny he earned on landscaping his estate near Halesowen in the West Midlands, celebrated 'the tangled vetch's purple bloom' in his work *Rural Elegance*, published in 1750. Early summer visitors to the Breckland region of Norfolk can see Shenstone's words brought vividly to life. Vast sweeps of purple milk-vetch, whose flowers look at a casual glance like those of clover, bring rich colour to the sandy hills.

Purple milk-vetch is found throughout Europe from the French Alps to northern Russia, but in Britain it is mainly confined to the eastern half of the island, from the Chilterns to northern Scotland. Even there, huge colonies like those in Breckland are rare, and the plant is uncommon in the west. In Ireland, it grows only on the Aran Islands.

Milk-vetches derive their common name from a country belief that they increase the milk yield of goats. Although they are related to the pea and some varieties of vetch are added to salads on the Continent, they are not generally noted for their food value to humans. Some European varieties of milk-vetch are cultivated as garden alpines.

Stems may trail, or climb with tendrils. Each short-stalked flower-head has up to six blooms. The bumble bee is a frequent pollinator. 12–40 in. (30–100 cm); flowers May–Aug.

Leaf has five to nine pairs of leaflets and a branching tendril.

Sepals are joined, forming a tube; teeth are shorter than remainder of tube. [× 2]

Common throughout the British Isles, bush vetch grows in grassy places, in hedges and as a garden weed.

Wood vetch
Vicia sylvatica

Scattered throughout the British Isles in rocky woods and thickets near the sea, wood vetch has up to 20 pale lilac-pink flowers in each head. It is a squat plant on shingle, but may climb to 8 ft (2·5 m) in woods.

Bush vetch *Vicia sepium*

Scrambling and sprawling over other plants, its twining tendrils forever reaching for new territory, the vetch has been familiar to man throughout his history. Its Latin name of *Vicia* occurs in early English as 'fitch'. Dialect forms include 'thetch', 'fitchacks' and even Yorkshire's 'twaddgers'. Among about 150 species of vetch, the most important to man has been the broad bean, *Vicia faba*. It was one of the earliest of all plants to be cultivated: evidence of its planting has been found on the site of an Iron Age lake-dwellers' settlement at Glastonbury, Somerset.

Bush vetch itself has no use to man, but like many other vetches it can be fed to livestock. Bumble bees, powerful enough to force their way to the tightly enclosed flower bases, are particularly attracted to its nectar.

Wood vetch, on the other hand, has larger and more accessible flowers that are often pollinated by wasps. It is a stronger climber, and may be taller than bush vetch. The pods of both species are black when ripe, but they can be told apart by their shape: a wood vetch pod is tapered at both ends; a bush vetch pod only at the beak. Another species, tufted vetch, looks similar but has brown pods.

127

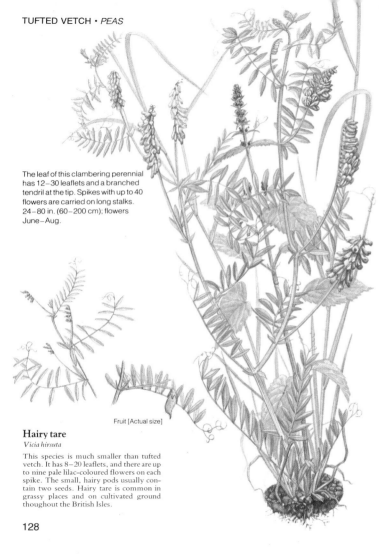

The leaf of this clambering perennial has 12–30 leaflets and a branched tendril at the tip. Spikes with up to 40 flowers are carried on long stalks. 24–80 in. (60–200 cm); flowers June–Aug.

Sepals are joined in a tube covering nearly half the flower. [× 2]

Smooth, almost square-ended pods hold up to six seeds. [Actual size]

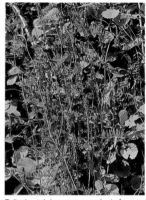

Tufted vetch is a common plant of grass-land, bushy places and hedgerows throughout most regions of Britain.

Fruit [Actual size]

Hairy tare
Vicia hirsuta

This species is much smaller than tufted vetch. It has 8–20 leaflets, and there are up to nine pale lilac-coloured flowers on each spike. The small, hairy pods usually contain two seeds. Hairy tare is common in grassy places and on cultivated ground thoughout the British Isles.

Tufted vetch *Vicia cracca*

Tall stems carrying spikes of up to 40 bright, bluish-purple flowers make tufted vetch one of the most distinctive plants to be seen scrambling among our British hedgerows. The plant climbs ladder-like by means of branched tendrils – a feature which distinguishes the vetches, vetchlings and peas from other British species of the pea family.

Occasionally, tufted vetch appears as a weed of gardens, where it is often allowed to grow because of its attractive appearance. Some gardeners even sow its seed to produce a display of colour in late summer in out-of-the-way corners.

A close relative of tufted vetch is the hairy tare, a member of an infamous family. Jesus told a parable (Matthew XIII, 30), about a man who sowed good seed in his field. 'But while men slept, his enemy came and sowed tares among the wheat. . . . when the blade was sprung up and brought forth fruit, then appeared the tares also.' In the 17th century when the Authorised Version of the Bible was published, most church-goers would instantly have recognised this plant, twining its way through crops of wheat, barley and oats, reducing yields and bringing further difficulties at harvest time.

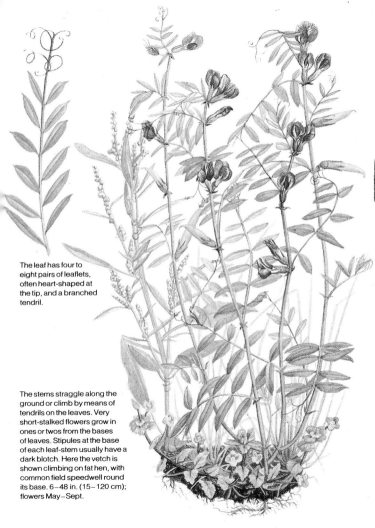

The leaf has four to eight pairs of leaflets, often heart-shaped at the tip, and a branched tendril.

The stems straggle along the ground or climb by means of tendrils on the leaves. Very short-stalked flowers grow in ones or twos from the bases of leaves. Stipules at the base of each leaf-stem usually have a dark blotch. Here the vetch is shown climbing on fat hen, with common field speedwell round its base. 6–48 in. (15–120 cm); flowers May–Sept.

Teeth at end of sepal tube are almost as long as the fused portion. [× 2]

Pods are smooth or slightly hairy, with a long beak and 4–12 seeds. [Actual size]

Common vetch grows in grassy places, hedges and tilled ground all over Britain, but is rarer in the north-west.

Common vetch *Vicia sativa*

Despite its name, this is not the most abundant of British vetches; although widespread, it is really common only in south-eastern England. Common vetch was introduced there from the Continent, where many hybrids had been bred for cattle food. In Britain the plant exists in two forms, the first with slender stems, pairs of narrow leaflets and flowers up to ⅝ in. (1·6 cm) long, the second with taller, stouter stems, broader and more oblong leaflets and flowers up to 1¼ in. (3 cm) long. It was the second form which was cultivated in England, where the seeds were commonly used as pigeon food in the 18th century.

Common vetch can be distinguished from the other British vetches, as it usually has a pair of flowers and two black-blotched stipules at the base of each leaf.

A form of common vetch that grows in North Africa and southern Europe produces two sorts of flowers – the normal, purple-petalled kind, and others which never open, and must fertilise themselves. These are grown on stems which are forced underground, where the flowers turn into rounded, whitish pods, each containing one or two seeds. Should normal seed production fail, this ensures a good chance of survival.

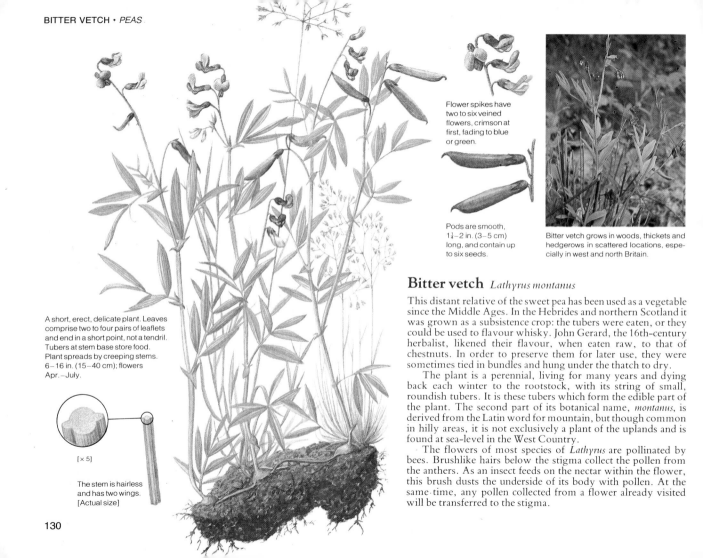

Flower spikes have two to six veined flowers, crimson at first, fading to blue or green.

Pods are smooth, 1¼–2 in. (3–5 cm) long, and contain up to six seeds.

Bitter vetch grows in woods, thickets and hedgerows in scattered locations, especially in west and north Britain.

A short, erect, delicate plant. Leaves comprise two to four pairs of leaflets and end in a short point, not a tendril. Tubers at stem base store food. Plant spreads by creeping stems. 6–16 in. (15–40 cm); flowers Apr.–July.

[× 5]

The stem is hairless and has two wings. [Actual size]

Bitter vetch *Lathyrus montanus*

This distant relative of the sweet pea has been used as a vegetable since the Middle Ages. In the Hebrides and northern Scotland it was grown as a subsistence crop: the tubers were eaten, or they could be used to flavour whisky. John Gerard, the 16th-century herbalist, likened their flavour, when eaten raw, to that of chestnuts. In order to preserve them for later use, they were sometimes tied in bundles and hung under the thatch to dry.

The plant is a perennial, living for many years and dying back each winter to the rootstock, with its string of small, roundish tubers. It is these tubers which form the edible part of the plant. The second part of its botanical name, *montanus*, is derived from the Latin word for mountain, but though common in hilly areas, it is not exclusively a plant of the uplands and is found at sea-level in the West Country.

The flowers of most species of *Lathyrus* are pollinated by bees. Brushlike hairs below the stigma collect the pollen from the anthers. As an insect feeds on the nectar within the flower, this brush dusts the underside of its body with pollen. At the same time, any pollen collected from a flower already visited will be transferred to the stigma.

Pods look flattened when ripe and sometimes have fine hairs. [Actual size]

Weak, spindly stems scramble by means of tendrils at leaf tips. Leaf-like stipules grow at base of leaf-stalk. 12–48 in. (30–120 cm); flowers May–Aug.

Five to twelve flowers are carried on a stalk that is longer than the leaves.

[× 5]

The stem is square in section and unwinged. [Actual size]

Meadow vetchling is common throughout the British Isles in grassy places; it is sometimes found in hedges or on banks.

Meadow vetchling *Lathyrus pratensis*

Farmers encourage this slender, scrambling plant to grow in their meadows, since the nodules on its roots fix nitrogen from the air and so increase the richness of the soil. Being relatively rich in protein, particularly in its seeds, it also contributes to the food value of pasturage or hay. The meadow vetchling has a creeping, underground rootstock, and on grassy banks such as railway embankments it often forms large clumps.

Although each leaf has a small, forked tendril for clambering up other plants, the meadow vetchling is not a great climber. Instead, the sharply angled stems arise from the rootstock in profusion, relying on each other and on surrounding plants for most of their support.

The numerous yellow flowers of meadow vetchling are visited mainly by bumble bees, which have tongues long enough to reach the nectar at the bottom of the long flower tube. The shape of the flowers has earned the plant the folk-names of 'lady's slippers' and 'old granny's slipper-sloppers'. Another name is yellow tare-tine; the word 'tare' is an old name for vetch, and does not necessarily mean a weed, as in the Biblical parable of the farmer whose enemy sowed tares among his corn.

131

The stalk bearing the flower-head is usually longer than the leaves, and carries three to eight flowers.

This scrambling plant climbs plants such as blackberries by means of big, branched tendrils at the tips of the leaves. 40–80 in. (100–200 cm); flowers June–Aug.

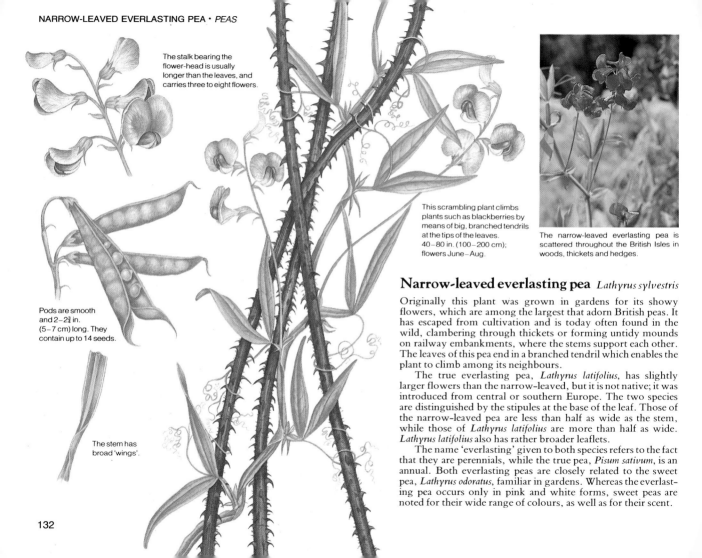

The narrow-leaved everlasting pea is scattered throughout the British Isles in woods, thickets and hedges.

Pods are smooth and 2–2¾ in. (5–7 cm) long. They contain up to 14 seeds.

The stem has broad 'wings'.

Narrow-leaved everlasting pea *Lathyrus sylvestris*

Originally this plant was grown in gardens for its showy flowers, which are among the largest that adorn British peas. It has escaped from cultivation and is today often found in the wild, clambering through thickets or forming untidy mounds on railway embankments, where the stems support each other. The leaves of this pea end in a branched tendril which enables the plant to climb among its neighbours.

The true everlasting pea, *Lathyrus latifolius*, has slightly larger flowers than the narrow-leaved, but it is not native; it was introduced from central or southern Europe. The two species are distinguished by the stipules at the base of the leaf. Those of the narrow-leaved pea are less than half as wide as the stem, while those of *Lathyrus latifolius* are more than half as wide. *Lathyrus latifolius* also has rather broader leaflets.

The name 'everlasting' given to both species refers to the fact that they are perennials, while the true pea, *Pisum sativum*, is an annual. Both everlasting peas are closely related to the sweet pea, *Lathyrus odoratus*, familiar in gardens. Whereas the everlasting pea occurs only in pink and white forms, sweet peas are noted for their wide range of colours, as well as for their scent.

132

Leaves are green above, white and hairy below. Pairs of small leaflets separate the bigger ones.

An upright plant. Its lower leaves have up to five pairs of big leaflets, with a lobed leaflet at the tip. 24–48 in. (60–120 cm); flowers June–Aug.

The flower has five sepals, bent back, and five petals. Stamens are long and numerous. [× 5]

Fruits are twisted spirally. [Actual size]

Meadowsweet is common throughout the British Isles, in wet parts of woods and meadows and in marshes and fens.

Dropwort
Filipendula vulgaris

Lower leaves have up to eight pairs of big leaflets. The flower cluster is broader than it is long; each flower has six sepals and six petals; and the fruits are not twisted.

Meadowsweet *Filipendula ulmaria*

A Tudor lady expecting a visit from Queen Elizabeth would have covered her floors with freshly cut meadowsweet, since this fragrant plant was the queen's favourite means of masking 16th-century smells. Meadowsweet has two distinct aromas, reflected in the plant's alternative name in Yorkshire of 'courtship and matrimony': the heady smell of the flowers is taken as representing courtship, while the sharper scent of the crushed foliage symbolises the reality of marriage.

The name of meadowsweet appears to describe the plant well, for it smells sweetly and grows in wet meadows. In fact, however, the name is a corruption of an older name, medesweete, given because the plant was used to flavour mead, the Anglo-Saxon drink made from fermented honey. In medieval days an infusion of meadowsweet was used to ease pain, to calm fevers and to induce sweating, for the sap contains chemicals of the same group as salicylic acid, an ingredient of aspirin.

The botanical name of *Filipendula* applied to meadowsweet and the related dropwort means literally 'hanging on a thread'. The word refers to the bitter tubers of dropwort which develop at a distance from the base of the plant on an elongated stem.

133

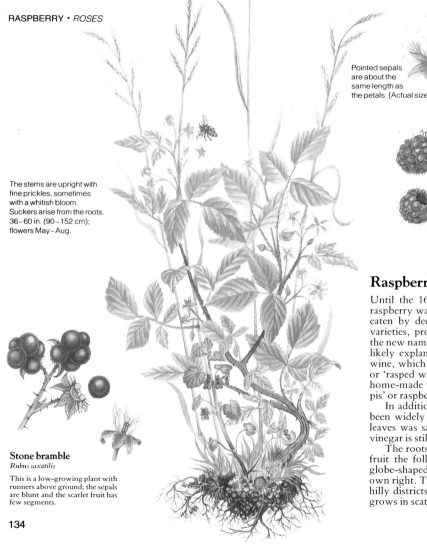

The stems are upright with fine prickles, sometimes with a whitish bloom. Suckers arise from the roots. 36–60 in. (90–152 cm); flowers May–Aug.

Pointed sepals are about the same length as the petals. [Actual size]

The red fruit has many segments and comes away from the conical core when ripe. [Actual size]

The raspberry grows wild in heathland and woods on uplands all over Britain, except parts of Cornwall and Wales.

Stone bramble
Rubus saxatilis

This is a low-growing plant with runners above ground; the sepals are blunt and the scarlet fruit has few segments.

Raspberry *Rubus idaeus*

Until the 16th century, the wild shrub now known as the raspberry was called the hindberry, presumably because it was eaten by deer. But with the arrival of more heavily fruited varieties, probably imported from the Continent, there arose the new name 'raspberry'; and nobody is certain why. The most likely explanation is that the berries were used for making a wine, which in appearance resembled the well-known *vin râpé*, or 'rasped wine', shipped from France. The ingredients of the home-made wine might therefore have become known as 'raspis' or raspberries.

In addition to providing a delicious fruit, the raspberry has been widely used in Britain as a medicine. An infusion of the leaves was said to ease the pangs of childbirth, and raspberry vinegar is still used to soothe colds and fevers.

The roots of the raspberry plant send up shoots, which bear fruit the following year. The fruits are complex, since each globe-shaped segment round its pip is technically a fruit in its own right. The related stone bramble is a much smaller plant of hilly districts, with fruits consisting of just a few segments. It grows in scattered colonies throughout the British Isles.

The fruit is black when ripe. Its many segments are attached to a core. [Actual size]

Sprawling, prickly, arched stems often take root to form new plants. Leaves have three to five leaflets, with white or grey hairy underside. The plant is seen growing with purple hedge woundwort; the pollinating insect is a hoverfly. Stems up to 36 in. (90 cm) long; flowers May–Sept.

Flowers are 1–1½ in. (2·5–4 cm) across, either white or pink. [Actual size]

Blackberries grow in woods, hedges and scrub all over England and Wales; less common in Scotland and Ireland.

Dewberry
Rubus caesius

This species has short, weak prickles and leaves which always have three leaflets. Fruits have only a few segments, larger than those of bramble and covered with a bluish bloom.

Blackberry *Rubus fruticosus*

The blackberry or bramble is one of the most familiar 'free foods' of our hedgerows. But it is a source of perplexity to botanists, for no fewer than 2,000 varieties, or micro-species, have been recorded; as a result, the brambles in one area often look rather different from those of another area.

According to old folklore, blackberries should not be eaten after Michaelmas (September 29) because the Devil then spits on them. The advice is sound, because the fruits become mushy and insipid about that time; but the miscreant which spits on them is not the Devil but the flesh-fly, which dribbles saliva on to the berries and is then able to suck up the juice.

Blackberry plants are a home for the shield bug (*Elasmucha grisea*), one of the few insects that looks after its young. Late in July a mother shield bug may be seen on a leaf with her 30–40 young; but at the first sign of danger, she herds them under the leaf while she stays bravely on top as a decoy for predators. Throughout the summer, young bramble leaves are mined by the larvae of the moth *Nepticula aurella*; their white, winding tunnels show where the larva emerged from its egg and ate its way onwards into the open.

135

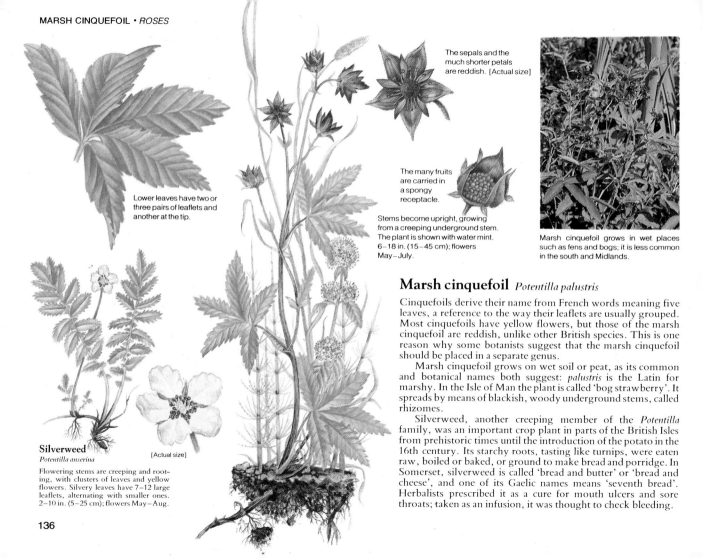

Lower leaves have two or three pairs of leaflets and another at the tip.

The sepals and the much shorter petals are reddish. [Actual size]

The many fruits are carried in a spongy receptacle.

Stems become upright, growing from a creeping underground stem. The plant is shown with water mint. 6–18 in. (15–45 cm); flowers May–July.

Marsh cinquefoil grows in wet places such as fens and bogs; it is less common in the south and Midlands.

Silverweed
Potentilla anserina

[Actual size]

Flowering stems are creeping and rooting, with clusters of leaves and yellow flowers. Silvery leaves have 7–12 large leaflets, alternating with smaller ones. 2–10 in. (5–25 cm); flowers May–Aug.

Marsh cinquefoil *Potentilla palustris*

Cinquefoils derive their name from French words meaning five leaves, a reference to the way their leaflets are usually grouped. Most cinquefoils have yellow flowers, but those of the marsh cinquefoil are reddish, unlike other British species. This is one reason why some botanists suggest that the marsh cinquefoil should be placed in a separate genus.

Marsh cinquefoil grows on wet soil or peat, as its common and botanical names both suggest: *palustris* is the Latin for marshy. In the Isle of Man the plant is called 'bog strawberry'. It spreads by means of blackish, woody underground stems, called rhizomes.

Silverweed, another creeping member of the *Potentilla* family, was an important crop plant in parts of the British Isles from prehistoric times until the introduction of the potato in the 16th century. Its starchy roots, tasting like turnips, were eaten raw, boiled or baked, or ground to make bread and porridge. In Somerset, silverweed is called 'bread and butter' or 'bread and cheese', and one of its Gaelic names means 'seventh bread'. Herbalists prescribed it as a cure for mouth ulcers and sore throats; taken as an infusion, it was thought to check bleeding.

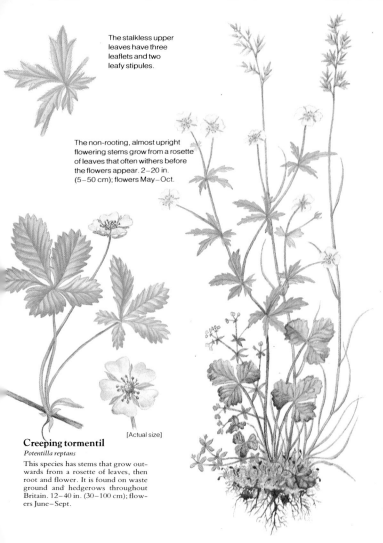

The stalkless upper leaves have three leaflets and two leafy stipules.

The non-rooting, almost upright flowering stems grow from a rosette of leaves that often withers before the flowers appear. 2–20 in. (5–50 cm); flowers May–Oct.

Flowers have four sepals and four petals. [Actual size]

Up to 20 fruits are produced on small, solid receptacle.

Tormentil is a plant of light acid soils, growing in grassland, fen and bogs, and especially on heaths, throughout Britain.

Creeping tormentil
Potentilla reptans
This species has stems that grow outwards from a rosette of leaves, then root and flower. It is found on waste ground and hedgerows throughout Britain. 12–40 in. (30–100 cm); flowers June–Sept.

[Actual size]

Tormentil *Potentilla erecta*

The widespread belief in the medicinal power of tormentil that existed in the 17th century was expressed by the dramatist John Fletcher when he wrote of

> This tormentil, whose vertue is to part
> All deadly killing poison from the heart

In the *Country Farme*, a book of rustic lore published in 1616, a powder or decoction of tormentil roots was recommended 'to appease the rage and torment of the teeth'. A local name for tormentil, blood root, refers to a red dye extracted from the roots and used to colour clothing. Tormentil roots were also used as an alternative to the oak bark in tanning hides, their highly astringent quality proving ideal for the purpose.

The tormentil's buttercup–like golden–yellow flowers secrete a nectar that attracts pollinating insects. In wet weather or at night, when the petals close up, the tormentil flower has the ability to pollinate itself.

Tormentil flowers almost always bear four petals. The smaller, but closely related creeping tormentil (*Potentilla reptans*), normally has five petals although a small proportion of them – approximately one in five – have six petals.

137

The fruit is fleshy and red when ripe. [Actual size]

Long runners root at intervals to form new plants. The lower leaves form a rosette. 2–12 in. (5–30 cm); flowers Apr.–July.

Flowers have sepals and petals in whorls of four or five. Petals are often longer than sepals. [Actual size]

Leaves have long stalks and three leaflets, bright green on top and pale below. [Actual size]

Wild strawberries are found in woods, scrub and grassland throughout the British Isles, especially on chalky soils.

Barren strawberry
Potentilla sterilis
This is easily mistaken for wild strawberry, but has blue-green leaves and gaps between petals. The fruit has yellowish achenes and is never fleshy.

Wild strawberry *Fragaria vesca*

In spite of the common belief, it is most unlikely that the strawberry got its name from the gardener's practice of putting straw beneath the berries to keep them clean and free of slugs. The name goes back to Anglo-Saxon days, before AD 1000, and is much older than the practice of cultivating strawberries. In old English, one meaning of straw was small particles of chaff; and the name may have been given to the scattering of pips (achenes) over the surface of the fruit. Another old meaning of straw was to strew over the ground, which is just what the wild strawberry does with its creepers.

The achenes are the equivalent of the juicy fruit segments of the raspberry or blackberry. The red flesh of the strawberry is the same structure as the central white core (receptacle) of a raspberry that is left on the plant when the fruit is picked. The receptacle of the unpalatable barren strawberry does not enlarge, and only dry achenes are produced.

Garden strawberries, originally raised in France in the 18th century, are hybrids between a North American and a Chilean species. The so-called Alpine strawberries, smaller and deliciously flavoured, are selected forms of the wild strawberry.

138

The numerous starry flowers have five notched petals. [× 2]

The grooved fruit has hooked spines around the top, used to disperse the seed. [× 2]

Stems are upright, unbranched and hairy, with yellow flowers in a spike. The plant is growing with cow parsley, dandelion and grass. 12–24 in. (30–60 cm); flowers June–Aug.

Agrimony is common in field margins, road verges and hedgerows over most of Britain, but is rare in north Scotland.

Fragrant agrimony

Agrimonia repens

This is a bigger and more branched species with fragrant leaves, which have sticky hairs underneath. Some of the spines on its fruit are bent back and not hooked.

[× 2]

Agrimony *Agrimonia eupatoria*

In the eyes of the ancients, this common flower of grassy places was nothing if not versatile – it was held to be a remedy against snake-bite, poor sight, loss of memory and liver complaints. An infusion produced from the leaves is still used as a stimulating alternative to tea. The genus name *Agrimonia* may come from the Greek for 'spot on the eye' or 'wild flower of the field'. The species name *eupatoria* may recall Mithradates Eupator, the king who resisted the Roman conquest of Asia Minor in the 1st century BC, and who introduced agrimony into medicine.

The plant was once believed to be associated with magic, being known as fairy's wand or fairy's rod in south-western England. Its widespread alternative common name, Aaron's rod, may have been introduced with church encouragement to supersede this relic of pagan belief. In more recent days, a strong yellow dye made from agrimony was used to colour wool.

Flies and bees are attracted to the slender spikes of flowers by a scent reminiscent of apricots. The fruits have a ring of hooks round the upper edge; these catch on to the fur of passing animals or the clothes of walkers, ensuring that the seed is distributed over a wide area.

Some leaves of this upright, hairy plant grow on stalks rising directly from the base, each bearing two to three unequal-sized pairs of leaflets. The upper leaves growing from the stem of the plant are usually three-lobed, with big, paired leaf-like stipules at the junction of stem and leaf-stalk. 12–24 in. (30–60 cm); flowers June–Aug.

The flowers are upright with turned-back sepals and spreading petals. [Actual size]

Single fruit [× 4]

The fruits are long-beaked, hooked and borne in a head. [Actual size]

Herb bennet is found throughout the British Isles in shady places that have damp but fertile soil.

Water avens

Geum rivale

This downy plant has nodding, orange-pink or – rarely – pale yellow flowers. The sepals are upright and purple, while the petals are twice the size of those of wood avens. The beaked fruit ends in a feathery point. It is commonest in northern Britain.

[× 2]

Herb bennet *Geum urbanum*

In the 15th century, herb bennet used to be hung over doors to stop the Devil crossing the threshold, for it was considered to be one of the most powerful charms against evil spirits. According to an early medical treatise of 1491, 'if a man carries the root about with him, no venomous beast can touch him'. The magical powers attributed to the plant seem to have derived from its association with St Benedict (or Bennet), founder of the Benedictine order of monks, after whom it is named. The roots of herb bennet have a delicate, clove-like aroma and were once used as a fly repellent and for flavouring ale.

The leaf-like stipules occurring where the upper leaf-stalks join the stem are a characteristic of herb bennet and some other members of the rose family. The hooked seeds spread by attaching themselves to the fur or feathers of animals and birds and to the clothing of passers-by.

Herb bennet is also known as wood avens. The related water avens is a widespread plant of ditches and wet ground. Its nodding flowers are usually orange-pink, with petals twice as big as those of herb bennet. When growing in the same area, the two often cross-pollinate to produce a variety of offspring.

Some stems are sprawling, others upright. Leaves rising from the roots are green on both sides; each leaf has 7–11 toothed lobes. The plant is shown growing with buttercups and grass. 2–18 in. (5–45 cm); flowers June–Sept.

The sepals are in two rings of four. There are no petals. [× 5]

The fruit is usually hairy, ripening in loose clusters. [× 5]

Lady's mantle grows all over the British Isles except the Channel Isles, but is less common in south-eastern England.

Alpine lady's mantle
Alchemilla alpina

This creeping plant is a smaller version of lady's mantle. The root leaves are deeply divided into five to seven lobes, green above and densely silver-haired below. The flowers are pale green and clustered.

Lady's mantle *Alchemilla vulgaris*

Medieval alchemists collected the dew from lady's mantle at dawn and used it in their experiments to manufacture gold from common metals. They called it 'celestial water', for obviously it had strange properties: lady's mantle leaves bore big pearls of dew when all other flowers had none. The reason for this is a process known as guttation. It occurs in conditions of high humidity when water cannot be lost from the leaves as vapour, and lady's mantle forces water out of the tiny leaf-holes through which it 'breathes'.

While the botanical name of the plant harks back to the alchemists, its common name refers to the Virgin Mary, to whom the plant is dedicated. Traditionally lady's mantle has been used for curing women's ailments, in particular for restoring sagging bosoms to their former shape and size.

Lady's mantle is not one plant but a name applied to several species, which vary in small but definite ways. An inconspicuous, low-growing plant, it is often found on grassy roadsides, especially in mountain areas, where it grows more luxuriantly. Alpine lady's mantle is common at over 2,000 ft (610 metres) in England and in grassy places on Scottish mountains.

141

Stipules form a leaf-like cup, enclosing the flower. [× 2]

The tiny green flower has four sepals and no petals. [× 15]

The fruit is oval. [× 15]

A sprawling, downy plant. The short-stalked leaves have three segments each lobed at the tip. It is shown growing with chickweed and bog pimpernel. ¾–8 in. (2–20 cm); flowers Apr.–Sept.

Common all over the British Isles, parsley piert grows on arable fields and bare wastelands, particularly in dry sites.

Parsley piert *Aphanes arvensis*

The name of parsley piert has nothing to do with parsley. It is a corruption of the French *perce-pierre*, meaning 'stone-piercer', and was given to the plant because of its habit of growing in shallow, stony soil and emerging between stones. As in the case of saxifrage (from the Latin meaning 'stone-breaker') it was wrongly assumed that the plant could pierce stones; and it was thought that a medicine made of parsley piert would break up stones in the bladder and kidneys. Old folk-names for the plant include 'colicwort' and 'bowel-hive-grass' (hive meant inflammation), showing that it was also used for intestinal ailments.

The 17th-century herbalist Nicholas Culpeper, recommended parsley piert for use in salads, although it would be difficult to gather sufficient quantities of such a tiny plant for a reasonable meal. Culpeper also recommends the plant to gentlemen for eating as a winter pickle in addition to the pickled samphire to which they were accustomed.

The genus name of *Aphanes* comes from a Greek word meaning unseen or unnoticed, which precisely describes this tiny plant. Nevertheless, parsley piert is a very common and widespread weed of cultivated ground, whether acidic or not.

Flower-head has an oblong outline. [Actual size]

Each flower has male and female parts. [× 5]

Fruit has four wings. [× 5]

Great burnet is not widespread but occurs frequently on damp grasslands in central England and Wales.

Salad burnet
Sanguisorba minor

The flower-head of this shorter species is round, smaller and has separate male, female and bisexual flowers.

Stems are upright and hairless. Leaves are composed of paired rows of toothed leaflets. 12–36 in. (30–90 cm); flowers June–Sept.

Great burnet *Sanguisorba officinalis*

This handsome plant may be in danger owing to the increasing efficiency of British farming. It grows in meadowland, particularly damp pastures and hilly areas, and is most common in central Britain.

Ancient herbalists believed in the doctrine of signatures – that plants advertise their medicinal powers by outward signs. In the case of great burnet, the dark crimson flower-heads suggested blood, and for centuries the plant was used to staunch wounds and as a remedy for internal bleeding. In more recent times a root, freshly dug up and peeled, was applied to burns to relieve the pain and encourage healing. Great burnet's blood-staunching reputation is preserved in its botanical name *Sanguisorba*, 'blood-absorbing'.

The flowers of great burnet are bisexual and produce abundant nectar for insect pollination. Salad burnet, which is much smaller in all its parts, has male-only flowers on the lower part of the head. These flower first, while the female and bisexual flowers higher up the head open later. This is a device commonly used by wind-pollinated plants to avoid self-fertilisation. As its name implies, salad burnet is eaten in salads.

143

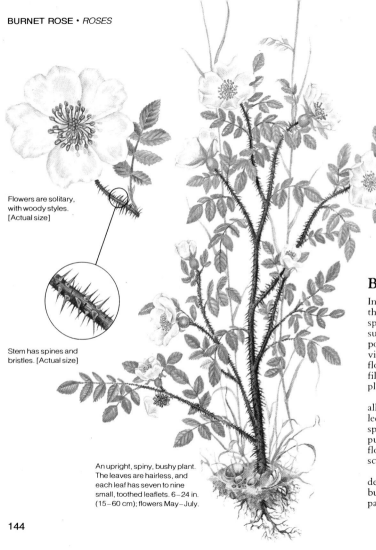

Flowers are solitary,
with woody styles.
[Actual size]

Stem has spines and
bristles. [Actual size]

An upright, spiny, bushy plant.
The leaves are hairless, and
each leaf has seven to nine
small, toothed leaflets. 6–24 in.
(15–60 cm); flowers May–July.

Fruits are round, with a
crown of long sepals.
[Actual size]

The burnet rose is found throughout
Britain on downland, heaths and dunes,
especially near the sea.

Burnet rose *Rosa pimpinellifolia*

In the shallow dunes and grassy sand-hills round Britain's coasts
the creamy-white flowers of the burnet rose – sometimes
splashed with pink – make a brave show in spring and early
summer. For many years, varieties of this flower have been
popular garden plants. Its rootstock suckers freely, spreading
vigorously underground from the main root and producing new
flowering stems at a distance from it. A single hybrid rapidly
fills out into a dense bush covering a large area, which makes the
plant popular with gardeners.

Botanists once called the burnet rose *Rosa spinosissima*, literally 'the spiniest rose'. The very large number of thorns, mingled with numerous stiff bristles, is a distinctive feature of the
species. Another characteristic, unique among wild roses, is the
purple-black swelling or 'hip' that forms on the end of the
flower-stalk after fertilisation. All other wild rose hips are red or
scarlet.

Both the common and the scientific names of the burnet rose
derive from the close resemblance of its leaves to those of the
burnet-saxifrage (*Pimpinella saxifraga*), which is a member of the
parsley family.

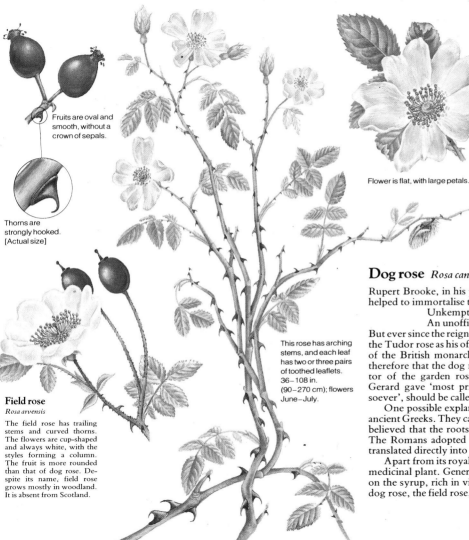

Fruits are oval and smooth, without a crown of sepals.

Thorns are strongly hooked. [Actual size]

Flower is flat, with large petals.

This rose has arching stems, and each leaf has two or three pairs of toothed leaflets. 36–108 in. (90–270 cm); flowers June–July.

Field rose
Rosa arvensis

The field rose has trailing stems and curved thorns. The flowers are cup-shaped and always white, with the styles forming a column. The fruit is more rounded than that of dog rose. Despite its name, field rose grows mostly in woodland. It is absent from Scotland.

The dog rose brightens hedgerows and scrubland throughout England and Wales. It is rare in Scotland.

Dog rose *Rosa canina*

Rupert Brooke, in his poem 'The Old Vicarage, Grantchester', helped to immortalise the dog rose:

> Unkempt about those hedges blows,
> An unofficial English rose.

But ever since the reign of Henry VII (1485–1509), who adopted the Tudor rose as his official emblem, the rose has been a symbol of the British monarchy and of England herself. It is curious therefore that the dog rose of the English hedgerow, the ancestor of the garden roses to which the 16th-century herbalist Gerard gave 'most principall place among all flowers whatsoever', should be called 'dog', suggesting 'of no worth'.

One possible explanation of this misnomer goes back to the ancient Greeks. They called the wild rose 'dog rose' because they believed that the roots could cure a man bitten by a mad dog. The Romans adopted the name, *Rosa canina*, which was then translated directly into English.

Apart from its royal connections, the dog rose was a valuable medicinal plant. Generations of children have been brought up on the syrup, rich in vitamin C, made from rose hips. Like the dog rose, the field rose, *Rosa arvensis*, is a vigorous climber.

145

Flowers are on long stalks
with finely lobed sepals.
The fruit is oval.

[Actual size]

The downy rose is an open shrub,
its long slender stems bearing
numerous pink or white flowers.

The downy rose is common in woods,
hedgerows and scrubland in England
and Wales but is rarer in Scotland.

Soft-leaved rose
Rosa villosa

A straight-branched rose with
grey-green young leaves and
straight thorns. Fruits are usually
crowned with five sepals.

[Actual size]

The arching stems have pale green young
leaves. The thorns are slightly curved.
36–72 in. (90–180 cm); flowers June–July.

Downy rose *Rosa tomentosa*

One Latin word, *tomentum*, provides a direct link between a
banquet in Imperial Rome and a downy rose growing in a
tangled hedgerow in modern Britain. Guests at a Roman banquet did not sit up at table but reclined on benches, propped up
on cushions which were stuffed with a soft filling, usually of
wool, known as *tomentum*. The same word was used by botanists as the basis for the species name of the downy rose, because
each leaf of the plant has two or three pairs of leaflets covered
with a soft, fine, downy growth.

The word rose has associations going back even further than
ancient Rome. In its Latin form *rosa*, it derives from a Greek
word for red, which is in turn traceable to a word meaning red in
Sanskrit, the literary language of ancient India.

Like many wild roses, including the very similar soft-leaved
rose, *Rosa villosa*, the downy rose is frequently attacked by a
species of wasp called *cynips* or gall-wasp. The gall-wasp punctures the plant and deposits its eggs, producing on the stem a
tufted growth called a gall caused by the larvae feeding on the
stem. On downy roses such galls are bright red and, as a result,
country people called them 'robin's pin-cushions'.

146

The fruit is purple, and does not spread out when ripe. [×2]

The fleshy, water-storing leaves are flat and shallow-toothed.

The clusters of upright, unbranched stems are often reddish. The pale green leaves are alternate. Growing in the same spot may be found hedge woundwort, with its darker leaves and spikes of purple flowers. 8–24 in. (20–60 cm); flowers July–Sept.

Rosy-red flowers are borne on long stalks in globe-shaped heads. [Actual size]

This succulent is a locally common plant of woods and hedges, found in most parts of Britain.

Orpine *Sedum telephium*

In late summer and early autumn, the flowers of orpine bring a rose-red flush to many woodlands. It is sometimes found in hedgerows, too, but orpine's large flower-heads and tall stems with fleshy leaves look out of place in a hedge, and it is no surprise to find that many plants are escapees from cultivation. The garden 'ice plant' is in fact of the same species as wild orpine.

Orpine's stems and leaves store water, enabling it to survive prolonged drought and withstand being picked. This power of resistance – which gives the plant its other common name of 'livelong' – is illustrated by an old country custom. A girl intending marriage would hang a pair of stems side by side in her house. If they grew together she would be happy with her chosen husband, but if they grew apart the outlook was bleak, and if one withered quickly – an unlikely contingency – death was in prospect. Orpine was also hung up as a fly repellent.

The name orpine derives from *orpiment*, an Old French name for 'a golden pigment'. Orpine has no gold about it; the name was originally given to wall-pepper, a yellow-flowered plant of the same genus, but after translation was given to a plant which was wrongly believed to be the same species.

147

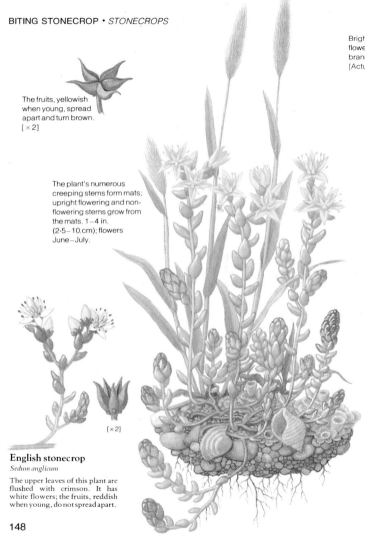

The fruits, yellowish when young, spread apart and turn brown. [× 2]

The plant's numerous creeping stems form mats; upright flowering and non-flowering stems grow from the mats. 1–4 in. (2·5–10 cm); flowers June–July.

Bright yellow flowers grow in branched clusters. [Actual size]

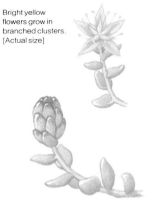

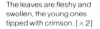

The leaves are fleshy and swollen, the young ones tipped with crimson. [× 2]

This succulent plant grows throughout Britain on grassland, shingle, dunes and walls, mainly on chalk and limestone.

Biting stonecrop *Sedum acre*

This diminutive plant has the alternative name of wall-pepper, from its peppery-tasting yellowish–green leaves. The smallest of the British yellow stonecrops, its star-like flowers spill out over walls, rocks and sand dunes forming a golden carpet during the summer. The short stalks are very numerous, some bearing flowers, others with overlapping, succulent leaves. The flowers, in a compact head, have broad-based petals.

Superstition claims that biting stonecrop, if planted on the roofs of houses, wards off thunderstorms. In olden days the plant was considered an excellent medicine for the cure of a variety of ills. It stopped bleeding, eased ulcers and prevented fevers. But it had to be used with care, for its juice could induce vomiting.

The closely related English stonecrop is the commonest of the white stonecrops. Found mostly in the west of Britain, it grows on short turf, rocks, dunes and in shingle, forming sprouting mats of stems. Its short, greyish leaves contrast with the yellowish–green leaves of biting stonecrop. The stem and the leaves are often tinged with red, especially in dry conditions. The white flowers may also have a pinkish tinge.

[× 2]

English stonecrop
Sedum anglicum

The upper leaves of this plant are flushed with crimson. It has white flowers; the fruits, reddish when young, do not spread apart.

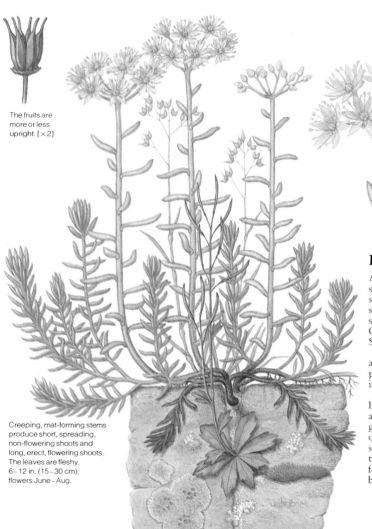

The fruits are more or less upright. [×2]

Bright yellow flowers grow in a single cluster at the top of the stem. [Actual size]

Creeping, mat-forming stems produce short, spreading, non-flowering shoots and long, erect, flowering shoots. The leaves are fleshy. 6–12 in. (15–30 cm); flowers June–Aug.

Reflexed stonecrop was introduced from Europe and is now naturalised, growing on rocks and walls throughout Britain.

Reflexed stonecrop *Sedum reflexum*

A dense head of flowers called a crop, and a habit of growing on stones – especially those of walls – give the group of plants called stonecrops their name. One of the group, reflexed stonecrop, is so called because the lower leaves of the flowering stem are sometimes curved back, or reflexed. It is an immigrant from the Continent, where it is found from Scandinavia to central Spain, Sicily and Albania.

With its large and striking bright yellow flowers, the plant is an attractive one that has been cultivated for many years. It produces an abundance of fertile seed, and can also propagate itself from small pieces that have been broken off.

Given this combination of characteristics, a plant is highly likely to be taken, or to take itself, beyond its native land, and also to spread beyond the garden fence. Reflexed stonecrop now grows in the wild in small quantities on old walls, rocks and other suitable habitats throughout Britain, especially in the south. At one time the leaves were eaten as a spring salad, and the 17th-century diarist John Evelyn recommended it as a plant for the kitchen garden. In the Middle Ages it was used to stop bleeding and to cure ulcers and sores.

149

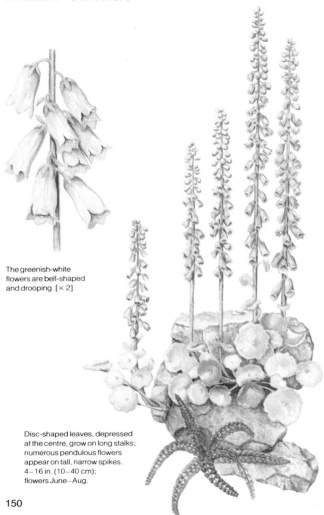

The greenish-white flowers are bell-shaped and drooping. [× 2]

Disc-shaped leaves, depressed at the centre, grow on long stalks; numerous pendulous flowers appear on tall, narrow spikes. 4–16 in. (10–40 cm); flowers June–Aug.

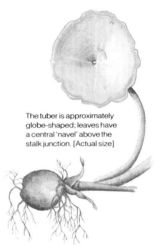

The tuber is approximately globe-shaped; leaves have a central 'navel' above the stalk junction. [Actual size]

The tall flower spike of navelwort and its dimpled leaves jut from walls and rock crevices in western Britain.

Navelwort *Umbilicus rupestris*

Anyone familiar with the high roadside banks of Devon and Cornwall will recognise navelwort, or wall pennywort as it is also called. It grows, often abundantly, between the stones in the banks; it is found, too, in rock crevices and on sea cliffs. The plant's size varies greatly according to its position. Lush, branched specimens spring from moist and shady surroundings, while much smaller plants cling to dry walls or the more exposed cliffs.

Navelwort is a fleshy perennial with disc-shaped leaves, each with a distinct dimple in the centre where leaf and stalk join. The flowers are in a long greenish spike, with the petals joined to form a tube. The plant's common and scientific names all refer to the unusual shape of the leaves – pennywort from their supposed resemblance to a penny, and navelwort to the central, navel-like dimple. The word *umbilicus* is Latin for 'navel', and *rupestris* means 'a plant that grows on rocks'.

Navelwort has a very westerly distribution, being found most abundantly in western England and Wales and western Scotland. It becomes rarer eastwards, and may be absent from parts of eastern England and Scotland.

The seed capsule splits to the middle or below when ripe. [× 2]

White flowers with conspicuous red anthers have two yellow spots at the base of each petal. The sepals are bent back. [× 2]

The plant has a rosette of toothed leaves at the base, but the upper parts of the stem are leafless. The low-growing leaves are less exposed to mountain winds, and their closeness to each other helps to conserve moisture. Up to 10 in. (25 cm); flowers June–Aug.

The leaf is short-stalked, toothed, and hairy on its top surface. [×2]

Starry saxifrage is a common plant found on wet, stony ground in the mountainous areas of the British Isles.

Starry saxifrage *Saxifraga stellaris*

Clinging to a narrow, rocky ledge high up in the mountains, the starry saxifrage seems to live up to its name and reach for the stars. Few plants have such a tenacious grip on life. Its tough, penetrating roots exploit the natural cracks and crevices in the rock and anchor it so firmly that it has gained the reputation, like other saxifrages, of being able to carve out its own foothold by actually cracking the stone. This belief, still widespread though erroneous, is reflected in the origin of the plant's scientific name *Saxifraga*; this combines the Latin words *saxum*, 'rock' and *frango*, 'break'.

In ancient medical lore the mythical stone-breaking properties of plants like the starry saxifrage were applied to curing stones in the body. It was believed that a decoction of the plant could crack kidney and gall stones. A 17th-century medical textbook, the *Physitian*, also recommends saxifrage roots, mixed with wine and vinegar, as a cure for the plague.

In the wild, the starry saxifrage is found only in the mountainous areas of Scotland, northern England, Wales and Ireland. Many other species of *Saxifraga* are popular plants of rockeries and alpine gardens.

151

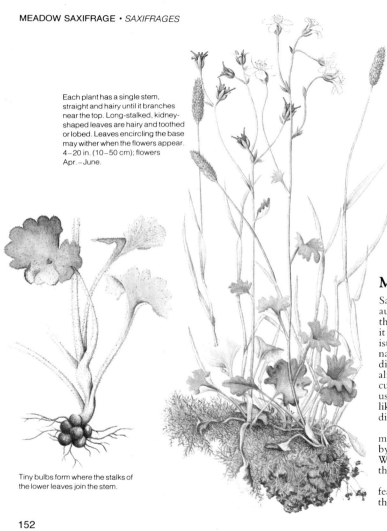

Each plant has a single stem, straight and hairy until it branches near the top. Long-stalked, kidney-shaped leaves are hairy and toothed or lobed. Leaves encircling the base may wither when the flowers appear. 4–20 in. (10–50 cm); flowers Apr.–June.

Flower has narrow white petals with green veins. [Actual size]

When ripe the long-horned fruit splits open at the top to release the seeds. [Actual size]

Non-acid, well-drained soils best suit this meadow plant, which is found in scattered locations, mainly in the east.

Tiny bulbs form where the stalks of the lower leaves join the stem.

Meadow saxifrage *Saxifraga granulata*

Saxifrage means 'stone-breaking', and according to certain authorities the flower was so named by the Romans because they found it growing in crevices of rocks and wrongly assumed it had broken them apart. But Pliny the Elder, a Roman naturalist of the 1st century AD, said the flower had been given this name because it had the medicinal power of breaking up a quite different sort of stone – a gallstone of the bile duct. This idea almost certainly arose from the ancient belief that plants with curative powers display a sign to indicate how they should be used. It was therefore deduced that a plant which grew stone-like brown bulbs round the base of its stem was intended to dissolve small stones in the body.

Once widespread in meadows over much of Britain, the meadow saxifrage has been driven from much of its old habitat by the intrusion of builders and by the uprooting of hedges. Where it has been left undisturbed, it still prospers, notably on the Breckland heaths of Norfolk.

The plant perpetuates itself by means of its most striking feature, the bulbs produced in the angle between the stem and the stalks of lower leaves.

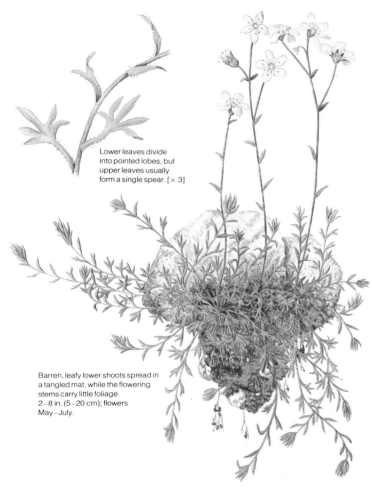

Lower leaves divide into pointed lobes, but upper leaves usually form a single spear. [× 3]

Barren, leafy lower shoots spread in a tangled mat, while the flowering stems carry little foliage. 2–8 in. (5–20 cm); flowers May–July.

Sepals do not bend back but remain upright. [× 3]

Fruit splits at the top when ripe. [× 3]

Rocky ground, or high, stony grassland with chalky soil best suit mossy saxifrage. It is common in parts of Wales.

Mossy saxifrage *Saxifraga hypnoides*

This low-lying plant can conceal its identity from highly experienced botanists by assuming widely diverse forms. In very moist sites it may be long and trailing, whilst in drier or more exposed areas it will form a wide, creeping mat. Mossy saxifrage can occasionally be found growing wild in more lowland sites, but generally it prefers the hills and the mountains, flourishing in Snowdonia, the Pennines, the Lake District and Scotland, sometimes as high as 4,000 ft (1,220 m) above sea-level. It is also found in some Irish mountains. This preference for upland places accounts for its alternative name of Dovedale moss.

Usually, mossy saxifrage grows on mountain ledges and screes where the soil is non-acid, and on open, grassy hillsides. A notable feature is that some of its branches are barren and others fertile, carrying attractive white flowers in groups of one to five. The nodding flower-buds are often pink-tipped. Like the meadow saxifrage, it frequently develops a cluster of bulbils between the stem and the stalks of lower leaves.

The creeping nature of mossy saxifrage and its showy, white flowers have made it a popular edging plant for herbaceous borders and a useful filling-in plant for rockeries.

153

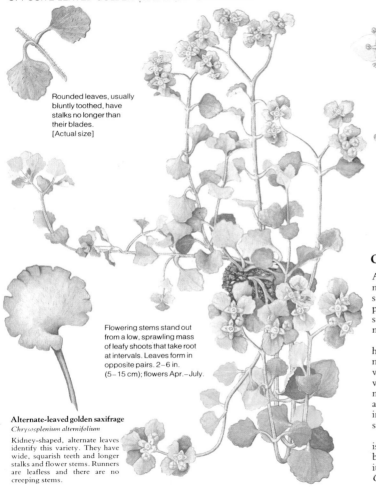

Rounded leaves, usually bluntly toothed, have stalks no longer than their blades. [Actual size]

Flowering stems stand out from a low, sprawling mass of leafy shoots that take root at intervals. Leaves form in opposite pairs. 2–6 in. (5–15 cm); flowers Apr.–July.

Alternate-leaved golden saxifrage
Chrysosplenium alternifolium
Kidney-shaped, alternate leaves identify this variety. They have wide, squarish teeth and longer stalks and flower stems. Runners are leafless and there are no creeping stems.

Flower has four sepals but no petals. A raised, lobed disc surrounds the styles. [× 4]

Fruit opens by splitting along the inner edge. [× 5]

This plant, which is found throughout Britain, favours wet and shady places on rocks, in woods or beside streams.

Opposite-leaved golden saxifrage *Chrysosplenium oppositifolium*

A gold-speckled, pale green mat spread beside a small stream or mountain rill signals that this plant has colonised the bank. The stems may creep until a large patch is formed, but as with many plants of such habitats, it varies in size from comparatively large specimens in lush, damp surroundings to small, dense tufts in more open, drier areas.

The bluntly toothed leaves are thin and crisp and, in fact, have in earlier times been eaten as a vegetable. The scientific name *Chrysosplenium* comes from two Greek words – *chrysos* which means gold, and *splene*, the spleen. The plant's leaves were believed to resemble a spleen in shape, and according to the medieval 'doctrine of signatures' should therefore be good for ailments of that part of the body when eaten or drunk in infusions. Another herb, the spleenwort, was held to have the same virtue, for the same reason.

Alternate-leaved golden saxifrage does not form mats, and is more robust than its relative. It is a plant of similar habitats, but occurs in more scattered locations. In mountain regions it can often be found growing further inside crevices than *Chrysosplenium oppositifolium*.

Casing of ripe fruit splits into four teeth. [Actual size]

Fringe of the modified stamen is tipped with yellowish glands. [× 4]

The flower stems, each with a single blossom, stand high above an abundance of long-stalked, heart-shaped base leaves. 4–12 in. (10–30 cm); flowers July–Oct.

Flower has veined petals and five fringed, modified stamens alternating with normal stamens. [Actual size]

Flower stem usually has a single stalkless leaf less than halfway up. [Actual size]

Grass-of-parnassus thrives on wet moorlands and marshy ground. It is common in Scotland and northern England.

Grass-of-parnassus *Parnassia palustris*

Mount Parnassus in Greece was sacred to Apollo, god of music. A place so bound up with Greek mythology was a fit home for so beautiful a plant as grass-of-parnassus, which was described by the Greek physician Dioscorides as growing on the slopes of the mountain in the 1st century AD. It is a plant with a short underground stem, from which arise the base leaves and the flowering stem.

Despite its name, grass-of-parnassus is not a grass, nor is it grass-like. Each stem bears a single large flower. It has five stamens which alternate around the centre of the flower, with the same number of delicately fringed modified stamens. The presence of these modified stamens, which are fringed with glands, distinguishes grass-of-parnassus from the saxifrages, with which it has sometimes been wrongly classified. The flower smells very faintly of honey. This scent, together with the veining of the petals, attracts insect pollinators.

In the past the plant was used as a herbal treatment for disorders of the liver, and an infusion of the leaves was claimed to aid digestion. Boiled in wine or water, the leaves were said to dissolve kidney stones.

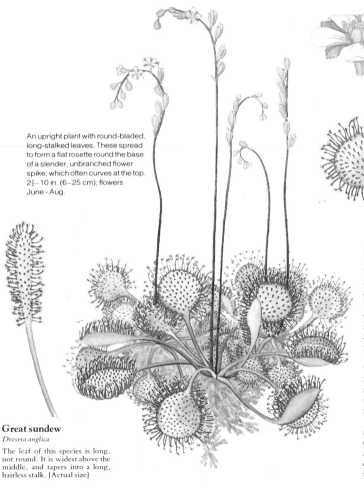

An upright plant with round-bladed, long-stalked leaves. These spread to form a flat rosette round the base of a slender, unbranched flower spike, which often curves at the top. 2½–10 in. (6–25 cm); flowers June–Aug.

Sundews have flower parts in groups of five to eight.

The leaf is covered with short, reddish, glandular hairs, while much longer hairs fringe the edges. [Actual size]

Sundews grow throughout Britain on wet heaths or boggy moorland. They digest insects to gain essential nutrients.

Great sundew
Drosera anglica

The leaf of this species is long, not round. It is widest above the middle, and tapers into a long, hairless stalk. [Actual size]

Round-leaved sundew *Drosera rotundifolia*

The sundew is a plant that feeds on insects, using its leaves to catch them. The leaf is covered with a multitude of red hairs, each tipped with a glistening droplet. Midges are attracted to these, mistaking them for water in which to lay their eggs, but once they touch the sticky fluid it holds them fast, while other hairs and the leaf-margins curl inwards to enclose them. Glands at the tips of the hairs then secrete juices that break down the soft parts of the insect's body into liquids to be absorbed by the leaf.

Several days later, the leaf uncurls and the husk of the insect is discarded. Once more, droplets appear on the leaf; and the trap is reset. It has been estimated that one sundew can catch as many as 2,000 insects in summer. This behaviour is an adaptation to the acid moorland soils where sundews grow. Because vital nutrients are lacking, the plant obtains them from insects.

Early observers mistook the fly-catching droplets for dew, and assumed that this plant, unlike almost all others, was capable of retaining its dew in full sunlight. So the sundew got its name, and also a reputation for magical properties; the 'dew' was much esteemed by medieval alchemists and herbalists, who claimed that it would burn off warts and excite lust in cattle.

The many-seeded berries are green or whitish when young, red when ripe. [Actual size]

Tendrils support the plant and help it to climb on grasses and other plants. The tendrils and the flower clusters shoot from the junction of the leaf and main stem. Leaves are usually five-lobed. Up to 120 in. (300 cm); flowers May–Sept.

Male flowers are larger than the females and are carried in long-stalked clusters. Each has four stamens but no style.

Female flower clusters are almost stalkless. Each flower has a three-lobed style but no stamens.

Bryony occurs frequently in hedgerows on well-drained soils. It is widespread in England, Wales and south Scotland.

White bryony *Bryonia dioica*

Fairground charlatans used to sell the swollen, twisted roots of white bryony as genuine mandrake roots, reputed from biblical times to hold magical powers as an aphrodisiac and a cure for sterility in women. But the infamous mandrake was a costly, rare plant, which had to be imported from the eastern Mediterranean, so unscrupulous folk dug up white bryony and sold it to the gullible.

Although an extract from the plant has been used in the treatment of rheumatism and as a drastic purgative, white bryony is poisonous, and dangerous taken in quantity. So, too, are its berries, which remain strung on thin stems in the hedges long after the leaves have withered. It is estimated that as few as 15 of them, if eaten, could kill a child.

The species climbs through hedges by means of tendrils, which arise at the base of the leaf-stalks; when the tips of the tendrils touch a twig, they wrap tightly around it. As the name *dioica*, 'two houses', implies, plants are either male or female. The common name refers to the colour of the roots and distinguishes this species from the unrelated black bryony, which is also found in British hedgerows.

157

[×2]

The stout, erect stem is square in section, with a rib at each corner. It is covered in hairs.

Flowers are in whorls of six, set in the angle between stem and small leaf-like bracts. The petals are lance-shaped, with darker veins. [Actual size]

This plant is found in fens and marshes, lake margins and slow-flowing rivers; it is common in southern England and Wales.

Stems are unbranched, or have a few short branches. The leaves are stalkless, the lower leaves in whorls of three and the upper leaves in pairs. The plant is seen growing with common reed. 24–48 in. (60–120 cm); flowers June–Aug.

Purple-loosestrife *Lythrum salicaria*

Water margins during the late summer bloom with a regal display of the rich reddish-purple flowers of purple-loosestrife. Testimony to the graceful, willow-like quality of its foliage is the species name *salicaria*, from the Latin *salix*, a willow.

Close examination of the flowers shows that although those of any one plant are the same, they may differ from plant to plant. Different plants may have any one of three sorts of flower, which vary in the positions of their male and female parts (stamens and stigmas). The stigma may project beyond the sepal tube, it may be level with the tips of the sepals, or it may be hidden inside. Each of the two whorls of stamens also vary in position. A bee feeding on the nectar of one sort of flower will receive a dusting of pollen on two parts of its tongue from the two whorls of stamens. This pollen will be in the right positions to be brushed onto the stigmas of the two other sorts of flower when the bee visits them. This arrangement makes sure that the flowers of one plant are fertilised only by pollen from another of the same species, ensuring the vigour of the species.

The juice of purple-loosestrife is rich in tannins, and has been used as an alternative to oak bark for tanning leather.

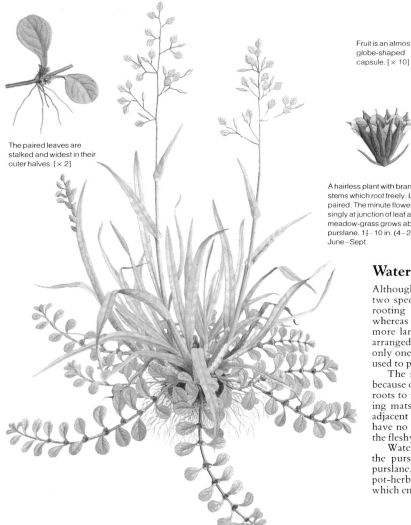

The paired leaves are stalked and widest in their outer halves. [× 2]

Fruit is an almost globe-shaped capsule. [× 10]

The tiny stalkless flowers usually have six pink petals, surrounded by brown sepals. [× 10]

A hairless plant with branched, creeping stems which root freely. Leaves are paired. The minute flowers are borne singly at junction of leaf and stem. Annual meadow-grass grows above the water purslane. 1½–10 in. (4–25 cm); flowers June–Sept.

This plant grows all over Britain on bare or open ground or on muddy pool margins, but never on chalky soil.

Water purslane *Lythrum portula*

Although this plant is closely related to purple loosestrife, the two species look very different. Water purslane has creeping, rooting stems and flowers only a millimetre or so across, whereas purple loosestrife is upright, with flowers ten times or more larger. The flower of purple loosestrife has 12 stamens arranged in two whorls, but that of water purslane often has only one whorl. These differences are so marked that botanists used to put water purslane in a separate genus, *Peplis*.

The stems of water purslane creep over the ground, and because of this the plant is often overlooked. The stems send out roots to form whole strings of connected plants. Dense, creeping mats are created in this way, and often these spread into adjacent water. However, the waterlogged condition seems to have no ill-effect on the plants. Sometimes both the stems and the fleshy leaves take on a reddish colour.

Water purslane, as its name suggests, resembles members of the purslane family. This includes spring beauty and pink purslane, and also common purslane and its cultivated variety, pot-herb purslane. Young leaves of this herb have a sharp taste which enhances green salads.

159

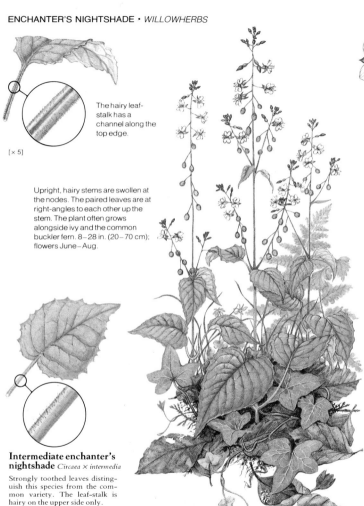

The hairy leaf-stalk has a channel along the top edge.

[× 5]

Upright, hairy stems are swollen at the nodes. The paired leaves are at right-angles to each other up the stem. The plant often grows alongside ivy and the common buckler fern. 8–28 in. (20–70 cm); flowers June–Aug.

The flower parts are arranged in pairs; the petals are deeply notched.

The flower-stalk droops with the ripe fruit, which is covered with hooked bristles.

Rich soils in woods and shady places throughout Britain are the setting for colonies of this nightshade.

Intermediate enchanter's nightshade *Circaea × intermedia*

Strongly toothed leaves distinguish this species from the common variety. The leaf-stalk is hairy on the upper side only.

Enchanter's nightshade *Circaea lutetiana*

In the 16th century, a Flemish botanist named Mathias De l'Obel tried to identify a magical plant which the early Greek physician Dioscorides had named after the mythical sorceress Circe. His first choice was the bittersweet, which supposedly acted as a good luck charm. But his choice later fell on the enchanter's nightshade, which still bears the botanical name of *Circaea lutetiana* – *lutetia* being the Roman name for Paris, where De l'Obel and other botanists worked. Before that, the Anglo-Saxons had used the plant – which they called *aelfthone* – as a protection against spells cast by elves.

Enchanter's nightshade differs from other willowherbs in that its fruit is not dispersed by the wind. Instead, the small hooks on the fruit catch onto the fur of an animal or the plumage of a bird. The fruit may then be carried for a considerable distance before being eventually shaken loose. The flowers are pollinated mostly by small flies, and the pale blooms stand out against the shade in which the plant usually grows.

Intermediate enchanter's nightshade is an almost sterile hybrid between enchanter's nightshade and the much rarer alpine enchanter's nightshade, *Circaea alpina*. It rarely sets fruit.

160

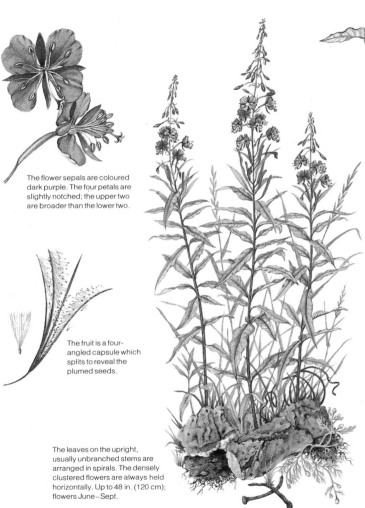

The flower sepals are coloured dark purple. The four petals are slightly notched; the upper two are broader than the lower two.

The fruit is a four-angled capsule which splits to reveal the plumed seeds.

The leaves on the upright, usually unbranched stems are arranged in spirals. The densely clustered flowers are always held horizontally. Up to 48 in. (120 cm); flowers June–Sept.

Long leaves are narrow at each end, like those of willow tree. They are hairless and have wavy, slightly toothed edges.

In autumn the white fluffy seed-heads of rosebay willowherb are a common sight on waste ground throughout Britain.

Rosebay willowherb *Epilobium angustifolium*

During the Second World War, the rosebay willowherb was one of the first plants to brighten London's bomb-sites. Its pretty, pink flowers became a cheering sight to people living in the East End and elsewhere, and the plant still colonises bare or waste ground. In Victorian times, however, the plant was often grown in gardens as an ornament, and it was by no means as widespread and abundant as it is today.

Rosebay willowherb spreads in two different and highly effective ways. In the autumn, its long fruit capsules split to release downy billows of seed. On a windy day, the air becomes thick with the clouds of seed as they are blown to new habitats. Once established at its new site, the plant can increase by means of its thick, woody roots, which spread horizontally. The roots send up new shoots at intervals and large, dense clumps of the plant are formed, to the exclusion of most other species. An exception to this is the foxglove, which is often found growing alongside the plant.

Rosebay willowherb thrives on disturbed ground, and frequently colonises ground that has been cleared by fire. One of its alternative common names is 'fireweed'.

161

The four notched petals are equal in size, and the sepals are green. [Actual size]

Seed [Actual size]

The fruit is a long, narrow capsule that splits open to release the plumed seeds.

The stems are upright, branched and hairy, with leaves in pairs. The flowers are solitary and held more or less erect at the junction of leaves and stem. 32–60 in. (80–152 cm); flowers July–Aug.

Stalkless, hairy leaves clasp the stem at the base and narrow towards the tip. The margins are sharp-toothed. [Actual size]

Great willowherb is found by the sides of streams, in marshes and in fenland throughout most of the British Isles.

Great willowherb *Epilobium hirsutum*

This tall, showy plant displays its rosy flowers in damp or wet places by the edges of rivers, streams or field-side ditches. It is able to spread by means of fleshy stems growing just under the surface of the mud or soil, and forms big, dense stands, which exclude and obliterate other plants.

Great willowherb has some delicious-sounding local names – codlins-and-cream, apple-pie and cherry-pie. While some have suggested that the reference to codlins (cooking apples) comes from the smell of the flowers or the crushed leaves, this alleged fragrance is undetectable to most noses. More probably the name refers to the young capsule, or 'codde' as the old herbalists called it, situated beneath the flower; this seems to have been confused with the better-known word 'codlin'. The botanical name of the species – *hirsutum*, or hairy – refers to the downy covering of the stem and leaves.

The flowers are usually pollinated by hoverflies or bees. Among the insects that feed on the foliage is the dark brown caterpillar of the elephant hawkmoth, with its four big eye-spots. It can be found in the lower leaves by day, and feeding on the top of the plant by night.

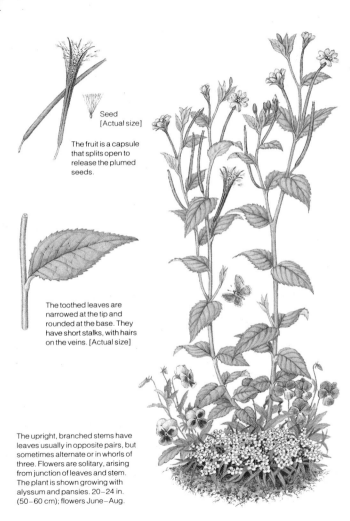

Seed
[Actual size]

The fruit is a capsule that splits open to release the plumed seeds.

The toothed leaves are narrowed at the tip and rounded at the base. They have short stalks, with hairs on the veins. [Actual size]

The upright, branched stems have leaves usually in opposite pairs, but sometimes alternate or in whorls of three. Flowers are solitary, arising from junction of leaves and stem. The plant is shown growing with alyssum and pansies. 20–24 in. (50–60 cm); flowers June–Aug.

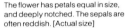

The flower has petals equal in size, and deeply notched. The sepals are often reddish. [Actual size]

Broad-leaved willowherb grows throughout Britain in shady places such as hedgerows, and as a weed in gardens.

Broad-leaved willowherb *Epilobium montanum*

Willowherbs belong to the same family as evening primroses and fuchsias, but the broad-leaved willowherb is a far less welcome resident in the garden. It is a weed, and its creeping stems root separately and remain in the ground when the plant is pulled out. Despite its unpopularity with gardeners, however, it had one friend in Nicholas Culpeper, the 17th-century herbalist, who believed that the dried and powdered roots of all willowherbs were a remedy for haemorrhages.

The drooping buds of the broad-leaved willowherb straighten up as the flowers open; the flowers have deeply notched purplish–pink petals. In the autumn the short, creeping stems are produced and lie on or just below the surface of the soil. The stems are covered with fleshy pink scales, or terminate in a tight rosette of leaves, and fatten to provide a winter food store for the next year's plants.

All willowherbs derive their common name from the likeness of the slender stems and narrow leaves to those of the willow tree, but the leaves of the broad-leaved willowherb are wider than others of the species. The leaves are usually opposite and grow out horizontally on short stalks.

163

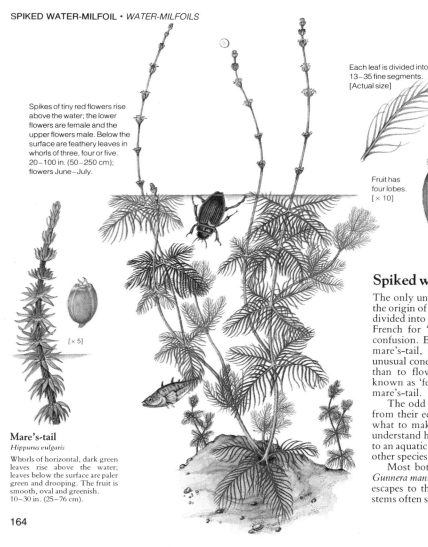

Spikes of tiny red flowers rise above the water; the lower flowers are female and the upper flowers male. Below the surface are feathery leaves in whorls of three, four or five. 20–100 in. (50–250 cm); flowers June–July.

Each leaf is divided into 13–35 fine segments. [Actual size]

Fruit has four lobes. [× 10]

Mare's-tail
Hippurus vulgaris

Whorls of horizontal, dark green leaves rise above the water; leaves below the surface are paler green and drooping. The fruit is smooth, oval and greenish. 10–30 in. (25–76 cm).

[× 5]

Spiked water-milfoil grows in lakes, ditches and streams, especially chalky ones, in scattered places in Britain.

Spiked water-milfoil *Myriophyllum spicatum*

The only unquestioned fact about the curious water-milfoils is the origin of their name; it refers to the way in which each leaf is divided into many fine segments, and derives from the Latin and French for 'a thousand leaves'. All else is disagreement and confusion. Early botanists thought that one water-milfoil, the mare's-tail, was the female form of the water horsetail, an unusual cone-bearing plant in fact more closely related to ferns than to flowering plants like the water-milfoils. It became known as 'female horse-tail', which was easily corrupted into mare's-tail.

The odd names given to the water-milfoils probably arose from their equally odd appearance: people were not quite sure what to make of them. Even botanists today do not entirely understand how these unusual plants, with their leaves adapted to an aquatic existence and their inconspicuous flowers, relate to other species.

Most botanists include the water-milfoils in a family with *Gunnera manicata*, a cultivated waterside plant which sometimes escapes to the wild in Britain. It is like a giant rhubarb, with stems often so high that it is possible to walk under the leaves.

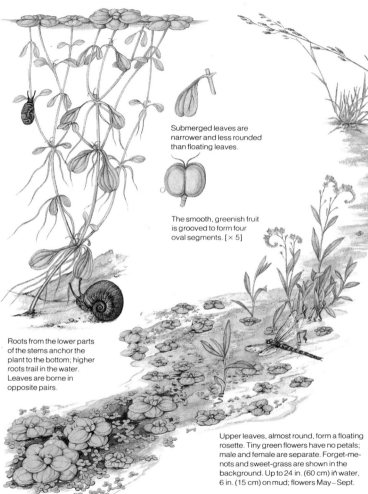

Submerged leaves are narrower and less rounded than floating leaves.

The smooth, greenish fruit is grooved to form four oval segments. [× 5]

Roots from the lower parts of the stems anchor the plant to the bottom; higher roots trail in the water. Leaves are borne in opposite pairs.

Upper leaves, almost round, form a floating rosette. Tiny green flowers have no petals; male and female are separate. Forget-me-nots and sweet-grass are shown in the background. Up to 24 in. (60 cm) in water, 6 in. (15 cm) on mud; flowers May–Sept.

Water starwort is common throughout the British Isles in ponds, ditches and slow-moving streams and on mud.

Water starwort *Callitriche stagnalis*

Water starworts have an almost chameleon-like capacity for changing their appearance, making it difficult to tell the different species apart. The form of the leaves varies with the depth and rate of flow of the water where the plant grows, and in some plants only the narrow underwater leaves are developed, not the broad-leaved floating rosettes. Moreover, water starworts found on mud or in wheel ruts grow only a few inches tall, and look very different from the same plants growing in ponds. The fruits of different species are grooved, keeled or occasionally winged, but as they are only a few millimetres long, it is difficult for the amateur to distinguish between them.

The minute flowers are borne singly at the base of the leaves in the floating rosettes, and are either male or female. Pollen is normally blown by the wind from the male stamens to the female stigmas, or is carried along on the surface of the water.

The botanical name *Callitriche* is derived from Greek and means 'beautiful hair', a reference to the hair-like growth of the stems and floating roots in deeper water. The species name *stagnalis* suggests that the plant grows in stagnant or still water, although in fact it also prospers in slow-moving streams.

165

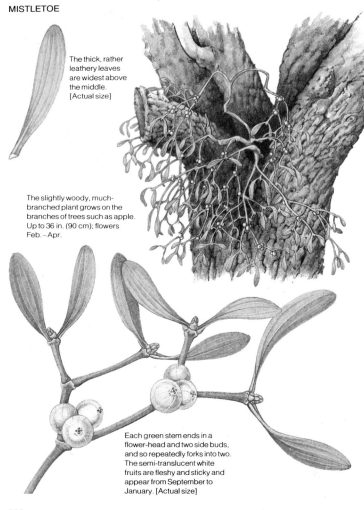

The thick, rather leathery leaves are widest above the middle. [Actual size]

The slightly woody, much-branched plant grows on the branches of trees such as apple. Up to 36 in. (90 cm); flowers Feb.–Apr.

Each green stem ends in a flower-head and two side buds, and so repeatedly forks into two. The semi-translucent white fruits are fleshy and sticky and appear from September to January. [Actual size]

The stalkless flowers are in whorls of three to five. [Actual size]

Mistletoe grows mainly on deciduous trees. It is common only in southern England and parts of the Midlands.

Mistletoe *Viscum album*

Every time a man kisses a girl under the mistletoe, he is perpetuating a magic ritual that has gone on for thousands of years. With the centuries, the ritual keeps changing its form: in the early 19th century, for instance, each young man given the privilege of a kiss had to pluck a berry from the twig, and once all the berries had gone there were no kisses for latecomers.

According to Pliny the Elder, writing 1,900 years ago, the Druids of Britain would cut down mistletoe with a golden sickle for use in their sacred rites. It was made to fall on to a white robe, as contact with the earth would have drained away the magic powers of this air-borne plant; and two white bulls were then sacrificed to ensure the potency of the magic. Pliny added that the plant had the power to make barren women fertile.

Mistletoe is a semi-parasite, living partly off a host tree into which it sinks its specialised roots, and partly off food produced with its own chlorophyll. It is spread by birds, which feed on the white berries, then wipe the sticky seeds off their beaks on to branches, where they take root. Mistletoe can be grown in gardens by securing the seed to a branch. The usual host trees are apple (particularly crab), hawthorn, poplar, lime and willow.

Leaves on flowering shoots are usually without lobes, although sometimes they have wavy edges. The ribbed fruits are black and resemble berries. [Actual size]

Leaves on non-flowering stems usually have three to five lobes. [Actual size]

A woody climbing plant whose stems have many fibrous, clinging, adhesive-covered roots, which enable them to ascend. The leaves are dark green and shiny, often with pale veins; they may be purplish in winter. Up to 100 ft (30 m); flowers Sept. – Nov.

Flowers are arranged in globular heads and are often pollinated by wasps. Each flower has five greenish petals.

Ivy is common in Britain, climbing trees, rocks and walls or creeping along the ground. It flourishes in deep shade.

Ivy *Hedera helix*

Clinging to a supporting tree or wall by fine rootlets that grow from the stem, ivy is one of the few native climbing plants to reach any great size. It clambers over ruins and old bridges, and is often cultivated to enhance the appearance of houses. It is also found in small, overshadowed town gardens, where variegated forms of the plant decorate the brick walls.

In the autumn, the plant's greenish-yellow flowers secrete abundant nectar, and they are pollinated by wasps and flies. The black berries that develop from the flowers in autumn are often eaten by birds, and at the same time of year caterpillars of the holly blue butterfly feed upon the leaves.

The use of ivy as a Christmas decoration arose through a superstition that house goblins were at their most malicious at Christmas-time. To guard against them, the custom arose of hanging ivy and holly on doors, beams and fireplaces. The plant's supposedly magical powers were put to various uses in different parts of Britain. In the Scottish Highlands, ivy was used to keep evil away from cows and their milk. In Shropshire, cups were made from parts of the thick, lower stems, from which children drank milk to ward off whooping cough.

EIGHT COMMON PARSLEYS

Members of the parsley family are easily recognisable by their umbrella-like heads of small flowers. Their leaves are divided into several distinct leaflets. This chart identifies – by leaf, flower or seed-pod – eight commonly confused species.

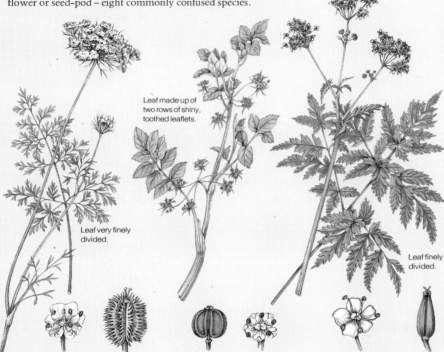

Leaf made up of two rows of shiny, toothed leaflets.

Leaf very finely divided.

Leaf finely divided.

Leaf has broad, lobed leaflets.

Petals notched, equal in size. Central flower of head often reddish. [× 3]

Fruit flat, ridged and spiny. [× 3]

Fruit oval and ridged. [× 4]

Flowers with equal-sized petals. [× 4]

Petals notched, and unequal in size on outermost flowers. [× 3]

Fruit long, smooth and conical. [× 2]

Fruit large, flat and slightly winged. [Actual size]

Petals notched, and unequal in size on outermost flowers of head. [Actual size]

Wild carrot
Daucus carota   Page 196

Fool's watercress
Apium nodiflorum   Page 181

Cow parsley
Anthriscus sylvestris   Page 175

Hogweed
Heracleum sphondylium   Page 195

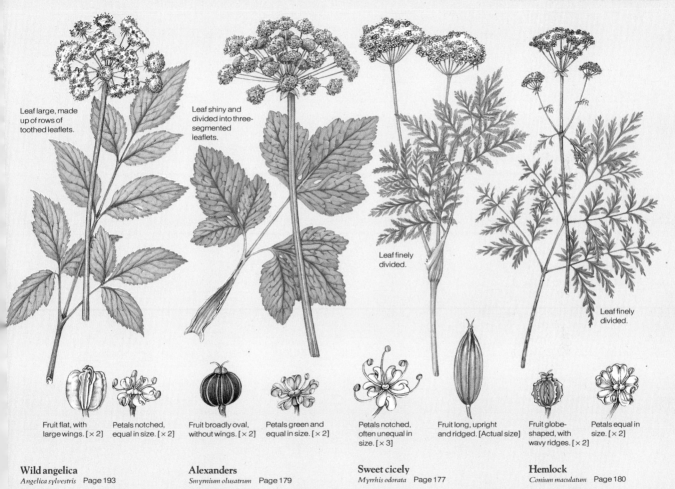

Leaf large, made up of rows of toothed leaflets.

Leaf shiny and divided into three-segmented leaflets.

Leaf finely divided.

Leaf finely divided.

Fruit flat, with large wings. [× 2]

Petals notched, equal in size. [× 2]

Fruit broadly oval, without wings. [× 2]

Petals green and equal in size. [× 2]

Petals notched, often unequal in size. [× 3]

Fruit long, upright and ridged. [Actual size]

Fruit globe-shaped, with wavy ridges. [× 2]

Petals equal in size. [× 2]

Wild angelica
Angelica sylvestris   Page 193

Alexanders
Smyrnium olusatrum   Page 179

Sweet cicely
Myrrhis odorata   Page 177

Hemlock
Conium maculatum   Page 180

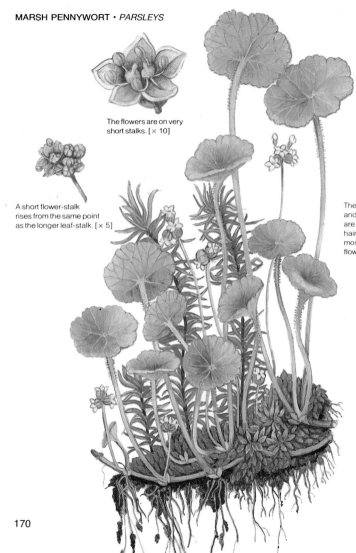

The flowers are on very short stalks. [× 10]

A short flower-stalk rises from the same point as the longer leaf-stalk. [× 5]

The fruits are round, ridged, and covered with brownish dots. [× 5]

The stem of marsh pennywort is creeping and rooting. The leaves are round, and are carried umbrella-like on sparsely hairy stalks. The plant often grows among mosses. $\frac{1}{2}$–10 in. (1·3–25 cm); flowers June–Aug.

Marsh pennywort is a plant of damp and wet places, usually on acid soils. It is common throughout Britain.

Marsh pennywort *Hydrocotyle vulgaris*

Marsh pennywort, in common with all the other pennyworts, derives its name from its round, penny-like leaves. It was once thought to cause liver rot in sheep, and folk-names such as 'white rot' and 'sheep rot' testify to this belief. John Fitzherbert in *The Boke of Husbandrie*, published in 1534, identifies it as one of the hazards that 'rotteth sheepe'. The association of marsh pennywort with sheep rot is reasonable, for the real culprit, liver fluke, thrives in the same marshy places as the plant.

Marsh pennywort may be found in abundance carpeting marshy and boggy areas throughout Britain. It is a prostrate, creeping plant, usually growing on sphagnum moss but sometimes floating freely on the water. The Latin name *hydrocotyle* means 'water cup', and probably refers to the leaf's cup-like shape. The flower-heads, clusters of tiny greenish-white flowers borne on short stalks, are completely overshadowed by the glossy green foliage: the flowers are so undistinguished that Fitzherbert thought the plant 'never beareth floure'.

The plant had some medicinal uses and was, according to the 17th-century herbalist Nicholas Culpeper, particularly useful 'to break the stone and void it'.

Bisexual stalkless flowers are found in the centre of the flower-head. [× 5]

The male flowers are stalked, and are located at the edge of the flower-head. [× 5]

The fruit is covered with hooked bristles. [× 5]

An upright hairless plant with umbrella-shaped flower-heads carried on tall stalks. The leaves have three to five lobes, shiny and deeply toothed, and grow on long stalks from the base. 8–24 in. (20–60 cm); flowers May–July.

The flower-head is made up of several smaller flower-heads.

Sanicle has a preference for limestone, forming carpets on chalky soils of beech and oak woods throughout Britain.

Sanicle *Sanicula europaea*

It is possible that the name sanicle is a contraction of Saint Nicholas, a saint who was, like the plant, credited with extraordinary curative powers: it is said he once restored to life two children who had been murdered and pickled in a pork tub. Another possible derivation is from the Latin *sanus*, meaning 'healthy'.

Whatever the derivation, it is clear that from earliest times sanicle has been associated with healing. In the Middle Ages it was commonly believed that 'he who keeps sanicle has no business with a doctor'. Henry Lyte, in his *Niewe Herball or Historie of Plantes*, published in 1578, states that 'The iuyce of Sanicle dronken, doth make whole and sound all inward, and outwarde woundes and hurtes'. Early herbalists list numerous conditions such as diseases of the throat, haemorrhaging and malignant ulcers in the mouth which will respond to treatment with a decoction or powder of the leaves and roots of sanicle.

The fruits of sanicle are covered with tiny hooks, and catch on to the fur of any passing animal, or on to the clothing of a passing man or woman. By this means the seeds may be spread miles from the parent plant.

171

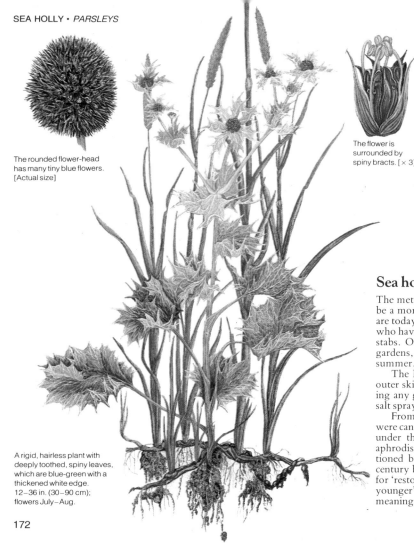

The rounded flower-head has many tiny blue flowers. [Actual size]

The flower is surrounded by spiny bracts. [× 3]

The oval fruit is covered with small hooks. [× 3]

Sea holly is found on sand and shingle beaches all round the coasts of the British Isles, and is grown in gardens.

A rigid, hairless plant with deeply toothed, spiny leaves, which are blue-green with a thickened white edge. 12–36 in. (30–90 cm); flowers July–Aug.

Sea holly *Eryngium maritimum*

The metallic-blue flowers and thistly leaves of sea holly used to be a more common sight on beaches and sand dunes than they are today. The plant has suffered from human users of the beach, who have rooted it out to save their feet and bodies from painful stabs. On the other hand, sea holly has found a new home in gardens, where it makes an unusual and showy display in late summer.

The leaves and stalks of sea holly have a thick cuticle, or outer skin; this is an adaptation to life on the seashore, preventing any great loss of water and protecting the plant against the salt spray.

From the 16th to the 19th centuries, the roots of sea holly were candied in Colchester, Essex, and sold as a popular delicacy under the name of 'eringoes'. They were thought to be an aphrodisiac, particularly for the elderly, and as such were mentioned by Falstaff in *The Merry Wives of Windsor*. In a 17th-century book of herbal remedies, eringoes were recommended for 'restoring the aged, and amending the defects of nature in the younger'. The name *Eryngium* comes from a Greek word, meaning a plant used to cure indigestion and wind.

Flowers on stalks of different lengths form an umbrella-shaped head.

The erect, purple-spotted stems are covered with short, stiff hairs, and are swollen at the junction of leaf-stalks and stem. The leaves divide into two or three lobes, and are downy on both sides. The plant is seen growing with hedge garlic and a roadside grass. 12–36 in. (30–90 cm); flowers June–July.

Flower has notched petals. [× 10]

Fruit is narrow and ridged, tapering towards the tip. [× 2]

Rough chervil is common in hedgerows throughout the British Isles, except for northern Scotland and western Ireland.

Rough chervil *Chaerophyllum temulentum*

The parsley family includes some of Britain's most poisonous plants, such as hemlock and cowbane, and should therefore be treated with caution. Rough chervil is no exception; its species name, *temulentum*, is derived from the Latin word for vertigo, and the effect of the plant on human beings is to simulate the staggering incapability of drunkenness.

With its big heads of flowers on stalks radiating like the spokes of an umbrella, rough chervil presents the typical appearance of a member of the parsley family. At first sight this makes the chervil difficult to distinguish from some of its cousins, but there are several ways in which they can be told apart.

One clue to the correct identification of rough chervil is its flowering time. It flowers midway between the other two familiar hedgebank and roadside parsleys, the first to flower being cow parsley, and the last being hedge parsley. On close examination, rough chervil is recognised by the conspicuous swelling where the leaf-stalks join the stem and by the purple spots on the stem. It is a characteristic plant of hedgebanks, which extend from the woodland edge and provide the half-light which is one of the richest habitats for plant growth.

173

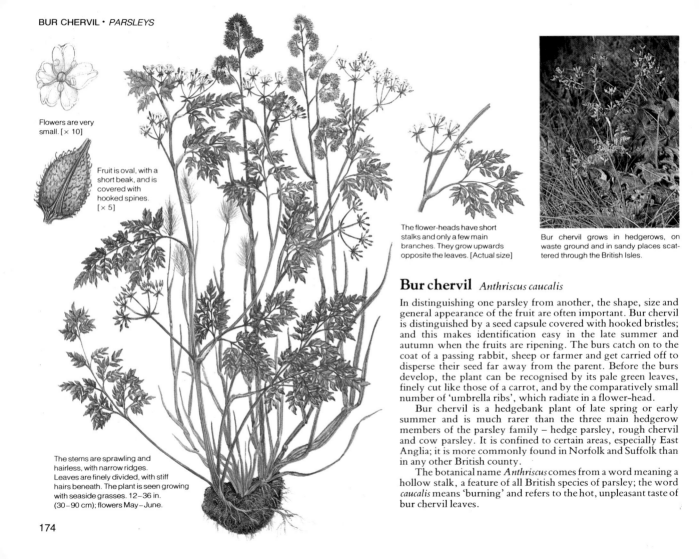

Flowers are very
small. [× 10]

Fruit is oval, with a
short beak, and is
covered with
hooked spines.
[× 5]

The flower-heads have short
stalks and only a few main
branches. They grow upwards
opposite the leaves. [Actual size]

Bur chervil grows in hedgerows, on
waste ground and in sandy places scattered through the British Isles.

The stems are sprawling and
hairless, with narrow ridges.
Leaves are finely divided, with stiff
hairs beneath. The plant is seen growing
with seaside grasses. 12–36 in.
(30–90 cm); flowers May–June.

Bur chervil *Anthriscus caucalis*

In distinguishing one parsley from another, the shape, size and
general appearance of the fruit are often important. Bur chervil
is distinguished by a seed capsule covered with hooked bristles;
and this makes identification easy in the late summer and
autumn when the fruits are ripening. The burs catch on to the
coat of a passing rabbit, sheep or farmer and get carried off to
disperse their seed far away from the parent. Before the burs
develop, the plant can be recognised by its pale green leaves,
finely cut like those of a carrot, and by the comparatively small
number of 'umbrella ribs', which radiate in a flower-head.

Bur chervil is a hedgebank plant of late spring or early
summer and is much rarer than the three main hedgerow
members of the parsley family – hedge parsley, rough chervil
and cow parsley. It is confined to certain areas, especially East
Anglia; it is more commonly found in Norfolk and Suffolk than
in any other British county.

The botanical name *Anthriscus* comes from a word meaning a
hollow stalk, a feature of all British species of parsley; the word
caucalis means 'burning' and refers to the hot, unpleasant taste of
bur chervil leaves.

Branches of the flower-head are hairless. There are small bracts under the flowers.

Chervil
Anthriscus cerefolium

The stem is hairy above the nodes. The flower-heads are on short stems, with downy branches and a few small bracts. Each fruit has a long slender beak.

The erect, furrowed stems are downy below but hairless above. Leaves are finely divided in toothed segments. 24–48 in. (60–120 cm); flowers Apr.–June.

Outer flowers in the flower-heads have petals of differing sizes. [× 5]

Each fruit is long, smooth and broad near the base and has a short beak. [× 2]

Cow parsley grows abundantly in hedges, wood edges and on wasteland. It is found in all parts of Britain.

Cow parsley *Anthriscus sylvestris*

Roadsides filled with flowering cow parsley, and the distinctive odour produced by masses of this plant, are richly evocative of the early days of spring. It is the commonest of the white hedgebank parsleys, and the earliest to flower. Almost certainly, the frothy appearance of large quantities of cow parsley gave rise to its picturesque folk-name of 'Queen Anne's lace'.

Not all the cow parsley's country names are so innocent in connotation, however, for despite its virginal whiteness it was called – among other things – 'adder's meat', 'devil's meat', and 'bad man's oatmeal'. The reason was probably that many similar-looking plants had harmful properties – for example hemlock and fool's parsley, both of which are poisonous, and both of which could resemble cow parsley to the apprentice herbalist. Cow parsley itself is completely innocuous, and the leaves, which often appear as early as December, have been fed to rabbits as greenstuff. Country children make pea-shooters of the hollow stems.

Chervil, a relative of cow parsley, is a popular herb, especially in France. It can be found in scattered localities throughout Britain, where it has escaped from cultivation.

175

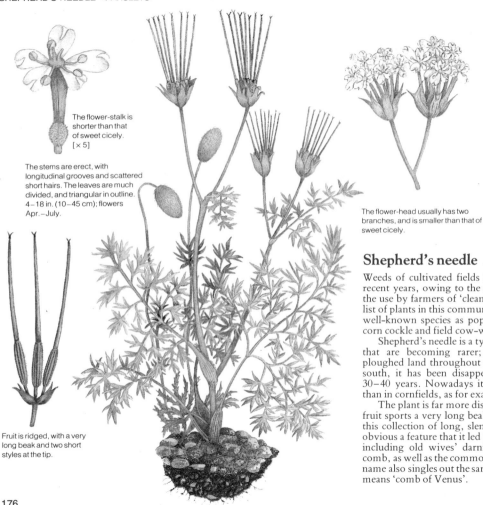

The flower-stalk is shorter than that of sweet cicely. [× 5]

The stems are erect, with longitudinal grooves and scattered short hairs. The leaves are much divided, and triangular in outline. 4–18 in. (10–45 cm); flowers Apr.–July.

Fruit is ridged, with a very long beak and two short styles at the tip.

The flower-head usually has two branches, and is smaller than that of sweet cicely.

Shepherd's needle is found on disturbed ground throughout Britain, though it is rare in Wales and the north.

Shepherd's needle *Scandix pecten-veneris*

Weeds of cultivated fields have suffered a dramatic decline in recent years, owing to the success of modern weed-killers and the use by farmers of 'clean' seed, untainted by weed seed. The list of plants in this community is a long one, ranging from such well-known species as poppies to less conspicuous plants like corn cockle and field cow-wheat.

Shepherd's needle is a typical member of this group of plants that are becoming rarer; once a fairly common weed of ploughed land throughout the British Isles, particularly in the south, it has been disappearing from cultivated ground for 30–40 years. Nowadays it exists on disturbed ground rather than in cornfields, as for example on cart tracks and footpaths.

The plant is far more distinctive in fruit than in flower. Each fruit sports a very long beak, often up to 2 in. (5 cm) long, and this collection of long, slender spikes sticking upwards was so obvious a feature that it led to a whole series of country names – including old wives' darning needles, hedgehogs and lady's comb, as well as the commoner shepherd's needle. The scientific name also singles out the same identification mark; *pecten-veneris* means 'comb of Venus'.

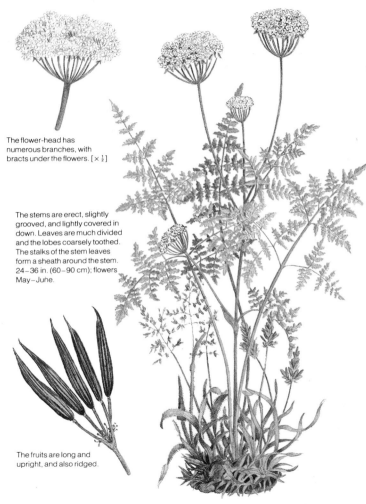

The flower-head has numerous branches, with bracts under the flowers. [× ½]

The stems are erect, slightly grooved, and lightly covered in down. Leaves are much divided and the lobes coarsely toothed. The stalks of the stem leaves form a sheath around the stem. 24–36 in. (60–90 cm); flowers May–June.

The fruits are long and upright, and also ridged.

Male flowers are borne on slender branches. [× 5]

Bisexual flowers are much larger than males, and are borne on stouter branches. [× 5]

Sweet cicely grows in shady and grassy places, under hedges and in woods. It is commoner in the north than the south.

Sweet cicely *Myrrhis odorata*

Anyone with a sense of smell can identify sweet cicely in the dark. When crushed, any part of the plant emits a strong fragrance of aniseed, reminiscent of aniseed balls and the strong French liquor *anis*. It is almost certain that sweet cicely was introduced into Britain for kitchen use, as it is so often found near old towns, villages and farms; however, it also grows in wild places, particularly in the north, where it is probably the commonest spring-flowering parsley. The strong flavouring of sweet cicely must have been highly prized in times when food often came to table less fresh than it does today.

The plant was also used medicinally. In the 16th century the naturalist John Gerard recommended the boiled roots, eaten with oil and vinegar, as a pick-me-up for elderly people 'dull and without courage'. In the next century Nicholas Culpeper, the herbalist, prescribed a big spoonful of unbruised seeds as a remedy for rheumatics and the 'falling sickness' (epilepsy).

A hundred years ago, sweet cicely found a new role in the Lake District as a polish for oak furniture which left not only a shiny surface but an agreeable smell as well. 'Cicely' is an adaptation of an old Greek name for the plant – *seseli*.

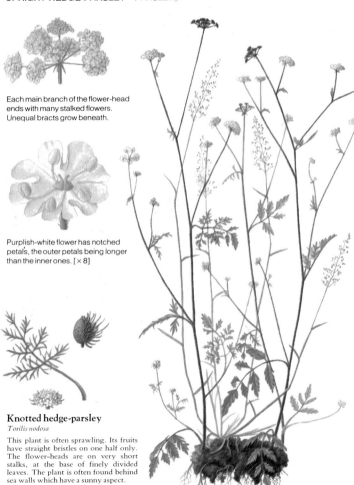

Each main branch of the flower-head ends with many stalked flowers. Unequal bracts grow beneath.

Purplish-white flower has notched petals, the outer petals being longer than the inner ones. [× 8]

Knotted hedge-parsley
Torilis nodosa

This plant is often sprawling. Its fruits have straight bristles on one half only. The flower-heads are on very short stalks, at the base of finely divided leaves. The plant is often found behind sea walls which have a sunny aspect.

The egg-shaped fruit is covered with curved, hooked spines and its styles are bent back. [× 5]

Stems are stiff and erect, with lines along them and hairs bent back sharply. Leaves have toothed lobes. The plant is shown with wood meadow-grass. 2–48 in. (5–120 cm); flowers July–Aug.

Hedge-parsley grows in woodland edges and hedges all over Britain, except in north Scotland.

Upright hedge-parsley *Torilis japonica*

One of nature's 'hitch-hikers', upright hedge-parsley spreads its seeds by tiny hooked bristles which become attached to a passing animal or person and eventually fall off at some distance from the parent plant. As a result it is a widespread plant commonly found on roadsides.

Upright hedge-parsley is one of three common roadside species of the parsley family. The other two are cow parsley and rough chervil, and all three flower in sequence: cow parsley from April until June, rough chervil in June and July, and upright hedge-parsley from July until September. They are very much alike in appearance, and this flowering sequence, which barely overlaps, is a useful first guide to identification.

The name *Torilis* is from a Greek word meaning 'to engrave', a reference to the furrowed look of the fruits. The plant has a number of English local names, such as 'Devil's nightcap', 'lace flower', 'pigs' parsley' and 'scabby head'. The species grows in most parts of Europe and North Africa and some parts of Asia. It extends as far east as Japan, hence the species name *japonica*. A near relative is knotted hedge-parsley, a rather less elegant plant with small, white flowers.

The greenish-yellow flower has curved-in petals and a short stalk. [× 5]

Fruit is dark brown and broadly oval, with ridged compartments. [Actual size]

Few bracts grow under the many-branched flower-head; sometimes they are absent altogether.

A plant with erect, grooved hairless stems. Its shiny, dark green leaves have three toothed, diamond-shaped leaflets, and the lower leaf-stalks form a sheath around the stem. The yellow flowers produce sharply ridged fruits. 18–60 in. (45–152 cm); flowers Apr.–July.

Alexanders often colonises waste ground near the sea and cliffs, showing its yellow flowers from spring onwards.

Alexanders *Smyrnium olusatrum*

The unusual name of alexanders is a reference to the fact that the plant is a herb of Macedonia, the country of Alexander the Great. In the 17th century its black seeds were sold in apothecaries' shops under the name of Macedonian parsley seeds, and the herbalist Nicholas Culpeper listed a variety of herbal uses including the power to cure flatulence and snake-bite. He also noted that 'it warmeth a cold stomach'.

The whole of the plant is edible, and the generic name *Smyrnium* is from the Greek word for myrrh, referring to its myrrh-like taste. The dark green leaves can be made into a white sauce, or used as a herb; the young stems can be cooked and eaten like asparagus; the flower-buds may be used in salads and the roots may be cooked as a substitute for parsnip. An old Irish recipe lists alexanders, watercress and nettles as ingredients for 'lenten pottage'.

Alexanders is a biennial plant whose yellowish flowers appear from April. It has become typical of seaside areas, where it may form large colonies on cliffs, such as those near Dover. Inland, although no longer cultivated, it is usually found near cultivated land in hedgebanks and on waste ground.

179

The flower-head is borne on side-branches or at the end of the stem.

Fruits are globular, with wavy ridges. [× 5]

The upright, smooth stems are greyish and covered with purple spots. Leaves are finely divided. 36–84 in. (90–210 cm); flowers June–July.

Male [× 5]

Female [× 5]

Male and female flowers are on separate flower-heads.

Hemlock is found by roads, streams and on waste ground throughout Britain. It is less common in the north.

Hemlock *Conium maculatum*

In the year 399 BC the Greek philosopher Socrates was accused of impiety on two counts: 'corruption of the young' and 'neglect of the gods whom the city worships and the practice of religious novelties'. He was found guilty, sentenced to death and drank a cup of hemlock, the poison used for judicial executions in ancient Greece.

Hemlock contains several poisonous alkaloid chemicals, the chief being coniine which derives its name from the Latin name of the plant. All parts of the plant are poisonous, but the seeds contain particularly high concentrations of coniine. Nicholas Culpeper, the 17th-century herbalist, recommended pure wine as an antidote to hemlock poisoning but this was not to be relied upon. Shakespeare's witches in Macbeth used a 'root of hemlock digg'd i' the dark' in their brew.

Hemlock resembles in appearance many other, harmless members of the parsley family. There have been several recorded deaths among children who by using the hollow stems for whistles and pea-shooters have absorbed enough poison to kill them. Hemlock can, however, be fairly easily identified by its smooth, purple-blotched stems and unpleasant, foetid smell.

The umbrella-shaped flower-heads are short-stalked or stalkless, and usually situated opposite a leaf. The branches are unequal in length.

The white flowers are smaller than those of true watercress, and bisexual. [× 7]

The sprawling stems are finely furrowed. Each leaf has two rows of lance-shaped or oval leaflets; they are shiny and stalkless, with toothed edges. The plant is shown growing with water mint. 12–36 in. (30–90 cm); flowers July–Aug.

The fruit is oval, longer than it is broad, and with five equal ridges. [× 10]

The white flowers of fool's watercress are typical of wet regions throughout Britain, except for northern Scotland.

Fool's watercress *Apium nodiflorum*

It is easy to mistake this plant for true watercress – hence its name. But the mistake is not a dangerous one. For although fool's watercress is not to everyone's taste it is certainly edible, and West Country people pick it for cooking with meat in pasties and pies. Fool's watercress is also sometimes confused with the lesser water-parsnip, although the lesser water-parsnip has many leaf-like bracts beneath the flower-head.

Fool's watercress with its small white flowers appears in marshy places, shallow ponds and ditches, and in still or moving water. It is at its most luxuriant in streams which rise from chalk or limestone, and which have a moderate flow.

The plant is also known as brooklime. This name may be derived from the Anglo-Saxon words *bruc*, or 'brook', and *lim* meaning 'a sticky substance', referring to the muddy habitat favoured by the plant. The present scientific name denotes several kinds of flower-head, but the plant was originally named *Helosciadum*, the Greek for 'a marsh plant with an umbrella head'. The 17th-century herbalist Nicholas Culpeper recommended fool's watercress as a 'diet drink' when mixed with other watercresses.

181

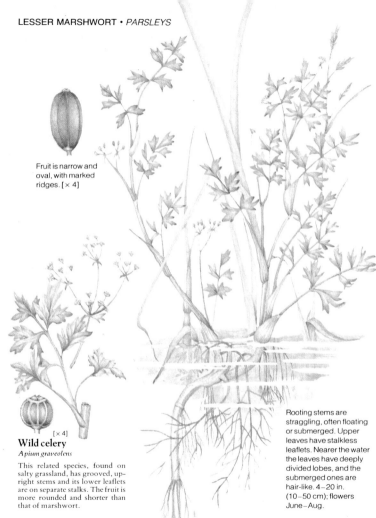

Fruit is narrow and oval, with marked ridges. [× 4]

[× 4]

Wild celery
Apium graveolens

This related species, found on salty grassland, has grooved, upright stems and its lower leaflets are on separate stalks. The fruit is more rounded and shorter than that of marshwort.

Rooting stems are straggling, often floating or submerged. Upper leaves have stalkless leaflets. Nearer the water the leaves have deeply divided lobes, and the submerged ones are hair-like. 4–20 in. (10–50 cm); flowers June–Aug.

Flowers are tiny and nearly stalkless. [× 5]

Each flower-head is carried on a long stem, opposite a leaf, and has two to four branches. [× 3]

Marshwort is locally common throughout Britain in lakes, ponds and ditches, especially in the south.

Lesser marshwort *Apium inundatum*

At first sight, this small and easily overlooked plant seems to bear little resemblance to other members of the parsley family; indeed, it is more easily confused with water-crowfoot, *Ranunculus aquatilis*. Closer examination of the flower-head, however, reveals that it has the umbrella-head construction of other parsleys, although the number of 'spokes' has been reduced to two or three and the flowers are very small.

Lesser marshwort is a perennial which grows in water, or just as often under water, sprawling far afield and rooting as it creeps. The leaves are of three types, with the segments becoming more divided as they go down the stem; those beneath the water are so thin and hairlike that they appear to be nothing but the skeleton of leaf-veins. Lesser marshwort is in danger of losing its marshy habitat as more land is drained.

Wild celery, common in scattered damp areas around the coast, is the ancestor of cultivated celery, which was derived from it by selective breeding. It has the well-known celery smell and the shiny green leaves of its cultivated relative, but is tough and wiry and lacks the size of the garden plant. Wild celery can also be found growing inland but is not very common there.

The flower-head is flat-topped, with 8–15 branches.

The tiny flowers have yellowish-green petals which curl inwards. [× 10]

The ridged fruits are often flattened on the sides. [× 5]

The stout upright stems are hairless. Leaves are much divided, shiny, bright green and often curled. It often grows with the pink-flowered thrift. 8–18 in. (20–45 cm); flowers June–Aug.

Wild parsley grows in grassy places close to walls and rocks, especially by the sea, but not in northern Scotland.

Corn parsley
Petroselinum segetum

The leaves of this species are divided into two rows of toothed leaflets, and the small flower-heads are borne on main branches of different lengths. The fruits are larger than those of wild parsley.

Wild parsley *Petroselinum crispum*

Any plant of this species that is found growing wild in Britain will have grown originally from domestic stock, for this is a common herb which has been valued for its culinary uses ever since the Greeks and Romans learned to savour its pleasantly aromatic flavour. The wild parsley differs from the cultivated form in lacking the deeply curled or frilled leaves which give a delicate, feathery quality to the kitchen-garden plant.

Parsley was introduced to Britain from the Mediterranean in the Middle Ages, and is used fresh or dried as a garnish or as a flavouring for soups, sauces, fish or meat. It is usually the principal herb in *bouquets garni* or *fines herbes*. Its scientific name derives from the Greek *petroselinon*, 'rock celery', and reflects the fact that wild parsley thrives on rocks and walls.

Numerous old wives' tales have attached themselves to this common plant. It should always, according to legend, be grown from seed planted on a Good Friday, and it should never be transplanted. It used to be thought bad luck to move to a new house where there was no parsley growing in the garden. The medicinal uses of parsley are limited, but its seeds were once considered a remedy for disorders of the digestive system.

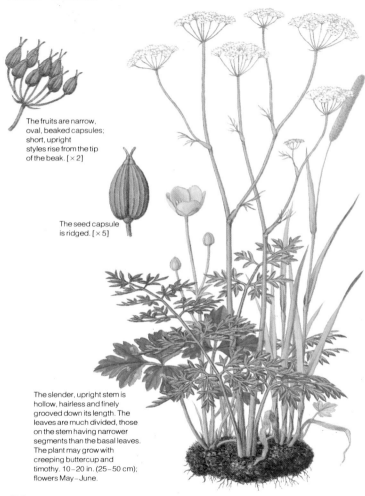

The fruits are narrow, oval, beaked capsules; short, upright styles rise from the tip of the beak. [×2]

The seed capsule is ridged. [×5]

The slender, upright stem is hollow, hairless and finely grooved down its length. The leaves are much divided, those on the stem having narrower segments than the basal leaves. The plant may grow with creeping buttercup and timothy. 10–20 in. (25–50 cm); flowers May–June.

Male flower [Actual size]

Female flower [Actual size]

Separate male and female flowers grow on the same head, which has 6–12 branches.

Pignut is a common plant of meadows and woods on light, dry, non-chalky soils in all districts of the British Isles.

Pignut *Conopodium majus*

Pignuts are one form of food growing wild in Britain that is still available for the gathering. In Shakespeare's day pignuts had apparently become a last resort for the starving. Meeting shipwrecked court servants in *The Tempest*, the monster Caliban offers his services to them with these words: 'I'll show thee the best springs; I'll pluck thee berries. . . . And I with my long nails will dig thee pig-nuts.'

Nowadays it is mainly children who enjoy chewing the brown, lumpy tubers, which they dig up from beneath the easily recognised, feathery leaves – provided, of course, that pigs have not rooted them up first. Pigs can smell the nuts, and they were once trained to nuzzle them out for human consumption, just as they are still taught to unearth truffles in France. In Ireland, the pignuts were thought to be the food of leprechauns.

It seems strange that this hardy and widespread relative of the carrot should not have been developed and improved as a staple root crop; but early attempts to cultivate it failed because of its reluctance to grow on ploughed land. The lower leaves of the pignut are as divided as those of the wild carrot, but unlike the carrot they usually wither before flowering starts.

The upright, usually rough stems are slightly ridged and have downy hairs. The leaves at the base consist of two rows of leaflets; stem leaves have narrower leaflets that are sub-divided. The leaf-stalks are like sheaths. 12–36 in. (30–90 cm); flowers July–Aug.

The style of the flower is much shorter than the petals. [× 5]

Fruit is globe shaped and shiny. [× 5]

The flower-head has 10–20 branches and becomes flatter-topped when in fruit.

Burnet-saxifrage grows in dry, grassy places in scattered localities throughout Britain, but is less common in the north.

Greater burnet-saxifrage
Pimpinella major

This species has a more prominently ridged stem. The leaves have larger leaflets, all in two rows, and the flower style is longer. It likes shady places.

[× 5]

Burnet-saxifrage *Pimpinella saxifraga*

Despite its name, burnet-saxifrage is, in fact neither a burnet nor a saxifrage; but a member of the umbrella-flowered parsley family. It got the name saxifrage (stone-breaker) around the 16th century because the apothecaries of the day thought that potions made from the plant would break up and remove kidney-stones and gall-stones. The stems and leaves were also used in preparations to staunch bleeding and heal wounds. In France, burnet-saxifrage has a common name which is uncomplimentary and more to the point: it is called *boucage* because its roots emit the offensive smell of the *bouc* (billy-goat).

Burnet-saxifrage is a slender plant with a preference for dry, grassy places on chalk and limestone soils; it is very much at home on the downs of southern England but is rarer in the north. Greater burnet-saxifrage prefers shady places on heavy, clay soils. It is a darker green than its smaller cousin, and the colour, together with the difference in shape of leaves and stem, serves to tell the two apart.

Greater burnet-saxifrage was once used for treatment of colic and indigestion, as well as for dissolving stones in the body. It is less common than *Pimpinella saxifraga*.

185

The fruit is egg-shaped and ridged with bent-back styles. [× 5]

The flower has notched petals and prominent stamens which give a yellowish colour to the flower-head. [× 5]

The flower-head has 10–20 branches and becomes flatter-topped when in fruit.

Ground elder is a troublesome weed of gardens and waste places near buildings throughout the British Isles.

Upright, grooved and hairless stems carry the white flower clusters. Each leaf has up to nine leaflets, usually grouped in twos or threes. The leaf-stalk is much longer than the leaf-blade. The plant is seen growing alongside rosebay willowherb. 12–24 in. (30–60 cm); flowers May–July.

Ground elder *Aegopodium podagraria*

This garden weed is not a native of Britain, but more of a guest that has outstayed its welcome. It was introduced from the Continent, presumably by somebody who wanted to eat it; the young leaves, boiled like spinach and eaten with butter, were once considered a delicacy. The blame has been variously laid on the Romans and on some unnamed medieval gourmet, but nobody knows for certain. What is sure is that when other vegetables became available and it was banished from the kitchen garden, the ground elder refused to go.

By the 16th century the plant had become a plague: the naturalist John Gerard complained that it 'groweth itselfe in gardens without setting or sowing, and is so fruitful in its increase, that where it hath once taken root, it will hardly be gotten out again, spoiling and getting every yeere more ground, to the annoying of better herbes'. Modern gardeners agree.

The name ground elder comes from the similarity of its leaves to those of the true elder, *Sambucus nigra*. In the Middle Ages and later, the plant was used for curing gout, whence comes its alternative name of 'gout weed' and its botanical name *podagraria* (*podagra* is Greek for gout).

186

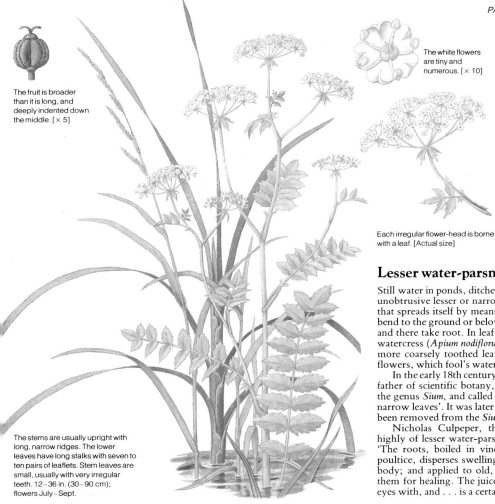

The fruit is broader than it is long, and deeply indented down the middle. [× 5]

The white flowers are tiny and numerous. [× 10]

Each irregular flower-head is borne with a leaf. [Actual size]

The stems are usually upright with long, narrow ridges. The lower leaves have long stalks with seven to ten pairs of leaflets. Stem leaves are small, usually with very irregular teeth. 12–36 in. (30–90 cm); flowers July–Sept.

Lesser water-parsnip is found in fens, ditches, canals and ponds throughout the British Isles, but is rare in Scotland.

Lesser water-parsnip *Berula erecta*

Still water in ponds, ditches, canals and fens is the habitat of the unobtrusive lesser or narrow-leaved water-parsnip. It is a plant that spreads itself by means of stolons – sprawling stems which bend to the ground or below the water under their own weight, and there take root. In leaf the plant is often mistaken for fool's watercress (*Apium nodiflorum*), but it can be distinguished by its more coarsely toothed leaves and the bracts below the lower flowers, which fool's watercress does not have.

In the early 18th century, Linnaeus (Karl Linné), the Swedish father of scientific botany, described the plant as belonging to the genus *Sium*, and called it *Sium augustifolium*, meaning 'with narrow leaves'. It was later known as *Sium erectum*, and has since been removed from the *Sium* genus and transferred to *Berula*.

Nicholas Culpeper, the 17th-century herbalist, thought highly of lesser water-parsnip's curative properties. He wrote: 'The roots, boiled in vinegar and applied in the form of a poultice, disperses swelling or inflammation in any part of the body; and applied to old, putrid sores, cleanses and disposes them for healing. The juice is good to bathe inflamed and sore eyes with, and . . . is a certain cure for jaundice.'

187

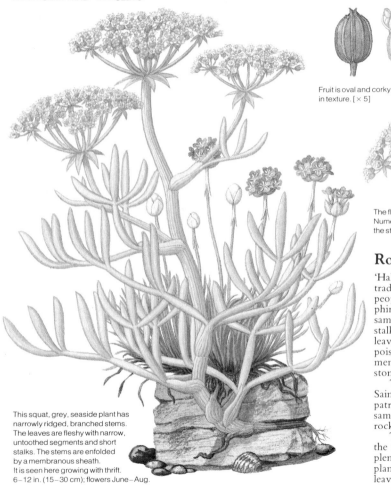

This squat, grey, seaside plant has narrowly ridged, branched stems. The leaves are fleshy with narrow, untoothed segments and short stalks. The stems are enfolded by a membranous sheath.
It is seen here growing with thrift.
6–12 in. (15–30 cm); flowers June–Aug.

Fruit is oval and corky in texture. [× 5]

The tiny flowers are yellowish-green. [× 5]

The flower-head has 8–20 branches. Numerous green bracts encircle the stem beneath the flower-head.

Rock samphire grows by the sea on cliffs, rocks, shingle or sand. It is most common in the south and west of Britain.

Rock samphire *Crithmum maritimum*

'Half way down hangs one that gathers samphire, dreadful trade!' – so wrote Shakespeare in *King Lear*, referring to the people who made a precarious livelihood collecting rock samphire from precipitous cliff faces. In Shakespeare's time, rock samphire was a popular vegetable. The thick, fleshy leaves and stalks were eaten, cooked in the same way as asparagus; the leaves were also pickled in vinegar. Like most of the non-poisonous species of the parsley family, the plant was recommended by herbalists as an aid to digestion, and also to relieve stones in the kidneys.

The common name samphire is a corruption of 'herbe Saint-Pierre', via the older name 'sampier'. St Peter was the patron saint of fishermen, and was also known as 'the rock'. The samphire's love of seaside habitats and exposed positions on rocks accounts for the dedication.

The fleshiness of the plant's leaves is an adaptation against the salty conditions of its habitat. Salt air, although containing plenty of moisture, tends to remove water from unprotected plants, and rock samphire resembles a desert-dwelling plant, its leaves covered with a thick, water-retaining skin.

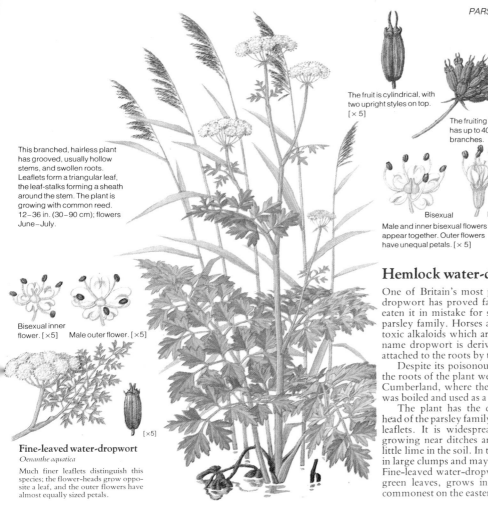

This branched, hairless plant has grooved, usually hollow stems, and swollen roots. Leaflets form a triangular leaf, the leaf-stalks forming a sheath around the stem. The plant is growing with common reed. 12–36 in. (30–90 cm); flowers June–July.

Bisexual inner flower. [×5]   Male outer flower. [×5]

[×5]

Fine-leaved water-dropwort
Oenanthe aquatica

Much finer leaflets distinguish this species; the flower-heads grow opposite a leaf, and the outer flowers have almost equally sized petals.

The fruit is cylindrical, with two upright styles on top. [×5]

The fruiting head has up to 40 branches.

Bisexual   Male

Male and inner bisexual flowers appear together. Outer flowers have unequal petals. [×5]

This poisonous plant, smelling of parsley, grows in or near fresh or brackish water, mainly in the south or west of Britain.

Hemlock water-dropwort *Oenanthe crocata*

One of Britain's most poisonous plants, the hemlock water-dropwort has proved fatal to a few unwary people who have eaten it in mistake for some other, harmless, member of the parsley family. Horses and cattle have also fallen victim to the toxic alkaloids which are present in all parts of the plant. The name dropwort is derived from the plant's tubers, which are attached to the roots by thread-like stalks.

Despite its poisonous character, small doses obtained from the roots of the plant were once used as a cure for gallstones. In Cumberland, where the plant was known as 'dead tongue', it was boiled and used as a poultice for the galled backs of horses.

The plant has the characteristic umbrella-shaped flower-head of the parsley family, together with glossy leaves and broad leaflets. It is widespread in the south and west of Britain, growing near ditches and streams, particularly where there is little lime in the soil. In those areas where it does occur it grows in large clumps and may form a conspicuous part of the scenery. Fine-leaved water-dropwort, with its paler and more graceful green leaves, grows in slow, still or stagnant water and is commonest on the eastern side of England.

189

Fruit is oval and ridged, with two spreading styles like horns on top. [× 5]

An upright, branched plant, with ribbed and lined stems. The leaves are divided into long, narrow segments. 12–36 in. (30–90 cm); flowers June–Sept.

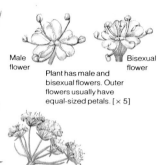

Male flower

Bisexual flower

Plant has male and bisexual flowers. Outer flowers usually have equal-sized petals. [× 5]

The flower-head has up to 15 slender branches, with bracts under both the main and the subsidiary heads.

This small-flowered plant is found in fresh water and brackish marshes, and is scattered in many parts of Britain.

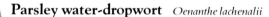

[× 2]   [× 2]

Tubular water-dropwort
Oenanthe fistulosa

The leaves of this species are less divided than those of parsley water-dropwort, and the flower-head has two to five branches, with no lower bracts. The outer flowers have petals of unequal size; the fruit is angular with long styles.

Parsley water-dropwort   *Oenanthe lachenalii*

Usually found growing in brackish marshland, parsley water-dropwort is a scattered but uncommon plant, found predominantly by the sea and occurring as far north as Inverness. In places it grows to a height of 3 ft (1 m).

The plant usually has a solid stem and cylindrical roots. Its generic name *Oenanthe* is derived from two Greek words meaning 'wine' and 'flower', alluding to the plant's vine-like smell. It is safest to leave the plant alone, for though not itself poisonous it is a close relative of the similar-looking hemlock water-dropwort which, if eaten, can cause death within a few hours. With careful examination, parsley water-dropwort can be distinguished from its poisonous relative by its long, narrow leaflets and greyish colour. Hemlock water-dropwort has wedge-shaped leaves, and is a deeper green.

Tubular water-dropwort, as its name implies, has a tubular stem. It is a small plant, often hard to detect among tall vegetation; its flower-head sometimes appears to be floating with no obvious connection to a plant. The flower-heads are very dense and have a flat-topped appearance. It is fairly common in central and southern Britain.

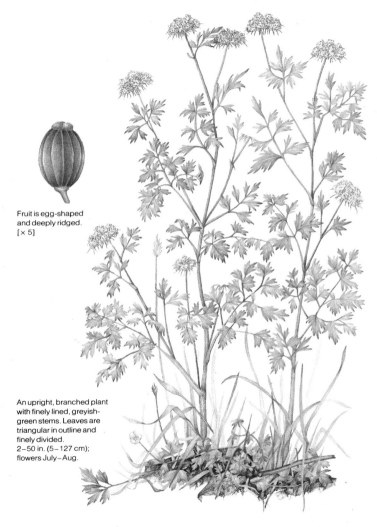

Fruit is egg-shaped and deeply ridged. [× 5]

An upright, branched plant with finely lined, greyish-green stems. Leaves are triangular in outline and finely divided. 2–50 in. (5–127 cm); flowers July–Aug.

Petals of flower may be slightly unequal in size. [× 5]

Long bracts are conspicuous, hanging underneath the flowers. [× 2]

Fool's parsley grows throughout most of Britain, but it is rarer in the north and absent from the far north of Scotland.

Fool's parsley *Aethusa cynapium*

People have sometimes mistaken this widespread plant for genuine parsley, which can be a dangerous error, for fool's parsley contains an alkaloid substance called coniine, which is the main active ingredient of hemlock. It is extremely poisonous to man and animals, and can be lethal if enough of it is eaten. The 16th-century herbalist John Gerard called the plant 'thinne leafed wilde Hemlock', drew attention to what he called its 'naughtie smell', and compared its properties to those of hemlock.

Fool's parsley is a hairless plant. It can be recognised by its umbrella-shaped heads of whitish flowers, which are always at the end of a branch, opposite a leaf. It is a weed of cultivated land, and is common in gardens in southern parts of Britain.

Its common name refers to those who consumed it in one form or another, and its botanical name *Aethusa* comes from the Greek word *aithos*, meaning 'fire'. This probably refers to the plant's fiery, acrid taste; although it has also been used to describe the shiny texture of the leaves. The plant's toxic qualities and general worthlessness are borne out by some of its alternative names, such as 'dog poison' in Somerset, 'devil's wand' in Dorset, and 'false parsley' in Shropshire.

191

The yellow flowers have narrow petals and few, if any, lower bracts. [× 10]

The fruit is narrowly oval and ridged, with short styles. [× 5]

The flower-heads consist of five to ten branches of unequal length, at the end of a stem.

An upright, branched plant with a lined stem. The lower stem leaves are much divided into very finely toothed, elliptical segments. The few upper leaves are small. 12–36 in. (30–90 cm); flowers June–Aug.

Pepper-saxifrage grows on roadsides and in meadows throughout Britain; in the north it is more localised and rare.

Pepper-saxifrage *Silaum silaus*

When this plant got its name it was a victim of mistaken identity, for it is neither very peppery, nor is it a saxifrage. It was known to the 17th-century herbalist Nicholas Culpeper as a means of breaking up stony deposits in the body – 'good to provoke urine, and serviceable in gravel distempers of the kidneys, as also in expelling wind'. Culpeper therefore classed it with the true saxifrages, which were said to have the same properties.

Culpeper also recorded that the plant's roots have a 'hot aromatic taste and smell', but he was almost certainly confusing the plant with one of the burnet saxifrages, which have a peppery root. The plants grow in similar places, and their roots resemble one another. Culpeper may have assumed that roots that looked alike must taste alike, even though the plants differ in many other respects.

The generic name *Silaum* applied to pepper-saxifrage is probably derived from the Latin word *sil*, meaning 'yellow ochre' and referring to the sulphurous yellow colour of its flowers. The plant is typical of areas of southern woodland and heaths such as the Weald of Sussex and Kent, where it is a food plant for the caterpillar of the swallowtail butterfly.

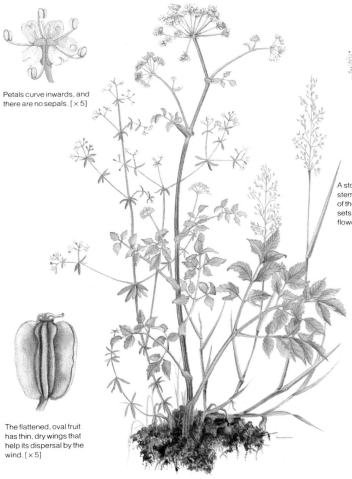

Petals curve inwards, and there are no sepals. [× 5]

The flower-head is situated at the end of a stalk arising from the angle between stem and leaf.

A stout, more or less hairless plant with a lined stem. Large leaves grow from the base, each of them roughly triangular in shape with many sets of leaflets. 12–60 in. (30–152 cm); flowers July–Aug.

This is a plant of wet woods, fens and damp meadows throughout Britain; it is also found on cliff tops.

The flattened, oval fruit has thin, dry wings that help its dispersal by the wind. [× 5]

Wild angelica *Angelica sylvestris*

A froth of white flowers, often tinged with pink, in a wood or beside a stream signals the presence of wild angelica. Often the whole of this tall, handsome plant seems to be flushed with purple. Close to, the decisive identifying feature becomes visible: the much-divided leaves, forming large swollen sheaths where they join the stem. The plant has a superficial similarity to hogweed, but hogweed is roughly hairy, while angelica is almost smooth.

Angelica received its name from the 'angelic', or heavenly, properties attributed to it. Herbalists knew it as a sovereign and universal remedy. The seeds and the root – said to be 'long, thick . . . warm and aromatic to the taste', and with 'a very agreeable smell' – were regarded as especially valuable. In early medical textbooks they were claimed to have a cordial and 'stomachic' effect (that is, aiding the digestion).

The 17th-century herbalist Nicholas Culpeper recommended angelica against 'all epidemical diseases'. But Culpeper also mentioned that the plant could be eaten as a candy, and it is in this form that it is best-known today, crystallised as a traditional decoration on cakes and other sweet foods.

193

Flowers are tiny and yellow, with the petals rolled inwards. [× 10]

The fruits are flat, oval and narrowly winged. [× 3]

An upright, rough-haired plant with furrowed, angled and usually hollow stems. Leaflets are arranged in two rows, and are oval, lobed and toothed. It may be seen growing with the purple flowers of greater knapweed, and with upright brome. 12–48 in. (30–120 cm); flowers July–Sept.

Flower-heads consist of 5–15 branches clustered at the end of a stem. [Actual size]

Wild parsnip is a tall plant, scattered all over Britain on dry, grassy and waste ground, particularly chalk and limestone.

Wild parsnip *Pastinaca sativa*

Above ground, wild parsnip is very similar to its kitchen-garden relation, which has developed from it after many generations of selective breeding. The root of wild parsnip, however, is much less well developed – indeed, it was described by the 16th-century herbalist John Gerard as 'small, hard, woodie, and not fit to be eaten'. But though useless in the kitchen, the root came into its own in the brew-houses of northern Irish farms: there the roots were brewed with hops in the same manner as malt, and the resulting liquor, fermented with yeast, was said to be extremely pleasant.

The plant had herbal uses as well. A strong decoction of the roots was claimed to be good for kidney disorders, and for dislodging obstructions of the intestines; and the oil in the seeds was administered as a cure for fever.

Many explanations have been offered for the derivation of the parsnip's name. Only one thing is sure – it comes from the Latin name for the plant, *pastinaca* – but that could have originated in *pastus* the Latin for 'pasture', one of the plant's habitats; or in the word *pastinare*, 'to dig', the root being the plant's most valuable part.

White or pink flower-head has up to 20 branches with small, bent-back bracts underneath. The flower-heads are a popular feeding site and mating ground for the soldier beetle.

Flowers from the outer edge of the head have very unequal-sized petals. [×2]

The fruit is large and flattened, with a slight wing. [×2]

This stout, upright plant is stiffly hairy and has ridged stems; its leaves have two rows of deeply lobed leaflets. It is shown with hawthorn. 24–72 in. (60–180 cm); flowers June–Sept.

The robust hogweed is a common sight on roadsides and in hedgerows, woods and grassy places throughout Britain.

Giant hogweed
Heracleum mantegazzianum

A much bigger plant than common hogweed, with stouter, sometimes purple-blotched stems reaching 13 ft (4 m), with flower-heads up to 24 in. (60 cm) across. The fruits are narrower than those of the common hogweed.

Hogweed *Heracleum sphondylium*

Children have long used the hollow stems of hogweed as pea-shooters. The plant is the most common species of the parsley family, and its flowers often have bright orange soldier beetles on them. The insects are especially common in July, when the large, flat flower-heads – called umbels – provide a feeding and mating ground for the insects. The flowers, with their rather unpleasant scent, also attract the less desirable carpet beetles, which may move on into houses and live in rugs and carpets.

Until fairly recently, hogweed was gathered for pig fodder, which gave rise to its common name. As well as providing food for swine, the young leaves were once considered a delicacy fit for humans as, when boiled, they taste very much like asparagus. The plant's generic name of *Heracleum* comes from the legendary Greek warrior-hero Heracles – known to the Romans as Hercules – who believed it had medicinal value.

The giant hogweed – and, to a lesser extent, common hogweed – contains a volatile substance which sensitises the skin and which can lead to blisters, especially in very hot weather. Both plants should therefore be treated with caution.

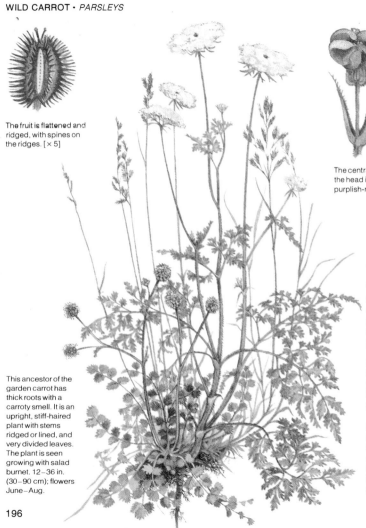

The fruit is flattened and ridged, with spines on the ridges. [× 5]

The central flower in the head is often purplish-red. [× 5]

The petals of the small, white flowers are often unequal in size. [× 10]

The fruiting head is concave; branches are crowded together.

Wild carrot grows in fields and grassy places, especially on chalk and near the sea, throughout most of the British Isles.

This ancestor of the garden carrot has thick roots with a carroty smell. It is an upright, stiff-haired plant with stems ridged or lined, and very divided leaves. The plant is seen growing with salad burnet. 12–36 in. (30–90 cm); flowers June–Aug.

Wild carrot *Daucus carota*

Wild carrot is a plant of downs and roadsides, and its leaves and flowers are a common sight in neglected vegetable gardens. The cultivated carrot has been bred from the wild form over many generations. Instead of producing a stout and totally inedible root at the end of the first season's growth, the cultivated form provides the succulent, fleshy kitchen carrot.

When the wild carrot begins to fruit, it is at its most distinctive. The fruits have long spines which attach themselves to the hair of any passing animal. The fruiting heads close up – particularly when it rains – and assume the shape of a bird's nest, by which name they are known in Somerset. The many much-divided bracts under the flower-heads are also distinctive.

In the 16th century, a concoction of the centrally placed red, or purplish-red, flowers of the wild carrot was held to be a certain remedy for the 'falling disease' – an old name for epilepsy. A century later, they were recommended for such diverse complaints as stitch, kidney stones and dropsy. The herbalist Nicholas Culpeper considered that they were also beneficial to would-be mothers, stating that they 'helpeth conception' when boiled in wine and drunk.

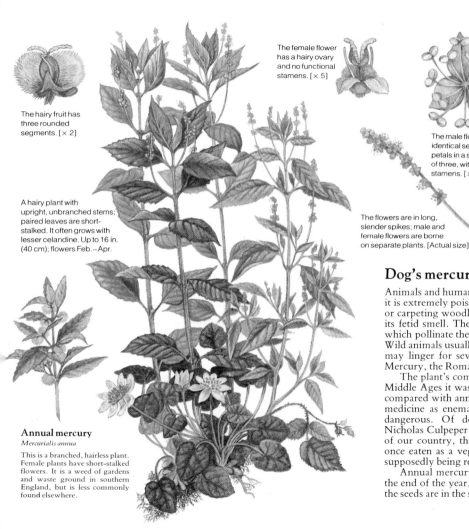

The hairy fruit has three rounded segments. [× 2]

The female flower has a hairy ovary and no functional stamens. [× 5]

The male flower has identical sepals and petals in a single whorl of three, with 8–15 stamens. [× 5]

A hairy plant with upright, unbranched stems; paired leaves are short-stalked. It often grows with lesser celandine. Up to 16 in. (40 cm); flowers Feb.–Apr.

The flowers are in long, slender spikes; male and female flowers are borne on separate plants. [Actual size]

Dog's mercury is a woodland plant, also found in shady places on mountains. It is absent from the Orkneys and Shetlands.

Annual mercury
Mercurialis annua

This is a branched, hairless plant. Female plants have short-stalked flowers. It is a weed of gardens and waste ground in southern England, but is less commonly found elsewhere.

Dog's mercury *Mercurialis perennis*

Animals and humans alike should beware of dog's mercury, for it is extremely poisonous. It is found in profusion under hedges or carpeting woodland floors, and often betrays its presence by its fetid smell. The purpose of the odour is to attract midges, which pollinate the female flowers when they crawl over them. Wild animals usually avoid the plant, and cattle that have eaten it may linger for several weeks before dying. It is named after Mercury, the Roman god of trade, its supposed discoverer.

The plant's common name derives from the fact that in the Middle Ages it was considered worthless, or fit only for dogs, compared with annual mercury, extracts of which were used in medicine as enemas and emetics. In fact both mercuries are dangerous. Of dog's mercury the 17th-century herbalist Nicholas Culpeper said: 'There is not a more fatal plant, native of our country, than this'. Surprisingly, annual mercury was once eaten as a vegetable in Germany, its poisonous qualities supposedly being removed by boiling the leaves.

Annual mercury is often found as a garden weed. It dies at the end of the year, but not before seeding profusely, and once the seeds are in the soil it re-appears annually for several years.

197

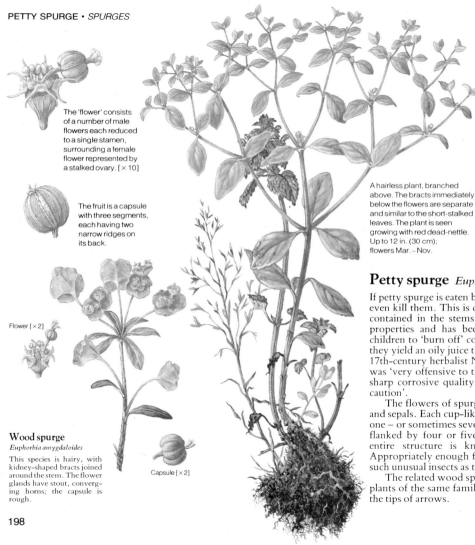

The 'flower' consists of a number of male flowers each reduced to a single stamen, surrounding a female flower represented by a stalked ovary. [× 10]

The fruit is a capsule with three segments, each having two narrow ridges on its back.

Flower [× 2]

Wood spurge
Euphorbia amygdaloides

This species is hairy, with kidney-shaped bracts joined around the stem. The flower glands have stout, converging horns; the capsule is rough.

Capsule [× 2]

A hairless plant, branched above. The bracts immediately below the flowers are separate and similar to the short-stalked leaves. The plant is seen growing with red dead-nettle. Up to 12 in. (30 cm); flowers Mar. – Nov.

Petty spurge is a common plant of waste and cultivated land, and is found growing throughout the British Isles.

Petty spurge *Euphorbia peplus*

If petty spurge is eaten by cattle or horses it can make them ill or even kill them. This is due to the poisonous, milky-white juice contained in the stems and leaves. The juice also has caustic properties and has been used by generations of adults and children to 'burn off' corns and warts. If the seeds are crushed, they yield an oily juice that can act as a strong purgative. But the 17th-century herbalist Nicholas Culpeper warned that the juice was 'very offensive to the stomach and bowels by reason of its sharp corrosive quality, and therefore ought to be used with caution'.

The flowers of spurges are most unusual, as they lack petals and sepals. Each cup-like structure contains a female flower and one – or sometimes several – very small male flowers. They are flanked by four or five glands which are often horned. This entire structure is known by botanists as a 'cyathium'. Appropriately enough for such an odd plant, it is pollinated by such unusual insects as the parasite ichneumon-wasp.

The related wood spurge is also full of caustic juice. In Africa plants of the same family have been used to provide poison for the tips of arrows.

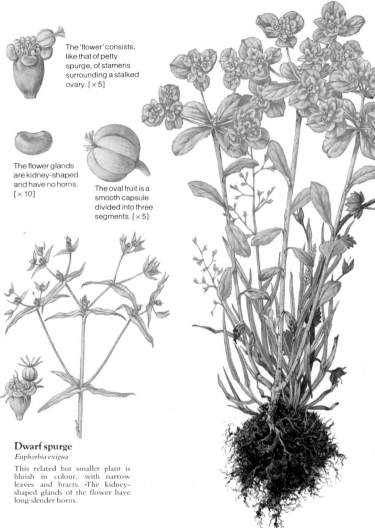

The 'flower' consists, like that of petty spurge, of stamens surrounding a stalked ovary. [×5]

The flower glands are kidney-shaped and have no horns. [×10]

The oval fruit is a smooth capsule divided into three segments. [×5]

The plant has a single stem or is branched near the base. Bracts below the flowers resemble the broadly oval, stalkless and finely toothed leaves. Up to 18 in. (45 cm); flowers Apr.–Oct.

Sun spurge is a common plant of cultivated ground, and grows abundantly throughout Britain.

Dwarf spurge
Euphorbia exigua

This related but smaller plant is bluish in colour, with narrow leaves and bracts. The kidney-shaped glands of the flower have long slender horns.

Sun spurge *Euphorbia helioscopia*

On a quiet autumn day, sun spurge may be heard as well as seen. Its seed capsules contain three seeds in separate compartments, and when the capsule is ripe it splits open with a crack and fires the seeds like a bursting grenade.

The sun spurge's unusual method of seed dispersal does not end when the seeds land on the ground. For they have a fleshy appendage containing an oil that ants find irresistible, and they gather up the seeds and carry them even further afield. Usually the ants eat only the oily part, and the seeds germinate where they have been left after their carriers have done with them. To attract insect pollinators, the plant has sweet-scented, kidney-shaped lobes on the petal-less flowers.

The genus was given the name *Euphorbia* after a man named Euphorbus, physician to King Juba of Mauretania, in the 1st century AD, who is said to have used the plant medicinally in North Africa. The species name *helioscopia* derives from two Greek words which together mean 'look at the sun', and probably refers to the flat-topped head of flowers which spreads out to be fully exposed to the sun. Dwarf spurge is a low, slender weed that particularly favours cornfields.

199

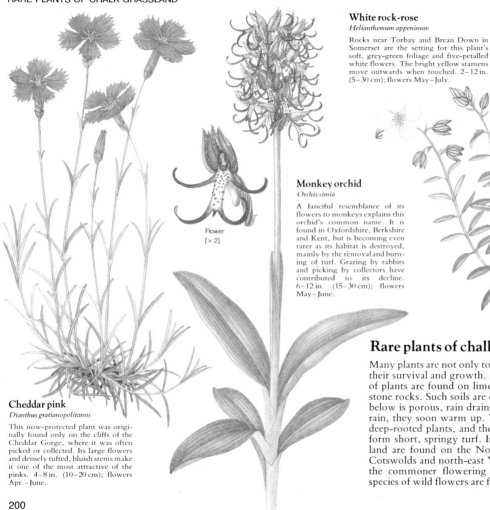

White rock-rose
Helianthemum appeninum

Rocks near Torbay and Brean Down in Somerset are the setting for this plant's soft, grey-green foliage and five-petalled white flowers. The bright yellow stamens move outwards when touched. 2–12 in. (5–30 cm); flowers May–July.

Flower
[× 2]

Monkey orchid
Orchis simia

A fanciful resemblance of its flowers to monkeys explains this orchid's common name. It is found in Oxfordshire, Berkshire and Kent, but is becoming even rarer as its habitat is destroyed, mainly by the removal and burning of turf. Grazing by rabbits and picking by collectors have contributed to its decline. 6–12 in. (15–30 cm); flowers May–June.

Cheddar pink
Dianthus gratianopolitanus

This now-protected plant was originally found only on the cliffs of the Cheddar Gorge, where it was often picked or collected. Its large flowers and densely tufted, bluish stems make it one of the most attractive of the pinks. 4–8 in. (10–20 cm); flowers Apr.–June.

Rare plants of chalk grassland

Many plants are not only tolerant of lime but depend upon it for their survival and growth. As a result, specialised communities of plants are found on lime-rich soils overlying chalk or limestone rocks. Such soils are often shallow, and because the rock below is porous, rain drains away through them quickly. After rain, they soon warm up. These soils do not favour trees and deep-rooted plants, and the dominant plants are grasses which form short, springy turf. In England, stretches of chalk grassland are found on the North and South Downs, and in the Cotswolds and north-east Yorkshire. As well as a profusion of the commoner flowering plants, several rare and colourful species of wild flowers are found in such areas.

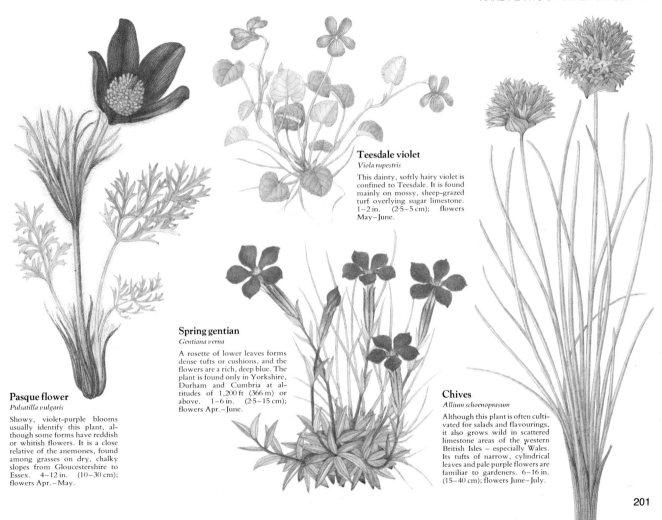

Teesdale violet

Viola rupestris

This dainty, softly hairy violet is confined to Teesdale. It is found mainly on mossy, sheep-grazed turf overlying sugar limestone. 1–2 in. (2·5–5 cm); flowers May–June.

Spring gentian

Gentiana verna

A rosette of lower leaves forms dense tufts or cushions, and the flowers are a rich, deep blue. The plant is found only in Yorkshire, Durham and Cumbria at altitudes of 1,200 ft (366 m) or above. 1–6 in. (2·5–15 cm); flowers Apr.–June.

Pasque flower

Pulsatilla vulgaris

Showy, violet-purple blooms usually identify this plant, although some forms have reddish or whitish flowers. It is a close relative of the anemones, found among grasses on dry, chalky slopes from Gloucestershire to Essex. 4–12 in. (10–30 cm); flowers Apr.–May.

Chives

Allium schoenoprasum

Although this plant is often cultivated for salads and flavourings, it also grows wild in scattered limestone areas of the western British Isles – especially Wales. Its tufts of narrow, cylindrical leaves and pale purple flowers are familiar to gardeners. 6–16 in. (15–40 cm); flowers June–July.

201

Spiked speedwell
Veronica spicata

The numerous blue flowers form a dense spike at the top of the stem; a single colony of plants may have many flowering stems. The plant is confined to the Breckland of East Anglia, but even there many plants have been destroyed by ploughing. 3–24 in. (7·5–60 cm); flowers July–Sept.

Flower has long stamens. [× 3]

Meadow saffron
Colchicum autumnale

Pink to pale purple flowers are produced in the autumn, when the plant is leafless; it is sometimes called autumn crocus. The plant is confined to meadowland around the Bristol Channel. Up to 10 in. (25 cm); flowers Aug.–Oct.

Fritillary
Fritillaria meleagris

The chequered purple flowers of fritillary were common in wet meadows early in the 20th century, but draining, ploughing and fertilisers have greatly reduced the number of sites where the massed blooms can be seen. 8–20 in. (20–50 cm); flowers Apr.–May.

Rare plants of cornfield and meadow

In former times, Britain's cornfields and meadows were richly endowed with flowers; the constantly disturbed and well-fertilised soils of arable land provided perfect conditions for a multitude of weed species. In more recent years, however, improved agricultural techniques such as seed cleaning and the use of selective weed killers, designed to eradicate species that taint food crops, have made some flowers very rare.

Agricultural advances today threaten even such formerly abundant cornfield species as poppies and cornflowers. Meadowland flowers, too, have suffered from more intensive farming, especially over-grazing. These include fritillary, spiked speedwell and meadow saffron.

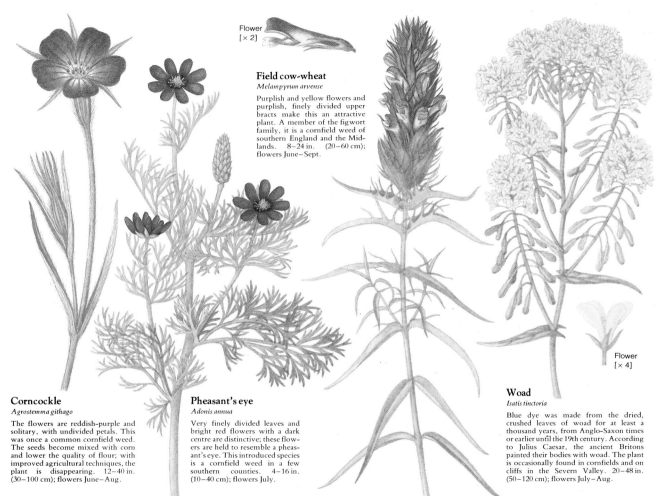

Flower
[× 2]

Field cow-wheat
Melampyrum arvense

Purplish and yellow flowers and purplish, finely divided upper bracts make this an attractive plant. A member of the figwort family, it is a cornfield weed of southern England and the Midlands. 8–24 in. (20–60 cm); flowers June–Sept.

Flower
[× 4]

Corncockle
Agrostemma githago

The flowers are reddish-purple and solitary, with undivided petals. This was once a common cornfield weed. The seeds become mixed with corn and lower the quality of flour; with improved agricultural techniques, the plant is disappearing. 12–40 in. (30–100 cm); flowers June–Aug.

Pheasant's eye
Adonis annua

Very finely divided leaves and bright red flowers with a dark centre are distinctive; these flowers are held to resemble a pheasant's eye. This introduced species is a cornfield weed in a few southern counties. 4–16 in. (10–40 cm); flowers July.

Woad
Isatis tinctoria

Blue dye was made from the dried, crushed leaves of woad for at least a thousand years, from Anglo-Saxon times or earlier until the 19th century. According to Julius Caesar, the ancient Britons painted their bodies with woad. The plant is occasionally found in cornfields and on cliffs in the Severn Valley. 20–48 in. (50–120 cm); flowers July–Aug.

203

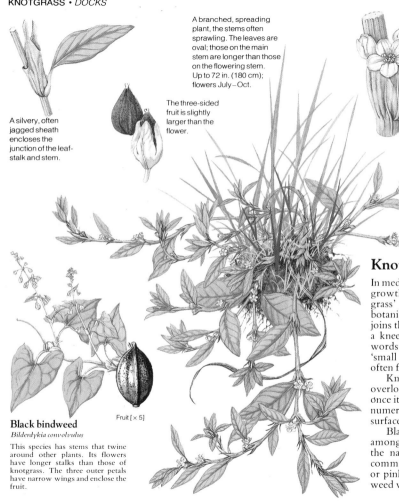

A silvery, often jagged sheath encloses the junction of the leaf-stalk and stem.

A branched, spreading plant, the stems often sprawling. The leaves are oval; those on the main stem are longer than those on the flowering stem. Up to 72 in. (180 cm); flowers July–Oct.

The three-sided fruit is slightly larger than the flower.

The pink or white flowers are in clusters of one to six at the bases of the upper leaf-stalks.

Knotgrass is a common weed throughout Britain. It often appears on waste ground and on rocky seashores.

Fruit [× 5]

Black bindweed

Bilderdykia convolvulus

This species has stems that twine around other plants. Its flowers have longer stalks than those of knotgrass. The three outer petals have narrow wings and enclose the fruit.

Knotgrass *Polygonum aviculare*

In medieval times it was thought that knotgrass would retard the growth of children, and Shakespeare refers to 'hindering knotgrass' in *A Midsummer Night's Dream*. Both its common and botanical names refer to the knotty swellings where each leaf joins the stem. In some species the stem bends at these joints like a knee: hence *Polygonum*, which is derived from two Greek words meaning 'many knees'. The species name *aviculare* means 'small bird' and comes from the fact that sparrows and finches often feed on the seeds.

Knotgrass is a common weed of cultivated ground, often overlooked because its flowers are very small. Like most weeds, once it is allowed to produce seed it will persist for years, and the numerous seeds can survive in the soil until brought to the surface by cultivation of the ground.

Black bindweed, another plant of cultivated ground, twines amongst the stalks of taller plants. Only its fruits are black, and the name was probably given to it to distinguish it from common bindweed (*Convolvulus arvensis*) which also has white or pink flowers. There is evidence to suggest that black bindweed was cultivated as a crop during the Bronze Age.

The silvery sheaths on the stem do not enclose the leaf-stalks.

A hairless, upright plant with unbranched stems. The leaves at the base have long stalks sheathing the stem, which has a single flower at its tip. Up to 8 in. (20 cm); flowers May–Aug.

Female flower

Male flower

The flowers are in pairs, one being male and one female.

The three-sided fruit is slightly longer than the flower.

Large patches of bistort are often found in damp meadows and other grassy areas throughout Britain.

Amphibious bistort
Polygonum amphibium

The leaves of the water-growing form, on the left, have longer stalks than those of the land-growing form. The fruits of both forms are similar. [× 5]

Bistort *Polygonum bistorta*

To most people *The Times* may seem an unusual ally of a common weed, but in 1971 the newspaper promoted a world championship contest for traditional puddings made from the young leaves of bistort. The pudding, known as Easter-ledge, is still made in the Lake District and in Yorkshire, and *The Times* competition attracted many entries from northern England.

Bistort derives its name from *bistorta*, Latin for 'twice twisted', and refers to the contorted shape of the underground stems. This snake-like shape has also led to local names 'snakeweed' and 'adderwort' for the plant. The root contains a high level of tannin, used for tanning leather, and its astringent properties were used in earlier times for arresting internal and external bleeding. It was also used to treat various infectious diseases. The 17th-century herbalist Nicholas Culpeper recommended it as a cure for toothache.

A similar plant, amphibious bistort, is able to adapt itself to growing both on land and water. In its land form it has almost upright stems, with hairy leaves which have short stalks. The aquatic plant has hairless, long-stalked leaves which float on the surface of the water.

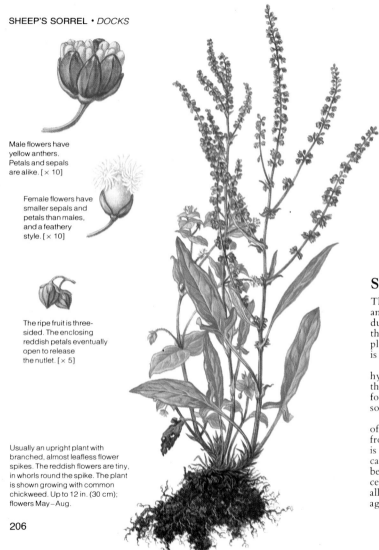

Male flowers have yellow anthers. Petals and sepals are alike. [× 10]

Female flowers have smaller sepals and petals than males, and a feathery style. [× 10]

The ripe fruit is three-sided. The enclosing reddish petals eventually open to release the nutlet. [× 5]

Usually an upright plant with branched, almost leafless flower spikes. The reddish flowers are tiny, in whorls round the spike. The plant is shown growing with common chickweed. Up to 12 in. (30 cm); flowers May – Aug.

The stalked leaf is shaped like a barbed spearhead, with basal lobes widespread or pointing forwards. A silvery sheath surrounds the stem and the base of the leaf-stalk.

Sheep's sorrel grows on heaths, grassy places and cultivated land throughout Britain, but rarely on chalky soil.

Sheep's sorrel *Rumex acetosella*

The small flowers of sheep's sorrel are dull and inconspicuous and have no noticeable scent or nectar. This economical design is due to the fact that the plant is pollinated not by insects, but by the wind. The male and female flowers are borne on separate plants, and the numerous males produce abundant pollen which is blown to the females.

As a family, sorrels are extremely variable in form and hybrids are often produced. This makes identification a job for the expert. But the ripe fruits – with their differing sizes and wart formations – provide useful 'identity tags'. The fruits of sheep's sorrel are small and without warts.

The plant's leaves contain the chemical calcium oxalate, a salt of oxalic acid, which has an acid taste; the name 'sorrel' comes from the old French word *'surele'*, meaning 'sour'. The leaf juice is poisonous if taken in excess, and it can cause milk fever in cattle. But an extract of the juice from fresh sheep's sorrel has been used to treat kidney and bladder ailments. The 17th-century herbalist Nicholas Culpeper declared that the leaves of all sorrels were very cooling, thirst-quenching and 'of great use against scurvy if eaten in spring as a salad'.

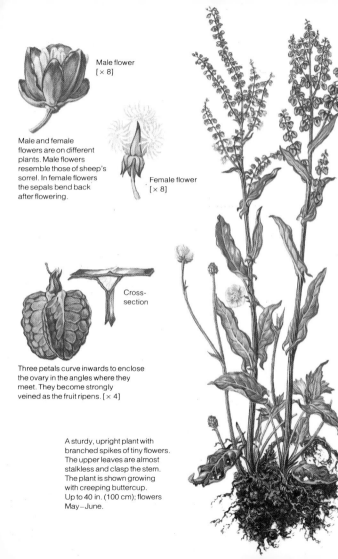

Male flower
[× 8]

Male and female
flowers are on different
plants. Male flowers
resemble those of sheep's
sorrel. In female flowers
the sepals bend back
after flowering.

Female flower
[× 8]

Cross-
section

Three petals curve inwards to enclose
the ovary in the angles where they
meet. They become strongly
veined as the fruit ripens. [× 4]

A sturdy, upright plant with
branched spikes of tiny flowers.
The upper leaves are almost
stalkless and clasp the stem.
The plant is shown growing
with creeping buttercup.
Up to 40 in. (100 cm); flowers
May–June.

The lance-shaped leaf
has two basal lobes
pointing backwards.
The sheath round the
stem and leaf base is
short and fringed.

The leaves of sorrel, a common plant of
grassland and open places in woods,
often turn crimson in late summer.

Sorrel *Rumex acetosa*

In Tudor times, sorrel was the most prized English vegetable. It
graced the table of Henry VIII, who is said to have held it in great
esteem. Sorrel leaves have a pronounced sourness, and were
used for flavouring in much the same way as lemons are used
today. The chopped leaves were the main ingredient in a green
sauce served with fish.

Another use for sorrel was the removal of ink or iron stains
from linen, and both the sharp taste and stain-removing properties are due to the presence of oxalic acid. The acid taste is
referred to in the species named *acetosa*, which is derived from
the Latin word *acetum*, meaning vinegar. The generic name
Rumex comes from the Latin *rumo*, 'to suck' – the Romans
sucked the leaves to assuage thirst. The sorrel's 'upstairs and
downstairs' uses have lapsed now, although the boiled leaves are
eaten in some parts of Ireland, and in Lapland the juice has been
used instead of rennet to curdle milk.

In late summer, sorrel adds a bright splash of red to the
grassy places where it grows. The colour comes from the leaves
and stems which frequently turn a beautiful crimson, and the
tiny flowers and fruits, too, become tinged with red.

207

The three-sided ripe fruit is enclosed by three petals, each strongly veined with a reddish swelling on the midrib. [× 5]

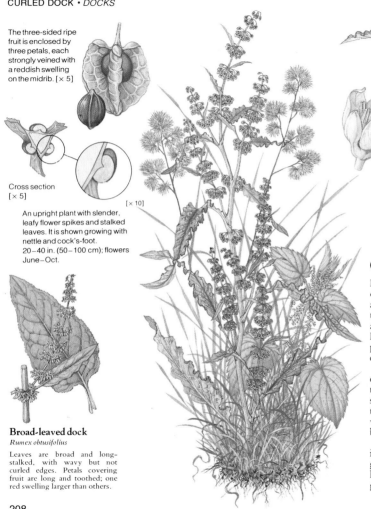

Cross section [× 5]

[× 10]

An upright plant with slender, leafy flower spikes and stalked leaves. It is shown growing with nettle and cock's-foot. 20–40 in. (50–100 cm); flowers June–Oct.

Broad-leaved dock
Rumex obtusifolius

Leaves are broad and long-stalked, with wavy but not curled edges. Petals covering fruit are long and toothed; one red swelling larger than others.

Most of the greenish flowers are bisexual and have anthers and stigmas. [× 10]

The lance-shaped leaves have curled and wavy edges.

Curled dock is a plant of waste ground and cultivated land, grassy places and pebbly beaches throughout Britain.

Curled dock *Rumex crispus*

In the same weedy places where nettles thrive, nature often obligingly provides its own 'medicine', the dock, whose leaves are still used by walkers in the country to neutralise the sting of the nettle. At one time, these leaves were applied as a dressing and used as a more general remedy for burns, scalds and blisters. In particular, workers in ironstone quarries who developed a peculiar sore on their forearms would rub the freshly cut surface of a dock root on the sore every third day until it was cured.

While they are still young, the leaves of curled dock, which eventually grow to 12 in. (30 cm) in length, are edible, although they taste rather bitter. In the United States they are sometimes sprinkled with vinegar and cooked with ham or bacon. Before the days of plastics and grease-proof paper, broad-leaved dock was one of several large-leaved British plants used to wrap butter; this is why the plant is also known as butter dock.

Curled dock is a troublesome weed in fields and gardens, for it is a tough perennial with a long, persistent root. The lazy gardener, pulling at the top of the plant, will find himself pulling loose only a handful of foliage, while the root remains in the ground to grow again.

The soft, hairy stem is cylindrical. The alternate leaves are stalked and untoothed. [× 3]

The reddish stems are often branched, and grow from crevices of walls or on the ground. The flowers form clusters at the base of each leaf-stalk. The plant is seen growing with dandelion and cock's-foot. Up to 28 in. (70 cm); flowers June – Sept.

Sepals enclose the ripe fruit. [× 3]

Three or more flowers form a cluster, the female towards the centre. [× 3]

Wall pellitory often takes root in cracks in old walls and rocks. It is locally common in England and Wales.

Wall pellitory *Parietaria diffusa*

South-western parts of the British Isles are the areas in which wall pellitory is most commonly seen, spilling out of the cracks and crevices in stones and smothering walls with a coating of pale pink. The plant appeared to early herbalists to be breaking up the stone, and so they came to the conclusion that it could be used to break up and dispel kidney or bladder stones in humans. In the 17th century the herbalist Nicholas Culpeper recommended the juice of wall pellitory, mixed with honey, for a multitude of aches, pains and coughs; he even claimed that it stopped the hair from falling out.

Wall pellitory belongs to the same family as the nettle; the leaves of both plants are similar in shape and arrangement, but wall pellitory lacks the stinging hairs of the nettle. Both species owe their success to man, whose building activities extended their habitat throughout the country. Whereas the nettle thrives on rubbish tips, the wall pellitory prefers walls; the generic name, *Parietaria*, comes from the Latin *paries*, meaning 'a wall'.

The plant is, however, quite common in more natural surroundings. It is often found amongst rocks and cliffs, and on drier soils, it grows at the bases of hedges and thickets.

209

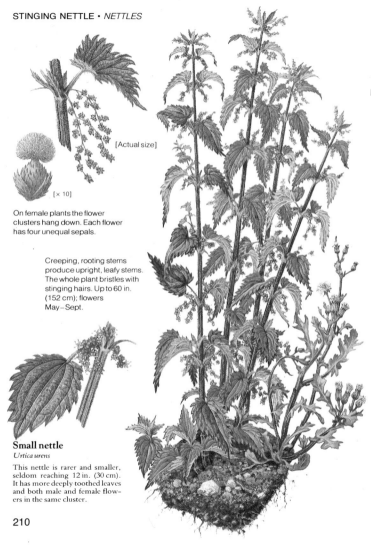

[Actual size]

[× 10]

On female plants the flower clusters hang down. Each flower has four unequal sepals.

Creeping, rooting stems produce upright, leafy stems. The whole plant bristles with stinging hairs. Up to 60 in. (152 cm); flowers May–Sept.

Small nettle
Urtica urens

This nettle is rarer and smaller, seldom reaching 12 in. (30 cm). It has more deeply toothed leaves and both male and female flowers in the same cluster.

210

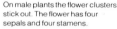

[Actual size]

[× 5]

On male plants the flower clusters stick out. The flower has four sepals and four stamens.

This is a common plant of hedgerows, woods, wasteland, and neglected gardens all over the British Isles.

Stinging nettle *Urtica dioica*

From prehistoric days mankind has needed, used and hated the stinging nettle. An enemy of the farmer and gardener, the bane of children's bare knees, and an instrument of torture with which medieval monks flagellated their bare backs, the plant has been reviled by one generation after another. Yet through the centuries it has been used for cloth, food and medicine. The bones of a Bronze Age Dane were found wrapped in fabric made from nettle stems, and as late as the last century nettle tablecloths and bed-linen were being used in Scotland.

Young nettle leaves are steamed in some country districts and used as a vegetable, while the dried leaves are made into nettle tea. The Roman belief that nettle stings cured rheumatism persists in Britain, and during the Second World War nettles were harvested to supply chlorophyll for medicines.

The mechanism that causes the stings is simple: on being touched, the tip of each hair breaks off and releases an acid which causes a painful rash. To spread pollen, the male nettle flowers have stamens kept bent over until maturity. They are then released with a flick, which tosses their pollen into the air and on to nearby female flowers.

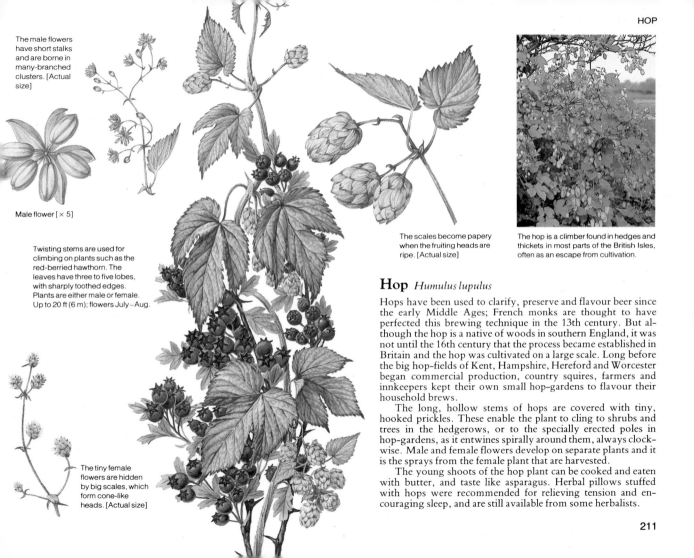

The male flowers have short stalks and are borne in many-branched clusters. [Actual size]

Male flower [× 5]

Twisting stems are used for climbing on plants such as the red-berried hawthorn. The leaves have three to five lobes, with sharply toothed edges. Plants are either male or female. Up to 20 ft (6 m); flowers July–Aug.

The tiny female flowers are hidden by big scales, which form cone-like heads. [Actual size]

The scales become papery when the fruiting heads are ripe. [Actual size]

The hop is a climber found in hedges and thickets in most parts of the British Isles, often as an escape from cultivation.

Hop *Humulus lupulus*

Hops have been used to clarify, preserve and flavour beer since the early Middle Ages; French monks are thought to have perfected this brewing technique in the 13th century. But although the hop is a native of woods in southern England, it was not until the 16th century that the process became established in Britain and the hop was cultivated on a large scale. Long before the big hop-fields of Kent, Hampshire, Hereford and Worcester began commercial production, country squires, farmers and innkeepers kept their own small hop-gardens to flavour their household brews.

The long, hollow stems of hops are covered with tiny, hooked prickles. These enable the plant to cling to shrubs and trees in the hedgerows, or to the specially erected poles in hop-gardens, as it entwines spirally around them, always clockwise. Male and female flowers develop on separate plants and it is the sprays from the female plant that are harvested.

The young shoots of the hop plant can be cooked and eaten with butter, and taste like asparagus. Herbal pillows stuffed with hops were recommended for relieving tension and encouraging sleep, and are still available from some herbalists.

211

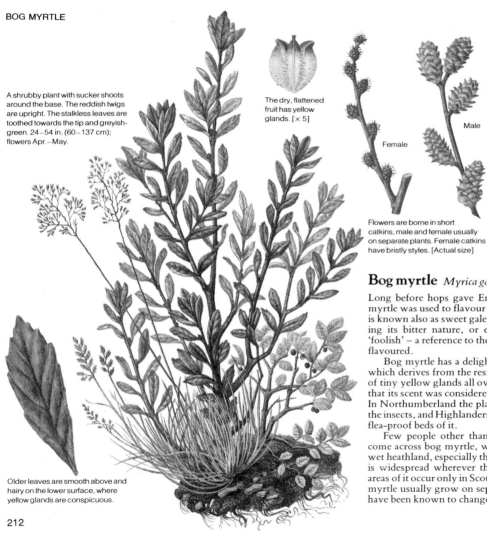

A shrubby plant with sucker shoots around the base. The reddish twigs are upright. The stalkless leaves are toothed towards the tip and greyish-green. 24–54 in. (60–137 cm); flowers Apr.–May.

The dry, flattened fruit has yellow glands. [× 5]

Female

Male

Flowers are borne in short catkins, male and female usually on separate plants. Female catkins have bristly styles. [Actual size]

Older leaves are smooth above and hairy on the lower surface, where yellow glands are conspicuous.

Bog myrtle grows in bogs, fens and wet heaths, often forming large, deliciously fragrant clumps.

Bog myrtle *Myrica gale*

Long before hops gave English beer its distinctive tang, bog myrtle was used to flavour the drink during brewing. The plant is known also as sweet gale, either from the word 'gall', indicating its bitter nature, or else from the Norse *gayr*, meaning 'foolish' – a reference to the intoxicating qualities of the drink it flavoured.

Bog myrtle has a delightful eucalyptus-like aromatic smell, which derives from the resinous substance exuded by hundreds of tiny yellow glands all over the plant. The name suggests also that its scent was considered similar to that of the myrtle shrub. In Northumberland the plant is known as flea wood – it repels the insects, and Highlanders used to make what they hoped were flea-proof beds of it.

Few people other than enthusiastic botanists are likely to come across bog myrtle, which grows in boggy areas, fens and wet heathland, especially those dominated by *Sphagnum* moss. It is widespread wherever there is extensive bogland, but large areas of it occur only in Scotland. Male and female catkins of bog myrtle usually grow on separate plants – but not always. Some have been known to change sex from year to year.

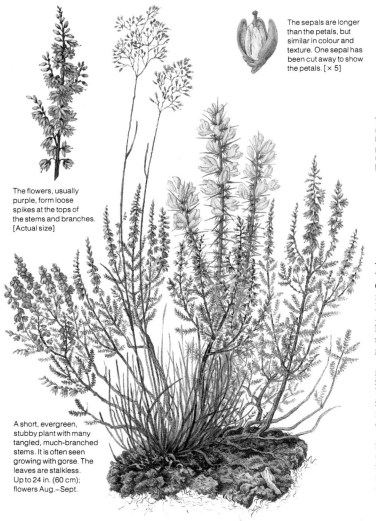

The flowers, usually purple, form loose spikes at the tops of the stems and branches. [Actual size]

A short, evergreen, stubby plant with many tangled, much-branched stems. It is often seen growing with gorse. The leaves are stalkless. Up to 24 in. (60 cm); flowers Aug.–Sept.

The sepals are longer than the petals, but similar in colour and texture. One sepal has been cut away to show the petals. [× 5]

The leaves of the flowering stems are borne in pairs. Each leaf has two pointed projections at the base and may be smooth or hairy. [× 10]

Tips of non-flowering stems have leaves in four tightly overlapping rows. [× 10]

Ling is a common plant of heaths and moors, and of bogs and woods with poor or acid soils all over the British Isles.

Heather *Calluna vulgaris*

Commonest of several species of heather that grow on the moors and heaths of Britain is the true heather, also known in England as 'ling'. This alternative name is derived from the Anglo-Saxon *lig*, meaning 'fire', and recalls the importance of heather in early times as fuel. In Scotland the word ling is not restricted to heather, but used to describe any rush or coarse grass growing on heathland.

Another use of heather in earlier days was the origin of its generic name *Calluna*, which comes from a Greek word meaning 'to brush'; stems of heather were often tied together in bundles to make brushes and brooms. Stems were also woven into baskets, and heather was used for thatching and as a bedding material. In the Scottish Highlands the walls of crofts were made of heather stems cemented together with peat.

Heather is an evergreen plant, and provides food for many forms of wild life. The tender young shoots form the main food of red grouse. Birds eat the ripe seeds, and the flowers provide nectar from which bees make delicious honey. Most heather flowers are purple, but on most moors there are isolated clumps of the rarer 'lucky' white heather.

213

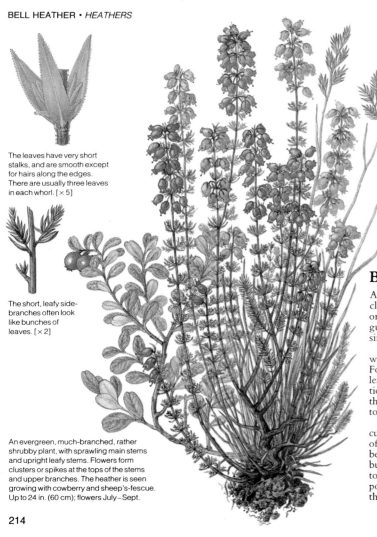

The leaves have very short stalks, and are smooth except for hairs along the edges. There are usually three leaves in each whorl. [× 5]

The short, leafy side-branches often look like bunches of leaves. [× 2]

An evergreen, much-branched, rather shrubby plant, with sprawling main stems and upright leafy stems. Flowers form clusters or spikes at the tops of the stems and upper branches. The heather is seen growing with cowberry and sheep's-fescue. Up to 24 in. (60 cm); flowers July–Sept.

The sepals are much shorter than the petals which form the bell-shaped flower. [× 5]

Bell heather is a common plant of drier heaths and moorland throughout Britain; it is also found in open woodland.

Bell heather *Erica cinerea*

Any walker crossing a tract of boggy land would do well to stay close to crops of bell heather, for in boggy areas the plant grows on the driest tussocks. Care must be taken, however, to distinguish the plant from cross-leaved heath, which is superficially similar but grows in wetter parts.

Throughout Britain, bell heather thrives on poor, sandy and well-drained soils, often in the midst of generally damp areas. For a plant of dampish habitats, the bell heather has unusual leaves, which appear to be adapted for extremely dry conditions. The edges of its leaves are tightly rolled and the leaves themselves have a very thick 'cuticle' or protective surface layer to conserve moisture.

Like most of the heathers, bell heather has been taken into cultivation. It is a gardener's delight – easy to grow, and giving of its best in places where the soil is poor in nutrients. The 'wild' bell heather is the most vividly coloured of the cultivated types, but there are many other varieties, ranging in colour from white to crimson. Since these varieties flower at different times, it is possible by choosing carefully to have bell heather flowering in the garden most of the year round.

Whorls of four leaves are spaced up the stem. [×2]

The short-stalked leaves are very hairy and also have long bristles, each tipped with a round gland. [×4]

An evergreen, shrubby plant with many tangled leaves, branched but without the clusters of tiny branchlets of bell heather. Up to 24 in. (60 cm); flowers July–Sept.

The drooping flowers form short, rounded heads at the tops of the stems or branches. The hairy sepals are much shorter than the petals. [×2]

As the fruits ripen, the dying flowers become upright.

Cross-leaved heath is common in bogs and on wet heath and moorland throughout Britain; it is rarer in drier areas.

Cross-leaved heath *Erica tetralix*

In many ways cross-leaved heath resembles bell heather, but it grows in slightly different locations. Whereas bell heather thrives in the drier parts of moorland areas, cross-leaved heath is found in the damp places and wet hollows near by. Only occasionally does the plant stray onto drier land.

Cross-leaved heath is also distinguished by its whorls of four thin leaves, which form a cross when looked at from above; the leaves of bell heather are in whorls of three. The plant's unusual leaf is the origin of its species name *tetralix*, incorporating the Greek word for four. The genus name *Erica* comes directly from the Greek *ereike*, which means 'heath' or 'heather'. In an adaptation suited to water conservation, the edge of the leaf is turned down and folded over to trap a layer of still air against the underside; this results in less evaporation of moisture than if air could move freely over the entire surface of the leaf.

A bush of cross-leaved heath, like all heathers, begins to sprawl with age. As the bush spreads outwards, branches will root and spread the bush even further. Although cross-leaved heath is a very brightly coloured plant, it has not shared the popularity of other heathers in cultivation.

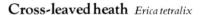

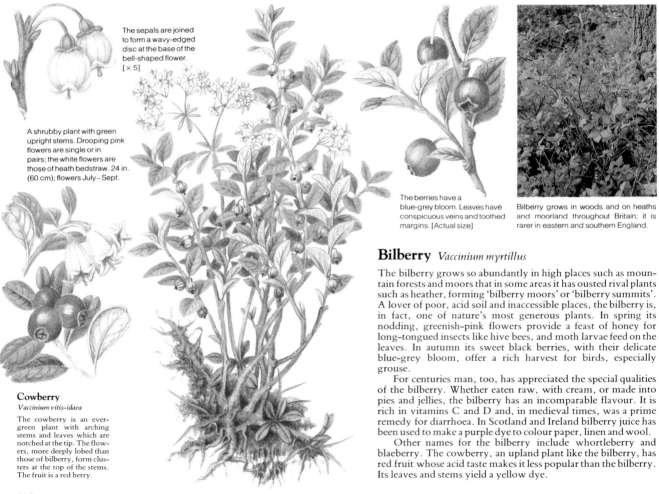

The sepals are joined to form a wavy-edged disc at the base of the bell-shaped flower. [× 5]

A shrubby plant with green upright stems. Drooping pink flowers are single or in pairs; the white flowers are those of heath bedstraw. 24 in. (60 cm); flowers July–Sept.

The berries have a blue-grey bloom. Leaves have conspicuous veins and toothed margins. [Actual size]

Bilberry grows in woods and on heaths and moorland throughout Britain; it is rarer in eastern and southern England.

Cowberry
Vaccinium vitis-idaea

The cowberry is an evergreen plant with arching stems and leaves which are notched at the tip. The flowers, more deeply lobed than those of bilberry, form clusters at the top of the stems. The fruit is a red berry.

Bilberry *Vaccinium myrtillus*

The bilberry grows so abundantly in high places such as mountain forests and moors that in some areas it has ousted rival plants such as heather, forming 'bilberry moors' or 'bilberry summits'. A lover of poor, acid soil and inaccessible places, the bilberry is, in fact, one of nature's most generous plants. In spring its nodding, greenish-pink flowers provide a feast of honey for long-tongued insects like hive bees, and moth larvae feed on the leaves. In autumn its sweet black berries, with their delicate blue-grey bloom, offer a rich harvest for birds, especially grouse.

For centuries man, too, has appreciated the special qualities of the bilberry. Whether eaten raw, with cream, or made into pies and jellies, the bilberry has an incomparable flavour. It is rich in vitamins C and D and, in medieval times, was a prime remedy for diarrhoea. In Scotland and Ireland bilberry juice has been used to make a purple dye to colour paper, linen and wool.

Other names for the bilberry include whortleberry and blaeberry. The cowberry, an upland plant like the bilberry, has red fruit whose acid taste makes it less popular than the bilberry. Its leaves and stems yield a yellow dye.

The evergreen short-stalked leaves are oval or almost oblong, dark green above and bluish or silvery below. The fruit is a red or a brown-spotted berry, and may be globular or pear shaped. [× 2]

The flowers have long, slender stalks; the petals curl back away from the stamens. [× 2]

The very slender, rooting stems lie on the ground, usually widely separated from one another. The leaves are also widely separated along the stems, which extend to 12 in. (30 cm) long. Flowers June–Aug.

Cranberries grow widely in bogs and wet heaths in scattered localities throughout Britain, especially with *Sphagnum* moss.

Cranberry *Vaccinium oxycoccos*

In her autobiographical *Journal Of Our Life In The Highlands*, Queen Victoria described with relish a dinner at Balmoral Castle that ended 'with a good tart of cranberries'. For centuries, the fruit of this little bog plant, with its distinctively sharp flavour, has been prized in Britain as a filling for pies, as jam, and, in the form of cranberry sauce, as an accompaniment to roast venison and turkey.

In medieval times the cranberry had a variety of names, including marsh-whort, fen-berry and moss-berry. It was not until the 19th century, when quantities of the American large cranberry, which has much bigger berries than the British variety, began to be imported that it received its current name. The large cranberry is occasionally found growing wild as an escape from cultivation. The plant is called 'cranberry' possibly because the unopened flower on its long, slender stalk resembles a crane's head and neck, or perhaps because the bogs and fens where it grows were favourite feeding grounds for cranes. In the lore of wild flowers, the cranberry is traditionally a cure for heart-ache. In spite of the disappearance of much marshland through agricultural drainage, it still thrives.

217

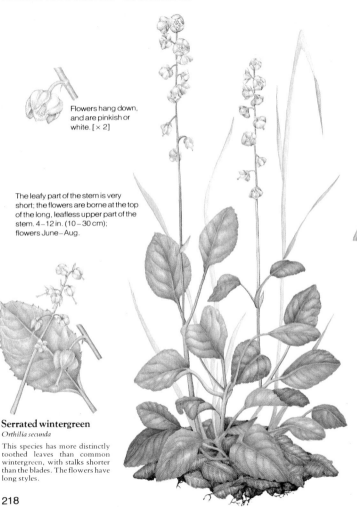

Flowers hang down, and are pinkish or white. [× 2]

The leafy part of the stem is very short; the flowers are borne at the top of the long, leafless upper part of the stem. 4–12 in. (10–30 cm); flowers June–Aug.

Serrated wintergreen
Orthilia secunda

This species has more distinctly toothed leaves than common wintergreen, with stalks shorter than the blades. The flowers have long styles.

The fruit is divided into five segments. [× 2]

The stalks of the rounded, toothed and glossy leaves are longer than the blades. [Actual size]

This plant of woods, moors, dunes and damp places in rocky areas is found locally in most parts of Britain.

Common wintergreen *Pyrola minor*

In medieval times wintergreen was valued for its supposed healing powers. People suffering from bladder or kidney ulcers, or from external wounds or haemorrhages, used its dry, cool leaves to bring relief. Midsummer is the best time for gathering this plant, which is still sometimes recommended for the treatment of muscular aches and pains. Wintergreen oil – which is now usually synthetically produced – can be used as an antiseptic or as an ingredient of embrocations. The oil taken from the leaves is also used as a flavouring for chewing-gum and sweets. In North America, mountain tea, an infusion of wintergreen leaves, is a popular beverage.

The wintergreen's drooping flowers, which have no nectar, are often pollinated by beetles. If they are not successfully pollinated by insects, the flowers sometimes pollinate themselves. After flowering, the globular fruits develop; the tiny seeds they contain are very light and are widely dispersed by the wind.

Wintergreens are rarely found in cultivation, as they are not easy to establish in a garden after transplanting. Serrated wintergreen is most commonly found in Wales and in the north.

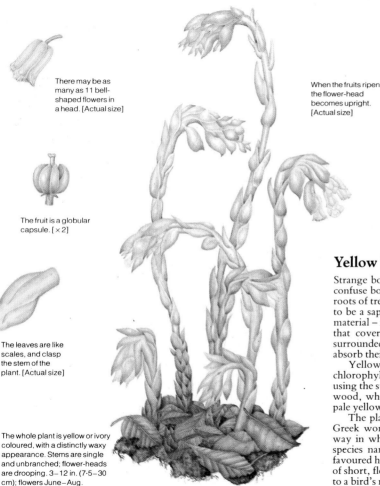

There may be as many as 11 bell-shaped flowers in a head. [Actual size]

The fruit is a globular capsule. [× 2]

The leaves are like scales, and clasp the stem of the plant. [Actual size]

The whole plant is yellow or ivory coloured, with a distinctly waxy appearance. Stems are single and unbranched; flower-heads are drooping. 3–12 in. (7·5–30 cm); flowers June–Aug.

When the fruits ripen, the flower-head becomes upright. [Actual size]

Yellow bird's-nest grows mainly in beech and pine woods. It is locally widespread throughout Britain.

Yellow bird's-nest *Monotropa hypopitys*

Strange both in its appearance and its habits, this plant used to confuse botanists. It was once believed to be a parasite upon the roots of trees such as beech and pine. However, it is now known to be a saprophyte. a plant that obtains its food from decaying material – in this case the thick layer of rotting vegetable matter that covers the woodland floor. The roots of the plant are surrounded by a mass of fungal threads which helps them to absorb their nutrients.

Yellow bird's-nest has none of the green pigment, chlorophyll, with which most plants manufacture their food using the sun's light: it is found growing in the darkest parts of a wood, where little light penetrates. The stout fleshy stems are pale yellow, turning brown in the autumn.

The plant's generic name, *Monotropa*, is derived from two Greek words meaning 'single' and 'to turn' – referring to the way in which the top of the stem is turned to one side. The species name means 'under pine', indicating the plant's most favoured habitat. The common name was inspired by the tangle of short, fleshy, branched roots, which bears some resemblance to a bird's nest.

219

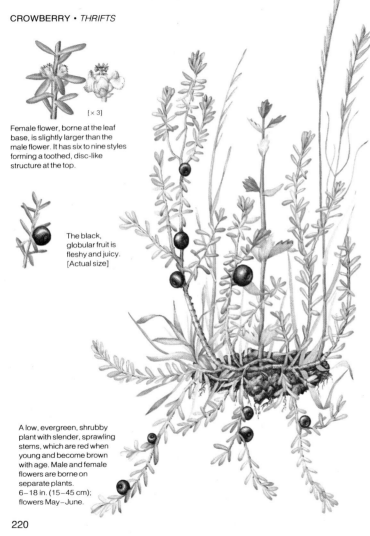

Female flower, borne at the leaf base, is slightly larger than the male flower. It has six to nine styles forming a toothed, disc-like structure at the top.

[× 3]

The black, globular fruit is fleshy and juicy. [Actual size]

A low, evergreen, shrubby plant with slender, sprawling stems, which are red when young and become brown with age. Male and female flowers are borne on separate plants. 6–18 in. (15–45 cm); flowers May–June.

[× 3]

Tiny, single flowers are borne at the base of each leaf; the male flower has three long stamens.

The edges of the smooth, oblong leaves are rolled inwards and almost meet. [× 4]

Crowberry, which grows on moors, mountains and drier bogs, is common in Scotland, northern England and Wales.

Crowberry *Empetrum nigrum*

Grouse, ptarmigan and other moorland birds feast on the black, glossy fruit of the crowberry when it ripens in late summer. The plant is also the main source of food for the caterpillars of several moths, including the black mountain, mountain burnet and broad-bordered white underwing. Humans can eat the berries too, but the taste is unpleasantly acid, and too many reputedly cause headaches. Perhaps that is the origin of the plant's name – 'the berry fit only for crows' – although it may also refer to the colour of the fruit.

Crowberry flourishes on the dry, sandy or peaty soil of rocky uplands, often alongside heather, cranberry and bilberry. The edges of the shiny leaves curl down and inwards to form a narrow tube, a device that reduces the loss of water by evaporation through the pores on the leaf surface. The plant's long, slender branches hug the ground and spread rapidly, choking out other plant life as they do so.

The crowberry is native to Britain, but occurs on moorlands and mountain-sides throughout Europe from Scandinavia to the Balkans and into Siberia. It is also widespread in North America, where it is sometimes called the crowpea.

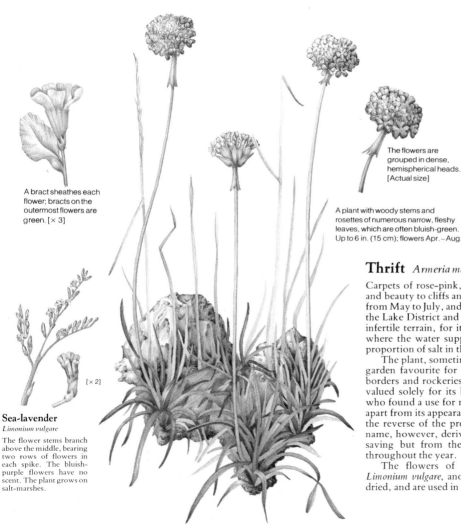

A bract sheathes each flower; bracts on the outermost flowers are green. [× 3]

The flowers are grouped in dense, hemispherical heads. [Actual size]

A plant with woody stems and rosettes of numerous narrow, fleshy leaves, which are often bluish-green. Up to 6 in. (15 cm); flowers Apr.–Aug.

[× 2]

Sea-lavender
Limonium vulgare

The flower stems branch above the middle, bearing two rows of flowers in each spike. The bluish-purple flowers have no scent. The plant grows on salt-marshes.

Thrift is common around the coast on drifts, salt-marshes and pastures throughout Britain.

Thrift *Armeria maritima*

Carpets of rose-pink, honey-scented thrift flowers add colour and beauty to cliffs and salt-marshes around the coast of Britain from May to July, and also appear on mountain tops in Scotland, the Lake District and western Ireland. Thrift is well adapted to infertile terrain, for it has long roots that reach down to levels where the water supply is constant, and it can tolerate a high proportion of salt in the soil.

The plant, sometimes called sea pink or rock rose, has been a garden favourite for more than 400 years, and is suitable for borders and rockeries. Since it was first cultivated, it has been valued solely for its beauty; even the 16th-century herbalists, who found a use for most plants, conceded that thrift has none apart from its appearance. In this century, the plant appeared on the reverse of the pre-decimal, 12-sided threepenny piece; its name, however, derives not from any association with money-saving but from the fact that it thrives, or remains green, throughout the year.

The flowers of thrift and of the similar sea-lavender, *Limonium vulgare*, another seaside plant, are 'everlasting' when dried, and are used in flower arranging.

221

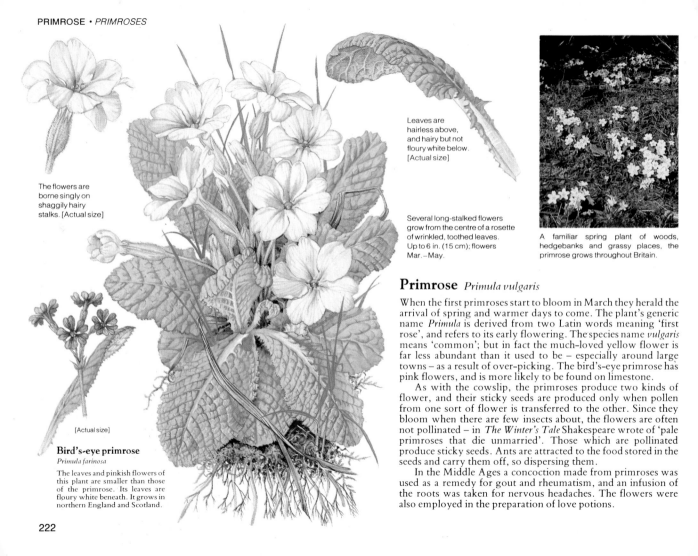

The flowers are borne singly on shaggily hairy stalks. [Actual size]

Leaves are hairless above, and hairy but not floury white below. [Actual size]

Several long-stalked flowers grow from the centre of a rosette of wrinkled, toothed leaves. Up to 6 in. (15 cm); flowers Mar.–May.

A familiar spring plant of woods, hedgebanks and grassy places, the primrose grows throughout Britain.

[Actual size]

Bird's-eye primrose
Primula farinosa

The leaves and pinkish flowers of this plant are smaller than those of the primrose. Its leaves are floury white beneath. It grows in northern England and Scotland.

Primrose *Primula vulgaris*

When the first primroses start to bloom in March they herald the arrival of spring and warmer days to come. The plant's generic name *Primula* is derived from two Latin words meaning 'first rose', and refers to its early flowering. The species name *vulgaris* means 'common'; but in fact the much-loved yellow flower is far less abundant than it used to be – especially around large towns – as a result of over-picking. The bird's-eye primrose has pink flowers, and is more likely to be found on limestone.

As with the cowslip, the primroses produce two kinds of flower, and their sticky seeds are produced only when pollen from one sort of flower is transferred to the other. Since they bloom when there are few insects about, the flowers are often not pollinated – in *The Winter's Tale* Shakespeare wrote of 'pale primroses that die unmarried'. Those which are pollinated produce sticky seeds. Ants are attracted to the food stored in the seeds and carry them off, so dispersing them.

In the Middle Ages a concoction made from primroses was used as a remedy for gout and rheumatism, and an infusion of the roots was taken for nervous headaches. The flowers were also employed in the preparation of love potions.

The fruits are hidden by the sepals. As the fruits develop, the flower-stalks become upright. [Actual size]

Leaves are finely hairy on both sides, but not floury white. [Actual size]

Oxlip
Primula elatior

A similar plant to the cowslip, but it has larger flowers in a one-sided head, and larger leaves. Also, the fruit is slightly longer than the sepals.

The flowers are drooping, and their petals less wide-spreading than those of the primrose. [Actual size]

Wrinkled, toothed leaves form rosettes from which rise one or more flower stems, each with up to 30 flowers in a head. 4–12 in. (10–30 cm), flowers Apr.–May.

Cowslip is a plant of meadows and chalky grassland throughout Britain, though it is less common in the north.

Cowslip *Primula veris*

According to legend, St Peter dropped the keys to Heaven when he learned that a duplicate set had been made. The keys landed somewhere in northern Europe, and the first cowslip sprang from the spot. The nodding, yellow flowers are thought to resemble the saint's 'bunch of keys' – which is another name for the cowslip in Somerset.

As with the primrose, there are two kinds of flower. One has the stigma showing in the flower centre, with the anthers placed further down the tube formed by the petals. The other has a ring of anthers in the flower centre, with the stigma further down the tube.

Both sorts of flower are visited by insects with long tongues, such as bees and moths, which seek the nectar from the base of the petal tube. The position of the stamens on one type of flower causes pollen to stick to the top of the insects' tongues, on which it is carried at the right height to be transferred to the stigma of a flower of the other type. The delicately perfumed cowslips are used to make one of the best and most potent of country wines. The oxlip, a woodland plant of southern and eastern England, is a hybrid between the cowslip and the primrose.

223

The five-petalled flowers, pink or purple but often very pale, are borne in whorls on stems rising above the water surface. There are three to eight flowers in each whorl.

The finely lobed leaves radiate from the stem in whorls.

The fruit stalks bend downwards; the fruit, hidden by the sepals, is a capsule with four teeth that open to release the seeds. [× 2]

The floating stems produce roots at intervals along their length. All the leaves are submerged. Up to 16 in. (40 cm); flowers May–June.

Water violets can occasionally be found growing wild in pools and ditches, and are planted in ornamental lakes.

Water violet *Hottonia palustris*

No other member of the primrose family growing in the British Isles is so completely aquatic as the water violet. The erect, completely leafless flower stems rise from the surface of the water to bear pink or pale purple flowers with deep yellow throats. They are usually pollinated by insects, but occasionally flowers are produced that never open, and are self-pollinating. After flowering, the fruit stalks bend downwards, and the capsules, each containing many small seeds, ripen in the water.

The plant's alternative names – featherfoil and millefolium – refer to the delicate pale green whorls of finely divided leaves that grow beneath the surface. The long roots growing from the floating stems are silvery–white, and glisten in the water.

The water violet is not a common plant in the wild, but is found most widely in the eastern counties. Being such a handsome plant, it is often grown in garden ponds and park lakes for its ornamental value. The origin of the common name is uncertain, since the plant does not belong to the same family as the familiar violets and pansies. The generic name was given to it in honour of Petrus Hotton, an 18th-century Dutch professor of botany; the species name means 'marshy' or 'swampy' in Latin.

The fruit is a globular capsule which splits into five parts when ripe. [× 2]

[× 2]

Chickweed wintergreen
Trientalis europaea

At the top of a single, un-branched stem are a whorl of large leaves and one or two white flowers. The fruit splits into five parts when ripe. The plant is found in mossy places, such as moors or pine woods. 4–10 in. (10–25 cm); flowers May–June.

The stalkless flowers are borne singly at the junction of leaf and stem. [× 2]

A plant with creeping, rooting stems and pairs of fleshy, stalkless leaves. It is shown growing with red fescue. 4–12 in. (10–30 cm); flowers June–Aug.

Sea milkwort is found on rocks, cliffs and in grassy salt-marshes around the British coast. Occasionally it occurs inland.

Sea milkwort *Glaux maritima*

This small, perennial plant is most commonly seen spreading a thick mat among the sand and shingle along the foreshores of Britain. It has adapted to life in the salt-marshes, where most plants cannot survive because the salt concentration prevents their roots from absorbing water. The sea milkwort solves this problem by storing water in its fleshy leaves, and by growing in a compact mat form, so reducing water loss by evaporation.

Each plant produces a large number of small flowers which usually pollinate themselves. They have no petals, and it is the pale pink sepals that give the flowers their colour. After flowering, the few seeds produced are shaken out from the capsule by the movement of the stems in the wind. The generic name *Glaux* is derived from a Greek word meaning 'bluish-green' – the colour of the small, oval-shaped leaves.

Chickweed wintergreen, a similar plant to sea milkwort but related neither to wintergreens nor to chickweeds, grows only in the north of England and in Scotland. It is a small herb and was once used for healing wounds and to cure blood poisoning. Its generic name *Trientalis* comes from the Latin for 'one-third of a foot' – the plant's average height.

225

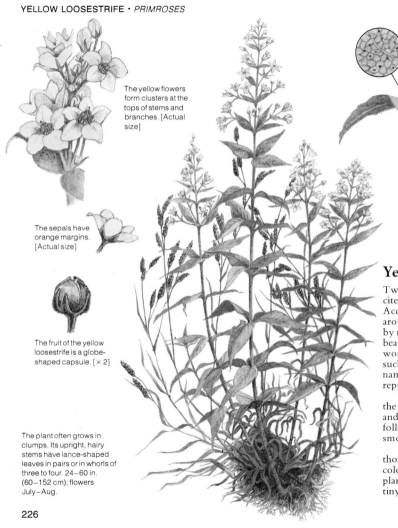

The yellow flowers form clusters at the tops of stems and branches. [Actual size]

The sepals have orange margins. [Actual size]

The fruit of the yellow loosestrife is a globe-shaped capsule. [× 2]

The plant often grows in clumps. Its upright, hairy stems have lance-shaped leaves in pairs or in whorls of three to four. 24–60 in. (60–152 cm); flowers July–Aug.

On its upper surface the leaf is dotted with tiny orange or black glands. [× 5]

The almost stalkless leaves are bright green above, bluish-green below. [Actual size]

Yellow loosestrife is a plant of fens and river and lake margins, scattered all over Britain except for north Scotland.

Yellow loosestrife *Lysimachia vulgaris*

Two stories dating back to the time of ancient Greece have been cited to explain this plant's botanical name of *Lysimachia*. According to one account, bunches of yellow loosestrife tied around the necks of draft animals would make them more docile by repelling insects that might otherwise irritate and unsettle the beasts. Hence people called the plant *Lysimachia* after two Greek words which together meant 'to loosen strife'. Other sources, such as the Roman writer Pliny the Elder, said that the plant was named after Lysimachus, an ancient king of Thrace, who was reputed to have discovered medicinal uses for the plant.

The 17th-century herbalist Nicholas Culpeper also thought the plant had healing properties. He recommended it for nose and mouth bleeding and for upset stomachs. Many people also followed his advice to burn the plant in their homes, since the smoke drove away troublesome flies and gnats.

Yellow loosestrife is found along river banks – including those of the Thames – in late summer, and often grows in large colonies. The flowers are scentless and contain no nectar; but the plant is pollinated by a number of wasps and one kind of bee, the tiny *Macropis labiata*.

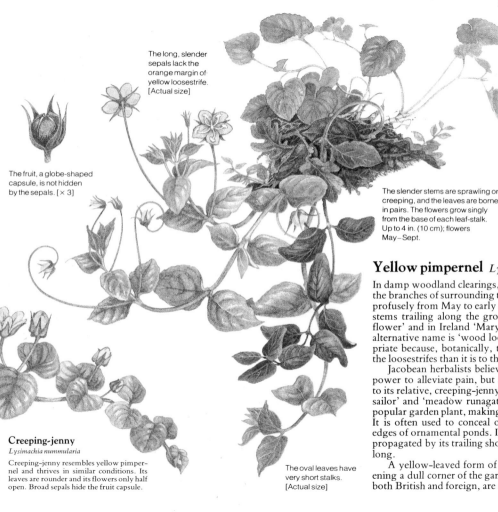

The long, slender sepals lack the orange margin of yellow loosestrife. [Actual size]

The fruit, a globe-shaped capsule, is not hidden by the sepals. [× 3]

The slender stems are sprawling or creeping, and the leaves are borne in pairs. The flowers grow singly from the base of each leaf-stalk. Up to 4 in. (10 cm); flowers May–Sept.

Yellow pimpernel grows in woods and shady hedges all over the British Isles, though it is rare in drier districts.

Yellow pimpernel *Lysimachia nemorum*

In damp woodland clearings, where the sunlight filters through the branches of surrounding trees, the yellow pimpernel flowers profusely from May to early autumn, its leafy, rapidly growing stems trailing along the ground. In Wiltshire it is called 'star flower' and in Ireland 'Mary's clover', though a more general alternative name is 'wood loosestrife'. This last name is appropriate because, botanically, the plant is more closely related to the loosestrifes than it is to the pimpernels.

Jacobean herbalists believed that yellow pimpernel had the power to alleviate pain, but attributed greater healing qualities to its relative, creeping-jenny, also called 'motherwort', 'roving sailor' and 'meadow runagates'. Creeping-jenny has become a popular garden plant, making useful, if vigorous, ground cover. It is often used to conceal old stonework, or to decorate the edges of ornamental ponds. It rarely produces fertile seeds and is propagated by its trailing shoots, which often grow several feet long.

A yellow-leaved form of creeping-jenny is useful in brightening a dull corner of the garden. Various other related species, both British and foreign, are also sometimes cultivated.

Creeping-jenny
Lysimachia nummularia

Creeping-jenny resembles yellow pimpernel and thrives in similar conditions. Its leaves are rounder and its flowers only half open. Broad sepals hide the fruit capsule.

The oval leaves have very short stalks. [Actual size]

227

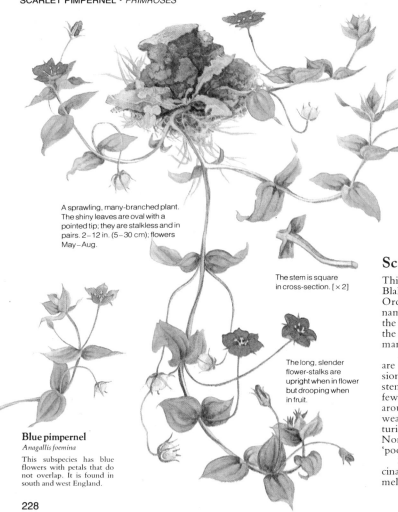

The red flowers have five overlapping petals.

A sprawling, many-branched plant. The shiny leaves are oval with a pointed tip; they are stalkless and in pairs. 2–12 in. (5–30 cm); flowers May–Aug.

The stem is square in cross-section. [× 2]

The fruit is a globular capsule, with a stalk that is longer than the leaves. [× 4]

The small, colourful scarlet pimpernel is common on cultivated land, waste ground and dunes throughout Britain.

The long, slender flower-stalks are upright when in flower but drooping when in fruit.

Blue pimpernel
Anagallis foemina
This subspecies has blue flowers with petals that do not overlap. It is found in south and west England.

Scarlet pimpernel *Anagallis arvensis*

This 'humble English wayside flower' was chosen by Sir Percy Blakeney – the foppish hero of *The Scarlet Pimpernel*, Baroness Orczy's novel of the French Revolution – as his undercover name when rescuing aristocrats from the guillotine. A rhyme in the book refers to him as 'that damned elusive Pimpernel'; but the flower itself is widespread throughout Britain, Europe and many other parts of the world.

Although its bright, starry flowers are usually scarlet, they are also sometimes coloured pink, white, lilac or blue. Occasionally plants are found with red and blue flowers on the same stem. The flowers contain no nectar or scent and are visited by few insects. They only open for a short time each day – from around 8 a.m. to 3 p.m. – and are always shut during dull or wet weather. Because of this, the plant has been regarded for centuries as a combined weatherglass and clock; it is known in Norfolk as 'change-of-the-weather', and in other counties as 'poor man's weatherglass' and 'shepherd's sundial'.

Scarlet pimpernel was once valued for its supposed medicinal qualities, and was thought to cure madness and dispel melancholy – hence its Somerset name of 'laughter bringer'.

This pimpernel is a plant of bogs, peaty places and damp grasslands in most of Britain except parts of southern Scotland.

The pink flowers are funnel-shaped and borne upright on long stalks from leaf axils.

The fruit is a globular capsule that splits round the middle. [× 2]

Chaffweed
Anagallis minima

The leaves of this species are alternate, with tiny stalkless flowers and fruit growing in the angles of the leaves. It grows in sandy areas on heaths and by the sea.

A slender, creeping plant with rooting stems and leaves in opposite pairs. It is shown growing with darker-flowered cranberry. 2–6 in. (5–15 cm); flowers June–Aug.

Bog pimpernel *Anagallis tenella*

The pale pink flowers of this small, delicate plant open in the sunshine and close in dull weather, like those of its more widespread and better-known relative, the scarlet pimpernel. Although the bog pimpernel can be found in wet places throughout much of Britain, like many other bog plants it is becoming less common because of the drainage and cultivation of its habitat for use as agricultural land. It often grows so densely as to form a mat.

The fruit-stalks hang downwards, and when the seeds are mature the capsule splits neatly around the middle. The top half, with the stigma still attached, falls away like a little hat, allowing the numerous tiny seeds to fall to the earth around the parent plant. The generic name *Anagallis*, from a Greek word that can be translated as 'delightful', was given to it by the ancient Greek physician Dioscorides. The common name 'pimpernel' is believed to come from 'bipinella', a diminutive of the Latin *bipinnis*, 'two-winged', referring to the leaves.

The related chaffweed is one of the smallest European plants, rarely growing over 2 in. (5 cm) high, and often not even reaching $\frac{1}{4}$ in. (2 cm). Its small size often helps to identify it.

229

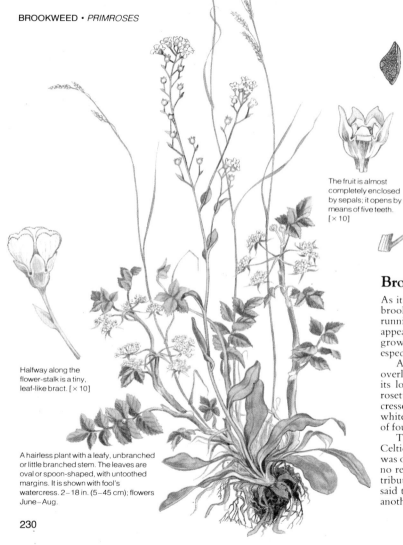

The seed is very small and conical and has one flat side. [× 20]

The fruit is almost completely enclosed by sepals; it opens by means of five teeth. [× 10]

The stalks bend in the middle when the fruits are ripe.

Halfway along the flower-stalk is a tiny, leaf-like bract. [× 10]

A hairless plant with a leafy, unbranched or little branched stem. The leaves are oval or spoon-shaped, with untoothed margins. It is shown with fool's watercress. 2–18 in. (5–45 cm); flowers June–Aug.

Brookweed is found in wet places, especially near the sea. It is scattered throughout Britain.

Brookweed *Samolus valerandi*

As its name suggests, brookweed is often found at the sides of brooks, particularly those that are connected to brackish streams running out to sea. But it is not solely a summer seaside plant, appearing on damp rocks and on cliffs above a beach. It also grows in ditches and marshy meadows in a few inland areas, especially in eastern England.

Although it is a fairly widespread plant, brookweed is often overlooked or wrongly identified. At first glance it seems – with its long, fleshy flower spikes and leafy stems arising from a rosette at the base – like a relative of the many small, white cresses of the cabbage family. But on closer inspection, the white flowers of brookweed are seen to have five petals instead of four. Furthermore, the petals are joined at the base.

The plant's generic name of *Samolus* may be derived from the Celtic words *san*, meaning 'health', and *mos*, 'a pig'; the plant was once regarded as a cure for various pig diseases, but there is no record of any such use today. Its species name *valerandi* is a tribute to the 16th-century herbalist Donre Valerand, who is said to have collected the plant on the Greek island of Samos – another possible derivation of its generic name.

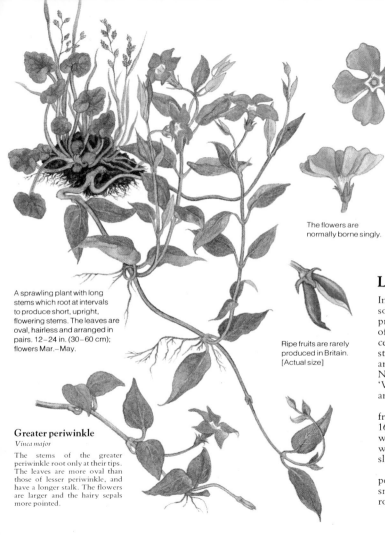

The petals are slightly unequal in size, and have a white ring around the centre of the flower.

The flowers are normally borne singly.

The seed is rough and blackish.

The sepals form a tube with five lance-shaped lobes.

This purple-flowered plant brightens copses, hedgebanks and woods. It is scattered throughout Britain.

A sprawling plant with long stems which root at intervals to produce short, upright, flowering stems. The leaves are oval, hairless and arranged in pairs. 12–24 in. (30–60 cm); flowers Mar.–May.

Ripe fruits are rarely produced in Britain. [Actual size]

Greater periwinkle
Vinca major

The stems of the greater periwinkle root only at their tips. The leaves are more oval than those of lesser periwinkle, and have a longer stalk. The flowers are larger and the hairy sepals more pointed.

Lesser periwinkle *Vinca minor*

In medieval England garlands or crowns of periwinkles were sometimes worn by people about to be executed. This was probably because the evergreen plant was regarded as a symbol of immortality. It was also used as a medicine, and a 17th-century writer declared that it 'hath an excellent virtue to staunch bleeding at the nose in Christians if made into a garland and hung about the neck'. Around the same time, the herbalist Nicholas Culpeper recommended it as a fertility aid, stating: 'Venus owns this Herb and saith that the Leaves eaten by Man and Wife together cause Love between them'.

The lesser periwinkle was probably introduced to Britain from the Continent, and its presence was recorded by a mid-16th-century herbalist, William Turner, who saw it growing wild in the West Country. It is also often found near habitation, where its dark green leaves and purple flowers, with their slightly asymmetrical lobes, make it conspicuous.

One plant which certainly came from abroad is the lesser periwinkle's 'big brother', the greater periwinkle. Like the smaller plant, it rarely produces ripe seed in Britain and it, too, roots very easily. It is seldom, if ever, seen far from civilisation.

231

The seed is marked with a net-like pattern. [× 10]

The ripe fruit is longer than the sepals and clearly visible. [× 2]

The petal tube extends beyond the long-toothed sepals. [× 3]

A hairless plant with a rosette of leaves at base of stem. The leaves are roughly oval or elliptical, with three to seven prominent veins. 2–12 in. (5–30 cm); flowers June–Oct.

The pink flowers of common centaury colour dunes and dry grassy places. It is common in England, rarer in Scotland.

Common centaury *Centaurium erythraea*

According to the Roman writer Pliny the Elder, common centaury was named after the centaur Chiron. This creature, part man and part horse, is said to have used the plant to cure himself of a wound inflicted by the nine-headed serpent Hydra. Nicholas Culpeper, like many other herbalists, remarked on the efficacy of common centaury against common wounds of all kinds and various diseases – it even, he claimed, removed freckles and facial blemishes. He concluded that this bitter herb was 'very wholesome but not very toothsome'.

Common centaury usually grows on poor soil, in dry grass-land, on dunes and at the edges of woods. Often it is extremely abundant. Where conditions are favourable it can be a large and graceful plant; when conditions are less suitable it can be very small. On chalky downs by the sea, common centaury grows in small clumps which look very unlike the normal plant. Before the enormous range of size and form displayed by the species was realised, different plants were sometimes treated as different species.

The size of slender centaury also varies; often the plant consists of no more than a single stem with one flower.

Slender centaury
Centaurium pulchellum

This widespread plant has no rosette of leaves at the base. Its red flowers have stalks, and the flowering spikes are less dense than those of the common centaury. The fruit is the same length as the sepal tube.

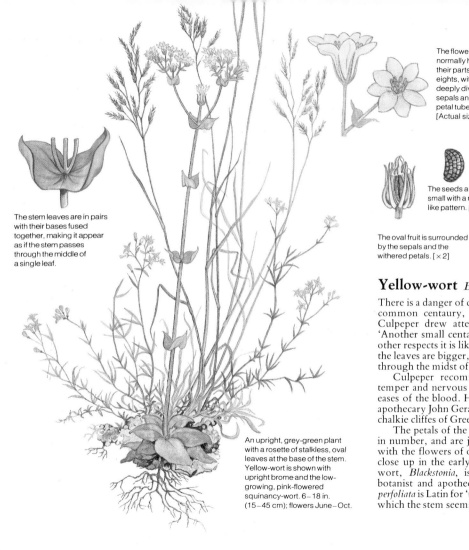

The stem leaves are in pairs with their bases fused together, making it appear as if the stem passes through the middle of a single leaf.

An upright, grey-green plant with a rosette of stalkless, oval leaves at the base of the stem. Yellow-wort is shown with upright brome and the low-growing, pink-flowered squinancy-wort. 6–18 in. (15–45 cm); flowers June–Oct.

The flowers normally have their parts in eights, with deeply divided sepals and a short petal tube. [Actual size]

The seeds are small with a net-like pattern. [× 10]

The oval fruit is surrounded by the sepals and the withered petals. [× 2]

The slender yellow-wort grows on chalk and limestone grassland and on dunes. It is fairly common in southern Britain.

Yellow-wort *Blackstonia perfoliata*

There is a danger of confusing the yellow-wort with the similar common centaury, and the 17th-century herbalist Nicholas Culpeper drew attention to this. He wrote that there was 'Another small centaury, which beareth a yellow flower; in all other respects it is like the former (common centaury), save that the leaves are bigger, and of a darker green, and the stalk passeth through the midst of them'.

Culpeper recommended yellow-wort as a cure for bad temper and nervous disorders, and common centaury for diseases of the blood. Half a century before that, the botanist and apothecary John Gerard recorded that yellow-wort grew on 'the chalkie cliffes of Greenhithe in Kent, and such like places'.

The petals of the yellow flowers vary between six and eight in number, and are joined at the base into a short tube. Along with the flowers of other members of the gentian family, they close up in the early afternoon. The generic name of yellow-wort, *Blackstonia*, is derived from an 18th-century London botanist and apothecary, John Blackstone. The species name *perfoliata* is Latin for 'through the leaves', and refers to the way in which the stem seems to pierce the leaves.

233

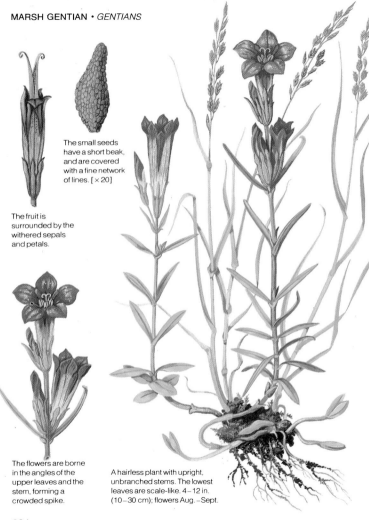

The small seeds have a short beak, and are covered with a fine network of lines. [× 20]

The fruit is surrounded by the withered sepals and petals.

The flowers are borne in the angles of the upper leaves and the stem, forming a crowded spike.

A hairless plant with upright, unbranched stems. The lowest leaves are scale-like. 4–12 in. (10–30 cm); flowers Aug.–Sept.

The petal tube is long, with a green stripe down each petal.

Marsh gentian is confined to scattered areas of bog and wet heath in England and Wales; it is rare, and becoming rarer.

Marsh gentian *Gentiana pneumonanthe*

It is unfortunate that so lovely a wild flower as the marsh gentian should be so rare in Britain. It can occasionally be found growing in wet heaths and bogs in Dorset, Kent and Dyfed, and sometimes as far north as Anglesey, Yorkshire and Cumbria. Never common in recent times, it is currently decreasing in numbers. The decline is probably caused by excessive collecting, current climatic changes, and the disappearance of the bogs where the plant grows as they are drained for cultivation.

The 16th-century herbalist John Gerard said of the marsh gentian: 'The gallant flowers hereof bee in their bravery about the end of August.' He recommended that it should be grown for the beauty of its flowers, but its root has long been important medicinally. Gerard claimed that it was useful against 'pestilent diseases' as well as the 'bitings and stingings of venomous beasts'.

More recently the root has been used to make a bitter tonic for jaded digestions. The active constituents that impart the bitter taste are two of the chemicals called glucosides – gentiin and gentiamarin. These are found in all gentians, so it does not matter which is used to make the tonic.

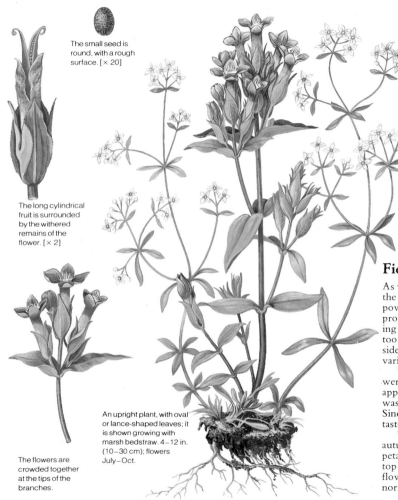

The small seed is round, with a rough surface. [× 20]

The long cylindrical fruit is surrounded by the withered remains of the flower. [× 2]

The flowers are crowded together at the tips of the branches.

An upright plant, with oval or lance-shaped leaves; it is shown growing with marsh bedstraw. 4–12 in. (10–30 cm); flowers July–Oct.

The parts of the flowers are in fours; the sepal tube has four lobes, the larger outer lobes nearly hiding the two inner ones. [× 2]

This plant of grassland and sand dunes is common in the north of Britain, but becoming very rare in the south and east.

Field gentian *Gentianella campestris*

As with other gentians, the field gentian was a major weapon in the early herbalist's armoury against the ills of the flesh. The powdered root was used to make medicines whose curative properties ranged from improving the digestion to counteracting the stings of venomous beasts. It was a principal ingredient, too, in a tonic called Stockton Bitters, probably after the Teesside town where it was first made. This was taken to treat a variety of complaints including dysentery and catarrh.

The name Stockton Bitters and a folk-name, 'bitter-root', were derived from the bitter taste of the root. This property was appreciated in Sweden, too, where the root of the field gentian was employed, instead of hops, to impart a bitter taste to beer. Since hops do not grow so far north, any plants with a bitter taste have always been highly prized by Swedish brewers.

The dull purple flowers are often confused with those of the autumn gentian; but there is one easy way to tell them apart. The petals of both gentians are fused into a tube, which divides at the top to produce star-shaped flowers. In the field gentian the flower is usually a four-pointed star, while the autumn gentian normally has five points.

235

The petal tube is about twice as long as the tube formed by the sepals. Each flower has a fringe of pale hairs in its throat. [× 2]

[× 2]

The fruit is cylindrical; petals and sepals remain attached after flowering. [× 2]

An upright plant, normally with several branches. The basal leaves are usually spoon-shaped; the stem leaves are oval or lance-shaped. The plant is seen growing with horseshoe vetch and upright brome. 2–12 in. (5–30 cm); flowers Aug.–Sept.

This plant, found mainly on dunes and in turf over chalk and limestone, is common except in south-western Scotland.

Early gentian
Gentianella anglica

This related species, which flowers in May or June, is usually a smaller plant than autumn gentian. It has narrower leaves, and the flowers are borne on long stalks. The petal tube is about twice as long as the sepals. It is an uncommon plant; one subspecies grows only on the cliffs of north Cornwall.

Autumn gentian *Gentianella amarella*

William Turner in his 16th-century herbal speaks of 'A kind of Gentian upon the playne of Salisberrye'. This was the autumn gentian, a native of this country and a very important find, because until then apothecaries had relied upon the supplies of great yellow gentian imported from alpine regions to treat a multitude of ailments and conditions, including cramps, king's evil (scrofula), the bites of mad dogs and venomous beasts, and loss of appetite. Nicholas Culpeper, the 17th-century herbalist, considered the field gentian and autumn gentian 'not a whit inferior in Vertue' to the imported species.

The name gentian was, according to the Roman writer Pliny the Elder, derived from that of Gentius, a king of the ancient Illyrians who was credited with discovering the plant's medicinal properties.

Autumn gentian is often found growing in damp hollows in sand-dunes which have their own local 'climate'. Plants rather like those of alpine pastures – grass of parnassus, marsh helleborine and dwarf alpine willows – are frequently seen alongside the gentian. The closely related early gentian is found almost exclusively on chalk downs south of the Thames.

236

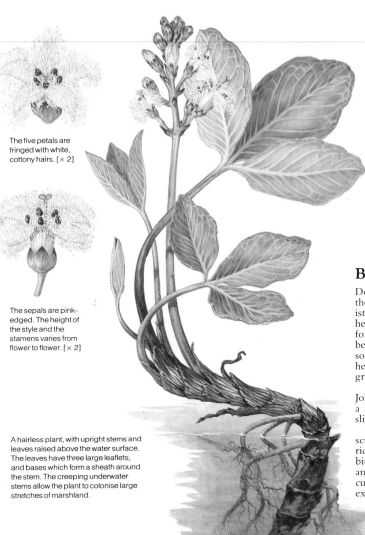

The five petals are fringed with white, cottony hairs. [× 2]

The sepals are pink-edged. The height of the style and the stamens varies from flower to flower. [× 2]

A hairless plant, with upright stems and leaves raised above the water surface. The leaves have three large leaflets, and bases which form a sheath around the stem. The creeping underwater stems allow the plant to colonise large stretches of marshland.

The fruit is crowned by a single style, which persists until the fruit is ripe. [× 2]

Bogbean flourishes in ponds, on lake edges, and in the wetter parts of bogs and fens. It is common throughout Britain.

Bogbean *Menyanthes trifoliata*

Despite its dull and unprepossessing name, the bogbean is one of the beauties of the British countryside. The 18th-century botanist William Curtis was so enraptured by the 'delicate native' that he compared it favourably with the most exotic and costly foreign bloom. He praised the fact that it cost nothing and could be cultivated without trouble, and was only sorry that it blossomed unseen 'and wastes its beauty in the desart air'. By 'desart' he meant the bogs, fens and marshes in which the bogbean grows, and which it sometimes comes to dominate.

Another admirer of the plant was the 16th-century herbalist John Gerard, who wrote: 'Towards the top of the stalks standeth a bush of feather-like flowers of a white colour, dasht over slightly with a wash of light carnation.'

In the Middle Ages, bogbean was recommended as a cure for scurvy, and the Irish considered that it purified the blood and got rid of boils. In the north of England, people sometimes used its bitter-tasting leaves to flavour beer. The leaves were also dried and put in herbal cigarettes – which were mostly made from the cured leaves of the coltsfoot plant – to improve the flavour. An extract from bogbean was prescribed as a general tonic.

237

COMMON FORGET-ME-NOTS

Most members of the forget-me-not family have bristly leaves and curved sprays of flowers. In some the flowers open purplish, only becoming blue with age. Five common species are here distinguished by their leaf shape and flower formation.

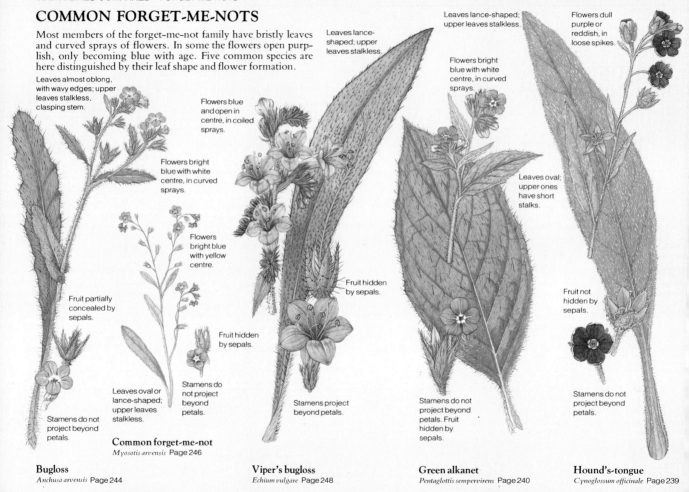

Leaves almost oblong, with wavy edges; upper leaves stalkless, clasping stem.

Flowers blue and open in centre, in coiled sprays.

Flowers bright blue with white centre, in curved sprays.

Flowers bright blue with yellow centre.

Fruit partially concealed by sepals.

Fruit hidden by sepals.

Leaves oval or lance-shaped; upper leaves stalkless.

Stamens do not project beyond petals.

Fruit hidden by sepals.

Stamens project beyond petals.

Stamens do not project beyond petals.

Common forget-me-not
Myosotis arvensis Page 246

Bugloss
Anchusa arvensis Page 244

Leaves lance-shaped; upper leaves stalkless.

Flowers bright blue with white centre, in curved sprays.

Leaves lance-shaped; upper leaves stalkless.

Flowers bright blue with white centre, in curved sprays.

Leaves oval; upper ones have short stalks.

Stamens do not project beyond petals. Fruit hidden by sepals.

Viper's bugloss
Echium vulgare Page 248

Green alkanet
Pentaglottis sempervirens Page 240

Flowers dull purple or reddish, in loose spikes.

Fruit not hidden by sepals.

Stamens do not project beyond petals.

Hound's-tongue
Cynoglossum officinale Page 239

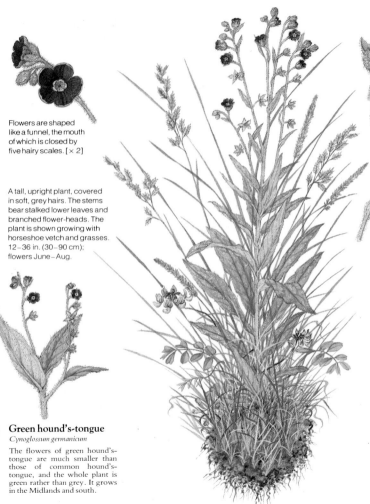

Flowers are shaped like a funnel, the mouth of which is closed by five hairy scales. [× 2]

A tall, upright plant, covered in soft, grey hairs. The stems bear stalked lower leaves and branched flower-heads. The plant is shown growing with horseshoe vetch and grasses. 12–36 in. (30–90 cm); flowers June–Aug.

Green hound's-tongue
Cynoglossum germanicum

The flowers of green hound's-tongue are much smaller than those of common hound's-tongue, and the whole plant is green rather than grey. It grows in the Midlands and south.

The fruit is not hidden by the sepals and consists of four nutlets. [Actual size]

Each nutlet is covered in short, barbed spines. [× 2]

As fruits ripen, flower spike grows longer and stalks curve down.

Common hound's-tongue grows on grassland at the edges of woods and by the sea throughout most of Britain.

Hound's-tongue *Cynoglossum officinale*

Until the 18th century, a person bitten by a mad dog was advised to bind the wound with the leaf of a hound's-tongue. According to Nicholas Culpeper, the 17th-century herbalist, it was also possible to ward off such attacks – and even to prevent dogs from barking at you – by placing a leaf under the big toe. The plant was said to 'tie the tongues of hounds' because of its distinctive and unpleasant smell, similar to that of rats and mice. The juice of the leaves, boiled in hogs' lard, was also used to prevent baldness, and as a treatment for burns, scalds and scabies.

The plant's generic name of *Cynoglossum* is derived from the Greek words for 'hound's-tongue'; it was the shape and texture of the leaves which gave rise to this name. Hound's-tongue is usually found on waste ground, or by roadsides and hedges. As well as applying it, or its juice, to the body, the distilled water of the roots and herbs used to be drunk as a remedy for ulcers and internal sores.

Green hound's-tongue is a closely related plant which, however, lacks the pungent smell of the common hound's-tongue, and is smooth instead of downy.

239

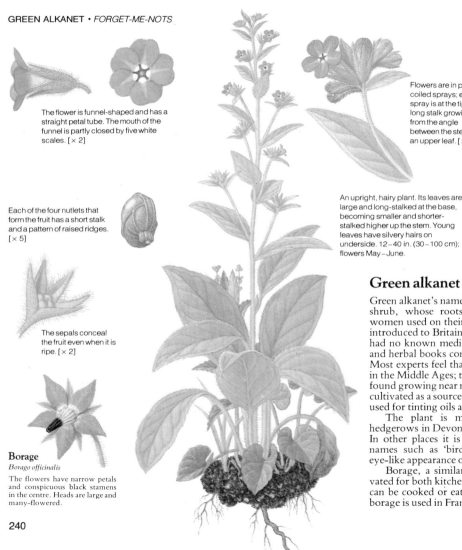

The flower is funnel-shaped and has a straight petal tube. The mouth of the funnel is partly closed by five white scales. [× 2]

Flowers are in pairs of coiled sprays; each spray is at the tip of a long stalk growing from the angle between the stem and an upper leaf. [× 2]

A plant of hedgerows and wood margins near habitation, green alkanet is widespread in south-west England.

Each of the four nutlets that form the fruit has a short stalk and a pattern of raised ridges. [× 5]

An upright, hairy plant. Its leaves are large and long-stalked at the base, becoming smaller and shorter-stalked higher up the stem. Young leaves have silvery hairs on underside. 12–40 in. (30–100 cm); flowers May–June.

The sepals conceal the fruit even when it is ripe. [× 2]

Green alkanet *Pentaglottis sempervirens*

Green alkanet's name goes back to the Arabic *al-henna*, or henna shrub, whose roots supplied the red dye which Egyptian women used on their hair and nails. It is uncertain when it was introduced to Britain, and why. Unlike many plants and herbs it had no known medicinal properties – and the early gardening and herbal books contained no reference to its virtues and uses. Most experts feel that green alkanet came from France or Spain in the Middle Ages; this is borne out by the fact that it was often found growing near medieval abbeys. At that time it was mainly cultivated as a source of red dye. More recently, alkanet has been used for tinting oils and cheap port wine.

The plant is most often found in damp woods and hedgerows in Devon and Cornwall, where it is possibly native. In other places it is probably an escape from gardens. Local names such as 'bird's-eye' and 'pheasant's-eye' refer to the eye-like appearance of the flowers.

Borage, a similar-looking plant to green alkanet, is cultivated for both kitchen and pharmacy use. The young green tops can be cooked or eaten raw in salads; and a drug derived from borage is used in France to treat fevers and nervous disorders.

Borage
Borago officinalis
The flowers have narrow petals and conspicuous black stamens in the centre. Heads are large and many-flowered.

Flowering branches are fairly short, and bear numerous long-stalked flowers. Top surface of upper leaves is covered with depressed scales.

The sprawling, rather fleshy, stems are purple with a whitish bloom. Oval leaves, greyish and hairless, usually lie in two rows along stem. Flower clusters are leafy and branched. The plant is shown growing with biting stonecrop. Up to 24 in. (60 cm); flowers June – Aug.

Young plants have rosettes of large, long-stalked leaves.

Flowers are bell-shaped, pink at first, becoming pink and blue. [× 4]

Fruit [Actual size]

Nutlet [× 2]

Ripe fruits are clearly visible within the spreading sepals. Each fruit is composed of four fleshy nutlets, their outer coats becoming papery as they mature.

This plant grows only on seaside shingle in scattered localities in Norfolk, North Wales, and north-western Britain.

Oysterplant *Mertensia maritima*

The leaves of this increasingly rare coastal plant are said to have the tangy flavour of oysters, so giving rise to its name. In the past, the leaves were either eaten raw or cooked as greens.

Seaside plants such as the oysterplant often have difficulty in obtaining and retaining enough water to live. One reason is the proximity of the sea, which creates a high concentration of salts in the soil. If the soil is saltier than the plants, the plants lose water to the soil and soon become dehydrated as a result. To counter this, seaside plants need a higher than normal salt content – hence the salty taste of the oysterplant. Seaside plants also lose water to the keen winds which blow across their exposed habitats. To reduce this water loss, the oysterplant has fleshy leaves which present the minimum surface area to the drying winds. The horny leaf surface also cuts down water loss caused by evaporation.

The oysterplant is usually found on the coastal shingle of north-west Scotland, but it seems to be decreasing in numbers in all its former haunts. Scientists are not certain what is causing this, but it does not appear to be the direct result of man's shoreline activities.

241

A tall, branched plant with hairs or bristles on its stem and leaves. The leaves at the base have long stalks, while those higher up have margins which continue down the stem to form a wing. The plant is seen growing with yarrow. 12–48 in. (30–120 cm); flowers May–June.

Blue comfrey

Symphytum × uplandicum

Narrow wings on the stem and blue or purplish flowers are distinctive. The plant, which flowers from June to August, is usually seen by roadsides and in hedges.

The nodding, bell-shaped flowers form coiled sprays; those at the base open first. They may be cream, white, purple or pink, but are always the same colour on any one plant.

Common comfrey is widespread throughout England and southern Scotland; it grows in damp places.

Common comfrey *Symphytum officinale*

Medieval herbalists used common comfrey for bone setting. The roots of the plant were dug up in the spring and grated to produce a sludge, which was packed around the broken limb. This hardened to a consistency similar to that of the plaster of Paris used today. Names for the plant reflect its former use; folk-names include 'knitbone' and 'boneset', and the common name comes from the Latin *conferre*, 'to bring together'.

In fact herbalists regarded common comfrey with a certain amount of wonder. They used it to draw splinters and to heal ruptures. John Gerard in the 16th century recommended that 'the slimie substance of the roote made in a posset of ale', should be 'given to drink against the paine in the back'. More recently the juice from the root has been mixed with sugar and liquorice to produce a linctus for coughs. Common comfrey can also be boiled like spinach and eaten as a vegetable.

The plant has a long petal tube, and only insects with long tongues can reach the nectar. Sometimes smaller bees bite through the side of the flower to obtain the nectar; when this happens the insect does not come into contact with the anther or the stamen and so pollination does not occur.

242

The flowers are grouped in coiled sprays, and are yellowish in colour. [Actual size]

The fruit is concealed by the sepals, which are narrower than those of common comfrey. [Actual size]

The upright, bristly stems have few or no branches. The middle leaves of the stem are larger than those near the base; the leaf margins continue down the stem to form a narrow wing. The plant is shown growing with bramble and ivy. 8–20 in. (20–50 cm); flowers June–July.

This plant of damp woods and hedgerows is found throughout Britain, but is more common in the north.

Soft comfrey
Symphytum orientale

This plant has white flowers, softly hairy stems and lower leaves larger than the rest. It is a very scattered plant of hedgebanks and grassy places.

Tuberous comfrey *Symphytum tuberosum*

Major differences between the two plants make it easy to distinguish tuberous comfrey from the related common comfrey. In the first place, they favour different parts of the country: tuberous comfrey is commonest in the north of England and Scotland, while common comfrey is most often seen in the south. Furthermore, tuberous comfrey has, as its name implies, a stout tuber-like root; above ground it is distinguished by a smaller, more slender outline, a stem that hardly branches at all, and flowers that are invariably yellowish in colour.

Cultivated varieties of comfrey make a striking addition to a garden. Any small piece of root will produce a plant; this makes the plant very difficult to eradicate if it spreads too far, for every last scrap of the very brittle root must be dug up to prevent it reappearing. As happens with all forget-me-nots, the tuberous comfrey's flowers quickly shrivel and die once picked.

Tuberous comfrey can be grown as fodder, though farm animals take time to get used to the taste, and its nutritive value is little higher than that of ordinary grass. Soft comfrey is a seldom-seen hedgerow plant that originated in Turkey. Its roots are slender and fleshy, unlike those of tuberous comfrey.

243

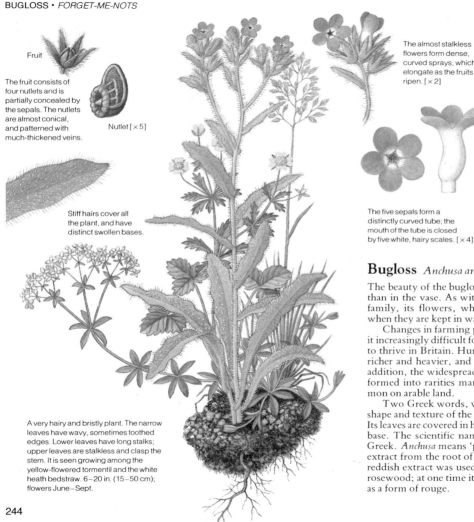

Fruit

The fruit consists of four nutlets and is partially concealed by the sepals. The nutlets are almost conical, and patterned with much-thickened veins.

Nutlet [× 5]

Stiff hairs cover all the plant, and have distinct swollen bases.

A very hairy and bristly plant. The narrow leaves have wavy, sometimes toothed edges. Lower leaves have long stalks; upper leaves are stalkless and clasp the stem. It is seen growing among the yellow-flowered tormentil and the white heath bedstraw. 6–20 in. (15–50 cm); flowers June–Sept.

The almost stalkless flowers form dense, curved sprays, which elongate as the fruits ripen. [× 2]

The five sepals form a distinctly curved tube; the mouth of the tube is closed by five white, hairy scales. [× 4]

Bugloss grows throughout Britain in arable fields and on heaths with sandy or chalky soils, especially near the sea.

Bugloss *Anchusa arvensis*

The beauty of the bugloss is to be appreciated in the field rather than in the vase. As with other members of the forget-me-not family, its flowers, when picked, wilt quickly and die, even when they are kept in water.

Changes in farming practice over the last 50 years have made it increasingly difficult for agricultural weeds such as the bugloss to thrive in Britain. Humus and fertiliser have made poor soils richer and heavier, and therefore less suitable for the plant. In addition, the widespread use of selective weedkillers has transformed into rarities many weeds which were previously common on arable land.

Two Greek words, which mean 'ox tongue' and refer to the shape and texture of the leaves, have given the bugloss its name. Its leaves are covered in hairs, which are unusually bulbous at the base. The scientific name for the species is also derived from Greek. *Anchusa* means 'paint' and is a reference to the use of an extract from the root of a related species, *Anchusa tinctoria*. This reddish extract was used to stain wood and to give an imitation rosewood; at one time it was even used by French society ladies as a form of rouge.

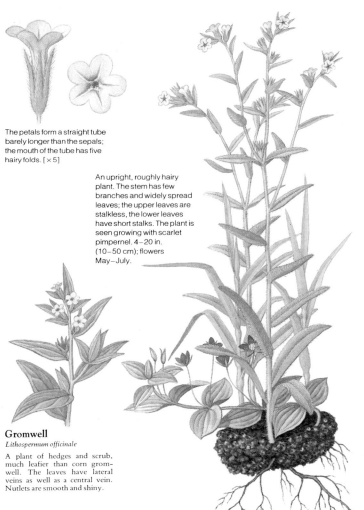

The petals form a straight tube barely longer than the sepals; the mouth of the tube has five hairy folds. [×5]

An upright, roughly hairy plant. The stem has few branches and widely spread leaves; the upper leaves are stalkless, the lower leaves have short stalks. The plant is seen growing with scarlet pimpernel. 4–20 in. (10–50 cm); flowers May–July.

Gromwell

Lithospermum officinale

A plant of hedges and scrub, much leafier than corn gromwell. The leaves have lateral veins as well as a central vein. Nutlets are smooth and shiny.

The conical, greyish-brown nutlets are conspicuously warty. [×5]

The flowers are in long, loose spikes which become even longer as the fruits develop. The fruit, consisting of four nutlets, is easily seen in the centre of the sepals. Leaves are narrow, with only the central vein apparent.

This plant is always found in and around arable land. It is common in England, but rare in the rest of Britain.

Corn gromwell *Buglossoides arvensis*

As its name suggests, corn gromwell is a plant of cultivated land. It used to be quite common, but since the introduction of selective weedkillers it has become much less widespread, in common with many other farmland weeds such as bugloss, corn cockle, cornflower and corn marigold.

As with many other weeds of arable land, the seeds of corn gromwell germinate almost continuously, enabling the plant to spread quickly wherever ideal conditions occur for it to do so. In this way corn gromwell, if not eradicated by weedkillers, can quickly gain a stranglehold over growing crops, competing for food and space and leaving the crops severely weakened.

The name gromwell is derived from two French words meaning 'grey millet', from the colour of the seeds. Until recently botanists included corn gromwell, together with true gromwell, in the genus *Lithospermum*, a name made up of two Latin words meaning 'stone seed', from the seed's hardness. Recently, however, the characteristics of corn gromwell have been recognised as resembling more closely those of the *Buglossoides* genus. Herbalists in the 16th and 17th centuries thought an infusion of the seeds dissolved stones in the kidneys.

245

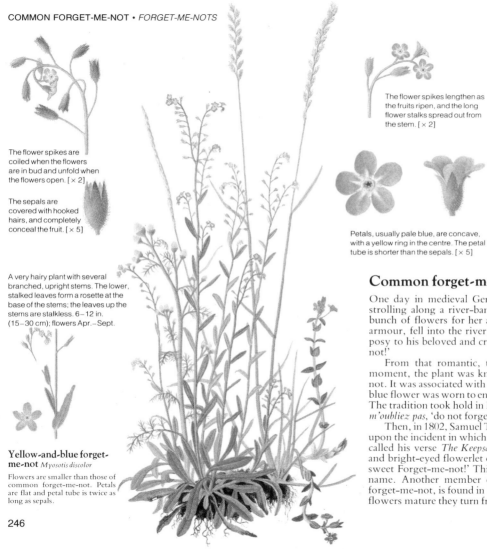

The flower spikes are coiled when the flowers are in bud and unfold when the flowers open. [× 2]

The sepals are covered with hooked hairs, and completely conceal the fruit. [× 5]

A very hairy plant with several branched, upright stems. The lower, stalked leaves form a rosette at the base of the stems; the leaves up the stems are stalkless. 6–12 in. (15–30 cm); flowers Apr.–Sept.

Yellow-and-blue forget-me-not *Myosotis discolor*

Flowers are smaller than those of common forget-me-not. Petals are flat and petal tube is twice as long as sepals.

The flower spikes lengthen as the fruits ripen, and the long flower stalks spread out from the stem. [× 2]

Petals, usually pale blue, are concave, with a yellow ring in the centre. The petal tube is shorter than the sepals. [× 5]

The blue or pinkish flowers of this plant are seen throughout Britain on dunes, cultivated land and in woods.

Common forget-me-not *Myosotis arvensis*

One day in medieval Germany, a knight and his lady were strolling along a river-bank. The knight bent down to pick a bunch of flowers for her and, overcome by the weight of his armour, fell into the river. As he was drowning he threw the posy to his beloved and cried: *Vergisz mein nicht!* – 'forget-me-not!'

From that romantic, tragic – and doubtless legendary – moment, the plant was known in Germany as the forget-me-not. It was associated with true love, and in the Middle Ages the blue flower was worn to ensure that a sweetheart stayed faithful. The tradition took hold in France, where the plant was called *ne m'oubliez pas*, 'do not forget me'; and *aimez-moi*, 'love me'.

Then, in 1802, Samuel Taylor Coleridge wrote a poem based upon the incident in which the knight supposedly drowned. He called his verse *The Keepsake*, and in it he spoke of: 'That blue and bright-eyed flowerlet of the brook/Hope's gentle gem, the sweet Forget-me-not!' This gave the plant its popular English name. Another member of the family, the yellow-and-blue forget-me-not, is found in Britain in open, grassy places. As the flowers mature they turn from yellow to a delicate blue.

246

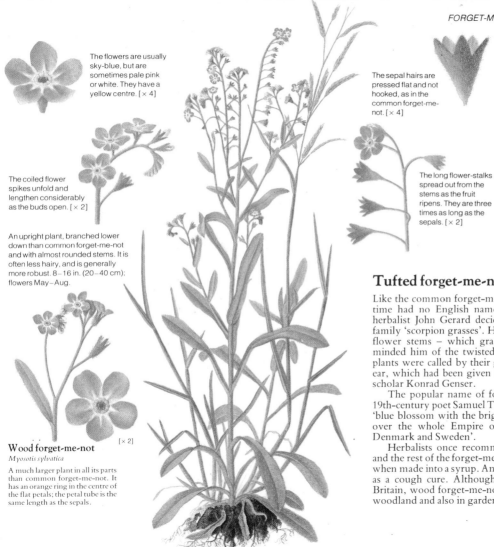

The flowers are usually sky-blue, but are sometimes pale pink or white. They have a yellow centre. [× 4]

The coiled flower spikes unfold and lengthen considerably as the buds open. [× 2]

An upright plant, branched lower down than common forget-me-not and with almost rounded stems. It is often less hairy, and is generally more robust. 8–16 in. (20–40 cm); flowers May–Aug.

The sepal hairs are pressed flat and not hooked, as in the common forget-me-not. [× 4]

The long flower-stalks spread out from the stems as the fruit ripens. They are three times as long as the sepals. [× 2]

The tufted forget-me-not raises its delicate flower-heads in marshy areas and beside water throughout Britain.

Wood forget-me-not
Myosotis sylvatica

A much larger plant in all its parts than common forget-me-not. It has an orange ring in the centre of the flat petals; the petal tube is the same length as the sepals.

[× 2]

Tufted forget-me-not *Myosotis laxa*

Like the common forget-me-not, this beautiful plant for a long time had no English name. Then, in the 16th century, the herbalist John Gerard decided to call all the members of the family 'scorpion grasses'. He did this because the plants' coiled flower stems – which gradually uncurl with maturity – reminded him of the twisted tails of scorpions. Until then, the plants were called by their genus name of *Myosotis*, or mouse-ear, which had been given to them by the 16th-century Swiss scholar Konrad Genser.

The popular name of forget-me-not was provided by the 19th-century poet Samuel Taylor Coleridge, who stated that the 'blue blossom with the bright yellow eye' had 'the same name over the whole Empire of Germany ... and, I believe, in Denmark and Sweden'.

Herbalists once recommended the tufted forget-me-not – and the rest of the forget-me-nots – as a cure for lung complaints when made into a syrup. An extract from the plant was also used as a cough cure. Although it is not particularly common in Britain, wood forget-me-not, as its name suggests, is found in woodland and also in gardens.

247

The flowers in their numerous curved sprays are pink in the bud and blue when open. The sprays elongate as the fruits develop. The funnel-shaped flowers have unequal lobes; stamens protrude from the open mouth of the funnel.

A roughly hairy plant, with the numerous basal leaves narrowing into stalks, and stalkless leaves up the stem. The flower spike is composed of numerous short sprays. Viper's-bugloss is sometimes seen among darnel fescue, sand sedge and sea bindweed. 12–36 in. (30–90 cm); flowers June–Sept.

A mass of whitish hairs partly obscures the green of the leaf surface when the plant is seen from a distance.

The long, slender sepals conceal the fruit, which consists of four nutlets. [× 2]

The angular nutlets are patterned with raised ridges. [× 5]

Preferring light, dry soils in grassy areas, viper's-bugloss is seen on cliffs and on dunes throughout England and Wales.

Viper's-bugloss *Echium vulgare*

A splash of blue on the foreshore is likely to signal the presence of viper's-bugloss, a plant whose colour is reflected in some of its other common names, such as 'bluebottle' and 'blue cat's-tail'. Farmers hate it for its deep, persistent roots, and call it 'blue devil'. Its most familiar name of viper's-bugloss recalls a time when the plant was used as a cure for snake-bite. Indeed to Dioscorides, the Classical writer on medicine, it was both a preventative and a remedy.

To the 17th-century herbalist William Coles, the stem of viper's-bugloss was 'speckled like a serpent's skin' – which, according to the widely accepted 'doctrine of signatures', was proof of its value against snake venom. A fancied resemblance of the dead flower-head with its ripe fruit to a snake's head reinforced the idea.

The herbalists found other uses for viper's-bugloss. An infusion of the seeds was said to drive away sadness and melancholy; it was also claimed to promote milk flow in nursing mothers, and to be effective against lumbago. The name 'bugloss' is derived from the Greek word for ox-tongue, and was applied to the plant because of its rough, tongue-shaped leaves.

The stalkless flowers are grouped into dense globular heads. The stems bear very small and inconspicuous scale-like leaves. [× 5]

The extremely slender stems of the common dodder are reddish and resemble threads; they twine around and over other plants such as ling, often in vast numbers. Flowers July–Sept.

[× 2]

Great dodder
Cuscuta europaea

This plant, similar to but somewhat larger than common dodder, grows almost exclusively on nettles and hops. The flowers are often whiter than those of common dodder.

Individual flower is bell-shaped, with short, rather blunt sepals and longer, paler petals. [× 5]

The fruit is topped by withering petals and stamens. [× 5]

Common dodder spreads on gorse, and is widespread in scattered localities throughout England and Wales.

Common dodder *Cuscuta epithymum*

When in flower, this strange plant can hide a small shrub completely from view under a mass of orange or rosy, intertwined, thread-like stems. When a seed germinates it produces a shoot that immediately begins to twine around the nearest plant; as it grows it produces suckers which penetrate the stem of the host, anchoring itself firmly. Once established, the root of the dodder withers and dies, and all its food requirements are drawn from the host plant through the suckers.

Common dodder grows on a wide variety of species, commonly on those of the pea family, and on heathers. Great dodder will usually grow only on nettles and hops. The common dodder's second scientific name is derived from two Greek words meaning 'upon thyme', referring to one of its hosts.

Dodder taken from a wild thyme plant was particularly valued by herbalists for its medicinal properties; the stems boiled in water were claimed to relieve a variety of complaints, including diseases of the liver and kidneys. Both species of dodder have been given numerous folk-names, among them 'hellweed' and 'devil's guts', probably applied by farmers who suffered the effects of their strangling stems on crops.

249

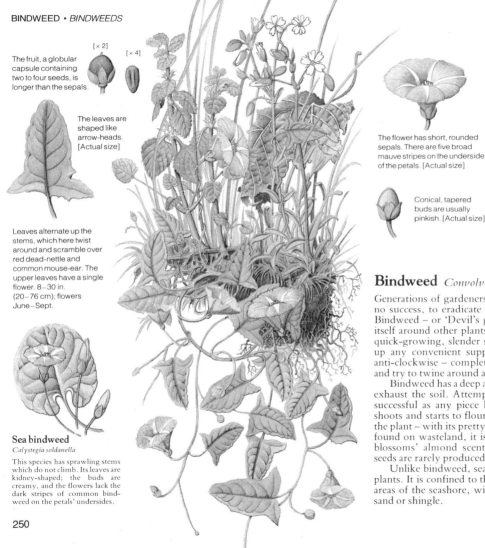

The fruit, a globular capsule containing two to four seeds, is longer than the sepals.

[× 2] [× 4]

The leaves are shaped like arrow-heads. [Actual size]

Leaves alternate up the stems, which here twist around and scramble over red dead-nettle and common mouse-ear. The upper leaves have a single flower. 8–30 in. (20–76 cm); flowers June–Sept.

Sea bindweed
Calystegia soldanella

This species has sprawling stems which do not climb. Its leaves are kidney-shaped; the buds are creamy, and the flowers lack the dark stripes of common bindweed on the petals' undersides.

The flower has short, rounded sepals. There are five broad mauve stripes on the underside of the petals. [Actual size]

Conical, tapered buds are usually pinkish. [Actual size]

Bindweed grows on farmland, derelict sites and grassy areas by the sea. It is common throughout most of Britain.

Bindweed *Convolvulus arvensis*

Generations of gardeners and farmers have tried, with little or no success, to eradicate this attractive but troublesome plant. Bindweed – or 'Devil's guts' as it is sometimes called – wraps itself around other plants and strangles them as they grow. Its quick-growing, slender stems trail over the ground and climb up any convenient support. The ends of the stems revolve anti-clockwise – completing a full circle in under two hours – and try to twine around anything they touch.

Bindweed has a deep and extensive root system, that tends to exhaust the soil. Attempts to dig up the plant are not always successful as any piece left in the soil quickly develops new shoots and starts to flourish as vigorously as before. Although the plant – with its pretty pink and white blooms – is commonly found on wasteland, it is also a typical corn-field flower. The blossoms' almond scent attracts many different insects, but seeds are rarely produced.

Unlike bindweed, sea bindweed does not fasten upon other plants. It is confined to the coast, where it trails over the higher areas of the seashore, with its stems often partly buried in the sand or shingle.

250

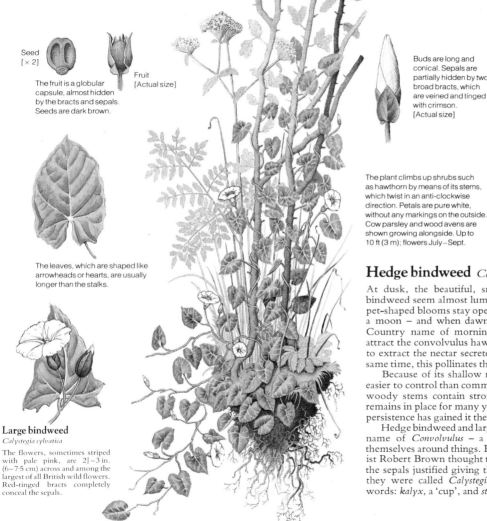

Seed
[× 2]

The fruit is a globular capsule, almost hidden by the bracts and sepals. Seeds are dark brown.

Fruit
[Actual size]

The leaves, which are shaped like arrowheads or hearts, are usually longer than the stalks.

Buds are long and conical. Sepals are partially hidden by two broad bracts, which are veined and tinged with crimson.
[Actual size]

The plant climbs up shrubs such as hawthorn by means of its stems, which twist in an anti-clockwise direction. Petals are pure white, without any markings on the outside. Cow parsley and wood avens are shown growing alongside. Up to 10 ft (3 m); flowers July – Sept.

This bindweed grows in hedges, on fenland and at the edges of woods, chiefly in the Midlands and southern England.

Large bindweed
Calystegia sylvatica

The flowers, sometimes striped with pale pink, are 2½–3 in. (6–7·5 cm) across and among the largest of all British wild flowers. Red-tinged bracts completely conceal the sepals.

Hedge bindweed *Calystegia sepium*

At dusk, the beautiful, snowy-white flowers of the hedge bindweed seem almost luminous in the fading light. The trumpet-shaped blooms stay open into the night – all night, if there is a moon – and when dawn comes they live up to their West Country name of morning glory. Although scentless, they attract the convolvulus hawk moth, which uses its long tongue to extract the nectar secreted at the base of the flower. At the same time, this pollinates the plant.

Because of its shallow roots, the hedge bindweed is much easier to control than common bindweed. Even so, its twining, woody stems contain strong fibres, and the plant frequently remains in place for many years. In some parts of the country its persistence has gained it the name of rope-bind.

Hedge bindweed and large bindweed once shared the generic name of *Convolvulus* – a reference to their ability to wrap themselves around things. But the 19th-century Scottish botanist Robert Brown thought the distinctive, large bracts covering the sepals justified giving the plants a new botanical name. So they were called *Calystegia*, which derives from two Greek words: *kalyx*, a 'cup', and *stege*, a 'covering'.

The petals are spreading or slightly curved in newly opened flowers; in old flowers they are folded back against the stalk. [× 2]

The leaves have a large oval blade with one to four short-stalked lobes below it. [Actual size]

Woody nightshade grows in woods and hedges and on beaches throughout Britain except for the north of Scotland.

The young fruits are green, turning yellow, then red when ripe. The flower-stalks curve as the fruits ripen.

Slender, rather woody stems scramble around vegetation such as brambles. 12–80 in. (30–200 cm); flowers June–Sept.

Woody nightshade *Solanum dulcamara*

This conspicuous ornament of Britain's woods and hedgerows puts on a brilliant display that lasts throughout the summer and late into the autumn. The blue-purple flowers bloom from early summer; in autumn the distinctive shiny berries ripen, often decorating the countryside with their deep red colours long after the leaves have begun to wither and fall.

Woody nightshade is a quick-growing plant which climbs by threading its pliant stems in and out of other plants for support; it has no prickles or tendrils with which to clutch other stems. When growing on sand-dunes and shingle beaches it looks very different, sprawling over the ground. This plant is sometimes mistaken for the highly poisonous deadly nightshade, though its berries are red rather than black. Woody nightshade berries, though not as poisonous as those of deadly nightshade, can cause sickness if eaten.

The plant's species name, *dulcamara*, is derived from two Latin words meaning sweet and bitter, and accounts for the plant's alternative common name of 'bittersweet'. Because of the presence of the toxic alkaloid solanine in the stem, leaves and berries, they taste bitter at first and then sweet.

A common weed on English wasteland, black nightshade is rarer in Wales and absent from most of Scotland.

The flowers are in unbranched, drooping heads, and the stalks are straight.

The flowers are smaller than those of woody nightshade. [× 2]

An upright, non-climbing plant. The leaves have a single blade, bluish-green above and paler beneath. Blue-flowered common field speedwell may sprawl around its base. Up to 24 in. (60 cm); flowers July–Sept.

The fruits are green when young, ripening to a dull black.

Black nightshade *Solanum nigrum*

So common is black nightshade on cultivated ground in Britain that it has earned the alternative name of garden nightshade. Large numbers of whitish, star-shaped flowers are produced during the summer, and the black berries that develop from them in the autumn are conspicuous.

The botanical name *Solanum* is derived from a Latin word meaning 'solace', and refers to the plant's medicinal properties. In former times the leaves were used to make compresses to ease the pain of burns and boils, and their juice was regarded as an excellent mouthwash. But, like the woody nightshade, black nightshade contains the poisonous alkaloid solanine. The amount can vary throughout the year, most of the poison being produced during a sunny spell.

Out of about 1,700 different species of *Solanum* found throughout the world, only the woody and black nightshades are native to the British Isles. The aubergine and the potato are close relatives. The foliage and berries of the potato plant contain the same poisonous substances as the nightshades, though the potato's tubers are harmless as long as they are not green; green tubers contain small quantities of the poison.

253

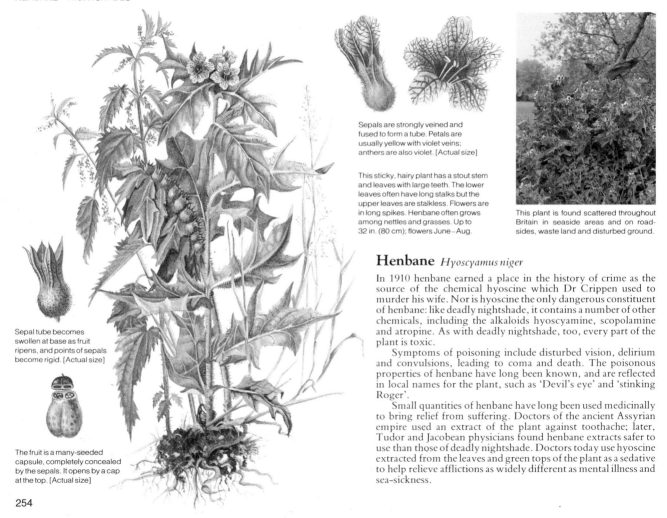

Sepals are strongly veined and fused to form a tube. Petals are usually yellow with violet veins; anthers are also violet. [Actual size]

This sticky, hairy plant has a stout stem and leaves with large teeth. The lower leaves often have long stalks but the upper leaves are stalkless. Flowers are in long spikes. Henbane often grows among nettles and grasses. Up to 32 in. (80 cm); flowers June–Aug.

This plant is found scattered throughout Britain in seaside areas and on roadsides, waste land and disturbed ground.

Sepal tube becomes swollen at base as fruit ripens, and points of sepals become rigid. [Actual size]

The fruit is a many-seeded capsule, completely concealed by the sepals. It opens by a cap at the top. [Actual size]

Henbane *Hyoscyamus niger*

In 1910 henbane earned a place in the history of crime as the source of the chemical hyoscine which Dr Crippen used to murder his wife. Nor is hyoscine the only dangerous constituent of henbane: like deadly nightshade, it contains a number of other chemicals, including the alkaloids hyoscyamine, scopolamine and atropine. As with deadly nightshade, too, every part of the plant is toxic.

Symptoms of poisoning include disturbed vision, delirium and convulsions, leading to coma and death. The poisonous properties of henbane have long been known, and are reflected in local names for the plant, such as 'Devil's eye' and 'stinking Roger'.

Small quantities of henbane have long been used medicinally to bring relief from suffering. Doctors of the ancient Assyrian empire used an extract of the plant against toothache; later, Tudor and Jacobean physicians found henbane extracts safer to use than those of deadly nightshade. Doctors today use hyoscine extracted from the leaves and green tops of the plant as a sedative to help relieve afflictions as widely different as mental illness and sea-sickness.

The fruit is a black, glossy berry, cupped by the spreading sepals. [Actual size]

The bell-shaped flowers are violet-brown with purple markings; the anthers are creamy coloured.

The long-stalked, rather drooping flowers are borne singly in the angle of leaf and stem.

Deadly nightshade, though rare, is found in hedges, woods and thickets on chalky soils, and sometimes near old buildings.

A tall plant with very large leaves and a few flowers. The leaves are often in pairs, one in each pair being larger than the other. Greater knapweed is shown growing beside it. Up to 60 in. (152 cm); flowers June–Aug.

Deadly nightshade *Atropa belladonna*

'Banish it from your gardens, and the use of it also,' implored the 16th-century herbalist John Gerard, 'being a plant so furious and deadly.' Then and now, deadly nightshade lives up to its name. Pheasants eat the berries with no apparent ill-effects, but just two or three of the dark, seductively shiny, cherry-like fruits can kill a child: a person merely suspected of having eaten a berry should be taken immediately to hospital.

Every part of this plant – a sinister member of the innocent-sounding potato family – is dangerous, including the dark purple, bell-like flowers. It contains atropine, solanine and hyoscyanine, all of them alkaloid poisons that attack the nervous system, making the heart race, the pulse weaken and the pupils of the eyes dilate. It is hardly surprising that the plant was associated with witchcraft and it attracted local names such as 'Devil's berries', 'Satan's cherries' and 'Devil's rhubarb'.

A 16th-century Venetian botanist thought that the scientific name *belladonna* ('beautiful woman' in Italian) referred to the use by fashionable ladies of a drug extracted from the plant to dilate their pupils. An alternative derivation is that the berries attracted the unwary, like a beautiful but treacherous woman.

255

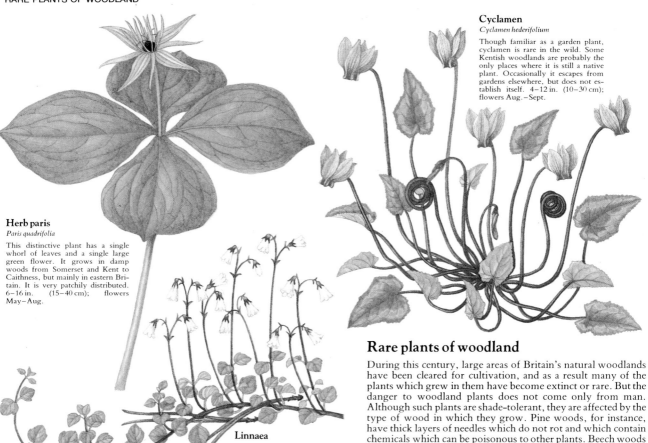

Cyclamen
Cyclamen hederifolium

Though familiar as a garden plant, cyclamen is rare in the wild. Some Kentish woodlands are probably the only places where it is still a native plant. Occasionally it escapes from gardens elsewhere, but does not establish itself. 4–12 in. (10–30 cm); flowers Aug.–Sept.

Herb paris
Paris quadrifolia

This distinctive plant has a single whorl of leaves and a single large green flower. It grows in damp woods from Somerset and Kent to Caithness, but mainly in eastern Britain. It is very patchily distributed. 6–16 in. (15–40 cm); flowers May–Aug.

Linnaea
Linnaea borealis

A creeping evergreen with pink flowers in pairs; found in eastern Scotland. 1–3 in. (2·5–7·5 cm); flowers June–Aug.

Rare plants of woodland

During this century, large areas of Britain's natural woodlands have been cleared for cultivation, and as a result many of the plants which grew in them have become extinct or rare. But the danger to woodland plants does not come only from man. Although such plants are shade-tolerant, they are affected by the type of wood in which they grow. Pine woods, for instance, have thick layers of needles which do not rot and which contain chemicals which can be poisonous to other plants. Beech woods are often found on poor soils and, because the leaves do not rot easily, the leaf mould which helps plants to grow is thin. Oak woods, on the other hand, tend to occur on rich soils and make generous amounts of leaf mould.

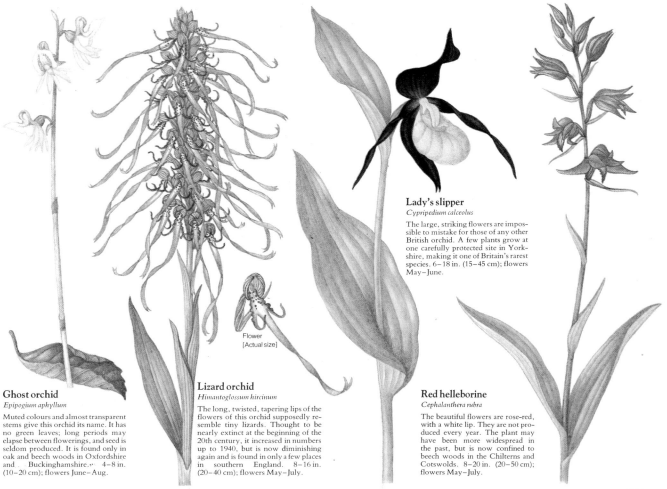

Lady's slipper
Cypripedium calceolus

The large, striking flowers are impossible to mistake for those of any other British orchid. A few plants grow at one carefully protected site in Yorkshire, making it one of Britain's rarest species. 6–18 in. (15–45 cm); flowers May–June.

Flower
[Actual size]

Ghost orchid
Epipogium aphyllum

Muted colours and almost transparent stems give this orchid its name. It has no green leaves; long periods may elapse between flowerings, and seed is seldom produced. It is found only in oak and beech woods in Oxfordshire and Buckinghamshire. 4–8 in. (10–20 cm); flowers June–Aug.

Lizard orchid
Himantoglossum hircinum

The long, twisted, tapering lips of the flowers of this orchid supposedly resemble tiny lizards. Thought to be nearly extinct at the beginning of the 20th century, it increased in numbers up to 1940, but is now diminishing again and is found in only a few places in southern England. 8–16 in. (20–40 cm); flowers May–July.

Red helleborine
Cephalanthera rubra

The beautiful flowers are rose-red, with a white lip. They are not produced every year. The plant may have been more widespread in the past, but is now confined to beech woods in the Chilterns and Cotswolds. 8–20 in. (20–50 cm); flowers May–July.

257

Alpine gentian

Gentiana nivalis

This upright, slender plant with brilliant, deep blue flowers is one of the rarest mountain plants in Britain; it grows on the southern edge of the Scottish highlands. 1–6 in. (2·5–15 cm); flowers July–Sept.

Diapensia

Diapensia lapponica

The exposed summit of a Scottish mountain is the only place in Britain where this tiny plant, which is primarily an Arctic species, can be found. Up to 2 in. (5 cm); flowers June–July.

Snowdon lily

Lloydia serotina

Although this slender plant is now very rare, it still grows on rock ledges in the mountains of North Wales. It is distinguished by fine leaves and white flowers with purple veins. 2–6 in. (5–15 cm); flowers in June.

Drooping saxifrage

Saxifraga cernua

Small red bulbils sometimes replace white flowers, which this plant does not always produce. The species, which is protected, grows at high altitudes in parts of the Grampians. 1–6 in. (2·5–15 cm); flowers in July.

Rare plants of mountain and moorland

Plants which grow at high altitudes face two main obstacles to survival. One is exposure to severe weather, the other is drought, since the available water is either in the form of ice, or else drains away rapidly. Most lowland species are unable to tolerate these conditions, and the flora of upland areas is consequently entirely different from that of other habitats.

Mountain species do not compete effectively with lowland species on their own ground, and remain confined to the uplands. A number of plants, especially mountain species such as diapensia, Snowdon lily and alpine gentian, live at the edge of their distribution range in the British Isles, and have to struggle to maintain a precarious foothold.

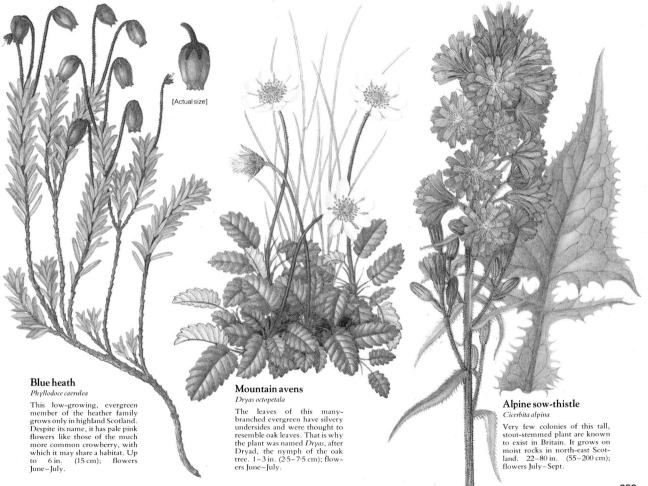

[Actual size]

Blue heath
Phyllodoce caerulea

This low-growing, evergreen member of the heather family grows only in highland Scotland. Despite its name, it has pale pink flowers like those of the much more common crowberry, with which it may share a habitat. Up to 6 in. (15 cm); flowers June–July.

Mountain avens
Dryas octopetala

The leaves of this many-branched evergreen have silvery undersides and were thought to resemble oak leaves. That is why the plant was named *Dryas*, after Dryad, the nymph of the oak tree. 1–3 in. (2·5–7·5 cm); flowers June–July.

Alpine sow-thistle
Cicerbita alpina

Very few colonies of this tall, stout-stemmed plant are known to exist in Britain. It grows on moist rocks in north-east Scotland. 22–80 in. (55–200 cm); flowers July–Sept.

Densely packed flowers usually form a single spike on each stem. The lower leaves have a narrowly winged stalk, covered in a down of soft white hairs. 12–80 in. (30–200 cm); flowers June–Aug.

Hairs on the filament are white; the anther is attached to it at an oblique angle. [Actual size]

The upper three stamens in each flower have hairy filaments, while the lower pair are almost smooth.

Upper leaves are stalkless, with margins that continue downwards to form wings on the stem.

The tall spikes of Aaron's rod are a common sight in waste places and on sunny banks throughout the British Isles.

[Actual size]

White mullein
Verbascum lychnitis

Flowers of this species are often white, and occur in a narrow branched spike. All the stamen filaments are hairy, and the anther is attached to it at right-angles. The leaf is dark green and almost hairless on top.

Aaron's rod *Verbascum thapsus*

In the Old Testament story, the rod of Levi on which Aaron's name was inscribed produced buds and blossoms when it was placed in the Tabernacle. Great mullein acquired its alternative name of Aaron's rod because its tall, straight flower spikes with individual flowers held close to the stem, have a narrow, staff-like appearance. The upward–pointing stem leaves act as a series of funnels, collecting moisture and directing it down towards the foot.

The downy, whitish coating on the leaves is made up of innumerable tiny branched hairs. Long before the introduction of cotton to Britain, this fluffy layer was scraped off and made into candle wicks. At country gatherings, the entire stem was burned as a flare. The folk-names 'candlewick plant' and 'high taper' derive from these uses.

Although most parts of mullein plants are poisonous, the dried flowers of both Aaron's rod and white mullein can be made into a pleasant-tasting medicine which was taken to relieve coughs and chills. Mixed with tobacco and smoked, the crushed leaves, which have an agreeable fruity scent, were thought to have the same virtue. The flowers yield a yellow hair dye.

The flower spike is looser than that of Aaron's rod, and sometimes branched. Five to ten flowers arise from the base of each bract. Leaves at the base are dark green on top and paler beneath, with long stalks. 20–48 in. (50–120 cm); flowers June–Sept.

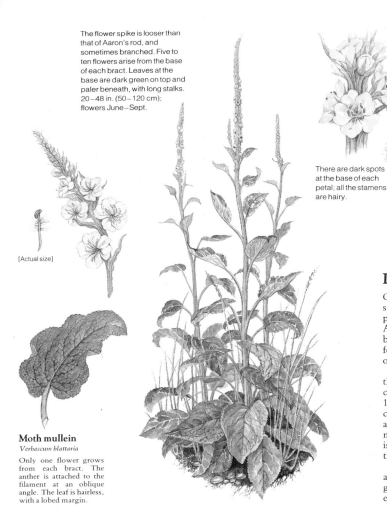

There are dark spots at the base of each petal; all the stamens are hairy.

Hairs on the filament are purple, and the anther is attached to it at right-angles. [Actual size]

[Actual size]

All leaves except those on the uppermost part of the stem have a long stalk.

Dark mullein grows on waysides and open banks. It is commonest in the south, rarer beyond the Midlands.

Moth mullein
Verbascum blattaria

Only one flower grows from each bract. The anther is attached to the filament at an oblique angle. The leaf is hairless, with a lobed margin.

Dark mullein *Verbascum nigrum*

On the chalky banks that are its favourite habitat, the flower spikes of dark mullein stand proud of most of the surrounding plants. The spikes can be distinguished easily from those of Aaron's rod, being more open and sometimes branched, and bearing rather smaller, darker leaves. The plant starts life by forming a rosette of leaves in its first year and dies after a display of flowers in the second year.

The soft, felted leaves of the mullein family gave these plants their name: it is derived from the Old French *moleine*, which comes in turn from the Latin word *mollis*, meaning 'soft'. The 17th-century herbalist Nicholas Culpeper suggested that a concoction made from the leaves of the species relieved chest ailments, including coughing and spitting of blood. All the mulleins are poisonous to animals, causing death if any quantity is eaten; fortunately, however, the unpleasant taste deters even the hungriest beasts.

There are several hundred species of mullein in the world, and some, such as *Verbascum phoeniceum*, are cultivated as rock-garden plants or in herbaceous borders. Sometimes these species escape to the wild, and are found naturalised on waste ground.

261

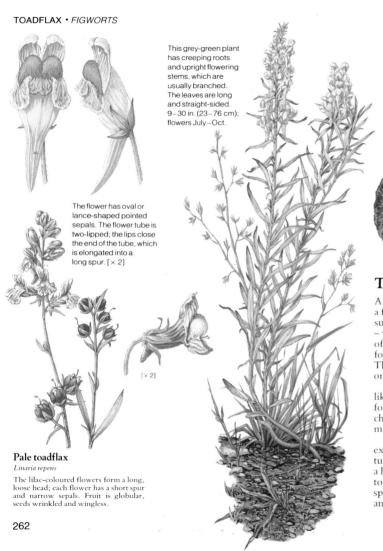

This grey-green plant has creeping roots and upright flowering stems, which are usually branched. The leaves are long and straight-sided. 9–30 in. (23–76 cm); flowers July–Oct.

The flower has oval or lance-shaped pointed sepals. The flower tube is two-lipped; the lips close the end of the tube, which is elongated into a long spur. [× 2]

[× 2]

The fruit is oval, and always more than twice as long as the sepals. [× 2]

The seeds are flattened and surrounded by a very broad, distinctive 'wing'. [× 10]

Toadflax flourishes in meadows, cultivated fields and waste ground. It is common throughout England.

Pale toadflax
Linaria repens

The lilac-coloured flowers form a long, loose head; each flower has a short spur and narrow sepals. Fruit is globular, seeds wrinkled and wingless.

Toadflax *Linaria vulgaris*

A sprinkling of yellow and orange toadflax along the borders of a field or country road is one of the everyday sights of an English summer. Its common name has a double derivation. The leaves – very narrow and spirally arranged up the stems – are like those of flax, and the plant was regarded as so useless as to be fit only for toads. The same word was applied to other worthless plants. Three species of toadflax are native to Britain; the flowers of one, pale toadflax, are lilac with violet stripes.

The unusual shape of the flowers caused toadflax to be likened to all manner of creatures, real and mythical. The folk-names 'lion's mouth', 'devil's head', 'weasel-snout', 'pig's chops' and 'squeeze-jaw', all refer to the way in which the mouth of the flower opens if its sides are squeezed.

The shape of the flower excludes all nectar-seeking insects except those most skilful and powerful. The mouth of the petal tube is closed by a fold of the lower lip called the palate, and only a heavy insect, such as a bee, can depress the palate to gain access to the tube. As the bee seeks the nectar at the tip of the flower's spur, pollen is exchanged between the stamens, the insect's body and the stigma.

The pale purple flower has narrow sepals and a short spur. [× 4]

Seeds are elongated and ridged. [× 15]

[× 4]

The fruit is oval and opens by several teeth. [× 4]

An upright, branched and hairy plant; its narrow, lance-shaped leaves grow mostly on alternate sides up the stem. 3–10 in. (7.5–25 cm); flowers May–Oct.

Though common on arable land in the south of England, small toadflax becomes rarer in the north.

Small toadflax *Chaenorhinum minus*

The small toadflax differs from the true toadflaxes in that its petal tube is not completely closed by the palate, or fold, of the lower lip. This 'open-mouthed' appearance is referred to in the botanical name *Chaenorhinum* which derives from two Greek words – *chaino*, meaning 'gaping', and *rynchos*, describing the snout-like appearance of the flower.

The small, purplish flowers of the small toadflax are a familiar sight on arable land in the southern counties of England. The plant has also adapted itself to growing in railway ballast. It is closely related to the snapdragon (*Antirrhinum majus*), which was introduced from the Mediterranean region as a garden flower and now grows wild on walls and chalk cliffs in many parts of the British Isles.

Sharp-leaved fluellen has flowers that are similar in shape to those of the small toadflax, but are yellow with a purple upper lip and a slender spur. Another difference between the two plants is the shape of the leaves; the small toadflax has slender, lance-shaped leaves, whereas the leaves of the sharp-leaved fluellen are broad and arrow-shaped with a flower rising from the base of each leaf.

Sharp-leaved fluellen
Kickxia elatine

A hairy plant growing 8–18 in. (20–45 cm) and flowering July–Oct. The flower has a long slender spur. The fruit opens by two tiny lids and the seeds are pitted.

263

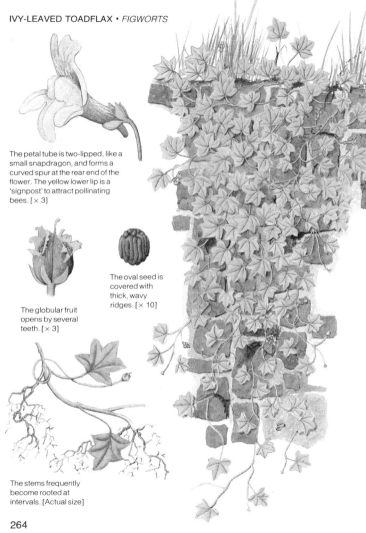

The petal tube is two-lipped, like a small snapdragon, and forms a curved spur at the rear end of the flower. The yellow lower lip is a 'signpost' to attract pollinating bees. [× 3]

The globular fruit opens by several teeth. [× 3]

The oval seed is covered with thick, wavy ridges. [× 10]

The stems frequently become rooted at intervals. [Actual size]

A hairless, sprawling plant with glossy, ivy-shaped alternate leaves scattered along the stems. 4–30 in. (10–76 cm); flowers May–Sept.

Walls throughout Britain are enhanced by this attractive plant. It is also seen on rocks or shingle.

Ivy-leaved toadflax *Cymbalaria muralis*

This delightful little plant, with its festoons of foliage and lilac-coloured, snapdragon-like flowers, grows on old walls throughout Britain. It is not a native species, but was introduced into London from the Mediterranean region in 1640 and soon became a favourite of garden rockeries. From there, it escaped to the wild.

The species is pollinated by bees. The stalks of the flowers first project from the foliage so that the flowers, which have a yellow honey-guide on the lower lip, are visible to the insect. After the flowers have been fertilised, the stalks gradually curve round until the capsules are firmly pushed into the cracks in the wall. When the seeds are released some remain to germinate on the wall, so guaranteeing continuous wall cover. The seeds are also provided with ridges that wedge them in place while the developing rootlet forces its way further into the crevice.

The stems bear numerous leaves that are often depressed in the middle like a cymbal, which gives the plant its generic name *Cymbalaria*. The common name comes from the shape of the leaf, which is lobed like ivy. In Italy the plant is popularly known as the 'Madonna's flower'.

The fruit is oval, pointed at the top, and has the remains of the style. [× 2]

The cylindrical seed is covered with numerous oval pits. [× 10]

The small flower is two-lipped, with the upper lip longer than the lower; the sepals have a very narrow, papery border. [× 5]

Water figwort
Scrophularia aquatica

A larger plant than common figwort, with square stems, conspicuously winged. The leaves often have extra leaflets. Sepals have a broad, papery band. The seeds have only a few large pits. [× 10]

Each branch has several flowers; the central one is the first to open.

An upright, mostly hairless plant. The square stem is unwinged; the oval, pointed leaves have sharp teeth. The plant is shown with wild angelica and reedmace. 24–36 in. (60–90 cm); flowers June–Sept.

Common figwort is found in wet places, especially woods by water. It is commonest in the south of England.

Common figwort *Scrophularia nodosa*

Numerous wasps are attracted to the unpleasant smelling, small reddish-brown flowers of the common figwort, which they pollinate as they feed on the nectar at the base of the petal tube. The tall flowering stems are produced each year from a small underground stem, called a rhizome. From this rhizome grow small nodules or tubers, which give the plant its species name of *nodosa*.

Medieval herbalists used common figwort in the treatment of the tubercular disease of scrofula, or king's evil: hence the generic name of *Scrophularia*. Scrofula affects the neck glands, and at one time the plant was known as 'throat-wort'. The leaves were also used as poultices to treat skin diseases, sores, abscesses and even gangrene. In Ireland figwort was regarded as 'Queen of Herbs' because of its supposed health-giving qualities.

Like common figwort, water figwort was used in the treatment of scrofula. It was also used to relieve toothache, and as a cosmetic; the distilled juice of the leaves was supposed to remove blemishes of the face and hands. According to the 17th-century herbalist Nicholas Culpeper, the juice was 'commended by some as good against the itch'.

265

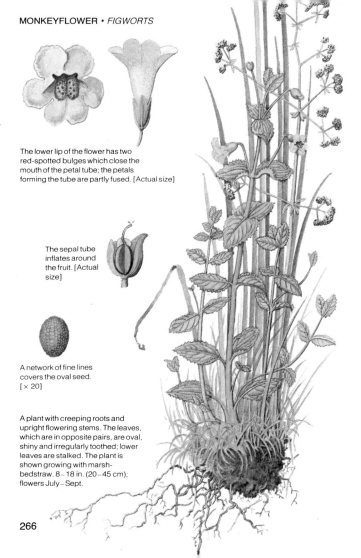

The lower lip of the flower has two red-spotted bulges which close the mouth of the petal tube; the petals forming the tube are partly fused. [Actual size]

The sepal tube inflates around the fruit. [Actual size]

A network of fine lines covers the oval seed. [× 20]

A plant with creeping roots and upright flowering stems. The leaves, which are in opposite pairs, are oval, shiny and irregularly toothed; lower leaves are stalked. The plant is shown growing with marsh-bedstraw. 8–18 in. (20–45 cm); flowers July–Sept.

The flowers are borne towards the tips of stems in the angle between stem and leaf.

Monkeyflower thrives locally in wet places throughout Britain, especially by streams and in marshy meadows.

Monkeyflower *Mimulus guttatus*

By 1812 the monkeyflower had been introduced into British gardens from Unalaska Island, off the coast of Alaska. The plant soon escaped from gardens, especially in the humid west of Britain, and by 1824 it was found growing wild near Abergavenny in Wales. Miles of new canals, which opened in the early 19th century, spread the species even further afield. Now the invasion of the country by the plant is so complete that it could easily be mistaken for a native.

The intricately folded petals, which can make the flower look like a grinning face, gave monkeyflower its common and botanical names. *Mimulus* is a Latin word, meaning 'little actor'; *guttatus* means 'spotted', after the numerous tiny red spots which often appear on the flower. Another species, which was introduced into Britain, *Mimulus luteus*, has much larger spots which have earned it the common name of 'blood-drop-emlets'.

In the plant's place of origin it often rains for more than 250 days a year. Not surprisingly, the monkeyflower thrives in wet places, along the edges of streams and other waterways. At the water's edge the stems project horizontally, turning up at the tips to hold the showy flowers above water.

The style persists on top of the fruit after flowering. The oval fruit grows longer than the tube formed by the sepals, and ripens to black before breaking open to release the seed. [× 2]

The seed is almost rectangular, with a net-like pattern of fine lines. [× 20]

The winged leaf-stalks are most prominent in leaves from the middle of the stem upwards. [Actual size]

An upright, hairy plant, usually without branches. At the base the oval or lance-shaped leaves form a rosette with gently toothed edges. The leaf-stalk becomes winged where it joins the stem. 24–60 in. (60–152 cm); flowers June–Aug.

Clusters of large flowers always hang at the top of the stem and on the same side. The petal tube is indistinctly five-lobed, with one large lobe on the bottom of the flower. [Actual size]

Foxglove is common throughout Britain; it grows in woods, on heaths, banks and rocks and on acid soils.

Foxglove *Digitalis purpurea*

While the name 'foxglove' conjures up a delightful image when interpreted literally, it is unlikely that the plant got its name from the belief that its bell-shaped flowers would make suitable gloves for foxes. Far more likely is the theory that the name comes from a series of corruptions in both the spelling and pronunciation of old words. For example, glove may be derived from the Anglo-Saxon *gliew* – a musical instrument with many small bells – and fox could be a corruption of 'folk's', meaning the 'little folk', or fairies. This theory is supported by the fact that in some parts of the British Isles, such as Somerset and Ireland, the plant is called 'fairy bells'.

Exploding the popular myth about the name, however, does not make the foxglove any less attractive. It is a stately plant, tall and upright with purple flowers hanging from a single, un-branched stem. There are 20–80 flowers on a single stem.

Foxglove is very poisonous, yet it yields the drug digitalis which is used in small doses in the treatment of heart complaints. This use was discovered in 1785 by the clinical investigator William Withering, though the way in which the drug acts by stimulating the heart was not understood at the time.

A hairless, creeping plant with upright, flowering stems. The short-stalked, paired leaves are slightly fleshy. They are oval, with a blunt tip and a toothed margin. The flower spikes grow from angles of the leaf and stem, and may contain up to 30 flowers. Brooklime may be found in company with the yellow-flowering celery-leaved buttercup. 8–24 in. (20–60 cm); flowers May–Sept.

The flower parts are in fours, with three petals more or less equal in size and one larger. The sepals follow the same pattern. There are only two stamens. [× 5]

The fruit is roughly heart-shaped, and a little shorter than the tube of sepals. There are lines on the valves. [× 5]

Brooklime is found in wet and muddy places throughout Britain. The stems may root in mud, or float in water.

Water speedwell
Veronica anagallis–aquatica

Leaves are stalkless, longer than those of brooklime, and oval or lance-shaped, with tiny teeth on the margins. The slightly smaller flowers are in longer spikes.

Brooklime *Veronica beccabunga*

Spikes of brooklime and water speedwell in summer make conspicuous splashes of blue on the banks of streams and beside other stretches of fresh water. As with many plants of wet and muddy places, the fleshy stems of brooklime creep along the ground, and each stem has a hollow centre. These air spaces allow oxygen and other essential gases to be transferred from the surface parts of the plant to the roots, which depend on the oxygen for their growth.

Both the common name and the botanical name (*beccabunga* is derived from the German *beck*, 'a stream') refer to the water-courses in which brooklime is found; 'lime' comes from the Latin *limus*, meaning 'mud'.

In the 17th century diet drinks made from brooklime were taken to purge the blood. The herbalists John Gerard and Nicholas Culpeper prescribed the plant as a cure for scurvy. Fried with butter and vinegar, full of 'hot and biting properties', it was said to relieve 'all manner of tumours, swellings and inflammations'. The plant's young, leafy shoots were also widely used in salads in Britain and northern Europe, even though the taste was rather bitter.

Flowers are grouped into long, loose spikes at the tops of the stems.

The petals are unequal in size, the upper ones being much the largest. [× 5]

The fruit is heart-shaped, longer than the sepals, and topped by a short style. [× 5]

A hairy creeping plant, often forming large mats, with upright flowering stems. The leaves are paired; they are oval, shallowly and bluntly toothed, narrowing at the base into short stalks. It is here seen growing with scarlet pimpernel. 4–12 in. (10–30 cm); flowers May–Aug.

Common speedwell is found in grassland, on heaths and in open woods, often on dry soils, throughout Britain.

Common speedwell *Veronica officinalis*

There are over 20 species of speedwell in the British Isles, most of them plentiful; but it is *Veronica officinalis*, also called heath speedwell, that has been given the name common speedwell. In fact, this species is probably less common than some of the other speedwells, as it is not particularly fond of cultivated or waste ground, but grows instead on the dry soils of heaths, grassland or woodland margins. With its creeping roots, common speedwell can form a living carpet of blue in such places.

The genus *Veronica* may have been dedicated to the saint of that name who is said to have wiped Christ's face on his way to the Cross, but some authorities claim that the name derives from two Greek words meaning 'I bring victory'. This is an allusion to the plant's supposed ability to cure a long list of ailments, from coughs and tuberculosis to wounds and leprosy.

The name 'speedwell', too, may have been a reference to the plant's curative powers; while the Latin word *officinalis* indicates that the plant was part of an apothecary's stock-in-trade. Alternatively, the common name may be rooted in the Irish version, 'speed-you-well': sprays of the plant were pinned to the clothing of a traveller to protect him against accidents.

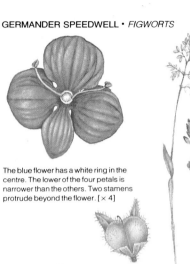

The blue flower has a white ring in the centre. The lower of the four petals is narrower than the others. Two stamens protrude beyond the flower. [× 4]

The heart-shaped fruit is shorter than the sepals and has both long hairs and short, downy hairs. [× 2]

Buxbaum's speedwell

Veronica persica

A plant most easily distinguished from germander speedwell by its single, long-stalked flower arising from the angle of stem and leaf. The lower petal is often very pale. The plant is very common on disturbed ground.

The stem has two lines of long hairs on opposite sides. The loose, long-stalked flower spike grows from the angle between stem and leaf.

The stems of this creeping plant root at intervals to produce upright flowering stems with triangular to oval, coarsely toothed leaves. The leaves are in opposite pairs, and have either a short stalk or none at all. 4–12 in. (10–30 cm); flowers Mar.–July.

Germander speedwell is a very common perennial, found on hedgebanks and in woods and grassy places.

Germander speedwell *Veronica chamaedrys*

Most explanations for the name 'speedwell' refer to the medicinal value attributed to some species of the plant. Among other uses, they were supposed to be good for healing wounds and clearing up respiratory complaints. According to another view, the name alludes to the fact that the flowers fall and blow away almost as soon as the plant is picked – the phrase 'speed well' was an equivalent of farewell or good-bye.

The flowers and fruits of germander speedwell have given rise to many local names and superstitions. Their fruits are heart-shaped, like those of shepherd's purse, so the name 'break-your-mother's-heart' was applied to both plants. Germander speedwell's small blue flowers, peering out of the foliage on a summer's day, reminded some folk of eyes – hence the alternative names of 'bird's-eye speedwell', or 'blue bird's eye'. If the flowers were destroyed, the birds would take their revenge, pecking out the eyes of the vandal, or of his or her mother.

Being similar in general appearance, many of the speedwells are easily confused. Another species that is now common on cultivated ground in Britain is Buxbaum's speedwell, a native of Iran and other parts of western Asia.

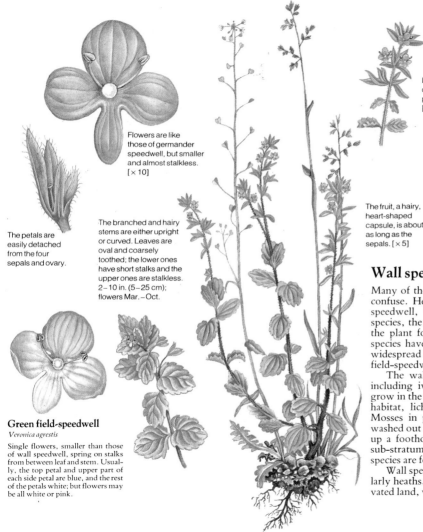

Flowers are like those of germander speedwell, but smaller and almost stalkless. [×10]

The petals are easily detached from the four sepals and ovary.

The branched and hairy stems are either upright or curved. Leaves are oval and coarsely toothed; the lower ones have short stalks and the upper ones are stalkless. 2–10 in. (5–25 cm); flowers Mar.–Oct.

Long flower spikes occupy the greater part of the stem. [Actual size]

The fruit, a hairy, heart-shaped capsule, is about as long as the sepals. [×5]

Wall speedwell is common in dry, usually bare places, including crevices in rocks and walls, throughout Britain.

Green field-speedwell
Veronica agrestis

Single flowers, smaller than those of wall speedwell, spring on stalks from between leaf and stem. Usually, the top petal and upper part of each side petal are blue, and the rest of the petals white; but flowers may be all white or pink.

Wall speedwell *Veronica arvensis*

Many of the common British species of speedwell are easy to confuse. Herbalists of former days thought that green field-speedwell, *Veronica agrestis*, was the male form of a different species, the germander speedwell, while others have mistaken the plant for Buxbaum's speedwell, *Veronica persica*. Several species have been introduced to the British Isles and are now widespread weeds, but both the wall speedwell and green field-speedwell are native species.

The wall speedwell is one of a small number of plants, including ivy-leaved toadflax and hairy rock-cress, that can grow in the crevices of old walls. In this seemingly inhospitable habitat, lichens and mosses are usually the first colonisers. Mosses in particular trap the fine particles of dust that are washed out of the atmosphere by the rain, so gradually building up a foothold for larger species. Crumbling mortar offers a sub-stratum similar to limestone scree slopes, where many wall species are found under more natural conditions.

Wall speedwell's natural habitat is on dry, bare soils, particularly heaths. Green field-speedwell is a common weed of cultivated land, where it flowers all the year round.

271

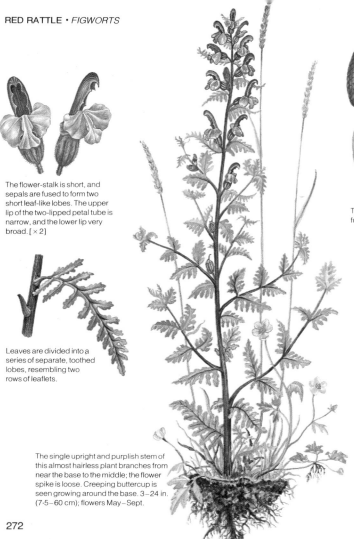

The flower-stalk is short, and sepals are fused to form two short leaf-like lobes. The upper lip of the two-lipped petal tube is narrow, and the lower lip very broad. [× 2]

Leaves are divided into a series of separate, toothed lobes, resembling two rows of leaflets.

The single upright and purplish stem of this almost hairless plant branches from near the base to the middle; the flower spike is loose. Creeping buttercup is seen growing around the base. 3–24 in. (7·5–60 cm); flowers May–Sept.

Egg-shaped seeds have a net-like patterning on their surface. [× 10]

The fruit is longer than the fused sepals. [× 2]

Red rattle flourishes in wet and grassy places throughout most of Britain; it is rarer in the south and in the Midlands.

Red rattle *Pedicularis palustris*

The noise produced by red rattle when its fruiting heads are shaken gives the plant its name. The seeds gradually shrink away from the walls of the fruit as the pod ripens and the tissue hardens. They jump about inside the pod and rattle like the beans inside the maracas of Caribbean bands.

Red rattle is one of a group of plants that are known as 'hemi-parasites', meaning that they live partly off other plants. Although red rattle has its own effective system for producing food from sunlight, water and carbon dioxide, its roots attach themselves to the roots of surrounding plants, particularly grasses. This ensures the plant of an adequate supply of water and necessary mineral salts, without the need for a large root system of its own; and the host plant is hardly harmed.

The plant is distributed throughout most of Britain, although it is much rarer in the south and east, and in the Midlands. According to the 17th-century herbalist Nicholas Culpeper, red rattle had great influence on the humours. He recommends that the plant should be boiled in wine and drunk when the uneasy balance in man of black bile, blood, choler and phlegm is threatened.

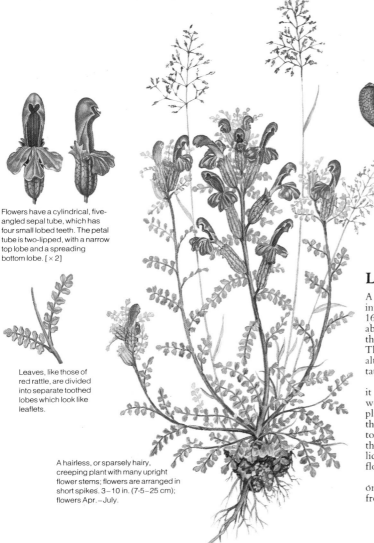

Flowers have a cylindrical, five-angled sepal tube, which has four small lobed teeth. The petal tube is two-lipped, with a narrow top lobe and a spreading bottom lobe. [× 2]

Leaves, like those of red rattle, are divided into separate toothed lobes which look like leaflets.

A hairless, or sparsely hairy, creeping plant with many upright flower stems; flowers are arranged in short spikes. 3–10 in. (7·5–25 cm); flowers Apr.–July.

The few kidney-shaped seeds have a net-like patterning. [× 10]

Curved and flattened fruit is about the same size as the sepal tube. [× 2]

Lousewort grows in bogs and marshes and on damp heathland. It is quite common throughout Britain.

Lousewort *Pedicularis sylvatica*

A long-held belief that lousewort was so called because it infested sheep and other animals with lice was supported by the 16th-century herbalist John Gerard in his writings. This alleged ability to promote attacks of lice is almost certainly the origin of the plant's scientific name too, *pedis* being the Latin for 'louse'. This appears a more probable explanation of the name than the alternative suggestion that lousewort was used to prevent infestation by the parasitic insect.

Whether the plant really spreads lice is unproved; however, it is likely that lousewort transmits liver-flukes, the parasitic worms which rot the livers of sheep. Lousewort thrives in damp places, which may well be submerged in water in the winter. In these conditions, snails carrying embryo liver-flukes often cling to vegetation and are transferred to sheep when they graze over the land. Sheep infested with liver-flukes are almost sure to have lice too, which, especially at the time of year when lousewort is flowering, spread rapidly through a flock.

Like red rattle, lousewort is a 'hemi-parasite', which battens on to the roots of grasses, extracting water and mineral salts from them. It often abounds in boggy areas and on heaths.

273

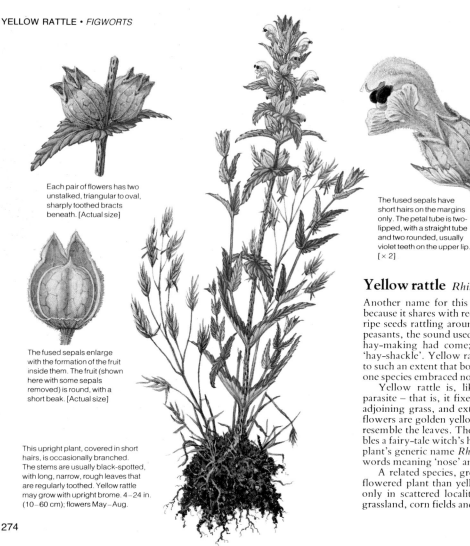

Each pair of flowers has two unstalked, triangular to oval, sharply toothed bracts beneath. [Actual size]

The fused sepals enlarge with the formation of the fruit inside them. The fruit (shown here with some sepals removed) is round, with a short beak. [Actual size]

This upright plant, covered in short hairs, is occasionally branched. The stems are usually black-spotted, with long, narrow, rough leaves that are regularly toothed. Yellow rattle may grow with upright brome. 4–24 in. (10–60 cm); flowers May–Aug.

The fused sepals have short hairs on the margins only. The petal tube is two-lipped, with a straight tube and two rounded, usually violet teeth on the upper lip. [× 2]

The golden flowers of yellow rattle are a common sight in grassy places throughout Britain. Large patches often form.

Yellow rattle *Rhinanthus minor*

Another name for this bright, attractive plant is 'rattle-box', because it shares with red rattle the sound effect produced by the ripe seeds rattling around inside the capsule. Among Swedish peasants, the sound used to be taken as a signal that the time for hay-making had come; a Somerset name for the plant was 'hay-shackle'. Yellow rattle occurs in a great variety of forms – to such an extent that botanists once thought that what is in fact one species embraced no fewer than six distinct plants.

Yellow rattle is, like red rattle and lousewort, a hemi-parasite – that is, it fixes its roots on to the root system of an adjoining grass, and extracts water and minerals from it. The flowers are golden yellow, with bracts underneath them which resemble the leaves. The shape of the petal tube, which resembles a fairy-tale witch's hooked, pendulous nose, gave rise to the plant's generic name *Rhinanthus*, which comes from two Greek words meaning 'nose' and 'flower'.

A related species, greater yellow rattle, is a bushier, larger-flowered plant than yellow rattle. It is very rare, being found only in scattered localities throughout Britain, such as chalk grassland, corn fields and occasionally sand-dunes.

The fruit is flattened, with a pronounced beak, and carries four seeds. [×5]

The seed is oval, with a small protuberance at one end. [×5]

A very variable plant, hairless or sparsely hairy. The stems are upright or sprawling, usually branched, with short stalked or stalkless leaves, untoothed, varying in shape from oval to narrowly lance-shaped. The flowers are borne in pairs, those on the same stem turned towards the same side. 3–24 in. (7·5–60 cm); flowers May–Oct.

Pairs of flowers arise in the angle between a bract and the stem. The petal tube is two-lipped, often with the mouth closed and the lower lip pointing forwards. [×2]

This plant of woods, heaths and grassy places is widespread throughout Britain, though it may be locally rare.

Common cow-wheat *Melampyrum pratense*

An old wives' tale said that pregnant women who ate flour made from the seeds of common cow-wheat would bear male children. Its common name is said to derive from the fact that the plant was much liked by cattle, and it was believed that any cows that were allowed to graze on it would produce only the finest and yellowest butter.

Despite its species name *pratense*, which means 'growing in meadows', common cow-wheat rarely grows in such conditions. It is a plant of woodlands, hedgerows and moorland; where it attaches itself to the roots of grasses to extract water and minerals. It is common in many parts of Britain, and is recognisable by its two-lipped yellow flowers, those on the same stem facing in the same direction.

The name *Melampyrum* comes from two Greek words, *melas*, 'black', and *pyros* 'wheat', because the plant has blackish, wheat-like seeds. Other species of *Melampyrum* were originally cornfield weeds, and flour produced from wheat contaminated by one species made a greyish, bitter-tasting bread. In the Isle of Wight, where the plant was once common, this was known as 'poverty bread'.

275

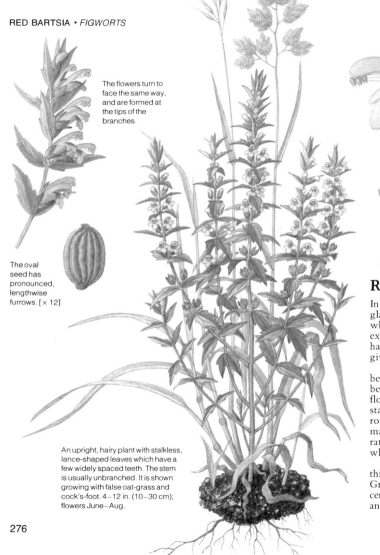

The flowers turn to face the same way, and are formed at the tips of the branches.

The oval seed has pronounced, lengthwise furrows. [× 12]

An upright, hairy plant with stalkless, lance-shaped leaves which have a few widely spaced teeth. The stem is usually unbranched. It is shown growing with false oat-grass and cock's-foot. 4–12 in. (10–30 cm); flowers June–Aug.

The stamens of the two-lipped flower protrude slightly from the top lip. [× 5]

The sepals are fused into a bell-shaped, four-toothed tube, about equal in length to the fruit.

The pinkish flowers of the red bartsia are found in fields, waste areas and roadsides throughout most of Britain.

Red bartsia *Odontites verna*

In terms of prettiness, the red bartsia has little appeal at first glance. It has a dusty appearance and tends to be overshadowed when surrounded by other, more colourful plants. But a close examination will reveal that the 'dust' is a covering of fine white hairs which, combined with the plant's often purplish tinge, give it a neglected air.

Red bartsia is an upright-growing plant with a single stem bearing toothed, unstalked leaves and pink flowers. Its lack of beauty is not even compensated for by an attractive scent, but its flowers are neatly formed with two open-mouthed lips and stamens that protrude like a tongue. It is a common plant of roadsides, grassy banks, corn fields and waste ground. Like many of its relatives, such as lousewort, red rattle and yellow rattle, it is a semi-parasite, living on the roots of grasses from which it extracts water and minerals.

Red bartsia was once considered a cure for toothache. From this it gained its generic name *Odontites*, which comes from the Greek word for tooth, *odons*. It was called bartsia by the 18th-century Swedish botanist Carolus Linnaeus, after a close friend and fellow Swede Dr Bartoch.

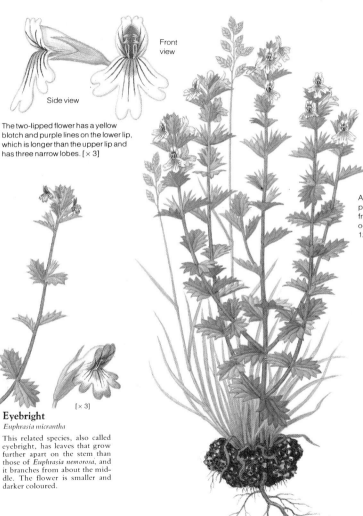

The two-lipped flower has a yellow blotch and purple lines on the lower lip, which is longer than the upper lip and has three narrow lobes. [× 3]

Side view

Front view

The sepals are fused into a tube with four pointed lobes, enclosing the capsule. [× 3]

The seed is narrowly oval, and has lengthwise furrows. [× 8]

An upright, sturdy plant often with a purplish tinge, branched usually from the base. The leaves are dark or occasionally purplish-green. Up to 12 in. (30 cm); flowers July–Sept.

Eyebright is a plant of downs, pastures, heaths and woods. It is common in England and Wales, and local in Scotland.

Eyebright *Euphrasia micrantha*

This related species, also called eyebright, has leaves that grow further apart on the stem than those of *Euphrasia nemorosa*, and it branches from about the middle. The flower is smaller and darker coloured.

[× 3]

Eyebright *Euphrasia nemorosa*

The belief that certain plants, because of their appearance or characteristics, could cure human ailments was widespread in the 18th century, so it is not surprising that this plant with its bright-eyed flower was thought to be good for poor eyesight. This belief was strengthened by the 17th-century botanist William Cole, who recorded in his book *Adam in Eden* that eyebright was the herb used by the linnet to clear its eyesight. Since short-sighted linnets are not easy to identify, few could argue with Cole's reasoning.

In fact, an extract made from eyebright and the herb golden seal is still used as an eye lotion. But medicinal uses apart, the plant is one of the most attractive found in the British countryside and is common from lowland moor to mountain peak. It occurs mostly on turf, particularly on chalky soil.

The generic name *Euphrasia* is derived from the Greek word *euphraino*, 'to gladden', probably a reference to the plant's reputed medicinal power in 'gladdening the eye'. More than 25 species occur throughout the British Isles; all are semi-parasites, growing successfully only where their roots attach themselves to other plants such as clover and plantains.

277

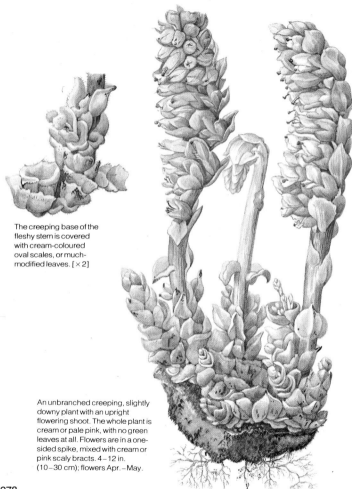

The creeping base of the fleshy stem is covered with cream-coloured oval scales, or much-modified leaves. [×2]

An unbranched creeping, slightly downy plant with an upright flowering shoot. The whole plant is cream or pale pink, with no green leaves at all. Flowers are in a one-sided spike, mixed with cream or pink scaly bracts. 4–12 in. (10–30 cm); flowers Apr.–May.

Each flower is on a short stalk, and has a tube of hairy sepals; the petals form a two-lipped flower which is usually purple-tinged. [Actual size]

The fruit is oval, with a pointed lip. [Actual size]

Toothwort is found growing near trees such as elm and hazel in damp woods and hedges. It is locally common.

Toothwort *Lathraea squamaria*

The deathly pallor of the stem, flowers and scales of the toothwort have given it the country name of 'corpse flower', in the belief that such a ghostly plant could only grow from a buried corpse. In fact it is a parasite, extracting nourishment from its host plant, usually a hazel tree, and without the need for chlorophyll, the pigment which gives other plants their greenness.

The toothwort attaches small, pad-like suckers to the roots of its host plant, which dissolve away the tissues until the main feeding elements in the root are reached. It then diverts the sap from the root to itself. The relationship between parasite and host plant is finely balanced: too much removal of nutrients will cause the host to die; too little, and the parasite becomes too weak to reproduce.

The scales below each of the pale pink or cream flowers are modified leaves and are tooth-shaped, giving the plant its common name. It occurs in clumps around the roots of the host tree, and is such an avaricious plant that it spreads underground and often gives the appearance that several plants are present, whereas there may be only one.

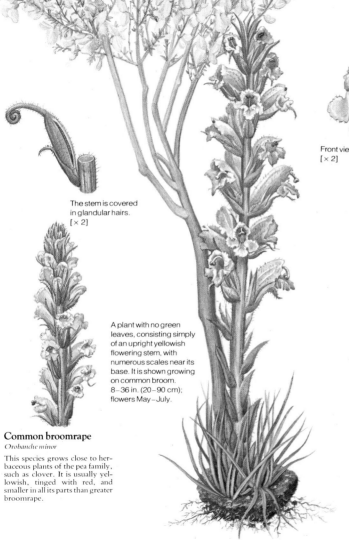

The stem is covered in glandular hairs.
[× 2]

A plant with no green leaves, consisting simply of an upright yellowish flowering stem, with numerous scales near its base. It is shown growing on common broom. 8–36 in. (20–90 cm); flowers May–July.

Common broomrape
Orobanche minor

This species grows close to herbaceous plants of the pea family, such as clover. It is usually yellowish, tinged with red, and smaller in all its parts than greater broomrape.

Front view
[× 2]

Side view
[Actual size]

The flowers have long, pointed bracts longer than the petal tube. The sepals form a tube of four equal lobes. Petals have fused to form a two-lipped tube; the lower lip is three-lobed, with the middle lobe larger than the others. Both lips have distinctly toothed edges.

Greater broomrape grows near shrubs such as gorse and broom; it is locally widespread throughout Britain.

Greater broomrape   *Orobanche rapum–genistae*

This parasitic close relative of toothwort takes its common name, as well as its sustenance, from its most usual victim. It is called broomrape because it is almost always found growing on broom. Much more rarely, gorse is the host. The second part of the name, rape, has been taken to mean that the swollen, tuber-like base of the plant resembles a turnip, *Brassica rapa*. The generic name *Orobanche*, which translates into English as 'vetch-strangler', indicates that various other members of the genus live on the vetches.

With its tall, stout, yellowish stems, greater broomrape is an imposing plant; but though widespread, it is nowhere common. Like toothwort, it has no need either of chlorophyll – which produces the natural green colour of plants – or of leaves, which are reduced to brown scales. Its tuber-like roots mean that it is usually perennial, though on rare occasions it may be annual. Greater broomrape produces huge numbers of very small seeds, for a parasite must disperse its seeds as widely as possible, to increase their chances of meeting a vulnerable host plant.

Common broomrape is a much more widespread plant, which can seriously damage the clover crops that it infests.

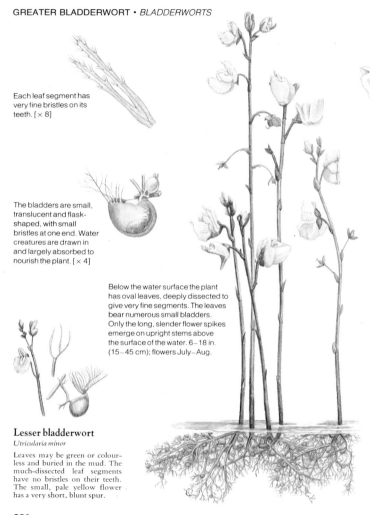

Each leaf segment has very fine bristles on its teeth. [× 8]

The bladders are small, translucent and flask-shaped, with small bristles at one end. Water creatures are drawn in and largely absorbed to nourish the plant. [× 4]

Below the water surface the plant has oval leaves, deeply dissected to give very fine segments. The leaves bear numerous small bladders. Only the long, slender flower spikes emerge on upright stems above the surface of the water. 6–18 in. (15–45 cm); flowers July–Aug.

Lesser bladderwort
Utricularia minor

Leaves may be green or colourless and buried in the mud. The much-dissected leaf segments have no bristles on their teeth. The small, pale yellow flower has a very short, blunt spur.

The bright yellow flowers are large, and have two-lipped sepals and petals. [Actual size]

The fruit is globular, with a short beak. [× 2]

Ponds, lakes and ditches with fairly deep water are the normal habitat of this plant, which occurs locally throughout Britain.

Greater bladderwort   *Utricularia vulgaris*

In summer the greater bladderwort speckles the surface of deep waters with its attractive, golden-yellow flowers. Beneath this display of innocent charm, however, there lies a sinister world where tiny bladders wait to trap and devour insects.

The greater bladderwort is rootless, and has adapted itself to conditions where natural mineral salts are lacking but can be obtained from living tissues. The small underwater leaves bear bladders which are oval and translucent and have a series of small hairs at one end. The bladders contain air, and when the hairs are brushed by an insect, such as a water flea, a trap-door is triggered to open and the insect is drawn into the bladder on the inrush of water. The trap-door closes again and the insect is left to die.

The plant does not secrete digestive juices to devour the insect, but absorbs the soluble products after it has decomposed. Then the bladder opens again and the water is pumped out, taking the remains of the insect with it, and the system is once more ready to trap the next unsuspecting victim. Greater bladderwort is found on deep lakes and ponds throughout Britain, but is rare in the north of England.

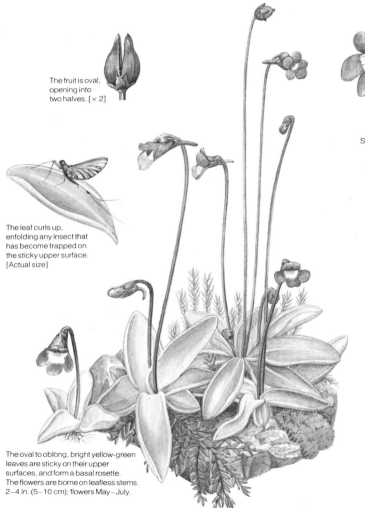

The fruit is oval, opening into two halves. [× 2]

The leaf curls up, enfolding any insect that has become trapped on the sticky upper surface. [Actual size]

The oval to oblong, bright yellow-green leaves are sticky on their upper surfaces, and form a basal rosette. The flowers are borne on leafless stems. 2–4 in. (5–10 cm); flowers May–July.

Front

Side

Spur

The flower is two-lipped, with the lobes of the bottom lip deep, each lobe much longer than it is broad. There is a long spur, either straight or slightly curved. [× 2]

This plant of bogs, damp heaths, moors and wet rocks is common throughout Britain except in the south.

Common butterwort *Pinguicula vulgaris*

Unlike the greater bladderwort, this insect-eating plant does not lurk below the water but spreads its yellow-green leaves invitingly on wet heaths, bogs and mountain rocks. Each leaf is curled at the edges, and when an insect lands on it sticky glands hold it fast while the leaf curls around it like a clutching hand. The victim's struggles to free itself from the gluey surface activate the leaf's mechanism. The leaf completely engulfs its victim and secretes digestive enzymes to break down the still-living body. Eventually the leaf opens again, and the dried remains of the insect are blown away by the breeze or are washed away by rain.

The common butterwort is an attractive plant with violet flowers on long stems; its other name is bog violet. The leaves radiate from the base of the plant in the form of a rosette.

As with other insect-eating plants, the butterwort extracts mineral salts, especially nitrates and phosphates, from its prey. It may have been used in curdling milk for butter at one time – hence its name – and it was said that butter from a cow that had eaten butterwort was good for a new-born child. The plant was also supposed to protect people from fairies and witches.

281

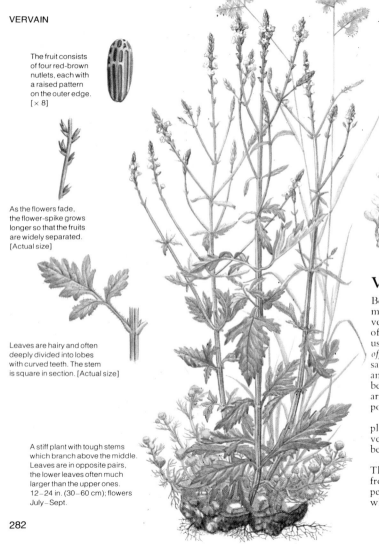

The fruit consists of four red-brown nutlets, each with a raised pattern on the outer edge. [× 8]

As the flowers fade, the flower-spike grows longer so that the fruits are widely separated. [Actual size]

Leaves are hairy and often deeply divided into lobes with curved teeth. The stem is square in section. [Actual size]

A stiff plant with tough stems which branch above the middle. Leaves are in opposite pairs, the lower leaves often much larger than the upper ones. 12–24 in. (30–60 cm); flowers July–Sept.

The petal tube is almost twice as long as the sepal tube; the upper two petals are slightly smaller than the others. [Rear view × 4]

Almost stalkless flowers are densely packed in long, slender spikes. [× 2]

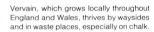

Vervain, which grows locally throughout England and Wales, thrives by waysides and in waste places, especially on chalk.

Vervain *Verbena officinalis*

Because of its tiny flowers, vervain is easy to overlook. But myth and medicine have not ignored the plant. People picking vervain should, according to early custom, bless it as a reminder of the legend that the plant grew on the hill at Calvary, and was used to staunch Christ's blood at the Crucifixion. In Latin, *officinalis* means 'of the apothecary's shop'; vervain has long been said to possess medicinal as well as magical powers, both to cure and to protect against infection and calamity. It was once believed that the plant could ward off plague, and that worn around the head it would act as a talisman against headaches and poisonous bites.

The generic name *Verbena* is a Roman term for those altar plants which were used during sacrifices. The Druids, too, used vervain when they cast their magic spells; however, it could also be used as an antidote to certain spells and forms of evil.

Several close relatives of vervain are cultivated in Britain. These include lemon verbena, *Aloysia triphylla*, a shrubby plant from South America whose fragrant leaves are used to make perfume and tea; and gardener's verbena, *Verbena × hybrida*, which is grown for its brightly coloured flowers.

Nutlet [× 10]

Sepal tube [× 4]

The fruit consists of four dry, flattened nutlets which are contained in the sepal tube.

The flowers form whorls at the base of each pair of leaves. [Actual size]

Sepals are sharply pointed. The upper two lobes of the flower are deeply notched; the lower two are spotted with purple. [× 4]

Gipsywort is common throughout England and Wales; it grows in damp places such as marshes and stream banks.

Leaves are short-stalked and lance-shaped, with long, narrow lobes; the lower lobes are sometimes divided down to the midrib. The stem is square in section. [Actual size]

A stiff, upright plant with branched stems, which usually form clumps. It has numerous pale leaves, which grow in opposite pairs up the stems. The plant is shown growing with water forget-me-nots. 12–40 in. (30–100 cm); flowers June–Sept.

Gipsywort *Lycopus europaeus*

Rogues masquerading as itinerant fortune-tellers and magicians used in past centuries to daub their bodies with a strong black dye produced from gipsywort, in order to pass themselves off as Egyptians and Africans. Swarthy looks were supposed to lend greater credibility to these vagabonds when they told fortunes; it was this use that gave the plant its names of gipsywort and Egyptian's herb.

The herbalist John Gerard had great faith in the dye, which was used to colour silk and wool. He maintained that cloth treated with gipsywort would hold its colour for ever. Occasionally the herb was also used as an astringent or as a sedative. However, unlike many members of the mint family, which contain sweet-smelling aromatic oils, gipsywort is completely odourless and is never used for cooking.

Gipsywort shares many of the characteristics of the mint family; its leaves sprout in pairs along the four-sided stem, and whorls of its flowers are often set far apart. However, it is easily distinguished from other members of the family by its lobed leaves and by its tight whorls of tiny white or pinkish flowers, each of which has two, rather than four, stamens.

283

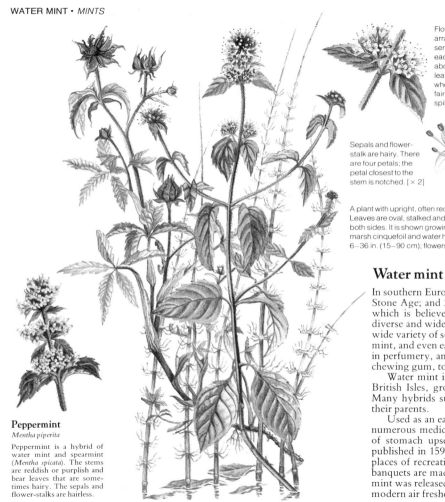

Flowers are arranged in a series of whorls, each immediately above a pair of leaves. The upper whorls form a fairly dense spike. [× 2]

Sepals and flower-stalk are hairy. There are four petals; the petal closest to the stem is notched. [× 2]

A plant with upright, often reddish stems. Leaves are oval, stalked and hairy on both sides. It is shown growing with marsh cinquefoil and water horsetail. 6–36 in. (15–90 cm); flowers July–Oct.

As its name implies, water mint is a plant of marshes, fens, swamps and other wet areas throughout Britain.

Peppermint
Mentha piperita

Peppermint is a hybrid of water mint and spearmint (*Mentha spicata*). The stems are reddish or purplish and bear leaves that are sometimes hairy. The sepals and flower-stalks are hairless.

Water mint *Mentha aquatica*

In southern Europe, the use of mint in cooking dates back to the Stone Age; and 2,000 years ago the Romans cultivated a plant which is believed to have been water mint. The mints are a diverse and widespread group containing many hybrids, with a wide variety of scents and flavours: there are apple mint, ginger mint, and even eau-de-cologne mint. They are used extensively in perfumery, and as flavourings in jelly, tea, sweets, liqueurs, chewing gum, toothpaste and medicine.

Water mint is the commonest of all the mint species in the British Isles, growing in almost any watery or damp place. Many hybrids such as peppermint have water mint as one of their parents.

Used as an early form of smelling salts, water mint also had numerous medicinal applications, particularly in the treatment of stomach upsets and earache. John Gerard in his *Herball*, published in 1597, said that people 'strowe it in chambers and places of recreation, pleasure and repose, and where feasts and banquets are made'. As they walked on the leaves, the scent of mint was released into the air – a 16th-century forerunner of the modern air freshener.

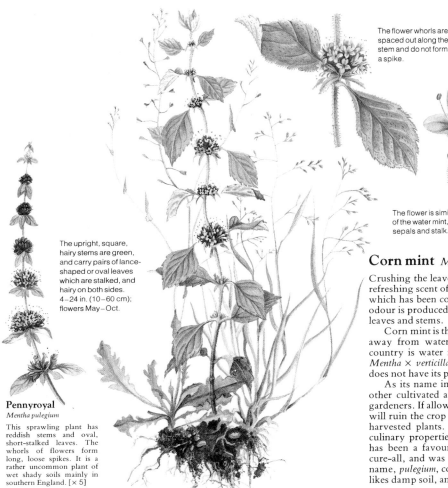

The flower whorls are spaced out along the stem and do not form a spike.

The flower is similar to that of the water mint, with hairy sepals and stalk. [× 5]

Corn mint is found in a variety of British habitats: on arable land, in damp places and in open areas in woods.

The upright, square, hairy stems are green, and carry pairs of lance-shaped or oval leaves which are stalked, and hairy on both sides. 4–24 in. (10–60 cm); flowers May–Oct.

Pennyroyal
Mentha pulegium

This sprawling plant has reddish stems and oval, short-stalked leaves. The whorls of flowers form long, loose spikes. It is a rather uncommon plant of wet shady soils mainly in southern England. [× 5]

Corn mint *Mentha arvensis*

Crushing the leaves of this mint produces not the characteristic refreshing scent of other species of mint, but a strong acrid smell which has been compared to that of over-ripe gorgonzola. The odour is produced by a volatile oil which the plant contains in its leaves and stems.

Corn mint is the commonest of British mints found growing away from water; the most widespread mint of any in this country is water mint. The two species hybridise to produce *Mentha × verticillata*, which is more robust than corn mint and does not have its pungent odour.

As its name implies, corn mint is a weed of cornfields and other cultivated areas, and as such it is a pest to farmers and gardeners. If allowed to grow in fields of peppermint, corn mint will ruin the crop by tainting the oil which is distilled from the harvested plants. Corn mint is a plant with no medicinal or culinary properties. By contrast, its close relative pennyroyal has been a favourite plant of the kitchen garden and a great cure-all, and was once also used to combat fleas. Its botanical name, *pulegium*, comes from the latin *pulex*, 'a flea'. Pennyroyal likes damp soil, and is now uncommon in the wild.

A tall, stiff, upright plant with leaves in opposite pairs. Small, non-flowering stems often grow from around the base. It is seen growing with eyebright and carline thistle. 12–24 in. (30–60 cm); flowers July–Sept.

Flowers, in crowded heads, are partly hidden by purplish, leaf-shaped bracts. [Actual size]

The upper lip of the flower has one notched lobe; the lower lip has three lobes. [× 5]

The fruit comprises four smooth, shiny nutlets which are completely concealed by the short, pointed sepals. [× 5]

Nutlet [× 10]

Marjoram grows on dry grassland scrub and hedgebanks on chalky soils. It is common in England and Wales.

Wild marjoram *Origanum vulgare*

The Roman poet Virgil wrote that when Venus, the goddess of love, carried Ascanius off to the groves of Idalin, she set him down on a bed of wild marjoram. A plant believed to have been chosen by the goddess was naturally regarded by the ancients as a symbol of happiness, and wedding couples were therefore crowned with it. The generic name *Origanum* comes from Greek words meaning 'mountain joy', and reflects the bright show of flowers that the plant presents on mountain-sides in Greece and other Mediterranean countries.

Cultivated species of marjoram are well known as kitchen-garden herbs and flavourings. Of these, pot marjoram, *Origanum onites*, and the less hardy sweet or knotted marjoram, *Origanum majorana*, are the two most commonly grown species.

Even though wild marjoram has been little used for cooking, its properties have not been neglected. Nicholas Culpeper in the 17th century recommended its dried and powdered leaves as a cure for a great many ills. The plant was popular for making herbal sachets and sweet-smelling powders. It yields a purple dye, once used to dye wool, and a juice which, when rubbed into furniture, imparts its fragrance to the wood.

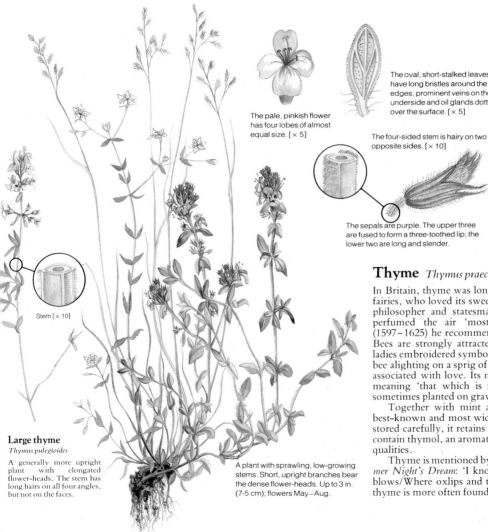

The pale, pinkish flower has four lobes of almost equal size. [× 5]

The oval, short-stalked leaves have long bristles around the edges, prominent veins on the underside and oil glands dotted over the surface. [× 5]

The four-sided stem is hairy on two opposite sides. [× 10]

The sepals are purple. The upper three are fused to form a three-toothed lip; the lower two are long and slender.

Stem [× 10]

The pale purple flowers of thyme are found throughout Britain on dry grassland such as heaths and dunes.

Thyme *Thymus praecox*

In Britain, thyme was long regarded as the favourite flower of fairies, who loved its sweet and delicate fragrance. The English philosopher and statesman Sir Francis Bacon wrote that it perfumed the air 'most delightfully', and in his *Essays* (1597–1625) he recommended it as a border for garden paths. Bees are strongly attracted to its nectar; in the Middle Ages ladies embroidered symbolic favours for their suitors showing a bee alighting on a sprig of thyme. But the plant was not always associated with love. Its name comes from the Greek *thumon*, meaning 'that which is included in a sacrifice', and it was sometimes planted on graves.

Together with mint and sage, thyme is one of Britain's best-known and most widely used culinary herbs. If dried and stored carefully, it retains its taste and smell for years. Its leaves contain thymol, an aromatic oil with antiseptic and preservative qualities.

Thyme is mentioned by Oberon in Shakespeare's *A Midsummer Night's Dream*: 'I know a bank whereon the wild thyme blows/Where oxlips and the nodding violet grows . . .' Large thyme is more often found on chalk downs than on heaths.

Large thyme
Thymus pulegioides

A generally more upright plant with elongated flower-heads. The stem has long hairs on all four angles, but not on the faces.

A plant with sprawling, low-growing stems. Short, upright branches bear the dense flower-heads. Up to 3 in. (7·5 cm); flowers May–Aug.

287

The upper lip of the flower has one notched lobe; the lower lip has three lobes, the middle one with a white patch. [× 2]

The leaves have small rounded teeth, and are very hairy when young. The stem is square. [× 2]

Nutlet [× 10]

Sepal tube [× 4]

The three upper sepals are much broader than the lower two. Four smooth nutlets are contained in the bulge towards the base of the sepal tube.

Basil thyme grows on arable land and in open grassy areas or especially on chalky soils amongst rocks.

Numerous hairy stems bear opposite pairs of small, short-stalked leaves. Whorls of up to eight flowers form loose flower-heads. The plant is seen growing among oats. 4–8 in. (10–20 cm); flowers May–Sept.

Basil thyme *Acinos arvensis*

This herb, sometimes simply called basil, has long been a cooks' favourite, either as a substitute for thyme which it resembles in scent and taste, or as a constituent of mixed herbs used for flavouring dishes. Sheep are particularly fond of it, and it is said that the flavour of its leaves is retained in their meat.

Medieval herbalists valued basil thyme as a cure for many ailments. They claimed that it would relieve sciatica and rheumatism, and would dispel bruises and make the skin white again. If burned or strewn on the ground it was believed to have the power to repel serpents, and was used as an antidote to their bites. The 16th-century herbalist John Gerard went even further and said that its 'seede cureth thee infirmities of the hart, taketh away sorrowfulness, from which cometh melancholie, and maketh a man merry and glad'.

But apart from its culinary and medicinal uses, basil thyme has the power to gladden with its appearance alone. It is one of the most attractive of wild flowers, with its violet, two-lipped flower showing a white patch on the lower lip. Its oval, hairy leaves are similar to those of the calamints, and it was once considered to be a member of that genus.

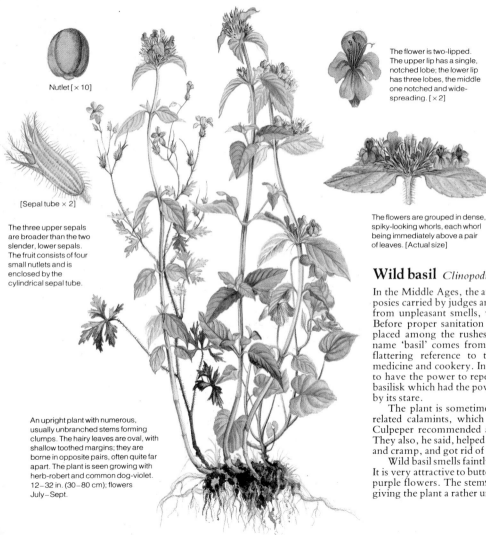

Nutlet [× 10]

[Sepal tube × 2]

The three upper sepals are broader than the two slender, lower sepals. The fruit consists of four small nutlets and is enclosed by the cylindrical sepal tube.

An upright plant with numerous, usually unbranched stems forming clumps. The hairy leaves are oval, with shallow toothed margins; they are borne in opposite pairs, often quite far apart. The plant is seen growing with herb-robert and common dog-violet. 12–32 in. (30–80 cm); flowers July–Sept.

The flower is two-lipped. The upper lip has a single, notched lobe; the lower lip has three lobes, the middle one notched and wide-spreading. [× 2]

The flowers are grouped in dense, spiky-looking whorls, each whorl being immediately above a pair of leaves. [Actual size]

The pink flowers of wild basil are seen near scrub, hedges and wood borders throughout England.

Wild basil *Clinopodium vulgare*

In the Middle Ages, the aromatic wild basil was included in the posies carried by judges and other officials to protect themselves from unpleasant smells, which they believed carried diseases. Before proper sanitation was introduced, wild basil was also placed among the rushes that were strewn upon floors. The name 'basil' comes from the Greek *basilikon*, or 'kingly' – a flattering reference to the plant's pungency and value in medicine and cookery. In even earlier times, the plant was said to have the power to repel serpents, particularly the legendary basilisk which had the power to kill all vegetable and animal life by its stare.

The plant is sometimes included amongst the very closely related calamints, which the 17th-century herbalist Nicholas Culpeper recommended as a cure for afflictions of the brain. They also, he said, helped to cure jaundice, leprosy, convulsions and cramp, and got rid of unsightly scars.

Wild basil smells faintly like thyme, especially when bruised. It is very attractive to butterflies, which seek the nectar in its pale purple flowers. The stems are tallish and often rather straggly, giving the plant a rather untidy appearance.

289

Flower spikes are made up of a series of whorls of flowers, with a pair of small stalkless leaves at the base of each whorl. [Actual size]

An upright plant with few branches. Leaves, in opposite pairs, are large and wrinkled, with coarsely toothed edges. The plant often grows alongside burnet-saxifrage and the yellow-flowered horseshoe vetch. 12–32 in. (30–80 cm); flowers May–Aug.

Meadow clary
Salvia pratensis
This rare plant of chalk grass-land has less coarsely toothed leaves and bigger flowers with curved upper lips.

The flower has a hood-shaped upper lip. The lower lip has a large pendulous central lobe and two small side lobes. [× 5]

The calyx has five sepals. The upper three are fused to form a broad lip. The sepal tube surrounding the fruit is very short. [× 5]

This plant is found on roadside banks and in areas of dry grassland. It is widespread in southern England.

Wild clary *Salvia verbenaca*

If the seed of wild clary is soaked in water, it exudes a slimy mucilage. In the 16th century the mucilage from one of these soaked seeds would be dropped into the eye by Cheshire folk to stop smarting and cure 'waterish humours, redness, inflammation and divers other maladies', according to the herbalist John Gerard. Because of this use, the plant's name became corrupted to clear-eye in late medieval times; but in fact clary derives from the Latin *sclarea*, the meaning of which is lost.

The flowers of wild clary are often small and pollinate themselves without opening; but other plants of the species produce normal, open flowers. The meadow clary, a rarer species, produces flowers of two sorts on different plants; one is female only, the other both male and female.

The best known relative of wild clary is the sage *Salvia officinalis*, principally known nowadays as a constituent of sage-and-onion stuffing but renowned in the past as one of the most useful herbs in the apothecary's shop. It was so esteemed in Asia as a prolonger of life that the early Dutch traders were able to obtain four pounds of tea for every pound of sage leaves they shipped to China.

Oval leaves are bright green, stalked, and borne in opposite pairs. Flower whorls are packed into a dense, oblong head. The plant is shown growing with salad burnet and grass. 2–12 in. (5–30 cm); flowers June–Sept.

Calyx has five sepals, the upper three fused to form a broad lip, the lower two partially fused, all covered with whitish hairs. [× 2]

The fruit is composed of four nutlets; each is smooth and has ridges running from top to base. [× 10]

Two-lipped flower has a hood-shaped upper lip and a spreading lower lip.

Selfheal grows in grassland, waste ground and open spaces in woods. It is widespread throughout Britain.

Cut-leaved selfheal
Prunella laciniata

This species is distinguished by its deeply lobed upper leaves, often whitish underneath, and white flowers. It grows in southern England.

Selfheal *Prunella vulgaris*

The old belief in the 'doctrine of signatures' – that every plant bore an outward sign of its value to mankind – led to the widespread reputation of this plant as a healer of wounds. The upper lip of its flower was clearly in the shape of a hook, and billhooks and sickles were the main causes of wounds in the medieval farming community. Selfheal was even made into a syrup for internal injuries.

Scholars identified the plant as the herb used by Dioscorides, the ancient Greek physician, to cure inflammation of the throat and tonsils; and its botanical name *Prunella* (or *Brunella*) originates from a German name for a sore throat. In England it was known as 'hook-heal', 'sickly-wort' and 'carpenter's herb'.

Selfheal is a native British plant, usually found among short grass where it raises its closely packed heads of bright purple flowers. Occasionally the flowers may be pink or white. Creeping stems spread the plant over wide areas, so that the flowers often carpet the ground along dry, grassy banks. Generally the flowers are pollinated by bees. The much rarer cut-leaved selfheal (*Prunella laciniata*) normally has creamy-white flowers and deeply divided leaves.

291

FOUR COMMON MINTS

Square stems, opposite leaves and tubular flowers that often have two lips distinguish the mint or dead-nettle family from any other. The colours of the flowers and their arrangement on the spike help to distinguish four otherwise similar species.

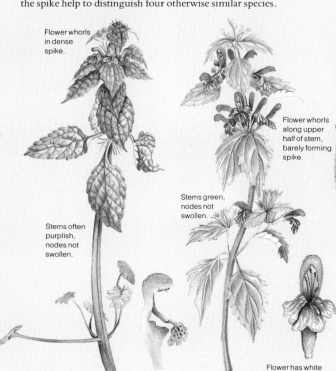

Flower whorls in dense spike.

Stems often purplish, nodes not swollen.

Flower whorls along upper half of stem, barely forming spike.

Stems green, nodes not swollen.

Flower has dark markings on lower lip.

Flower has white markings on lower lip.

Flower whorls in loose spike.

Stems often purplish, nodes not swollen.

Flower has white markings on lower lip.

Flower whorls in loose spike.

Stems green; nodes swollen, covered with red-tipped hairs.

Flower has dark markings on lower lip.

Red dead-nettle
Lamium purpureum Page 299

Black horehound
Ballota nigra Page 296

Hedge woundwort
Stachys sylvatica Page 294

Common hemp-nettle
Galeopsis tetrahit Page 293

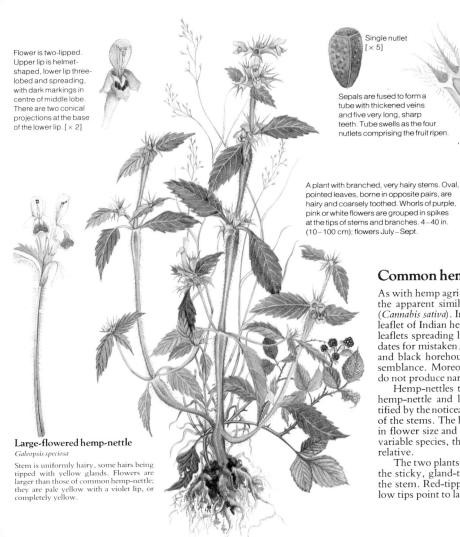

Flower is two-lipped. Upper lip is helmet-shaped, lower lip three-lobed and spreading, with dark markings in centre of middle lobe. There are two conical projections at the base of the lower lip. [× 2]

Single nutlet [× 5]

Sepal tube [× 2]

Sepals are fused to form a tube with thickened veins and five very long, sharp teeth. Tube swells as the four nutlets comprising the fruit ripen.

A plant with branched, very hairy stems. Oval, pointed leaves, borne in opposite pairs, are hairy and coarsely toothed. Whorls of purple, pink or white flowers are grouped in spikes at the tips of stems and branches. 4–40 in. (10–100 cm); flowers July–Sept.

Common hemp-nettle is mainly a plant of arable land; but it sometimes grows in woods and fens and on wet heathland.

Large-flowered hemp-nettle
Galeopsis speciosa

Stem is uniformly hairy, some hairs being tipped with yellow glands. Flowers are larger than those of common hemp-nettle; they are pale yellow with a violet lip, or completely yellow.

Common hemp-nettle *Galeopsis tetrahit*

As with hemp agrimony, hemp-nettle was so named because of the apparent similarity of its leaves to those of Indian hemp (*Cannabis sativa*). In fact a leaf of hemp-nettle looks like a single leaflet of Indian hemp, which has leaves composed of five such leaflets spreading like the fingers of a hand. More likely candidates for mistaken identity are the purple-flowered dead-nettles and black horehound, to which hemp-nettle has a greater resemblance. Moreover, the hemp-nettles, unlike Indian hemp, do not produce narcotic resin or medicinal oils.

Hemp-nettles tend to be tall, robust plants; and common hemp-nettle and large-flowered hemp-nettle are easily identified by the noticeably swollen, often almost egg-shaped, nodes of the stems. The hemp-nettles usually differ from one another in flower size and colour, but common hemp-nettle is a rather variable species, the flowers sometimes resembling those of its relative.

The two plants can be distinguished positively by looking at the sticky, gland-tipped hairs just below the swollen nodes of the stem. Red-tipped hairs indicate common hemp-nettle; yellow tips point to large-flowered hemp-nettle.

An upright, hairy plant with large stem leaves borne in opposite pairs. The whorls of the flowers form rather loose spikes. The heart-shaped, long-stalked leaves have coarsely toothed margins. The plant is shown growing with tufted vetch and grasses. 12–40 in. (30–100 cm); flowers July–Aug.

The sepals form a tube with five long, pointed teeth. [× 5]

Flower has concave upper lip and three-lobed, white-marked lower lip. [× 2]

The leaves just below the flower whorls are shorter and narrower than the other stem leaves.

A common plant of woods, hedges and shady places throughout Britain, hedge woundwort usually grows on richer soils.

Betony
Stachys officinalis

Betony is a much less hairy plant than hedge woundwort, with a well-marked basal rosette of long-stalked, oblong leaves. There are few stem leaves. The flowers have a long tube and a flat upper lip; the lower lip has no white markings.

Hedge woundwort *Stachys sylvatica*

Since the days of the ancient Greeks, woundworts have been used to treat wounds and to stem bleeding. Hedge woundwort and its close relative betony were often applied as a poultice, which was made from the green parts of the plants. The effectiveness of the treatment can be gauged by the attention given to the plants. A number of early medical works were entirely devoted to the uses of woundworts and betony, which seem to have been regarded as almost universal cure-alls. An old Italian proverb advises anyone who is unwell: 'Sell your coat and buy betony.'

As well as poultices, ointments and infusions were made with the leaves; and the flowers were made into conserves. Modern experiments have shown that the volatile oil contained in hedge woundwort does indeed have antiseptic qualities.

Betony was widely cultivated in physic gardens and monastery gardens, and it can still be found on their former sites. It was also planted in churchyards to ward off evil spirits, and it was said that serpents would fight to the death if placed inside a ring of betony. Hedge woundwort was kinder to animals, and toads were supposed to enjoy living in its shade.

Sepals are fused to form a five-toothed tube, which swells very little as the four nutlets of the fruit ripen.

A hairy, unbranched or sparsely branched plant with many stem leaves but no rosette at the base. The finely toothed leaves are in opposite pairs. The plant is seen growing with marsh-marigold. 16–40 in. (40–100 cm); flowers July–Sept.

The two-lipped flower is pale purple or mauve, with a concave upper lip and a white-marked, spreading lower lip.

Whorls of flowers form a loose spike at the top of the stem.

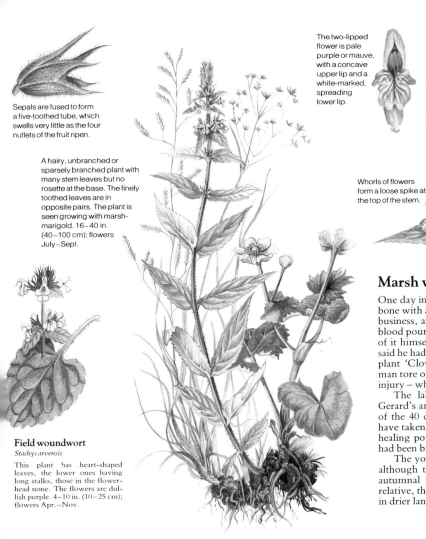

Ditches, swamps and fens are the usual home of this common British plant, but it is also found on arable land.

Field woundwort
Stachys arvensis

This plant has heart-shaped leaves, the lower ones having long stalks, those in the flower-head none. The flowers are dullish purple. 4–10 in. (10–25 cm); flowers Apr.–Nov.

Marsh woundwort *Stachys palustris*

One day in the 16th century a labourer in Kent cut his leg to the bone with a scythe. The herbalist John Gerard was in the area on business, and he offered to heal the wound free of charge. With blood pouring from him, the man replied that he could take care of it himself by applying the plant marsh woundwort. Gerard said he had never heard such a 'clownish answer' and dubbed the plant 'Clown's woundwort'. He looked sceptically on as the man tore off a piece of his shirt and tied clumps of the plant to the injury – which was 'very large and wide'.

The labourer applied fresh poultices each day and, to Gerard's amazement, the wound was healed in a week – instead of the 40 days which a more orthodox herbal method would have taken. From then on, Gerard was a staunch believer in the healing powers of marsh woundwort, using it on people who had been badly wounded in tavern brawls.

The young shoots can be cooked and eaten like asparagus – although they have an unpalatable smell. To some tastes the autumnal tubers are pleasant when boiled. Unlike its larger relative, the field woundwort has no healing qualities and grows in drier land, especially on non-chalky soils.

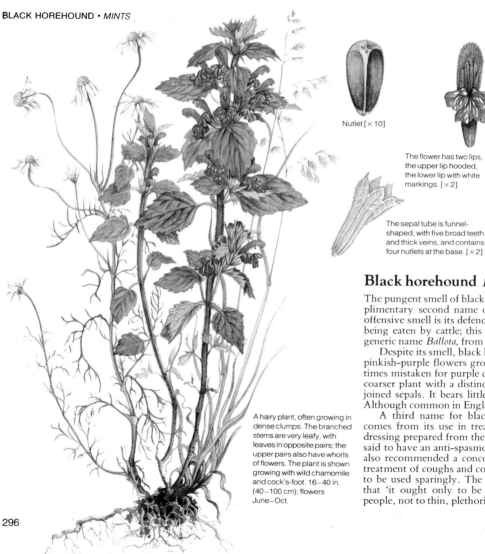

A hairy plant, often growing in dense clumps. The branched stems are very leafy, with leaves in opposite pairs; the upper pairs also have whorls of flowers. The plant is shown growing with wild chamomile and cock's-foot. 16–40 in. (40–100 cm); flowers June–Oct.

Nutlet [×10]

The flower has two lips, the upper lip hooded, the lower lip with white markings. [×2]

The sepal tube is funnel-shaped, with five broad teeth and thick veins, and contains four nutlets at the base. [×2]

The purple flower-heads of black horehound are a common sight in hedgerows in England and Wales.

Black horehound *Ballota nigra*

The pungent smell of black horehound has earned it the uncomplimentary second name of 'stinking roger'. But the plant's offensive smell is its defence mechanism, for it protects it from being eaten by cattle; this quality has given rise to the plant's generic name *Ballota*, from the Latin *ballo*, 'to reject'.

Despite its smell, black horehound is an attractive plant with pinkish-purple flowers growing from a leafy stem. It is sometimes mistaken for purple dead-nettle, but is a larger and rather coarser plant with a distinctive funnel shape to the tube of the joined sepals. It bears little resemblance to white horehound. Although common in England and Wales, it is rare in Scotland.

A third name for black horehound is 'madwort', which comes from its use in treatment of bites from mad dogs. A dressing prepared from the plant's leaves, mixed with salt, was said to have an anti-spasmodic effect on the patient. Herbalists also recommended a concoction made from the plant for the treatment of coughs and colds; but it was a powerful medicine, to be used sparingly. The herbalist Nicholas Culpeper wrote that 'it ought only to be administered to gross, phlegmatic people, not to thin, plethoric persons'.

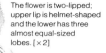

The flower is two-lipped; upper lip is helmet-shaped and the lower has three almost equal-sized lobes. [×2]

Nutlet is brown and somewhat spade-shaped. [×5]

Yellow archangel is usually found on heavier soils in woodlands in England and Wales. It is rare in Scotland.

The sepals form a tube with five teeth. The tube is about twice as long as the four enclosed nutlets. [×2]

Flowering stems are leafy and upright. The oval, stalked leaves are hairy, irregularly toothed and borne in opposite pairs. The plant is seen growing with common dog violet and sanicle. 8–24 in. (20–60 cm); flowers May–June.

Yellow archangel *Lamiastrum galeobdolon*

This plant is closely related to the red and white dead-nettles which, because they flower close to April 27, the day dedicated to the Archangel Michael, are sometimes called red archangel and white archangel. Yellow archangel flowers later in the year, but shares the holy nickname of the dead-nettles because of its similarity to them. It also shares their reputation as guardians against evil spirits and spells, and for protecting cattle against a black magic disease known as elf-shot.

Many parts of the yellow archangel strongly resemble the white dead-nettle, but its striking yellow flowers, with red streaks on the lower lip and a red style, are a major point of difference. The flowers and bruised leaves give off a strong, unpleasant smell.

Whereas the dead-nettles are common plants of waste and cultivated land, yellow archangel is a plant of woodlands and hedgerows and is less widespread. It is common on heavy soils in England and Wales, but is rare in southern England and south-east Ireland and is absent in other areas. It appears to have no herbal uses, but a form of yellow archangel with silver-marked leaves is cultivated in gardens.

297

Flower is white, with black anthers under hooded upper lip. Lower lip has two small lateral lobes and a large, deeply notched middle lobe. [× 2]

Sepal tube [× 2]

Nutlet [× 5]

Sepals are fused to form a five-toothed tube. The tube is a little longer than the four nutlets forming the fruit.

White dead-nettle is a common plant of roadsides, hedgebanks and waste places throughout Britain.

White dead-nettle *Lamium album*

Almost any hedgerow, roadside, or corner of waste ground may provide a home for a patch of white dead-nettle, with its characteristic rings of large white flowers. These flowers rely on bumble bees for pollination, and they possess a number of features to accommodate these visitors. The flower has two distinct lips; the lower lip forms a landing platform on which the bee alights, while the hooded upper lip conceals and protects the stamens. As the bee probes into the tube of the flower, the top of its abdomen brushes the stamens and becomes covered in pollen which will be carried to the style of another flower, so pollinating it.

The bee's reward for its endeavours is the copious supply of nectar it finds at the bottom of the flower tube. The white dead-nettle is an important food plant for bees, particularly early in the year, before most other nectar-producing plants flower.

In full flower, white dead-nettle could never be confused with the true or stinging nettle, but before the flowers have formed it does bear a close resemblance to that plant. However, it lacks the stinging hairs of the true nettle; the names 'dead' or 'blind nettle' refer to its inability to inflict injury.

The upright stems often grow in large clumps; their wrinkled, almost heart-shaped leaves are in opposite pairs. The plant is shown with cleavers and black bindweed. 8–24 in. (20–60 cm); flowers May–Dec.

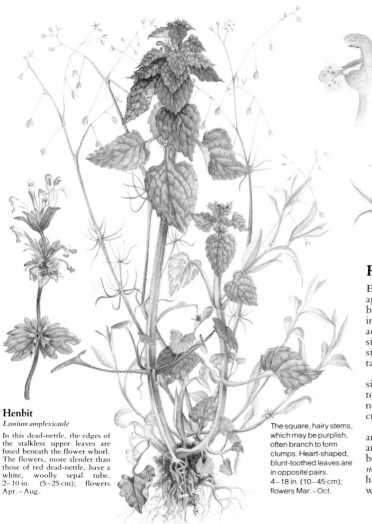

The two-lipped flower is pinkish-purple. The upper lip is hooded; the lower lip has two small lateral lobes, and a large deeply notched middle lobe with darker markings. [× 2]

The sepals are fused to form a tube with five slender teeth enclosing the four nutlets which form the fruit. [× 2]

Red dead-nettle is a very common plant of waste and cultivated ground. It is widespread throughout Britain.

Red dead-nettle *Lamium purpureum*

Early in the year red and white dead-nettle are very similar in appearance; only when the flowers appear does the distinction become obvious, for those of red dead-nettle are pinkish-purple in colour. Furthermore, the red dead-nettle varies in shape according to the habitat in which it is growing. Plants in open situations are short and spreading, while those in shady places or sites where competition for light from other plants is intense, are taller, more upright, and often less-brightly coloured.

Both red and white dead-nettle were used by country folk in similar ways. They were boiled and eaten as a pot-herb, or used to make pig-swill; and they had a variety of medicinal uses, notably against the 'King's Evil' or scrofula, a form of tuberculosis that caused skin eruptions.

Two other dead-nettles are common in Britain. Henbit, another weed of cultivated areas, is smaller than red dead-nettle, and has stalkless upper leaves fused together to form a dish beneath each whorl of flowers. Spotted dead-nettle, *Lamium maculatum*, is widely grown for its attractive foliage, each leaf having a broad silvery band down the centre. It is seen in the wild as an escape from gardens.

Henbit
Lamium amplexicaule

In this dead-nettle, the edges of the stalkless upper leaves are fused beneath the flower whorl. The flowers, more slender than those of red dead-nettle, have a white, woolly sepal tube. 2–10 in. (5–25 cm); flowers Apr.–Aug.

The square, hairy stems, which may be purplish, often branch to form clumps. Heart-shaped, blunt-toothed leaves are in opposite pairs. 4–18 in. (10–45 cm); flowers Mar.–Oct.

299

The flower has two notched lips, the lower lip having darker markings. [× 2]

Large mauve flowers appear in whorls, usually of two to four, on the same side of the stem. [Actual size]

The sepals are fused to form a tube with five short, broad teeth. [× 3]

Ground-ivy is common in waste places, woods and grassland throughout Britain, particularly on damp, heavy soils.

Creeping stems root at intervals; the flowering branches are upright. The long-stalked leaves are kidney-shaped or almost round, unlike the leaves of true ivy. 4–12 in. (10–30 cm); flowers Mar.–May.

Ground-ivy *Glechoma hederacea*

Like the true ivy, ground-ivy remains green all the year unless the leaves are cut down by severe frost. The size and appearance of the plant vary according to the conditions in which it grows: in full sun, the leaves often have purplish edges. When bruised they have a minty smell, but fainter and less pleasing.

Until hops were introduced to England in the 16th century, leaves of ground-ivy, or gill, were added to ale during brewing to clear the fermenting liquid and sharpen the flavour – a use that is commemorated in the name 'alehoof', given to the plant in the West Country and parts of Yorkshire. Even when hops had become widespread, liquor flavoured with ground-ivy was still sold as an alternative to beer in some inns and taverns. Jonathan Swift, author of *Gulliver's Travels*, complained in 1767: 'I was forced to . . . dine for tenpence upon gill-ale, bad broth and three chops of mutton.'

Another drink, called 'gill tea', was made by infusing the faintly mint-scented leaves with boiling water and adding honey. The concoction was reputed to alleviate coughs and other chest disorders, and until the last century was sold by street vendors in London.

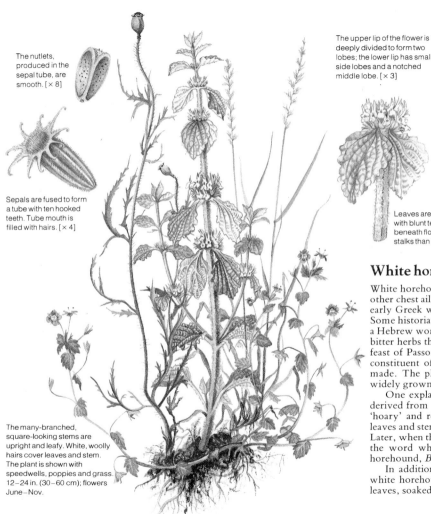

The nutlets, produced in the sepal tube, are smooth. [× 8]

Sepals are fused to form a tube with ten hooked teeth. Tube mouth is filled with hairs. [× 4]

The many-branched, square-looking stems are upright and leafy. White, woolly hairs cover leaves and stem. The plant is shown with speedwells, poppies and grass. 12–24 in. (30–60 cm); flowers June–Nov.

The upper lip of the flower is deeply divided to form two lobes; the lower lip has small side lobes and a notched middle lobe. [× 3]

Leaves are wrinkled, usually with blunt teeth. Those beneath flowers have shorter stalks than lower ones.

White horehound grows on downland, waste ground, and by roadsides as far north as Inverness in Scotland.

White horehound *Marrubium vulgare*

White horehound has been used in the treatment of coughs and other chest ailments since the days of the ancient Egyptians; and early Greek writers recommended it as an antidote to poison. Some historians believe its Latin name, *Marrubium*, comes from a Hebrew word meaning 'bitter juice', and that it was one of the bitter herbs that Jews were formerly required to eat during the feast of Passover. An extract made from its crushed leaves is a constituent of horehound pastilles and syrup, which are still made. The plant is grown in many country gardens, and is widely grown as a medicinal herb in the south of France.

One explanation for the plant's unusual name is that it is derived from the Anglo-Saxon words *hare*, meaning 'white' or 'hoary' and referring to the thick, woolly hairs covering the leaves and stem, and *hune*, the Saxon name for this type of plant. Later, when the sense of the Anglo-Saxon words was forgotten, the word white was added; this distinguishes it from black horehound, *Ballota nigra*.

In addition to its medicinal value to humans, the juice of white horehound reputedly cures canker worm in trees. The leaves, soaked in fresh milk, make a fast-acting fly-killer.

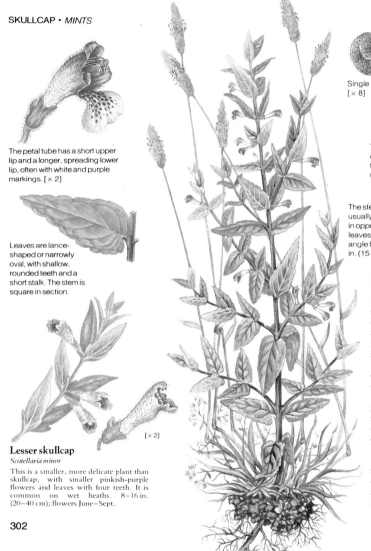

The petal tube has a short upper lip and a longer, spreading lower lip, often with white and purple markings. [× 2]

Leaves are lance-shaped or narrowly oval, with shallow, rounded teeth and a short stalk. The stem is square in section.

Lesser skullcap
Scutellaria minor
This is a smaller, more delicate plant than skullcap, with smaller pinkish-purple flowers and leaves with four teeth. It is common on wet heaths. 8–16 in. (20–40 cm); flowers June–Sept.

[× 2]

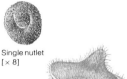

Single nutlet
[× 8]

The hairy sepal tube has a distinctive scale or projection on the top. It contains four warty nutlets. [× 4]

The stems are simple or branched, usually upright. The leaves are borne in opposite pairs, and the upper leaves have a single flower in the angle between leaf and stem. 6–20 in. (15–50 cm); flowers June–Sept.

Skullcap grows in wet places by streams, and in fens and water-meadows throughout the British Isles.

Skullcap *Scutellaria galericulata*

Sufferers from nervous disorders might be advised to take skullcap in tablet form, for the plant produces a volatile oil, called scutellarin, which is one of the best treatments for such afflictions ever discovered. The plant is dried, powdered and infused in boiling water to make a strong tonic, which calms spasms and hysteria, and relieves epilepsy and St Vitus's dance. However, care must be taken; it is a powerful drug, and an overdose might induce the very symptoms which, at correct dosages, it alleviates.

Although a North American species, Virginian skullcap, gives the best results, both British species make acceptable substitutes. These two plants, which are less flamboyant in colour than the American ones, resemble each other closely except in size.

The five sepals of the plant fuse together to form a curious two-lipped tube, the back of which bears a broad, pouch-like scale. The scale is a characteristic feature of all skullcaps, and distinguishes them from other members of the mint family. It is also the origin of the plant's names: the Latin word *scutellum* means 'a disc-shaped pouch'.

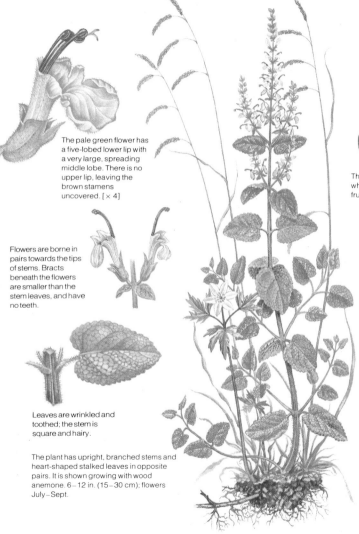

The pale green flower has a five-lobed lower lip with a very large, spreading middle lobe. There is no upper lip, leaving the brown stamens uncovered. [× 4]

Flowers are borne in pairs towards the tips of stems. Bracts beneath the flowers are smaller than the stem leaves, and have no teeth.

Leaves are wrinkled and toothed; the stem is square and hairy.

The plant has upright, branched stems and heart-shaped stalked leaves in opposite pairs. It is shown growing with wood anemone. 6–12 in. (15–30 cm); flowers July–Sept.

The sepal tube is swollen at the base and has a very broad upper tooth and four shorter, narrower lower teeth. [× 4]

The four nutlets which form the fruit are smooth. [× 8]

Wood sage grows on dry soils in woods, grassland, heaths and dunes throughout the British Isles.

Wood sage *Teucrium scorodonia*

In taste and smell, wood sage resembles hops, and not surprisingly it has been used as a substitute for them in some areas. The plant gives a bitter flavour, and is said to clarify beer very quickly, although it leaves the liquid with a strong colour. In Jersey, where it was used for brewing, it was called ambroise, possibly after ambrosia, the fabled food of the ancient gods.

Teucer, an ancestor of the kings of Troy, used wood sage as a medicine, and the plant now honours his name. Later it was believed for a time that wounded deer could be cured by eating it; which explains one of the plant's folk-names, 'hind-heal'. Until recent times people from around Dursley in Gloucestershire would pick the leaves every spring and dry them to prepare a tea which they believed would protect them from rheumatism.

Wood sage has also been called wood garlic; however, the name is more appropriate to the related wood germander, which emits a penetrating odour of garlic when its leaves are bruised. The 19th-century gardener Gertrude Jekyll appreciated the charm of the much-neglected wood sage, and thought it worthy of a place in the garden. The plant is not a true sage, although, like sages, it belongs to the mint family.

303

The blue flower is two-lipped, but the upper lip is so short as to appear absent, leaving the blue stamens uncovered. The lower lip has two small side lobes and a large notched central lobe. [×2]

Nutlet [×8]

The five sepals are fused to form a short bell-shaped tube with five longer teeth. The tube conceals the fruit, which comprises four nutlets.

Bugle is a common woodland plant throughout Britain, and is sometimes also found growing in damp meadows.

A plant with long, leafy rooting stems. Leaves are opposite, but form a rosette at the base of an upright stem. The plant is shown growing with greater bird's-foot-trefoil. 4–12 in. (10–30 cm); flowers May–July.

Bugle *Ajuga reptans*

Creeping, rooting stems allow the bugle to spread through surrounding vegetation to form large mats, when its blue flowers and glossy–green or sometimes bronzed leaves create a striking impression. The cold of winter kills the stems, but wherever they have touched the ground and rooted, a new plant is formed.

Bugle was one of the many plants regarded by medieval herbalists as a cure-all. Nicholas Culpeper, in his *Complete Herbal* published in the 17th century, advised readers to 'keep a syrup of it . . . always by you', as it healed all kinds of wounds, thrusts and stabs, as well as ulcers and broken bones. It was also highly recommended for combating the delirious tremblings brought on by excessive drinking, and has been called one of the mildest and best narcotics in the world.

Both the Latin name *Ajuga* and the English name bugle appear to be corruptions of one or other of the plant's earlier names 'abuga', 'abija' and 'bugula'. A more fanciful suggestion concerning the origin of the name bugle is that it comes from *bugulus*, a thin glass pipe used in embroidery whose shape resembled that of the bugle flower.

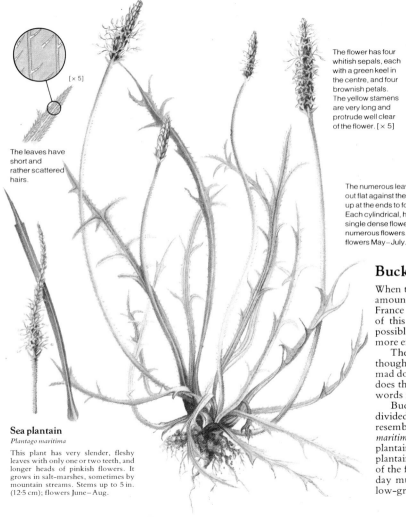

[× 5]

The leaves have short and rather scattered hairs.

The flower has four whitish sepals, each with a green keel in the centre, and four brownish petals. The yellow stamens are very long and protrude well clear of the flower. [× 5]

The numerous leaves at first grow out flat against the ground, then turn up at the ends to form a bowl shape. Each cylindrical, hairy stem has a single dense flower-head containing numerous flowers. Up to 4 in. (10 cm); flowers May – July.

Buck's-horn plantain usually grows on sand, gravel and rocks on open ground, especially in areas near the sea.

Sea plantain
Plantago maritima

This plant has very slender, fleshy leaves with only one or two teeth, and longer heads of pinkish flowers. It grows in salt-marshes, sometimes by mountain streams. Stems up to 5 in. (12·5 cm); flowers June – Aug.

Buck's-horn plantain *Plantago coronopus*

When the seeds of this plantain become wet, they exude a large amount of mucilage – a gummy substance which was used in France to stiffen muslins and other woven fabrics. The purpose of this mucilage in nature is not yet fully understood; one possible advantage is that it may enable the seed to take up water more effectively, as the sticky seeds adhere to the ground.

The leaves were used in medicine to treat wounds, and were thought powerful enough to be effective against the bite of a mad dog. The common name refers to the shape of the leaves, as does the species name *coronopus*, which comes from two Greek words meaning 'crow's foot'.

Buck's-horn plantain can usually be recognised by its divided leaves. But occasionally the leaves are undivided, and resemble the strap-shaped leaves of the sea plantain, *Plantago maritima*, with which it is sometimes confused. On buck's-horn plantain, however, the leaves have one to three veins, and on sea plantain they have three to seven faint veins. Sea plantain is one of the few plants that can survive in a salt-marsh, where twice a day much of the vegetation is inundated with sea water. It is low-growing on saturated mud, taller in less salty parts.

305

Leaf section [× 5]

Thin, oval leaves narrow into a long stalk. Three to five conspicuous veins run up each leaf. Leaves are covered with silky hairs.

The numerous leaves grow from the base of the plant, forming a rather upright rosette. The flower-heads are raised well above the leaves. 18 in. (45 cm); flowers Apr.–Aug.

Each furrowed, silkily hairy stem carries a single dense, dark and many-flowered head. [× 2]

Flower has four white sepals, each with a brown keel in the centre, and four brownish petals. The long stamens are white or pale yellow. [× 5]

Ribwort grows in grassy areas on non-acid soils, including pastures, lawns and roadside verges.

Ribwort *Plantago lanceolata*

The ribwort became common in the British Isles at a time when the tree cover began to be cleared by Stone Age farmers, from about 5,000 years ago. Evidence that the plant flourished widely at that time has been obtained from analysis of the pollen found preserved in peats and lake sediments. It is still one of the commonest plants throughout the British Isles – and the rest of Europe too.

Most of the new growth of the ribwort sprouts from the bottom of the plant. This characteristic enables it to survive heavy grazing by cattle in a pasture, or mowing by gardeners in a lawn. Even if the top of the plant is removed, the ribwort will still flourish.

In various parts of the country, children still play centuries-old games with ribwort. In one game, the stalk is held between thumb and forefinger, with the bottom of the stalk looped around the back of the flower-head. By pulling sharply on the loop the flower-head is 'fired' and can travel a considerable distance. Ribwort can also be used to play a form of conkers. Local names for the plant include 'fighting cocks' or 'kemps', from the Anglo-Saxon *cempa*, 'a warrior'.

[× 5]

Broad, oval leaves narrow into a short stalk. Five to nine conspicuous veins run up each blade. Leaves are covered with whitish hairs, giving hoary appearance.

Stalks radiate from the flat rosette of leaves at the plant base. The plant is seen growing with horseshoe vetch and grasses. 12 in. (30 cm); flowers May–Aug.

Great plantain
Plantago major

Leaves are big, broad and almost hairless. Flower-heads are long and pale green. Great plantain grows in well-trodden places, such as garden paths, waysides and lawns. 6 in. (15 cm); flowers May–Sept.

Flower has four whitish sepals, each with a green keel, and four white or colourless petals. Long purplish stamens have white anthers. [× 5]

Each hairy stalk carries a single, light-coloured, densely flowered head. [Actual size]

Hoary plantain grows on chalky grass-land and lime-rich meadows, but is rarer in the north of England and Scotland.

Hoary plantain *Plantago media*

The hoary plantain is unusual among the British plantains in producing a delicate scent, which attracts numerous bees to pollinate the flowers. This need to attract pollinating insects is probably the reason why the hoary plantain is the beauty of the species – all others, including the great plantain, are pollinated by the wind and do not need the attention of insects.

The great plantain has a long flower spike – hence its alternative common name of 'rat's-tail' – which produces an abundance of seeds. These are ideal for caged birds and are still sold in some bird markets. In the wild, during the cold winter months, sparrows will fight among themselves for rat's-tails. The plant has two other common names, 'birds' meat' and 'canary flower', both illustrating the fact that birds are fond of these seeds.

Plantains share the botanical name *Plantago*, derived from the Latin *planta*, meaning 'sole of a foot', which describes the shape of the broader-leaved species. Like all other plantains, the hoary plantain and its close relative the great plantain are able to survive crushing or tearing, since new growth takes place at the protected base of the plant.

307

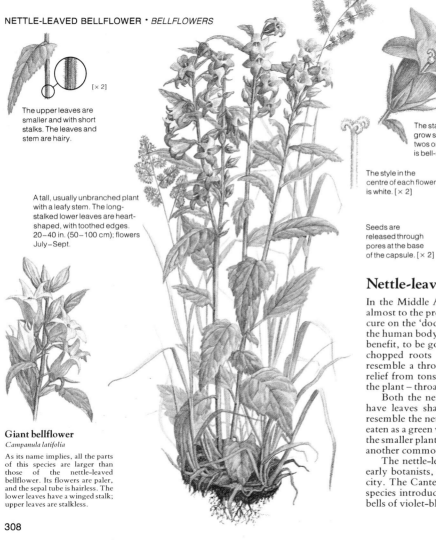

[× 2]

The upper leaves are smaller and with short stalks. The leaves and stem are hairy.

A tall, usually unbranched plant with a leafy stem. The long-stalked lower leaves are heart-shaped, with toothed edges. 20–40 in. (50–100 cm); flowers July–Sept.

The stalked flowers grow singly or in twos or threes. Tube is bell-shaped.

The style in the centre of each flower is white. [× 2]

Seeds are released through pores at the base of the capsule. [× 2]

This woodland and hedgerow plant is usually found on heavy soils, and grows as far north as the River Tay.

Giant bellflower
Campanula latifolia

As its name implies, all the parts of this species are larger than those of the nettle-leaved bellflower. Its flowers are paler, and the sepal tube is hairless. The lower leaves have a winged stalk; upper leaves are stalkless.

Nettle-leaved bellflower *Campanula trachelium*

In the Middle Ages – and in some parts of the country down almost to the present day – people who fell sick often relied for a cure on the 'doctrine of signatures'. If a plant resembled part of the human body, then it had clearly been put on earth for man's benefit, to be good for that part of the body. So it was that the chopped roots of the bellflower, whose flower was held to resemble a throat, were used in a gargle that was said to give relief from tonsilitis and sore throats. Two popular names for the plant – throat-wort and husk-wort – reflect this old belief.

Both the nettle-leaved bellflower and the giant bellflower have leaves shaped like those of the nettle. The plants also resemble the nettle in that the young shoots can be cooked and eaten as a green vegetable. Sometimes the bell-shaped flowers of the smaller plant hang in clusters like a peal of bells, giving rise to another common name for the plant, 'bats-in-the-belfry'.

The nettle-leaved bellflower was called Canterbury bell by early botanists, as it grew in abundance in the woods near that city. The Canterbury bell cultivated in gardens, however, is a species introduced from Italy, and is distinguished by its wide bells of violet-blue, pink or white.

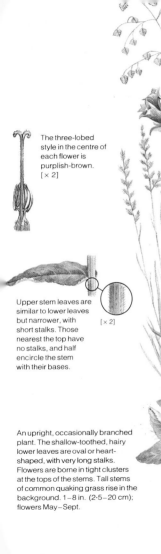

The three-lobed style in the centre of each flower is purplish-brown. [× 2]

Upper stem leaves are similar to lower leaves but narrower, with short stalks. Those nearest the top have no stalks, and half encircle the stem with their bases. [× 2]

An upright, occasionally branched plant. The shallow-toothed, hairy lower leaves are oval or heart-shaped, with very long stalks. Flowers are borne in tight clusters at the tops of the stems. Tall stems of common quaking grass rise in the background. 1–8 in. (2·5–20 cm); flowers May–Sept.

The stalkless flower is violet or blue, and has a bell-shaped petal tube with five lobes. The sepal tube is hairy.

Seeds are released through pores at the top of the capsule. [Actual size]

A plant of grassy places, the clustered bellflower is common locally in England, Wales and southern Scotland.

Clustered bellflower *Campanula glomerata*

The botanical name of this plant exactly describes the shape and arrangement of its flowers. The Latin word *campanula* means 'little bell'; and *glomerata*, 'clustered', indicates the way in which the flowers are gathered in heads at the tips of the stems.

The clustered bellflower is sometimes grown as a garden plant, but when cultivated becomes rather coarse and over-sized, reaching 20 in. (50 cm) or more. The species is seen at its best in the wild, on dry, chalky soils where its flowers appear at their brightest, and are very large in relation to the size of the plant.

Bellflowers are pollinated in an unusual way, in that their pollen is not transferred directly from the stamens to a visiting insect. While the flowers are in a tight bud, the five stamens deposit their pollen on to the hairy outsides of the stigmas, which are pressed tightly together to form a spike. An insect crawling inside a newly opened flower is dusted by pollen from the outsides of the stigmas. After a few days, the stigmas curve apart, so that the flower can be pollinated by other insects entering the bell. If the flower is not pollinated, the stigmas curl back on to their own pollen, so that the flower pollinates itself.

309

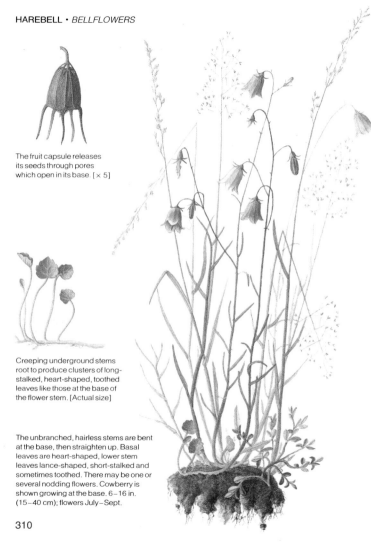

The fruit capsule releases its seeds through pores which open in its base. [× 5]

Creeping underground stems root to produce clusters of long-stalked, heart-shaped, toothed leaves like those at the base of the flower stem. [Actual size]

The unbranched, hairless stems are bent at the base, then straighten up. Basal leaves are heart-shaped, lower stem leaves lance-shaped, short-stalked and sometimes toothed. There may be one or several nodding flowers. Cowberry is shown growing at the base. 6–16 in. (15–40 cm); flowers July–Sept.

Upper stem leaves are very narrow, untoothed and without stalks.

The three-lobed style in the flower centre is light blue. [× 2]

The pale blue flower has a broad, five-lobed petal tube in the shape of a bell. Sepals are very small, slender and hairless. [Actual size]

Harebells grow in dry, grassy places, often on poor, shallow soils, in sites scattered over most of Britain.

Harebell *Campanula rotundifolia*

The light blue flowers of the harebell, dancing in summer breezes on their fine, hanging stems, are among the most colourful sights encountered by walkers. These are the bluebells of Scotland, linked with magic in folklore and given curious names like 'witches' thimbles', 'fairy bells' and 'old man's bells' – the old man being the Devil.

Although the common name of harebell is given to *Campanula rotundifolia* in England, in Scotland it is known as the bluebell; the Scots call the English bluebell, *Hyacinthoides non-scriptus*, the wild hyacinth. The botanical name *rotundifolia*, 'with rounded leaves', can lead the observer astray; for the heart-shaped leaves which grow at the base of the stem often wither by the time the plant is in flower, leaving only the lance-shaped foliage of the middle and upper stem.

The bell-shaped flowers hang and nod, but as the fruit develops the stalks become more upright and pores develop at the base of the fruit-capsule, just large enough to allow a few seeds to pass through at a time. When the capsule sways in the wind on its wiry stem, the seeds are shaken out, and are carried off to widely dispersed growing sites.

The round flower-head, held in a cup of oval, green bracts, contains many bright blue or occasionally white flowers. [× 2]

The hairy sepal tube is almost globe-shaped, with five slender teeth. Petals are long and strap-like. [× 5]

Two valves open at the top of the capsule, between the teeth of the sepal tube, to release the seeds. [× 5]

A hairy plant, sheep's-bit has many slightly spreading stems, leafy on their lower halves and leafless on their upper halves. Each stem bears a single flower-head on its tip. 2–20 in. (5–50 cm); flowers May–Aug.

The leaves are more or less oblong, with toothed or wavy edges. [Actual size]

Sheep's-bit grows in scattered localities throughout Britain, preferring lime-free sites on rough pasture, heaths and cliffs.

Sheep's-bit *Jasione montana*

Although this plant is often called sheep's-bit scabious, it does not belong to the scabious family, but to the bellflowers. Its leaves are arranged in a spiral pattern around the stem, rather than in opposite pairs like a true scabious, and the stigma has three lobes instead of two.

The name sheep's-bit refers to the way the plant is cropped, or 'bit', by sheep in the rough pastures where it frequently grows. The bright blue flowering heads have given the plant its alternative country names of 'blue bonnets', 'blue cap' and 'blue buttons'. It shares the last name with devil's-bit (*Succisa pratensis*), which is similar in appearance but prefers damper ground and has a deeper blue, purple or mauve flower.

The flowering heads of sheep's-bit, like those of the daisy and the scabious, consist of tiny flowers, or florets, surrounded by a ring of green scales. To wasps and other insects which pollinate the plants these florets appear as one large flower, making them more alluring. After pollination, each floret produces a capsule which eventually opens by means of two valves near the apex, to release the seeds. When the leaves or stem of sheep's-bit are bruised they emit a strong, disagreeable smell.

311

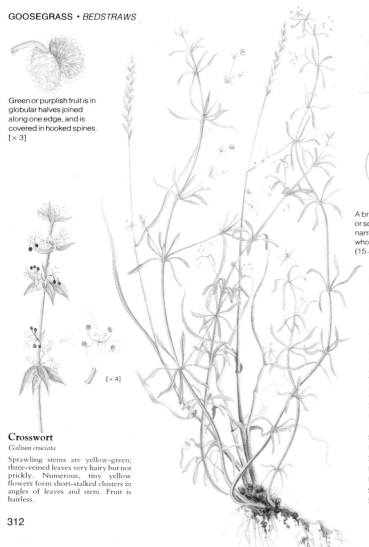

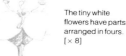

Green or purplish fruit is in globular halves joined along one edge, and is covered in hooked spines. [× 3]

The tiny white flowers have parts arranged in fours. [× 8]

The square stem has backward-pointing spines along its angles. [× 3]

A bright green plant with sprawling or scrambling, branched stems. The narrow, single-veined leaves grow in whorls of six to eight. 6–48 in. (15–120 cm); flowers June–Aug.

Hedges, wasteland, peaty places and shingle are the habitats of this plant, which is common throughout Britain.

[× 4]

Crosswort
Galium cruciata

Sprawling stems are yellow-green; three-veined leaves very hairy but not prickly. Numerous, tiny yellow flowers form short-stalked clusters in angles of leaves and stem. Fruit is hairless.

Goosegrass *Galium aparine*

As its common name implies, goosegrass is a favourite food of geese, and in some regions it is fed to goslings after hatching. The plant has other uses, too, and over the centuries has collected a varied reputation and two other names.

Under the name of cleavers, goosegrass is a missile in children's games: when thrown, its hooked seeds cling or 'cleave' to clothing or hair. In the late 16th century the plant's juices were used as a slimming aid, and the herbalist John Gerard wrote that 'women do usually make potage of cleavers with a little oatmeal to cause lanknesse, and to keep them from fatnesse'. A third name, scurvy grass, refers to the plant's use in the treatment of scurvy and other diseases of the skin.

Goosegrass is a relative of coffee and quinine, so it is not surprising to find that it has medicinal properties. At one time the seeds of goosegrass were collected and roasted as a substitute for coffee. The young shoots are also edible and can be picked in the spring and cooked in soups as a vegetable. Shepherds are said to have used the stems and leaves for straining the hair out of sheep's milk. Crosswort, a related plant with honey-scented flowers, is found in open woodlands and scrub.

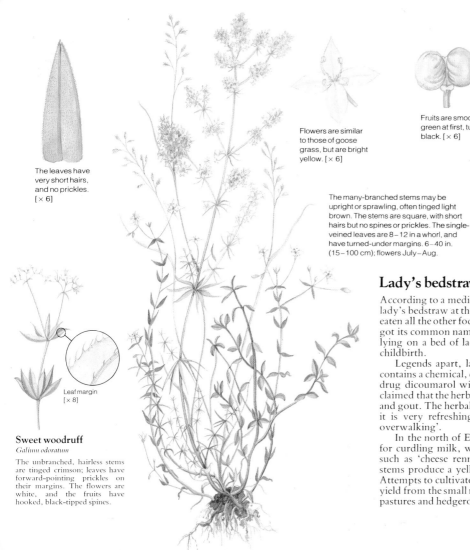

The leaves have very short hairs, and no prickles. [× 6]

Flowers are similar to those of goose grass, but are bright yellow. [× 6]

Fruits are smooth, green at first, turning black. [× 6]

The many-branched stems may be upright or sprawling, often tinged light brown. The stems are square, with short hairs but no spines or prickles. The single-veined leaves are 8–12 in a whorl, and have turned-under margins. 6–40 in. (15–100 cm); flowers July–Aug.

This common, widespread plant grows in grassland, in hedgebanks and on old-established sand-dunes.

Sweet woodruff
Galium odoratum

The unbranched, hairless stems are tinged crimson; leaves have forward-pointing prickles on their margins. The flowers are white, and the fruits have hooked, black-tipped spines.

Leaf margin [× 8]

Lady's bedstraw *Galium verum*

According to a medieval legend, the Virgin Mary lay on a bed of lady's bedstraw at the inn in Bethlehem because the donkeys had eaten all the other fodder in the stable. From this legend the plant got its common name, and it also led to the belief that a woman lying on a bed of lady's bedstraw would have a safe and easy childbirth.

Legends apart, lady's bedstraw has many practical uses. It contains a chemical, called coumarin, which when made into the drug dicoumarol will prevent blood from clotting. Herbalists claimed that the herb was a remedy for urinary diseases, epilepsy and gout. The herbalist Joseph Miller wrote that 'a bath made of it is very refreshing to wash the feet of persons tired with overwalking'.

In the north of England the yellow flowers were once used for curdling milk, which has given rise to several local names such as 'cheese rennet' and 'cheese running'. The leaves and stems produce a yellow dye, and the roots produce a red dye. Attempts to cultivate the plant for the red dye failed because the yield from the small roots was too low, and it is found mostly on pastures and hedgerows.

313

The pale lilac flower emerges in four parts from a very long petal tube. [× 6]

The halves of the fruit fuse down one edge. The fruit is hairy. [× 6]

A bushy plant with many spreading stems. The narrow oval leaves are in whorls of four on the lower parts of the stem and of five to six on the upper parts. 2–16 in. (5–40 cm); flowers May–Oct.

Stalkless flowers cluster at the top of the stem. [× 2]

[× 4]

Edges and lower surface of the leaf have prickles which point forwards.

The square stem of the plant may have short prickles, pointing downwards. [× 8]

Tangled stems of field madder are frequently seen on arable and waste ground throughout Britain.

Field madder *Sherardia arvensis*

At one time the red dye extracted from the slender, coloured roots of the field madder was used to colour cloth. But the yield was not enough to warrant large-scale cultivation of the plant; furthermore, the colour of the dye is not as brilliant as that obtained from the true madder, *Rubia tinctorum*, which used to be cultivated as long ago as Anglo-Saxon times. Today, the production of such vegetable dyes has been almost completely superseded by synthetic products derived from coal-tar and the petrochemical industries.

Field madder is one of the few British members of the bedstraw family to have lilac or pinkish flowers. It is usually pollinated by flies. The plant's close relative squinancywort, *Asperula cynanchica*, also has pinkish-lilac blooms. It differs from field madder in that it is hairless and more slender; it grows only on dry, chalky pastures and dunes.

Squinancywort was first recorded in Britain by the 16th-century Flemish botanist Mathias De l'Obel, and was used to make a gargle which supposedly cured quinsy, or tonsillitis. Its roots also contain a red dye which has occasionally been used by artists and craftsmen, especially in Sweden.

Bright red berries, which contain several seeds, are crowned with the remains of the sepals. [Actual size]

The flower has a long tube with a four-lobed upper lip and a tongue-like lower lip. Stamens extend beyond the mouth of the flower, which is yellow, orange or purplish, and white inside. [Actual size]

Climbing stems of honeysuckle, with their fragrant, exotic-looking flowers, are familiar in woods, hedgerows and thickets.

Honeysuckle climbs by twining round other shrubs such as hawthorn, but often trails close to the ground. The oval, short-stalked leaves are dark green on top and bluish below. Stems are reddish-purple and become woody over the years. Up to 20 ft (6 m); flowers June–Sept.

Honeysuckle *Lonicera periclymenum*

At dusk on a summer's evening the scent of honeysuckle perfumes the air in woodlands and hedgerows. Small wonder that the 17th-century diarist Samuel Pepys called it 'the trumpet flower' whose bugles 'blow scent instead of sound'.

Honeysuckle, also called woodbine, is a climbing plant which entwines itself around young trees and saplings. So tight are its clockwise coils that it can deform the trunk into a 'barley-sugar' shape. Its dense growth prompted William Shakespeare to write in *Much Ado About Nothing*: 'Honeysuckles, ripened by the sun, forbid the sun to enter.' Honeysuckle leaves are among the first to appear in woods, sometimes as early as December, and the flowers appearing in June deepen in colour after being pollinated by insects that feed on the nectar lying deep within the flower tube.

Such a profusely growing plant did not escape the attention of herbalists, who used its flowers in potions for headaches, lung diseases and asthma. Honeysuckle has romantic associations, too; there is an old superstition that if honeysuckle is brought into the house, a wedding will follow, and that its flowers placed in a girl's bedroom will bring her dreams of love.

315

The flower-head almost forms a cube, with one flower on each side face and one flower on top. [× 2]

The top flower on a head has two sepals, four petals and eight stamens. [× 3]

Each side flower (seen here from beneath) has three sepals and five petals; it has ten stamens. [× 3]

The long-stalked leaves arising from the base of the stem are divided into three, each division being stalked and two or three-lobed. These lobes may be further divided. The stem leaves are similar but smaller. 2–4 in. (5–10 cm); flowers Apr.–May.

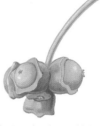

The stem often droops with the weight of the fruits, which are arranged like the flowers: one on each side of a head, and one at the tip. [× 2]

Moschatel is a plant of woods and hedgebanks and rocky mountain places, locally common throughout Britain.

Moschatel *Adoxa moschatellina*

So small and insignificant is this plant that it has been given the generic name *Adoxa*, which comes from the Greek words *a doxa* meaning 'without glory'. It is the solitary species of a whole family – the *Adoxaceae*.

The plant's common name, moschatel, refers to its scent which is musk-like, though it has also been likened to that of almond and elder blossom. The scent is stronger at dusk when the dew falls, or in damp weather, and it attracts insects which suck nectar secreted by a ring at the base of the stamens. The insects pollinate the flowers, but the flowers seldom produce seeds and the plants usually spread by sending up shoots from their spreading rootstock.

The flower-head of moschatel consists of five flowers – four facing outwards and one upwards. The four outward-facing flowers have given the plant another name, 'town-hall clock', but in Cheshire it is known as 'five-faced bishop' after a church dignitary of bygone times who was constantly changing his mind. Moschatel is such a strange plant that in the past it has defied classification, and at one time some botanists placed it with the buttercups.

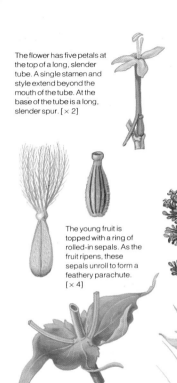

The flower has five petals at the top of a long, slender tube. A single stamen and style extend beyond the mouth of the tube. At the base of the tube is a long, slender spur. [× 2]

The young fruit is topped with a ring of rolled-in sepals. As the fruit ripens, these sepals unroll to form a feathery parachute. [× 4]

The stalkless upper leaves are sometimes toothed, and may be joined at their bases around the stem. [Actual size]

An upright, bluish-green plant with oval, stalked lower leaves. The flower-head consists of branched clusters, each with numerous flowers. 12–32 in. (30–80 cm); flowers June–Aug.

Although the flowers are usually red, a white form is quite common. [Actual size]

This plant is found on old walls, dry banks, cliffs and waste places, especially in south-western England.

Red valerian *Centranthus ruber*

In the summer, red valerian adds a splash of colour to rocks, old walls, quarries and cliffs. The roots bury themselves in holes and crevices, giving the plant a firm anchorage. It was introduced from the Mediterranean in the 16th century as a garden plant, but has escaped and become naturalised, growing wild in many parts of Britain.

Butterflies and other long-tongued insects visit the sweet-scented flowers and suck the nectar from the base of the tubes. The flowers are pollinated in the process, and the seeds which develop have small, hairy parachutes on which they are carried away by the wind. The generic name *Centranthus* is derived from the Greek words *kentron* and *anthos*, meaning 'spur' and 'flower'; it refers to the horn-shaped projection on the side of the flower tube. The species name *ruber* is Latin for 'red', although the plant sometimes has white flowers.

Red valerian does not possess the medicinal properties attributed to the true valerian (*Valeriana officinalis*). But its young leaves can be used in green salads if they are first boiled to mitigate their bitter taste, and in France a soup is sometimes made from its roots.

317

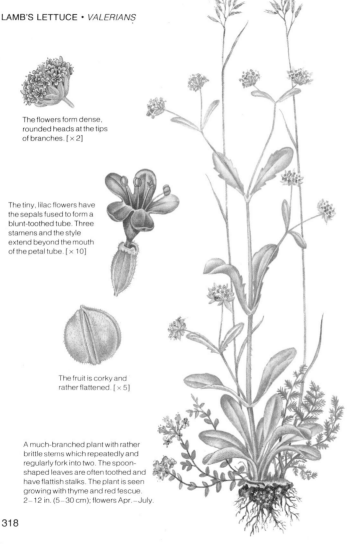

The flowers form dense, rounded heads at the tips of branches. [× 2]

The tiny, lilac flowers have the sepals fused to form a blunt-toothed tube. Three stamens and the style extend beyond the mouth of the petal tube. [× 10]

The fruit is corky and rather flattened. [× 5]

A much-branched plant with rather brittle stems which repeatedly and regularly fork into two. The spoon-shaped leaves are often toothed and have flattish stalks. The plant is seen growing with thyme and red fescue. 2–12 in. (5–30 cm); flowers Apr.–July.

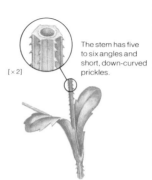

[× 2]   The stem has five to six angles and short, down-curved prickles.

Lamb's lettuce grows locally on dry soils all over the British Isles, on hedgebanks, rocks, dunes and arable land.

Lamb's lettuce *Valerianella locusta*

It is easy to overlook this small, dainty plant, whose generic name means 'little valerian'. It was given this name by an 18th-century botanist, John Miller. Before that time it was called *Lactuca agnina*, or 'lamb's lettuce', which survives as its common name today. The name may have originated because the plant appears at lambing time, or else because it was a favourite food of lambs.

Lamb's lettuce – or cornsalad as it is also known – used to be grown in England for use in winter salads. This custom came from the Continent and was probably spread by visiting foreigners, especially Frenchmen, who were extremely fond of the plant's young leaves. Although the leaves contain few calories, they are rich in vitamins and mineral salts.

Weeds of the valerian family such as lamb's lettuce are fairly common in England. Their tiny, purple flowers appear between April and June, but are often hidden by the large, green, leaf-like bracts. The flowers are probably self-pollinated, after which the fruits develop. It is by looking at the fruits that the various plants – among them smooth-fruited cornsalad, broad-fruited cornsalad and keeled cornsalad – can be told apart.

The young fruit is topped by inrolled sepals, which unfurl as the fruit ripens and form a feathery parachute. [× 3]

An upright plant with few branches. The main stem is angular, and usually hairy towards the bottom. The dense flower-heads at the tops of the stems are branched. The lower leaves have long stalks; those near the top are stalkless. 8–60 in. (20–152 cm); flowers June–Aug.

Male flower-head

Female flower-head

Marsh valerian
Valeriana dioica

This plant of marshy places, usually smaller than common valerian, has creeping, rooting stems at the base of the flowering stem. The lowest leaves have very long stalks and a single, rounded blade. The male flowers are bigger and lighter coloured than the female.

The curved flower tube has a pouch towards the base. The style and three stamens extend beyond the tube. [× 4]

The leaves are divided into pairs of opposite leaflets, stalked and toothed. The leaf stem is hairy.

Valerian grows throughout the British Isles in rough grassland, usually on damp soils. White-flowered forms are common.

Common valerian *Valeriana officinalis*

During the First World War the juice of fresh valerian roots was used to calm people who had been upset by air-raids. For many years before that, herbalists had used the juice as a sedative for those stricken with epilepsy or St Vitus's dance. The 17th-century herbalist Nicholas Culpeper recommended the plant for 'nervous affections, such as headaches, trembling, palpitations, vapours and hysteric complaints'.

Culpeper warned that the roots had a 'strong and disagreeable smell', but this only occurs after they have been dried. The smell – which has been compared to that of new leather – attracts animals, especially cats. In the Middle Ages the scent was well enough liked for the dried roots to be used as a spice and a perfume. They were also placed in drawers to keep linen smelling 'fresh'. The roots of the closely related marsh valerian are smaller and have a less pungent smell.

The genus name, *Valeriana*, may be derived from the Latin word *valere*, meaning 'healthy'; or it may have come from an early herbalist named Valerius who was the first person to use the plant medicinally. In some continental countries, particularly Germany, valerian tea is taken for the nerves.

319

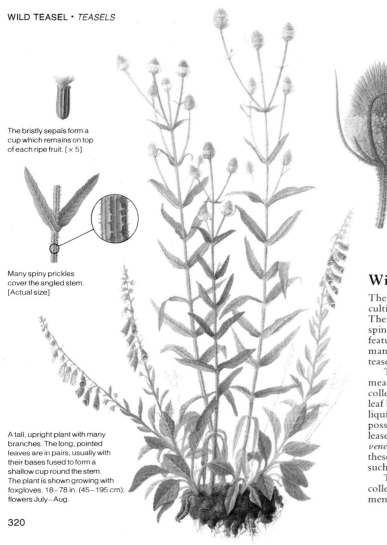

The bristly sepals form a cup which remains on top of each ripe fruit. [× 5]

Many spiny prickles cover the angled stem. [Actual size]

A tall, upright plant with many branches. The long, pointed leaves are in pairs, usually with their bases fused to form a shallow cup round the stem. The plant is shown growing with foxgloves. 18–78 in. (45–195 cm); flowers July–Aug.

The flower is pink or white and has four petals at the top of a long, slender tube. [× 2]

The dense, prickly flower-head is surrounded by curved, spiny bracts.

Wild teasel grows in rough pastures and copses, and by streams and roads all over the British Isles as far north as Perth.

Wild teasel *Dipsacus fullonum*

The teasel family is probably best known in the form of the cultivated fuller's teasel, which is used in the textile industry. The cultivated plants differ from the wild teasels in that the spines on the ends of the bracts curve back to form hooks. This feature is exploited to raise the nap of woollen cloth in the manufacture of fabrics such as velour and cashmere. Fuller's teasel is grown for this purpose in Somerset.

The botanical name *Dipsacus* is derived from a Greek word meaning 'to thirst', and refers to the way in which rainwater collects in the cup-like structures formed around the stem by the leaf bases. Insects sometimes become trapped and drown in this liquid. Their bodies are broken down by bacteria, and it is possible that the plant derives benefit from the nutrients released. The Roman names for teasel, *labrum veneris* or *lavacrum veneris*, 'Venus's lip' or 'Venus's basin', probably also refer to these 'cups'. There are many vivid and descriptive folk-names such as 'brush and comb' and 'Johnny-prick-the-finger'.

The teasel was not much used by herbalists, but the water collected in the stems was considered beneficial, and an ointment produced from the roots was used to cure warts.

Fruit is crowned by a scaly cup from which five shiny black sepals project. The fruit is furrowed and hairy. It is dispersed mainly by wind. [× 2]

Leaves become more divided and shorter-stalked towards the top of the stem, where they are divided into slender segments and are almost stalkless.

The stems branch at the base and send up long, slender flower-stalks. The long-stalked lower leaves have oval, toothed blades. The plant is shown growing with meadowsweet, purging flax and grass. 6–28 in. (15–70 cm); flowers July–Aug.

Outer flower [× 2]   Inner flower [× 2]

Rounded flower-heads are cupped by lance-shaped bracts. Petals of flowers at the edge of the head are larger than those of flowers close to the centre.

Small scabious thrives on pastures and banks on dry chalky soils throughout England, Wales and southern Scotland.

Small scabious *Scabiosa columbaria*

In the summer, butterflies and bees are frequent visitors to the button-like flower-heads of the small scabious. Hard, shiny fruits develop from the pollinated flowers. Water drains away very rapidly through the porous chalky soils in which the small scabious grows, but the plant is well adapted to a dry habitat; its roots are very long, growing deep into the soil to a level where water is more plentiful, even in times of drought.

The first part of the plant's botanical name, and its common name, are supposed to be derived from a Latin word meaning itch. This flower, like its relative the field scabious, was once thought by herbalists to be a remedy for skin conditions. The juice from scabious plants was prescribed for a host of complaints, from wounds and sores to dandruff and unwanted freckles.

The second part of the botanical name, *columbaria*, is derived from the Latin for dove or pigeon. This may refer either to the finely divided leaves, resembling the bird's feet, or to the dove-coloured flowers. *Scabiosa columbaria* is also grown as a garden plant. The many cultivated species of scabious include dwarf varieties and have colours varying from white to crimson.

321

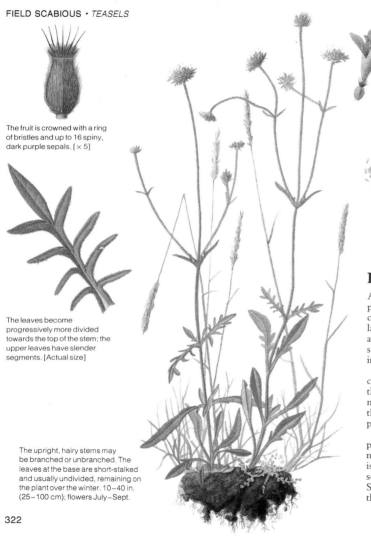

The fruit is crowned with a ring of bristles and up to 16 spiny, dark purple sepals. [× 5]

The leaves become progressively more divided towards the top of the stem; the upper leaves have slender segments. [Actual size]

The upright, hairy stems may be branched or unbranched. The leaves at the base are short-stalked and usually undivided, remaining on the plant over the winter. 10–40 in. (25–100 cm); flowers July–Sept.

Outer flower Inner flower

Flowers have four unequal petals, those of the outer flowers being much larger than those of the inner ones. [× 2]

The flat, circular flower-head contains numerous lilac or blue flowers.

Field scabious is found in dry fields and pastures and on grassy banks and roadsides throughout Britain.

Field scabious *Knautia arvensis*

As many as 50 individual flowers may make up one of the purplish-blue flower-heads of field scabious that stand out conspicuously in fields all over Britain. Field scabious is the largest and most attractive of several related plants; all are named after the reputation the juice once enjoyed for curing scabies (the scab or itch) and other diseases of the skin. It was drunk in an infusion, or applied externally in the form of an ointment.

The dull green leaves of field scabious form the diet of the caterpillars of several butterflies and moths. Sheep and goats eat the plant, but cattle dislike it. To prevent self-pollination, the male stamens wither before the female stigmas mature, but at their peak they stand up erect, giving the impression of pins in a pin-cushion.

In many counties the plant is known by names such as 'lady's pin-cushions' and 'pins-and-needles'. A West Country folk-name, 'bachelor's buttons' – shared by around 20 other flowers – is probably connected with the continental custom of using scabious buds to tell a girl which of her suitors she should marry. She would give each bud the name of an eligible young man, then wait to see which developed into the finest flower.

All the flowers in a head are of equal size. Flowers are violet, sometimes white, with four approximately equal-size petals at the top of a funnel-shaped tube. [× 4]

The fruit is crowned with four triangular green lobes and four to five reddish-black, spiny sepals. [× 5]

The flower-head forms an inverted cup shape above two whorls of oval, hairy bracts. [Actual size]

Devil's-bit scabious grows in marshes and fens, damp woodland, meadows and pastures, all over Britain.

The stems are upright and slender, with few branches. Spearwort and marsh horsetail grow alongside. 6–40 in. (15–100 cm); flowers June–Oct.

Devil's-bit scabious *Succisa pratensis*

The Devil was so furious at the success of this plant in curing all sorts of ailments that he bit away part of the root, hoping to put an end to its good works. According to the legend, he left the plant with the abruptly shortened root it has today, but failed to destroy its curative properties. Nicholas Culpeper, the 17th-century herbalist, prescribed a concoction made from the boiled root for snake-bite, swollen throats, wounds and the plague.

The long-stemmed flower-heads of devil's-bit scabious present a striking display in the fields of every county in the British Isles, growing at both high and low altitudes. It is easy to mistake the plant for a member of the daisy family (*Compositae*), to which it is closely related; for as in the daisy, each flower-head consists of numerous individual flowers, clustered together and giving the impression of a single flower. Unlike the flowers of the field scabious and small scabious, the outer flowers of devil's-bit scabious are not noticeably bigger than the inner ones.

The caterpillars of several butterflies and moths use the devil's-bit scabious as a food plant. They include the marsh fritillary butterfly and the narrow-bordered bee hawk moth.

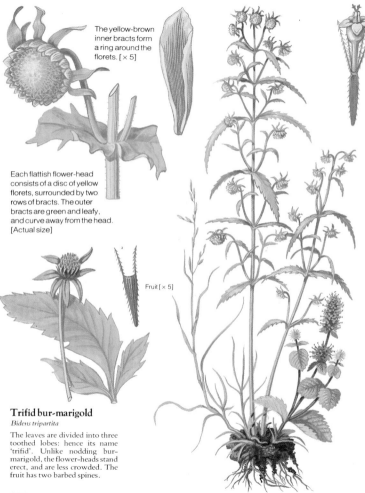

The yellow-brown inner bracts form a ring around the florets. [× 5]

Each flattish flower-head consists of a disc of yellow florets, surrounded by two rows of bracts. The outer bracts are green and leafy, and curve away from the head. [Actual size]

Each floret has five triangular petals at the top of a long tube. The fruit below each is four-sided, with a row of spines down each angle. Four barbed spines project from the tip. [× 5]

Fruit [× 5]

This upright, sparsely hairy plant has slightly fleshy stems and numerous drooping flower-heads. The toothed leaves, borne in opposite pairs, are long, lance-shaped and stalkless. The plant is shown growing with water mint. 3–24 in. (7·5–60 cm); flowers July–Sept.

Nodding bur-marigold grows by still water, especially in soil flooded in winter. It is locally common throughout Britain.

Trifid bur-marigold
Bidens tripartita

The leaves are divided into three toothed lobes: hence its name 'trifid'. Unlike nodding bur-marigold, the flower-heads stand erect, and are less crowded. The fruit has two barbed spines.

Nodding bur-marigold *Bidens cernua*

By ponds and streams the nodding bur-marigold can be seen drooping its flower-heads as if ashamed of their drab, brown and yellow flowers. It is an undistinguished plant of the daisy family to which it belongs, and would pass unnoticed among plants of a brighter hue.

The unscented flowers consist of a head of many disc florets, and many flower-heads are crowded together. When the seeds of bur-marigold develop they have small, barbed spines or burs – four in number in the case of nodding bur-marigold – which attach themselves to the fur of passing animals or the clothing of people. This ensures that the seeds are widely distributed. The generic name *Bidens*, which means 'two teeth', is more suited to trifid bur-marigold, of which the seed has only two spines.

Nodding bur-marigold is particularly characteristic of areas where the ground is under water for most of the winter but dries out in the summer. It is usually found growing on banks rather than at the water's edge, and is commonest in the south of England, though scattered. For medicinal purposes the whole plant is infused and is said to be useful for dropsy and gout. It has also been used to treat various diseases affecting the lungs.

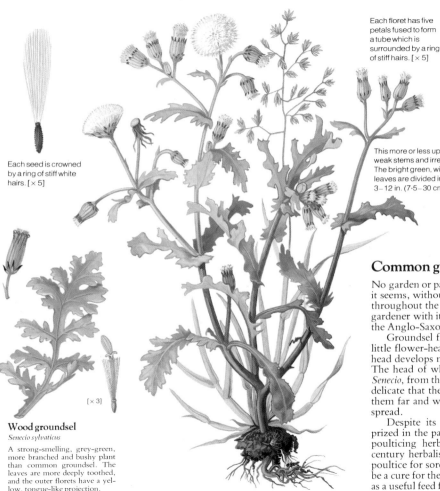

Each seed is crowned by a ring of stiff white hairs. [× 5]

Each floret has five petals fused to form a tube which is surrounded by a ring of stiff hairs. [× 5]

This more or less upright plant has weak stems and irregular branches. The bright green, widely spaced leaves are divided into toothed lobes. 3–12 in. (7·5–30 cm); flowers all year.

[× 3]

Wood groundsel

Senecio sylvaticus

A strong-smelling, grey-green, more branched and bushy plant than common groundsel. The leaves are more deeply toothed, and the outer florets have a yellow, tongue-like projection.

Groundsel is a very common weed of any cultivated ground or waste place. It is abundant throughout Britain.

Common groundsel *Senecio vulgaris*

No garden or patch of cultivated ground in Britain is complete, it seems, without the inevitable groundsel. It is found as a weed throughout the British Isles, and is the despair of the suburban gardener with its ability to spread rapidly: its name comes from the Anglo-Saxon *grondeswyle*, meaning 'ground glutton'.

Groundsel flowers from January to December, its compact little flower-heads looking like tiny shaving brushes, and each head develops many seeds with a parachute of fine white hairs. The head of white hairs has given the plant its generic name *Senecio*, from the Latin *senex*, 'old man'. These parachutes are so delicate that the slightest breeze will keep them aloft and carry them far and wide – the main reason for the plant's ability to spread.

Despite its unpopularity with gardeners, groundsel was prized in the past for its medicinal properties; it was used as a poulticing herb as early as Anglo-Saxon times. The 17th-century herbalist Nicholas Culpeper also recommended it as a poultice for sore skin, and among its other virtues it was said to be a cure for the staggers in horses. Nowadays it is better known as a useful feed for rabbits and canaries.

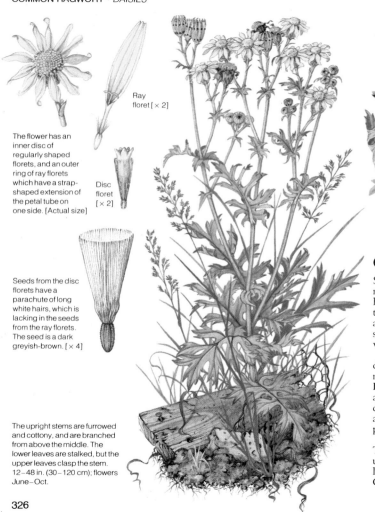

The flower has an inner disc of regularly shaped florets, and an outer ring of ray florets which have a strap-shaped extension of the petal tube on one side. [Actual size]

Ray floret [× 2]

Disc floret [× 2]

Seeds from the disc florets have a parachute of long white hairs, which is lacking in the seeds from the ray florets. The seed is a dark greyish-brown. [× 4]

The upright stems are furrowed and cottony, and are branched from above the middle. The lower leaves are stalked, but the upper leaves clasp the stem. 12–48 in. (30–120 cm); flowers June–Oct.

The leaves are noticeably divided, giving the appearance of two rows of divided leaflets.

Common ragwort is a weed of waste ground, roadsides and neglected pastureland. It grows throughout Britain.

Common ragwort *Senecio jacobaea*

St James, the patron saint of horses, is remembered in the species name *jacobaea* borne by common ragwort. It was once mistakenly believed that an infusion made from the plant, and administered in small doses, provided a cure for staggers, a disease that affects the brain and spinal cord of horses. Because of its supposed power, the plant was given the name of the saint. It was also said to begin flowering on the saint's day, July 25.

The striking plant, with its dark green leaves and yellow, daisy-like flowers, is very often a pest of agricultural land: the neglect of a pasture will often give rise to a large crop of ragwort. It is no friend of the livestock farmer either, as its leaves contain an alkaloid poison which can remain in plants that have been dried with hay. In this condition it is eaten unnoticed by farm animals, and its active ingredient destroys their livers over a period of months.

The name ragwort refers to the cut or ragged-looking leaves. The Scots have named this plant 'stinking Billy', from its unpleasant odour when bruised. The 'Billy' alluded to is William, Duke of Cumberland, ruthless victor of the Battle of Culloden in 1746.

A plant with almost hairless stems, sprawling at the base but becoming upright and branched. The lower leaves narrow into a thin stalk; the bases of the upper leaves clasp the stem. 8–12 in. (20–30 cm); flowers May–Dec.

The leaf is usually deeply divided into a few narrow lobes.

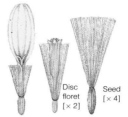

Ray floret [× 2]

Disc floret [× 2]

Seed [× 4]

There are usually 13 outer ray florets, each with a broad, bright yellow extension. The disc florets have a regular structure. Both florets produce seeds with parachute hairs.

The pointed bracts around the flower-head have black tips. [Actual size]

Rare only in northern Britain, this plant grows on walls, roadsides and railway banks, and on waste and arable land.

Oxford ragwort *Senecio squalidus*

Just as some plants today have taken to motorway embankments as a new habitat, so Oxford ragwort spread with the railway boom of the 19th century. It was an introduced plant, found only on old walls in Oxford – where it was abundant, having escaped from the city's Botanic Garden – and at Bideford in Devon. Then it suddenly began to spread along the line of the Great Western Railway, which was opened between Oxford and London in 1844. It is likely that the seeds, which have the 'parachute' of hairs associated with many of the daisy family, were swept along in the turbulence created by the locomotives.

After its initial 'break-out' the plant became very common, its expansion coinciding very closely with the growth of the railway network. Another factor that helped Oxford ragwort to multiply is its prolific flowering: it begins to flower in May and will continue to do so until December, one plant in that time producing up to 10,000 seeds.

Oxford ragwort is noticeable for its bright yellow flowers, which are similar to those of common ragwort. The 19th-century clergyman-naturalist C. A. Johns claimed Oxford ragwort was the prettiest of British ragwort species.

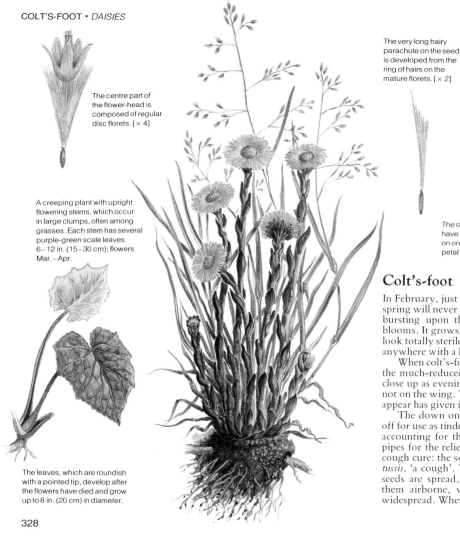

The centre part of the flower-head is composed of regular disc florets. [× 4]

A creeping plant with upright flowering stems, which occur in large clumps, often among grasses. Each stem has several purple-green scale leaves. 6–12 in. (15–30 cm); flowers Mar.–Apr.

The leaves, which are roundish with a pointed tip, develop after the flowers have died and grow up to 8 in. (20 cm) in diameter.

The very long hairy parachute on the seed is developed from the ring of hairs on the mature florets. [× 2]

The outer florets have an extension on one side of the petal tube. [× 4]

Colt's-foot inhabits all kinds of disturbed or thinly covered ground, often growing on clay. It is abundant throughout Britain.

Colt's-foot *Tussilago farfara*

In February, just when winter is at its hardest and it seems that spring will never come, a single sunny day will bring colt's-foot bursting upon the scene in an explosion of sulphur-yellow blooms. It grows in the bleakest of situations – waste places that look totally sterile, dry banks where little else grows, and indeed anywhere with a little loose soil. It strongly prefers clay.

When colt's-foot is flowering no leaves are visible, except for the much-reduced scales on the flowering stems. The flowers close up as evening approaches, when would-be pollinators are not on the wing. The plant's habit of flowering before the leaves appear has given it the folk-name of 'son-before-father'.

The down on the underside of the leaves was once scraped off for use as tinder. Colt's-foot leaves – which are hoof-shaped, accounting for the plant's name – were dried and smoked in pipes for the relief of asthma, and their juice was regarded as a cough cure: the scientific name *Tussilago* comes from the Greek *tussis*, 'a cough'. The 'parachutes' of colt's-foot, by which the seeds are spread, need only the slightest of draughts to keep them airborne, which helps to explain why the plant is so widespread. When the outer wall decays the seed is released.

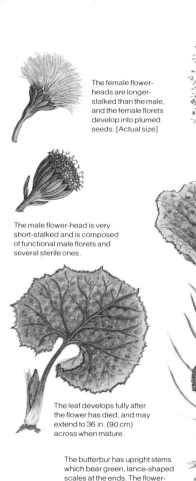

The female flower-heads are longer-stalked than the male, and the female florets develop into plumed seeds. [Actual size]

The male flower-head is very short-stalked and is composed of functional male florets and several sterile ones.

The leaf develops fully after the flower has died, and may extend to 36 in. (90 cm) across when mature.

The butterbur has upright stems which bear green, lance-shaped scales at the ends. The flower-heads are borne at the end of the stem. 6–12 in. (15–30 cm); flowers Mar.–May.

The seed is cylindrical, with a whitish parachute of hairs. [× 5]

This creeping plant is widespread and has a liking for damp ground by streams, copses, roadsides and ditches.

Butterbur *Petasites hybridus*

According to tradition, the large leaves of this liver-coloured plant were used for wrapping butter – which is how it got its English name. The leaves can grow to almost 36 in. (90 cm) across and have a dense felting of hairs underneath. The genus name, *Petasites*, comes from the Greek *petusos*, a broad-brimmed hat, and the 16th-century herbalist John Gerard wrote that the leaf 'is bigge and large inough to keepe a man's head from raine, and from the heat of the sunne'.

The male butterbur is common throughout Britain, but the female plant is usually only found in Yorkshire, Lancashire, Cheshire, Derbyshire and Lincolnshire. Occasionally, however, single female flowers occur on an otherwise male plant, and it is presumably from these that sufficient seed is produced to assist the butterbur's spread to new localities. But it also spreads to cover large areas by means of its creeping, underground roots.

In the Middle Ages, the plant's roots were powdered and used to remove spots and skin blemishes. The herbalist Nicholas Culpeper thought that rich gentlewomen should preserve the roots for their poor neighbours, who 'cannot help themselves'.

329

The flower-stalk is leafless and hairy. Each solitary flower-head has a yellow disc surrounded by a ring of white rays. [× 2]

Seeds are small, oval and downy, with flattened ends. [× 10]

Oval or spoon-shaped leaves form a rosette at the base of this downy plant. Each leaf is broader above the base and rounded at the end, and has many small teeth. 8–24 in. (20–60 cm); flowers Aug.–Sept.

Yellow disc florets are short and broad, with a five-lobed petal tube. [× 10]

On one side of the petal tube, ray florets have a long, strap-like extension, which is white or occasionally tinged pink. [× 5]

The daisy is a very common perennial; it thrives in short grassland, and especially on lawns, throughout the British Isles.

Daisy *Bellis perennis*

Countless writers from Chaucer onwards have written in praise of the humble daisy. In his Prologue to *The Legend of Good Women*, Chaucer said that the daisy was his favourite flower, and that every morning in May he would rise early and wander in the meadows to look at the only plant which could 'soften all my sorrow'. The poet Shelley likened daisies to earthbound stars: 'Those pearled Arcturi of the Earth, the constellated flower that never sets.'

The very name of the daisy – derived as it is from 'day's eye' – is a reminder of the plant's resemblance to a small sun, which opens very early in the morning and closes in the evening. The flowers also close in dull weather when fewer pollinating insects are active.

It is ironic that the daisy, whose generic name *Bellis* is derived from the Latin for 'beautiful', is often regarded as a pernicious weed, especially when it grows on lawns. The 17th-century herbalist Nicholas Culpeper believed, however, that the reason why nature had made the daisy common was that it was such a useful plant. 'Boiled in asses milk,' he wrote, 'it is very effectual in consumptions of the lungs'.

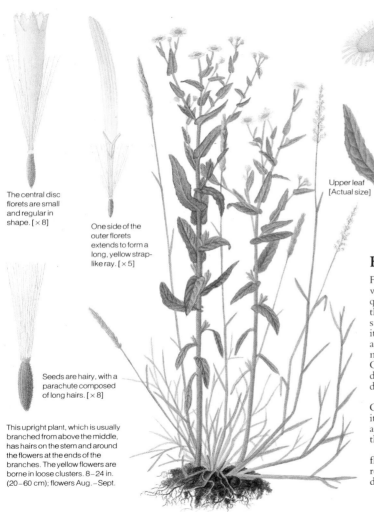

The central disc florets are small and regular in shape. [× 8]

One side of the outer florets extends to form a long, yellow strap-like ray. [× 5]

Seeds are hairy, with a parachute composed of long hairs. [× 8]

This upright plant, which is usually branched from above the middle, has hairs on the stem and around the flowers at the ends of the branches. The yellow flowers are borne in loose clusters. 8–24 in. (20–60 cm); flowers Aug.–Sept.

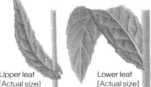

Each flower consists of a cluster of florets forming a central disc, surrounded by a ring of ray florets. [× 2]

Upper leaf [Actual size]

Lower leaf [Actual size]

Lower leaves narrow into a stalk; upper leaves are heart-shaped at the base and clasp the stem.

Fleabane grows on marshy ground, meadows and ditches; it is common throughout most of Britain.

Fleabane *Pulicaria dysenterica*

For centuries the leaves of fleabane, when dried and burned, were said to give off a vapour which drove fleas away. This quality must have made the plant highly prized in times when thousands of fleas swarmed among the rushes and sweet-smelling grasses which were laid on the floors of houses. Even in its unburned state the plant, when sprinkled on the ground, apparently acted as an insecticide, though in a slightly different manner: 'The smell,' said the 17th-century herbalist Nicholas Culpeper, 'is supposed delightful to insects and the juice destructive to them, for they never leave it till the season of their deaths'.

Apart from commending its effectiveness against insects, Culpeper had nothing good to say about the plant. He described it as 'an ill-looking weed', and its flowers as 'small, very poor and of a dirty yellow'. The Romans, however, must have held the plant in higher esteem, for they used it to make wreaths.

The generic name *Pulicaria* refers to the plant's power against fleas, *pulex* being Latin for 'flea'. The species name *dysenterica* recalls a time when fleabane was used as a medicine against dysentery.

331

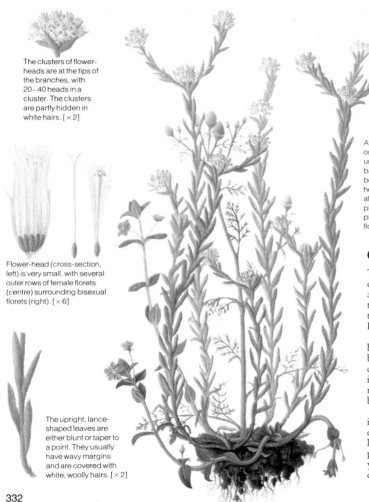

The clusters of flower-heads are at the tips of the branches, with 20–40 heads in a cluster. The clusters are partly hidden in white hairs. [× 2]

Flower-head (cross-section, left) is very small, with several outer rows of female florets (centre) surrounding bisexual florets (right). [× 6]

The upright, lance-shaped leaves are either blunt or taper to a point. They usually have wavy margins and are covered with white, woolly hairs. [× 2]

The seeds are covered in small projections, with a 'parachute' of one ring of hairs. [× 5]

A thickly hairy plant with upright or slightly sprawling stems, unbranched or branched at the base. Further branches arise below the main cluster of flower-heads. It is shown growing alongside the dark green pineapple weed and scarlet pimpernel. 2–12 in. (5–30 cm); flowers July–Aug.

Common cudweed grows on heaths, in dry fields and pastures and by roadsides in England and southern Scotland.

Common cudweed *Filago vulgaris*

The unusual structure of common cudweed often makes it difficult to tell whether the plant is in flower. The flower-heads are very small, and are sunk into the silver-grey hairs that cover the plant. The inconspicuous yellow flowers are also masked by the spreading side branches. The genus name *Filago*, from the Latin *filium*, 'thread', refers to the plant's hairy covering.

The cottony covering gives the plant its common name, too; but in the 17th century some English farmers believed it must be beneficial to cattle that had stopped ruminating, or had 'lost their cud'. The plant has been used as a cure for human ailments, too: in Roman times, its juice was recommended as a cure for mumps, and in the 17th century Nicholas Culpeper said its bruised leaves quickly healed a fresh wound.

Cudweed leaves were sometimes placed between a horse and its rider to prevent chafing – in Northumberland the plant was called 'chafeweed'. An alternative name for the plant in Scotland, 'son-afore-the-father', arose from a description of the plant by the 16th-century herbalist John Gerard, who said its young flowers 'overtop those that come first, as many wicked children do unto their parents'.

The seed is usually hairless; rarely there are hair-like projections. [×20]

Leaves are narrow and broader above the middle. They end in a blunt or pointed tip, and are very hairy on both sides. [×2]

An annual plant with upright or sprawling stems which are much branched from the base and covered in dense, woolly hair. The clusters of flower-heads are shorter than the surrounding leaves. It is shown growing with heath and grass. 1½–8 in. (4–20 cm); flowers July–Aug.

[×6]

[×20]

[×20]

The flowers are in dense clusters of three to ten oval heads. Each head (left) is mainly composed of female florets (centre), with a few bisexual florets in middle of head (right).

Marsh cudweed is found in damp places, frequently on acid soils. It is common throughout the British Isles.

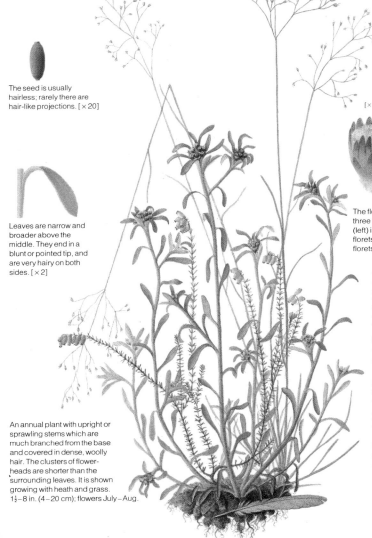

Marsh cudweed *Filaginella uliginosa*

Like common cudweed, this widespread plant is densely covered with silver-grey hairs. Until recently, botanists gave it the genus name of *Gnaphalium*, from a Greek word for 'wool'. The English name 'cudweed', or 'cotton-weed', refers to the all-over, cottony hairs. The leaves, which are longer than those of the common cudweed, are broader towards the ends and cottony on either side.

The plant is small and undistinguished and is often found growing on rutted tracks; in puddles; on damp heaths; in wet, sandy areas, especially where the water has stood throughout the winter; or any place where the vegetation is generally dismal. It is also frequently seen at waysides and is sometimes known as 'wayside cudweed'.

Marsh cudweed is not often visited by pollinating insects. It is an annual species and, as with many other annuals that rely on seed for the production of new plants, self-pollination ensures a reliable supply of fertile seed. This can lead to offspring which may be less adaptable to changed conditions; but the occasional transference of pollen from another plant ensures the introduction of some necessary 'new blood'.

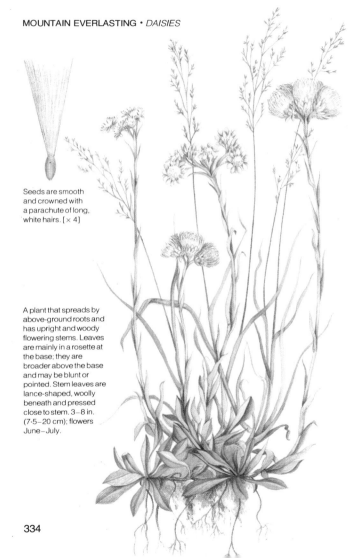

Seeds are smooth and crowned with a parachute of long, white hairs. [× 4]

A plant that spreads by above-ground roots and has upright and woody flowering stems. Leaves are mainly in a rosette at the base; they are broader above the base and may be blunt or pointed. Stem leaves are lance-shaped, woolly beneath and pressed close to stem. 3–8 in. (7·5–20 cm); flowers June–July.

Male flower-heads are smaller than the females, and consist of florets ringed by bracts. The bracts resemble ray florets. [× 2]

The female plant has a cluster of flower-heads at end of stem. They consist of many female florets, surrounded by pink or white woolly bracts. [× 2]

Mountain everlasting is found on heath-land and on dry pasture and mountain slopes. It is common locally in the north.

Mountain everlasting *Antennaria dioica*

There are two reasons why this attractive plant, with leaves that are grey-green on top and silvery beneath, has earned the name of 'everlasting'. Firstly, it is a perennial, which springs up year after year on the same spot. Secondly, its flowers when gathered in summer have been dried for use in the winter as an unusual room decoration. However, the plant has become relatively scarce, especially in southern England.

The species name of *dioica*, literally 'double house' in Greek, means that male and female flowers are produced on separate plants; some sterile bisexual flowers occur rarely with the male flower-heads. After the production of fertile seeds, the flowers drop away, revealing the seed with its white parachute of hairs. As well as producing seeds, the plant can also reproduce by means of leafy creeping stems that root at the nodes.

The generic name *Antennaria* is derived from antenna – the Latin name for the feeler of an insect. This may have referred to the supposed resemblance of the hairs of the seed parachute to insect antennae. The alternative common name for the plant of mountain cat's-foot comes from the soft appearance and feel of the leaf, stem and flower.

Flower-heads are short-stalked, and borne at the ends of branches. The narrow, surrounding bracts are greenish-yellow. [× 2]

The brown seeds have short hairs and are crowned with a white parachute of long hairs. [× 4]

An upright plant with rounded, sometimes branched stems, which are downy or hairless. The toothed leaves of the basal rosette are wider above the middle. They taper into a short stalk, whilst the stem leaves are oval and narrow, with few teeth. 2–24 in. (5–60 cm); flowers July–Aug.

The central disc florets have a regularly lobed petal tube. [× 4]

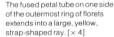

The fused petal tube on one side of the outermost ring of florets extends into a large, yellow, strap-shaped ray. [× 4]

Goldenrod is common on mountains and in woods, hedgerows and dunes throughout much of Britain.

Goldenrod *Solidago virgaurea*

Among the dark rocks of upland Britain the blaze of colour of goldenrod in flower makes a startling contrast with its sombre surroundings. Its recorded history goes back to 16th-century London, where there were numerous sword fights and knife stabbings. Goldenrod was much in demand medicinally as a herb for healing wounds; it was applied externally as an ointment or drunk as a hot beverage. Some early herbalists also recommended it to those whose kidneys were not functioning properly, or who suffered from mouth or throat ulcers.

Large quantities of goldenrod were imported in Elizabethan times at the hugely inflated price for those days of half a crown ($12\frac{1}{2}$p) an ounce. The boom lasted until the plant was found growing wild on the southern slopes of Hampstead Heath. After that, to quote the 16th-century herbalist John Gerard, 'no man will give half a crowne for a hundredweight of it . . . esteeming no longer of any thing (how precious soever it be) than whilest it is strange and rare'.

The generic name *Solidago* comes from the Latin verb *solidare* – 'to make whole or heal' – a reference to the healing powers once attributed to the plant.

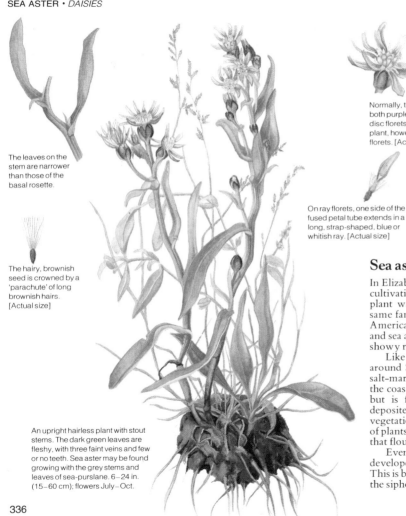

The leaves on the stem are narrower than those of the basal rosette.

The hairy, brownish seed is crowned by a 'parachute' of long brownish hairs. [Actual size]

An upright hairless plant with stout stems. The dark green leaves are fleshy, with three faint veins and few or no teeth. Sea aster may be found growing with the grey stems and leaves of sea-purslane. 6–24 in. (15–60 cm); flowers July–Oct.

Normally, the flower comprises both purple ray florets and yellow disc florets. One variety of the plant, however, has only disc florets. [Actual size]

On ray florets, one side of the fused petal tube extends in a long, strap-shaped, blue or whitish ray. [Actual size]

On disc florets there are five regular lobes at the top of the fused petal tube. [Actual size]

Sea aster is a plant of salt-marshes, and is also found on sea cliffs. It is common around the British coastline.

Sea aster *Aster tripolium*

In Elizabethan times many plants were taken from the wild into cultivation. One of those that became very popular as a garden plant was sea aster. However, when another member of the same family, the Michaelmas daisy, was imported from North America, it too was found to grow well in British conditions, and sea aster was gradually replaced as a garden plant by its more showy relative.

Like the Michaelmas daisy, sea aster is usually at its best around St Michael's Day, September 29, when whole areas of salt-marsh take on a blue tinge. The plant is common all round the coasts of Britain. Occasionally it grows on rocks and cliffs, but is found usually on salt-marshes – areas where mud, deposited by the sea, has been overgrown by a distinctive type of vegetation. Sea aster is probably the most attractive of the group of plants – which includes glassworts, seablite and sea-purslane – that flourish here at the mercy of the tides and winds.

Even though sea aster can grow in water, the plant has developed very fleshy leaves, like those of a plant of dry places. This is because it must retain as much fresh water as it can against the siphoning-off effect of salt water.

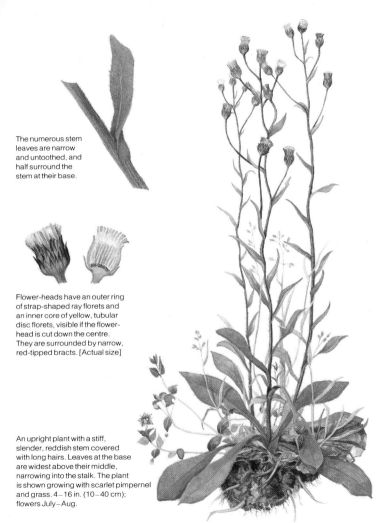

The numerous stem leaves are narrow and untoothed, and half surround the stem at their base.

Flower-heads have an outer ring of strap-shaped ray florets and an inner core of yellow, tubular disc florets, visible if the flower-head is cut down the centre. They are surrounded by narrow, red-tipped bracts. [Actual size]

An upright plant with a stiff, slender, reddish stem covered with long hairs. Leaves at the base are widest above their middle, narrowing into the stalk. The plant is shown growing with scarlet pimpernel and grass. 4–16 in. (10–40 cm); flowers July–Aug.

In ray florets, the petal tube extends on one side to form an upright, pale purple ray. [Actual size]

Female floret   Bisexual floret

Outer disc florets are female. Inner disc florets are bisexual, with a five-lobed petal tube. [Actual size]

Blue fleabane springs up on dry, grassy places, banks, walls and dunes, especially on chalk. It is locally common.

Blue fleabane *Erigeron acer*

Despite its name, blue fleabane has flower-heads that are pale purple at the rim and pale yellow in the centre; from a distance, however, the overall effect is blue. Each flower-head, borne singly on a fairly long branch, has a multitude of tiny florets, the outermost purple ring remaining upright rather than spreading.

When the top inch or so of soil is newly turned on chalk grassland, blue fleabane is one of a number of species that will rapidly spring up, either from seeds left dormant in the soil for years or from those carried in by the wind. It is an annual plant and, as with most annuals, a favourable habitat can bring about a massive increase in numbers by enabling the species to force two flowering generations in one growing season. The later seedlings, which do not have time to flower in their first season, behave as biennials and flower in the following year.

Long tufts of fine white hairs, tinged with red, form on each fruiting head, eventually serving as parachutes to disperse seeds. These give the plant its botanical name of *Erigeron*, from the Greek *eri*, 'early', and *geron*, 'old', because its white beard suggests premature old age. The common name of fleabane refers to the burning of the plant in the past to smoke out fleas.

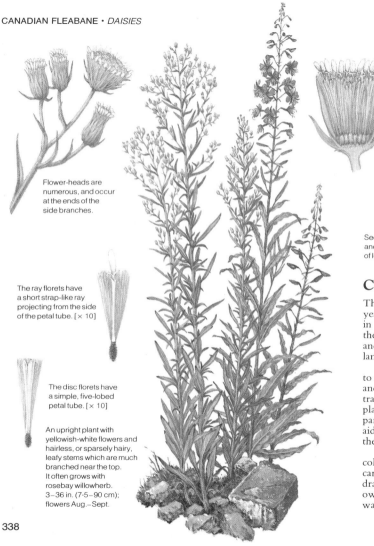

Flower-heads are numerous, and occur at the ends of the side branches.

The ray florets have a short strap-like ray projecting from the side of the petal tube. [× 10]

The disc florets have a simple, five-lobed petal tube. [× 10]

An upright plant with yellowish-white flowers and hairless, or sparsely hairy, leafy stems which are much branched near the top. It often grows with rosebay willowherb. 3–36 in. (7·5–90 cm); flowers Aug.–Sept.

The flower-heads are composed of ray florets and disc florets. The surrounding bracts are narrow, with papery margins. [× 5]

Seeds are yellowish and downy, with a parachute of long hairs. [× 10]

Canadian fleabane is a common sight on roadsides especially on light soils in south and south-east England.

Canadian fleabane *Conyza canadensis*

This wayside plant was unknown in Britain until about 200 years ago, when some seeds reached here from North America in a consignment of goods unloaded at London docks. Since then the plant has become firmly established all over southern and south-eastern England, though it is still absent from Scotland and Ireland.

The early success of Canadian fleabane as a coloniser was due to a large extent to the development of the railways in the 1830s and 1840s. The expanses of ballast between and alongside the tracks provided a new and unexploited habitat into which the plant soon moved. Its seeds are small and light and have a parachute of hairs, and the draughts caused by passing trains aided their dispersal. As the railway network extended through the countryside, so Canadian fleabane followed in its wake.

It is in much the same way that Canadian fleabane is today colonising motorway verges. The air currents caused by passing cars and lorries are doing the same job of seed dispersal as the draughts caused by passing trains in the last century. The plant owes its name to the use in Classical times of a related plant to ward off fleas and midges.

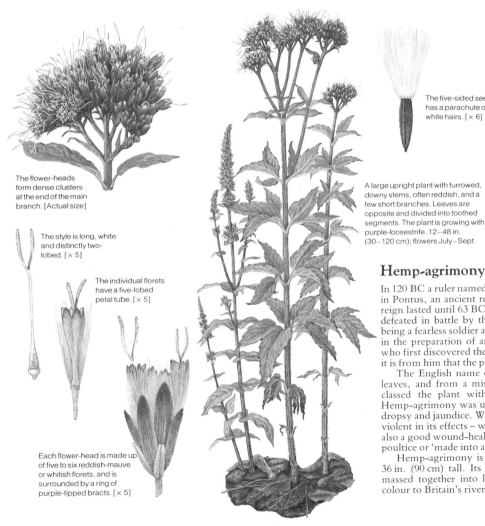

The flower-heads form dense clusters at the end of the main branch. [Actual size]

The style is long, white and distinctly two-lobed. [× 5]

The individual florets have a five-lobed petal tube. [× 5]

Each flower-head is made up of five to six reddish-mauve or whitish florets, and is surrounded by a ring of purple-tipped bracts. [× 5]

The five-sided seed has a parachute of white hairs. [× 6]

A large upright plant with furrowed, downy stems, often reddish, and a few short branches. Leaves are opposite and divided into toothed segments. The plant is growing with purple-loosestrife. 12–48 in. (30–120 cm); flowers July–Sept.

Hemp-agrimony is a plant of marshes, stream banks and wet woodland, common in England but rarer in Scotland.

Hemp-agrimony *Eupatorium cannabinum*

In 120 BC a ruler named Mithradates VI Eupator came to power in Pontus, an ancient region of north-eastern Asia Minor. His reign lasted until 63 BC when he committed suicide after being defeated in battle by the Roman general Pompey. As well as being a fearless soldier and a great king, Mithradates was skilled in the preparation of antidotes to poison. It was Mithradates who first discovered the medicinal uses of hemp-agrimony, and it is from him that the plant gets its generic name.

The English name of the plant comes from its hemp-like leaves, and from a mistake by early herbalists who wrongly classed the plant with true agrimony, *Agrimonia eupatoria*. Hemp-agrimony was used as a purge, an emetic and a cure for dropsy and jaundice. Writers described it as a 'rough medicine' – violent in its effects – which had to be used with caution. It was also a good wound-healing herb, and could be applied direct as a poultice or 'made into an ointment with hog's lard'.

Hemp-agrimony is a large, handsome plant, usually over 36 in. (90 cm) tall. Its reddish stems and its tiny pink florets massed together into large flat-topped heads add a splash of colour to Britain's riversides.

339

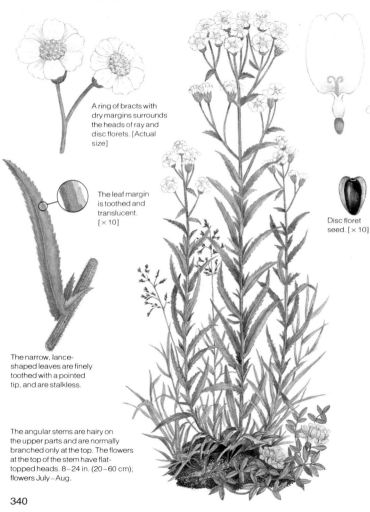

A ring of bracts with dry margins surrounds the heads of ray and disc florets. [Actual size]

The leaf margin is toothed and translucent. [× 10]

The narrow, lance-shaped leaves are finely toothed with a pointed tip, and are stalkless.

The angular stems are hairy on the upper parts and are normally branched only at the top. The flowers at the top of the stem have flat-topped heads. 8–24 in. (20–60 cm); flowers July–Aug.

On the outer ray florets the petal tube is extended on one side to form a broad white ray with a three-lobed end. [× 5]

The centre disc florets are more regularly shaped than the outers, with a five-lobed petal tube. [× 5]

Ray floret seed. [× 10]

Seeds from the ray florets are oblong, those from the disc florets are heart-shaped.

Disc floret seed. [× 10]

The petals of the sneezewort add colour to damp grassland throughout Britain. The plant grows on acid or heavy soils.

Sneezewort *Achillea ptarmica*

Toothache sufferers in the Middle Ages often turned to this acrid, native plant to relieve their pain. According to the 17th-century herbalist Nicholas Culpeper they held the roots in their mouths and this helped the toothache 'by evacuating the rheum'. Culpeper also recommended sneezewort for those with stuffy heads, saying that 'the powder of the herb stuffed up the nose, causes sneezing, and cleanses the head'.

The name of the species, *ptarmica*, comes from the Greek word *ptarmos*, which means 'sneezing'. The plant was first recorded in England – in the fields of Kentish Town, now part of North London – by the 16th-century herbalist John Gerard, who said that its smell was enough to make a man sneeze.

Sneezewort is a greyish perennial with a creeping root. The flower-heads have greenish-white disc florets and 8–13 oval ray florets. Although the plant is mainly found growing wild, it has been cultivated in gardens for its attractive, creamy-white blooms. A larger variety with extra florets in the flower has been bred; it is known as 'bachelor's buttons'. The leaves of sneezewort – with their hot, biting taste – are sometimes used to counteract the 'coldness' in green salads.

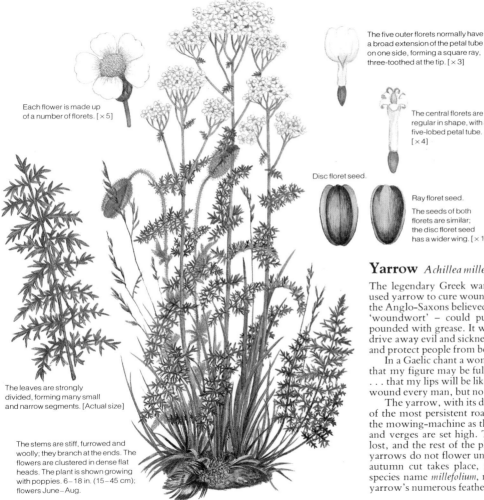

Each flower is made up of a number of florets. [× 5]

The five outer florets normally have a broad extension of the petal tube on one side, forming a square ray, three-toothed at the tip. [× 3]

The central florets are regular in shape, with a five-lobed petal tube. [× 4]

Disc floret seed.

Ray floret seed.

The seeds of both florets are similar; the disc floret seed has a wider wing. [× 10]

The leaves are strongly divided, forming many small and narrow segments. [Actual size]

The stems are stiff, furrowed and woolly; they branch at the ends. The flowers are clustered in dense flat heads. The plant is shown growing with poppies. 6–18 in. (15–45 cm); flowers June–Aug.

The flat white flower-heads of yarrow are common in hedges and on banks and roadsides throughout Britain.

Yarrow *Achillea millefolium*

The legendary Greek warrior-hero Achilles was said to have used yarrow to cure wounds made by iron weapons. In Britain, the Anglo-Saxons believed that the plant – sometimes known as 'woundwort' – could purge and heal such wounds, when pounded with grease. It was also used, especially in Ireland, to drive away evil and sickness; to increase physical attractiveness; and protect people from being hurt by the opposite sex.

In a Gaelic chant a woman says: 'I will pick the green yarrow that my figure may be fuller . . . that my voice will be sweeter . . . that my lips will be like the juice of the strawberry . . . I shall wound every man, but no man shall harm me.'

The yarrow, with its deep, water-gathering tap roots, is one of the most persistent roadside plants. Its basal rosette escapes the mowing-machine as the cutting-blades used on grass banks and verges are set high. This means that only the flowers are lost, and the rest of the plant remains and grows again. Also, yarrows do not flower until after the spring cut and, when the autumn cut takes place, most of the plants are seeding. The species name *millefolium*, meaning 'thousand leaf', refers to the yarrow's numerous feathery leaves.

Flower-head is flat and solitary with a yellow central disc and white rays which droop as the flower ages.

A hairless plant with upright or sprawling branched stems. The long leaves are deeply divided into numerous slender lobes. The terminal segments of the leaf end in a sharp point. The plant is seen growing with dandelion. 6–24 in. (15–60 cm); flowers July–Sept.

Corn chamomile
Anthemis arvensis

The leaves of this species are divided into broader segments than those of scentless mayweed and pineapple weed; the terminal segments are short and oblong, rather than long and pointed. This downy, slightly scented plant is common throughout Britain.

One side of the outer florets develops into a large, white, strap-like ray. [×5]

The central disc florets have five lobes at the top. [×5]

Seeds, which are almost oblong and up to twice as long as broad, have two dark brown oil glands at the top of the outer side. [×4]

This weed abounds on waste and cultivated land, and on sand, shingle, rocks and walls throughout Britain.

Scentless mayweed *Matricaria maritima*

Despite its name, scentless mayweed does not flower in May, but from July onwards. Its name is derived not from the month of May but from the Old English word for a maiden, and refers to the use once made of the plant for the treatment of female complaints. Similarly the generic name *Matricaria* comes from the Latin word *matrix*, 'a womb'. The species name *maritima* was given to the plant because the first specimen to be properly described was a fleshy-leaved form with larger flowers, which grew on the coast.

Scentless mayweed abounds in all sorts of disturbed areas. Frequently it colonises agricultural wasteland and new cuttings and embankments, especially on recently constructed motorways. Places like these provide ideal habitats for many annual and perennial weeds.

The species is so variable that different races can be recognised; some of these are almost certainly no more than the results of different environments, but others differ more fundamentally. Superficially, corn chamomile resembles scentless mayweed, although it has a faint smell; it grows in scattered localities throughout Britain, especially on chalky soils.

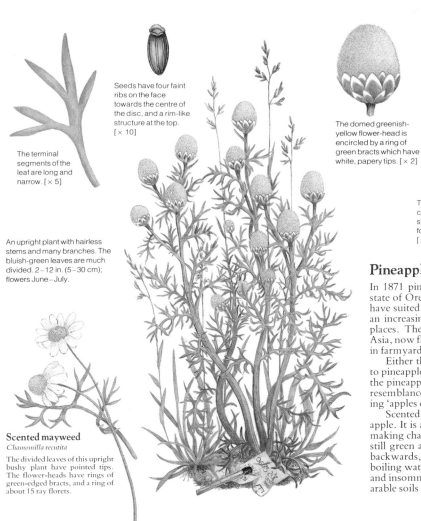

The terminal segments of the leaf are long and narrow. [× 5]

Seeds have four faint ribs on the face towards the centre of the disc, and a rim-like structure at the top. [× 10]

An upright plant with hairless stems and many branches. The bluish-green leaves are much divided. 2–12 in. (5–30 cm); flowers June–July.

The domed greenish-yellow flower-head is encircled by a ring of green bracts which have white, papery tips. [× 2]

The flower-head is composed solely of small disc florets with four-lobed tubes. [× 12]

Pineapple weed grows by the sides of roads and on waste places. It is increasingly common throughout Britain.

Scented mayweed
Chamomilla recutita

The divided leaves of this upright bushy plant have pointed tips. The flower-heads have rings of green-edged bracts, and a ring of about 15 ray florets.

Pineapple weed *Chamomilla suaveolens*

In 1871 pineapple weed was introduced into Britain from the state of Oregon in North America. Conditions in these islands have suited the plant well, for it has spread rapidly and become an increasingly abundant annual weed of waysides and waste places. The flower, which is probably a native of north-east Asia, now flourishes throughout Britain, especially on paths and in farmyards and trampled gateways.

Either the resemblance of the plant's rounded flower-heads to pineapples, or a strong aroma of pineapple or apple, has given the pineapple weed its name. The generic name confirms these resemblances: *Chamomilla* is derived from Greek words meaning 'apples on the ground'.

Scented mayweed has an even more pronounced scent of apple. It is also known as wild chamomile, and can be used for making chamomile tea. In July and August, when the bracts are still green and the white ray florets are just beginning to bend backwards, the flower-heads are picked, dried and infused in boiling water. The resultant tea is taken as a cure for indigestion and insomnia. Scented mayweed is common on sandy or loamy arable soils and in waste places throughout England and Wales.

343

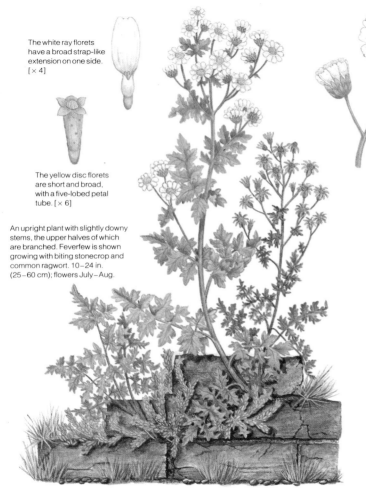

The white ray florets have a broad strap-like extension on one side. [× 4]

The yellow disc florets are short and broad, with a five-lobed petal tube. [× 6]

An upright plant with slightly downy stems, the upper halves of which are branched. Feverfew is shown growing with biting stonecrop and common ragwort. 10–24 in. (25–60 cm); flowers July–Aug.

The long-stalked flower-heads are surrounded by downy oblong or lance-shaped bracts.

The seeds are ribbed, with a short papery border. [× 10]

The white daisy-like flowers of feverfew adorn waste ground, hedgebanks and walls throughout most of Britain.

Feverfew *Tanacetum parthenium*

It is unlikely that feverfew – almost certainly an introduction from the Continent – would have come to Britain were it not for its value as a medicinal plant. The 17th-century herbalist Nicholas Culpeper stated that 'it grows wild in many places of the country, but is for the most part nourished in gardens'. The common name is derived from the Latin *febrifuga*, meaning that the plant was thought to be effective in driving away fevers.

The plant had many other medicinal uses too, for instance, as a remedy for headaches and as a cure for feminine complaints, especially those connected with childbirth. Culpeper wrote that it 'does a woman all the good she can desire of a herb'. The species name *parthenium* comes from the Greek *parthenos*, meaning 'maiden', which points to the plant's use against feminine ills. Some experts say, however, that the name is a reference to the plant's virginal white flowers.

Once grown commercially as a drug, feverfew is now regarded as no more than a noxious weed to be rooted out, but it is very persistent and hard to eradicate. It is especially common on walls, from where it spreads readily even though its seeds lack 'parachutes' of hairs to catch the wind.

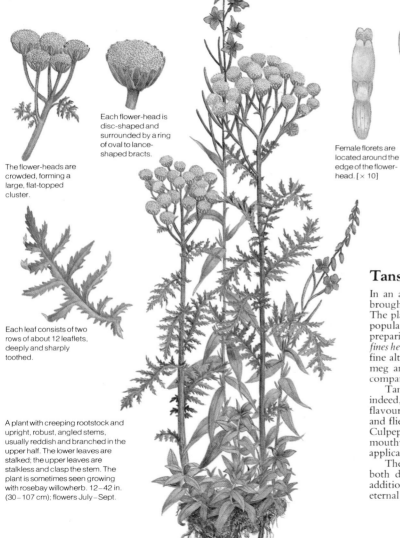

The flower-heads are crowded, forming a large, flat-topped cluster.

Each flower-head is disc-shaped and surrounded by a ring of oval to lance-shaped bracts.

Each leaf consists of two rows of about 12 leaflets, deeply and sharply toothed.

A plant with creeping rootstock and upright, robust, angled stems, usually reddish and branched in the upper half. The lower leaves are stalked; the upper leaves are stalkless and clasp the stem. The plant is sometimes seen growing with rosebay willowherb. 12–42 in. (30–107 cm); flowers July–Sept.

The seeds are oval and cylindrical, with five ribs. [× 10]

Female florets are located around the edge of the flower-head. [× 10]

The florets in the centre of the flower-head are bisexual. [× 10]

The bright yellow flowers of tansy are a familiar sight in waste places, roadsides and hedgebanks throughout Britain.

Tansy *Tanacetum vulgare*

In an age with a less-sensitive palate than the present, tansy brought together two arts: gardening and omelette-making. The plant's dark green leaves are strongly aromatic, and were popular as a flavouring, particularly for egg dishes. French chefs preparing an omelette used the leaves much in the same way as *fines herbes* today. When baking a cake, cooks regarded tansy as a fine alternative to very expensive imported spices such as nutmeg and cinnamon. At Easter, tansy cake was popular until comparatively recent times.

Tansy's spicy savour is too overwhelming for modern tastes; indeed, its scent is so strong that even at the time it was in use as a flavouring it was also used as a repellent, to keep mice from corn and flies from meat. In the 17th century the herbalist Nicholas Culpeper recommended it as a preventer of miscarriages, a mouthwash, an eye lotion, and a cosmetic, among many other applications.

The genus name *Tanacetum* and the common name tansy are both derived from the Greek word for immortality, for in addition to its other virtues, the plant was believed to confer eternal life on those who drank an infusion of it.

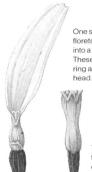

One side of the white florets is elongated into a tapered ray. These florets form a ring around the flower-head. [× 5]

The centre disc florets have five equal lobes to the petal tubes. [× 5]

The deeply divided upper leaves are often narrower than the lower ones, and their bases clasp the stem.

A sparsely hairy, or hairless, upright plant with large daisy-like flowers. The lower leaves are long-stalked and broadly toothed. The plant is shown growing with yarrow. 8–24 in. (20–60 cm); flowers June–Aug.

The ox-eye daisy grows on most moderately good soils. It is common in the south but rarer in Scotland.

Corn marigold
Chrysanthemum segetum

The corn marigold is shorter than the ox-eye daisy, reaching 6–18 in. (15–45 cm), and has bright yellow flower-heads. It is hairless, and its leaves are rather fleshy. It is an annual plant, thriving abundantly on newly cultivated land.

Ox-eye daisy *Leucanthemum vulgare*

Throughout the summer the ox-eye daisy transforms grassy areas, from meadows to railway embankments and roadsides, into graceful carpets of white and gold. It is also known as the marguerite, moon-daisy or dog-daisy. The flower-heads are solitary, and have an outer ring of white ray florets surrounding a central golden button of disc florets. They may be up to 2 in. (5 cm) in diameter. The plant has branched or unbranched stems, and glossy, dark green leaves.

In former times an extract obtained by boiling ox-eye daisies was used in salves and medicines to cure a variety of ailments, among them diseases of the chest and liver. Juice from the stems was used as drops for runny eyes.

The cultivated marguerite, or Shasta daisy (*Leucanthemum maximum*), is a related species from the Pyrenees. It has larger flower-heads than the ox-eye daisy, between 2 and 3 in. (5–7·5 cm) in diameter, and is widely grown in gardens. Another related species is the corn marigold, which grew abundantly in cornfields throughout Britain before selective weed-killers were introduced. Its seeds will lie dormant for years in undisturbed ground, flowering when the land is turned again.

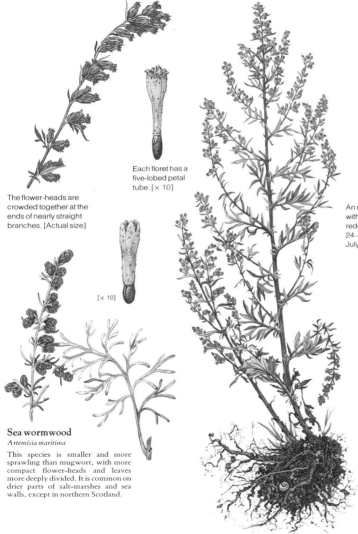

The flower-heads are crowded together at the ends of nearly straight branches. [Actual size]

Each floret has a five-lobed petal tube. [× 10]

[× 10]

The stem leaves are nearly stalkless, and clasp the stem; all leaves are covered with short, white, cottony hairs. [× 2]

An upright plant, often forming tufts, with sparsely hairy stems that are reddish, angled and grooved. 24–48 in. (60–120 cm); flowers July–Sept.

Mugwort is a plant of roadsides, waste places and hedgerows. It is common throughout the British Isles.

Mugwort *Artemisia vulgaris*

This dusty looking plant with its unromantic name seems ordinary enough, but it has often been written about by poets. For instance, Edward Thomas in *The Brook* described how 'there was a scent like honeycomb from mugwort dull' – a reference to the plant's aromatic odour. From Anglo-Saxon times, too, mugwort was associated with sorcery. On Midsummer's Eve it was said to secrete a 'coal' beneath its roots which would give protection from lightning, plague and carbuncles to anyone who dug it up and kept it. An old couplet tells of the plant's medicinal properties:

> If they'd drink nettles in March and mugwort in May,
> So many fine maidens would not turn to clay.

Mugwort has been used instead of hops to impart a bitter taste to beer. At the turn of the century Cornish folk made an infusion of its dried leaves when they could not afford tea. On the Continent today mugwort is used as a herb to stuff geese. It also serves as a moth repellent when laid in clothes.

Leaves of mugwort have also been burned to fumigate the sick-room, but it is only slightly aromatic compared with its pungent relative sea wormwood.

Sea wormwood
Artemisia maritima

This species is smaller and more sprawling than mugwort, with more compact flower-heads and leaves more deeply divided. It is common on drier parts of salt-marshes and sea walls, except in northern Scotland.

347

Oval seeds are fringed with short hairs. [×2]

Lower leaves are oblong-oval, nearly hairless on top and sparsely cottony underneath. The leaf-stalk is hollow.

The upright stems are furrowed, reddish and woolly, with several spreading branches. Leaves are arranged spirally up the stem. The plant is seen growing with grasses. 24–48 in. (60–120 cm); flowers July–Sept.

[×2]

Greater burdock
Arctium lappa

This is a larger, sturdier plant, with blunter-tipped and oval to heart-shaped lower leaves. The leaf stalk is long and solid, and the flower-heads are bigger. Each floret has a five-lobed petal tube, but unlike lesser burdock, the narrow waist of the tube is longer than the upper part.

The red-purple florets have a five-lobed petal-tube, broad at the top with a narrow waist of equal length beneath. [×2]

Stalkless flowers form a short-stalked head with rings of hooked bracts surrounding it. [×2]

This familiar plant of waste ground, road-sides, dry woods and clearings is common in all parts of the British Isles.

Lesser burdock *Arctium minus*

The vigorous aspect and broad leaves of burdock made it a favourite plant of landscape painters for adding foreground colour and perspective. The 17th-century herbalist Nicholas Culpeper wrote of it as being well known to small boys, who threw the bur-like buds and flower-heads at one another in play. They stick to clothing and also to animal fur, for the bracts are hooked. In this way the seeds may be spread over large areas. The adhesive habit of the burs accounts for many of the folk-names of this plant, which include 'bachelor's buttons' and 'sticky buttons'.

Burdock and its relatives, such as greater burdock, had less frivolous roles to play as well. Medicinally, they were nothing if not versatile. The juice was said to counteract the bites of snakes and rabid dogs, to soothe burns, and the flow of urine; the leaves were applied to sores and ulcers; and the seeds were prescribed for sciatica. The young stalks of burdock, peeled and chopped, found their way into the kitchen as a salad ingredient, or boiled and eaten with melted butter, or added to meat broth. Its large leaves have led the plant to be mistaken for rhubarb, and account for its alternative name of wild rhubarb.

The very spiny leaf-base clasps the stem, and the leaf edges run into the stem wing. [Actual size]

The fawn seed is covered in crosswise wrinkles. It has a parachute of whitish hairs. [× 2]

This upright, very prickly plant has a cottony, branched stem with a spiny wing all the way up except for a short section just below the flower-heads. All leaves are dissected and spiny. 12–48 in. (30–120 cm); flowers June–Aug.

Florets are reddish-purple or white, the petal tube being divided into five lobes. [× 2]

Each upright flower-head is egg-shaped and surrounded by narrow bracts, each ending in a weak spine. There are normally three to five flower-heads in a group. [Actual size]

The light green stems and leaves of this thistle are common in damp, grassy places in southern Britain.

Musk thistle

Carduus nutans

This relative of welted thistle has more deeply dissected leaves and longer spines. The big, drooping, cup-shaped flowers are usually solitary; they have a surround of spiny bracts, the outer ones bent backwards.

Welted thistle *Carduus acanthoides*

Difficult though it is to distinguish between the different kinds of thistle, the welted thistle presents fewer problems than most. It does not have strong spines, and its leaf blades are wide and soft. This is an unusual, if not unique, feature among thistles. Another tell-tale feature is the wing, or welt, that runs down the stem, giving the plant its common name.

As with several other species of thistle the flowers provide food, in the form of nectar, for many sorts of butterfly, including the rare painted lady. On a sunny day in high summer it is not unusual to see clouds of butterflies rising from clumps of welted thistle. The welted thistle favours damp, lowland countryside. The musk thistle, on the other hand, prefers higher, drier, chalky soils; it gets its name from the strong musky odour of its flowers.

Man has never regarded thistles as much more than a nuisance. Few had any medicinal value attributed to them in past times. Stories that the seeds of the welted thistle, with their silky plumes, were used to stuff pillows and mattresses are hard to credit, for it would take an enormous number of seeds to fill the smallest pillow adequately.

349

Smooth, dark brown seed has a parachute of long, brownish hair. [× 5]

Male flower-head and floret.

Flower-heads have numerous florets, surrounded by spine-tipped bracts closely pressed to the heads. [Actual size]

Female flower-head and floret.

Spear thistle
Cirsium vulgare

Spiny leaf-bases partly wing the stem of this upright plant. Flower-heads are usually bigger than those of the creeping thistle. Spine-tipped bracts, surrounding each flower-head, stick outwards.

Bases of upper leaves clasp the stem.

The roots of this creeping plant shoot up furrowed, upright stems to form large clumps. Spiny leaves are oblong to lance-shaped. 12–60 in. (30–152 cm); flowers July–Sept.

Often a troublesome weed, creeping thistle is abundant all over Britain in fields, roadsides and waste places.

Creeping thistle *Cirsium arvense*

The flowers of the creeping thistle have a sweet, musky odour which is most attractive to butterflies – including the rare painted lady. In midsummer, clouds of butterflies of many types can be seen feeding from the flowers of this thistle, and they are the usual pollinators of the plant. Most plants of the creeping thistle produce only male or female flowers. In order for seed to be produced, male and female plants have to be growing close enough together for a butterfly to be able to transfer pollen from one to the other.

This thistle does not depend only on seed for reproduction, however, but also spreads by means of the creeping root system, which sends up new plants some distance away from the parent plant. This causes problems for farmers and gardeners who find the thick, white growth hard to eradicate as it is resistant to weed-killers and very hard to dig up.

Creeping thistle is sometimes attacked by the thistle gall fly, which lays its eggs in the stem near the top of the plant. The plant then produces an oval gall, or swelling, around the eggs. There are several chambers within the gall, each containing a single egg. A larva emerges from each hatched egg.

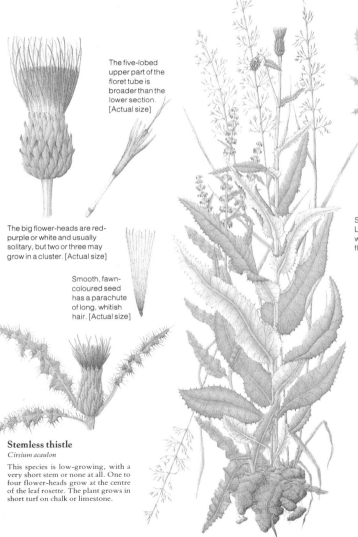

The five-lobed upper part of the floret tube is broader than the lower section. [Actual size]

The big flower-heads are red-purple or white and usually solitary, but two or three may grow in a cluster. [Actual size]

Smooth, fawn-coloured seed has a parachute of long, whitish hair. [Actual size]

Stemless thistle
Cirsium acaulon

This species is low-growing, with a very short stem or none at all. One to four flower-heads grow at the centre of the leaf rosette. The plant grows in short turf on chalk or limestone.

Some leaves may be dissected, with two rows of lobes.

Stem upright, mostly unbranched. Leaves lance-shaped, undersides white. 18–48 in. (45–120 cm); flowers July–Aug.

An upland plant of damp meadows, scrub and open woodland, this thistle grows from Scotland to South Wales.

Melancholy thistle *Cirsium helenium*

Drooping buds that stir in the wind give the melancholy thistle a rather sad appearance, which gave the plant its name and also suggested to early herbalists, on the principle of like driving away like, that it would provide a cure for melancholia. The Greek physician Dioscorides, who wrote five books on medicine, considered that the thistle made an effective charm against sadness, and in the 17th century Nicholas Culpeper claimed that a potion made by steeping the leaves of the plant in wine 'expels superfluous Melancholy out of the Body, and makes a man as merry as a cricket'.

The thistle, which has no prickles on the stem, has a white underside to its leaves which gave rise to its alternative name of 'fish belly'. It has been familiar for centuries in damp places, in mountainous regions and in grassy, limestone areas. Yet it was not officially recorded until the 16th century, after the French nature writer Charles de l'Ecluse had been told of its 'discovery' in Ingleborough in North Yorkshire.

The low-growing stemless thistle, also known as the dwarf or ground thistle, is common in northern England and in parts of north Wales, especially on grazing land.

Flower-heads are in clusters of two to five, and have two rings of bracts. The outer bracts are lance-shaped and cottony with a green or purple tinge, and a spine at the top. The inner bracts are narrow, straw-yellow in colour and are usually seen spread out.

The old flower-spikes can be seen for many months after the seed has dispersed.

A stiff, upright plant with a branched, flowering stem. The broad-based leaves clasp the stem and are lobed and divided; the lobe margins bear many weak spines. The leaves have soft prickles. 4–24 in. (10–60 cm); flowers July–Oct.

The floret consists of a five-lobed petal tube. [× 4]

The seed is crowned by a parachute of many-branched, rust-coloured hairs. [× 2]

This yellow-flowered thistle grows in grassland and scrub, mainly on chalk or limestone, throughout lowland Britain.

Carline thistle *Carlina vulgaris*

When the army of the 8th-century Frankish king Charlemagne was stricken with plague, it is said that he prayed to God for help. An angel carrying bow and arrows appeared and told the monarch to shoot an arrow: the plant upon which the missile landed would cure the disease. The arrow came to rest on this plant, which from then on was known as the 'carolina', or 'carline thistle', a corruption of Charlemagne's name. It has camphor-like properties, and was later used by herbalists as an antiseptic.

In Anglo-Saxon times, the thistle was known as 'boar's throat' because the prickly appearance of the flower-heads was thought to resemble the rough hair around a boar's throat. At that period it was used as a charm against bad luck and ill health. The flowers expand in dry weather and close in moist weather, and in some country areas they were pinned over cottage doors to be consulted as a kind of barometer. They are also used in dried flower arrangements.

Carline thistle sometimes grows on dry, sandy and lime-rich pastureland. It is difficult to eradicate, and has caused trouble and expense to farmers.

352

The stem is covered with white, woolly hairs and is winged along its length; the wing bears strong spines, and the edges of the leaves are joined to the wing.

Florets are pale purple, or occasionally white. The petal tube has five long, thin lobes. [× 2]

The grey-brown seed has a ladder-like pattern of wrinkles, and a parachute of pale red or brownish hairs, up to twice the length of the seed. [× 2]

This large plant has an upright stem, with short branches rising from above the middle. The stalkless leaves are large, cottony on both sides, and have lobes bearing strong spines. 18–60 in. (45–152 cm); flowers July–Sept.

Flower-head is large and usually solitary. The green rings of bracts are cottony and tipped with large yellowish spines, which may be bent back.

Despite its other name of Scottish thistle, this robust plant is more often seen in England and Wales.

Cotton thistle *Onopordon acanthium*

As the heraldic emblem of Scotland, the cotton thistle – also known as the Scottish thistle – has a long ancestry. The early kings of Scotland used the thistle as their personal heraldic device; but it had been accepted as a national emblem by 1503, when William Dunbar wrote a poem called *The Thistle and the Rose* to celebrate the marriage of King James III of Scotland to Princess Margaret of England. In 1687 James II instituted the Order of the Thistle as a distinctively Scottish order of knight-hood. This order is now the oldest of all surviving British orders of knighthood except the Order of the Garter.

Its symbolic importance apart, many different practical uses have been found for the cotton thistle. On the Continent, an oil made from its seeds is used for cooking and as a fuel for lamps. In 16th-century England, the cotton fibres and down from the stem were collected for stuffing mattresses and pillows.

The cotton thistle has also been used as a medicine and as a food. Herbalists once believed that a concoction made from the plant's stem cured cancer, rickets and nervous complaints. Whether or not they have any curative effect, the stems can certainly be peeled and boiled, then eaten with butter.

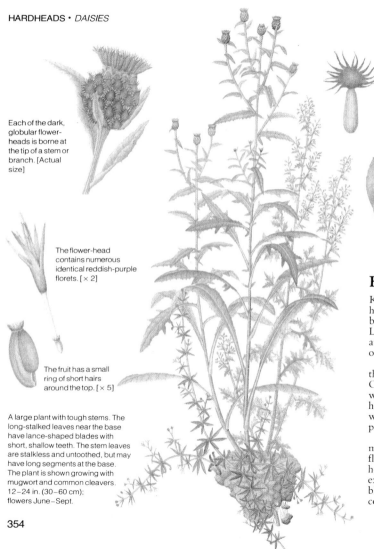

Each of the dark, globular flower-heads is borne at the tip of a stem or branch. [Actual size]

The flower-head contains numerous identical reddish-purple florets. [× 2]

The fruit has a small ring of short hairs around the top. [× 5]

A large plant with tough stems. The long-stalked leaves near the base have lance-shaped blades with short, shallow teeth. The stem leaves are stalkless and untoothed, but may have long segments at the base. The plant is shown growing with mugwort and common cleavers. 12–24 in. (30–60 cm); flowers June–Sept.

Overlapping bracts cover the lower part of each flower-head. Each bract has a feathery, dark brown or blackish appendage.

The grooved stem is scattered with rough hairs. [× 2]

Hardheads, or black knapweed, is found on waysides throughout Britain. It is also common on grasslands and cliffs.

Hardheads *Centaurea nigra*

Knob-like flower-heads have given this plant its names of hardheads and knapweed – 'knap' meaning a knob – and their blackish patterning is responsible for the species name of *nigra*, Latin for 'black'. The generic name of *Centaurea* was probably attached to the plant because Chiron, wisest among the centaurs of Greek myth, was said to use the plant to heal wounds.

The anthers of hardheads develop before the stigmas, and so the flowers progress from a male phase to a female phase. Occasionally both anthers and stigmas are fertile at once, and when this occurs the flowers can pollinate themselves. Usually, however, they are cross-pollinated by the many different insects which visit them. The seeds, attached to hairs which form tiny parachutes, are later dispersed by the wind.

According to folklore, hardheads can be used to foretell a maiden's future. A girl must pick the expanded florets off a flower-head, then put the remainder of the flower-head inside her blouse. After an hour she should take it out again and examine it: if the previously unexpanded florets have now blossomed, it is a sure sign that the man she will marry is shortly coming her way.

Each of the flower-heads is borne at the tip of a stem or branch. The florets are reddish-purple; those on the outer row are larger than the others, and rather spreading.

Inner florets are long and slender. [× 2]

The fruit is crowned with stiff, whitish hairs about the same length as the fruit itself. [× 2]

An upright, hairy plant, usually branched above the middle. The lower leaves are stalked, and have blades divided into numerous toothed segments. Upper leaves are similar but stalkless. Up to 12–36 in. (30–90 cm); flowers July–Sept.

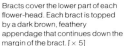

Bracts cover the lower part of each flower-head. Each bract is topped by a dark brown, feathery appendage that continues down the margin of the bract. [× 5]

The grooved stem is scattered with hairs. [× 2]

This thistle-like plant is found on roadsides, dry grassland and cliffs throughout Britain, especially on chalky soils.

Greater knapweed *Centaurea scabiosa*

It is easy to confuse greater knapweed with hardheads, since both have flower-heads shaped like knobs, which gave knapweed its common name. Greater knapweed is a larger plant, but perhaps the best way to distinguish the two is to compare the shapes of the bracts which enclose the flower-heads. The appendages which top the bracts of hardheads are triangular or circular, whereas those of greater knapweed are shaped like horseshoes. Since the bracts of greater knapweed do not overlap completely the pale green bases of the bracts can be seen.

According to the 17th-century herbalist Nicholas Culpeper, greater knapweed 'is good for those who are bruised by any fall, blows, or otherwise, by drinking a decoction of the herb roots in wine, and applying the same outwardly to the place'. For years the plant was used to treat wounds, ruptures, bruises, sores, scabs and sore throats.

The medicinal properties of the plant partly explain its scientific name, for *scabiosa* comes from a Latin word meaning an irritating roughness of the skin. Another reason suggested for this name is that greater knapweed resembles and often grows alongside the plant called scabious.

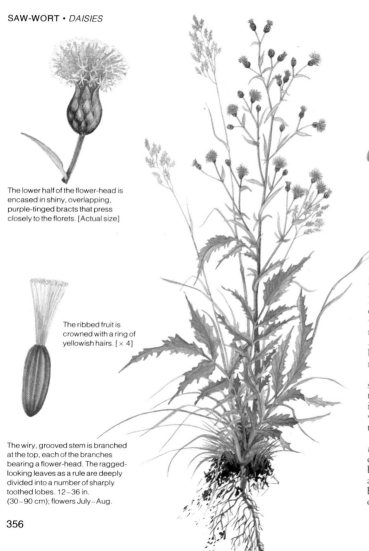

The lower half of the flower-head is encased in shiny, overlapping, purple-tinged bracts that press closely to the florets. [Actual size]

The ribbed fruit is crowned with a ring of yellowish hairs. [× 4]

The wiry, grooved stem is branched at the top, each of the branches bearing a flower-head. The ragged-looking leaves as a rule are deeply divided into a number of sharply toothed lobes. 12–36 in. (30–90 cm); flowers July–Aug.

The purplish florets have a five-lobed petal tube. All florets in the flower-head are alike. [× 2]

This plant is found in clearings and rides in woods, along woodland edges, and in grassy places on chalky soil.

Saw-wort *Serratula tinctoria*

Like woad and dyer's greenweed, saw-wort was once an ingredient of dye. Its leaves were mixed with alum, and the resulting yellow-green dye was used to colour woollen cloth. The species name *tinctoria* is Latin for 'pertaining to dyers'. The generic name *Serratula* is derived from a Latin word meaning 'a little saw', and both this and the plant's common name describe the toothed margins of the leaves.

The toothed leaves caused herbalists to recommend crushed saw-wort for healing wounds: the ancient 'doctrine of signatures' held that the shape of a plant, or part of a plant, indicated its usefulness in relieving the sufferings of mankind. Saw-wort was also regarded as good for checking dysentery, vomiting and the flow of blood.

Of about 40 different species belonging to the genus *Serratula*, saw-wort is the only one to be found in Britain. It grows in damp meadows and open woods, usually in lowland districts, but nowhere in Britain is it very common. The plant is similar in appearance to the knapweeds, to which it is closely related; it can be distinguished from them by the absence of fringes or prickles on the overlapping bracts that surround each flower-head.

The flower-heads are borne in clusters of two or three in the angles of the upper leaves and stems. [× 2]

The stiff, grooved stems have branches rising at a steep angle. The stalked lower leaves may be toothed, or more deeply divided into triangular lobes. The upper leaves are stalkless, with the base clasping the stem. The plant is shown growing beside the white flowers of yarrow. 12–48 in. (30–120 cm); flowers July–Oct.

The bright blue florets have the petal tube extended to form a long strap. [× 5]

The fruit is crowned with a ring of ragged-edged scales. [× 10]

Chicory grows in fields and on roadsides, especially on chalky soils in England and Wales; it is rare in Scotland.

Chicory *Cichorium intybus*

For at least three centuries the leaves of this native of the Orient have been prized in continental Europe as a vegetable and as animal fodder. However, it is the thick, fleshy roots that are the main reason for growing chicory: they are dried, roasted, ground, and then either added to some blends of coffee to strengthen the flavour, or used on their own as a coffee substitute. Chicory seeds are sometimes sown with grass-seed mixtures for the beneficial effect that the long, penetrating tap roots of the chicory plants have in breaking up the soil.

Chicory, or wild succory as it is sometimes known, has a very long flowering season, and may be seen still blooming in late autumn when most summer flowers have long since faded. Normally, only a few of the flowers are in bloom at any one time. They open with the sun in the morning and close about midday; in dull weather they stay closed. This habit led country folk to believe that water distilled from the flowers was good for dim sight and inflammation of the eyes.

The cultivated endive, *Cichorium endivia* ssp. *endivia*, widely grown as a salad ingredient, may be told from chicory by its less deeply lobed leaves and its larger fruits.

357

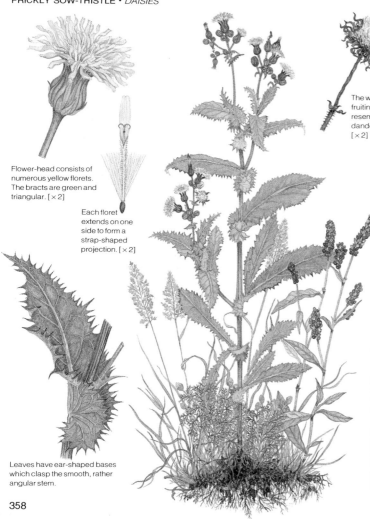

Flower-head consists of numerous yellow florets. The bracts are green and triangular. [×2]

Each floret extends on one side to form a strap-shaped projection. [×2]

Leaves have ear-shaped bases which clasp the smooth, rather angular stem.

The white, fluffy fruiting head resembles a small dandelion 'clock'. [×2]

The brown fruit is crowned with a ring of long hairs. [×2]

An upright plant with few branches. The lower leaves are spiny-toothed and curled at the margins, and narrowed into stalks at the base. Flower-heads are clustered. The plant is shown growing with redshank and pineapple weed. 8–60 in. (20–152 cm); flowers June–Aug.

This weed is widespread throughout Britain. It is found near walls, and on dunes and disturbed ground.

Prickly sow-thistle *Sonchus asper*

It was once believed that the juice which flows from cuts in the stem or root of the prickly sow-thistle increased the milk yield of sows. Even nursing mothers were said to benefit from drinking the white milky fluid or latex. This latex is also produced by dandelions, to which the prickly sow-thistle is related, and by a large group of plants within the daisy family, including lettuce and chicory.

The prickly leaves, which resemble those of the true thistle, may deter some animals from eating this plant. The leaves are glossy green, unlike the dark grey-green leaves of the commoner smooth sow-thistle, with which it often grows. The young leaves of prickly sow-thistle are quite succulent in spite of their spiny teeth, and have been used in salads or as pot-herbs.

Prickly sow-thistle flourishes wherever man has disturbed the soil – in gardens, on waste ground or among crops. Both the prickly and smooth sow-thistles are visited by insects, particularly bees and hoverflies, which pollinate the flowers. Each fruit is surrounded by two rows of white hairs which act as parachutes and carry the seeds in the breeze long distances away from the parent plants.

The brown fruit is crowned with a ring of long hairs. [×2]

An upright plant with few branches. Lower leaves have a triangular terminal lobe, with two or more oval lobes beneath. The stalk is winged. The plant is seen growing with cocksfoot, field pennycress and red dead-nettle. 8–60 in. (20–152 cm); flowers June–Aug.

All leaves have spiny-toothed, uncurled margins and two projections at the base which clasp the smooth stem. Upper leaves are stalkless.

Floret forms a strap-like projection on one side, lighter yellow than that of prickly sow-thistle. [×2]

The flowering and fruiting head consists of many yellow florets. The bracts which cover the lower part of the flower-head are green and triangular. [×2]

Smooth sow-thistle is a common weed of waste and cultivated land and roadsides, often growing by walls.

Smooth sow-thistle *Sonchus oleraceus*

According to the Roman historian Pliny the Elder, a dish of the strength-giving smooth sow-thistles was eaten by the legendary Greek hero Theseus before he slew the Minotaur – the creature, part man, part bull, that lived in a Cretan labyrinth. For centuries, the leaves of the plant have been boiled like spinach, or taken raw in winter salads.

As well as humans, animals have fed upon the leaves, and the plant has such local names as 'rabbit's meat', 'swine thistle', 'dog's thistle' and 'hare's lettuce'. Traditionally, the leaves are thought to revive and strengthen such creatures when they are overcome by heat, or – in the case of the supposedly gloomy hare – stricken with melancholy.

The 17th-century botanical writer William Coles said that sows, because of 'a certain natural instinct', knew that the juice in the plant's hollow stems would increase their milk yield after they had given birth to a litter of pigs. Smooth sow-thistle flourishes on most soils, including those which have been disturbed or burned. It was one of the first plants to grow in the new earth raised from the Pacific Ocean after an earthquake in Hawkes Bay, New Zealand, in 1931.

YELLOW-FLOWERED DAISIES

In such a large flower family as the daisies, many members are superficially alike. Those with yellow flowers can be told apart by the arrangement of their flower-heads, the pattern of their lower leaves, and their fruits.

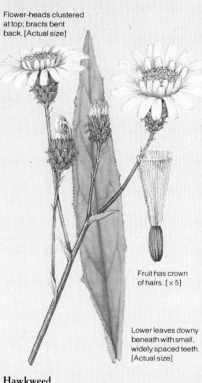

Flower-heads clustered at top; bracts bent back. [Actual size]

Fruit has crown of hairs. [× 5]

Lower leaves downy beneath with small, widely spaced teeth. [Actual size]

Hawkweed
Hieracium umbellatum Page 367

Many small flower-heads; bracts erect. [Actual size]

Fruit has no crown or parachute of hairs. [× 5]

Lower leaves have toothed terminal lobes; smaller lobes below. [Actual size]

Nipplewort
Lapsana communis Page 362

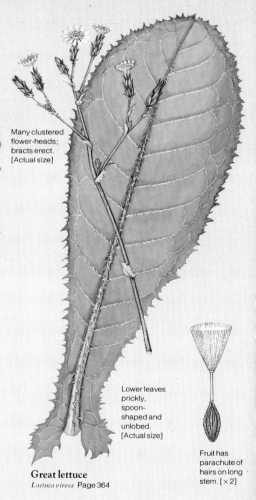

Many clustered flower-heads; bracts erect. [Actual size]

Lower leaves prickly, spoon-shaped and unlobed. [Actual size]

Fruit has parachute of hairs on long stem. [× 2]

Great lettuce
Lactuca virosa Page 364

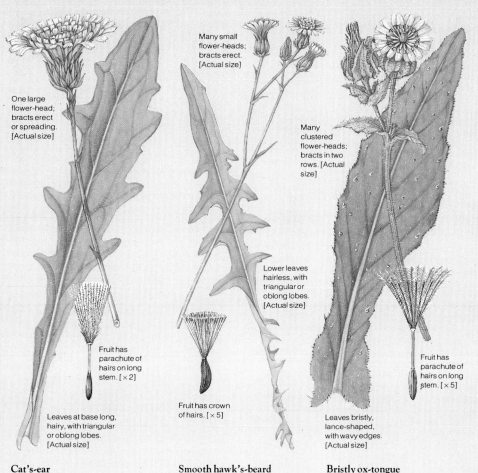

One large flower-head; bracts erect or spreading. [Actual size]

Many small flower-heads; bracts erect. [Actual size]

Many clustered flower-heads; bracts in two rows. [Actual size]

One large flower-head; outer bracts spreading, inner bracts erect. [Actual size]

Fruit has parachute of hairs on long stem. [×2]

Lower leaves hairless, with triangular or oblong lobes. [Actual size]

Leaves at base long, hairy, with triangular or oblong lobes. [Actual size]

Fruit has crown of hairs. [×5]

Fruit has parachute of hairs on long stem. [×5]

Leaves bristly, lance-shaped, with wavy edges. [Actual size]

Fruit has parachute of hairs on long stem. [×2]

Leaves hairless, with triangular, toothed lobes. [Actual size]

Cat's-ear
Hypochoeris radicata Page 366

Smooth hawk's-beard
Crepis capillaris Page 365

Bristly ox-tongue
Picris echioides Page 363

Dandelion
Taraxacum officinale Page 368

361

The numerous flower-heads, each ringed by lance-shaped bracts, form many-branched clusters.

The petal tube of the floret is extended on one side to form a five-toothed strap. [× 5]

The fruits are brown, ribbed and curved, and do not have a crown of hairs at the top. [× 5]

An upright plant with the stem much branched above the middle. Branches grow upwards at a steep angle. The upper leaves are broadly oval with toothed margins and short stalks. The plant is shown growing with herb-robert and grasses. 8–36 in. (20–90 cm); flowers July–Sept.

The lower leaves have a large, toothed terminal lobe with several smaller lobes, or a wing, along the stalk below it.

Nipplewort is a common plant of road-sides, waste ground, hedges and wood margins throughout Britain.

Nipplewort *Lapsana communis*

The so-called 'doctrine of signatures' is typified in the powers men have attributed to this plant, which takes its very name from the resemblance of its closed buds to nipples. This similarity led to the ancient belief that the plant would cure sore or ulcerated nipples. In the 16th century, Prussian apothecaries prescribed nipplewort for such diseases and called it *papillaris*, from the Latin word *papilla*, or 'teat'.

Nipplewort is a native plant, which is known to have been growing in Britain in Stone Age times. Its pale yellow flower-heads are rather insignificant, particularly as they are open for only part of the day, closing in the middle of the afternoon and not opening at all in bad weather. Bees and flies pollinate the flowers, but if pollination is unsuccessful, self-pollination may sometimes occur.

The nipplewort's slender, wiry and hollow stems are very tough, with none of the milky sap found in many other plants of the daisy family. A leaf discoloration sometimes occurs due to attack by a fungus, *Puccinia lapsanae*. In country areas, nipplewort is often known as 'dockorene', and at one time was eaten in salads. It is sometimes found growing as a garden weed.

Each flower-head is ringed by many slender bracts, surrounded in turn by three to five broad, curved triangular bracts. [Actual size]

The yellow florets have the petal tube extended on one side to form a strap with five small teeth at the tip. The outermost florets are purplish on the outside. [× 4]

The stems, leaves and flower-heads of this tall, irregularly branched plant are covered with stiff bristles. The leaves are lance-shaped, with wavy edges, the lower ones narrowing into a short stalk. The plant is shown growing with common nettle. 12–36 in. (30–90 cm); flowers June–Oct.

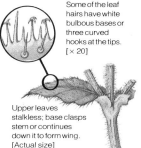

Some of the leaf hairs have white bulbous bases or three curved hooks at the tips. [× 20]

Upper leaves stalkless; base clasps stem or continues down it to form wing. [Actual size]

This plant is locally common in lowland England, Wales and southern Scotland on roadsides and waste ground.

Bristly ox-tongue *Picris echioides*

Bristle-like hairs growing from small white spots on the leaves make this plant easily identifiable. It is a fairly robust plant, which is found most commonly in hedgebanks and in field borders in the south of England. The short-stalked flower-heads are large and bright yellow in colour, growing in irregular clusters at the top of the stem. The fruiting head looks like a small dandelion 'clock'.

Bristly ox-tongue is a close relative of the sow thistles, for which it is often mistaken because of its similar appearance, but is less common. Its generic name, *Picris*, is derived from the Greek word for 'bitter' and refers to the sticky white juice which exudes from the broken stem and has an extremely bitter taste. The species name, *echioides*, refers to the leaves and stems which are rough and prickly. Despite their unpalatable appearance, however, they were once eaten after being boiled and were said to have a pleasant taste. They were also used for making pickle.

A related plant, hawkweed ox-tongue, *Picris hierocioides*, is as common as bristly ox-tongue and grows in similar habitats. It can be distinguished from bristly ox-tongue by its flower-heads, which have smaller, narrower bracts covered in blackish hairs.

363

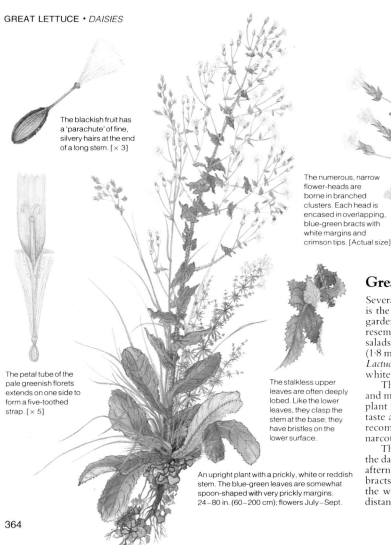

The blackish fruit has a 'parachute' of fine, silvery hairs at the end of a long stem. [× 3]

The petal tube of the pale greenish florets extends on one side to form a five-toothed strap. [× 5]

The stalkless upper leaves are often deeply lobed. Like the lower leaves, they clasp the stem at the base; they have bristles on the lower surface.

The numerous, narrow flower-heads are borne in branched clusters. Each head is encased in overlapping, blue-green bracts with white margins and crimson tips. [Actual size]

An upright plant with a prickly, white or reddish stem. The blue-green leaves are somewhat spoon-shaped with very prickly margins. 24–80 in. (60–200 cm); flowers July–Sept.

Great lettuce prefers chalky soils, and is found in grassy areas by roads and canals. It often occurs near the sea.

Great lettuce *Lactuca virosa*

Several species of wild lettuce grow in Britain, and great lettuce is the most common. It is not known from which species the garden lettuce came, but certainly the great lettuce bears little resemblance to the plant which has so long been a favourite in salads. For one thing, it can reach a height of well over 6 ft (1·8 m). Both the common name of lettuce and its generic name, *Lactuca*, derive from the Latin word for milk, and refer to the white juice that flows from the stems when they break.

The species name *virosa* also refers to the juice of the plant, and means 'poisonous'. It has a hot and bitter taste – indeed, the plant is sometimes known as acrid lettuce for this reason. Both taste and smell reminded herbalists of opium, leading them to recommend an infusion of the plant in wine as a pain-killer and narcotic.

The pale greenish–yellow flowers are open for only part of the day, opening late in the morning and closing during the early afternoon. Tiny 'parachutes' of hairs form on the fruits; the bracts then curl back, allowing the fruits to be wafted away by the wind, so dispersing the seeds they contain a considerable distance from the parent plant.

Flower-heads are borne in branched clusters. Each head is surrounded by two rows of lance-shaped bracts, the outer row being much shorter than the inner. [Actual size]

A rosette of lower leaves surrounds the stems. The lower leaves are long, slender, and divided into triangular lobes. 8–36 in. (20–90 cm); flowers June–Sept.

The petal tube of the bright yellow florets extends on one side to form a five-toothed strap. The outermost florets are often reddish beneath. [× 5]

The fruit is ribbed and crowned with a 'parachute' of soft, white hairs. [× 5]

Smooth hawk's-beard grows in pastures and other grassy areas, and on heaths and waste places throughout Britain.

Smooth hawk's-beard *Crepis capillaris*

The small size of the bright yellow flower-heads of smooth hawk's-beard distinguishes it from other hawk's-beards; they measure just over ½ in. (1·3 cm) across and are the smallest flowers of the species. Of several different types of hawk's-beards growing in the British Isles, smooth hawk's-beard is the most common; it appears in meadows and waysides and sometimes on walls and on the roofs of cottages.

The flower-heads bloom at the beginning of June and continue in blossom well into the autumn. They appear in loose bunches at the ends of green or purplish stems, and attract many bees and flies. The small forms of the plant that are found on heaths frequently lack stem leaves. After pollination, fruits develop which are compressed at the top, giving the fruiting head a distinctive triangular shape. The tuft of hairs that surrounds each fruit catches the wind, so encouraging the dispersal of the seeds within the fruit.

A related species called pink hawk's-beard, *Crepis rubra*, bears numerous pale pink flowers, deepening at the centres. The plant came to Britain from south-eastern Europe, and is often cultivated in gardens.

The orange fruit has a parachute of unbranched hairs and feathery hairs at the end of the long stem. The surface of the fruit is scaly. [×2]

The stem below the flower-heads bears numerous tiny, dark, scale-like bracts. [×2]

The overlapping bracts of the flower-heads are bristly along the midribs. [Actual size]

The yellow floret has the petal tube elongated on one side to form a five-toothed strap. [×2]

The hairy leaves radiate from the base of the stem; they are wavy and edged with oblong or triangular teeth. The sparingly branched stem carries several flower-heads. 8–24 in. (20–60 cm); flowers June–Sept.

Cat's-ear brightens pastures, grassy dunes and waysides throughout Britain; but it also invades lawns.

Cat's-ear *Hypochoeris radicata*

The cheerful bright yellow flower-heads of cat's-ear, up to 1½ in. (4 cm) across, are displayed from June onwards and attract many kinds of insects, particularly bees. The flower flourishes in meadows and fields, on waste ground and along roadsides. It has wiry stems, roughly hairy leaves, and a very long, unbranched root which is white and exudes a milky sap if broken.

The plant's generic name, *Hypochoeris*, comes from two Greek words: *hypo* meaning 'under', and *choiros*, 'a pig', because pigs are said to relish the plant's roots as food. The species name, *radicata*, refers to the leaves which are said by botanists to be 'radical' because they all arise from the root. The English name, cat's-ear, was given because it was thought that the small scale-like bracts dispersed spirally up the flower-stems resembled the ears of a cat. Gardeners are not fond of the plant as its hairy leaves evade the lawn-mower, and the flower-stems often have to be removed by hand.

Two other species of cat's-ear grow in the British Isles – the smooth cat's-ear *Hypochoeris glabra*, and the spotted cat's-ear, *Hypochoeris maculata*. But these are far less widespread than the common cat's-ear.

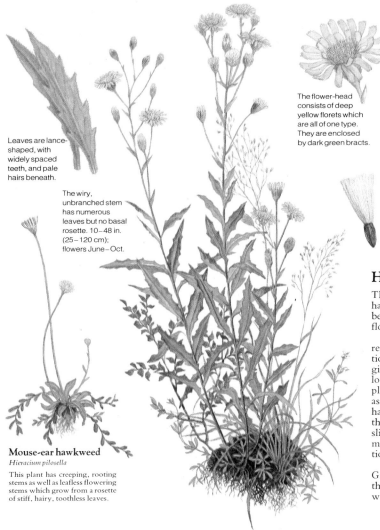

Leaves are lance-shaped, with widely spaced teeth, and pale hairs beneath.

The flower-head consists of deep yellow florets which are all of one type. They are enclosed by dark green bracts.

The wiry, unbranched stem has numerous leaves but no basal rosette. 10–48 in. (25–120 cm); flowers June–Oct.

The floret has the petal tube extended on one side to form a five-toothed strap. [×2]

The ribbed fruit is crowned with a ring of long hairs mingled with shorter, stiffer hairs. [×5]

Hedges, roadsides and open woods are the likeliest places to spot hawkweed, which is common in lowland areas.

Mouse-ear hawkweed
Hieracium pilosella

This plant has creeping, rooting stems as well as leafless flowering stems which grow from a rosette of stiff, hairy, toothless leaves.

Hawkweed *Hieracium umbellatum*

This tall, erect plant is one of the most widespread species of hawkweed found in the British Isles. As with many plants belonging to the daisy family, the fairly large, bright yellow flower-heads close up in the early afternoon.

Many species of hawkweed have an unusual method of reproduction. Most of their seed is produced without fertilisation – by a process known as apomixis. As a result each plant can give rise to a line of true-breeding descendants, and plants in one locality tend to look the same as each other, but different from plants in other localities. It is possible to treat these populations as individual species, and some botanists recognise about 300 hawkweed species in the British Isles, and possibly 20,000 throughout the world. The differences between the species is so slight, however, that only an expert can tell them apart. The mouse-ear hawkweed has a more normal method of reproduction, and recognition of this species is easier.

The plant's botanical name, *Hieracium*, comes from the Greek *hierax*, meaning 'a hawk'. It was believed in olden days that hawks ate the plant to obtain the milky juice contained within, which sharpened their eyesight.

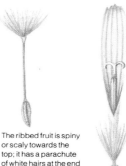

The ribbed fruit is spiny or scaly towards the top; it has a parachute of white hairs at the end of a long stem. [× 2]

On one side of the bright yellow florets the petal tube extends to form a five-toothed strap. [× 2]

In April and May dandelions show their golden heads in abundance in grassland and on banks and waste ground.

Long leaves are deeply divided into triangular, often toothed lobes and form a flat rosette at the base of the plant. Several long-stalked flower-heads may grow upright from the rosette. 2–12 in. (5–30 cm); flowers Mar–Oct.

Dandelion *Taraxacum officinale*

The resemblance of the sharp, pointed lobes of dandelion leaves to the teeth of a lion give the flower its common name. Dandelion is a corruption of the French words *dent de lion*, or 'lion's tooth'. It is one of the most common weeds in Britain, and a constant source of annoyance to gardeners. Yet growing wild it can be seen as a beautiful plant, and its sun-like flower-heads bloom early in the year when little else is on show.

The flower-heads contain up to 200 individual florets, which close up at night or in dull weather, or if picked and put in a vase. Generations of children have 'told the time' by counting the number of puffs needed to blow away all the fruits on their small parachutes – and so have unwittingly helped the plant to disperse its seeds.

In the past, dandelion drinks and broths were recommended for a variety of illnesses, from jaundice to consumption. Although no longer used medicinally, the plant still has its uses. The leaves have a high content of vitamins A and C and, when young, are tasty in salads. A delicious country wine can be made from the florets, and the dried and ground roots can be used as a coffee substitute.

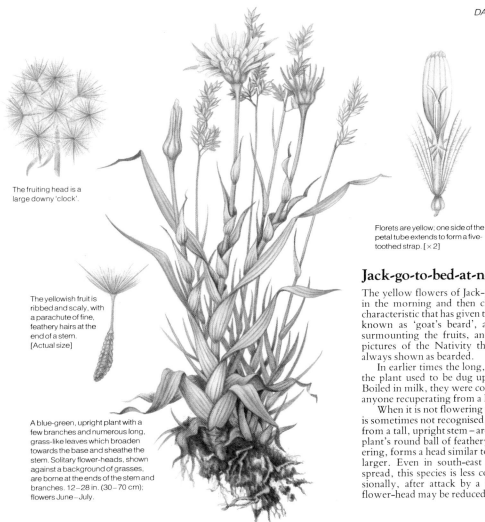

The fruiting head is a large downy 'clock'.

The yellowish fruit is ribbed and scaly, with a parachute of fine, feathery hairs at the end of a stem. [Actual size]

A blue-green, upright plant with a few branches and numerous long, grass-like leaves which broaden towards the base and sheathe the stem. Solitary flower-heads, shown against a background of grasses, are borne at the ends of the stem and branches. 12–28 in. (30–70 cm); flowers June–July.

Florets are yellow; one side of the petal tube extends to form a five-toothed strap. [× 2]

Jack-go-to-bed-at-noon grows by roadsides, on waste ground and dunes, and in meadows and grassland.

Jack-go-to-bed-at-noon *Tragopogon pratensis*

The yellow flowers of Jack-go-to-bed-at-noon open very early in the morning and then close around midday – an unusual characteristic that has given the plant its common name. It is also known as 'goat's beard', after the tufts of long silky hairs surmounting the fruits, and as 'Joseph's flower', because in pictures of the Nativity the husband of the Virgin Mary is always shown as bearded.

In earlier times the long, brown, sweet-tasting tap-roots of the plant used to be dug up, cooked, and eaten like parsnips. Boiled in milk, they were considered to be an excellent tonic for anyone recuperating from a long illness.

When it is not flowering or in fruit, Jack-go-to-bed-at-noon is sometimes not recognised, as its long, narrow leaves – arising from a tall, upright stem – are very grass-like in appearance. The plant's round ball of feathery fruits, which develops after flowering, forms a head similar to the familiar dandelion 'clock', but larger. Even in south-east England, where it is most widespread, this species is less common than the dandelion. Occasionally, after attack by a fungus called *Ustilago tragopogi*, a flower-head may be reduced to a mass of black powder.

369

The flower parts are arranged in threes; each of the lilac or white petals has a yellow blotch at the base. [× 2]

The numerous flattened seeds are arranged in a flat-headed fruit. [× 5]

Seed [× 5]

The stout stem is much branched at the top, each branch bearing many flowers. 8–40 in. (20–100 cm); flowers June–Aug.

The long-stalked flowers are arranged in whorls around the stem and branches, with several small, pointed bracts at the base of each whorl.

Water-plantain grows in mud by ponds and slow-flowing rivers throughout Britain, except in the extreme north.

Arrowhead
Sagittaria sagittifolia

A plant with large, arrow-head-shaped leaves above water, and flowers which are twice the size of those of water-plantain. There are few flower whorls; the lower ones consist of female flowers, and the upper ones of male flowers. 12–36 in. (30–90 cm); flowers July–Aug.

Water-plantain *Alisma plantago–aquatica*

When in flower the water-plantain makes an impressive show, its tall, graceful flowering stems growing up above the leaves and bearing a pyramid of numerous delicate, pale lilac blooms. The flowers remain closed all morning, opening at the beginning of the afternoon and shutting again in the early evening. Each flower secretes several tiny droplets of nectar in a ring at the base of the stamens. Flies, attracted by these, become covered with pollen as they move from drop to drop, helping to pollinate the flower as they do so.

In spite of its name, this plant is no relative of the plantains; it is so called because of the similarity of its leaves to those of some species of plantains. The base of the stem appears almost bulb-like, because of the thick, fleshy stalks of the broad, oval leaves which arise from it.

Arrowhead grows in habitats similar to those of the water-plantain, but its distribution is more scattered. The leaves below the surface in water-growing plants are long and slender. Others that float on the surface are broader, and very like those of water-plantain; but it is the leaves that grow clear of the water, with their distinctive shape, that give the plant its name.

The flower parts are arranged in threes. The sepals are smaller and narrower than the petals. [× 2]

The sepals and petals persist around the fruit, which is divided into six segments. [× 3]

An upright plant with unbranched stems, here seen growing alongside reedmace. The leaves grow in a rosette from the base. Up to 60 in. (152 cm); flowers July–Aug.

The long, slender, greyish-green leaves are triangular in cross-section. [× 2]

Flowers form a single cluster at the top of each stem. The flower-stalks are of unequal length and grow from the same point on the stem.

This typical plant of water-margins is locally common in England, rare in Wales and absent from Scotland.

Flowering-rush *Butomus umbellatus*

A splash of magnificent pink, dark-veined flowers beside still or running water indicates the presence of a clump of graceful flowering-rush. It grows naturally in most parts of Europe, but its beauty has led to its being cultivated in gardens. *Butomus* is not a true rush; it is, in fact, one of a kind – the only species of its genus. Its common name probably derives from a habit of growing in wet places, alongside the grass-like true rushes. The long, slender leaves, too, are rush-like, growing to about the same height as the flowers. The leaves are often twisted, with the bases sheathing the stem.

The flowering-rush has underground creeping stems called rhizomes. These remain alive during the winter, and from them spring the flowering stems and basal leaves. *Butomus* is therefore a perennial. In parts of Russia the fleshy rhizomes are eaten.

The flowering stem, or scape, is leafless; though at the base of the flower-head there are several leaf-like bracts. Both leaves and stems are smooth and hairless. There are between six and nine stamens on each flower, which is bisexual. After pollination the style remains attached to the developing fruit until it is ripe. Each of the segments of the fruit contains many tiny seeds.

371

The flower parts are arranged in threes. The petals and inner surface of the sepals are a translucent white. They open wide as the flower matures. [× 5]

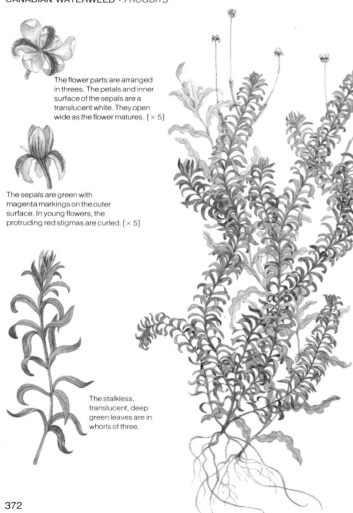

The sepals are green with magenta markings on the outer surface. In young flowers, the protruding red stigmas are curled. [× 5]

The stalkless, translucent, deep green leaves are in whorls of three.

The plant's leafy stems are completely submerged and grow roots along their lengths. Canadian waterweed often grows with the paler-leaved curled pondweed. Stems extend to 36 in. (90 cm); flowers July – Sept.

The flowers of the Canadian waterweed decorate slow-moving fresh water. It is widespread throughout Britain.

Canadian waterweed *Elodea canadensis*

This invader from Canada spread so luxuriantly when it first gained a foothold in Britain that it blocked the Thames in several places. It first appeared in Europe in 1836, when it was recorded in Ireland, and by 1842 it was spreading across the lake of Duns Castle in Berwickshire. Thereafter its progress was aided by botanists, who had no inkling of how explosive its growth would be.

In 1849 a small scrap was introduced into an aquarium in the Oxford Botanic Garden; it soon escaped to thrive and proliferate in the ditches and ponds around the city, and nine years later the plant was growing profusely in the Thames as far downstream as Reading. When the river started to become blocked with long stems, alarm was felt about the damage that might be caused; but, in fact, the danger was almost over.

By the late 1860s the plant's remarkable expansion was coming to an end; nobody knows why. Nowadays it is widespread in ponds, streams, rivers and ditches all over the British Isles, but seldom in such quantities as to cause a serious nuisance. Nevertheless its formidable reputation lives on in the name it won in Worcestershire – 'drain devil'.

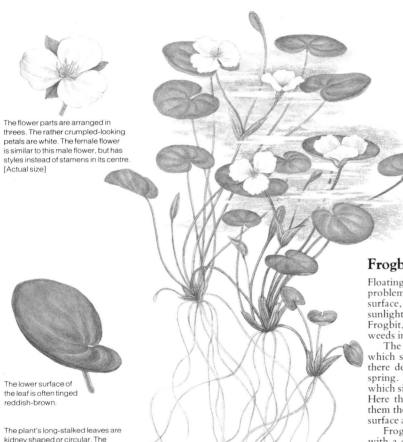

The flower parts are arranged in threes. The rather crumpled-looking petals are white. The female flower is similar to this male flower, but has styles instead of stamens in its centre. [Actual size]

The fruit is smooth, oval and dark green. [Actual size]

The floating frogbit holds its flowers above the water in ponds and ditches. It grows in chalky places.

The lower surface of the leaf is often tinged reddish-brown.

The plant's long-stalked leaves are kidney shaped or circular. The flowers are long-stalked, with two to three males in a cluster and the females solitary. Both leaves and roots are bunched at the nodes of the stem. Flowers July–Aug.

Frogbit *Hydrocharis morsus-ranae*

Floating water-weeds growing in still water are faced with a problem of survival in the British winter. To remain on the surface, where they need to float in summer to catch the sunlight, means likely destruction by ice in hard weather. Frogbit, which is one of the few fairly large, floating water-weeds in Britain, solves the problem in two ways.

The first method of ensuring survival is to produce seeds which sink to the bottom of the pond or lake in autumn and there develop into young plants; these rise to the surface in spring. The second method is to grow special winter buds, which sink and become buried in the comparatively warm mud. Here they remain dormant until the warmth of spring gives them the signal to grow into tiny plantlets, which float up to the surface and begin a new season's life.

Frogbit has a relative called water soldier (*Stratiotes aloides*), with a different survival technique. In late summer its leaves become covered with a chalky substance, which eventually becomes so heavy that the whole plant sinks to the bottom. In spring new leaves are formed without the chalky coating; the plant is now lighter and buoyant, and it rises to the surface.

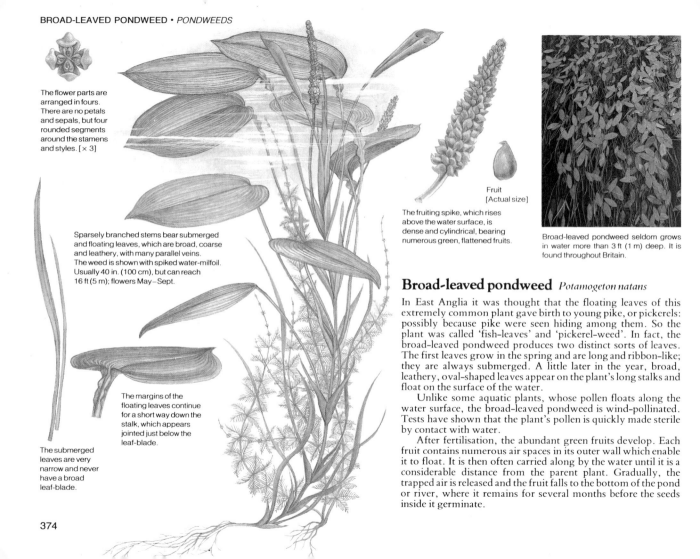

The flower parts are arranged in fours. There are no petals and sepals, but four rounded segments around the stamens and styles. [× 3]

Sparsely branched stems bear submerged and floating leaves, which are broad, coarse and leathery, with many parallel veins. The weed is shown with spiked water-milfoil. Usually 40 in. (100 cm), but can reach 16 ft (5 m); flowers May–Sept.

The margins of the floating leaves continue for a short way down the stalk, which appears jointed just below the leaf-blade.

The submerged leaves are very narrow and never have a broad leaf-blade.

Fruit [Actual size]

The fruiting spike, which rises above the water surface, is dense and cylindrical, bearing numerous green, flattened fruits.

Broad-leaved pondweed seldom grows in water more than 3 ft (1 m) deep. It is found throughout Britain.

Broad-leaved pondweed *Potamogeton natans*

In East Anglia it was thought that the floating leaves of this extremely common plant gave birth to young pike, or pickerels: possibly because pike were seen hiding among them. So the plant was called 'fish-leaves' and 'pickerel-weed'. In fact, the broad-leaved pondweed produces two distinct sorts of leaves. The first leaves grow in the spring and are long and ribbon-like; they are always submerged. A little later in the year, broad, leathery, oval-shaped leaves appear on the plant's long stalks and float on the surface of the water.

Unlike some aquatic plants, whose pollen floats along the water surface, the broad-leaved pondweed is wind-pollinated. Tests have shown that the plant's pollen is quickly made sterile by contact with water.

After fertilisation, the abundant green fruits develop. Each fruit contains numerous air spaces in its outer wall which enable it to float. It is then often carried along by the water until it is a considerable distance from the parent plant. Gradually, the trapped air is released and the fruit falls to the bottom of the pond or river, where it remains for several months before the seeds inside it germinate.

Curled pondweed is widespread and common throughout Britain. It grows in ponds, streams and canals.

The flower parts are arranged in fours; the petal-like segments are larger than in broad-leaved pondweed. [× 3]

The fruiting spike is roughly oval, with a curved stem. The fruits have a prominent beak which is as long as the rest of the fruit. [× 2]

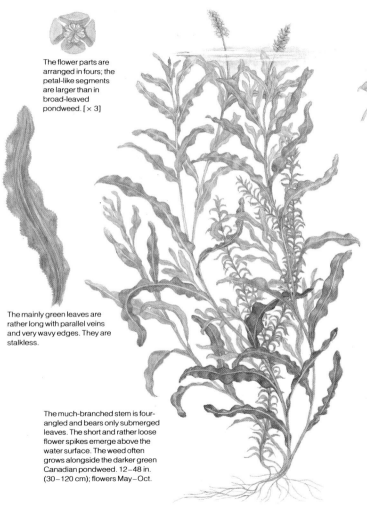

The mainly green leaves are rather long with parallel veins and very wavy edges. They are stalkless.

The much-branched stem is four-angled and bears only submerged leaves. The short and rather loose flower spikes emerge above the water surface. The weed often grows alongside the darker green Canadian pondweed. 12–48 in. (30–120 cm); flowers May–Oct.

Curled pondweed *Potamogeton crispus*

With its twin rows of delicate, shiny and translucent leaves, curled pondweed is easily the most beautiful water-weed in Britain. It grows in still and slow-moving water and its many-forked stems make good hiding places for fish – some of which, such as carp, feed upon the plant. Crustaceans also eat the thin, wavy-edged leaves.

Although the submerged leaves are usually a pale green, they are sometimes brown or reddish; this depends upon the depth of water in which the plant is growing. The plant's first botanical name, *Potamogeton*, comes from two Greek words – *potamos*, meaning 'river', and *geiton*, 'neighbour' – a reference to the watery habitat in which the curled pondweed grows. The species name *crispus* refers to the curled leaves.

Curled pondweed is one of some 24 different water-weeds found in Britain. The plants are sometimes extremely difficult to tell apart. However, the stems and leaves can vary greatly, according to the depth and movement of the water and the age of the individual plant. Other distinguishing features are the various vein patterns and shapes of the tips of the leaves. Even so, identification remains a problem, due to the numerous hybrids.

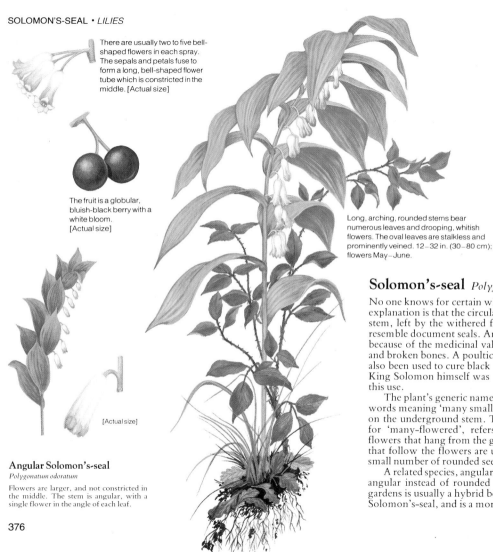

There are usually two to five bell-shaped flowers in each spray. The sepals and petals fuse to form a long, bell-shaped flower tube which is constricted in the middle. [Actual size]

The fruit is a globular, bluish-black berry with a white bloom. [Actual size]

Long, arching, rounded stems bear numerous leaves and drooping, whitish flowers. The oval leaves are stalkless and prominently veined. 12–32 in. (30–80 cm); flowers May–June.

[Actual size]

Angular Solomon's-seal
Polygonatum odoratum

Flowers are larger, and not constricted in the middle. The stem is angular, with a single flower in the angle of each leaf.

Solomon's-seal is a woodland plant found in most parts of England and Wales, but is common only in the south.

Solomon's-seal *Polygonatum multiflorum*

No one knows for certain why Solomon's-seal is so called. One explanation is that the circular scars on the underground rooting stem, left by the withered flowering shoots of previous years, resemble document seals. Another theory is that the name arose because of the medicinal value of the plant in 'sealing' wounds and broken bones. A poultice made from its powdered roots has also been used to cure black eyes and other bruises. The biblical King Solomon himself was traditionally said to have approved this use.

The plant's generic name *Polygonatum* is derived from Greek words meaning 'many small joints', and alludes to the swellings on the underground stem. The species name *multiflorum*, Latin for 'many-flowered', refers to the little clusters of tubular flowers that hang from the gracefully curving stems. The fruits that follow the flowers are unpleasant-tasting. Each contains a small number of rounded seeds.

A related species, angular Solomon's-seal, which is rarer, has angular instead of rounded stems. The plant seen growing in gardens is usually a hybrid between Solomon's-seal and angular Solomon's-seal, and is a more vigorous plant than its parents.

376

The three sepals and petals are fused to form a short, bell-shaped flower tube. [× 2]

Lily-of-the-valley grows wild in dry woods on chalky soils in England, parts of Wales and scattered localities in Scotland.

The fruits are bright red, globular berries. [Actual size]

The leaves are broad, oval and rather leathery. The flowering stem has numerous, drooping white flowers, all hanging on the same side of the stem. Lily-of-the-valley spreads principally by means of rhizomes, or underground rooting stems. 6–8 in. (15–20 cm); flowers May–June.

Lily-of-the-valley *Convallaria majalis*

This beautifully named plant is a familiar sight in British gardens, but it also grows wild, forming large patches of pure white on the woodland floor. It first blooms in May, when the nodding, bell-shaped flowers begin to exude their delightful sweet scent to attract insects. If they are not successfully pollinated in this way, the plants can pollinate themselves.

Fruits are not often produced, and the plant spreads mainly by sending up new shoots from its creeping rootstock. However, scarlet berries do sometimes develop early in the autumn.

Lily-of-the-valley has been cultivated for more than 500 years, its broad leaves making useful ground cover for shady parts of a garden. The virginal colour of the flowers was supposed to represent purity, but this was also believed to be an unlucky plant – it was said that anyone who planted it would die within a year. The flowers still impart their fragrance to perfumes and soaps, and were once also used as an ingredient of snuff. Medicinal properties, too, were attributed to the plant. According to the 16th-century herbalist John Gerard, 'it without doubt strengthens the brain, and renovates a weak memory'. Other herbalists prescribed it for eye inflammations.

377

The fruit is a capsule surrounded by the remains of the flower. It contains brown seeds with a tail at either end. [× 2]

Long, slender, often curved leaves rising from the base of the plant surround the upright, leafy stem, which has a flower spike at the top. It is shown growing with cotton grass. 2–16 in. (5–40 cm); flowers July–Sept.

Stem leaves are much shorter than those growing from the base and sheathe the stem. [Actual size]

After flowering, the petals, sepals, ovary and flower-stalk all take a deep orange colour. [× 2]

The petals and sepals are similar and the six stamens are woolly with orange tips. [× 2]

Bog asphodel is a plant of bogs, moors and mountain places in Britain, except for south-eastern England.

Bog asphodel *Narthecium ossifragum*

In the 16th century, the women of Lancashire collected bog asphodel from the moors and used it to dye their hair yellow. This gave it the local name of maiden hair. The attraction of the plant is understandable, for in July the fragrant flowers are a mass of golden-yellow on the bogs and green moors. In autumn the fruits cloak the bogs in a deep orange mantle. It also grows in mountainous districts, and has been recorded at altitudes above 3,000 ft (900 m).

Bog asphodel grows on wet ground and sends out thick, underground stems, which spread easily in the loose soil and form large patches. After flowering, the fruit capsules develop, and contain several pale yellow seeds with long tails at each end which help the seeds to float during periods of flooding.

The second part of the plant's name, *ossifragum*, comes from two Latin words meaning 'bone-breaking'. The name was given because it was once thought that bog asphodel was the cause of cruppany, or brittleness of the bones, in sheep that ate it. This has been shown to be untrue, and it is probable that the bone weakness is caused by the absence of mineral salts in the soil where the plant grows.

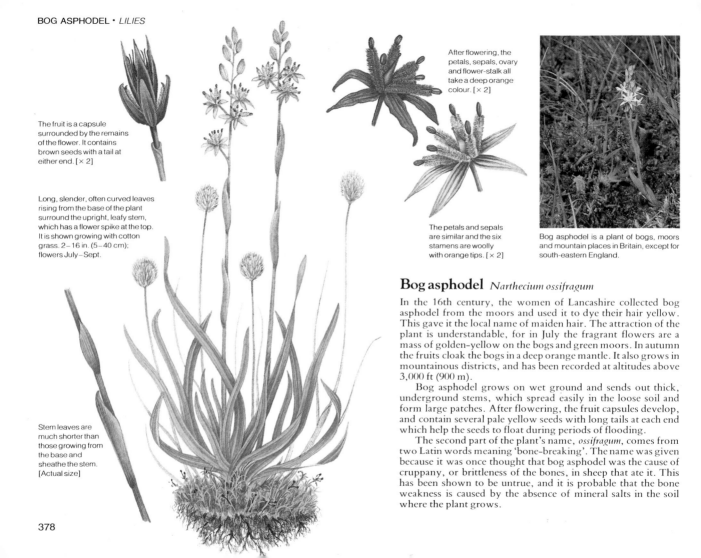

378

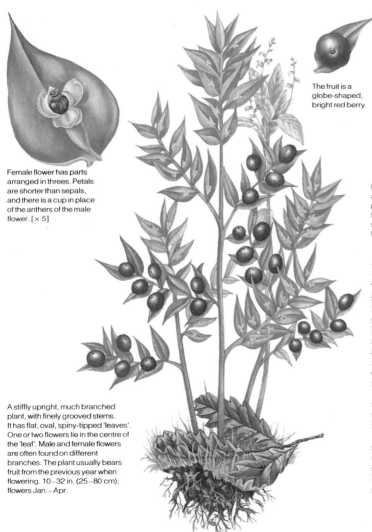

Female flower has parts arranged in threes. Petals are shorter than sepals, and there is a cup in place of the anthers of the male flower. [× 5]

The fruit is a globe-shaped, bright red berry.

Male flowers have a similar arrangement of sepals and petals to that of the female flower, but the central globe-shaped structure bears three anthers. [× 5]

Butcher's-broom grows mainly among rocks and in dry woods throughout southern England and Wales.

A stiffly upright, much branched plant, with finely grooved stems. It has flat, oval, spiny-tipped 'leaves'. One or two flowers lie in the centre of the 'leaf'. Male and female flowers are often found on different branches. The plant usually bears fruit from the previous year when flowering. 10–32 in. (25–80 cm); flowers Jan.–Apr.

Butcher's-broom *Ruscus aculeatus*

There are few stranger plants in Britain than butcher's-broom. It is unlike most others because it has no true leaves; instead, it has leaf-like structures which are really flattened stems. These stems, which botanists call cladodes, have evolved to function as leaves in creating energy to fuel the plant's life processes. They are dark green, thick and rigid, and since they are not shed in the autumn, butcher's-broom appears to be evergreen. The tiny male and female flowers are borne on the cladodes in the angles of small papery bracts. If the greenish flowers have been pollinated, large red berries develop containing the seeds.

Butcher's-broom is so colourful that it is often dried and used to decorate homes during the winter months. It is sometimes also planted in shrubberies. As with asparagus, to which it is closely related, the young shoots can be eaten as a vegetable.

According to tradition, bundles of mature branches were sold to butchers for sweeping their blocks, so giving the plant its common name. The 17th-century herbalist Nicholas Culpeper suggested that drinking a potion made from the roots of butcher's-broom, and using a poultice made from the berries and leaves, helped broken bones to knit together.

379

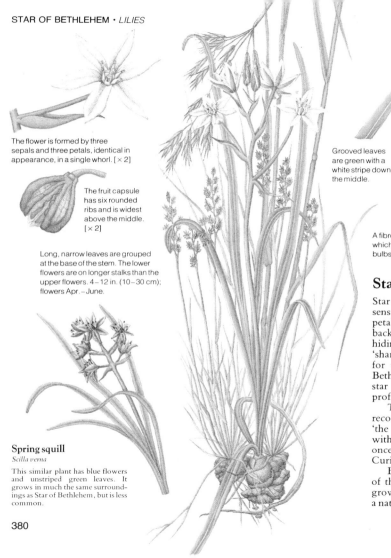

The flower is formed by three sepals and three petals, identical in appearance, in a single whorl. [× 2]

The fruit capsule has six rounded ribs and is widest above the middle. [× 2]

Long, narrow leaves are grouped at the base of the stem. The lower flowers are on longer stalks than the upper flowers. 4 – 12 in. (10 – 30 cm); flowers Apr. – June.

Spring squill
Scilla verna

This similar plant has blue flowers and unstriped green leaves. It grows in much the same surroundings as Star of Bethlehem, but is less common.

Grooved leaves are green with a white stripe down the middle.

A fibrous sheath covers the bulb, which grows bulbils, or smaller bulbs, round its base. [Actual size]

The Star of Bethlehem is a delicate flower scattered in grassy places in England and Wales, but found rarely in Scotland.

Star of Bethlehem *Ornithogalum umbellatum*

Star of Bethlehem is one of nature's shyest plants. Ultra-sensitive to the level of light, it curls up its pretty, star-like petals, which are white but have a central green stripe down the back, after the middle of the day or earlier if the sky is overcast, hiding its face from the world. 'Betty-go-to-bed-at-noon', 'shamefaced maiden' and 'eleven o'clock lady' are all local names for the plant that reflect this behaviour. The name Star of Bethlehem is a reference not only to its shape – it is likened to the star of the Nativity – but also to the fact that it grows in profusion in Palestine.

The 17th-century British medical writer William Salmon records in his *Pharmacopoeia Londoniensis*, published in 1678, that 'the root serves for meat or food being roasted in embers, mixt with honey'. In the Middle East, pilgrims journeying to Mecca once carried dried Star of Bethlehem bulbs to eat on the way. Curiously, however, the raw bulbs are poisonous to cattle.

Botanists are uncertain whether Star of Bethlehem is a native of the British Isles; in the Breckland district of East Anglia it grows in such quantities that it is difficult to believe that it is not a native plant. In plant lore, it is a symbol of purity.

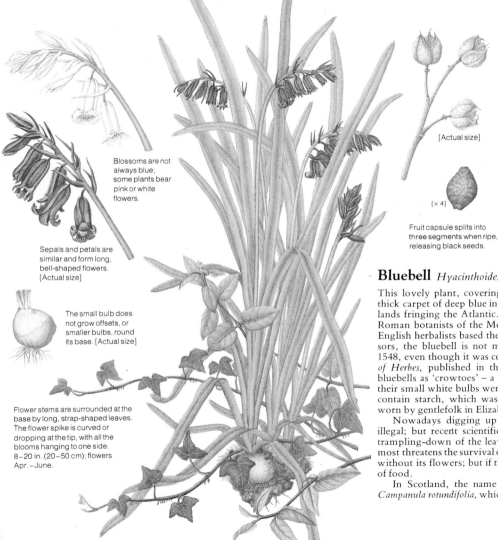

Blossoms are not always blue; some plants bear pink or white flowers.

Sepals and petals are similar and form long, bell-shaped flowers. [Actual size]

The small bulb does not grow offsets, or smaller bulbs, round its base. [Actual size]

Flower stems are surrounded at the base by long, strap-shaped leaves. The flower spike is curved or dropping at the tip, with all the blooms hanging to one side. 8–20 in. (20–50 cm); flowers Apr.–June.

[Actual size]

[× 4]

Fruit capsule splits into three segments when ripe, releasing black seeds.

Bluebells are common in most parts of Britain, blooming in woods, hedges and scrubland, on sea-cliffs and mountains.

Bluebell *Hyacinthoides non-scriptus*

This lovely plant, covering Britain's woodland floors with a thick carpet of deep blue in the springtime, is native only to the lands fringing the Atlantic. It was unknown to the Greek and Roman botanists of the Mediterranean world; and as the early English herbalists based their work on these classical predecessors, the bluebell is not mentioned in British herbals before 1548, even though it was certainly abundant then. In his *Names of Herbes*, published in that year, William Turner refers to bluebells as 'crowtoes' – a common folk-name – and says that their small white bulbs were used to make glue. The bulbs also contain starch, which was used to stiffen the elaborate ruffs worn by gentlefolk in Elizabethan times.

Nowadays digging up bluebell bulbs for any purpose is illegal; but recent scientific research has shown that it is the trampling-down of the leaves by heavy-footed sightseers that most threatens the survival of the bluebell. The plant can survive without its flowers; but if the leaves are crushed, it dies for lack of food.

In Scotland, the name bluebell is given to the harebell, *Campanula rotundifolia*, which has paler, less curved petals.

381

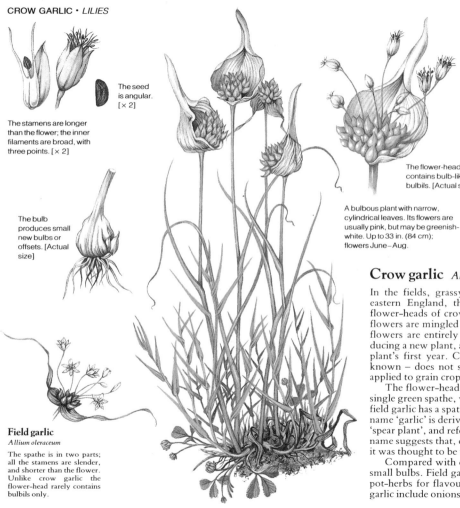

The stamens are longer than the flower; the inner filaments are broad, with three points. [× 2]

The seed is angular. [× 2]

The bulb produces small new bulbs or offsets. [Actual size]

The flower-head usually contains bulb-like bulbils. [Actual size]

A bulbous plant with narrow, cylindrical leaves. Its flowers are usually pink, but may be greenish-white. Up to 33 in. (84 cm); flowers June–Aug.

Crow garlic is a troublesome weed of fields and grassy banks in England and Wales, but is rarer in Scotland.

Crow garlic *Allium vineale*

In the fields, grassy banks and hedgerows of southern and eastern England, the stiff, upright stems and purplish-pink flower-heads of crow garlic are a common sight. Usually, the flowers are mingled with tiny bulbs, or bulbils. Sometimes the flowers are entirely replaced by bulbils, each capable of producing a new plant, although they are too small to flower in the plant's first year. Crow garlic – or wild onion, as it is often known – does not succumb to the usual selective weedkillers applied to grain crops, so farmers regard it as a serious pest.

The flower-heads of crow garlic are initially protected by a single green spathe, which becomes papery as it opens; whereas field garlic has a spathe in two parts, each with a long point. The name 'garlic' is derived from two Anglo-Saxon words meaning 'spear plant', and refers to the shape of the leaves. The common name suggests that, compared with its relative cultivated garlic, it was thought to be worthless – fit only for crows.

Compared with cultivated garlic, the wild garlics have very small bulbs. Field garlic and crow garlic have both been used as pot-herbs for flavouring meat dishes. Other relatives of crow garlic include onions, chives, leeks and shallots.

Field garlic
Allium oleraceum

The spathe is in two parts; all the stamens are slender, and shorter than the flower. Unlike crow garlic the flower-head rarely contains bulbils only.

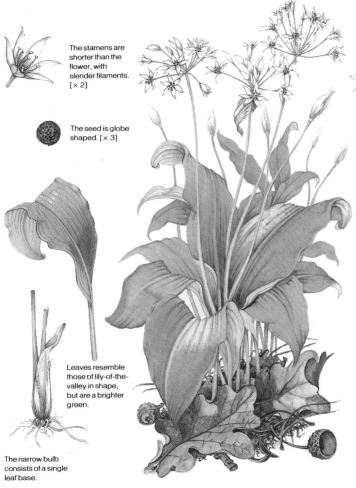

The stamens are shorter than the flower, with slender filaments. [× 2]

The seed is globe shaped. [× 3]

Leaves resemble those of lily-of-the-valley in shape, but are a brighter green.

The narrow bulb consists of a single leaf base.

Flower-head contains flowers only, never bulbils. [Actual size]

A bulbous plant with white flowers and broad, flat leaves; it is often seen growing in large clumps. Up to 18 in. (45 cm); flowers Apr.–Aug.

Ramsons grows in woods and shady places throughout Britain; in the north it may grow in more exposed parts.

Ramsons *Allium ursinum*

At its most prolific, ramsons can be found carpeting the floor of deciduous woodlands anywhere in the British Isles, accompanying bluebells and celandines in a profusion of colour. The name 'ramsons' is very similar to that used in Germany and some Scandinavian countries – *rams* – and is probably derived from an older word meaning 'rank'. This refers to the odour and strong flavour the plant imparts to the milk of any cow that eats it.

The species name *ursinum* is derived from the Latin *ursus*, meaning 'a bear'. Some authorities say that it refers to the shape of the leaves, supposedly resembling a bear's ears; others suggest that it signifies inferiority to cultivated garlic – a garlic fit only for bears to eat. The chopped and cooked leaves have, however, been used to flavour dishes and sauces.

The garlic that is most widely used to flavour food, especially in southern Europe, is *Allium sativum*, cultivated garlic. This plant is of such antiquity that its place of origin is unknown. It has been grown in England since the early 16th century, occasionally escaping to the wild. Cultivated garlic was used during the First World War as an effective antiseptic: the juice from the bulbs was applied to sterilised swabs of *Sphagnum* moss.

383

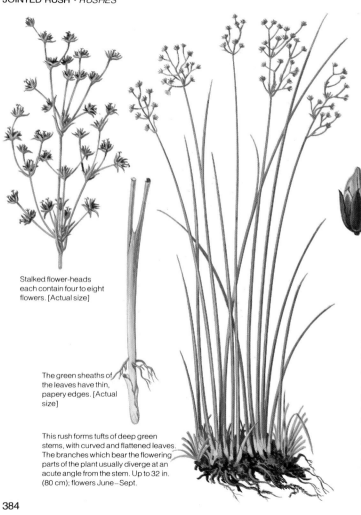

Stalked flower-heads each contain four to eight flowers. [Actual size]

The green sheaths of the leaves have thin, papery edges. [Actual size]

This rush forms tufts of deep green stems, with curved and flattened leaves. The branches which bear the flowering parts of the plant usually diverge at an acute angle from the stem. Up to 32 in. (80 cm); flowers June–Sept.

Flowers are dark brown or almost black. Petals and sepals are similar, although the inner ones have a broad, colourless edge. [× 5]

The fruit is a long, oval capsule which narrows above the middle.

Jointed rush grows on wet, acid soils in meadows and on moors, especially those that are grazed or mown.

Jointed rush *Juncus articulatus*

At first glance jointed rush, like other members of the rush family, looks very like a grass or a sedge; but in fact, like all rushes, it is closely related to the lily family. Rushes and lilies usually have three petals, three sepals and six stamens to each flower, whereas the individual flowers of grasses and sedges are much simplified. The flowers of the rush, with petals and sepals like tiny papery scales, are however much less showy than those of the lily.

The leaves of the jointed rush are hollow and divided inside by about 20 walls. These distinctive partitions or joints, which can be felt by a finger, have given this rush its name. Like its relatives, the jointed rush is a perennial; in the spring upright flowering stems shoot from the plant's underground root, or rhizome, which has kept alive all winter.

After the flower has been pollinated by wind-borne pollen, shining, blackish capsules develop. Each of these is larger than the petals, which still remain on the rush, and contains about 40 seeds. Since the outer layers of the seeds become sticky when wet, they cling to the fur and feet of animals, or to birds' feathers, and are carried away from the parent plant.

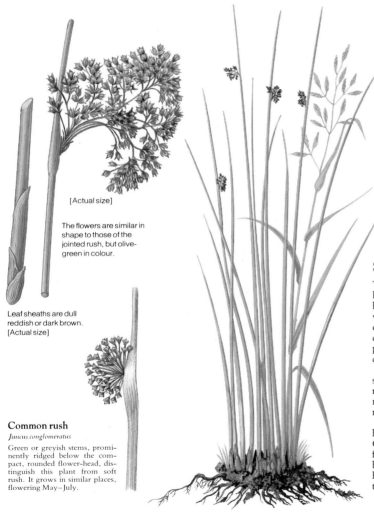

[Actual size]

The flowers are similar in shape to those of the jointed rush, but olive-green in colour.

Leaf sheaths are dull reddish or dark brown. [Actual size]

Flower [× 4]

The cylindrical leaves of this stiff, upright plant are very similar to the yellowish stems, which form dense tufts. The loose, rounded flower-head is borne on one side of the stem, some way from the top. 12–60 in. (30–152 cm); flowers June–Aug.

Soft rush is common throughout Britain; it grows in wet places, especially on acid soils, and in grassland, woods and bogs.

Common rush

Juncus conglomeratus

Green or greyish stems, prominently ridged below the compact, rounded flower-head, distinguish this plant from soft rush. It grows in similar places, flowering May–July.

Soft rush *Juncus effusus*

The name 'rush' comes from a Germanic word meaning 'to bind' or 'to plait', and reflects the extent to which rushes have been used through the centuries for various types of basket-work. Before the days of carpets, rushes were used for strewing on the stone floors of houses to provide protection against the cold. The shiny stems of rushes are filled with a spongy white pith which used to be scraped out and made into wicks for candles.

In the 17th century, a concoction made by immersing the seeds of soft rush in water and then mixing them with wine was recommended as a cough cure; but in recommending this medicine the herbalist Nicholas Culpeper urged care, as the mixture can result in headaches and drowsiness.

Soft rush and common rush are very similar; for both species have upright shoots and finely ridged stems, and grow in tufts. One of the best ways to distinguish them is to compare their flower-heads. Whereas the heads of the soft rush have stalks and branches and grow in loose clusters, those of the common rush have very short branches and form dense domes on the side of the stem.

385

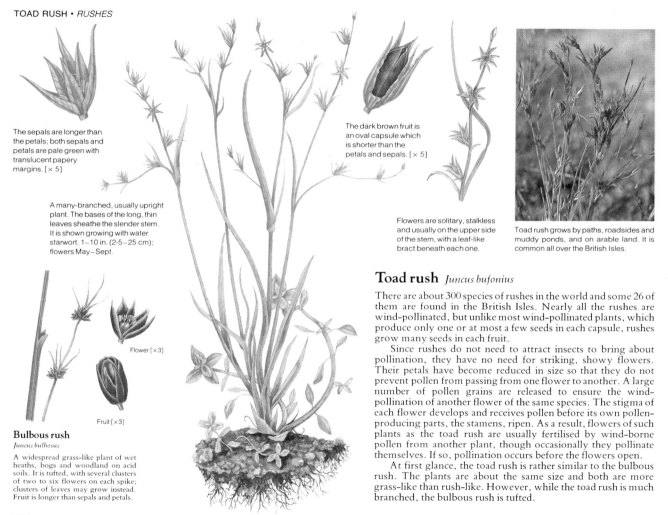

The sepals are longer than the petals; both sepals and petals are pale green with translucent papery margins. [× 5]

A many-branched, usually upright plant. The bases of the long, thin leaves sheathe the slender stem. It is shown growing with water starwort. 1–10 in. (2·5–25 cm); flowers May–Sept.

The dark brown fruit is an oval capsule which is shorter than the petals and sepals. [× 5]

Flowers are solitary, stalkless and usually on the upper side of the stem, with a leaf-like bract beneath each one.

Toad rush grows by paths, roadsides and muddy ponds, and on arable land. It is common all over the British Isles.

Flower [×3]

Fruit [×3]

Bulbous rush
Juncus bulbosus

A widespread grass-like plant of wet heaths, bogs and woodland on acid soils. It is tufted, with several clusters of two to six flowers on each spike; clusters of leaves may grow instead. Fruit is longer than sepals and petals.

Toad rush *Juncus bufonius*

There are about 300 species of rushes in the world and some 26 of them are found in the British Isles. Nearly all the rushes are wind-pollinated, but unlike most wind-pollinated plants, which produce only one or at most a few seeds in each capsule, rushes grow many seeds in each fruit.

Since rushes do not need to attract insects to bring about pollination, they have no need for striking, showy flowers. Their petals have become reduced in size so that they do not prevent pollen from passing from one flower to another. A large number of pollen grains are released to ensure the wind-pollination of another flower of the same species. The stigma of each flower develops and receives pollen before its own pollen-producing parts, the stamens, ripen. As a result, flowers of such plants as the toad rush are usually fertilised by wind-borne pollen from another plant, though occasionally they pollinate themselves. If so, pollination occurs before the flowers open.

At first glance, the toad rush is rather similar to the bulbous rush. The plants are about the same size and both are more grass-like than rush-like. However, while the toad rush is much branched, the bulbous rush is tufted.

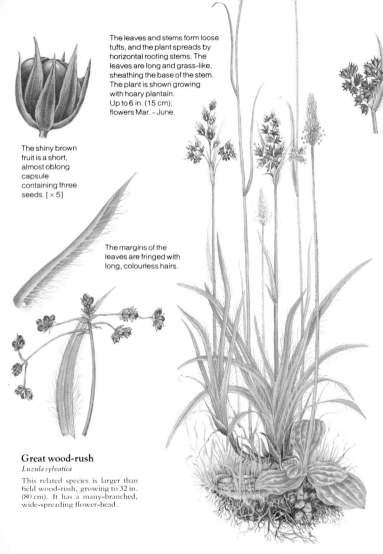

The leaves and stems form loose tufts, and the plant spreads by horizontal rooting stems. The leaves are long and grass-like, sheathing the base of the stem. The plant is shown growing with hoary plantain.
Up to 6 in. (15 cm); flowers Mar. – June.

The shiny brown fruit is a short, almost oblong capsule containing three seeds. [× 5]

The margins of the leaves are fringed with long, colourless hairs.

The flower-head is composed of up to six clusters of small, chestnut-brown flowers.

The anthers are yellow, conspicuous and much longer than their stalks. [× 5]

The field wood-rush – also known as cuckoo grass – is a common plant of all grasslands throughout Britain.

Great wood-rush
Luzula sylvatica

This related species is larger than field wood-rush, growing to 32 in. (80 cm). It has a many-branched, wide-spreading flower-head.

Field wood-rush *Luzula campestris*

When shining after rain or covered with dew in the morning, wood-rushes are thought to look as if alight with glow-worms. So, at least, goes the traditional explanation for their generic name, *Luzula*, said to be derived from the Italian word for a glow-worm, *lucciola*. The crowded appearance of its flower-heads has given the plant the alternative name of 'sweep's brush'. Although they are called wood-rushes, species such as the field wood-rush are plants of open ground. However, oak woodlands on acid soils are the favoured habitat of the great wood-rush, with its leaves of up to a foot long.

Though wood-rushes are members of the same family as the rushes, they differ in several ways. The leaves of rushes are hairless, while the wood-rushes have long, soft hairs at the edges of their leaves. In both, the base of the leaf forms a sheath that clothes the stem. In the wood-rushes the edges of the sheath overlap, but not in the rushes.

Both genera of plants are wind-pollinated, but while the two produce similar flowers, the pods of rushes contain many seeds, and those of the wood-rushes have only three. Ants are very partial to the seeds of wood-rushes, which contain a rich oil.

387

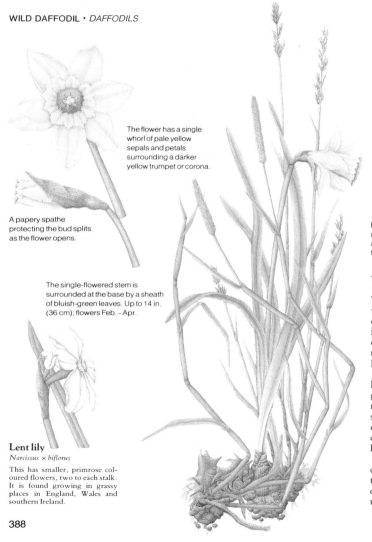

The flower has a single whorl of pale yellow sepals and petals surrounding a darker yellow trumpet or corona.

A papery spathe protecting the bud splits as the flower opens.

The single-flowered stem is surrounded at the base by a sheath of bluish-green leaves. Up to 14 in. (36 cm); flowers Feb.–Apr.

Lent lily
Narcissus × biflorus

This has smaller, primrose coloured flowers, two to each stalk. It is found growing in grassy places in England, Wales and southern Ireland.

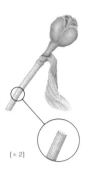

[× 2]

Fruit splits into three parts when ripe. The papery spathe remains attached. The stem is slightly flattened, with two sharp edges.

The wild daffodil is a native of damp woods and grasslands in England and Wales and has spread to Scotland.

Wild daffodil *Narcissus pseudonarcissus*

The daffodil, today one of the most familiar of garden plants, was once as common in the wild. It was widespread in the 16th century; since then, however, the clearance of woodland, the improvement of pasture and increased soil drainage have all combined to reduce the wild daffodil's numbers. It has declined, too, as a result of people digging up the bulbs for their gardens. Nowadays, the species is protected by law.

The name daffodil is very old. According to Greek mythology, *asphodelus* was a name originally given to a plant which grew in the meadows of the Underworld. Today, that name is reserved for a plant in the lily family; meanwhile, the alternative spellings asphodilus, affodilus and affadyl have evolved into the common name daffodil. Further to confuse the picture, a species of wild daffodil has been given the names 'Lent lily' or 'Easter lily', though it is no lily.

The bulb of the daffodil has narcotic properties. In small doses it is a purgative and emetic, and it was recommended by the 17th-century herbalist Nicholas Culpeper for use against all obstructions in the body. Mixed with barley meal, the ground-up bulb has been used to aid the healing of wounds.

Strap-shaped bluish-green leaves grow at the base of each stem, which bears a single drooping blossom. The flower's three spreading sepals are longer than its three green-tipped petals. 6–10 in. (15–25 cm); flowers Jan.–Mar.

[× 2]

The double-lobed covering that protected the young bud stays on the plant as the fruit capsule develops on its long stalk. The stem is not flattened, but cylindrical.

Clumps of snowdrops – often in woodlands – are scattered throughout England, Wales and southern Scotland.

Summer snowflake
Leucojum aestivum

The summer snowflake is twice as tall as the snowdrop and flowers in April–May. It grows in wet meadows and willow thickets in south-east England. Each stem has several flowers, with petals and sepals the same size.

Snowdrop *Galanthus nivalis*

One of the more vivid local names for the snowdrop is the 'snow-piercer', for this exactly describes how the familiar early spring flower pushes its head above the snow or earth to brighten the gloomy February woodlands. A small leaf-like spathe, or protective sheath, covers the tip of the flowering stem and enables the snowdrop flower to force its way up through the snow.

The snowdrop provides an early feast for bees which in turn pollinate the flowers. Nectar is secreted by the green-spotted inner petals of the snowdrop and, as the bee forages, it brushes onto the female stigma some of the pollen adhering to its body after visits to other flowers.

In the past, the snowdrop, sometimes confused with the similar but later-flowering summer snowflake (*Leucojum aestivum*), was also known as 'the fair maid of February'. This refers to an old custom connected with the Feast of Purification of St Mary, celebrated on February 2. Village maidens would gather bunches of snowdrops and wear them as symbols of purity. The snowdrop's generic name of *Galanthus* derives from two Greek words meaning 'milk' and 'flower'.

389

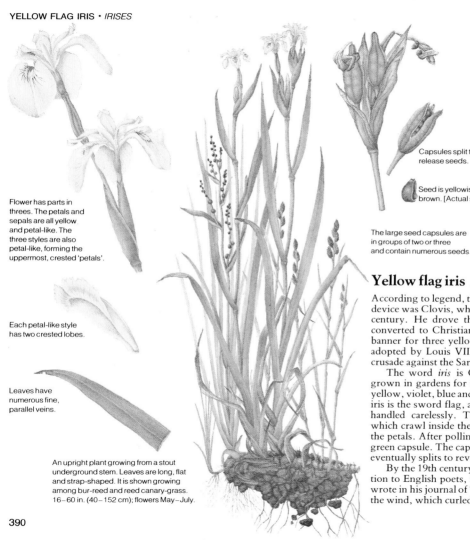

Flower has parts in threes. The petals and sepals are all yellow and petal-like. The three styles are also petal-like, forming the uppermost, crested 'petals'.

Each petal-like style has two crested lobes.

Leaves have numerous fine, parallel veins.

An upright plant growing from a stout underground stem. Leaves are long, flat and strap-shaped. It is shown growing among bur-reed and reed canary-grass. 16–60 in. (40–152 cm); flowers May–July.

Capsules split to release seeds.

Seed is yellowish-brown. [Actual size]

The large seed capsules are in groups of two or three and contain numerous seeds.

Yellow flag is a plant of wet ground or shallow water. It grows in marshes and woods and near rivers and streams.

Yellow flag iris *Iris pseudacorus*

According to legend, the first person to wear the iris as a heraldic device was Clovis, who became king of the Franks in the late 5th century. He drove the Romans out of northern Gaul, was converted to Christianity, and changed the three toads on his banner for three yellow irises. Six centuries later, the iris was adopted by Louis VII in the *fleur-de-lys* which he wore in his crusade against the Saracens – 'lys' is a corruption of 'Louis'.

The word *iris* is Greek for 'rainbow', and the plants are grown in gardens for their showy flowers in various shades of yellow, violet, blue and white. Another name for the yellow flag iris is the sword flag, as its leaves are sharp-edged and can cut if handled carelessly. The plant is mainly pollinated by bees, which crawl inside the flowers to reach the nectar at the base of the petals. After pollination, the petals fall off to reveal a large, green capsule. The capsule stalk begins to bend, and the capsule eventually splits to reveal a mass of yellowish-brown seeds.

By the 19th century, the yellow flag was a source of inspiration to English poets, including Gerard Manley Hopkins, who wrote in his journal of 'Camps of yellow flag flowers blowing in the wind, which curled over the grey sashes of the long leaves'.

The fruit is a green capsule, which turns brown and splits into three parts when ripe. The bright red seeds remain attached to the split capsule for some time.

The shiny, dark green leaves have numerous parallel veins.

This upright plant grows from an underground stem. The long, stiff leaves are evergreen, and grow in flat sprays. 12–32 in. (30–80 cm); flowers May–July.

The purplish flower has parts in groups of three, as in the yellow flag. The parts include three large, petal-like, yellowish styles.

The tip of each style has two lobes. [× 2]

Stinking iris is a plant of open woods, hedgebanks and sea-cliffs, and is widely distributed on chalky soil.

Stinking iris *Iris foetidissima*

For such an attractive plant, the stinking iris has an unjustly unflattering name. Its description as 'stinking' refers to the smell emitted when the dagger-like leaves are crushed or bruised. But not everyone is offended by the smell: it has been likened to that of beef, so providing one of the plant's alternative names, 'roast beef plant'.

The flower of the stinking iris is distinctive, with its blue-grey and purple-grey 'pencilling' marks. These have given rise to such local names as 'dragon's tongue' in Kent; 'adder's mouth' and 'blue devil' in Somerset; and 'snake's meat' in Devon. The three sepals and three petals are all petal-like, so that botanists call them 'tepals'. A bee visiting the flower uses one of the outer tepals as a landing platform. The three styles, or female parts, are also petal-like, and are situated above the broad tepals. Any pollen adhering to the bee's body from a previous visit to a flower brushes on to the stigma, and the stamens dust the insect with fresh pollen.

Gardeners often use this iris to brighten up a damp, shady corner during the winter months. A variegated form of the plant is also cultivated, often beside water.

391

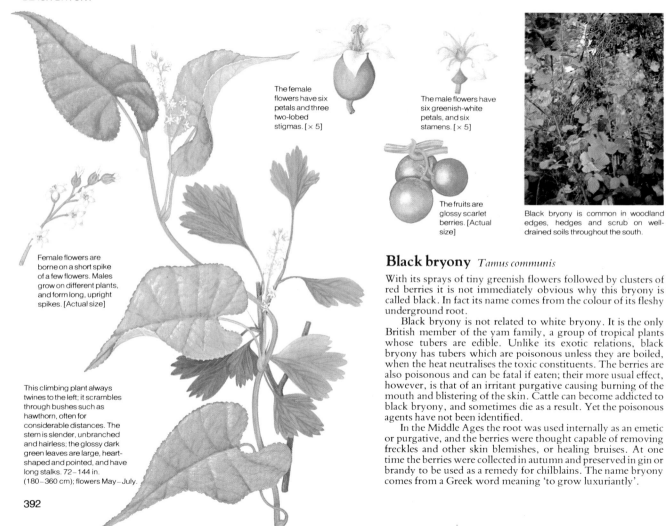

The female flowers have six petals and three two-lobed stigmas. [× 5]

The male flowers have six greenish-white petals, and six stamens. [× 5]

The fruits are glossy scarlet berries. [Actual size]

Black bryony is common in woodland edges, hedges and scrub on well-drained soils throughout the south.

Female flowers are borne on a short spike of a few flowers. Males grow on different plants, and form long, upright spikes. [Actual size]

This climbing plant always twines to the left; it scrambles through bushes such as hawthorn, often for considerable distances. The stem is slender, unbranched and hairless; the glossy dark green leaves are large, heart-shaped and pointed, and have long stalks. 72–144 in. (180–360 cm); flowers May–July.

Black bryony *Tamus communis*

With its sprays of tiny greenish flowers followed by clusters of red berries it is not immediately obvious why this bryony is called black. In fact its name comes from the colour of its fleshy underground root.

Black bryony is not related to white bryony. It is the only British member of the yam family, a group of tropical plants whose tubers are edible. Unlike its exotic relations, black bryony has tubers which are poisonous unless they are boiled, when the heat neutralises the toxic constituents. The berries are also poisonous and can be fatal if eaten; their more usual effect, however, is that of an irritant purgative causing burning of the mouth and blistering of the skin. Cattle can become addicted to black bryony, and sometimes die as a result. Yet the poisonous agents have not been identified.

In the Middle Ages the root was used internally as an emetic or purgative, and the berries were thought capable of removing freckles and other skin blemishes, or healing bruises. At one time the berries were collected in autumn and preserved in gin or brandy to be used as a remedy for chilblains. The name bryony comes from a Greek word meaning 'to grow luxuriantly'.

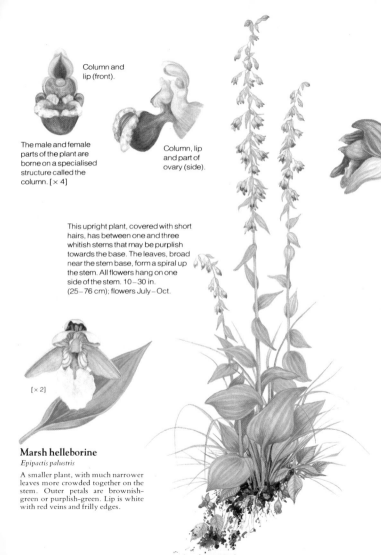

Column and lip (front).

The male and female parts of the plant are borne on a specialised structure called the column. [× 4]

Column, lip and part of ovary (side).

This upright plant, covered with short hairs, has between one and three whitish stems that may be purplish towards the base. The leaves, broad near the stem base, form a spiral up the stem. All flowers hang on one side of the stem. 10–30 in. (25–76 cm); flowers July–Oct.

Front

Side

The petals are green or purple, with the lowest forming a heart-shaped lip. [× 2]

[× 2]

Marsh helleborine
Epipactis palustris

A smaller plant, with much narrower leaves more crowded together on the stem. Outer petals are brownish-green or purplish-green. Lip is white with red veins and frilly edges.

Common helleborine is a plant of woodland and woodland edges, found locally throughout most of Britain.

Common helleborine *Epipactis helleborine*

As many as 100 flowers may bloom on a single crowded flower spike of this woodland orchid. Their colours – and especially those of the large lower lip – vary from green to deep purplish-red. Broad stem leaves give the plant its alternative common name of broad-leaved helleborine. Its short, thick roots are often heavily infected with a fungus which actually benefits the orchid by supplying it with increased water and mineral salts.

Pollination takes place from July to August, when the plant flowers. The stamens are modified to form two pollinia, which rest on a sac-like structure containing a 'glue'. This structure is easily ruptured by an insect in search of nectar, and the glue, which sets hard on exposure to air, cements the pollinia to the creature's head. At the next flower it visits, the pollen from the pollinia becomes smeared on to the sticky stigma. Cross-fertilisation is necessary for setting seed in this species of orchid, and self-pollination never occurs.

While common helleborine is mainly an orchid of hedgerows and woodlands – especially beech woods on chalk-lands in southern England – the related marsh helleborine is more likely to be found in wet and boggy areas of Britain.

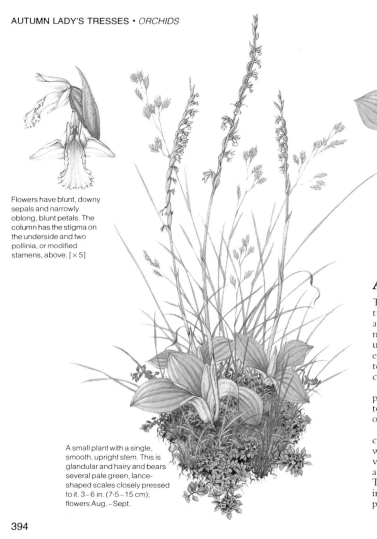

Flowers have blunt, downy sepals and narrowly oblong, blunt petals. The column has the stigma on the underside and two pollinia, or modified stamens, above. [× 5]

A small plant with a single, smooth, upright stem. This is glandular and hairy and bears several pale green, lance-shaped scales closely pressed to it. 3–6 in. (7·5–15 cm); flowers Aug.–Sept.

At the base of the stem is a rosette of oval, hairless leaves from which the following year's flower spike will grow.

The plant is found on dunes, dry meadows and other dry grassy places, usually on chalky soil.

Autumn lady's tresses *Spiranthes spiralis*

This curious little plant differs from all other orchids except the two other species of lady's tresses in having its white flowers arranged spirally up the stem. Although it grows in fairly large numbers on downland and dry pastureland, it is so small that it usually has to be searched for. Its flowers are fragrant in the evening. Autumn lady's tresses, which was known by this name to the herbalist William Turner as long ago as 1548, is locally common in southern Britain, becoming rarer northwards.

The bluish-green leaves form a rosette at the base of the plant, and these die back in June before the flowering spike arises to produce its flowers in August. The spike always grows from one side of the rosette.

Autumn lady's tresses is a plant especially of short turf, as it can survive constant mowing and will suddenly appear in a year when grass cutting is infrequent. Like many orchids, it is very variable in its appearance. One year it may be growing in abundance, while the next year not a single flower may be seen. This may be due to the varying activity of the fungus which infects the roots and provides the mineral salts necessary for plentiful growth.

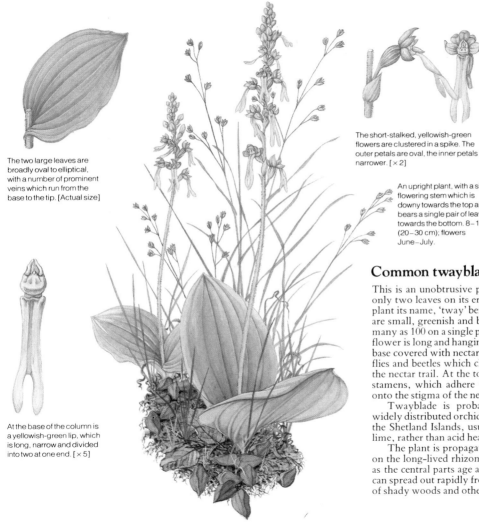

The two large leaves are broadly oval to elliptical, with a number of prominent veins which run from the base to the tip. [Actual size]

At the base of the column is a yellowish-green lip, which is long, narrow and divided into two at one end. [× 5]

The short-stalked, yellowish-green flowers are clustered in a spike. The outer petals are oval, the inner petals narrower. [× 2]

An upright plant, with a single flowering stem which is downy towards the top and bears a single pair of leaves towards the bottom. 8–12 in. (20–30 cm); flowers June–July.

The plant is common throughout Britain in damp woods and meadows; it is also found in scrubland and sand-dunes.

Common twayblade *Listera ovata*

This is an unobtrusive plant, but very distinctive in that it has only two leaves on its erect stem; it is these leaves that give the plant its name, 'tway' being an archaic form of two. The flowers are small, greenish and borne in large numbers – sometimes as many as 100 on a single plant. The bright yellow-green lip of the flower is long and hanging, with the groove in the centre and the base covered with nectar. It is pollinated by small insects such as flies and beetles which climb up the centre of the lip, following the nectar trail. At the top, they touch the pollinia, or modified stamens, which adhere to their heads; pollen is then brushed onto the stigma of the next plant they visit.

Twayblade is probably Britain's commonest and most widely distributed orchid. It is found throughout Britain, except the Shetland Islands, usually preferring soils which are rich in lime, rather than acid heathlands.

The plant is propagated both by seed and by buds that form on the long-lived rhizome. The buds produce flowering shoots as the central parts age and die. A whole colony of twayblades can spread out rapidly from one single plant, to cover large areas of shady woods and other grassy places with its flowers.

395

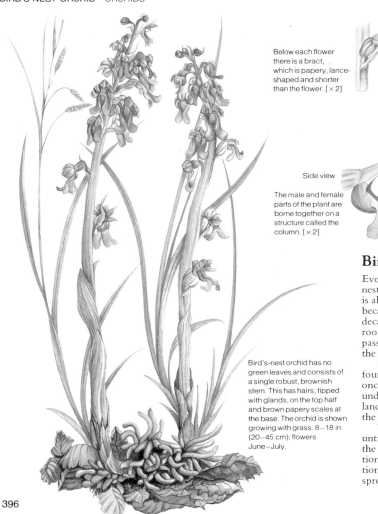

Below each flower there is a bract, which is papery, lance-shaped and shorter than the flower. [×2]

A long, two-lobed lip hangs down in front of the yellow-brown flower. The flower has short, oval petals. [×2]

Side view

Front view

The male and female parts of the plant are borne together on a structure called the column. [×2]

Bird's-nest orchid has no green leaves and consists of a single robust, brownish stem. This has hairs, tipped with glands, on the top half and brown papery scales at the base. The orchid is shown growing with grass. 8–18 in. (20–45 cm); flowers June–July.

This orchid grows in deeply shaded beech woodland locally throughout Britain, often on chalk or limestone.

Bird's-nest orchid *Neottia nidus-avis*

Even in the darkest woodland, the flowering spikes of bird's-nest orchid may poke up through masses of leaf litter. The plant is able to grow in places where very little light ever penetrates, because it has the ability to use for food such unlikely material as decaying leaves. A fungus, which grows closely around the roots of the plant, absorbs nutrients from the rotting humus and passes them to the plant. In exchange, the fungus takes some of the plant's nutrients.

Under a heavy canopy of beech trees, where it is usually found, bird's-nest orchid is sometimes the only plant to grow once the leaves have matured. Sometimes the plant is found under hazel or oak, and even occasionally in more open woodland. In the south of England it is only locally scattered, and in the north it is even less common.

The roots of the plant are densely matted and look like an untidy bird's nest. This strong resemblance is the origin of both the scientific and the common names: 'bird's-nest' is a translation of the Latin *nidus-avis*. New plants are produced by pollination or by shoots which spring from the tips of these roots and spread the original plant.

All the leaves are hooded at the tip, are unspotted and very finely toothed.

The outer petals of the small flowers are spreading and have rolled-up margins. The lip has a long spur protruding backwards from its base.

[× 10]

Pollen grains are bound into pollinia, which are attached to column by short stalks.

Fragrant orchid is a grassland plant, especially on chalk and limestone. It is also found in fens and marshes.

A plant with upright, hairless stems, often tinged purple at the top. The leaves are long and narrow, and those at the base normally have a blunt tip. They have prominent keels. The plant is shown growing with sheep's fescue. 6–16 in. (15–40 cm); flowers June–Aug.

Fragrant orchid *Gymnadenia conopsea*

Although the fragrant orchid grows abundantly in Britain, its numbers fluctuate dramatically from year to year. Sites that one year are ablaze with the clove-scented flowers may in the following year have no more than a dozen plants showing their slender heads. This fluctuation is typical of many orchids; in the case of the fragrant orchid it is apparently due to the periodic failure of seedlings to establish themselves.

The flowers are usually rosy or reddish-pink and normally have a distinct bluish or lilac sheen. They are extremely attractive to moths and also to some butterflies. The long, tapering spur indicates that the plant also attracts other long-tongued insects. As the insect's tongue penetrates the flower it brushes the pollinia, which stick to it and are removed as the tongue is withdrawn. The pollinia swivel round as the insects are in flight, ending up in a position which makes it easy for them to be pushed onto the stigma of the next flower that is visited.

The fragrant orchid has large underground tubers which are infected with a fungus that helps the plant to obtain mineral salts. In exchange for these, it provides the fungus with the nutrients that it needs to survive.

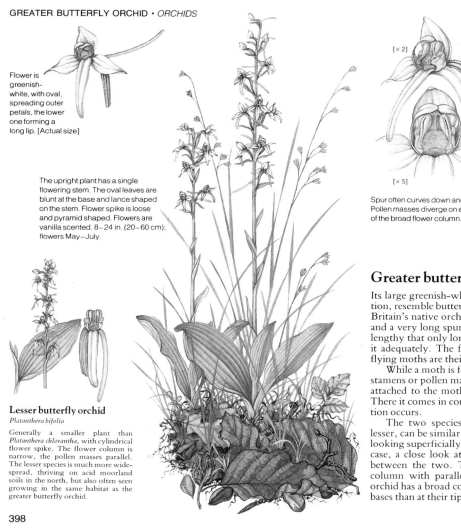

Flower is greenish-white, with oval, spreading outer petals, the lower one forming a long lip. [Actual size]

The upright plant has a single flowering stem. The oval leaves are blunt at the base and lance shaped on the stem. Flower spike is loose and pyramid shaped. Flowers are vanilla scented. 8–24 in. (20–60 cm); flowers May–July.

Lesser butterfly orchid
Platanthera bifolia

Generally a smaller plant than *Platanthera chlorantha*, with cylindrical flower spike. The flower column is narrow, the pollen masses parallel. The lesser species is much more widespread, thriving on acid moorland soils in the north, but also often seen growing in the same habitat as the greater butterfly orchid.

[× 2]

[× 5]

Spur often curves down and forward. Pollen masses diverge on either side of the broad flower column.

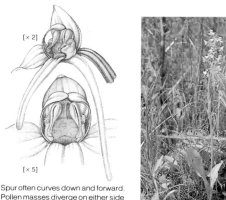

Greater butterfly orchids are found in woods and pastures throughout Britain, especially on chalky soil.

Greater butterfly orchid *Platanthera chlorantha*

Its large greenish-white flowers, which, given a little imagination, resemble butterflies, make this one of the most attractive of Britain's native orchids. Each flower has a long lip in the front, and a very long spur. This can be up to 1 in. (2·5 cm) long – so lengthy that only long-tongued butterflies and moths can reach it adequately. The flowers show up well at night, and night-flying moths are their most frequent visitors.

While a moth is feeding, its head touches one of the modified stamens or pollen masses, known as pollinia. The mass becomes attached to the moth's head, and is carried to another flower. There it comes in contact with the flower's stigma, and pollination occurs.

The two species of butterfly orchid, the greater and the lesser, can be similar in size, a large specimen of the lesser species looking superficially like a small specimen of the greater. In this case, a close look at the centre of the flowers will distinguish between the two. The lesser butterfly orchid has a narrow column with parallel pollinia, whereas the greater butterfly orchid has a broad column with the pollinia further apart at their bases than at their tips.

398

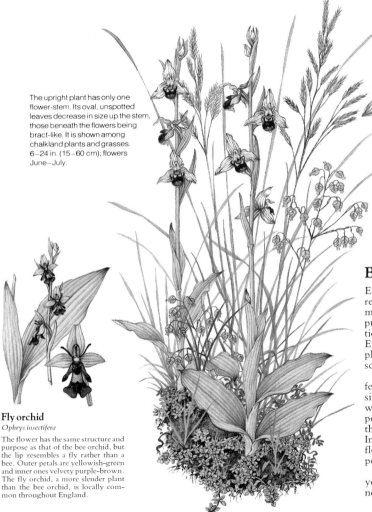

The upright plant has only one flower-stem. Its oval, unspotted leaves decrease in size up the stem, those beneath the flowers being bract-like. It is shown among chalkland plants and grasses. 6–24 in. (15–60 cm); flowers June–July.

Bee-like lip

Inner petals

The pale pink outer petals are oval-oblong; inner petals are pinkish-green. [Actual size]

Bee orchids thrive on dunes and on turf, especially on chalk and limestone, in all Britain except northern Scotland.

Fly orchid
Ophrys insectifera

The flower has the same structure and purpose as that of the bee orchid, but the lip resembles a fly rather than a bee. Outer petals are yellowish-green and inner ones velvety purple-brown. The fly orchid, a more slender plant than the bee orchid, is locally common throughout England.

Bee orchid *Ophrys apifera*

Each curious flower of this plant appears to have a bumble bee resting on it, taking nectar. In fact, the 'bee' is the beautifully marked lip of the flower, and this elaborate charade has the purpose of attracting a real bee, which will bring about pollination. However, in the case of British bee orchids, unlike other European species, this ruse is nearly always superfluous – the plants usually pollinate themselves before any bee appears on the scene.

The ruse depends on the fact that the false bee resembles a female bumble bee. A male of the same species, attracted by the siren-like lure of this 'female', lands on the lip and tries to mate with it. As it does so, the flower's two pollen masses, the pollinia, become attached to its head. Eventually, frustrated by the lack of response, the bee flies off, taking the pollinia with it. In its over-excited state, it is likely to try to mate with another flower; if it does so, the pollinia touch the flower's stigma and pollination occurs.

The bee orchid varies enormously in numbers from year to year. A location that produces hundreds in one year may have none at all in the following year.

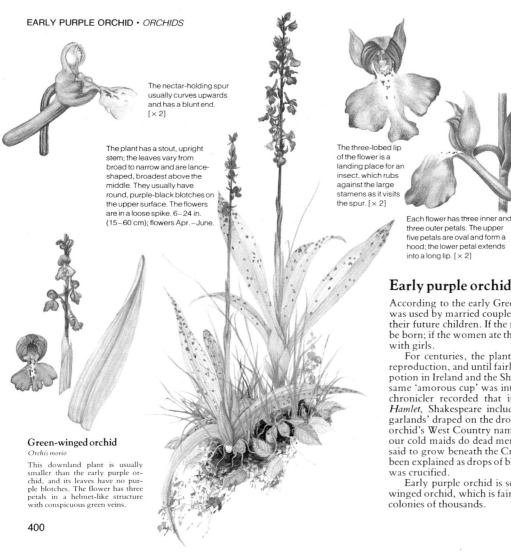

The nectar-holding spur usually curves upwards and has a blunt end. [× 2]

The plant has a stout, upright stem; the leaves vary from broad to narrow and are lance-shaped, broadest above the middle. They usually have round, purple-black blotches on the upper surface. The flowers are in a loose spike. 6–24 in. (15–60 cm); flowers Apr.–June.

The three-lobed lip of the flower is a landing place for an insect, which rubs against the large stamens as it visits the spur. [× 2]

Each flower has three inner and three outer petals. The upper five petals are oval and form a hood; the lower petal extends into a long lip. [× 2]

This orchid is frequently found in woodlands. It is widespread throughout Britain, especially on lime-rich soil.

Green-winged orchid

Orchis morio

This downland plant is usually smaller than the early purple orchid, and its leaves have no purple blotches. The flower has three petals in a helmet-like structure with conspicuous green veins.

Early purple orchid *Orchis mascula*

According to the early Greek physician Dioscorides, this plant was used by married couples in Thessaly to determine the sex of their future children. If the men ate the large tuber, boys would be born; if the women ate the small tuber, they would be blessed with girls.

For centuries, the plant has been associated with love and reproduction, and until fairly recently it was employed as a love potion in Ireland and the Shetland Isles. In the 17th century, the same 'amorous cup' was introduced to New England, where a chronicler recorded that it 'wrought the desired effect'. In *Hamlet*, Shakespeare included the plant among the 'fantastic garlands' draped on the drowned body of Ophelia. He used the orchid's West Country name of 'long purples' and added, 'But our cold maids do dead men's fingers call them'. The plant was said to grow beneath the Cross, and the spots on its leaves have been explained as drops of blood which fell from Christ when he was crucified.

Early purple orchid is sometimes confused with the green-winged orchid, which is fairly widespread, and is often found in colonies of thousands.

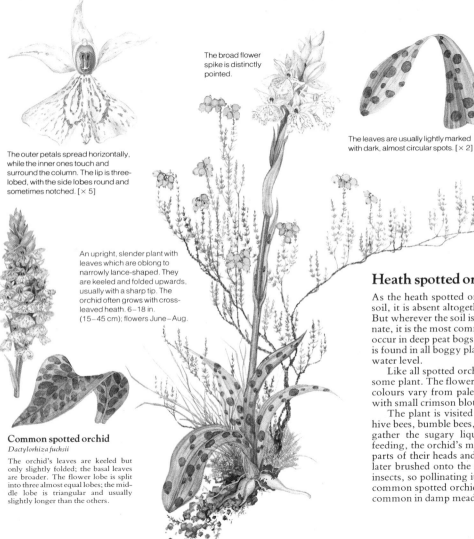

The outer petals spread horizontally, while the inner ones touch and surround the column. The lip is three-lobed, with the side lobes round and sometimes notched. [× 5]

The broad flower spike is distinctly pointed.

The leaves are usually lightly marked with dark, almost circular spots. [× 2]

An upright, slender plant with leaves which are oblong to narrowly lance-shaped. They are keeled and folded upwards, usually with a sharp tip. The orchid often grows with cross-leaved heath. 6–18 in. (15–45 cm); flowers June–Aug.

This orchid adds colour to heaths, moors and bogs. It is widespread on damp acid soils, but rare in the Midlands.

Common spotted orchid
Dactylorhiza fuchsii

The orchid's leaves are keeled but only slightly folded; the basal leaves are broader. The flower lobe is split into three almost equal lobes; the middle lobe is triangular and usually slightly longer than the others.

Heath spotted orchid *Dactylorhiza maculata*

As the heath spotted orchid rarely grows on chalky or neutral soil, it is absent altogether from large tracts of the countryside. But wherever the soil is acid and heath-like conditions predominate, it is the most common of all orchids. Although it does not occur in deep peat bogs, it will grow on *Sphagnum* moss – which is found in all boggy places – provided it is reasonably above the water level.

Like all spotted orchids, the heath spotted orchid is a handsome plant. The flower spike is dense with large flowers whose colours vary from pale pink to pale purple and even to white, with small crimson blotches.

The plant is visited by a large number of insects, including hive bees, bumble bees, hoverflies and several other flies, which gather the sugary liquid in the spur. While the insects are feeding, the orchid's modified stamens, called pollinia, stick to parts of their heads and are carried off by the insects. They are later brushed onto the stigma of another flower visited by the insects, so pollinating it. The plant's grassland equivalent is the common spotted orchid, which tends to avoid acid soils and is common in damp meadows and on marshes.

Long, thread-like spur has a pointed tip and is the same length as the ovary. [× 2]

Young flower-heads are pyramid-shaped. Mature heads are more open.

The plant is upright and hairless, with a slightly angled upper stem. The pointed leaves are narrow, oblong or lance-shaped, becoming smaller near top of stem. This orchid is often found growing with yellow-flowering horseshoe vetch. 8–18 in. (20–45 cm); flowers June–Aug.

Outer petals are curved. Inner petals form a head over the column. [× 2]

This orchid grows on chalk and limestone grassland and is locally common in most of Britain, but rare in northern Scotland.

Pyramidal orchid *Anacamptis pyramidalis*

The pure pink flowers of the pyramidal orchid are one of the delights of chalk downland in mid-July, when the blooms are at their colourful best. It is one of the last of the downland orchids to flower, and has a wide range of colour shading, which can often be seen even within a comparatively small area. Sometimes the plant is mistaken for the equally attractive fragrant orchid, whose flowers are more lilac-pink in colour; but the pyramidal orchid can easily be distinguished by its distinctive, pyramid-shaped spikes of flowers.

The flower has an abundant supply of nectar in its long spur; this attracts day and night-flying butterflies and moths. The scent is 'foxy', with a distinct musky overtone.

As with other orchids, there is a complex and beautifully adapted pollination mechanism. The modified stamens, or pollinia, stick to the tongue of the insect. They straighten during the insect's flight and are pushed directly onto the stigma of the next flower to be visited. In this way, up to 95% of the flowers produce viable seed, bearing out the contention by the 19th-century naturalist Charles Darwin that the pyramidal orchid is finely adapted for insect pollination.

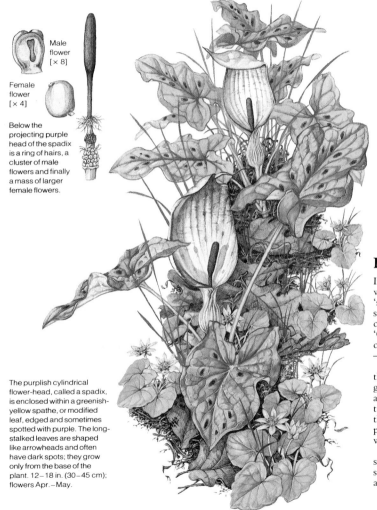

Male flower [× 8]

Female flower [× 4]

Below the projecting purple head of the spadix is a ring of hairs, a cluster of male flowers and finally a mass of larger female flowers.

The purplish cylindrical flower-head, called a spadix, is enclosed within a greenish-yellow spathe, or modified leaf, edged and sometimes spotted with purple. The long-stalked leaves are shaped like arrowheads and often have dark spots; they grow only from the base of the plant. 12–18 in. (30–45 cm); flowers Apr.–May.

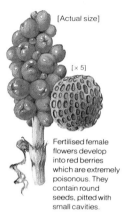

[Actual size]

[× 5]

Fertilised female flowers develop into red berries which are extremely poisonous. They contain round seeds, pitted with small cavities.

Lords and ladies is a common plant of woods and hedgerows throughout Britain, particularly on chalk and limestone.

Lords and ladies *Arum maculatum*

In the Middle Ages, this unusually shaped flower was connected with the act of making love. Its various local names – such as 'sweethearts', 'silly lovers' and 'Adam and Eve' – often had a sexual connotation. In the 16th century it was also known as cuckoo pintle, which was later abbreviated to cuckoo pint. 'Cuckoo' probably referred to the supposedly lustful male cuckoo, although some authorities think it came from 'cuckold' – a man whose wife has been unfaithful to him.

The flowers are contained in a broad, sheathing hood, called the spathe. Inside there is a club-like structure, the spadix. It gives off a smell of decay which, together with its slight heat, attracts flies. The insects crawl down inside the spathe and are trapped by the backward pointing hairs on the spadix. They then crawl around pollinating the flowers, at the same time picking up pollen from the flowers, until they die, or else escape when the spadix withers after pollination.

The roots of lords and ladies were gathered for their high starch content, and in Elizabethan times this was used for stiffening the high, pleated, linen ruffs that were then fashionable. The poisonous berries can be fatal if eaten by children.

403

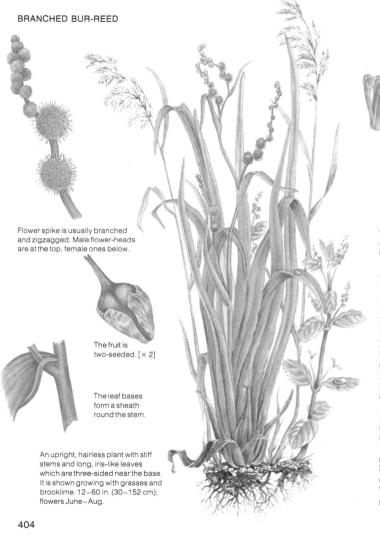

Flower spike is usually branched and zigzagged. Male flower-heads are at the top, female ones below.

The fruit is two-seeded. [× 2]

The leaf bases form a sheath round the stem.

An upright, hairless plant with stiff stems and long, iris-like leaves which are three-sided near the base. It is shown growing with grasses and brooklime. 12–60 in. (30–152 cm); flowers June–Aug.

Each flower in the rounded female flower-head is simply a stigma and styles, surrounded by papery scales. [× 3]

The male flower is very simple with several stamens and a ring of papery scales at the base. [× 5]

This is a common plant of mud or shallow water in ponds, ditches, slow-moving rivers and marshes all over Britain.

Branched bur-reed *Sparganium erectum*

Four of the world's 15 species of bur-reeds grow in the British Isles. Their flowers are tiny, and grow in globe-like flower-heads. Each head has numerous flowers of one sex only and the male heads grow above the female ones. The female heads produce beaked fruits, which give them a bur-like appearance; it is from this feature that the plants get their name. As bur-reeds are wind-pollinated, they have no need to attract insects by producing colourful, conspicuous flowers. Their flowers have minute greenish scales instead of petals, but what they lack in attractiveness they make up for in numbers.

Bur-reeds are found in standing or running water and in marshes. They often grow in pure stands, which provide sheltered nesting and roosting places for wildfowl. The ripe fruits of the plants contribute much of the birds' diet in autumn.

Branched bur-reed has several leafy branches in each flower spike. Male and female unstalked flower-heads occur on each branch, the females being larger than the males. Male heads usually outnumber female heads, which may be reduced to one. The four species of the plant in Britain are distinguished by slight differences in the shape and colour of their fruits.

Male flower-heads consist of numerous clusters of stamens. [× 5]

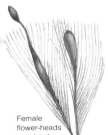

Female flower-heads consist of numerous slender, hairy, florets. [× 5]

A very robust plant with an upright stem and narrow, straight-sided upright leaves that rise above the top of the flower. The female flower-head is brown and sausage-shaped; the male flower-head, with a bract at its base, rises from the top of the female flower-head. 54–90 in. (137–230 cm); flowers June–July.

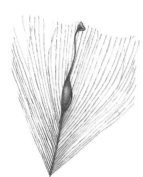

The fruit is single-seeded, with a surrounding parachute of long hairs. [× 5]

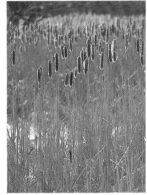

Large clumps of reedmaces appear in swampy ground throughout Britain, most commonly in the south.

Reedmace *Typha latifolia*

A Victorian artist's error turned this plant into an 'impostor'. When Sir Lawrence Alma-Tadema painted 'Moses in the Bulrushes' from the biblical story, he in fact showed the child's cradle among a clump of reedmaces – much more spectacular plants than the bulrush, which has few leaves and is topped by several clusters of flower-heads. The reedmace was so named because of its mace-like appearance, but although it is sometimes called by that name, it is still – wrongly – the bulrush to most people. The names false bulrush or 'cat's-tail' are also used.

There are two species of reedmaces in Britain, the greater (*Typha latifolia*) and the lesser (*Typha angustifolia*). Both rise from thick underwater roots, but the lesser has narrower leaves and is paler in colour. The female flower-head of the greater reedmace is about 6 in. (15 cm) long or more, and has thousands of tiny, tightly packed flowers. In the greater reedmace, the male flower-head is borne immediately above the female, but in the lesser there is a stem about 4 in. (10 cm) long between them.

In the past, the fluffy seeds were used to stuff mattresses. Baskets and chairs were woven from the leaves, which, being waterproof, were also used for making reed boats.

405

FIVE COMMON SEDGES

Sedges differ from grasses in having solid, often three–sided stems, and also in having no flap of tissue – the ligule – at the junction of leaf-blade and sheath. Differences in flower-head, leaf and stem distinguish one sedge from another.

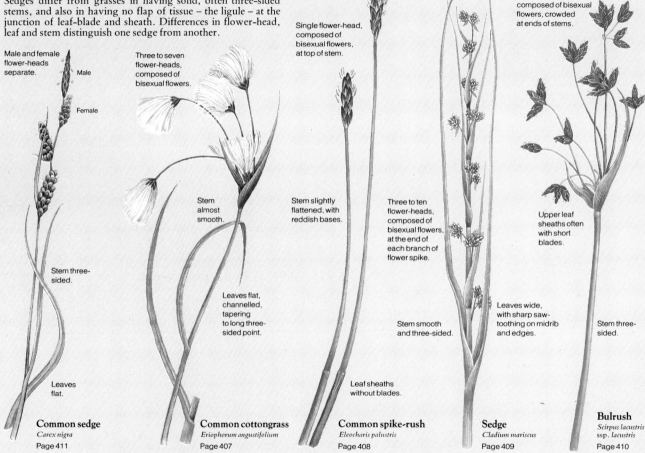

Male and female flower-heads separate.

Male

Female

Stem three-sided.

Leaves flat.

Three to seven flower-heads, composed of bisexual flowers.

Stem almost smooth.

Leaves flat, channelled, tapering to long three-sided point.

Single flower-head, composed of bisexual flowers, at top of stem.

Stem slightly flattened, with reddish bases.

Leaf sheaths without blades.

Three to ten flower-heads, composed of bisexual flowers, at the end of each branch of flower spike.

Stem smooth and three-sided.

Flower-heads, composed of bisexual flowers, crowded at ends of stems.

Leaves wide, with sharp saw-toothing on midrib and edges.

Upper leaf sheaths often with short blades.

Stem three-sided.

Common sedge
Carex nigra
Page 411

Common cottongrass
Eriophorum angustifolium
Page 407

Common spike-rush
Eleocharis palustris
Page 408

Sedge
Cladium mariscus
Page 409

Bulrush
Scirpus lacustris
ssp. *lacustris*
Page 410

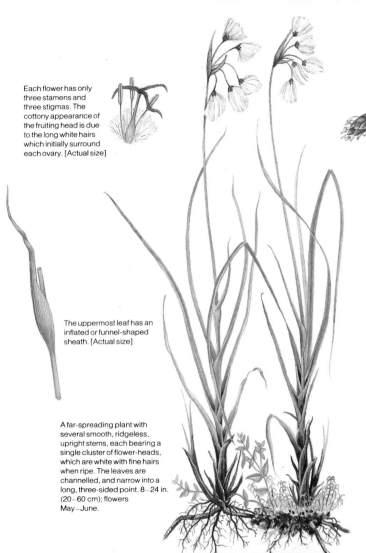

Each flower has only three stamens and three stigmas. The cottony appearance of the fruiting head is due to the long white hairs which initially surround each ovary. [Actual size]

The uppermost leaf has an inflated or funnel-shaped sheath. [Actual size]

A far-spreading plant with several smooth, ridgeless, upright stems, each bearing a single cluster of flower-heads, which are white with fine hairs when ripe. The leaves are channelled, and narrow into a long, three-sided point. 8–24 in. (20–60 cm); flowers May–June.

The many, long-stalked flower-heads consist of spirally arranged flowers.

This plant is widespread in bogs and swampy ground, but land drainage is reducing its range.

Common cottongrass *Eriophorum angustifolium*

One of the characteristic features of British peat bogs is the spattering of little tufts of what looks like pure white cotton-wool. These tufts are the cottongrasses, a small group of plants which thrives in such damp places. Despite their name, they are not grasses but close relations of the sedges, and can mostly be recognised as such by their three-sided stems.

There are four native species of cottongrass in Britain, but the most usual and most easily recognised is the common cottongrass. This has a head of several nodding flowering spikes, and its stems and leaves are three-sided only at their tips. Below the tips, the stems are cylindrical and the leaves are flattish. The strands that make up the ball of cottonwool begin as short hairs surrounding the ovary. After pollination of the flower and ripening of the fruit, they elongate until they form a fluffy ball. Earlier in the year, when the leaves are fresh and there are no balls of cottonwool, the plants can be hard to recognise against a background of dull green vegetation.

The fluffy heads of cottongrasses were once used for making candle wicks. They are still excellent for stuffing pillows and mattresses if enough can be collected.

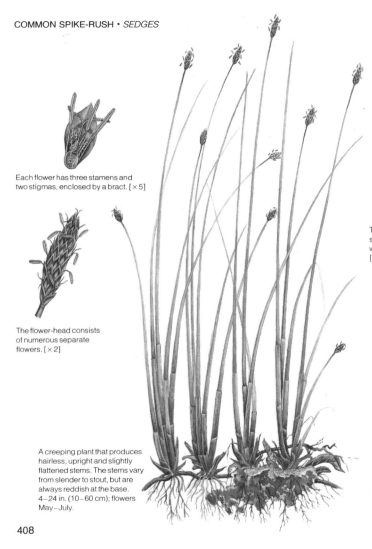

Each flower has three stamens and two stigmas, enclosed by a bract. [× 5]

The flower-head consists of numerous separate flowers. [× 2]

A creeping plant that produces hairless, upright and slightly flattened stems. The stems vary from slender to stout, but are always reddish at the base. 4–24 in. (10–60 cm); flowers May–July.

The fruit is smooth, or minutely pitted, yellow to deep brown in colour and with a cap-like top. [× 5]

The sheaths encasing the stems are yellowish-brown, with a squared-off end. [Actual size]

The slender and erect common spike-rush is found in ditches, marshes and on the edges of ponds throughout Britain.

Common spike-rush *Eleocharis palustris*

There are seven kinds of spike-rushes in the British Isles; and the common spike-rush, as its name suggests, is by far the most abundant and widespread of them. Two of the plants – *Eleocharis parvula* and *Eleocharis austriaca* – are extremely rare and have to be specially sought out. The remainder, including the common spike-rush, can be found in all kinds of damp, sandy or peaty places, such as mud-flats, fens and bogs.

The various spike-rushes are mostly leafless, the common spike-rush among them. It has stiff, often much-tufted stems and short, solitary spikelets. The base of the spike is half-circled by the lowest scale on the spike. In this it differs from the smaller slender spike-rush (*Eleocharis uniglumis*), in which the corresponding spike encircles the base. In two of the five most frequently seen species of spike-rush – needle spike-rush (*Eleocharis acicularis*), and few-flowered spike-rush (*Eleocharis quinqueflora*) – the lowest scale of the spike is at least half as long as the spike itself.

Common spike-rush, and the other rushes, are closely related to the true sedges of the *Carex* genus. However, their stems are cylindrical or four-sided instead of three-sided.

Each flower-head has very reduced flowers which normally have two stamens and three stigmas. The uppermost flowers are sometimes male only. [× 4]

Bisexual flower [× 4]

The leaves are keeled, with sharp saw-toothing on both the keel and leaf margins. [× 2]

A sturdy, far-spreading plant with cylindrical or triangular hollow stems. The evergreen leaves are long, wide and flat, the tops often becoming withered. Young leaves have a triangular point. 30–108 in. (76–270 cm); flowers July–Aug.

Flower-heads are arranged in a many-branched flower spike.

The seed is oval, dark brown and shiny and has a sharp point. [× 5]

Sedge is a plant of swamps and fens. It is scattered throughout Britain, but is absent from northern Scotland.

Sedge *Cladium mariscus*

The name sedge comes from an ancient Indo-European word which means 'to cut'. Of all the 75 or more plants classed as sedges in Britain, only this plant, *Cladium mariscus*, has a true claim to the name. This is because the saw-like edges of the plant's leaves can easily cut into the flesh. The leaves sometimes grow as long as 9 ft (2·75 m) and can live for up to two to three years. Sedge does not decay easily and, by accumulating dead foliage, it forms large beds which keep out most other plants.

In the past, sedge made a major contribution to the economies of Cambridgeshire, Norfolk and Suffolk. It was used to form the ridging along the top of reed-thatched roofs; indeed, when it was used in Scotland in this way it was known as thack – a Scottish form of 'thatch'. For centuries it was harvested every fourth year, which kept it in a healthy state of growth. But the former fenland practice of harvesting sedge every other year for making hay had an adverse effect upon the plant, and many acres of it perished.

Hundreds of years of drainage also resulted in a serious loss of sedge. Today, very little of the eastern lowlands is dominated by this once extremely characteristic plant.

409

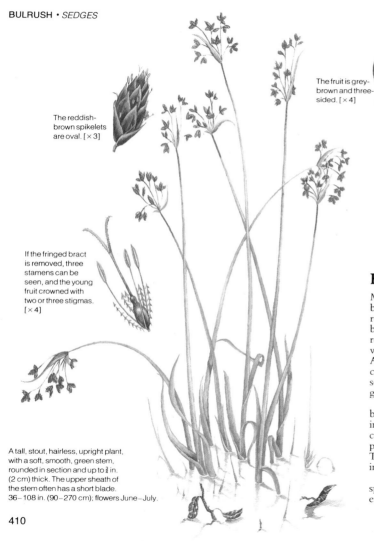

The reddish-brown spikelets are oval. [× 3]

If the fringed bract is removed, three stamens can be seen, and the young fruit crowned with two or three stigmas. [× 4]

A tall, stout, hairless, upright plant, with a soft, smooth, green stem, rounded in section and up to ¾ in. (2 cm) thick. The upper sheath of the stem often has a short blade. 36–108 in. (90–270 cm); flowers June–July.

The fruit is grey-brown and three-sided. [× 4]

The flower spike is a dense, sometimes branched, mass of flower-heads.

Bulrushes grow throughout Britain in lakes, ponds and rivers, normally where there is a large quantity of silt.

Bulrush *Scirpus lacustris* ssp. *lacustris*

Medieval man called this plant 'bull rush' because it was much bigger and more impressive than other rushes, and bulrush it has remained. Like the rather similar but leafy clubrushes, the bulrushes – including true bulrush, *Scirpus lacustris* – are close relatives of the sedges. They are leafless or almost leafless plants with stems that are either cylindrical or triangular in section. Although true bulrush may be entirely without leaves, its creeping stem – the rhizome – may produce tufts of leaves, sometimes submerged. Its stems are green, whereas those of glaucous bulrush have a bluish tinge.

The flower-head of bulrush is tuft-like and unobtrusive: the big, cigar-shaped spike popularly associated with the bulrush is in fact the female flower-head of reedmace, or false bulrush. The confusion was originally caused by the fame of a Victorian painting, 'Moses in the Bulrushes', in which the artist Alma-Tadema showed reedmace, not bulrushes. There are no petals; instead, bulrushes have short, barbed bristles.

In Norfolk, the bulrush was at one time particularly widespread, and until it virtually vanished through over-exploitation, it was regularly harvested for making rush mats.

Male flower is a bract with three stamens. [× 3]

There are normally two or three male flower-heads, the lowest of which is usually the smallest. Very rarely, a male spike may have a few female flowers at the base.

The fruit is smooth and oval, with a very short beak. [× 3]

The female flower has two styles and a dark brown or blackish bract. [× 3]

The one to four female flower-heads may be closely clustered, or more widely separated.

Common sedge is found in wet, grassy areas, or beside water, usually on acid soil. It is plentiful throughout Britain.

Common sedge *Carex nigra*

After the innumerable hawkweeds and brambles, the sedges grouped together under the scientific name *Carex* form the largest single group of flowering plants in Britain: there are about 75 species, out of a world total of perhaps 1,000. To complicate the picture further, different populations of one kind are often dissimilar in such features as their size, the length of their spikelet stems or the shape of their fruit.

A feature of many sedges, including this species, is that the flowers are reduced to a single scale, called a glume, enclosing the stamens or ovary, and are bunched together in spikes. Each spike normally contains only male or female flowers. Common sedge is not too difficult to distinguish from other species because, as its name *nigra* indicates, the scale-like glumes are blackish. The small fruits which develop in autumn are brown; these fruits, called nutlets because they are quite hard, are hairless in common sedge, and slightly flattened.

Other characteristics that help to identify common sedge are its creeping manner of growth (the stems of many other sedges grow close together in tufts), and the two feathery styles on top of the ovary (other sedges may have three).

A creeping, hairless plant with three-angled stems, smooth above and rough below. The leaves may be longer or shorter than the stems, and often have rolled-up margins in dry conditions. 3–30 in. (7.5–76 cm); flowers May–July.

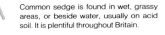

411

A robust plant with broad, yellow-green leaves, keeled on the back, and drooping flowers. Largest of the woodland sedges, its leaves grow to 1 in. (2·5 cm) wide. 36–54 in. (90–137 cm); flowers May–June.

Four or five drooping female flower spikes occur at intervals along the upper stem.

The elliptical or oval, three-sided fruit is greeny-brown and has a short, slightly notched beak.

Single male flower spike occurs at top of stem.

River banks and damp woodlands are the setting for the pendulous sedge. It is widespread, except in Scotland.

Pendulous sedge *Carex pendula*

This distinctive and handsome plant is often found in shady corners of gardens, among trees and shrubs or beside a pond. As its name suggests, it is easily recognisable by its drooping flower spikes which, when fully matured, resemble reddish-brown catkins.

In its wild state the pendulous sedge grows in damp woodlands and on the shady banks of streams. It is well scattered throughout most of the British Isles, but occurs rarely in Scotland. The plant has stout stems with long, rough-edged leaves almost 1 in. (2·5 cm) wide and coloured yellowish-green on top and bluish-green underneath. The stems are triangular, with sharp edges.

The numerous flower spikes grow from the top third of the stem, and only the topmost spike is male. Each spike grows from the base of a leaf which forms a sheath around the stem, and there are usually four or five female flower spikes to each stem. The spikes grow straight upwards at the beginning of their growth and start to droop as they mature, reaching a length of 3–6 in. (7·5–15 cm) by the end of the season. The sword-like base leaves also begin to droop as they grow taller.

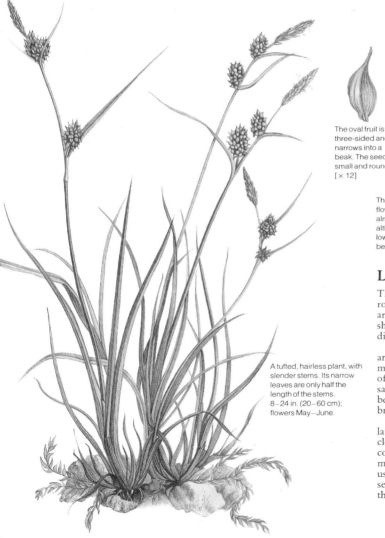

A tufted, hairless plant, with slender stems. Its narrow leaves are only half the length of the stems. 8–24 in. (20–60 cm); flowers May–June.

The oval fruit is three-sided and narrows into a beak. The seed is small and round. [× 12]

The short female flower-heads are almost stalkless, although the lowest one may be short-stalked.

The tiny flowers on the male flower-head consist of scales and stamens only.

The bristly heads of this sedge are frequently seen in wet places such as fens, almost always on soils rich in lime.

Long-stalked yellow sedge *Carex lepidocarpa*

This sedge is a fairly large-tufted plant, with triangular or almost round stems which grow to about 24 in. (60 cm) tall. The leaves are channelled, leaving a groove in the inner face, with the sheath at the base containing fibres that persist after the leaf has died and frayed.

At the top of the flowering stems are several spikes, which are usually well spaced. The uppermost, long-stalked spike is male; the lower, usually stalkless spikes are female. At the base of each female spike is a leaf-like bract. The bracts are about the same length as the group of spikes. When the sedge is in fruit, the beaked nutlets that are borne on the female spikes give them a bristly appearance.

There are several sedges in the yellow-sedge group. The large yellow sedge (*Carex flava*) has golden-yellow fruits, closely crowded spikes and very long bracts. It is a rare plant, confined to north Lancashire and west Yorkshire. In the common yellow sedge (*Carex demissa*) the top two female spikes are usually much closer together than on the long-stalked yellow sedge, with a third female spike much further away. This species thrives on damp, acid soils.

413

Male flower consists of a purplish-brown bract with a translucent margin and three stamens. [× 5]

There are two to three male flower-heads on each stem. [Actual size]

The fruit is oval or elliptical; it is covered in fine hairs, and has a short beak. It can be yellow-green, reddish or almost black. [× 5]

A creeping, hairless, grey-green plant with upright three-sided stems. The leaves are rough and shorter than the stem, and have a slight keel. Towards the top they become flat, pale green above and grey-green underneath. 4–18 in. (10–45 cm); flowers May–June.

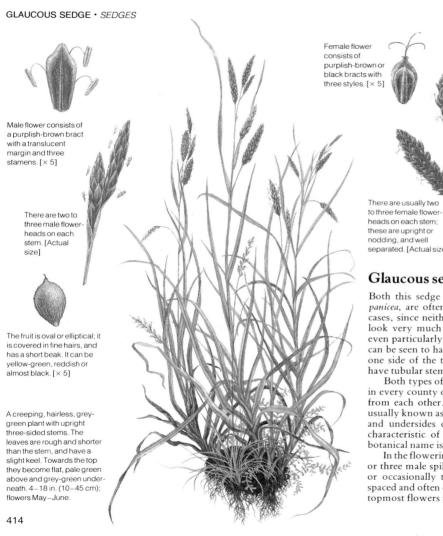

Female flower consists of purplish-brown or black bracts with three styles. [× 5]

There are usually two to three female flower-heads on each stem; these are upright or nodding, and well separated. [Actual size]

Glaucous sedge is found on dry chalky grassland, and in damp clayey woods, bogs and marshes.

Glaucous sedge *Carex flacca*

Both this sedge and one other closely related species, *Carex panicea*, are often called carnation grass – a misnomer in both cases, since neither is a grass. Though grasses and sedges may look very much alike, they are quite different plants and not even particularly closely related. Looked at from above, sedges can be seen to have three rows of leaves, each corresponding to one side of the three-sided stem. Grasses, on the other hand, have tubular stems with alternate leaves in two rows.

Both types of 'carnation grass' are very common, occurring in every county of the British Isles, but they are quite different from each other. To avoid confusion *Carex flacca* is therefore usually known as glaucous sedge because of its colour: the stems and undersides of the leaves are of the bluish-green colour characteristic of garden carnations and pinks, for which the botanical name is glaucous.

In the flowering parts of glaucous sedge there are usually two or three male spikes, rarely only one, and below these are two, or occasionally three, female spikes. These are quite widely spaced and often drooping, on rather thin stalks. Sometimes the topmost flowers in a female spike are male.

FOUR COMMON GRASSES

With their slender blades and much–simplified flowers, grasses appear insignificant and indistinguishable from each other. Closer examination, however, reveals a range of diverse structures. The distinguishing features of four species are shown.

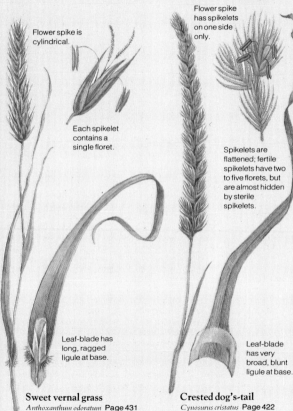

Flower spike is cylindrical.

Each spikelet contains a single floret.

Leaf-blade has long, ragged ligule at base.

Sweet vernal grass
Anthoxanthum odoratum **Page 431**

Flower spike has spikelets on one side only.

Spikelets are flattened; fertile spikelets have two to five florets, but are almost hidden by sterile spikelets.

Leaf-blade has very broad, blunt ligule at base.

Crested dog's-tail
Cynosurus cristatus **Page 422**

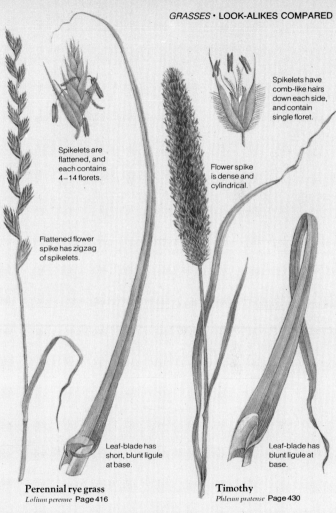

Spikelets are flattened, and each contains 4–14 florets.

Flattened flower spike has zigzag of spikelets.

Leaf-blade has short, blunt ligule at base.

Perennial rye grass
Lolium perenne **Page 416**

Spikelets have comb-like hairs down each side, and contain single floret.

Flower spike is dense and cylindrical.

Leaf-blade has blunt ligule at base.

Timothy
Phleum pratense **Page 430**

415

The flattened spikelets contain 4–14 florets. [× 2]

A short, membranous ligule is found at the base of the leaf-blade – which has two claw-like lobes clasping the stem. [× 5]

The stem of the flower spike is wavy and has numerous spikelets set edge-on to it. [× 2]

Perennial rye grass thrives on damp, rich soils. Cultivated throughout Britain, it also grows on roadsides and waste ground.

Perennial rye grass *Lolium perenne*

For more than 300 years British farmers have been growing perennial rye grass for grazing and making hay. New pastures are sown either with pure rye grass or mixtures of rye grass and clover. Since it has been cultivated, many new strains have been developed; they range from short-lived grasses with little foliage, to the very persistent, tall, leafy forms ideal for pasture.

The top third of the plant consists of the flower spike. The spikelets – the groups of narrow, green scales enclosing the tiny flowers – are stalkless and set singly on alternate sides of the stem. Another very common and widespread rye grass – Italian rye grass – differs from the perennial form in that each scale in the spikelet has a long bristle at the tip.

A third and much rarer kind of rye grass is darnel (*Lolium temuleutum*): in fact the name *Lolium*, though applied by botanists to the whole genus, means 'darnel' in Latin. Darnel is possibly the tare – the weed mentioned in the Bible, as for instance in the parable explaining how everything evil on earth will be gathered up by angels at the end of time and burned like tares. Another similar grass, called couch, quickly reaches plague proportions on farmland and is difficult to eradicate.

Couch
Elymus repens

The spikelets of this aggressive plant are similar to those of perennial rye grass, but are set broadside on to the stem. The grass is common on cultivated and waste ground.

This tufted plant has a smooth, upright stem. The leaf-blades are folded when young, and the young basal leaf-sheaths are pinkish-brown. 4–36 in. (10–90 cm); flowers May–Aug.

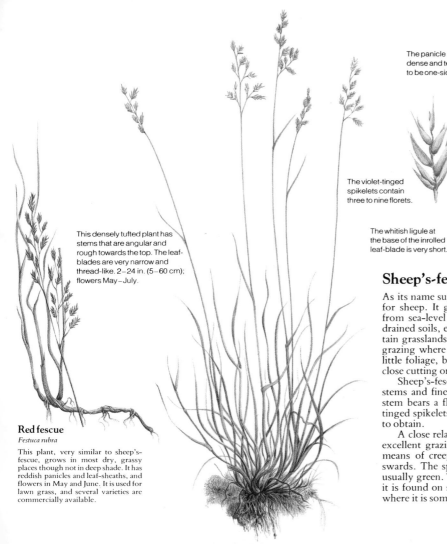

This densely tufted plant has stems that are angular and rough towards the top. The leaf-blades are very narrow and thread-like. 2–24 in. (5–60 cm); flowers May–July.

The panicle is short, dense and tends to be one-sided.

The violet-tinged spikelets contain three to nine florets.

The whitish ligule at the base of the inrolled leaf-blade is very short.

Sheep's-fescue is common throughout Britain on poor, well-drained soils such as heaths, moors and mountain pastures.

Red fescue
Festuca rubra

This plant, very similar to sheep's-fescue, grows in most dry, grassy places though not in deep shade. It has reddish panicles and leaf-sheaths, and flowers in May and June. It is used for lawn grass, and several varieties are commercially available.

Sheep's-fescue *Festuca ovina*

As its name suggests, sheep's-fescue is a valuable pasture grass for sheep. It grows abundantly throughout the British Isles, from sea-level to nearly 4,000 ft (1,220 m), on poor but well-drained soils, especially limestone and chalk. On hill or mountain grasslands it is often the dominant grass, providing good grazing where lusher vegetation does not flourish. It produces little foliage, but is hardy and drought resistant and can stand close cutting or heavy grazing.

Sheep's-fescue is a densely tufted plant with stiff, upright stems and fine, hair-like leaves which are tightly rolled. Each stem bears a flowering head – the panicle – which has violet-tinged spikelets. Its seed is useful for lawn grass, but is difficult to obtain.

A close relative of sheep's-fescue is red fescue. It, too, is an excellent grazing grass, and unlike sheep's-fescue spreads by means of creeping shoots, called rhizomes, and forms thick swards. The spikelets are sometimes reddish or purplish, but usually green. There are a number of variants of red fescue, and it is found on salt-marshes, meadows, heaths and sand dunes, where it is sometimes known as sand fescue.

417

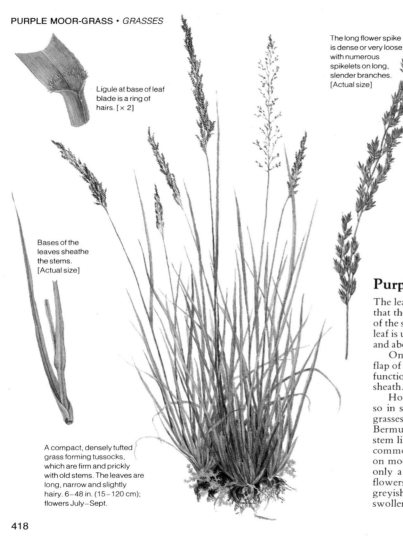

Ligule at base of leaf blade is a ring of hairs. [× 2]

The long flower spike is dense or very loose, with numerous spikelets on long, slender branches. [Actual size]

Bases of the leaves sheathe the stems. [Actual size]

Each small spikelet, on a long, slender branch, has one to four pointed purple florets. [× 2]

A compact, densely tufted grass forming tussocks, which are firm and prickly with old stems. The leaves are long, narrow and slightly hairy. 6–48 in. (15–120 cm); flowers July–Sept.

Moor-grass often covers large areas in marshes and fens and on wet moors and commons throughout Britain.

Purple moor-grass *Molinia caerulea*

The leaves of grasses are unusual among the flowering plants in that they have no stalks. Each leaf joins the stem at a node – one of the swellings occurring at intervals along the stem. There the leaf is usually wrapped tightly around the stem to form a sheath and above this the leaf broadens out into a blade.

On the inside, where sheath and blade join, there is a small flap of tissue – the ligule, which is generally whitish in colour. Its function is probably to prevent water from getting inside the sheath.

However, in rare cases a line of hairs forms the ligule. This is so in seven grasses found in Britain. Three of these are cord grasses, which grow only on salt-marshes. Another is the rare Bermuda grass, with flower spikes arranged at the top of the stem like the fingers of a hand. The fifth is the feathery-headed common reed of waterside places. The other two are both found on moors and heaths. One is heath grass, which is small, with only a few spikelets. The other is purple moor-grass, which flowers from July to September, later than heath grass. It has greyish-green leaves, is much taller, and has many spikelets and swollen bases to its stems.

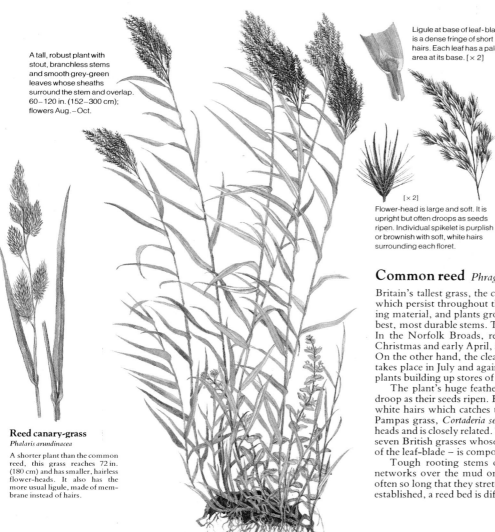

A tall, robust plant with stout, branchless stems and smooth grey-green leaves whose sheaths surround the stem and overlap. 60–120 in. (152–300 cm); flowers Aug.–Oct.

Ligule at base of leaf-blade is a dense fringe of short hairs. Each leaf has a pale area at its base. [× 2]

[× 2]

Flower-head is large and soft. It is upright but often droops as seeds ripen. Individual spikelet is purplish or brownish with soft, white hairs surrounding each floret.

Common reed grows in thick clusters at the edges of rivers, lakes and brackish waters throughout Britain.

Reed canary-grass
Phalaris arundinacea

A shorter plant than the common reed, this grass reaches 72 in. (180 cm) and has smaller, hairless flower-heads. It also has the more usual ligule, made of membrane instead of hairs.

Common reed *Phragmites australis*

Britain's tallest grass, the common reed, has tough, stiff stems which persist throughout the winter. These make ideal thatching material, and plants growing in brackish water produce the best, most durable stems. The wide, tough leaves are also used. In the Norfolk Broads, reeds for thatching are cut between Christmas and early April, as cutting later destroys new shoots. On the other hand, the clearing of waterways choked by reeds takes place in July and again before mid-August to prevent the plants building up stores of food for next year's growth.

The plant's huge feathery heads stand erect, but they may droop as their seeds ripen. Each floret has a dense fringe of silky white hairs which catches the wind and takes the seed with it. Pampas grass, *Cortaderia selloana*, a garden species, has similar heads and is closely related. The common reed is also one of only seven British grasses whose ligule – normally a scale at the base of the leaf-blade – is composed of hairs.

Tough rooting stems of the common reed form tangled networks over the mud on which they grow. The stems are often so long that they stretch right across a waterway, and once established, a reed bed is difficult to get rid of.

Rough meadow-grass
Poa trivialis

This grass can be distinguished from all other
meadow-grasses by the
roughness of its stems to the
touch, except above the uppermost leaves, where the
stems are smooth.

The loosely tufted stems
sometimes root at the nodes.
The flower-heads are roughly
triangular in outline. 1½–12 in.
(4–30 cm); flowers
throughout year.

The ligule, up
to ⅛ in. (5 mm)
long, is thinly
membranous.
[× 4]

Each spikelet
has closely
overlapping
florets. [× 5]

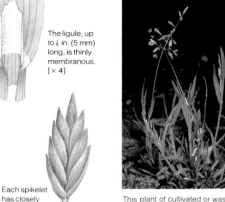

This plant of cultivated or waste ground,
grassland, roadsides and paths, is common throughout the British Isles.

Annual meadow-grass *Poa annua*

There is perhaps no commoner grass in the world than *Poa
annua*. It grows on any soil, from sand to clay, throughout the
temperate regions of both hemispheres, and on mountains in the
tropics. It tolerates both damp and dry situations. Over much of
its range it was introduced from Europe in seed mixtures.
Although described as an annual – a plant which completes its
entire life cycle in a single year – annual meadow-grass often
continues growing through a mild winter, and may survive for
several years. It flowers throughout the year and, given fair
weather, can produce fertile seed at any time.

A lawn full of annual meadow-grass is nearly always green,
because of the continual output of fresh seeds and replacement of
dying plants. Because many of the individual plants are short-
lived, *Poa annua* cannot produce the even, thick turf of a true
perennial grass, but it may grow abundantly on shaded lawns or
on lawns where other grasses are severely cut back or killed.

Rough meadow-grass, which is also very common,
flourishes best on wetter, heavier soils. A related species is the
famous Kentucky blue grass, which is known as smooth
meadow-grass in Britain.

The ligule at the base of the leaf-blade is membranous with a slightly ragged tip. [× 2]

The flower-heads are one-sided, with branches often close together. [Actual size]

Compressed spikelet is green or purplish, with two to five florets. The spikelets are in clusters. [× 5]

Cock's-foot is a grass of meadows, pastures and roadsides throughout the British Isles. It is cultivated on pastures.

A densely tufted grass, but with few flowering stems. The pointed leaves, folded at first, open out to greyish-green blades. 6–54 in. (15–137 cm); flowers June–Sept.

Old leaf-bases protect young shoots in winter.

Cock's-foot *Dactylis glomerata*

The dense flowering head of this grass, fancifully said to resemble the foot of a cockerel, is a familiar sight on roadside verges and wasteland. The grass is also cultivated, for although cock's-foot is tough and coarse it is valued by farmers as a pasture and hay grass.

The flowering head consists of a number of short branches, each with bunches of spikelets on short, individual branches. The spikelets are similar to those of fescue grasses, to which cock's-foot is closely related. The name *Dactylis* derives from the Greek word *dactylos*, 'finger', which alludes to the spikelet arrangement.

The majority of British grasses are difficult to identify when not in flower, but cock's-foot is an exception. At the start of the season there are two kinds of shoot; tall, cylindrical ones that will flower during the season, and shorter, sterile shoots consisting only of leaves and destined to flower the following year. The sterile shoots are distinctly flattened on one side, so that the sheaths which bear the leaves are V-shaped in cross-section. The leaves, which are rough-edged and flat, have a keel running along the middle, rather like the underside of a boat.

421

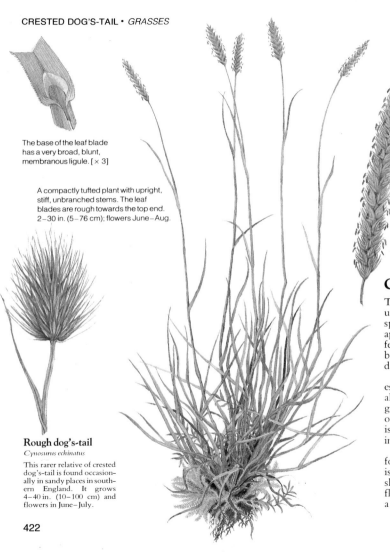

The base of the leaf blade has a very broad, blunt, membranous ligule. [× 3]

A compactly tufted plant with upright, stiff, unbranched stems. The leaf blades are rough towards the top end. 2–30 in. (5–76 cm); flowers June–Aug.

Flower-head is long and spike-like.

A cluster of spikelets consists of fertile spikelets with brown stamens, and barren spikelets.

Crested dog's-tail is common throughout Britain; it is particularly widespread in meadowland and in disused pasture.

Rough dog's-tail

Cynosurus echinatus

This rarer relative of crested dog's-tail is found occasionally in sandy places in southern England. It grows 4–40 in. (10–100 cm) and flowers in June–July.

Crested dog's-tail *Cynosurus cristatus*

This grass, recognisable by its long, spike-like flower-head, is unique among British grasses in having two different sorts of spikelet. One sort is sterile and gives the flower-head its spiky appearance; the other sort is fertile, bearing brown stamens. The fertile spikelets are hidden behind the sterile ones. The plant's botanical name means, literally, crested dog's-tail – *cynosurus* is derived from the Greek words *kuon* 'dog' and *oura* 'tail'.

Crested dog's-tail is found throughout the British Isles, especially in the older and well-established grasslands, and in almost any kind of soil. It is not particularly useful as a fodder grass because it is leafy only at the base, with a high proportion of wiry stem, which makes it suitable only for sheep grazing. It is a hardy plant, able to withstand cold and drought, and is often included in seed mixtures for pastures and lawns.

A rarer grass of this type, rough dog's-tail, is sometimes found on waste and cultivated ground, especially near the sea. It is rare in northern Britain. It is a Mediterranean weed and has shorter and broader flower-heads than crested dog's-tail. The florets are tipped with rough bristles which give the flower-head a spiky appearance.

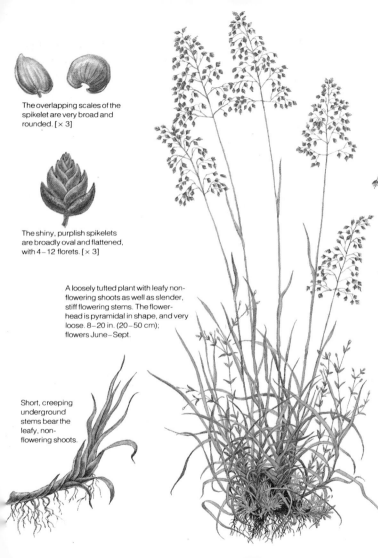

The overlapping scales of the spikelet are very broad and rounded. [× 3]

The shiny, purplish spikelets are broadly oval and flattened, with 4–12 florets. [× 3]

A loosely tufted plant with leafy non-flowering shoots as well as slender, stiff flowering stems. The flower-head is pyramidal in shape, and very loose. 8–20 in. (20–50 cm); flowers June–Sept.

Short, creeping underground stems bear the leafy, non-flowering shoots.

The drooping spikelets are suspended on fine, hair-like stalks.

Quaking grass, named for its trembling flower-heads, is found in pastures and on dry, grassy banks throughout Britain.

Quaking grass *Briza media*

Triangular, purplish-green flower-heads drooping from hair-like stalks readily identify quaking grass, but it has another and unique characteristic – when the wind blows, it rattles. It requires sharp ears, however, to catch the tiny sound made by the dryish and papery scales on the spikelets rubbing and scraping together when caught in a breeze.

It is the trembling of the spikelets that gives the plant its name, and it is also known as rattle grass, shivering grass, cow quakes, and by a variety of folk-names such as 'doddering dickies' or 'dillies', and 'didder'. The fine stalks have given rise to names like maiden's hair and lady's hair grass. The generic name *Briza* comes from the Greek *britho*, meaning 'I balance', because of the delicately suspended spikelets.

When flattened, the scales that make up the spikelets are almost circular. The flowers are often dried and used for floral decorations. Quaking grass is common throughout the British Isles, particularly in the south, and is often found in pastures with other grasses. But because it has so little foliage, it is of no importance as fodder. Most of the few flat, pointed leaves grow on non-flowering shoots that rise from the creeping rootstock.

Slender, slightly
spreading stems and
bright green blades form
loose, leafy patches. The
leaf sheaths are purplish;
the blades are smooth
above and rough below.
The flower-heads are
sparingly branched, with
few spikelets. 8–24 in.
(20–60 cm); flowers
May–July.

Each spikelet has a
single fertile floret and
one stalked, barren
floret, contained
within two petal-like
glumes. [× 4]

The ligule at the base of
the leaf-blade is short
and membranous, and
extends to form a sharp
bristle on the side opposite
the blade. [× 4]

Wood melick, a common woodland and
hedgerow plant, often covers the ground
in the open areas of beech woods.

Wood melick *Melica uniflora*

The delicate flower-heads of wood melick signal the presence of
a curiosity among British grasses – a plant strange both for its
habitat and for the structure of its flowers. Wood melick grows
best on the edges of clearings and on the banks of streams in
dense woodland – it is one of the few grasses that will survive in
beech woodland, and then only on its less sun-starved fringes. It
is found in hedgerows as well, and other plants that do well in
such places – for example, foxglove and red campion – grow
beside it.

Wood melick's flowers are unusual, too. Most other grass
species have spikelets with several fertile florets – pairs of scales,
each enclosing a flower – but as its species name *uniflora* suggests, wood melick's spikelet has only one fertile floret. This in
itself is not unusual – the bents, timothy, cat's-tails and fox-tails
all have only one – but on the wood melick's spikelet there is
also, above the single fertile floret, a mass of empty, sterile scales
forming a knob-like lump.

After the wind has pollinated the flowers, the seeds ripen,
and the scales that enclose them become hard and shiny. This
gives the seed the appearance of a tiny nut.

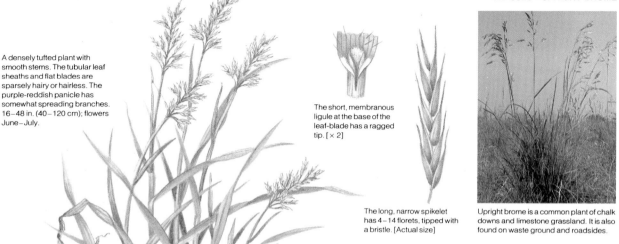

A densely tufted plant with smooth stems. The tubular leaf sheaths and flat blades are sparsely hairy or hairless. The purple-reddish panicle has somewhat spreading branches. 16–48 in. (40–120 cm); flowers June–July.

The short, membranous ligule at the base of the leaf-blade has a ragged tip. [× 2]

The long, narrow spikelet has 4–14 florets, tipped with a bristle. [Actual size]

Upright brome is a common plant of chalk downs and limestone grassland. It is also found on waste ground and roadsides.

Ligule [× 5]

Wood brome
Bromus ramosus

The stems and leaves are very hairy and the flower-head is loose and drooping. The ligule is blunt, and the base of the leaf-blade has two narrow, ear-like projections.

Upright brome *Bromus erectus*

Hay-fever sufferers have no love for upright brome; for of all the plants that grow in Britain this grass probably produces the largest and most irritating clouds of pollen. Like all grasses, upright brome depends on the wind to transfer pollen from one plant to another; and the quantities of pollen spread by whole hillsides covered in upright brome are prodigious. However, the plant is confined to the chalk or limestone hills of the south and east.

Benjamin Stillingfleet, the 18th-century botanist who gave many British grasses including brome their names, must have thought that the brome family resembled oats; for brome is the English version of the Greek word for oats, *bromos*. It is a misnomer, however, for only sterile brome, a grass of roadsides and wasteland, looks anything like the cereal plant. Brome grasses are characterised by a loose, nodding, or sometimes upright, flower-head, and by a hairy appendage on top of the ovary.

Unlike upright brome, wood brome is widespread throughout most of Britain. It grows in damp and shady places in deciduous woods and hedgerows, and on roadsides.

425

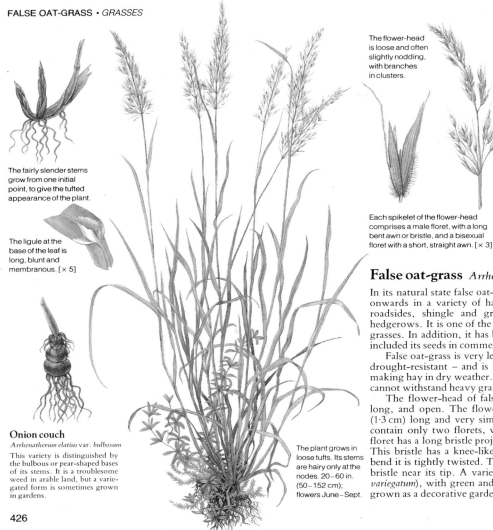

The fairly slender stems grow from one initial point, to give the tufted appearance of the plant.

The ligule at the base of the leaf is long, blunt and membranous. [× 5]

Onion couch

Arrhenatherum elatius var. *bulbosum*

This variety is distinguished by the bulbous or pear-shaped bases of its stems. It is a troublesome weed in arable land, but a variegated form is sometimes grown in gardens.

The plant grows in loose tufts. Its stems are hairy only at the nodes. 20–60 in. (50–152 cm); flowers June–Sept.

The flower-head is loose and often slightly nodding, with branches in clusters.

Each spikelet of the flower-head comprises a male floret, with a long bent awn or bristle, and a bisexual floret with a short, straight awn. [× 3]

False oat-grass is found on roadsides, waste ground and in rough grassland and hedgerows throughout Britain.

False oat-grass *Arrhenatherum elatius*

In its natural state false oat-grass is found flowering from June onwards in a variety of habitats, including rough grassland, roadsides, shingle and gravel beaches, waste ground and hedgerows. It is one of the most abundant of all Britain's wild grasses. In addition, it has been spread by man, who formerly included its seeds in commercial seed mixtures.

False oat-grass is very leafy, fast-growing, deep-rooted and drought-resistant – and is therefore of considerable value for making hay in dry weather. It does not, however, live long, and cannot withstand heavy grazing.

The flower-head of false oat-grass is up to 12 in. (30 cm) long, and open. The flower-bearing spikelets are up to $\frac{1}{2}$ in. (1·3 cm) long and very similar to those of the true oat. They contain only two florets, which are not identical. The lower floret has a long bristle projecting from halfway down its back. This bristle has a knee-like bend at the centre, and below the bend it is tightly twisted. The upper floret has a short, straight bristle near its tip. A variegated form of false oat-grass (var. *variegatum*), with green and white-striped leaves, is sometimes grown as a decorative garden plant.

The soft, greyish-green stems and leaves form tufts or loose mats, many with non-flowering stems. The flower-heads often appear pinkish on one side and white on the other, and have numerous spikelets. 8–24 in. (20–60 cm); flowers June–Sept.

The outer scales of the spikelet more or less hide the two florets, the upper of which has a hooked awn, or bristle. [× 5]

The ligule at the base of the leaf is fairly short and membranous, with a squarish tip. [× 5]

The stems and nodes are covered with short, greyish hairs. [× 2]

Yorkshire fog is a grass of meadows, pastures and waste ground. It is common throughout Britain and Europe.

Creeping soft-grass
Holcus mollis

The stems are slightly hairy or else smooth, except for the nodes, which have long hairs. The awn, or bristle, of the upper floret is not so curved as in Yorkshire fog. The grass sends out extensive roots which may be 100 ft (30 m) in length within a square foot of soil.

Yorkshire fog *Holcus lanatus*

The changing colours of its bushy flower-heads make Yorkshire fog one of the most attractive of Britain's common grasses. The flowers are a delicate pinkish-green in July, deepening to purple as they mature and fading in autumn to a fine greyish-white. The grass is found in all kinds of surroundings, from rough grassland through meadows and pastures to open woodland, and it can tolerate a wide variety of soils from heavy loams to sands. Though generally regarded as a weed, the grass when young provides grazing for animals, particularly on poor soils.

In North Country dialect 'fog' is any coarse winter grass that grows after the hay has been cut. The word may have come from the Old Norse *fogg*, meaning a long, limp, damp grass: a good description of Yorkshire fog. Its stems and leaves are covered with short velvety hairs, and in North America it is aptly known as velvet grass.

Creeping soft-grass is very like Yorkshire fog, and it, too, is a winter food for farm beasts; but it is most often found in woods and among scrub, and commonly grows on acid soils. As its name suggests, it may often be found carpeting the ground and is a troublesome weed in sandy fields.

427

The stems are stiff and the leaves greyish-green, with overlapping sheaths and rolled blades. The long panicles contain numerous spikelets. Shoots grow from creeping stems. 24–48 in. (60–120 cm); flowers June–Aug.

If the bracts are removed from the floret, three stamens can be seen, and the young fruit crowned with two stigmas. [× 3]

The base of each blade has a long, firm, sharply pointed ligule. [Actual size]

Each spikelet contains a single floret. [× 3]

Marram grass is commonly found on sand-dunes around the coast of Britain. It is often planted to bind the sand.

Marram grass *Ammophila arenaria*

A familiar sight at the seaside is the tufted marram grass which covers so many sand-dunes. The coarse foliage – which can prick and scratch – has very long roots which help to bind the dunes and so prevent wind erosion. It is extensively planted to fix bare dunes; when this has happened, other plants can move in, after which the marram grass eventually disappears.

The botanical name of this grass relates to its habitat: *Ammophila* comes from two Greek words meaning 'to like sand', and the Latin *arenaria* refers to sand which was destined for the Roman arenas. 'Marram' comes from two old Norse words, *marr* and *halmr*, meaning 'sea reed':

The leaves of marram grass are long and narrow and, in dry weather, they roll up lengthwise. Their bluish undersides are exposed to the weather and are smooth and glossy. The upper surfaces – which are on the inside when the leaves are furled – are ribbed and grooved with hairs along the ribs. The combination of ridges, furrows and hairs, in addition to its ability to roll up, helps to reduce the plant's water loss. The roots can be used for weaving; hence the alternative name of 'mat grass'. In Anglesey the leaves were used for thatching.

428

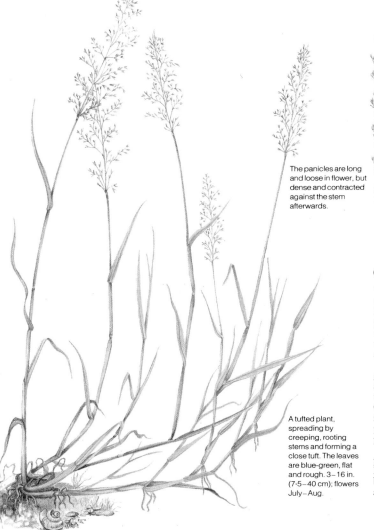

The panicles are long and loose in flower, but dense and contracted against the stem afterwards.

A tufted plant, spreading by creeping, rooting stems and forming a close tuft. The leaves are blue-green, flat and rough. 3–16 in. (7·5–40 cm); flowers July–Aug.

Floret has three stamens, and two styles on ovary.

Each spikelet contains one floret. [× 10]

The ligule at the base of each leaf blade is rather blunt and membranous.

This very common grass is found in all parts of Britain, particularly in wet lowland areas and open ground.

Creeping bent *Agrostis stolonifera*

The word 'bent' comes from an Old English word *beonet* which originally described various kinds of stiff, coarse grass. Today, however, the description 'bent' is confined to members of the plant group called *Agrostis*, the Greek word for 'grass', most of which are slender and delicate. More than 100 species are known world-wide, but only five are found in Britain: creeping bent, and brown, bristle, black and common bent.

Some bents can be identified with the help of a magnifying glass. In creeping bent, black bent and common bent the ligule – a short white membrane at the point where the leaf blade joins the sheath – is blunt, while in the other bents it is pointed. Creeping bent, which is also called white bent, is distinguished from black bent and common bent by the fact that its spreading panicle closes up after flowering. In the other two bents the panicle stays open.

Another name for creeping bent is *fiorin*. This Irish name was popularised in the 19th century by the Irish cleric William Richardson, who urged Irish farmers to improve their meadows by planting the grass widely. Today, however, farmers regard it as a weed, though dwarf varieties are used in lawns.

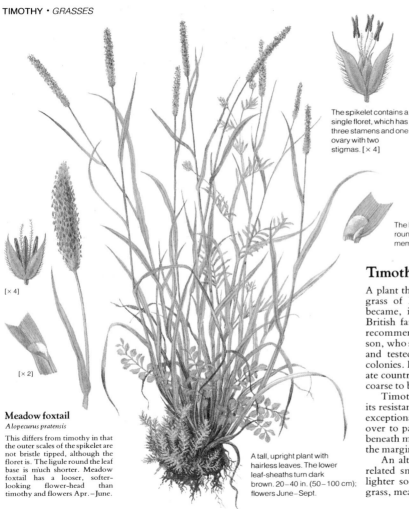

The spikelet contains a single floret, which has three stamens and one ovary with two stigmas. [× 4]

The stem bends at the base and the lower nodes are swollen. [× 2]

The blunt ligule, or flap, round the leaf base is membranous. [× 2]

Timothy is common throughout Britain. It is used for grazing and hay, and grows on roadsides and waste ground.

[× 4]

[× 2]

Meadow foxtail
Alopecurus pratensis

This differs from timothy in that the outer scales of the spikelet are not bristle tipped, although the floret is. The ligule round the leaf base is much shorter. Meadow foxtail has a looser, softer-looking flower-head than timothy and flowers Apr.–June.

A tall, upright plant with hairless leaves. The lower leaf-sheaths turn dark brown. 20–40 in. (50–100 cm); flowers June–Sept.

Timothy *Phleum pratense*

A plant that for centuries had been no more than an unregarded grass of Britain's water-meadows and low-lying grasslands became, in the mid-18th century, a major source of hay to British farmers. The transformation came about through the recommendation of an American agriculturist, Timothy Hanson, who suspected the plant's value as an excellent fodder grass, and tested and proved his theories in the North American colonies. It was named after him and was taken to most temperate countries – although some authorities believe it is a little too coarse to be especially palatable to cattle.

Timothy is particularly fond of heavy soil, and is noted for its resistance to cold and drought. Some strains of the grass are exceptionally leafy. When fields containing timothy are given over to pasture instead of hay, it tends gradually to disappear beneath more vigorous kinds of grass, and then survives only in the margins of the fields.

An alternative name for timothy is meadow cat's-tail; the related small, or purple cat's-tail (*Phleum bertolonii*), prefers lighter soils and grows on chalk downland. Another similar grass, meadow foxtail, grows in wetter places.

The flower-head is spike-like with short branches. It turns from green or purplish to yellow. [Actual size]

The fibrous ligule, or flap, at the base of the leaf-blade is long and rather ragged at the top. The leaf-sheath is bearded at the junction with the blade. [× 5]

This grass forms tufts of stiff, smooth, unbranched stems and finely pointed, flat leaves. 8–40 in. (20–100 cm); flowers Apr.–July.

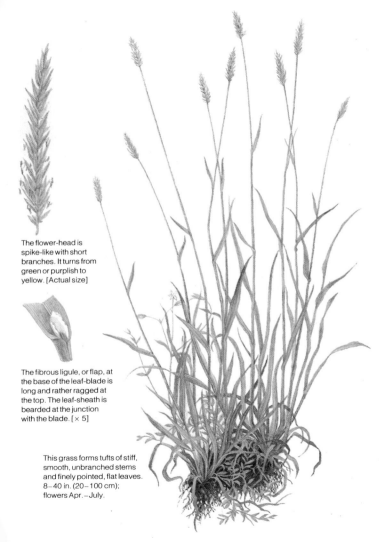

The feathery styles protrude from the barely opened tip of the floret. Later the purplish anthers will emerge from the tip and dangle outside the floret [× 2]

Sweet vernal grass is common on heaths, moors and pastures and in woods throughout the British Isles.

Sweet vernal grass *Anthoxanthum odoratum*

Sweet indeed is the scent of sweet vernal grass, for it is the source of that most pleasant of country smells – new-mown hay. The odour comes from a chemical called coumarin, which also occurs in sweet woodruff, melilot and the South American tonka bean; it is from the South American Indian name for the tonka bean, *cumari*, that the chemical takes its name.

Sweet vernal grass begins to flower early in the year, as the description vernal implies, and at one time its seeds were included in seed mixtures for pastures because of its fragrance. However, the high proportion of stem to leaves makes it lacking in nourishment, and in any case cattle do not find it appetising. Nevertheless the grass is so common that it survives in nearly every meadow.

The grass once proved popular for bonnet-making. For this purpose it was cut when thin and green, boiled for ten minutes in water and then dried in the sun. After a week of drying it turned a fine gold colour and was ready for weaving into bonnets. Whenever a bonnet made of sweet vernal grass became damp it gave off the smell of new-mown hay. Sweet vernal grass has also been used for scenting newly laundered linen.

431

WILD FLOWERS
PAST AND PRESENT

The history of Britain's flowers

From earliest times to the present day, changes in the distribution and diversity of Britain's flowers have run parallel to the geological, climatic and social changes taking place in the land. As one generation of plants has succeeded another, flowers have colonised new ground and retired from ground which is no longer suitable for them, advancing or retreating from one area to another as surely as any species of animal.

Some 30,000 years ago ice still covered much of the land that would later become Britain. South of the ice sheet grew a few hardy flowers, similar to those Arctic species such as mountain avens which still grow in the Scottish mountains. When the ice began its final retreat, about 15,000 years ago, new species spread out across the bare land. The first to appear were herbaceous plants with efficient methods of seed-dispersal, similar to the annual weeds of today.

Behind them came slower-growing shrubs and trees, which gradually became well-established. By the time the sea swept through the Straits of Dover and severed Britain from the Continent about 7,500 years ago, an extensive forest of broad-leaved trees blanketed much of the land, oak and elm being among the most common species. The forest canopy was so dense that relatively few herbaceous plants could survive beneath it, and wild flowers in general were much rarer than they are today.

By examining the layers of pollen in lake sediment and peat, and by dating them according to the quantities of radioactive carbon they contain, scientists can tell that elm trees began to become much scarcer after about 3000 BC, and wild flowers became more abundant. Neolithic people spreading northwards were beginning to clear the forests, using trees for fuel and building materials and making clearings where they could cultivate crops and graze animals. Herbaceous plants spread into the clearings; ribwort and common nettle were among the flowers which started to become widespread at about this time.

Clearing the forests

The reduction of the forests, and the consequent spread of wild flowers, became more rapid after about 500 BC, when the Celts, with more sophisticated agricultural techniques, began arriving in Britain. By the time the Romans arrived, there was already extensive cultivation of corn on the farmland that had been carved from the forest over the preceding 3,000 years, particularly in the chalkland and limestone hills of central and southern England. Large herds of cattle also grazed the pastures. The corn fields provided a habitat for many flowers which are common today, including fat hen, good King Henry and black bindweed. Some of these had been used as subsidiary food crops

by neolithic people, and may even have been deliberately introduced for that purpose.

The Romans probably introduced more corn-field weeds in the supplies of corn imported from the Continent to feed the invading legions. Corn marigold, corncockle and scarlet pimpernel may have arrived in this way. The extensive Roman roads provided an opportunity for the rapid spread of flowers characteristic of trodden pathways, such as greater plantain. These flowers still flourish in similar localities. The Romans also encouraged further cultivation of land for crops, as well as introducing new cultivated plants such as rye. In the warmer southern regions of the country they planted vines, mulberries, figs and plums, as well as vegetables such as peas and radishes. Herbs, including fennel and dill, were much prized, and some of the pot herbs which the Romans introduced, such as alexanders and ground elder, are now very widespread.

Grasslands and heaths

Although the ground cultivated by the Celts and Romans was extensive, it was largely restricted to lighter soils and higher ground. It was left to the Anglo-Saxons to clear many of the valleys, using eight-ox ploughs to turn the heavy, clay soil. Much of the farmland of the chalk and limestone hills was abandoned, and in many places beech woodland took over the cultivated ground. Elsewhere sheep continued to graze, keeping the land clear of trees and helping to create chalk and limestone grassland, with its characteristic plants.

Almost all the grasslands and heaths of modern Britain, with their rich profusion of flowers, are largely artificial habitats, created originally by man's destruction of the forests. The most notable exception is grassland on high mountains, above the level where trees are able to grow. Even when forest covered most of the rest of the land, flowers such as bilberry, heath bedstraw and mat-grass grew in these places.

A few other areas, such as the sugar limestone regions of Teesdale, were probably also always devoid of trees, for the soil formed on the crumbling rocks was constantly eroded by wind and rain. The flowers which grow there now – mountain avens and Teesdale violet on the turfy hummocks, drooping saxifrage in the wetter parts – are probably the same as those which first colonised the area in the wake of the retreating ice.

The unstable shingles and sands of the coast have probably also remained treeless ever since the ice retreated. It was from coastal habitats such as these, as well as from mountain habitats, that species spread out into the land newly cultivated by man, to form the original vegetation of grassland and heath. Grazing animals, and later the rabbits introduced by the Normans, ate the seedlings of trees, and so prevented them from recolonising the land.

Most of the remaining forest was destroyed during the 16th and 17th centuries to provide timber for boat building or charcoal for the smelting of iron ore. By the end of the 17th century, many iron smelters had to move to Scotland to find an adequate supply of wood. At about the same time a new habitat was appearing; and it was one which encouraged not only the growth of trees and shrubs, but also that of flowers as well.

Britain's hedgerows

Hedgerows are now such a characteristic feature of the British landscape that it is hard to imagine the countryside without them. Originally some of them may have been narrow belts of surviving woodland left as windbreaks, or they may have marked boundaries between areas of land being used for different purposes. Some were planted to enclose the open field systems of the Anglo-Saxon villages. But between the late 18th and late 19th centuries the Parliamentary Land Enclosures Acts brought about the planting of hedgerows to enclose many millions of acres of wasteland, common pasture and open fields. Some trees were left in the newly planted hedgerows, including elm and ash; and many species of flowers, such as garlic mustard and cow parsley, found new homes there.

The number of trees and shrubs in a hedgerow is a rough guide to its age. Hedgerows gain on average one new woody species each century, so a hedge with as many as 12 different trees or shrubs may date from the Anglo-Saxon period. In recent years many hedgerows have been destroyed to make large fields which are more suitable for the operation of modern farm machinery. Between 1946 and 1970 an estimated 4,500 miles of hedgerow were destroyed each year. When a hedgerow is lost, so too is the rich profusion of grasses and herbaceous plants which flourish in and around it.

Some flowers have suffered from man's activities while others have benefited from them. Few flowers can grow in the intensively planted commercial timber forests which are now so characteristic of many areas of Scotland and Wales. The draining of the East Anglian fens created some of the richest agricultural land in Britain, but many of the flowers which were once abundant in the region – species of water margins and marshy ground, such as arrowhead – are now much rarer. Oxford ragwort, by contrast, is now widespread and common, but a century ago it hardly occurred outside Oxford. It had been introduced to Oxford Botanic Gardens from Sicily, but soon the seeds with their parachutes of hairs drifted over the walls. The flowers colonised the bare embankments of the newly opened Great Western Railway and spread rapidly eastwards, the turbulent air created by passing trains helping to disperse the seeds.

Elsewhere, however, the clearing of wasteland and the intensive cultivation of ground using modern agricultural methods has led to a decline in the number and variety of wild flowers. More efficient seed-cleaning techniques and the use of selective weed-killers has resulted in wholesale destruction. Many once-common corn-field flowers, including pheasant's eye and field cow-wheat, have today become rare.

In search of wild flowers

The search for wild flowers is a trail which starts in any garden and leads out into the wildest and most beautiful countryside which Britain has to offer. For most people the greatest satisfaction lies in being able to name the plants which they find, since a flower's name is the key to all further information about it. At the same time, looking for flowers is a hobby which can be combined with a great variety of other forms of recreation, such as hiking, climbing, painting, photography or even studying the insects which pollinate flowers.

Few hobbies require so little equipment. A hand lens of about 10× magnification is useful for examining in detail some of the smaller flowers, particularly when the arrangement of the petals or the structure of the inner parts of the flower are important identification features. A field sketchbook in which to note as many details as possible about a flower's appearance and the habitat where it grows serves as an invaluable aid to memory when trying to identify unfamiliar species.

Flowers and the law

Many flowers have a very restricted distribution – some grow only in one or two small areas, others are thinly scattered about the country. The present rarity of some of these species is a direct result of man's activities. The Cheddar pink, for instance, was picked and dug up by generations of admirers, and consequently it is now one of Britain's rarest flowers. The Snowdon lily has been brought close to extinction in North Wales by avid gardeners collecting its bulbs.

To prevent any further destruction of wild flowers, the Conservation of Wild Creatures and Wild Plants Act of 1975 made it a criminal offence for anyone to uproot a wild plant without the express permission of the owner or occupier of the land on which it grows. In addition, special provision has been made for some of the rarest flowers, including many of those illustrated on the pages about rare plants in this book; and it is now illegal to collect any part of these plants, even the seeds. The species protected in this way are listed in a leaflet entitled 'A Code of Conduct for the Conservation of Wild Flowers', available from the Botanical Society of the British Isles, c/o British Museum (Natural History), Cromwell Road, London, SW7 5BD.

Conservation of plants is only effective if people follow a code of conduct in the countryside. Avoid damaging plants in any way, and never pick flowers without a good reason. Many species are uncommon because they can only survive in a particular habitat. So it is just as important to protect the habitat as it is to protect the plants themselves. Take extra care when walking in an area where a rare species grows: it is easy to damage young, non-flowering plants without even seeing them, and compression of the soil by excessive trampling may prevent future seedlings of the species from becoming established.

In the case of some very rare but well-known flowers, it has been known for so many enthusiasts to come to see a plant that they have worn a trail right up to it. This may result finally in the destruction of the plant, when an uninformed visitor following the trail picks its flower without realising what it is.

It is also dangerous to introduce foreign species to areas where they did not grow before. Species that are transported to new areas in this way may be removed from the natural conditions that keep their numbers in check. The resulting population explosion can change the natural vegetation over a large area, and the introduced plant may cause a decline among less-rapidly reproducing species.

There are many examples of species which have been taken from one part of the world to another and have become established as weeds in this manner. One instance of this happening was the rapid spread of Canadian waterweed when it was introduced to Britain in the 19th century.

Pineapple weed was introduced from North America in the 19th century, and spread rapidly along farm tracks and roadsides. Now it grows abundantly beside motorways, one of a great variety of species which have successfully colonised the thousands of acres of grassland which the motorway verges provide.

Where to find wild flowers

Probably the first wild flowers which most people encounter are the so-called weeds of gardens and waste ground, such as groundsel, shepherd's purse, scarlet pimpernel and annual meadow-grass. These plants are adapted to colonising bare ground as rapidly as possible. Most of them are annuals; they germinate, grow, flower and fruit all in the same year. They produce abundant seed, so that one plant has the potential to produce several hundred in the space of a year. The speed with which weeds can colonise the verges of a new road shows the efficiency of this method of reproduction.

Another area where weeds grow in abundance is around the edges of arable fields. However, some once-familiar species of arable ground, such as cornflower and corncockle, are today becoming rare due to modern methods of agriculture.

The flowers that grow on pastures are quite different from the flowers of arable fields. Among the many grasses, such as timothy and meadow foxtail, there is a wealth of other species; the selection depends on the nature of the underlying rocks and how wet the soil is. Wet meadows beside meandering rivers are the ideal habitat for cuckoo flower, marsh-marigold and lousewort, and the handsome chequered flowers of fritillary may also be seen.

The chalk grassland of southern England is an area of particular botanical interest. Its typical plants include the delicate nodding flowers of quaking grass, the bright blue of clustered bellflowers and many of Britain's most interesting orchids, including the bee orchid. Further north in England, similar plants can be found on hills of the harder limestone rocks. Other grassland species include mountain pansy, common rock-rose and common milkwort.

Soils above chalk and limestone are alkaline. In regions of sandstone, shale or granite they tend to be more acid, and this difference is reflected in the species which grow there. In general, acid heaths and moorlands are poorer than alkaline grasslands in the number of species which they support. Along with grasses such as fescues and purple moor-grass, there are many species of the heather family, including bell heather and bilberries. Around the edges of springs and streams, the leaves of the insect-eating butterworts and sundews spread out in wait for their prey.

Woodland flowers

British woodlands cover only a fraction of their former acreage, but they still provide homes for a great number of species. In spring the floor of a deciduous woodland is richly carpeted with bluebells, primroses, celandines, lords and ladies and occasional wild daffodils. Unfortunately, much woodland is of recent origin and poorly managed; the stems of ivies and clematis intertwine with the tangled woodland growth, and on lime-rich soil dog's mercury spreads across the shadowed ground. In beech woods, the dense foliage screens out most of the sunlight, and a thick blanket of partly rotted leaves covers the ground. But even in the darkest parts of the wood, some plants still grow; bird's-nest orchid, for instance, needs no light, for it feeds on decomposed leaves. Hellebores and several species of orchids grow around the clearings.

Pine woodlands are usually found on acid soils. In the commercial plantations which cover many Scottish hillsides the trees are packed so tightly together that the ground beneath them is almost sterile. This is in stark contrast with natural pine woodland, which is more open, with clearings supporting the growth of species such as foxglove.

Hedgerows are an extension of woodland, and many flowers which grow at the edges of woods also flourish along the hedgerows. Black and white bryonies twine through the hedge, together with hops, vetches and the arching stems of brambles and dog roses.

Flowers of the waterside and coast

The flowers that grow in and alongside rivers, streams or lakes are able to survive with completely waterlogged roots. These include purple-loosestrife, flag iris, figworts, monkeyflower, reedmace and rushes. The Lake District and the Norfolk Broads are particularly rich in such species.

In the water are the true aquatic plants. Those of still or slow-moving water include water-lilies, water violet and the insect-eating bladderwort, while in more swiftly flowing waters there are various species of water crowfoots.

Cliffs, sandy shores and salt-marshes have their own characteristic flowers, which are capable of surviving in the heavily salt-laden air. The flowers at the top of the cliffs may be similar to those growing on inland heath and chalk grassland, though among the kidney vetches and rock-roses there will also be thrifts, sea campions and perhaps spring squills. On steep, rocky parts of the cliff, flowers such as samphire and sea plantains grow, and in the south there may be brilliant masses of Hottentot-figs.

Along the upper tide-line of a sandy or pebbly shore, sea-purslane and restharrow bind the loose sand or pebbles and a foothold is provided for horned poppy. Higher up, sea bindweed festoons the tussocks of marram grass, between prickly tufts of sea holly and viper's-bugloss.

On salt-marshes, immersed twice daily by the sea, the dark green foliage of seablites and glassworts sets off the pastel colours of sea aster and sea-lavender.

Keeping records

When setting off in search of wild flowers, always take a field guide: it is much better to examine and identify plants in the place where they are growing, rather than to pick them for identification at home, so destroying the flowers. If necessary, record in a sketchbook the general appearance of the plant, together with details about the shape and arrangement of its leaves, the colour, number and relative size of its petals, the number of its stamens and, if possible, the sort of fruit it bears.

Photographing flowers is another way of keeping a permanent record without having to destroy any part of the flowers.

A single-lens reflex camera is the most suitable for photographing flowers, because of the ease of framing and focusing. Extra lenses or extension tubes may be necessary for taking really close-up shots.

Correct exposure is essential for bringing out all the details of the flower. Many cameras have a built-in light meter which measures the amount of light coming through the lens. However, holding a separate meter close to the flower may give more accurate readings. The light reflected by a flower is often brighter than the light reflected by its surroundings, and a meter reading taken of the flower and its background from a distance may result in a picture where the flower is over-exposed and details of the petals are lost. It is then often wise to under-expose the picture by a half or a whole f-stop.

When photographing really small flowers, depth of field – the range of distances over which the picture is in focus – may cause problems. To obtain the maximum depth of field, it is necessary to use the smallest possible aperture of the lens. This affects the exposure, and must be compensated for by allowing a longer exposure time, by using a faster film, or by using a flash. Many of the best flower pictures are taken on a bright morning or early evening, when the air is at its most still; for when a photograph is being taken using a long exposure, the slightest breath of wind may move the flower and blur the photograph.

Pressing and preserving flowers

Among the Victorians, pressing wild flowers was a very popular pastime, but the desire to collect uncommon species brought many plants close to extinction. Before pressing wild flowers today, make certain that they are common species, and use scissors or cutters to collect them in order to avoid causing any damage to the rootstock. Arrange the cut flowers between thin sheets of paper, sandwich these between pieces of thick, absorbent card, then clamp the whole stack between perforated wooden boards or frames.

Other methods of preserving flowers include drying them in sand, powdered silica gel or powdered borax. In the silica-gel technique, the cut flowers are placed upright in a tin or plastic container, and florist's silica gel is carefully sifted around the plant. With care it is possible to preserve the petals and all other parts of the flower in their natural positions. Once the silica gel completely covers the plant, the container is sealed to prevent the gel from absorbing water from the air. After one to five days, depending on the species, the flowers will be dry, and should last for months or years.

Wild flowers in your garden

Many wild flowers make good garden plants. For example, the tall, silvery cotton thistle makes a fine display when planted with foxgloves against a background of tall shrubs or trees. As an added attraction, goldfinches particularly enjoy the seed-heads of thistles, and swing from the flower-stalks as they feed. The seeds or bulbs of many wild flowers, including cotton thistle and foxglove, are available commercially. Even such rarities as gentians, pasque flowers, lilies and fritillaries can be bought in gardening shops.

Some places to see rare plants

The following areas are particularly notable for the rare flowers which grow there.

Caenlochan National Nature Reserve Grampian and Tayside.

A large upland area with many species typical of marshy ground and soil on lime-rich rock, including mountain avens. In some parts of the mountains the snow only melts for a brief period in the summer, when the plants grow and flower.

Cavenham Heath National Nature Reserve, Foxhole Heath, Lakenheath Warren Norfolk and west Suffolk.

The best remaining examples of Breckland grass heath, with a rich abundance of flowers including spiked speedwell and other rarities. Arable land near by is a refuge for some of the now-rare weeds of arable fields.

Great Ormes Head Gwynedd.

A peninsula jutting out to form the headland of Conwy Bay, with limestone cliffs, rocks

and grassland. It supports a mixture of sea-side plants and plants of lime-rich grassland.

Meall Nan Tarmachan National Nature Reserve and Ben Lawers Tayside.

One of the most important botanical localities in Britain, rich with species of the high mountains, such as alpine gentian. The only other places where some of these flowers can be seen are in the Alps and the Arctic regions of Europe. The main habitats of the reserve are heath, grassland, peat bogs, scree slopes and cliffs.

Mole Gap to Reigate Escarpment (including Box Hill) Surrey.

Part of the North Downs, with a rich selection of chalk grassland species including bee orchid and many other orchids. There are also areas of acid heath, scrub and woodland, with characteristic flowers.

Snowdon Gwynedd. Part of the Snowdonia National Park.

Acidic heath and grassland on ancient volcanic rock, with flowers such as mossy saxifrage. There are also lime-rich cliffs here and near by where Snowdon lily and other rare species grow, and many characteristic plants of high mountains.

Upper Teesdale Cumbria and Durham.

The areas of sugar limestone are famous for the rare flowers they support, such as Teesdale violet. There are also many interesting species that are characteristic of acid grassland, peat bogs, pools and running water, including drooping saxifrage.

West Lizard and Kynance Cove Cornwall.

One of the most famous areas in Britain for wild flowers, partly owned by the National Trust and leased to the Cornwall Naturalists' Trust. The unusual soils built on serpentine and schistose rocks support many rare plants.

Wicken Fen Cambridge.

One of the last remaining examples of the wet fenlands which once covered much of East Anglia, preserved in its natural state by the National Trust. Many of the species found here are now extremely rare elsewhere in the British Isles.

Societies to join

The following are the most important societies concerned with wild flowers. BOTANICAL SOCIETY OF THE BRITISH ISLES, c/o British Museum (Natural History), Cromwell Road, London, SW7 5BD. The foremost society for people interested in British flowers, whether amateurs or professionals. County Naturalists' Trusts and Natural History Societies. Contact local libraries for the addresses of local societies, or write to the Council for Nature, c/o Zoological Gardens, Regent's Park, London, NW1 4RY. These societies are especially useful for anyone interested in the conservation of plants locally. WILD FLOWER SOCIETY, Rams Hill House, Horsmonden, Tonbridge, Kent. A useful organisation for amateurs new to the study of wild flowers. Competitions are organised to hunt and record wild flowers.

Glossary

Alternate Term used to describe leaves or buds which arise singly on alternate sides of the stem, instead of occurring in OPPOSITE pairs.
Anther The part of the STAMEN that contains the POLLEN grains.
Awn A bristle-like appendage, most often found projecting from the LEMMA of grass flowers.
Axil The upper angle between a stem and a leaf or BRACT.

Basal Term used to describe leaves arising at the base of the stem.
Bract A SCALE-like or leaf-like organ, with a flower or flower-head arising from its AXIL.
Bulb An underground organ consisting of a short stem and a bud enclosed by numerous, fleshy, SCALE-like leaves or leaf-bases.
Bulbil A small BULB arising above ground in the AXIL of a leaf or BRACT.

Calyx All the SEPALS of a flower.
Column An organ of an orchid flower consisting of the joined STIGMA, STYLE and STAMENS.
Corolla Term used to describe all the PETALS of a flower.

Entire Term used to describe leaves or leaflets with edges which are neither toothed nor LOBED.

Filament The stalk of the STAMEN, which supports the ANTHER.
Floret A small flower, usually part of the flower-head of species of daisy or grass.

Glume One of the lowest pairs of BRACTS in a grass SPIKELET.

Keel A raised or sharply folded edge, resembling the keel of a boat. The term is usually used to describe the lower petals in most species of pea.

Leaflet A single part of a leaf that is divided into separate, leaf-like parts.
Lemma The lower of the top pair of BRACTS in a grass SPIKELET.
Ligule A thin flap of tissue such as that between the leaf-blade of a grass and the point where it joins the stem.
Lobed Term used to describe leaves which are deeply divided into segments, or lobes.

Nectary The part of a flower or plant that secretes nectar.

Opposite Term used to describe leaves or buds which arise in pairs at the same level on the stem.
Ovary The part of the female reproductive organs of a flower which contains the bodies that will develop into seeds after fertilisation.

Palea The upper BRACT of the top pair of bracts in a grass SPIKELET, enclosing the OVARY and STAMENS.
Panicle A branched flower-head, each branch bearing numerous individual stalked flowers.
Perfoliate A leaf, or pair of leaves, whose base entirely surrounds the stem, so that the stem appears to pass through it.
Perianth All the SEPALS and petals of a flower.

Petals The parts of a flower immediately inside the SEPALS. A few flowers lack petals altogether.
Pollen Grains produced in the ANTHERS, necessary to produce fertile seeds in the OVARY.
Pollinia Mass of pollen formed by pollen grains adhering to one another.

Rhizome An underground stem, often thick and fleshy.
Rosette A cluster of leaves at ground level, with a flower-stem arising from the centre.

Scale A thin plate of tissue, usually small and like membrane or chaff.
Sepals The outermost parts of a flower that protect the flower in bud. Sepals are usually green or brown.
Spadix A slender, spike-like flower-head, usually surrounded by a sheath or SPATHE.
Spathe A sheath enclosing a flower-head, sometimes resembling a single, large PETAL.
Spikelet Part of a branched flower-head containing stalkless flowers. In particular, a spikelet is the basic unit of a grass flower-head, comprising two GLUMES and one or more FLORETS. Each floret consists of two BRACTS enclosing an OVARY and STAMENS.
Stamen The male reproductive organ of a flower, made up of the ANTHER and the FILAMENT.
Stigma The pollen-receptive part of the female reproductive organs of a flower.
Stipule A SCALE-like or leaf-like appendage at the base of some leaf stalks.

Style The part of the female reproductive organs of a flower which connects the STIGMA to the OVARY.

Tube The joined lower parts of the SEPALS or PETALS of some flowers. The tube may have parallel sides, or one end may be wider than the other.

Umbel A flower-head in which all the flower-stalks arise from a single point. Many species of parsley have branched umbels, with several small umbels arising from a single point.

Whorl A cluster of three or more leaves or buds arising at the same level on the stem.

Index

Page numbers in **bold type** denote full-page illustrated entries. Page numbers in roman type denote additional references to these flowers in 'look-alike' comparative charts, or shorter illustrated profiles of less common species.

Acknowledgments

Artwork in *Wild Flowers of Britain* was supplied by the following artists:

3, 8–9 Barbara Walker · 10–15 Wendy Brammal · 16–17 Jim Russell · 18–19 Stephanie Harrison · 20–21 Peter Wrigley · 22–27 Victoria Goman · 28–29 Colin Emberson · 30–37 Helen Cowcher · 38–45 Colin Emberson · 46–47 Norman Lacey · 48–53 Shirley Hooper · 54–59 Wendy Brammal · 60–61 John Rignall · 62–65 Colin Emberson · 66–69 Paul Wrigley · 70–73 Stuart Lafford · 74–81 Victoria Goman · 82–95 Wendy Brammal · 96–107 Leonora Box · 108–21 Shirley Hooper · 122–3 Line Mailhe · 124–5 Leonora Box · 126–31 Helen Cowcher · 132–41 Stuart Lafford · 142–3 Frankie Coventry · 144–5 Stuart Lafford · 146–9 John Rignall · 150–7 Paul Wrigley · 158 Colin Emberson · 159 Josiane Campan · 160–9 Colin Emberson · 170–1 Marie-Claude Guyetand · 172–5 Frankie Coventry · 176–7 Wendy Brammal · 178–9 Sarah Fox-Davies · 180–1 Line Mailhe · 182–3 Shirley Hooper · 184–9 John Rignall · 190–1 Shirley

Hooper · 192–3 Brenda Katte · 194–5 Leonora Box · 196–7 Barbara Walker · 198–9 Guy Michel · 200–3 Victoria Goman · 204–5 Colin Emberson · 206–7 Guy Michel · 208–9 Colin Emberson · 210–11 Guy Michel · 212–15 Marjory Saynor · 216–17 Marie-Claire Nivoix · 218–21 Shirley Hooper · 222–5 Colin Emberson · 226–33 Barbara Walker · 234–5 Philippe Coute · 236–7 Guy Michel · 238–9 Colin Emberson · 240–1 John Rignall · 242–3 Josiane Campan · 244–5 John Rignall · 246–9 Josiane Campan · 250–1 Roger Hughes · 252–3 Line Mailhe · 254–5 Brenda Katte · 256–9 Victoria Goman · 260–1 Leonora Box · 262–3 Guy Michel · 264–7 Roger Hughes · 268–9 Marie-Claire Nivoix · 270–3 Stuart Lafford · 274–5 Guy Michel · 276–7 John Rignall · 278–83 Helen Cowcher · 284–301 Brenda Katte · 302–3 Stuart Lafford · 304–5 Brenda Katte · 306–7 Sarah Fox-Davies · 308–9 Helen Cowcher · 310–11 Sarah Fox-Davies · 312–13 Brenda Katte · 314–15 Colin Emberson · 316–17 Philippe Coute · 318–19 Stuart

Lafford · 320–3 Sarah Fox-Davies · 324–5 Philippe Coute · 326–7 Colin Emberson · 328–9 Maurice Esperance · 330–3 Sarah Fox-Davies · 334–5 Brenda Katte · 336–7 Delyth Jones · 338–9 Guy Michel · 340–5 Wendy Brammal · 346–7 Guy Michel · 348–55 Helen Senior · 356–7 Line Mailhe · 358–9 Derek Rodgers · 360–3 Colin Emberson · 364–5 Line Mailhe · 366–7 Leonora Box · 368–9 Marie-Claire Nivoix · 370–1 Roger Hughes · 372–5 Leonora Box · 376–7 Line Mailhe · 378–9 Stuart Lafford · 380–1 Helen Senior · 382–3 Colin Emberson · 384–5 Philippe Coute · 386–7 Stuart Lafford · 388–91 Helen Senior · 392–3 Line Mailhe · 394–5 Colin Emberson · 396–7 Brenda Katte · 398–9 Colin Emberson · 400–1 Brenda Katte · 402–3 Colin Emberson · 404–11 Stuart Lafford · 412–13 Brenda Katte · 414–15 Leonora Box · 416–17 Brenda Katte · 418–19 Leonora Box · 420–1 Brenda Katte · 422–3 Leonora Box · 424–5 Marie-Claire Nivoix · 426–7 Leonora Box · 428–9 Brenda Katte · 430–1 Leonora Box · 432–3 Jim Russell

Names of photographic agencies are in capital letters. The following abbreviations are used:
NHPA – Natural History Photograph Agency
NSP – Natural Science Photographs
OSF – Oxford Scientific Films
SLBI – South London Botanical Institute

18, 19 Heather Angel · 20 NHPA/M. Savonius · 21 BRUCE COLEMAN/J. Markham · 22 BRUCE COLEMAN/P. Ward · 23 Oleg Polunin · 24 OSF/G. A. Maclean · 25 Oleg Polunin · 26 OSF/G. A. Maclean · 27 Heather Angel · 28 OSF · 29, 30 Heather Angel · 31 OSF/G. A. Maclean · 32 A–Z COLLECTION/M. B. Jones · 33 A–Z COLLECTION/M. Nimmo · 34 Robin Fletcher · 35 Ron & Christine Foord · 36 NHPA/D. M. Manners · 37 NHPA/Stephen Dalton · 40, 41, 42 NSP/G. A. Matthews · 43 SLBI · 44 A–Z

COLLECTION/G. A. Matthews · 45 Oleg Polunin · 46 A–Z COLLECTION · 47 NSP/G. A. Matthews · 48 SLBI · 50 NSP/P. H. Ward · 51 SLBI · 52 Ron & Christine Foord · 53 A–Z COLLECTION/M. B. Jones · 54, 55 A–Z COLLECTION/M. Nimmo · 56 Heather Angel · 57 Gerald Wilkinson · 58 Ron & Christine Foord · 59 Heather Angel · 60 Robin Fletcher · 61 NSP/G. A. Matthews · 62 BRUCE COLEMAN/J. Markham · 63 A–Z COLLECTION/M. Nimmo · 64 AQUILA/A. W. Cundall · 65 BRUCE COLEMAN/H. G. Heyer · 66 Robin Fletcher · 67 Ron & Christine Foord · 68 Heather Angel · 69 NSP/G. A. Matthews · 70 BRUCE COLEMAN/S. C. Bisserot · 71 SLBI · 72 Oleg Polunin · 73 NSP/G. A. Matthews · 74 BRUCE COLEMAN/S. C. Porter · 75 SLBI · 77 A–Z COLLECTION · 78, 79 Heather Angel · 80 SLBI · 81 Heather Angel · 82 NSP/G. A. Matthews · 83 OSF/G. A. Maclean · 84 A–Z COLLECTION/G. A. Matthews · 85 SLBI · 86 Ron & Christine Foord · 87 OSF/G. A. Maclean · 88 NSP/G. A. Matthews · 89 Ron & Christine Foord · 90 Harry Smith Collection · 91 A–Z COLLECTION/M. Nimmo · 92 Brian Hawkes · 93 Heather Angel · 94 Oleg Polunin · 95 Brian Hawkes · 96 Ron & Christine Foord · 97 SLBI · 98 Heather Angel · 99 ARDEA/A. Paterson · 100 Ron & Christine Foord · 101 David Sutton · 102 Ron & Christine Foord · 103 A–Z COLLECTION/W. F. Davidson · 104, 105 Robin Fletcher · 106 David Sutton · 107 Robin Fletcher · 108 Ron & Christine Foord · 110 A–Z COLLECTION/W. F. Davidson · 111 OSF/G. A. Maclean · 112 NSP/G. A. Matthews · 113 Brian Hawkes · 114 Ron & Christine Foord · 115 NSP/G. A. Matthews · 116 OSF/G. A. Maclean · 117 Heather Angel · 118 Robin Fletcher · 119 BRUCE COLEMAN/S. C. Porter · 120 Anthony Huxley · 121 Ron & Christine Foord · 122 Heather Angel · 123 M. King & M. Read · 125 OSF/G. A. Maclean · 126 Ron & Christine Foord · 127 NSP/G. A. Matthews · 128 Robin Fletcher · 129 ARDEA/R. Gibbons · 130 NSP/A. W. Cundall · 131 Anthony Huxley · 132 BRUCE COLEMAN/Bruce Coleman · 133, 134 NSP/G. A. Matthews · 135, 136, 137 Heather Angel · 138 NSP/A. W. Cundall · 139 Robin Fletcher · 140 A–Z COLLECTION/W. F. Davidson · 141 Heather Angel · 142 A–Z COLLECTION/M. B. Jones · 143 Heather Angel · 144 Anthony Huxley · 145 BRUCE COLEMAN/J. Markham · 146 Ron & Christine Foord · 147 SLBI · 148 A–Z COLLECTION/M. Nimmo · 149 A–Z COLLECTION/M. B. Jones · 150 Robin Fletcher · 151 Brian Hawkes · 152 Heather Angel · 153 Ron & Christine Foord · 154 Heather Angel · 155 Brian Hawkes · 156 Heather Angel · 157 Gerald Wilkinson · 158 Heather Angel · 159 Robin Fletcher · 160 NSP/G. A. Matthews · 161 Gerald Wilkinson · 162 NSP/M. Chinery · 163 A–Z COLLECTION/M. B. Jones · 164, 165, 166, 167 Heather Angel · 170, 171 Robin Fletcher · 172 Alan Beaumont · 173 OSF · 174 SLBI · 175 Heather

Angel · 176 JACANA/R. Volot · 177 ARDEA/John Mason · 178 A–Z COLLECTION/M. Nimmo · 179 Robin Fletcher · 180 OSF/G. A. Maclean · 181 A–Z COLLECTION/M. Nimmo · 182 ARDEA/John Mason · 183 Ron & Christine Foord · 184 Heather Angel · 185 ARDEA/Ake Lindau · 186 A–Z COLLECTION/M. Nimmo · 187 SLBI · 188 Heather Angel · 189 NSP/G. A. Matthews · 190 OSF/G. A. Maclean · 191 JACANA/M. Viard · 192 A–Z COLLECTION/W. F. Davidson · 193 BRUCE COLEMAN/J. Markham · 194 NSP/G. A. Matthews · 195 Eric Hosking · 196 Heather Angel · 197 Robin Fletcher · 198, 199 Ron & Christine Foord · 204 Heather Angel · 205 A–Z COLLECTION/M. Nimmo · 206 NSP/G. A. Matthews · 207 AQUILA/Tom Leach · 208 BRUCE COLEMAN/B. & C. Calhoun · 209 Heather Angel · 210 BRUCE COLEMAN/Neville Fox-Davies · 211 Gerald Wilkinson · 212 A–Z COLLECTION/M. Nimmo · 213 Robin Fletcher · 214 BRUCE COLEMAN/J. Markham · 215 ARDEA/I. R. Beames · 216 Robin Fletcher · 217 ARDEA/R. Gibbons · 218 Robin Fletcher · 219 BRUCE COLEMAN/S. C. Porter · 220, 221, 222 Heather Angel · 223 BRUCE COLEMAN/S. C. Porter · 224 Heather Angel · 225 Robin Fletcher · 226 Eric Hosking · 227, 228, 229 Heather Angel · 230 Oleg Polunin · 231 NSP/G. A. Matthews · 232 Robin Fletcher · 233 Heather Angel · 234 Robin Fletcher · 235 ARDEA/J. Mason · 236 NSP/A. W. Cundall · 237 Neville Fox-Davies · 239 Robin Fletcher · 240 A–Z COLLECTION/G. A. Matthews · 241 Robin Fletcher · 242 Gerald Wilkinson · 243 SLBI · 244 David Sutton · 245 JACANA/C. de Klemm · 246 BRUCE COLEMAN/Bruce Coleman · 247 Heather Angel · 248 Eric Hosking · 249 Heather Angel · 250 John Vigurs · 251 Heather Angel · 252, 253 Brian Hawkes · 254 OSF · 255 A–Z COLLECTION/M. Nimmo · 260 OSF/G. A. Maclean · 261 Robin Fletcher · 262 AQUILA/E. A. Janes · 263 SLBI · 264 A–Z COLLECTION/M. Nimmo · 265 BRUCE COLEMAN/J. Markham · 266 David Sutton · 267 Robin Fletcher · 268 NSP/G. A. Matthews · 269 Robin Fletcher · 270 Heather Angel · 271 Ron & Christine Foord · 272 ARDEA/B. L. Sage · 273 Brian Hawkes · 274 Heather Angel · 275 Gerald Wilkinson · 276 A–Z COLLECTION/M. Nimmo · 277 BRUCE COLEMAN/J. Markham · 278 BRUCE COLEMAN/S. C. Porter · 279 SLBI · 280 Heather Angel · 281 Ron & Christine Foord · 282 JACANA/Noailles · 283 Heather Angel · 284 A–Z COLLECTION/M. Nimmo · 285 NSP/G. A. Matthews · 286 NHPA/E. A. Janes · 287 BRUCE COLEMAN/S. C. Porter · 288 ARDEA/R. Gibbons · 289 NSP/G. A. Matthews · 290 A–Z COLLECTION/F. Collet · 291 ARDEA · 293 A–Z COLLECTION/W. F. Davidson · 294 A–Z COLLECTION/G. A. Matthews · 295 Heather Angel · 296 NSP/P. J. K. Burton · 297 BRUCE COLEMAN/S. C. Porter · 298 NHPA/Brian

Hawkes · 299 Heather Angel · 300 AQUILA/E. A. Janes · 301 Oleg Polunin · 302, 303 Heather Angel · 304 Robin Fletcher · 305 A–Z COLLECTION/F. Collet · 306 ARDEA/R. Gibbons · 307 Brian Hawkes · 308 BRUCE COLEMAN/S. C. Porter · 309 Heather Angel · 310 NSP/G. A. Matthews · 311 Ron & Christine Foord · 312 NSP/P. J. K. Burton · 313, 314 Robin Fletcher · 315 BRUCE COLEMAN/J. Markham · 316 NHPA/K. G. Preston-Mafham · 317 Heather Angel · 318 NSP/G. A. Matthews · 319 Robin Fletcher · 320 Brian Hawkes · 321 ARDEA · 322, 323 Robin Fletcher · 324 NSP/G. A. Matthews · 325 BRUCE COLEMAN/J. Burton · 326 NSP/G. A. Matthews · 327 Heather Angel · 328 NHPA/G. Cambridge & J. Bain · 329 NHPA/K. G. Preston-Mafham · 330 Robin Fletcher · 331 Brian Hawkes · 332 Ron & Christine Foord · 333 NSP/G. A. Matthews · 334 Heather Angel · 335 Robin Fletcher · 336 A–Z COLLECTION/G. A. Matthews · 337, 338 Heather Angel · 339 Ron & Christine Foord · 340 Robin Fletcher · 341 ARDEA/Ake Lindau · 342 Robin Fletcher · 343 OSF/R. W. Whiteway · 344 OSF/G. A. Maclean · 345 NSP/G. A. Matthews · 346 BRUCE COLEMAN/Neville Fox-Davies · 347 SLBI · 348 ARDEA/J. A. Bailey · 349 A–Z COLLECTION/M. Nimmo · 350 Robin Fletcher · 351 ARDEA/R. Gibbons · 352 Robin Fletcher · 353 Gerald Wilkinson · 354 NSP/G. A. Matthews · 355 Heather Angel · 356 Robin Fletcher · 357 BRUCE COLEMAN/F. Sauer · 358 Gerald Wilkinson · 359 AQUILA/A. W. Cundall · 362 A–Z COLLECTION/G. A. Matthews · 363 Heather Angel · 364 Ron & Christine Foord · 365 A–Z COLLECTION/M. Nimmo · 366 A–Z COLLECTION/M. B. Jones · 367 JACANA/C. de Klemm · 368 BRUCE COLEMAN/J. Burton · 369, 370 Robin Fletcher · 371 A–Z COLLECTION/G. A. Matthews · 372 ARDEA/R. Gibbons · 373 NSP/G. A. Matthews · 374 BRUCE COLEMAN/Neville Fox-Davies · 375 ARDEA/C. Nardin · 376 Alan Beaumont · 377 Eric Crichton · 378 Ron & Christine Foord · 379 Robin Fletcher · 380 BRUCE COLEMAN/S. C. Porter · 381 AQUILA/A. Cooper · 382 Ron & Christine Foord · 383 Heather Angel · 384, 385 NSP/G. A. Matthews · 386 SLBI · 387 OSF/G. A. Maclean · 388 AQUILA/A. J. Bond · 389 Heather Angel · 390 Robin Fletcher · 391 A–Z COLLECTION/G. A. Matthews · 392 Brian Hawkes · 393 NHPA/K. G. Preston-Mafham · 394 Robin Fletcher · 395 Heather Angel · 396 NHPA/J. & M. Bain · 397 ARDEA/R. Gibbons · 398 Robin Fletcher · 399 Oleg Polunin · 400 Robin Fletcher · 401 AQUILA/A. Hems · 402 ARDEA/J. & S. Bottomley · 403 NSP/G. A. Matthews · 404 Jill Gardiner · 405 BRUCE COLEMAN/W. Brooks · 407, 408 Heather Angel · 409 ARDEA/J. Mason · 410 NSP/G. A. Matthews · 411 A–Z COLLECTION/M. B. Jones · 412 PITCH/F. Charmoy · 413 ARDEA/J. Mason · 414 OSF/G. A. Maclean · 416 JACANA/F. Winner · 417 A–Z

COLLECTION/M. Nimmo · 418 ARDEA/I. R. Beames · 419 BRUCE COLEMAN/J. Burton · 420 Ron & Christine Foord · 421 BRUCE COLEMAN/J. Markham · 422 Oleg Polunin · 423 OSF · 424, 425, 426 SLBI · 427 ARDEA/R. Gibbons · 428 ARDEA · 429 A–Z COLLECTION/M. Nimmo · 430 Gerald Wilkinson · 431 ARDEA/R. Gibbons · 432 A–Z COLLECTION/M. Nimmo

The publishers acknowledge their indebtedness to the following books which were consulted for reference:

British Sedges by A. C. Jermy and T. G. Tutin (Botanical Society of the British Isles) · *British Wild Flowers* by John Hutchinson (Pelican) · *British Wild Flowers* by Patricia Lewis (Eyre and Spottiswoode) · *The Concise British Flora in Colour* by W. Keble Martin (Ebury Press/Michael Joseph) · *Culpeper's Complete Herbal* by Nicholas Culpeper (Foulsham) · *A Dictionary of English Plant Names* by Geoffrey Grigson (Allen Lane) · *Drawings of British Plants* by Stella Ross-Craig (G. Bell and Sons) · *English Names of Wild Flowers* by John G. Dony, Franklyn Perring and Catherine M. Rob (Butterworths/Botanical Society of the British Isles) · *The Englishman's Flora* by Geoffrey Grigson (Phoenix House) · *A Field Guide in Colour to Wild Flowers* by Dietmar Aichele (Octopus Books) · *Flora Europaea* (Vols. 1–5) ed. T. G. Tutin (Cambridge University Press) · *Flora of the British Isles* by A. R. Clapham, T. G. Tutin and E. F. Warburg; illustrations by Sybil J. Roles (Cambridge University Press) · *Flowers of Europe: A Field Guide* by Oleg Polunin (Oxford University Press) · *Flowers of the Field* by Rev. C. A. Johns (Routledge and Kegan Paul) · *Food for Free* by Richard Mabey (Collins) · *Gardener's Magic and Other Old Wives' Lore* by Bridget Boland (The Bodley Head) · *Grasses* by C. E. Hubbard (Penguin) · *Grasses, Sedges and Rushes* by M. Skytte Christiansen (Blandford Press) · *Hedgerow Plants* by Molly Hyde (Shire Publications) · *A History of British Gardening* by Miles Hadfield (John Murray) · *The History of the British Vegetation* by Winifred Pennington (English Universities Press) · *A Modern Herbal* by N. Grieve (Penguin) · *The Observer's Book of Grasses, Sedges and Rushes* edited by W. J. Stokoe, A. Laurence Wells (Frederick Warne) · *The Oxford Book of Wild Flowers* by B. E. Nicholson, S. Ary and M. Gregory (Oxford University Press) · *Plant Galls* by Arnold Darlington (Blandford Press) · *The Pocket Guide to Wild Flowers* by David McClintock and R. S. R. Fitter (Collins) · *Pollination of Flowers* by Michael Proctor and Peter Yeo (Collins) · *Wild Flowers* by John Gilmour and Max Walters (Collins) · *Wild Flowers of Britain* by Roger Phillips (Pan) · *The Wild Flowers of Britain and Northern Europe* by Richard Fitter, Alastair Fitter and Marjorie Blamey (Collins)

Printing, paper and binding
SIR JOSEPH CAUSTON & SONS LTD, EASTLEIGH · HAZELL WATSON & VINEY LTD, AYLESBURY
KONINKLIJKE NEDERLANDSE PAPIERFABRIEKEN NV, MAASTRICHT · MULLIS MORGAN LTD, LONDON
VANTAGE PHOTOSETTING LTD, ROWNHAMS, SOUTHAMPTON · WINTERBOTTOM PRODUCTS LTD, WEASTE